Enterprise Mac Administrator's Guide

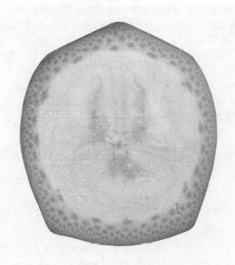

Charles S. Edge Jr.,
Beau Hunter,
Zach Smith

Apress®

Enterprise Mac Administrator's Guide

ISBN-13 (pbk): 978-1-4302-2443-3

ISBN-13 (electronic): 978-1-4302-2444-0

Printed and bound in the United States of America 9 8 7 6 5 4 3 2 1

Trademarked names may appear in this book. Rather than use a trademark symbol with every occurrence of a trademarked name, we use the names only in an editorial fashion and to the benefit of the trademark owner, with no intention of infringement of the trademark.

Lead Editor: Michelle Lowman
Technical Reviewers: Joe Kissell, Dee-Ann LeBlanc, and Brad Lees
Editorial Board: Clay Andres, Steve Anglin, Mark Beckner, Ewan Buckingham, Tony Campbell, Gary Cornell, Jonathan Gennick, Michelle Lowman, Matthew Moodie, Jeffrey Pepper, Frank Pohlmann, Ben Renow-Clarke, Dominic Shakeshaft, Matt Wade, Tom Welsh
Project Manager: Debra Kelly
Copy Editors: Katie Stence and Sharon Terdeman
Composition: ContentWorks, Inc.
Indexer: Ann Rogers/Ron Strauss
Artist: April Milne

Distributed to the book trade worldwide by Springer-Verlag New York, Inc., 233 Spring Street, 6th Floor, New York, NY 10013. Phone 1-800-SPRINGER, fax 201-348-4505, e-mail orders-ny@springer-sbm.com, or visit http://www.springeronline.com.

For information on translations, please e-mail info@apress.com, or visit http://www.apress.com.

Apress and friends of ED books may be purchased in bulk for academic, corporate, or promotional use. eBook versions and licenses are also available for most titles. For more information, reference our Special Bulk Sales–eBook Licensing web page at http://www.apress.com/info/bulksales.

To Lisa & Emerald, with love
—Charles S. Edge Jr.

Dedicated to my wife, Monica, who, despite completely losing me to the world of bits and bytes for the last six months, has been a source of constant support.
—Beau Hunter

Contents at a Glance

Contents

About the Authors

■**Charles S. Edge Jr.** is the Director of Technology at 318, which is based in Santa Monica, California, and is the largest Mac consultancy in the United States. At 318, Charles leads a team of more than 40 engineers and has worked with network architecture, security, and storage for various vertical and horizontal markets. Charles maintains the 318 corporate blog at 318.com/techjournal as well as a personal site at krypted.com.
Charles is the author of a number of titles on Mac OS X Server and systems administration topics, including three titles from Apress for Mac OS X 10.6. He has spoken at a variety of conferences including DefCon, Black Hat, LinuxWorld, Macworld, MacSysAdmin, and the Apple WorldWide Developers Conference. Charles is the developer of the SANS course on Mac OS X Security and coauthor of its best practices guide to securing Mac OS X as well. Charles now lives in Minneapolis, Minnesota, with his wife, Lisa, and sweet little daughter, Emerald.

■**Beau Hunter** has worked professionally with Apple technologies since 1999 and has supported businesses running the Mac OS for more than 10 years. Throughout this time, he has developed a strong skill set supporting and securing Apple OS X Server in multiple capacities: clustered web and database solutions, cross-platform integration, high-performance SANs, high-capacity backup systems, automation, and cross-platform mass deployment and integration.
Beau has spoken at numerous events, including Macworld 2009, and has been confirmed to speak at Macworld 2010. In his free time he can be found writing Python and PHP, playing PC games, and rooting for the Seattle Seahawks. In November 2009, Beau and his wife, Monica, will be returning to their true home— Seattle, Washington.

■**Zack Smith** has worked as an IT consultant his entire adult life. He has consulted for insurance companies, entertainment companies, medical organizations, and governmental agencies. Zack is an Apple Certified Trainer and as such has taught Apple's Security Best Practices and many other Apple Certified System Administrator–level classes, such Mac OS X Deployment and Mac OS X Directory Services, at Apple and various market centers in Boston, Virginia, Los Angeles, and Cupertino. . Zack has spoken at Macworld San Francisco and at smaller venues as well, such as IT user groups. Zack is the author of a set of open source IT administration software and scripts and has long-term plans to be a full-time Objective-C developer. When not attending IT and security conferences or traveling for work at 318, Zack can be found in Portland, Oregon, with his partner in crime, Anna, and dog, Watson.

About the Technical Reviewers

■**Joe Kissell** is Senior Editor of *TidBITS*, a Web site and e-mail newsletter about the Mac and the Internet, and the author of numerous print and electronic books about Mac software, including *Take Control of Mac OS X Backups* and *Take Control of Upgrading to Snow Leopard*. He is also a Senior Contributor to *Macworld* and was the winner of a 2009 Neal award for Best How-To Article.

Joe has worked in the Mac software industry since the early 1990s and previously managed software development for Nisus Software and Kensington Technology Group. He was named one of MacTech's 25 most influential people in the Mac community for 2007. When not writing about Macs, Joe likes to cook, travel, watch movies, and practice tai chi. He also runs a number of Web sites, including JoeKissell.com and the popular *Interesting Thing of the Day* (itotd.com). Joe lives in Paris with his wife, Morgen Jahnke, and their cat, Zora.

■**Dee-Ann LeBlanc** has been Into computers since she first got her hands on one and shortly after had her first Apple computer. Since then she's done help desk work, technical consulting, computer books and articles, and technology journalism covering a variety of platforms. Her specialties include Linux, open source, OS X, and content management systems.

■**Brad Lees** has more than 12 years of experience in application development and server management. He has specialized in creating and initiating software programs in real estate development systems and financial institutions.

His professional career has been highlighted by his positions as Information Systems Manager at The Lyle Anderson Company of Scottsdale, Arizona; Product Development Manager for Smarsh; Vice President of Product Development for iNation; and Information Technology Manager at The Orcutt/Winslow Partnership, the largest architectural firm in Arizona, based in Phoenix.

A graduate of Arizona State University, Tempe, Brad and his wife, Natalie, reside in Phoenix with their four children.

Acknowledgments

I'd like to first and foremost thank the Mac OS X community. This includes everyone from the people that design the black box to the people that dissect it and finally the people that help others learn to dissect it. We truly stand on the shoulders of giants. Of those at Apple that need to be thanked specifically: Schoun Regan, Joel Rennich, Greg Smith, JD Mankovsky, David Winter, Stale Bjorndal, Cawan Starks, Eric Senf, Jennifer Jones, and of course the one and only Josh Wisenbaker. A special thanks to Randy Saeks for his contribution to the title and to Michael Bartosh without whom any of the directory services content in this title likely would not have been possible. Also, thanks to the crew at 318 for their hard work. Without you guys I would never have been able to take the time to complete this book!

Finally, a special thanks to the fine staff at Apress for tuning this book to be a well-oiled machine of prose and code. This especially includes Clay Andres for getting the book kick-started and, of course, Debra Kelly, the best whip cracker I have had the joy of working with to date. Thanks also to my coauthors, Beau and Zack, for tirelessly working with me to meet our deadlines — it was a fun ride!

Charles S. Edge Jr.

Introduction

In the beginning was the command line. You can automate anything and everything in Mac OS X, but knowledge of the command line will be required to fully automate your deployment and integrate Mac OS X in the enterprise while maintaining a low total cost of ownership. This isn't to say you can't integrate Mac OS X into a large organization en masse without using the command line — you can.However, from automation to troubleshooting, opening up a terminal window will be key to keeping your sanity, if only from time to time. But don't fear the terminal, and know that the fundamental tasks required and the fundamental methodologies with Windows deployments are the same as with Mac OS X.

If you are reading this book, then you are likely charged with integrating Macs into your environment, whether kicking and screaming (which we hope this book will change) or as the sponsor. The message that you take away from this book is hopefully that you can do anything you want to with Mac OS X, from deploying 10,000 machines overnight to building a petabyte worth of storage to house all sorts of data for your Macs, provided you are not averse to learning a little bit of command line to achieve your goals. The power and flexibility of Mac OS X along with the best of the open source community is right at your fingertips to help along the way.

The first question many in IT ask when told about the need to use the command line is, "But isn't Mac OS X supposed to be easy to use." It is. But we're not talking about just using the Mac. We're talking about building and managing a complicated IT infrastructure, which at some point requires staff that is tooled with the mastery of the internals of each platform for which they are tasked as the steward. As such, the more you learn about internals, the more you learn about the basics, the more you can automate, the more you learn about what goes on under the hood, the more you can master management en masse, and, ultimately, the more appropriately you will be able to address issues and concerns on an enterprise-wide scale as they arise. To take this a step further, the more you learn about managing a second platform (no matter what the platform is), the better you will be at managing others. But drastic reduction in Total Cost of Ownership is possible with OS X compared to other platforms for a variety of reasons. And since users are typically happier on a Mac, who wouldn't want a happier user base combined with lower recurring costs.

Paradigm Shifts

Just as when enterprise computing was young, you will need to rethink some of your strategies to accommodate for a wider variety of platforms, resulting in a paradigm shift of sorts. But luckily you are not alone, and the jump is not as bad as many seem to think. There are a number of resources to help you through the process. From web sites to books, from Apple engineers to third-party providers/channel partners, from e-mail lists to user groups, you are not on an island. And while it is not fully open source, the Mac platform is a largely community-driven affair. One of our contributions to that community is this book, where we take on the lofty task of bridging the gap between your enterprise and your Mac.

The fundamentals of designing a Mac-based enterprise are the same as with any other platform — the specifics are not. In any enterprise organization you will need to perform a mass deployment, whether all at once or a refresh cycle performed on an ongoing basis. Every enterprise will also need centralized servers that provide a number of services to hosts on the network, including directory services, shared storage, groupware, and application servers. But the software that provides the needs of an enterprise is often different with the Mac than with other platforms. This isn't to say that the functionality of solutions already in use in many organizations cannot be extended to cover Mac OS X. But in some cases it is going to garner a higher return on investment to prop up an entire infrastructure to support the Mac while in others you are best to leave your existing solutions in place and extend them to the Mac.

Mac OS X is a standards-compliant operating system — to a point. Given the support of a number of standards, Mac OS X can be integrated into a primarily Microsoft environment. This includes support for Active Directory, Exchange support (either through Entourage or natively with ActiveSync), DFS, SMB/CIFS, and NFS. Many Microsoft-centric solutions will work out of the box. But when compared to the features available to Windows-based users, you may find yourself frustrated with integrating systems on a large scale. Users may also be frustrated with certain features that are missing when moving from Mac to Windows. Ultimately some of these features can even result in needing to purchase a third-party solution, deploying a thin client-based solution, or using virtualization solutions to ease the pain of integration, be it temporarily or permanently.

None of these obstacles are insurmountable. Through each release of Mac OS X, the system has become more and more enterprise friendly. And with each subsequent release you can expect that trend to continue. But don't expect to be able to do business as usual; expect to slightly alter your way of thinking to a more open model of computing. That shift toward openness, once you get right down to it, will make the process far easier and far more rewarding and in the end will lead you to a new paradigm in how you deal with enterprise computing.

Measure Twice, Cut Once

This likely goes without saying, but here goes: Before you deploy and integrate on a large scale, test. Before you test, plan. The more you plan, the less work you will ultimately have to do. What do you need to plan for? In our experience, it all starts with directory services. This is why the very first chapter of the book jumps into directory services, and from there we cover further integration in the same order that most organizations build out that infrastructure. It varies between environments, but if you go through each chapter and take into account the technologies introduced, then you will be able to plan more holistically.

Mac OS X is a great platform and suitable for a bevy of uses, but not the right fit for providing a number of network services. Therefore, throughout the book you will find information for integrating with existing infrastructure that may or may not be more suitable given your shift in platforms (however extensive that shift may be). Aside from infrastructure, the Mac systems you are planning to deploy and support require users to be productive on them, something they may not be able to do within the confines of Mac OS X. The book ends with virtualization and thin client solutions that can be leveraged to provide services that otherwise would not be available to the Mac platform.

Application Availability

While the book covers virtualization, the best deployments are going to be those that don't require any applications to be virtualized. If your organization has invested in leveraging a consumer model — a mixture of using cloud services and migrating client-based software into intranets — then the Mac is more likely going to be able to take on your software with ease. But if you are using a number of proprietary products that do not come with a Mac OS X client, then you may need to use some form of virtualization to bridge the gap.

Long term, though, you need a plan to migrate to applications that are cross platform in order to keep the costs for your Mac OS X clients at a minimum. There are a number of sites available to help you find software for the Mac, most notably versiontracker.com. But there will be times when the Mac software is not as advanced or well kept as the Windows versions. This can lead to frustration from end users who possibly once championed the platform. In this case you may have to virtualize the software or an entire operating system in order to achieve parity. But this is where testing on a per-group basis will become key to planning your deployment.

When testing, make sure each user in your pilot thoroughly tests each piece of software. Find the biggest power users in a group and ask them to be your testers. Their voices will often be heard the loudest when things don't go well. But if you can keep them involved in the process and communicate with them along the way, once you achieve success you will often have the best proponent you could ask for.

How This Book Is Organized

Sandwiched between chapters on directory services and virtualization there are a variety of other topics that have been near and dear to organizations big and small as they grapple with integrating Mac OS X. These topics have been broken down into a number of chapters, each playing a critical role and requiring specialized planning. A summary of the chapters, aimed at guiding your planning and deployment:

Chapter 1 - **Directory Services** is a critical aspect of Mac OS X integration. In this chapter we cover how to set up a directory services environment using Open Directory, Apple's own directory service solution. Whether you are an Active Directory environment, eDirectory, or some other variant of a supported directory service, you will need to become acquainted with the fundamentals of implementing Open Directory. Additionally, Open Directory can be leveraged to work with Active Directory, providing a compelling framework for policy management.

Chapter 2 - **Directory Services Clients** are as critical as directory services themselves. In this chapter, the focus is on how to configure the directory services client from the command line, allowing you to deploy complex and automated binding scripts. The script examples provided with Chapter 2 will, at a minimum, help to get any mass deployment of Mac OS X in motion, saving a considerable amount of time and giving a glance into best practices that can be applied to further automation topics that will arise throughout the book.

Chapter 3 - **Active Directory** deserves a dedicated chapter. Why? The binding process, while part of the directory services framework, is considerably different than that of the other directory services modules. The third-party solutions, requirements, roadblocks to a successful integration, and the methodology are just that different from the other directory services modules. These differences should show the considerable amount of development taken on by Apple in order to provide such a feature-rich Active Directory solution.

Chapter 4 - **Storage** is a requirement for any business. Sure, some pundits say that eventually storage will all be in the cloud, but it's not yet. And you need to automatically mount, log into, and configure storage in such a way that your Mac clients can connect to it, use it for home directories, synchronize it, and even share it out themselves if need be.

Chapter 5 - **Messaging and Groupware** mean productivity. In this chapter we look at the options for typing your Mac OS X clients into shared groupware services hosted on Microsoft Exchange and Mac OS X Server. We also look into implementing groupware-oriented policies in the environment and automatically configuring groupware applications as part of your deployment process.

Chapter 6 - **Mass Deployment**. Whether it's imaging, deploying the image, or automating the tasks that enable you to be closer and closer to the one-touch image, this chapter is all about providing a step-by-step process to accomplishing these tasks. However, over the past few years a number of solutions have emerged to make mass deployment infinitely easier for administrators. Therefore, of the tasks we follow through the steps, we will use a different solution for each, allowing you to see a spectrum of options.

Chapter 7 - Mac OS X has a rich **Client Management** framework. In this chapter we look at local and directory services–based deployments of policies and explore the options for extending existing solutions to cover client management.

Chapter 8 - By **Automating Administrative Tasks**, you as an IT professional (or the manager of an IT professional) will be freed up to take on enhancing how your business interacts with technology (or you'll learn to fish, sleep nights, etc.). In this chapter we take a deep look into scripting and other forms of automation. This is where mastery of the command can become absolutely critical.

Chapter 9 - **iPhones** are cool. They're popular and gaining a considerable footprint in the enterprise space, given the penchant for synchronizing with Microsoft Exchange and the robust Objective-C development platform. But how do you deploy and manage thousands of the things? And while you're doing that, how do you use the features for connecting to standard enterprise application sets? In this chapter we help you get there and introduce you to some tools and techniques to ease the burden.

Chapter 10 - **Virtualization**. You just can't do everything on the Mac that you can do in Windows XP, Windows 7, Linux, or any other operating systems you can think of. Therefore, we give you a whole chapter of virtualization and thin client best practices and deployment techniques to ease the burden of your now doubled operating system footprint if you embark on this convoluted journey.

Chaos Theory

There is no magic bullet for your deployment. Most environments are going to be different in some way, shape, or form from every other environment out there. But provided there is industry-standard infrastructure (and most vendors have long since moved into providing industry standards) then rest assured that there is some way to make your Mac clients integrate fairly seamlessly into the enterprise. Therefore, while we don't have a magic bullet to offer, we do have a plethora of options for a given situation, options you can use to cut costs, reduce required human capital, and free up IT staff for creating value to businesses rather than living in the IT cost center.

## Chapter 1

Directory Services

A **directory service** is the software that stores, organizes, and provides access to information in a directory. In the context that we will use the term throughout this book, we mean a database of users, groups, computers, and network devices such as printers. The directory service supplies that database to client computers. In most enterprise, educational, and larger institutions, common directory service implementations range from Microsoft's Active Directory (AD) to Novell's eDirectory, as well as the open source Open LDAP. Most modern directory services are based on standards developed in the public forum.

The most common standard architectural guidelines are defined in the X.500 model "The Directory: Overview of concepts, models and services." While the concepts and roots of most directories are complex, by their very nature they share the simple goal of unified user management, authentication, and authorization. Directory servers with different origins thus find many commonalities in their structure and accessibility. The Lightweight Directory Access Protocol (LDAP), which is utilized by nearly every major directory service system, is a testament to this need for accessibility, as we will discuss later in this chapter. Put simply, any system engineered for large-scale centralized authentication must inherently allow disparate clients to participate, otherwise it is doomed to a finite growth potential.

In Mac OS X, there are a number of plug-ins that allow you to leverage a variety of different directory services. Each computer must at least contain a local directory service database to establish a baseline of system-critical data, such as users, groups, and even some configuration data. If every Mac OS X computer sold required an enterprise directory service just to login, Apple stores would not be popping up like Starbucks in cities around the United States. Local authentication is a cornerstone of all modern operating systems, and often the gateway for small and medium businesses to grow into larger directory systems over time. A common misconception is that Apple's *Open Directory* terminology is applied only to its enterprise-class authentication services. In reality, the same term refers to those local or client standards implemented in local accounts. In fact, in previous operating systems, Apple even had the same technology running on Open Directory masters, such as 10.2 netinfod and 10.3 Password Server. This concept of architecting what amounts to miniature directory servers into the base operating system allows for later migration to larger directory service systems without much reeducation of entry-level system administrators. The best example of this is Apple's parental controls system that, at its base, leverages the same technology used to manage thousands of Mac OS X in enterprise environments every day. Due to such forethought, clients can also be configured out of the box to utilize a variety of other external directory services; support for several network-based directory service systems is provided without the installation of any additional software.

This chapter starts with an explanation of how the local directory service works. Once we have explained how local users can be managed, we will move on to discuss LDAP, the industry-standard directory database used to supply directory services. Next, we will cover various types of binding to directory servers from Mac OS X that let end users log into their computers using a centralized username and password. Finally, we will look at building external accounts and show how to build a directory service based on Apple's Open Directory.

Local Accounts

In Mac OS X, System Preferences are similar to Control Panel in Windows, and they allow you to configure a wide range of settings. The information you set in these panes is stored in files throughout the operating system. Local directory service configuration is accessed through the Accounts preference pane, which provides the ability to add local user and group accounts. Accounts can also be added to groups, assigned a type, and a few other options can be set.

To access a System Preferences pane, click on the Apple in the top left corner of the screen and then on System Preferences, or launch the application directly from the /Applications folder. You will then be shown all of the System Preferences available. Next, click on Accounts and you'll see the list of Accounts on the left side of the screen. As you click through each one, you will see the options for that account on the right side of the screen. To make changes in this area, you must first authenticate to System Preferences by clicking on the lock in the lower left corner of the Preferences window. For the authentication to succeed, the user must be a member of the local directory service's admin group.

> **TIP:** The /etc/authorization file is used to determine which users are able to attain elevated privileges for a variety of operations. In a standard OS X environment, the admin group will be able to obtain escalation for all authorization rights. However, this file can be modified to provide very granular administrative access to users. For instance, to manage users via the System Preference pane, a non-admin group could be specified under system.preferences.accounts, which would then give its members administrative access solely to the Accounts pane of System Preferences.

Creating Accounts

To add an account, first click on the lock icon in the Accounts System Preferences pane, then click on the plus sign to create an account. In the Account: field you'll see the five options shown in Figure 1-1, which indicate the basic account types for Mac OS X. These include:

- Administrator: Administrative accounts, accounts with elevated privileges; can open System Preference panes and perform most tasks.

- Standard: Standard User accounts; cannot open System Preference panes and cannot perform administrative tasks.

- Managed With Parental Controls: Standard User accounts with policies applied to them.

- Sharing Only: Accounts that cannot log onto the local system but can access resources via file sharing protocols.

- Group: A group of user accounts.

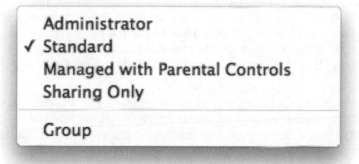

Figure 1-1. *Contextual menu for account types*

Once you have selected an account type, enter a full name in the Name: field and a short name in the Short Name: field. For example, the full name might be John Doe and the short name jdoe. By default, the short name is generated from the full name in lower case with spaces removed. The full name is primarily used for display purposes and can be changed at will. The short name has additional system-level functions. Notably, it is used to name a user's home directory when first created, though that directory can be changed to a different location that does not correspond to the short name (such as a "mystuff" folder on a external drive).

The short name is used for other purposes as well, such as establishing a primary email mailbox for the user or for linking scheduled items through cron. Because of this, setting the initial short name demands some consideration. It's also worth noting that the short name cannot easily be edited in the prominent user interface, and though right-clicking on a user account and choosing Advanced Options allows you to edit this name (as seen in Figure 1-3), doing so has other repercussions, such as loss of group membership (such as admin); possible loss of preference data if an application stores configuration data based on the short name; or disassociation of the user's home folder. In most cases when you plan to modify a user's short name, you will also want to rename his home directory to coincide. This is merely for cosmetic reasons and is not a necessity. You can change short name jdoe to psherman and still utilize the original home directory stored at /Users/jdoe. If you do change the home directory to /Users/psherman, you should make sure you rename the user's home folder on the file system to match the new path specified (in this case, from the original home directory value /Users/jdoe to /Users/psherman).

Next, enter the password the user will use in the Password: field and then enter it again into the Verify: field. The small key icon in this dialog box will reveal the Password Assistant, an interface that assists users with choosing strong passwords by supplying them with visual feedback. This functionality is available as a stand-alone program using third party applications available on the Internet, and can also be accessed via the Keychain Access application when you create a new password item. Optionally, you can enter a hint as to what the password is in the Password Hint: field. If a password hint is set for a user, it will be displayed when the user fails to authenticate when logging in. Here you can also check the box to enable FileVault, which encrypts the contents of the user's profile or home folder.

When you are satisfied with your settings, click on the Create Account button. You have now created your first Mac OS X user. If you are done making changes, you should close the lock options available in the Security system preference pane, which will cause the System Preference to forget your previous authentication each time the application is reopened during your timed session. Alternatively, if you forget to close the lock, the elevated privileges will time out.

Granting Administrative Privileges

As noted earlier, you can choose to make a user an administrator of the local computer when you create an account. To elevate an existing account to an administrative account, you can simply check the Allow user to administer this computer checkbox, as shown in Figure 1-2. To set up basic policies for an account, you can click on the Open Parental Controls button for any non-administrator account and enable them. (We will cover more in-depth policies on local and network directory services accounts further in Chapter 7, Client Management.)

Figure 1-2. *Making a user an administrator*

As mentioned previously, you can also edit some slightly more advanced settings from within the Accounts System Preference pane. These settings are accessible by control-clicking on the account name and then clicking on Advanced Options, which brings up a screen similar to the one in Figure 1-3. This screen lets you change the values for various attributes of the accounts, including Short Name, User ID, default group, path to the home folder, default shell and the generated ID for the account. You can also add aliases using the plus sign; this allows the same account to authenticate using multiple names in the authentication dialogs throughout the operating system. We will discuss these attributes later in the chapter.

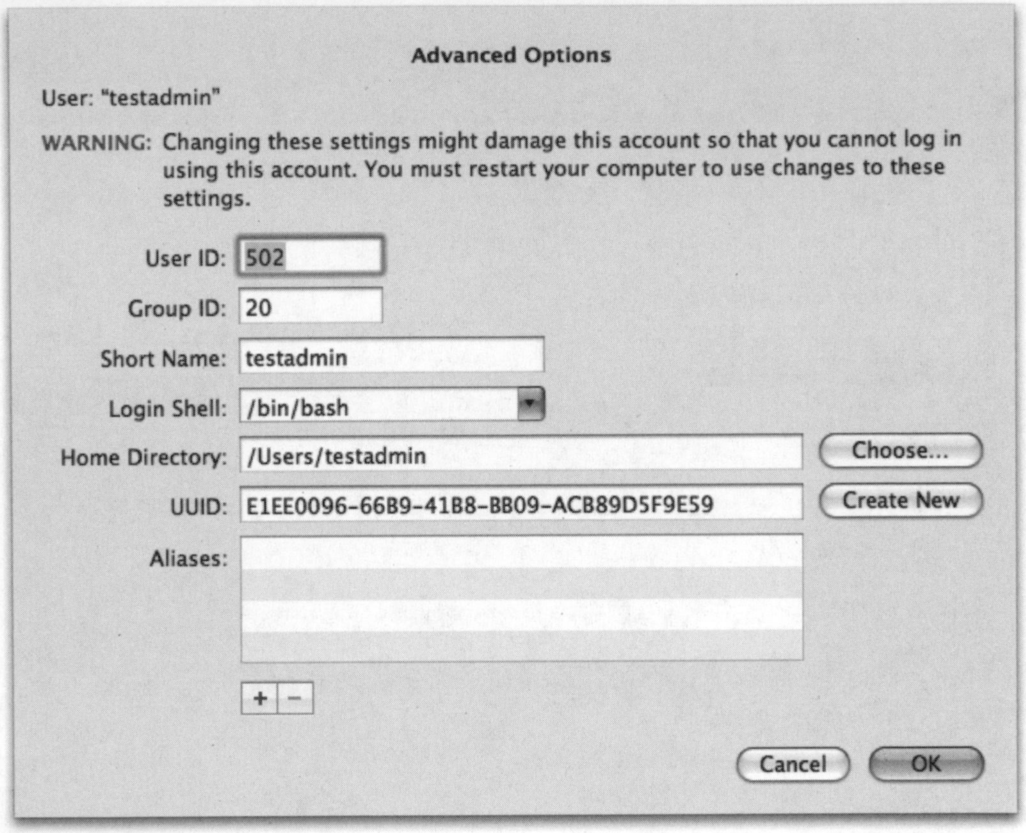

Figure 1-3. *Advanced account options*

The Root Account

In a Unix, BSD, or other *nix environments, the root account can do things that even standard administrators typically can't do. A root account can be a security risk, which is why Apple has disabled root by default, but it is an account you may find you need to enable from time to time. If you are new to administering Mac OS X from the command line, you may wish to enable the root account for certain GUI operations that would otherwise use the command line, such as renaming a home folder or editing a configuration file owned by root.

To enable the root account, open the Directory Utility application found on the Accounts pane of System Preferences (version 10.6), or in the /Applications/Utilities folder (version 10.5). As with most secure operations in Mac OS X, you will need to authenticate to perform this action using the lock in the corner of this window. Then click on the Edit menu and select Enable Root User, which will display the screen shown in Figure 1-4. Next, enter the password that will be assigned to the root user and click on OK.

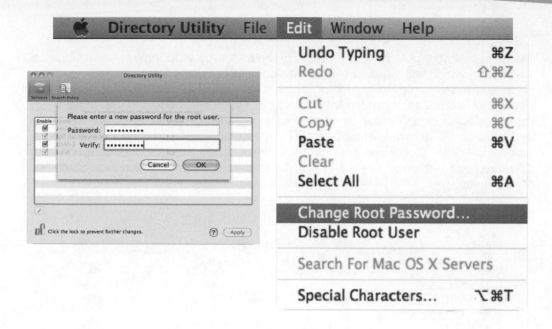

Figure 1-4. *Enabling Root in Directory Utility*

You can also enable the root account using the command line. The dsenableroot command can be used to enable the root user and assign it a password. To enable root, enter:

dsenableroot

First you will be prompted for the current user password; this user must be an administrative account. You will then be prompted twice, first for a password to assign the root account and then to verify the password. On success you'll see the following success code:

dsenableroot:: ***Successfully enabled root user.

To disable the root account, enter:

dsenableroot -d

TIP: It is best to leave the root account disabled when you do not need it. If you do enable it, do so only temporarily.

How the Local Directory Service Works

The local directory data resides primarily in the folder found at /private/var/db/dslocal. This folder, which will require elevated privileges to access, contains numerous files pertaining to the computer's directory service configuration. For instance, accounts for Users and Groups are stored in flat property list (.plist) files nested in the /private/var/db/dslocal/nodes/Default directory. Users are stored in /private/var/db/dslocal/nodes/Default/users while groups are stored in /private/var/db/dslocal/nodes/Default/groups. Every local user and group account has a corresponding .plist file found in these directories, as seen in Figure 1-5, which shows the contents of /private/var/db/dslocal/nodes/Default/.

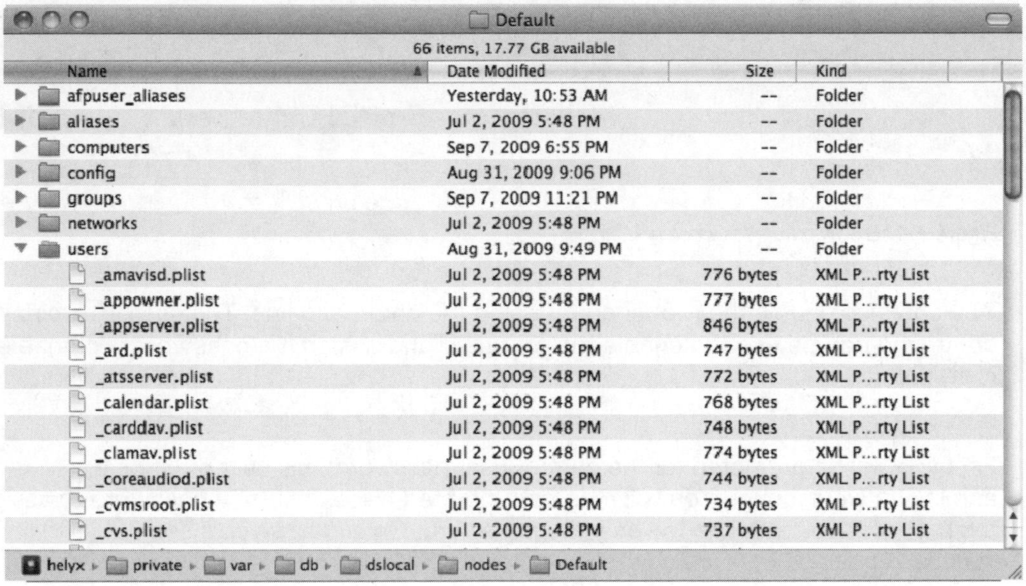

Figure 1-5. *Contents of a dslocal node*

The above output is trimmed, but each folder will contain a plist file for each respective user, computer, or group in the local directory. Accounts that begin with an underscore (_) are hidden service users and groups. For example, the web server uses the_www account, which obtains user settings from the _www.plist file. The _www user can't log in because the account has no shell or password. If you created a new user in the above section, look in the /private/var/db/dslocal/nodes/Default/users directory and you should see a .plist file with a name that corresponds to the new user's short name.

Inside a .plist file there are a number of attributes containing data about a given user or group. Looking at local users and groups from a Microsoft Windows perspective, files in the local directory node resemble registry keys for local accounts. Examine the .plist file for the user created earlier and look for the key called authentication_authority.

```
<key>authentication_authority</key>
<array>
                    <string>;ShadowHash;</string>
</array>
```

This key specifies the service that will be utilized to authenticate the user. Notice that it says ShadowHash, which indicates that the system will use a local file called a hash file to authenticate the user. Mac OS X password hash files contain copies of a user's password in multiple formats; this Rosetta Stone allows for different services to authenticate a user with their own native password encryption type. If this were not the case, the password would need to be stored in a much less secure reversible hash in order to support the various authentication schemes out there. It also should be noted that for ShadowHash users, any network service that does not support SHA-1 (Secure Hash Algorithm 1) or NTLM (NT LAN Manager) authentication will require cleartext authentication; SSL is highly recommended in these scenarios.

In the user's plist file, you will also see a generateduid key, which is used to track the user account even if the short name is changed. GeneratedUIDs are based on a standard called the Universally Unique IDentifier (UUID), which is a complex, programmatically generated string of characters that will never be duplicated in our lifetime. A UUID is unique across time and space for every user.

If you look in the /private/var/db/shadow/hash directory, you will find a file that is named using the value of this key. This means that even if a user account's username is changed, the password will still be tied to that account. Moreover, it prevents stale password files from collecting, which would happen if passwords were based on the short name. In 10.4 and later, the password hash file will contain at least a SHA-1 salted hash for the user, which is a secure, unrecoverable password type. If Windows file-sharing services are enabled for the user, it will also contain the respective NTLM hash for that user, which is used by our Windows file-sharing components. Apple has struggled to implement the best balance of security and functionality in regard to password hashes. While hashes for Windows file sharing require NTLM, the NTLM hash type is more susceptible to common password attacks, which makes its recoverability more feasible. Apple only enables the NTLM hash when Windows file-sharing users are specifically configured for SMB/Windows sharing access in the System Preferences Sharing pane. Storing passwords in a hash file allows for a consistent password file location, with flexible extensibility for other password hashes such as NTLM. In the above example, the authentication_authority record, which has a value of ;ShadowHash;, tells the local directory service to consult the user's local hash file when the user attempts to authenticate.

The data from the account property lists can be managed by modifying the text files directly. For example, if you want to change a user's picture, you could alter the picture key. However, editing property lists directly can be pretty cumbersome, so Apple has provided a host of commands that can be used to manage and query data from the local directory node and other directory services plug-ins without having to read raw XML-style property list data. Some commands have GUI equivalents while others do not. Here are some of the commands:

- dirt: used to test authentication in 10.4 and 10.5, tests authentication, for example dirt -u zsmith -p 'd0gc4t'. The only GUI equivalent would be the login window or an authentication screen. As of 10.6, the dirt utility is no more; the dscl utility now performs this role.

- dscacheutil: looks up information stored in the Directory Services cache and flush various caches

- dscl: used to edit and browse directory services settings, such as user accounts, group accounts, and search policies (the order in which Mac OS X looks up account information in each directory service). The closest GUI equivalents would be the Accounts System Preference pane and the Directory Utility. This command is covered in more depth in the next section.

- dseditgroup: used to edit, create, and delete groups or to add or remove group members.

- dsenableroot: manages the root user account (enable, disable, and reset the root password). The GUI equivalents are the Change Root Password and Enable Root User or Disable Root User options in the Edit menu of Directory Utility.

- dserr: prints a description of Directory Services-related errors, example dserr 14090. Once you have the error code, you can use the man page for DirectoryService to look up the meaning of each error (or Google for more information on the specific errors, but quote errors if there is a – in front of the number).

- dsexport: exports directory services data. Similar functionality is available using the Export feature of Workgroup Manager, a tool distributed as part of Mac OS X Server.

- dsimport: imports directory services data. Similar functionality is available using the Import feature of Workgroup Manager.

- dsmemberutil: looks up UUIDs and group information and flush group cache, for example dsmemberutil flushcache.

- dsperfmonitor: run performance monitors of the directory services plugin, useful with debugging operations, for example dsperfmonitor -dump.

- id: look up a user identity, including group memberships, for example id zsmith.

You can learn more about these commands by viewing their manual pages using the "man" command line program. For instance, the following command looks up the manual page for the dscl tool:

```
man dscl
```

For more information about the command line, use their manual pages—that is, man "command".

In many enterprises, one of the first differences that cross-platform administrators notice is that by default, domain administrators from a directory service are not administrators of local Mac OS X client computers (although, as we illustrate in Chapter 3, Active Directory, you can make Enterprise Admins or any other group administrators of Mac OS X clients). To mimic this functionality, it is possible to nest a network directory service group inside of the local administrators group, thereby granting local administrator rights to all network members of that group. This is very handy in large environments where administrator access may need to be limited to subsets of administrators. This technique is covered in more detail in Chapter 7, Client Management.

While we recommend having all of your admins use their own unique network credentials for administrative tasks, it is always recommended to maintain at least a single dedicated local administrative account on Mac OS X systems to ensure that you always have administrative access to your client nodes. To create these local administrative accounts, you can use the Setup Assistant or the Accounts System Preference pane. This is common in monolithic imaging environments (imaging is covered further in Chapter 6, Mass Deployment), but it's not entirely scalable in most cases. You can also use dscl in a scripted fashion.

dscl

For a number of tasks, dscl is the gateway to directory services. This can include viewing existing information from local or network directory services, augmenting settings for the local directory service node, or altering how the directory services daemon functions, Including the priority that is given to each directory domain, or entry in a plug-in.

From an enterprise management perspective, perhaps the most useful aspect of dscl is that it can be used to automate account creation and editing. To create a local account using the command line (and thus be able to script the process), dscl is the preferred command. Dscl is an interactive tool that can, in its simplest form, be used by simply typing dscl at a command-line prompt. To see all of the directory services plug-ins that are enabled on the system, type ls at the prompt:

```
> ls
Active Directory
BSD
Local
Search
Contact
```

You can use `dscl` as any given user if you're only interested in reading account information. However, in order to alter the contents of a database, you will need elevated privileges. To invoke `dscl` with elevated privileges, prepend the command with `sudo` as follows:

```
sudo dscl
```

The `sudo` command can be prepended to any command to force it to run with root privileges. When using `sudo`, you will be prompted for the currently logged-in user's password, and that user must be an administrator. The `sudo` command will cache credentials for 5 minutes after successful authentication, so if you have recently used it, you will not need to retype your password.

At this point, you should be in an interactive command-line environment and see a > on the screen, so we'll prepend each command with a > so that our screen matches yours. The first step in the process of creating a new account is to add a user to the database, which will create a new .plist file for the account. This can be done with the –create `dscl` command followed by the path to the record being created. In the following example, we will create an empty account called *corpadmin*.

```
> -create /Local/Default/Users/corpadmin
```

A property list is made up of keys. In the above example, we did not specify any keys. The `dscl` command created the record and, therefore, a file in the form of the corpadmin.plist file has manifested in /var/db/dslocal/nodes/Default/users. In order for the corpadmin account to be viable, we now need to create a number of keys that tell the directory services daemon about this user. These keys make up the attributes for the account. A list of commonly used user attributes can be seen in Table 1-1.

Table 1-1. *Basic User Attributes*

Attribute	Purpose
UniqueID	An integer id unique to this user.
PrimaryGroupID	Denotes the primary group of the user.
GeneratedUID	A universally unique identifier for the user.
NFSHomeDirectory	Absolute path to the user's home directory.
RealName	The user's full name.
RecordName	The user's short name.
UserShell	The user's default shell.

To create our own user by hand, we will need to assemble the required attributes, let's enter what in the Account add screen from the Accounts System Preference pane would be the Name: field: *RealName*. We will use the –create the key to do this. Because there is a space in our name, let's put what will go into the record in quotes:

```
> -create /Local/Default/Users/corpadmin RealName "Corporate Administrator"
```

Next, we'll give our user a User ID using the UniqueID key. This ID should be unique (as the name implies), and so no other accounts should have the same ID. We will again use the –create command:

```
> -create /Local/Default/Users/corpadmin UniqueID 1500
```

Now we'll set up a Default Group ID (GID), which has an attribute of PrimaryGroupID. We're going to set the PrimaryGroupID to the Staff group, which has a group number of 20:

```
> -create /Local/Default/Users/corpadmin PrimaryGroupID 20
```

> **CAUTION:** As with most things that happen at the command line, dscl is unforgiving with regard to typos, including spaces, and so on. But it does support tabbed auto-completion, which is awesome.

We also need to give the account a default shell to use if it is going to do anything meaningful. The default shell is the shell used when a Terminal.app window is first opened. The attribute for a default shell is UserShell. The contents of this key should be any shell on the system, including /bin/zsh, /bin/tcsh, or the default with Mac OS X, /bin/bash. To prevent users from utilizing a shell account, assign /usr/bin/false as their shell, which will immediately terminate any attempts at a shell session, as well as disable access to the terminal application. This also prevents an account from logging in via loginwindow, in which case /usr/bin/true is a completely acceptable substitute. To set the shell attribute, create the UserShell key using the following command:

```
> -create /Local/Default/Users/corpadmin UserShell /bin/bash
```

Every user needs a home directory. Even the root account has one (/var/root by default). The home directory doesn't need to reference a path that currently exists as the first time the user logs into a system the home directory will be created and assigned appropriate permissions. The attribute for the home directory is NFSHomeDirectory:

```
> -create /Local/Default/Users/corpadmin NFSHomeDirectory /Users/corpadmin
```

Because we're creating an administrative user, we also need to add the account to the admin group. Here, we'll use the –append dscl command rather than –create because we're augmenting an existing key rather than creating one. We'll follow it with the relative path of the admin group and then the attribute that we'll be editing and finally the payload of the actual edit. To add the corpadmin user to the administrative users group:

```
> -append /Local/Default/Groups/admin GroupMembership corpadmin
```

> **TIP:** If you know the value of an attribute, it is best to use the –merge option here; if you don't, you can use –append.

Next you'll give your new user a password using the `passwd` option, typing a password once the following command is run:

```
> -passwd /Local/Default/Users/corpadmin
```

By now, the account should be listed in the local directory service. To make sure, we'll use the `-list` option:

```
> -list /Local/Default/Users
```

Once the account has been recognized by the local directory services node, you can look at information that was not in the original property list, such as the GeneratedUID, using `dscl`:

```
> -read /Local/Default/Users/corpadmin GeneratedUID
```

The `dscl` command is also very useful in troubleshooting. In the above command we were looking for a specific attribute, but if we wanted to see all of the attributes for our new corpadmin account we could simply run the following:

```
> -read /Local/Default/Users/corpadmin
```

Changing Accounts En Masse

If you have `ssh` or Apple Remote Desktop (ARD) access, you can push out a variety of changes to an account. Once an account has been created, any of the attributes can be changed en masse, using `dscl`. For example, if you wanted to reset the corpadmin password to MYSECRETPASSWORD, the following command could be sent to each machine in your enterprise:

```
sudo dscl . -passwd /Users/corpadmin MYSECRETPASSWORD
```

> **NOTE:** If you change the password as a non-administrative user, you need to enter the actual user's password to do so.

Or if you wanted to move the user's home folder into the /var directory (so it can live with and be friends with root), you could use the following (assuming you put the original home folder into /Users/corpadmin):

```
sudo dscl . -change /Users/corpadmin NFSHomeDirectory /Users/corpadmin /var/corpadmin
```

Notice that in the above command we used the -change dscl command rather than -edit. Also notice that in both of these examples, we used dscl along with the . operator rather than using dscl interactively. By using the . operator, we ended up with a different relative path to the user record; it is a shortcut to the Local/Default node. The attribute then appears as:

```
NFSHomeDirectory: /var/corpadmin
```

Account Creation Scripts

New accounts can also be created using scripts. These scripts will also leverage dscl, along with the . operator (no point in complicating things by trying to script against an interactive command-line environment). To get started, let's create a script called adduser.sh on our desktop, and then take the commands we used in the above section to create our user attributes and put them into a script, replacing the > with dscl . and removing /Local/Default:

```
#!/bin/bash
user="corpadmin"
dscl . -create /Users/$user
dscl . -create /Users/$user RealName "Corporate Administrator"
dscl . -create /Users/$user UniqueID 1100
dscl . -create /Users/$user PrimaryGroupID 20
dscl . -create /Users/$user NFSHomeDirectory /Users/corpadmin
dscl . -create /Users/$user UserShell /bin/bash
dscl . -passwd /Users/$user 'MYSECRETPASSWORD'
```

There is a serious problem with the above script: it has the administrative password in it. To get around this, you can also create an account by copying the authentication files, which contain the hashed password, directly to the client system.

Parachuting Accounts into Clients

Next, we're going to look at what we call performing a *file drop* to create a user account. File drops are when we simply copy files into appropriate directories to achieve a task. In this example, we're going to take an administrative account we created on our own system, using either the command line or the Accounts System Preferences pane. We're going to grab the .plist file that makes up the account and the password file from /var/db/dslocal/nodes/Default, and then take the corresponding password hash for the account from /var/db/shadow/hash; (The name of that hash, remember, is based on the generated UID.) We'll simply copy all of these to the same destinations folders on the client that they were in at the source (the .plist file goes into the /var/db/dslocal/nodes/Default/users directory and the password hash file goes into the /var/db/shadow/hash directory of the target hosts).

Since we've been using `dscl`, the directory services daemon has been keeping track of our actions. However, if we aren't using `dscl` and we're file-dropping an account, we either need to wait for the next restart on the system or restart the directory services daemon. To restart the daemon, use the `killall` command with the pattern of DirectoryService:

```
sudo killall DirectoryService
```

Hiding Administrative Accounts

Hiding an administrative account can help keep users in organizations from tampering with or disabling user accounts, and help maintain a secure channel for administrators to remotely administer the system. There are a variety of ways to obscure the presence of an administrative account in Mac OS X. For example if the only admin account on a Mac OS X client is Administrator with Admin as the short name (case sensitive), then the admin account won't show up at the login window. However, it will not be hidden in the Accounts System Preference pane. If you have multiple admin accounts, you can suppress them from the login window by adding them to the HiddenUsersList array in com.apple.loginwindow.plist, using the following command:

```
defaults write /Library/Preferences/com.apple.loginwindow HiddenUsersList -array-add ↵
mysecretadmin
```

You can also simply file-drop a new com.apple.loginwindow.plist file into /Library/Preferences/com.apple.loginwindow.plist.

But these methods simply suppress the admin account from a list of users at login, and don't truly hide the account. Here's another way to hide the accounts. You can set the any user's account (either existing or new) with a Unique ID of any integer below 500. To create a new admin user, you can copy an existing user from /var/db/dslocal/nodes/Default/users and alter the NFSHomeDirectory, RealName, and UniqueID keys to be unique (not that a home directory has to be unique, but it should be. And, as noted, the new UniqueID should be an integer below 500 in order to be hidden). You could also create a new account called `secrethiddenuser` with a password of `secrethiddenuserspassword` using `dscl`, with the following script:

```
#!/bin/bash

dscl . -create /Users/secrethiddenuser

dscl . -create /Users/secrethiddenuser RealName "Hidden Admin"

dscl . -create /Users/secrethiddenuser NFSHomeDirectory /Users/hidden

dscl . -create /Users/secrethiddenuser UserShell /bin/bash

dscl . -create /Users/secrethiddenuser UniqueID 150
```

```
dscl . -create /Users/secrethiddenuser PrimaryGroupID 20
```

```
dscl . -passwd /Users/secrethiddenuser 'secrethiddenuserspassword'
```

Although this will create a new, hidden user account, it is fairly straightforward to view the contents of the /var/db/dslocal/nodes/Default/users directory and look for files that are neither listed in the accounts System Preference pane nor included with a default install of Mac OS (including _amavisd, _amavisd, _appowner, _appserver, _ard, _atsserver, _calendar, _clamav, _cvs, _cyrus, _devdocs, _eppc, _installer, _jabber, _lp, _mailman, _mcxalr, _mdnsresponder, _mysql, _pcastagent, _pcastserver, _postfix, _qtss, _sandbox, _securityagent, _serialnumberd, _spotlight, _sshd, _svn, _teamsserver, _tokend, _unknown, _update_sharing, _usbmuxd, _uucp, _windowserver, _www, _xgridagent, _xgridcontroller, daemon, nobody, root and the default user applications).

Some will choose to create a hidden user account in an entirely separate directory services node. This can be done by copying the current directory services node (/var/db/dslocal/nodes/Default) into a new folder located in /var/db/dslocal/nodes, and then restarting the DirectoryService daemon (killall DirectoryService). After restarting DirectoryService, use Directory Utility to specify a custom search path, and then add the new node. This can also be done using dscl to alter the /Search node). The downside of creating a new directory services node is that it is fairly straightforward to find the node's information using Directory Utility, and if you are attempting to be a stealthy admin, you have just increased the surface space of your hidden account.

Raw Mode

If you edit the directory services daemon while it is not running (for example, if you're scripting against a bare-metal system for future imaging), you will need to do so in raw mode, specified by the flag -f. Raw mode allows you to specify the location of the directory services domain that you will be working against, useful when working against any non-running systems programmatically. Thus the commands would become the following:

```
VOL=/Volumes/newimagehd
dscl -f "$VOL/var/db/dslocal/Nodes/Default" -raw . -create /Users/corpadmin
dscl -f "$VOL/var/db/dslocal/Nodes/Default" -raw . -create RealName "Corporate Admin"
dscl -f "$VOL/var/db/dslocal/Nodes/Default" -raw . -create NFSHomeDirectory
/Users/corpadmin
dscl -f "$VOL/var/db/dslocal/Nodes/Default" -raw . -create UserShell /bin/bash
dscl -f "$VOL/var/db/dslocal/Nodes/Default" -raw . -create UniqueID 1500
dscl -f "$VOL/var/db/dslocal/Nodes/Default" -raw . -create PrimaryGroupID 1500
dscl -f "$VOL/var/db/dslocal/Nodes/Default" -raw . -passwd corpadmin
MYUBERSECRETPASSWORD
```

Set Search Paths

The Search Path in Mac OS X client can be used to define where your system can search for directory services information, whether local or shared. The search policy defines which directory services nodes will be searched and in what order. To set the search path, you need to switch from LSPSearchPath to CSPSearchPath for your SearchPolicy. To do so, use the following command:

```
sudo dscl /Search -change / SearchPolicy dsAttrTypeStandard:LSPSearchPath ↵
dsAttrTypeStandard:CSPSearchPath
```

To switch back to using only a local policy, just run the following command:

```
sudo dscl /Search -change / SearchPolicy dsAttrTypeStandard:CSPSearchPath ↵
dsAttrTypeStandard:LSPSearchPath
```

Create Additional Local Directory Nodes

The local directory service is not limited to one directory tree to store property lists. You can have a number of different directory trees, much like you can bind to a number of different directory services. This opens up the ability to not only hide an administrative user from the GUI but also to hide that user from those who might not realize how to traverse multiple local directory nodes. Moreover, it allows you to store a directory node on a shared volume or external disk (which would, of course, error when those are not reachable and would not have the flexibility of an actual network-based directory service).

First, we'll make a copy of the local directory services information store we've been working on throughout this chapter. For the following example, we'll copy it into the same nodes folder that Mac OS X uses by default, but rather than call our node Default, we'll call it NEW:

```
sudo cp -prnv /var/db/dslocal/nodes/Default /var/db/dslocal/nodes/NEW
```

The DirectoryService daemon will look in the nodes directory for any newly created nodes when it is started up. So let's go ahead and restart the daemon with the following:

```
sudo killall DirectoryService
```

Now open up Directory Utility.app and click on the Search Policy tab, authenticate using the lock in the lower left hand corner of the screen, and then change the Search: field to *Custom path*, as shown in Figure 1-6.

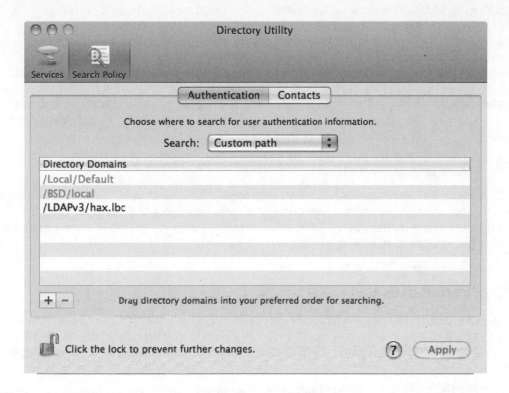

Figure 1-6. *Changing the Search Path*

Next, click on the add icon (indicated by a +) and then add NEW from the list of available directories. The Default node will always be first in the search path and can't be removed. If accounts happen to be in multiple nodes, the one that appears higher in the Search Policy will be authenticated first. Therefore, keep in mind that if you have an account called corpadmin in your Default local directory service node, one in Active Directory (which we will cover in Chapter 3), and one in your secondary local directory service node, the one in the Default directory service node will always be utilized for lookups and authentication; the other nodes will never be consulted.

External Accounts

External Accounts are similar to Mobile Accounts (which we will cover in Chapter 7). Beyond the fact that the home directory resides on external media, the account operates like a standard account, with the addition of an .account file.

Creating an external account is facilitated by the createmobileaccount command. So rather than letting the operating system decide whether it wants to invoke the createmobileaccount dialog at the loginwindow, we're going to force the issue by manually running the command, which is located in /System/Library/Coreservices/ManagedClient.app/Contents/Resources directory. Note that this is not in your default PATH, meaning you must always type the full path to the command or modify your shell preferences. The -n, -p and -h flags define the username, password and home directory of the account. So assuming your USB drive is called JUMPDRIVE, the following would create an external account on the USB drive:

```
./createmobileaccount -n mobileadmin -p 'MYSECRETPASSWORD' -h ↵
/Volumes/JUMPDRIVE/Users/mobileadmin
```

At this point we're pretty much done. We could also have enabled FileVault by using the -e flag and/or run the command verbosely (great for troubleshooting issues during account creation) by using the –v flag. Now, use ls –al to verify that your new external account can write to the volume.

Open Directory

Open Directory is the network directory services implementation that is native to Mac OS X. Mac OS X Server leverages a number of open source products with a little bit of Apple's special sauce to form Open Directory. Open Directory provides client systems with a centralized location for accounts, passwords, mount points, and the like.

Like the FSMO (Flexible Single Master of Operation) roles in Active Directory, Open Directory is made up of a number of parts. Open Directory utilizes LDAPv3 to store data, Kerberos to provide single sign-on, Apple Password Server to securely store passwords, and SASL (Simple Authentication and Security Layer) to provide authentication integration with other services.. Each of these components is accessible using standard protocols, and each can therefore be integrated with other standard directory services such as Active Directory and Novell's eDirectory, typically using what is commonly referred to as a triangle topology. In the most common triangle configuration, the three points of the triangle are represented by the client system, Apple's Open Directory, and Active Directory. In such a setup, Active Directory is used for authentication, while Open Directory provides management capabilities. As an alternative to a triangle setup, augmented records can be used to virtually extend a single service's capabilities. A triangle is most useful when not all of the attributes needed by Mac OS X for policy management are available by the primary directory service (the NFSHomeDirectory attribute, for example).

LDAP

A directory is a logically grouped collection of objects with attributes organized in a hierarchical fashion. LDAP directories can track anything from users and groups to computers, printers, and mount points on servers. The LDAP implementation for Mac OS X Server is slapd. The slapd process uses a number of schema files, located in the directory /etc/openldap/schema, to define the structure of the directory services database. These schema files include the object classes and attributes that the LDAP server presents to LDAP clients. Attributes are the same as those located in property list files, as noted earlier in this chapter. An ObjectClass is a set of attributes.

New schema files can be added, thus extending the functionality of LDAP and therefore Open Directory. Schema files can also be augmented to include new attributes. When you enhance the metadata stored for objects in LDAP, it is therefore typically referred to as extending the schema.

Kerberos

Kerberos is the gold standard with regard to single sign-on. Active Directory, Open Directory, and a variety of other solutions use Kerberos. Mac OS X clients also run a Kerberos server to secure peer-to-peer networks. With Kerberos, users and servers verify one another's identity, which helps to prevent a number of sophisticated (and some not so sophisticated) exploits when users are attempting to authenticate to services.

Kerberos makes use of a Key Distribution Center (KDC) that consists of two parts, an Authentication Server (AS) and a Ticket Granting Server (TGS). Kerberos works through the use of tickets and principals. A ticket is a session-based key that is used to obtain various service principals to provide access to a respective service. The KDC maintains a database of three types of principals: user; host; and service. These principals are sensitive, shared only between the KDC and the device, service, or user that corresponds to the principal. Upon requesting access to a particular Server Service (SS), say file services over AFP (Apple Filing Protocol), the user must first obtain what is referred to as a Ticket Granting Ticket (TGT). The TGT is obtained by properly authenticating with the Authentication Server. Once a user has a TGT, it can be presented to the TGS to obtain service tickets; in this case a user would request the afpserver service ticket. Once the user is granted this ticket from the TGS, the ticket is presented to the afpserver, which validates the ticket and the session. Assuming no problems are found, the server then grants the user access to the service. The ability to provide the TGT proves an entity's identity. By default, the TGT has a lifetime of 10 hours, which can be renewed without re-authenticating. Once the ticket has expired, the user must re-authenticate to obtain a new TGT and active service principals.

Apple's implementation of the MIT Kerberos Key Distribution Center (KDC) is krb5kdc. Apple has modified Kerberos to handle communication with the Apple Password Server, which is responsible for building and replicating the Kerberos Database. Clients who are using Open Directory for authentication (known as binding) will be automatically configured to use Kerberos using special entries provided and updated by the LDAP server. You can manually initiate this auto-configuration by using the kerberosautoconfig command. The Apple Active Directory service plug-in was developed to provide interconnectivity with Microsoft's Active Directory and also supports Kerberos auto-configuration for bound client using DNS entries known as Service (SRV) records. This automatically generated configuration file is stored at /Library/Preferences/edu.mit.Kerberos and /etc/krb5.conf. This file can be manually edited by removing auto-generation comments from the top of the file. More on Kerberos clients in Chapter 2.

Users can specify multiple Kerberos realms by editing this file, or in 10.5 by using /System/Library/CoreServices/Kerberos.app and choosing Edit ➤ Edit Realms as in Figure 1-7.

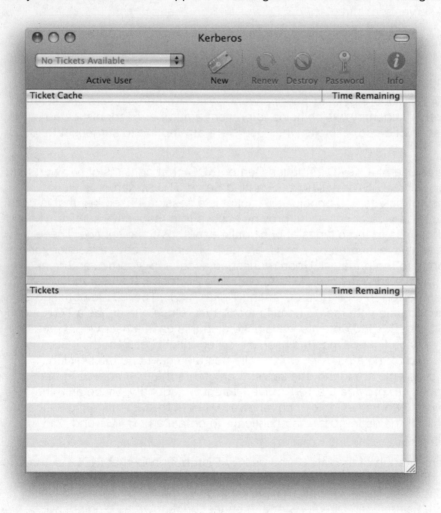

Figure 1-7. *Editing realms in Kerberos.app*

TIP: The Kerberos.app utility was removed in 10.6 and replaced with a new utility, Ticket Viewer.app. Unfortunately, Ticket Viewer has limited functionality compared to Kerberos.app, and it does not have the ability to edit REALMS. However, The Kerberos.app can be copied to a 10.6 machine and continue to function.

One of the most critical aspects of Kerberos configuration is time. If a client is more than 5 minutes apart from its KDC server, authentication will fail. The time value is normally best synchronized using the Network Time Protocol (NTP). To enable the NTP service on the Mac OS X server configured as your Open Directory master, mark the NTP check box in the General settings section of the Server Admin Application. This setting can then be pushed out using scripts or applications such as Apple Remote Desktop (an example of changing this setting is available in the Send Unix Command Templates section of the Apple Remote Desktop Admin software).

The systemsetup command can be used to set the NTP server:

```
systemsetup -setnetworktimeserver time.apple.com
```

This client setting can be configured manually in the Date & Time pane of the System Preferences; note that multiple time servers are supported when separated by a space. You can manually initiate time synchronization by using:

```
sudo ntpdate -u
```

In addition to authenticating the identity of a host in a Kerberos environment, safeguards are also put into place to protect the authenticity of each service running on a system In the form of a Service Principal. In order for a client to obtain tickets and authenticate with a daemon, the client will request a ticket using a TGT and a name constructed from the daemon/hostname:port. This information, in the form of Service Principals, can be viewed in Mac OS X by using the klist command from a Mac OS X host.

```
klist
Kerberos 5 ticket cache: 'API:Initial default cache'
Default principal: acid@WALLCITY.ORG

Valid Starting      Expires            Service Principal
07/06/09 13:12:40  07/06/09 23:12:40  krbtgt/WALLCITY.ORG@WALLCITY.ORG
        renew until 07/07/09 13:12:40
```

To access information regarding Kerberos tickets using a graphical interface, open Keychain Access from /Applications/Utilities, click on the Keychain Access menu item and then on Kerberos Ticket Viewer.

Setting up Open Directory Using Server Admin

Open Directory begins with the Open Directory Master. The Open Directory Master houses the Password Server and Kerberos KDC roles. It also provides a centralized repository for Open Directory Replicas to use for synchronizing the contents of the LDAP and password server databases. Much like with Active Directory (although oddly enough, less so), Open Directory needs DNS.

> **CAUTION:** It is highly recommended that you not use a ".local" domain name for Open Directory. The .local domain space is already being utilized by Bonjour for zero-configuration networking. Kerberos must be manually configured in domains utilizing .local name spaces.

Before you upgrade a server to an Open Directory Master, first check that the IP address that Open Directory will be running on matches the information contained in your network's DNS zones for the server and vice-versa. Start out with the changeip command located at /usr/sbin. This command utilizes a number of support scripts found in the /usr/libexec/changeip directory. In its most basic form, changeip can be called with the –checkhostname flag and can be run as follows:

```
/usr/sbin/changeip -checkhostname
```

With any luck, the script will return a success. But if it doesn't, stop and fix your DNS. changeip will fail if either forward or reverse DNS resolution fails to properly map out to the same respective values. Do not promote an Open Directory Master that does not have perfect DNS as reported by the changeip command.

First you need to display the Open Directory service on the server. To do so, open Server Admin from the /Applications/Server/ directory and click on the name of the server in the SERVERS list on the left side of the screen (adding it if it's not there). Then click on Settings from the toolbar and navigate to the Services tab, checking the box for Open Directory. Click on Save and then Open Directory will appear in the SERVERS list for your server (see Figure 1-8).

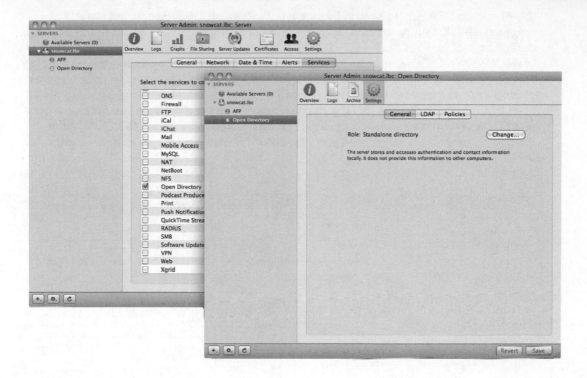

Figure 1-8. *Enable the Open Directory Service in Server Admin*

Next, we're going to promote the server to an Open Directory master. To do so, click on Open Directory and fire up the Service Configuration Assistant by clicking on the Change button. The first option will be the role that the server will be fulfilling. Here, select Open Directory Master and click on the Continue button.

You will then be prompted to specify the required information for the Open Directory administrator account. This account will be used to administer the shared domain, although it will not be granted local administrative rights to computers bound to the domain. By default, the Directory Administrator account has a name of Directory Administrator, a Short Name of diradmin, and a User ID of 1000. This information is editable, and the administrator name probably should be obscured for increased security by changing to a value specific to your environment, such as *corpdiradmin*. Since Open Directory policies can be bypassed by administrative accounts, choosing a common administrator short name represents a significant chink in the armor. Once you have entered information about the desired account into the required fields, type the password first in the Password field and again in the Verify field. While setting up a new Open Directory Master, you will also be prompted to specify the LDAP search base and the Kerberos REALM, as seen in Figure 1-9. By default, OS X Server will enter a machine-specific entry for both. That is, when promoting server myhost.myco.com, the default search base is dc=myhost,dc=myco,dc=com, and the Kerberos realm would be MYHOST.MYCO.COM. In many cases, it may be undesirable to include the host name in a company-specific domain. If myhost is ever retired, its hostname will still be forever etched into your directory system. To avoid this, remove the hostname specific values from both the search base and the realm. Thus, in the previous example, the desired search base would be dc=myco,dc=com, and the realm would by MYCO.COM. After specifying these values, proceed with the setup by clicking on the Continue button.

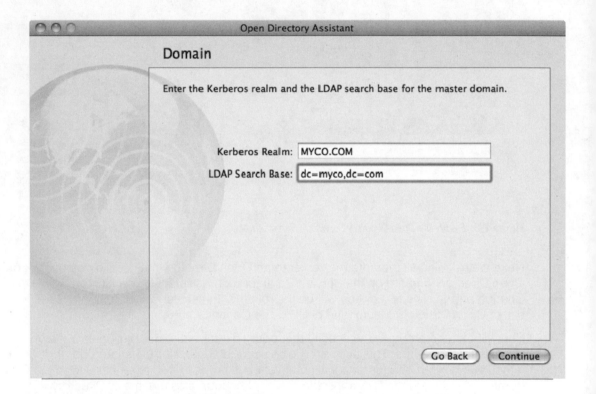

Figure 1-9. *Specify Kerberos REALM and LDAP Search Base*

Next you'll see the Confirm screen. Review the contents, which should mirror what was entered in the preceding screens. When you are satisfied with the settings, click Finish and Mac OS X Server will finish configuring Open Directory for you (see Figure 1-10).

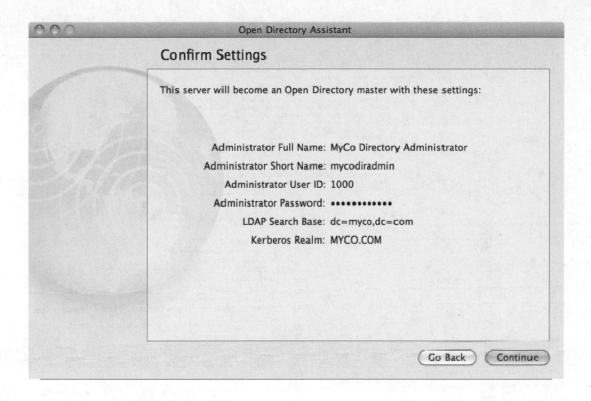

Figure 1-10. *Confirm final settings*

Now you can verify that all components of Open Directory are properly functional with your Open Directory setup by going into Server Admin, clicking on the Open Directory service listed in the SERVERS list, and then clicking on the Overview button in the Server Admin toolbar. In a standard Open Directory setup, LDAP, Password Server, and Kerberos should all be running. In a triangle environment with Active Directory, typically the AD Kerberos system is utilized. In such setups, it is normal for Kerberos not to be running. Should any of the services fail to start, consult the Open Directory logs found in Server Admin under the logs tab of the Open Directory service (as shown in Figure 1-11). Look for any errors and make corrections as needed.

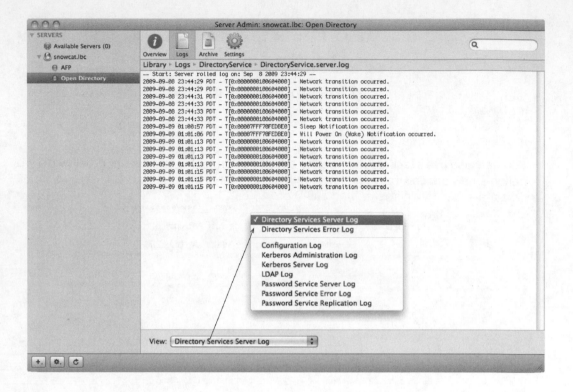

Figure 1-11. *Open Directory logs*

Setting up Open Directory from the Command Line

Setting up LDAP, Kerberos, the Password Server, SASL, and creating a directory services administrative account could seem daunting if you were to do it manually. But as with many tasks, Apple has made setup easier if you choose to go the command-line route. This functionality is provided by using the `slapconfig` command binary, the same tool utilized by the Server Admin application.

NOTE: For the Active Directory guru readers, slapconfig can be thought of as being similar to dcpromo, but with many, many more options, and therefore similar to dcpromo only from the perspective of promoting and destroying a directory server! In addition to promotion, slapconfig can also be used to configure various Open Directory settings, replication, and global password policies.

To create an Open Directory master using the command line, you could simply run the following command:

```
slapconfig -createldapmasterandadmin
```

In the above example, the default values presented in all of the Server Admin screens from the previous section were used. The Name of the account was set to *Directory Administrator* and the Short Name was set to *diradmin*. The password was set to the same value as the password for the administrative account that ran the command, and the Unique ID was set to *1000*.

You can also use slapconfig to define custom settings. In the command below,we will define a new administrative account with a short name of corpodadmin, a full name of Corporate OD Administrator, and a UID of 1100:

```
slapconfig -createldapmasterandadmin corpodadmin "Corporate OD Administrator" 1100
```

There are still a couple of default settings that slapconfig is using during the Open Directory Master promotion process. These include the search base suffix and the Kerberos realm. According to Microsoft, "A search base (the distinguished name of the search base object) defines the location in the directory from which the LDAP search begins." The search base suffix is, by default, derived using the DNS name of the server. To obtain the search base suffix for a given Open Directory Master, you can run the slapconfig command with the –defaultsuffix query.

The realm is the name of the Kerberos realm that will be used. This, too, is generated based on an enumeration of the server's host name (are you starting to put together why DNS is so important?). However, it can be customized during the –createmasterandadmin process.

Demoting an Open Directory Master

Demoting an Open Directory Master can be done using either the command line or Server Admin.

If demotion is done at the command line, the following command would get the job done:

```
slapconfig -destroyldapserver
```

Set up an Open Directory Replica

An Open Directory Replica can be set up using Server Admin. Once you have opened the application, connect to the server that is destined to perform the Replica role. Under the Open Directory service, select the Settings tab. This tab will specify the current role of the server. To promote the server to a Replica, simply click the Change button, and specify the role Open Directory Replica. The interface will then query you for information about the Open Directory system to connect to. Specifically, you will need to specify the Open Directory Master's IP/DNS name, the root user's password, and the Open Directory admin's short name and password. After specifying this information and continuing, the server will contact the Open Directory master and begin replicating all of the relevant databases. This process does involve taking the Open Directory Master's LDAP database offline during initial setup, so plan accordingly. In a typical scenario, it will be offline for roughly a minute. That being said, it is always a good idea to perform this operation during non-peak times.

If the server that you're promoting to replica status is not already in the role of a stand-alone server, it's a good idea to demote it to stand alone before it is configured as a replica. However, it's an even better idea to start off with a nice clean server as your replica, so this situation should be completely avoidable.

Replicas can also be created using the `slapconfig` binary. From the replica, run the command with the syntax:

```
slapconfig –createreplica myodmaster.myco.com myodadmin
```

Removing a Replica

Removing a Replica from an Open Directory environment should be done any time you are decommissioning a server running as an Open Directory replica. You should first attempt to do this using the Server Admin tool. Simply open Server Admin and connect to the OD Replica. Under the Open Directory service, click on the Settings tab, where you'll see the Server's role, listed as Open Directory Replica. Click on the Change button, and select Stand Alone Server. This will require you to enter various credentials that will facilitate the proper demotion between the OD master and the replica in question. When that's done, the replica will be removed from the system.

For a variety of reasons, you may not be able to remove a replica from Open Directory using Server Admin. When that happens, try doing so using `slapconfig`. For example, if the replica has an IP address of 192.168.53.249, the command would be:

```
slapconfig -removereplica 192.168.53.249
```

Using Workgroup Manager to Create New Users

Using Workgroup Manager, you can create Open Directory users and alter attributes for their user accounts. You can also add computers, configure automounts, and perform other tasks. In this module we will create a user. As a prerequisite, you will want to have a functional Open Directory Master.

To create a new Open Directory user, open Workgroup Manager. As you can see in Figure 1-12, you will see the "domain" that you are connected to listed in the directory bar (below the toolbar). If the credentials that you provided in Workgroup Manager do not have Directory admin rights, you will not be authenticated to the domain and you'll need to authenticate. To do so, click on the lock icon on the directory bar. You will be asked for a username and a password. The default username is *diradmin*, although this might have been customized (and should be!) when the Open Directory Master was created. Type the username and password in the Authenticate to directory: dialog box and then click on the Authenticate button. If the authentication is successful, you'll notice that the directory bar will appear, also shown in Figure 1-12 (and with an open lock on the right-hand side). As per standard OS X behavior, you will not be able to make any changes to the selected directory if the lock is not open.

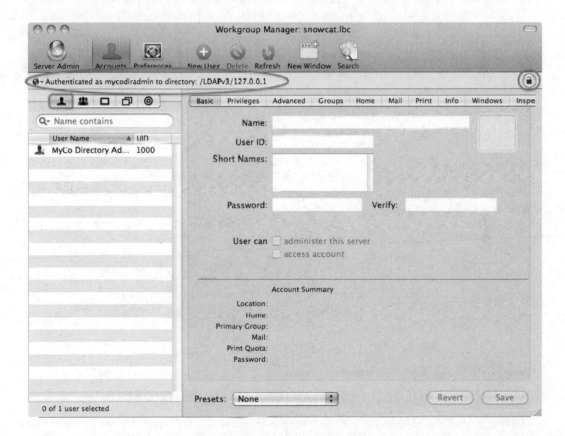

Figure 1-12. *Ensure proper directory is selected and you are authenticated to create a user*

Once you are authenticated to Open Directory, you can create a user account. To do so, click on the New User button in the toolbar, or select New User from the Server menu.

Next, fill in the general user information using the Basic tab of the New User window. You can customize the Short Name at this point (but not in the future without a complicated process), apply a Name (the user's full name in most cases) and enter a password. While you can change the User ID, it is wise to simply stick with the one that is automatically applied in this field.

Next, click on the Groups tab. Here you will add any groups that the user should be a member of. To do so, click on the plus sign (+) and then drag the group into the Other Groups: field from the resultant floating menu of users and groups (see Figure 1-13).

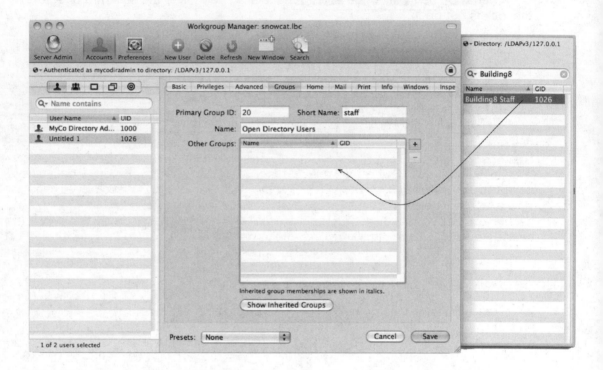

Figure 1-13. *Assign users to the appropriate groups*

Next, click on the Info tab and fill in any other pertinent information you would like to track, including the user's physical address, phone information, email address, and so on. In addition to the information that is easily accessible about a user, you can also access data that at first glance seems hidden by enabling the Inspector, which allows you to view raw directory information. To enable the Inspector, open Workgroup Manager and click on the Workgroup Manager menu (immediately to the right of the Apple menu). Then check the box for *Show "All Records" tab and inspector* and click OK to save the changes (see Figure 1-14).

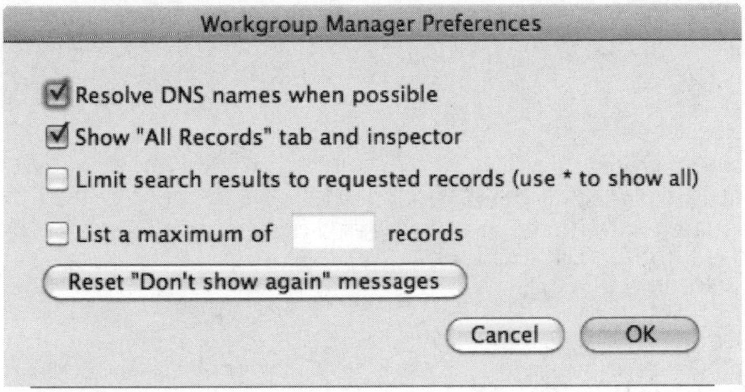

Figure 1-14. *Enable the All Records tab and Inspector in Workgroup Manager*

You will now be able to view a far more detailed account of what is hosted in your directory service. When you are viewing information using the Inspector, you will be able to change information that should not be changed unless you know exactly what you are doing, so be very careful. However, it is worth noting that with the Inspector you can view a far more detailed account of the data stored in each record of the LDAP database. Once you have enabled the Inspector, you will see the Inspector tab in your new test account. Click it to see the information now available.

Backing up Open Directory

While much attention is placed on files and folders on a many servers, an integral part of rebuilding a server from scratch is not just having a back up of data, it's also having a back up of the accounts and permissions references that go along with that data. Manually backing up Open Directory is a straightforward process. Simply click on the Archive tab of the Open Directory service in Server Admin. From there, you can choose a directory to save the OD archive to. After you've chosen a destination path, the Archive button will become enabled. Click on this button to specify a name and a password for the OD archive. Be sure not to place any whacks (/) in the name of the Archive, or the process will silently fail, leaving you with a false sense of security. As always with any backup routine, an occasional spot-check is necessary to be absolutely certain that you have clean data. In this case, you can simply mount the produced disk-image file by double-clicking on it, and verify that data has been written to it. The OD Archive process is decently broad. It archives both Network and Local directory services databases, launchd.plist files for relevant services, as well as numerous configuration files and preferences.

One limitation of the Server Admin archive process is that it is a manual process, which can often be a detriment to the consistency of an important function. To back up Open

Directory with a script can be easier and more reliable. You can do this from the command line by scheduling the following script with cron or launchd:

```perl
#!/usr/bin/perl -w

use strict;

my $archive_password = 'MYPASSWORD';
my $archive_path = '/Volumes/Data/backups/opendirectory/';

my $max_keep_time = 1; # MONTHS TO KEEP ARCHIVES AROUND

my @date = localtime();
my $year = $date[5] + 1900;
my $month = sprintf("%.2d",$date[4] + 1);
my $day = sprintf("%.2d",$date[3]);

my $filename = $year.$month.$day;
my $archive_file = $archive_path.$filename;

print "Archiving to $archive_file...\n";

if (open(CMD,"|/usr/sbin/serveradmin command")) {
  print CMD "dirserv:backupArchiveParams:archivePassword = $archive_password\n" ;
  print CMD "dirserv:backupArchiveParams:archivePath = $archive_file\n";
  print CMD "dirserv:command = backupArchive\n";
  close(CMD);
  print "Archive successful.\n";
} else {
  print "Error: $!\n";
  exit;
}

$month -= $max_keep_time;
if ($month < 1) {
  $month = 12;
  $year--;
}

my $expire_date = sprintf("%.4d%.2d%.2d",$year,$month,$day);

print "Cleaning up old archives...\n";

if (opendir(DIR,$archive_path)) {
  while (my $file = readdir(DIR)) {
    chomp($file);
    next unless ($file =~ /^\d{8}\.sparseimage$/i);
    my $file_date = $file;
    $file_date =~ s/[^0-9]//g;
    if ($file_date < $expire_date) {
      print "Removing ".$archive_path.$file."\n";
      unlink($archive_path.$file);
    }
  }
```

```
    print "Cleanup successful.\n";
} else {
    print "Error: $!\n";
}
```

Troubleshooting Directory Services

Directory Services Debug Logs

When you're trying to troubleshoot issues with Directory Services on Mac OS X sometimes the best thing you can do is put the `directoryservices` daemon into debug mode. To do so, we must send a USR1 signal to the daemon using the following command:

```
killall -USR1 DirectoryService
```

By default errors get trapped into this file:

```
/Library/Logs/DirectoryService/DirectoryService.error.log
```

But when in debug mode using -USR1, you can see more specific errors here:

```
/Library/Logs/DirectoryService/DirectoryService.debug.log
```

You can then use commands such as `tail` and `more` in conjunction with `grep` to isolate issues to specific strings such as ADPlugin. Alternatively, you can enable API logging if you choose to send the -USR2 signal. For debugging then, the logs will get written into the /var/log/system.log file.

To disable verbose logging, you can just restart the Directory Services daemon if you originally sent a -USR1 signal to DirectoryService. If you used -USR2, debugging information will automatically stop writing to the log after 5 minutes.

Cache

In some cases, you may find that certain lookup tools, such as `id`, return data which differs from what is stored in the directory. This is typically caused by stale data stored in the local machine's cache. While this cache will eventually expire and update, it may be desirable to manually flush the cache. In version 10.4, this was accomplished using lookupd:

```
lookupd -flushcache
```

Unfortunately, lookupd has gone to tech heaven, abandoned after 10.4. Introduced with 10.5, the tool `dscacheutil` allows for more cache-specific functionality than `lookupd`. For example, using -cachedump allows you to dump an overview of the cache contents. The -cachedump command has a slew of flags to get pretty granular with the output, such as -entries and -buckets. The –configuration command allows you to access detailed information about your search policy, and -statistics allows you to view detailed information on the statistics of calls.

Here are some examples of using these commands:

dscacheutil –flushcache to empty the DNS Cache Resolver;

dscacheutil -cachedump -entries user to dump cache with user entries;

dscacheutil -q user to look up all users on a system;

dscacheutil -q user –a name jdoe to look up data for user jdoe.

The dscacheutil tool is also one of two command-line utilities that allow you to query a group for direct membership (querying raw membership attributes with dscl is the other). However, this functionality is somewhat limited as dscacheutil does not consistently recurse through nested group membership. It does, however, work with basic membership. For instance, to list members of the group admin, you could use:

```
dscacheutil -q group –a name admin
```

Verifying Authentication

There are a number of ways that you can test authentication in OS X, and the exact process will vary based upon the version of the OS that you are running. Naturally, you can verify authentication for a user by attempting to login to a bound Mac OS client. The main problem with this type of testing is that it is fairly inefficient; if you don't have a spare client to test with, a trip to the login window likely requires you to logout. On top of this, home directory problems can prevent a successful login, so it is not always an accurate test.

If the target user has a default shell assigned, you can test authentication using the su command in any version of OS X. Simply open up a new shell and type su testuser. You will be prompted to enter the user's password. Provided that you entered in accurate credentials, you will be granted a shell under the new user. You can use the id tool to verify.

```
bash-3.2$ su testuser
Password:
bash-3.2$ id
uid=1078(testuser)
```

This is not the only means to do this, however. In 10.5 a new utility, dirt, was introduced solely for the purpose of testing authentication. The dirt utility is unique to Leopard and can be used to test Directory Service user resolution and authentication. You can use dirt to test authentication for users residing in local, LDAP, or Active Directory nodes. The -u flag uses the username from the node you are testing against. The dirt command tests whether an account exists in any node and can be used with the following structure:

```
dirt -u corpadmin –n '/Active Directory/domainname'
```

This would result in the following output if the account is located in Active Directory:

```
User username was found in:
/Active Directory/domainname
```

> **NOTE:** The -p flag can also be used to test passwords. You can also specify the node in Directory Services you would like to test.

In addition to lookups, the `dirt` tool can be used to test authentication. For instance, to test authentication for user *jdoe*, use the following command:

```
dirt -u jdoe
```

After running this command, you will be prompted for the password, which can also be specified when invoking the command using the –p flag. Once you provide a password, the tool will output whether or not authentication succeeded, as well as some user data.

> **NOTE:** Unfortunately, when using `dirt` the password is always (unnecessarily!) echo'd out in clear text, so make sure you only use this tool when there are no prying eyes around.

Unfortunately, the `dirt` utility is not included with 10.6. Not all is lost, though: this functionality was rolled into Apple's other directory services tool, `dscl`. To test authentication using dscl, 10.6 introduces the –authonly flag, which must be called with at least a username. The password can be supplied optionally after the username:

```
$ dscl /Search -authonly testuser "MySuperSecretPassword"
Password:
$
```

As this shows, if you provide the correct password, the dscl utility will exit with a 0 status and will return you directly to your shell prompt with no feedback. This indicates a successful authentication. If authentication is not successful, you will be greeted with an eDSAuthFailed error:

```
$ dscl /Search -authonly testuser "MySuperPass"
Authentication for node /Search failed. (-14090, eDSAuthFailed)
<dscl_cmd> DS Error: -14090 (eDSAuthFailed)
```

Notice also in the previous example that we are calling `dscl` specifically with the /Search search path. We could specify an explicit node to authenticate against:

$ dscl /LDAPv3/odm.myco.com –authonly testuser "MySuperSecretPassword"

Summary

In this chapter, we discussed the role Directory Services plays in a networked computing environment. That is, the Directory Services act as the unifying glue, allowing user and group membership to be utilized across an unlimited number of clients. Directory services are the core of any enterprise organization; without the ability to centrally manage users, support requirements would balloon. Directory services enable a group of otherwise ad -hoc computers to operate with similar parameters. They enable centralized authentication, allowing users from multiple computers and multiple platforms to authenticate against a single database, creating a more user-friendly and ultimately more secure system.

In the next chapter, we will further explore directory services, with a specific focus on integrating OS X client desktops with Apple's Open Directory platform. Later, in Chapter 3, we will discuss integrating OS X client desktops with Microsoft's Active Directory system.

## Chapter 2

Directory Services Clients

In Chapter 1, we discussed Directory Services and the various types of information that a Directory Service can provide. In contrast, this chapter focuses on utilizing a centralized Directory Service for user and group resolution and authentication. Utilizing a centralized Directory Service is absolutely essential to the efficient management of your fleet of computers and eliminates the need to synchronize user and group databases across all of your computers.

Lightweight Directory Access Protocol (LDAP) is the building block for most modern directory services solutions. Whether you are using Microsoft's Active Directory or Apple's Open Directory, to a large degree the basis for their implementation lies in the LDAPv3 specification. As such, LDAP in this context consists of a communication protocol, a data scheme that is used to store directory information, and the replication infrastructure to distribute that data across multiple remote data stores. Because Mac OS X is built from the ground up to accommodate for LDAP, there are myriad of options in terms of automation and management functionality that can be provided to Mac OS X clients. This isn't to say that you can't leverage the same LDAP structures built in Chapter 1 in order to provide directory services to Microsoft Windows, but the context for this chapter will focus primarily on Mac OS X directory service clients. In Chapter 9, we will look at providing some aspects of directory services to Windows clients.

When a client is added to a directory services environment this is often referred to as binding. There are two general types of binding that can be performed by an OS X client. The first kind is referred to as a trusted, or authenticated, bind. With a trusted bind the client computer creates a representative computer object in the LDAP store, which contains the same AuthenticationAuthority record familiar to an OS X user account. From here on, the computer itself must use a locally stored key to authenticate to the directory in order to receive directory data. By authenticating, the computer proves that it is a member of the network, and thereby has certain elevated access, based on the trust relationship created at bind time. Trusted binding requires a password to establish this trust. The second type of binding is not necessarily binding at all; it simply involves configuring the client so that it should query a certain directory server for certain data, such as user names, passwords, and even policies. This type of bind is sometimes referred to as an anonymous bind. In these configurations, a client computer need not have an associated computer object in LDAP.

In Chapter 1, I covered setting up and using localized directory services. In Chapter 2, I'm going to dive into leveraging the Mac OS X Open Directory environment and other non-Microsoft based directory services solutions that leverage LDAP in order to provide a centralized directory service to client computers. I will begin by looking at binding to LDAP and then delve into the topics that will allow you to automate LDAP, mass deploy LDAP settings, and realize the full potential of your directory services solution. This chapter will end with a cursory glance at leveraging both NIS and BSD flat files for those environments still committed to 1990s style networking (although I refuse to cover Banyan Vines for posterities sake).

The Lay of the Land

Directory Utility is the application used to bind to Open Directory and other directory servers. When you first open Directory Utility, you will notice the Directory Utility shows a status indicator that it is looking for Mac OS X Servers. If you have an LDAP environment broadcasting via Bonjour, then in many cases it will discover the server and allow you to easily perform an unauthenticated bind. This is common, for example, with environments based on Mac OS X Server 10.5 Standard, where Apple was trying to make the setup of these fairly complicated environments as zero-configuration as possible.

If you completed the default Open Directory setup as described in Chapter 1, after a few moments the Looking for Mac OS X Servers indicator will disappear once the query fails. To disable the automatic search feature, click on the Preferences menu of Directory Utility and then uncheck the box for Look for Mac OS X Servers at Launch. You can also set the preference from the command line (for example, if you were pushing it out via Apple Remote Desktop) using the defaults command, by pushing a new ~/Library/Preferences/com.apple.DirectoryUtility.plist file to clients, or by using com.apple.DirectoryUtility.plist as part of your managed preferences environment. The following command uses the defaults command to edit the boolean "No SBS Assistant" key of the com.apple.DirectoryUtility.plist file to be a 0, which disables the feature:

```
defaults write com.apple.DirectoryUtility "No SBS Assistant" 0
```

While the Looking for Mac OS X Servers process may fail, this isn't to say that you can't leverage Bonjour to help locate directory servers. Bonjour Browser is a tool from TildeSoft (http://www.tildesoft.com) that can be used to find a variety of services. To use Bonjour Browser, download it and drag the application bundle to your /Applications directory then open it and wait for the list of hosts and services to populate. Once populated, you will see a screen similar to the one in Figure 2-1. Here you can find the _ldap.tcp. entry and then browse other information on this host. It will show the port that LDAP is running on along with the IP address that is running it.

Figure 2-1. *Bonjour Browser*

NOTE: Instead of enumerating the address you will bind to, you can also simply look at the IP address or hostname of your LDAP server as well.

Once you have found your LDAP servers, it is important to make sure you can communicate with the hosts. LDAP runs on port 389 (636 with SSL). There are two fairly straightforward ways that you can check that you can communicate with LDAP. The first is to scan the port. To do so, open Network Utility and click on the Port Scan tab. Enter the host name or IP address in the Please enter an Internet or IP address to scan for open ports field, check the box for Only test ports between 389 and 389, then click on Scan (see Figure 2-2).

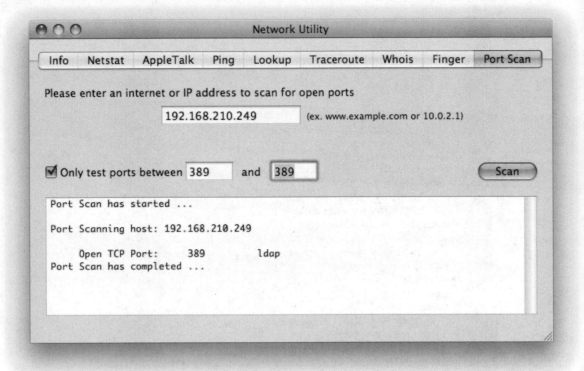

Figure 2-2. *Network Utility*

As a sanity check, many organizations will choose to verify that the Open Directory Master is accessible by a client prior to attempting to bind. You can also script against the same tool that Network Utility uses to perform port scans, called stroke. To use stroke, you will need to cd into the Network Utility application bundle using the command:

```
cd /Applications/Utilities/Network\ Utility.app/Contents/Resources/
```

Once you are in this directory, you will need to provide stroke with an IP address (or name), followed by a port range—specifying the lowest port first, a space, and then the last. Use the same number twice if your range is only a single port. For example, if you want to port scan port 389 on your own system you could use the following (assuming a working directory of /Applications/Utilities/Network Utility.app/Contents/Resources):

```
./stroke 127.0.0.1 389 389
```

If your Open Directory Master were named seldon.company.com, then you could use the following code to check availability, by DNS name of the LDAP service on the server:

```
./stroke seldon.company.com 389 389
```

Because the name seldom.company.com has to resolve, you're actually able to check whether a DNS error occurs and whether you can communicate over port 389 to the host in one command. If you plan to use stroke a lot, you may want to create a symlink to the binary in a directory that is specified in your environment's PATH, you can then use it without needing to change your working directory:

```
ln -s /Applications/Utilities/Network\ Utility.app/Contents/Resources/stroke
/usr/bin/stroke
```

> **NOTE:** If you can scan port 389 (or port 636, if you are using SSL) from the server using localhost (127.0.0.1) then it typically stands to reason that if you cannot access port 389 on the server from a client via IP or DNS that you likely have a network problem that is preventing connectivity—even if the server requires authentication to enumerate the directory tree it should still listen over the LDAP port for said authentication.

The second way to check that LDAP is available to your client systems is to telnet into port 389 of the host running the LDAP service. There are a number of services that can be tested in this manner, including most web servers and SMTP. For each service you would simply follow telnet by the name (or IP address) of the host you are testing and then the port, as follows:

```
telnet seldom.company.com 389
```

At this point, you should receive a response similar to the following, which by virtue of the Connected line shows that you were indeed able to communicate with port 389:

```
Trying 192.168.210.249...
Connected to 192.168.210.249.
Escape character is '^]'.
```

You can also go a step further and use a third party tool to query an LDAP server, without performing any custom configurations of Mac OS X. LDapper is an application that will allow you to authenticate to and display information accessible through LDAP. LDapper has a number of options that mirror various settings within LDAP, and so becomes a good tool for figuring out what LDAP settings to use when configuring the

Directory Utility for binding. The ability to enter different settings and quickly obtain results makes LDapper a great tool for enumerating an LDAP environment and is very helpul for troubleshooting connectivity problems.

To use LDapper, first download it from `http://carl-bell-2.baylor.edu/~Carl_Bell/stuff.html`. Once the dmg file has been downloaded, drag the LDapper application bundle into your /Applications directory. From here, open LDapper by double-clicking on it and then select Preferences from the LDapper menu, as shown in Figure 2-3.

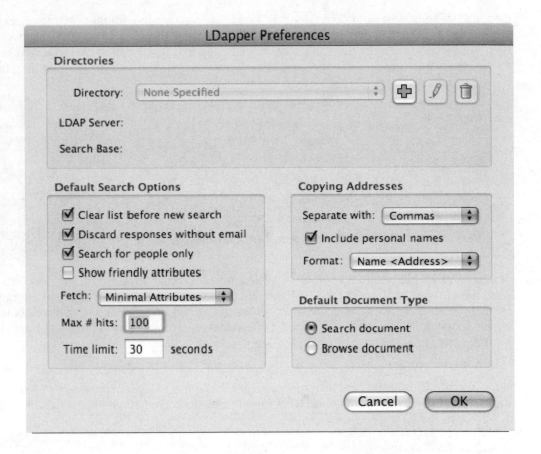

Figure 2-3. *LDapper Preferences*

Next, click on the Plus sign and then enter a friendly name (to remember the specific server by) into the Directory Name: field and then enter a server's hostname or IP address into the LDAP Server: field. Finally, type the Search Base. If you are using Open Directory, you can find the Search Base by opening Server Admin and then clicking on the Open Directory listing in the SERVERS list for the Open Directory Master (see Figure 2-4).

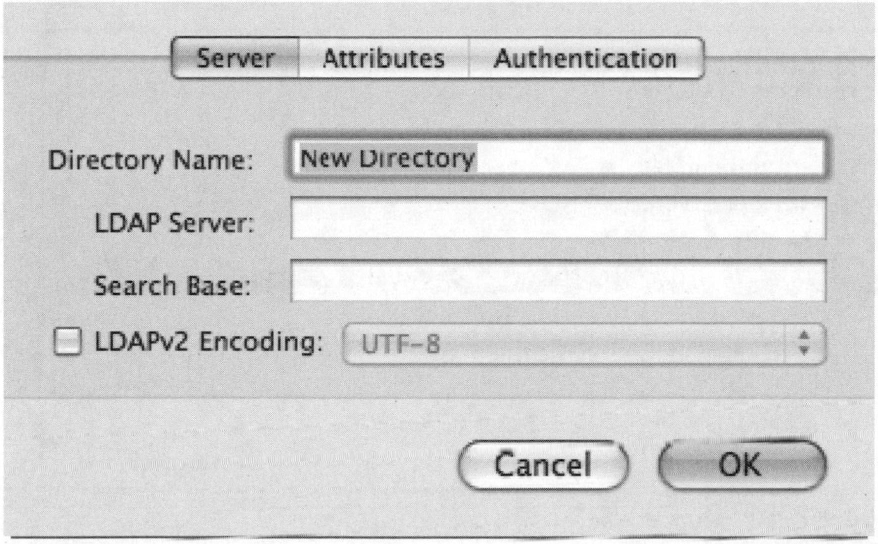

| Server | Attributes | Authentication |

Directory Name: New Directory

LDAP Server:

Search Base:

☐ LDAPv2 Encoding: UTF-8

Cancel   OK

Figure 2-4. *LDapper add server dialog*

TIP: With many LDAP implemenatations you can determine the search base by querying it with the ldapsearch utility, using the syntax: ldapsearch -h ldap.myco.com -x -a never -s base namingContexts.

There are a few more options to LDapper as well. In order to use Authentication, click on the Authentication tab and enter a username that can read information from the directory service in the Identification: field and a password in the Password: file. Additionally, if you are using custom mapped attributes, click on the Attributes tab to enter the pertinent information. Once you are satisfied with all of your options, click on the OK button and you should be able to browse records for your LDAP environment, as shown in Figure 2-5.

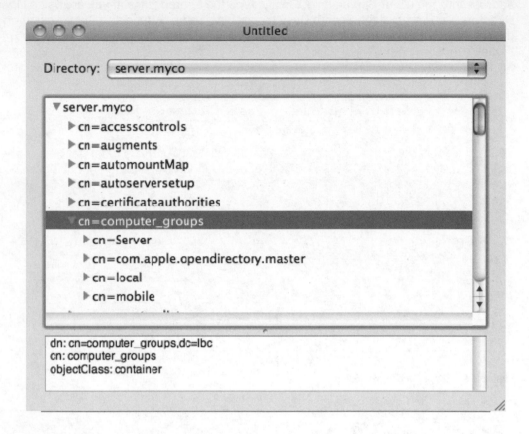

Figure 2-5. *Browsing an LDAP server with LDaper*

From the command line, you can do much of the same tasks, using the ldapsearch tool. Using ldapsearch you have many more options, likeSASL, output to ldif, and LDAP version.

Basic Binding

As mentioned earlier, there are two types of binding that can be performed. The first is trusted binding, where the computer and the directory service share a key, which allows each to trust the other. When a host performs a trusted bind, it creates a computer record in the directory database. Based on the record in the database and the key, the computer is then granted certain access to directory services information that it might not have otherwise been provided. For example, in a number of environments the directory service is configured to only allow a system to perform LDAP queries if it has successfully authenticated. This is a good way to lock down a system.

In an anonymous or non-trusted bind, the directory server does not necessarily have representative data for the anonymous computer. Thus, in order for an anonymous/untrusted bind to function, the LDAP server must provide anonymous access to its store. However, the ability remains to perform an untrusted bind but authenticate using an LDAP user. For such a setup, the user credentials used to authenticate to the LDAP server are cached locally. This technically qualifies as an authenticated bind. However, it differs in that a trusted bind utilizes a pre-shared key stored in the computer object on the LDAP server. While certainly authentication, supplying user credentials does not qualify as computer-level authentication.

When a client is bound to a directory service, the directory service must trust the client in such a way that the client will be able to access (and in some cases update) certain records in the LDAP database. This may simply be the computer's own entry in Open Directory or it may be an entire computer list.

In OS X, the Directory Utility application (found in /Applications/Utilities/) is the primary graphical interface to manage directory service bindings. However, the tool does not provide a facility to actually query directory data.

Unfortunately, there is no graphical utility for browsing directory data in OS X. However, as mentioned in Chapter 1, dscl is a very handy command-line tool for querying and modifying the contents of bound directory services. dscl will also play a substantial part in preparing a system for binding and automation with regard to the actual bind process. However, another common command that you'll leverage throughout this chapter will be dsconfigldap, the tool used to perform LDAP binding operations and configure LDAP options.

Plug-ins

Directory Utility uses a number of plug-ins to provide functionality for various directory services solutions. Most notable are the defacto plug-in for Active Directory or the LDAPv3 plug-in used for Open Directory. As you work through this chapter, you will be using the LDAPv3 plug-in, but you could easily be using the Quest, Likewise, or Centrify plug-ins, according to your required task.

Plug-ins are developed in the form of .dsplug files. The default plug-ins that Apple includes are located in the /System/Library/Frameworks/DirectoryService.framework/Versions/A/Resources/Plugins directory, which is where Likewise (discussed further in Chapter 3) stores its plug-in as well. Third party plug-ins are typically installed in the /Library/DirectoryServices/PlugIns directory of a computer, which is where you will find plug-ins for Quest and products from Thursby.

To enable a plug-in in the Directory Utility, you will open Directory Utility from /Applications/Utilities and then click on services, as shown in Figure 2-6.

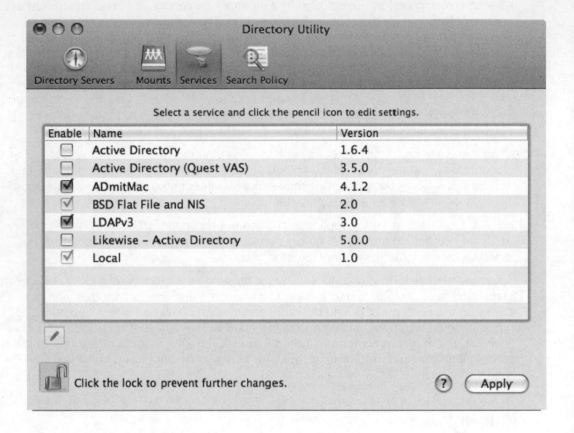

Figure 2-6. *Directory Utility Services*

You can also enable and disable plug-ins from the command line. To do so, you will augment the DirectoryService.plist in the/Library/Preferences/DirectoryService/ folder, likely using the `defaults write` command. In order to read or write to the property list file, you will need to run the command with root privileges. To start, you can simply read the file with defaults and see what keys already exist that you can work with:

```
$sudo defaults read /Library/Preferences/DirectoryService/DirectoryService
{
    "Active Directory" = Inactive;
    AppleTalk = Active;
    BSD = Active;
    Version = "1.1";
}
```

To enable a particular plug-in (LDAPv3 is enabled by default), you can simply set the value to Active and then restart your DirectoryService daemon:

```
$sudo defaults write /Library/Preferences/DirectoryService/DirectoryService "LDAPv3"↵
 "Inactive"
$sudo killall DirectoryService
```

Or, if you're feeling constructive, maybe you want to enable a plug-in, following the same modus operandi:

```
$sudo defaults write /Library/Preferences/DirectoryService/DirectoryService ↵
"Active Directory" "Active"
$sudo killall DirectoryService
```

> **NOTE:** You can also work with third party plug-ins in the same fashion. The list here should always mirror the list that you see in Directory Utility.

In earlier versions of OS X, enabling or disabling plug-ins through this method could be a little inconsistent. A reboot will typically ensure the setting is properly applied.

Unauthenticated Dynamic Binding

Each Mac OS X client with an automatic search policy can connect to a shared LDAP directory that is provided dynamically using the DHCP protocol, which I will call unauthenticated dynamic binding. This can be useful in controlling settings for properly configured client computers while they are guests on your network. For example, if you just want to point them at a Software Update Server, manage proxy settings, or deploy application restrictions, you can also utilize this setup to provide your client systems that support DHCP-supplied LDAP (also known as Option 95) with LDAP settings en masse if you do not have a framework in place for management. For this reason, in certain instances unauthenticated dynamic binding can be attractive as a means to an end to install mass deployment tools and configure LDAP settings in environments where security of the directory service itself is not a major concern. In environments where security of the directory service is a concern, unauthenticated dynamic binding can be leveraged with a strategy to automate the move into a more secure environment, allowing for more zero touch integration on actual client systems.

When the computer starts, it can get the address of an LDAP directory server from DHCP service. The DHCP service of your Mac OS X Server can supply an LDAP server address in the same way it supplies the addresses of DNS servers and a router/default gateway. If you are hosting your DHCP for your Mac clients using Mac OS X Server, then you would configure the LDAP servers by clicking on the DHCP listing for the server that runs your DHCP service in the SERVERS list of Server Admin. Next, click on Subnets in the DHCP toolbar (as shown in Figure 2-7). From here, if you double-click on your DHCP scope entry for the scope you would like to use DHCP for, you will notice an

LDAP tab on the bottom portion of the screen. Here, enter the server's DNS name or IP address and the Search Base as its listed in the Open Directory service.

If the port is not 389, go ahead and enter the port into the Port: field as well. Finally, if you are using SSL and the certificate has been accepted, you can click on the LDAP over SSL checkbox as well. If you are using SSL and the certificate has not been accepted, it will need to be before the client system will be able to access LDAP. Once you are satisfied with all of your settings, click on Save and then Start DHCP to start the service.

If the server is not a Mac, you can still supply LDAP DCHP information. For Linux, you would add the following lines to your dhcpd.conf-Server:

```
option ldap-server code 95 = text;
option ldap-server "ldap://seldon.company.com:389/dc=seldon,dc=company,dc=com";
```

NOTE: For more information on Option 95 (and other unused Options), see RFC 3679.

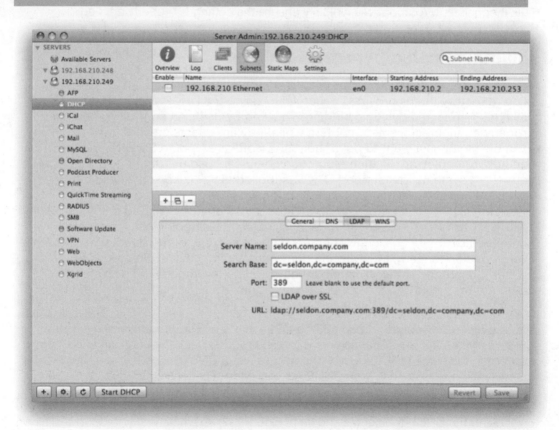

Figure 2-7. *Providing LDAP information via DHCP*

If you wish to obtain LDAP information from a client computer using DHCP, you will first need to enable DHCP-supplied LDAP. To do so, open Directory Utility and click on the Show Advanced Settings button. Then click on the Services icon in the application toolbar. Here, you will see the LDAPv3 entry. Click on the lock icon and enter the username and password for an administrative account on the system. From here, double-click on the LDAPv3 entry, check the box for Add DHCP-supplied LDAP servers to automatic search policies, and then click on the OK button.

Next, test logging in using an account stored only in the directory services to verify that providing LDAP settings over DHCP is functioning as intended. If you cannot authenticate, open dscl and test whether you can read accounts from the directory server. If you cannot, then verify that the directory server that was supplied by DHCP is listed in the LDAPv3 tree of dscl. If it is not, then troubleshoot the DHCP environment. Start by verifying that you are receiving an IP address. If so, look for multiple scopes or a different DHCP server that may be supplying an address to your system.

If you wish to script the enablement of receiving LDAP information over DHCP, you can use the dscl command to edit the /Search/dsattrTypeStandard:DCHPLDAPDefault key as follows:

```
dscl -q localhost -create /Search dsAttrTypeStandard:DHCPLDAPDefault on
```

> **NOTE:** Clients that are using a trusted bind cannot also use a DHCP-supplied LDAP directory setup.

Enabling unauthenticated dynamic binding on client machines has some pretty serious repercussions. By enabling this setting, you are essentially telling client computers to trust any LDAP server provided by DHCP. If the DHCP packet comes from an untrusted source, then the client machine can easily be compromised. In environments where security is a concern, or where a client machine will potentially connect to public networks, this setup should be avoided.

Unauthenticated Static Binding

While you can set up LDAP clients through DHCP, most organizations don't choose this as their standard. Option 95 is the standardized configuration option for supplying LDAP information over DHCP. Use of Option 95 is fairly rare and most client systems are setup statically. As previously mentioned, setting up LDAP clients will be done by using either the Directory Utility application or the dsconfigldap command, if you wish to do so programmatically. To set up a client for unauthenticated static binding using Directory Utility, open the tool from /Applications/Utilities (/System/Library/CoreServices in 10.6), then click on the Show Advanced Settings button in the lower right-hand corner of the screen. Next, use the lock icon in the lower-left corner of the screen to authenticate in order to make changes to the Directory Utility. Once authenticated, click on Services and then double-click on LDAPv3 to see the LDAP Configuration screen, as shown in Figure 2-8.

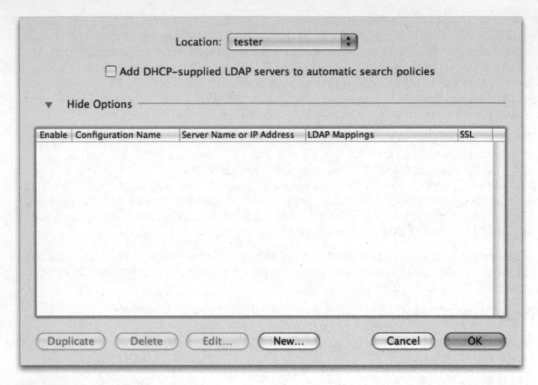

Figure 2-8. *LDAP configuration screen*

Next, click on the New… button and then click on Manual, as shown in Figure 2-9. If you were to enter the Server Name or IP address in the appropriately named field, you would be performing a trusted bind.

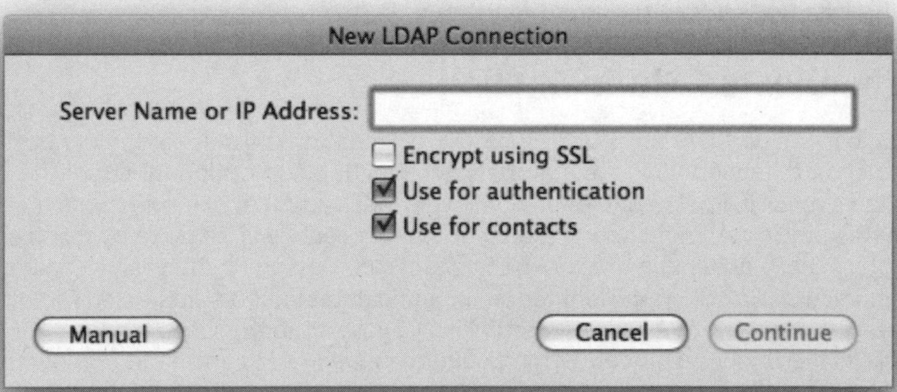

Figure 2-9. *New LDAP Connection dialog box*

Now enter a name for the configuration in the Configuration Name field, as shown in Figure 2-10. This name has nothing to do with the LDAP configuration other than a friendly name to help you remember which configuration does what task in environments with multiple configurations. The only consideration for this value is that it helps to keep it consistent across all of your clients. Click on the Server Name or IP Address field and type the name or DNS host name of the Open Directory Master. Then, click on LDAP Mappings and select the appropriate item from the drop down list. If the server is an Open Directory Master, you would select Open Directory Server, although you can also simply leave the field set to From Server. Also, highlight the SSL checkbox if an SSL certificate was enabled for the Open Directory server (assuming you have chosen to accept the certificate).

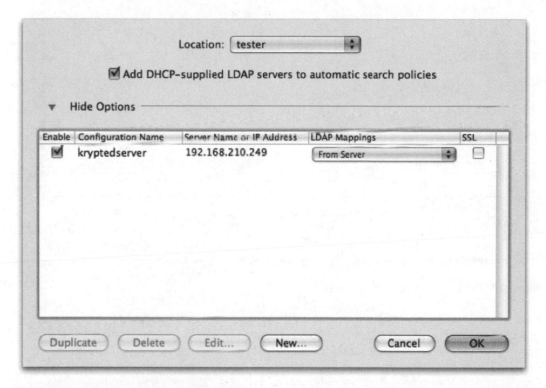

Figure 2-10. *Populated configurations for LDAP*

Once you are satisfied with your settings, click on OK. Next, you will need to add the new directory service configuration to your search path by setting the Search: field to Custom Path. To do this, you will specify a custom search path and then add the new service to the list of Search Domains. To do so, click on the Search Policy icon in the Directory Utility toolbar. From the Authentication tab, click on the plus sign (+) below the list of Domains, as shown in Figure 2-11. Next, select the newly added listing and then click on the Add button.

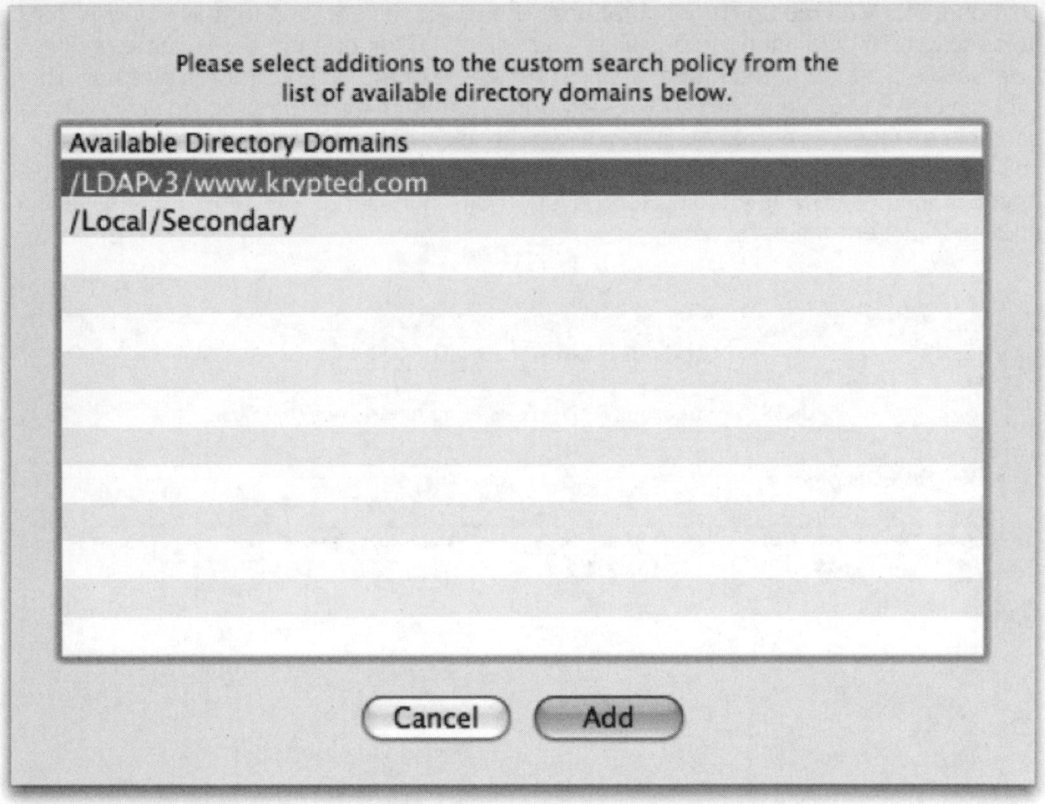

Please select additions to the custom search policy from the
list of available directory domains below.

Available Directory Domains
/LDAPv3/www.krypted.com
/Local/Secondary

Cancel   Add

Figure 2-11. *Select a Directory Domain to add.*

Now, click on the Apply button. You should see your new domain listed in the search policy (see Figure 2-12). You should now be able to use dscl to test whether the client can read information from the LDAP database. When you open dscl, you will be able to navigate to the LDAPv3 container and then to the text entered in the preceding Configuration Name field. Alternatively, you can do a simple one line non-interactive query with the tool to test our new directory service's functionality:

```
$dscl /LDAPv3/www.krypted.com list /Groups
```

Provided the previous command returns valid data, you have verified that you can browse the new directory services domain, and that you have completed an unauthenticated static bind.

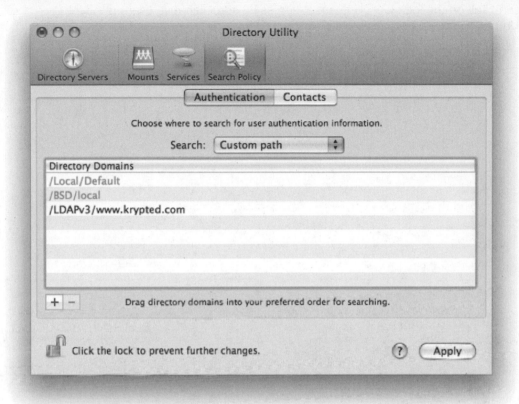

Figure 2-12. *The Authentication search path*

NOTE: Provided you are using a monolithic imaging solution, you can push out the image with an unauthenticated static binding en masse.

Trusted Static Binding

We saved the most common method of binding for last. This isn't because it is the least important, but because it is (or at least can be) the most complicated in terms of integration. If you built an Open Directory environment using the default settings for Open Directory, then by default you can use unauthenticated static binding or trusted static binding for client access. Of the two, trusted static binding is the most secure. If you are going to touch each client system (either manually or using a script), you might as well go ahead and make for as secure a solution as possible, given that it is not much more work (if any) to deploy a trusted bind-based solution.

Trusted static binding to LDAP can be achieved using a few different ways. The first is to use Directory Utility. Simply open the Directory Utility from /Applications/Utilities and then click on the lock icon, authenticating as an administrative user on the local computer you are using to bind. The resulting window is shown in Figure 2-13.

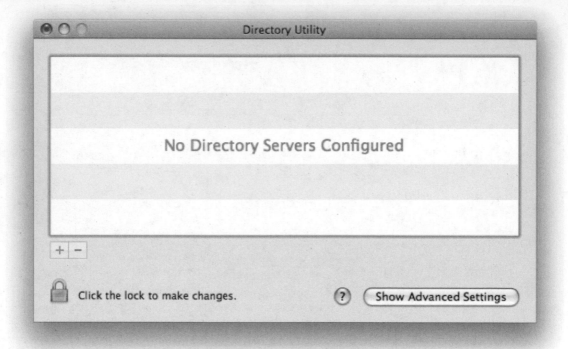

Figure 2-13. *Directory Utility*

Next, click on the plus sign (+). The dialog box will default with the Add a new directory of type: field set to Open Directory; enter the IP address or host name of the Open Directory Master (or a Replica) and optionally choose to enable SSL. Once you are satisfied with your entries, click on the OK button as shown in Figure 2-14.

Figure 2-14. *Directory Utility Add Server dialog box*

If the directory services configuration is successful, you have successfully bound. When using an unauthenticated static bind, you needed to set the Search Policy to custom. However, with a trusted static bind, the Search Policy is set as part of the bind operation. Although it's never a bad idea to check the search domains list and verify operation, this step will not need to be done.

> **NOTE:** If you are using a monolithic imaging solution you cannot push out the image with a trusted static binding en masse. You will need to script the trusted static bind into the post-installation automation tasks that you will use as part of your deployment.

Pushing Out SSL Certificates

As mentioned, using SSL as part of your directory services integration helps to make it as secure as possible. If that's the case, why doesn't everyone do it? It's an extra few steps that aren't absolutely necessary. If you would like to use SSL on your clients, for Open Directory or any other service, then on a per-host basis you typically need to trust a certificate, unless it was granted from a certificate authority. In order to get a certificate from a certificate authority you have to pay money. Additionally, the added complexity is not something many administrators will deal with, if not required. As of 10.5, Open Directory is additionally onerous when utilizing SSL with directory services. By default, the LDAP client utilized by the directory services daemon has no RootCA trusts. That is, even certs signed from a valid certificate authority will be rejected with the default configuration.

Overall, it isn't that hard to use SSL. Since Chapter 1 covered doing so on the server side, we're going to move into managing SSL on the client side. As you probably guessed, you can manage SSL from the GUI or from the command line, which makes for better automation. However, setting up our CA trust requires command-line interaction.

In order to configure our client to use SSL for directory services, you must first copy your rootCA pem file to your client. This certificate can be exported from the Keychain if it has been accepted or obtained from an administrator of the Certificate Authority (CA). This file must contain the certificate for each CA in the cert chain, and is often referred to as a cert bundle. If your Open Directory's SSL cert was signed by an intermediate CA, then your rootCA file must contain the certificate of that intermediate CA as well as the root CA certificate. Apple commonly installs certificates in the directory /etc/certificates, so this is a common place to store this file. It is best to avoid spaces in the path to this file, including the filename.

If your Open Directory implementation utilizes a certificate signed by a recognized Certificate Authority then you can utilize a certificate bundle preinstalled on all OS X machines. If your host recognizes the certificate authority, it will not require acceptance—specifically, the certificate-bundle file utilized by curl and located at: /usr/share/curl-ca-bundle.crt.

Once this file has been installed on the client, you can verify proper validation of the chain against your Open Directory server by utilizing the openssl command-line utility:

```
$openssl s_client -connect www.myhost.com:636 -CAfile /etc/certificates/rootCA.crt |↵
 grep "Verify"
```

You are looking for the value specified by the string Verify Return Code:. If the command succeeded, you will see the output:

```
Verify return code: 0 (ok).
```

If a non-zero value is returned, then there is a problem with your bundle file. You will need to rerun the command without the grep filter and decipher the problem from its output.

Once you have the pem file installed and tested, the next step is to configure your DirectoryService LDAP client to utilize this CA file. To do so, you need to edit the file located at /etc/openldap/ldap.conf. When viewing this file, take note of the key TLS_REQCERT. This key represents the primary change between Leopard and Tiger. In Leopard, the value of this key was changed from never to demand. With no associated TLS_CACERT or TLS_CACERTDIR values configured, you will fail to trust any certs presented.

To establish a trust, add a TLS_CACERT entry, pointing toward the cert bundle that you just installed as shown in the following code (run with root privileges):

```
echo "TLS_CACERT /etc/certificates/ldapCA.crt" >> /etc/openldap/ldap.conf
```

Once done, restart the Directory Services daemon:

```
killall DirectoryService
```

After modifying your file, restart Directory Services to read in the new values. At this point, you are ready to perform an SSL-enabled OpenDirectory connection.

If you are utilizing your own internal Certificate Authority, you will also want to import the CA file into the Keychain framework for utilization by Cocoa applications. To do this from the GUI then you will do so using Keychain Access, located in /Applications/Utilities, as shown in Figure 2-15. SSL certificates can be installed for a given users account or system-wide. Mac OS X uses a number of keychains to store all of the SSL certificates that have been installed on the system or a users account in an encrypted format. This separation between userlandspace and system-wide space is important. Local user accounts store keychains in ~/Library/Keychains, with the default keychain for a user called login.keychain. The system keychain is stored in /Library/Keychains and by default called System.keychain. There is one more directory worth noting, /System/Library/Keychains, which for the purpose of this chapter should not be altered.

To install an SSL certificate using either the login.keychain (for the user) or the System.keychain (global for all users on the host), simply drag the .cer or .crt file to the entry under Keychains and when prompted authenticate. If you do not yet have a .cer or .crtfile, learning how to export one will help you to have one to deploy, assuming, of course, you have at least one machine that has the public key installed. To export an SSL certificates public key, click on the certificate you wish to export and then drag it to the location where you would like to store it.

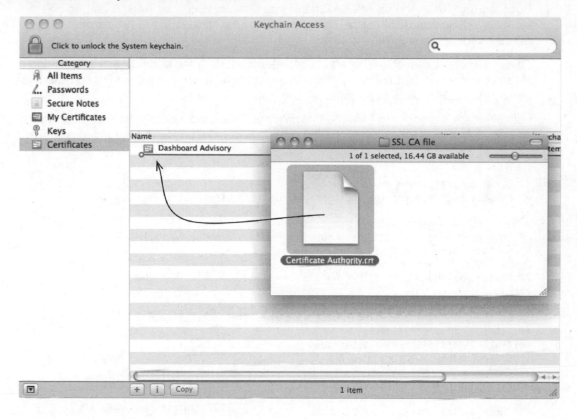

Figure 2-15. *Add root Certificate to Keychain Access*

As mentioned previously, you can also import keys programmatically. To do so for Tiger, you would copy the crt or certfile to the local system. For example, if you have a number of scripts that use a temporary folder called .tmp then you could use the following script, assuming you have the files stored in that directory. (To get them there, you can use curl to pull them off a web page or cp to pull them off a share point.) Next, copy the /System/Library/Keychains/X509Anchors into the users home folder, update it to include the certificate, and then push it back up to the correct location (replacing mycertname.crt with the actual name and path of your certificate):

```
cp /System/Library/Keychains/X509Anchors ~/Library/Keychains
certtool i "mycertname.crt" k=X509Anchors
cp ~/Library/Keychains /System/Library/Keychains/X509Anchors
```

To programmatically install certificates in 10.5, you must utilize the security framework (run as root).

```
security add-trusted-cert -d "/etc/certificates/rootCA.crt"
```

This command will add the specified certificate to the admin domain, effective for all users. Once added to this Keychain, GUI applications, such as Safari and Mail, will properly trust certificates signed by our CA. Oddly enough, the LDAP client in Address Book actually uses the same LDAP facility as DirectoryService. Thus, to set up SSL lookups in Address Book, previous methodology for configuring the previous /etc/openldap/ldap.conf file applies.

This is a rather exhaustive procedure between importing the certificate(s) into our local file system for use by LDAP, importing the certificate(s) into the Keychain, and then configuring LDAP settings to establish the trust.

Luckily, there is a script to facilitate this process. This script will take a specified pem file, so copy it into a specified directory, import into keychain, and update the ldap.conf file:

```
PATH=/bin:/usr/bin:/usr/sbin

## Setup our vars.:
## myName: NameUsed for logging (default SSLPackageInstaller)

myName="SSLPackageInstaller"
## resourceDir: pathToDirectory containing our cert to be installed
## (default same folder as script)
resourceDir="${dirname "${0}"}"
## Cafile: filename of our cert-bundle to be installed (as well as final destination
name)
CAfile="ldcintChainCABundle.pem"
## certStore: Path to the local cert directory (/etc/certificates)
certStore="/etc/certificates"
certPath="${certStore:?}"/"${CAfile}"
importForCurl=1

logger -s "${myName}: started. Build: $build"

## Check system version (script currently only supports 10.5+)
isSnowLeopard=$(sw_vers | grep -c 10.6)
isLeopard=$(sw_vers | grep -c 10.5)
isTiger=$(sw_vers | grep -c 10.4)
if ( [ ${isLeopard} -eq 0 ] && [ ${isSnowLeopard} -eq0 ] ); then
  logger -s "${myName}: Script currently only supports 10.5, or 10.6!!!"
  exit 1
fi

## Verify we were given a valid cert file, if not we bail.
## See CERTIFICATE EXTENSIONS section of x509 manpage
if [ -f "${resourceDir}"/"${CAfile:?}" ]; then
        goodCert=$(openssl verify -purpose any "${resourceDir}"/"${CAfile}" | egrep -c ↵
"^OK\$")
fi
if [ "$goodCert" -eq 0 ]; then
        logger -s "${myName}: Certificate failed validation!!"
        exit 2
fi

## Make sure our local certStore directory exists, make it if it doesn't
test -d "${certStore:?}" || mkdir -p "${certStore}"
```

```
## test for a pre-existing cert with the same name, if it's there move on,
## otherwise install ours.
test -f "${certPath:?}" || cp "${resourceDir}"/"${CAfile:?}" "${certPath:?}"
if [ $? != 0 ]; then
        logger -s "${myName}: Certificate transfer failed!! Copying $resourceDir/$CAfile ↵
 to $certPath"
        exit 3
fi


## Import the cert into keychain using the security framework
security add-trusted-cert -d "${certPath}"
## Modify the TLS_CACERT attribute of the local ldap.conf file to consult our
## newly installed cert bundle
if ( [ ${isLeopard} -eq 0 ] && [ ${isSnowLeopard} -eq0 ] ); then
        if [ `egrep -c "^TLS_CACERT" /etc/openldap/ldap.conf` != 0 ]; then
                escapedPath=`echo "${certPath}" | perl -p -e 's/\///\\\\//g'`
                perlCommand="perl -p -i -e 's/(^TLS_CACERT\s)(.*)/\$1${escapedPath}/g'"
                eval ${perlCommand:?} /etc/openldap/ldap.conf
        else
                printf "TLS_CACERT %s\n" ${certPath} >> /etc/openldap/ldap.conf
        fi
fi

exit 0
```

Custom LDAP Settings

Now that you can bind using the default method in Directory Utility, let's look at a way to set a little bit more information. The alternative method to performing a trusted static bind to Open Directory, or another LDAP server without using the command line, is to open Directory Utility and click on the lock to allow changes. Next, click on the Services icon in the Directory Utility application and then double-click on LDAPv3. From here, click on the New… button, but unlike the section on unauthenticated static binding go ahead and enter a hostname or IP address to bind to in the Server Name or IP Address field, as shown in Figure 2-16.

These options are as follows:

- Use for Authentication, which allows users to authenticate into local resources using the bound directory service.

- Define whether or not you want to supply Contacts to client systems using the Contacts tab of Search Policy in much the same way that you used the Authentication tab.

- Encrypt using SSL, one of the best ways to securely configure Open Directory (assuming, of course, that you have an SSL certificate and have followed the procedures previously outlined).

Next, click on the Continue button. Once you have updated the Search Policy, you should be able to test authentication using the aforementioned dirt (10.5) or dscl (10.6) utilities.

Figure 2-16. *New LDAP connection*

Now that you are bound, open Directory Access from /Applications/Utilities and click on the Services icon in the Directory Utility toolbar again. From here, click on the name of the server you recently bound to and then click on the Edit... button toward the bottom of the screen. Here, you can set a variety of options about how the LDAPv3 Plug-in functions, outlined in Figure 2-17. These include the following:

- *Configuration name:* the friendly name entered earlier in this chapter. If the wizard was used this will be the same as the Server Name or IP Address: field.

- *Server name or IP address:* the location of the LDAP server.

- *Open/close times out in:* number of seconds that the server will cancel an open or close event for the LDAP connection.

- *Query times out in:* number of seconds that a Query for a record will time out if the record has not yet been found.

- *Re-bind attempted in:* number of seconds to wait before reconnecting to the LDAP server if there is no response.

- *Connection idles out in:* number of minutes before an idle connection disconnects from the LDAP server.

- *Encrypt using SSL:* whether the connection will use SSL (likely set at bind time).

- *Use custom port:* uses a custom TCP port (other than 389 or 636).

- *Ignore server referrals*: server referrals aid the LDAP plug-in in finding information, but can cause latency in lookups and long wait times for logins.

- *Use LDAPv2*: uses the LDAPv2protocol rather than the LDAPv3 protocol, for backward compatibility.

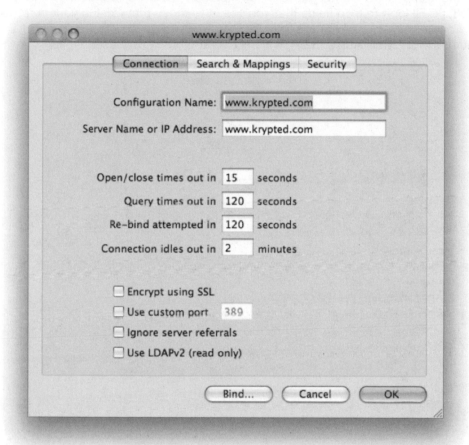

Figure 2-17. *Advanced LDAP settings*

NOTE: Apple has chosen the most appropriate values for the time out settings. However, if you have fairly latent connections then you may choose to increase the values, or if your directory servers are saturated then you may choose to lower them. Additionally, laptop users who are frequently out of the office may have a better user experience with lower values configured to reduce timeouts. Use caution when changing them though, as they are optimized for a standard Open Directory environment.

Now, click on the Search & Mappings tab. Through the interface found under this tab, you can configure the maps between standard Mac OS X attributes and those available via other LDAPv3 servers. (This can be seen through the Inspector in Workgroup Manager or using a standard read on a record in dscl, as explained in Chapter 1.) In some cases, this is only the difference between, for example, CreationTimestamp in OS X and createTimestamp in an LDAP object. As shown in Figure 2-18, you'll look to map fields that you see fit to those that exist in your current LDAP environment. Using the Access this LDAPv3 Server drop-down menu, you can select one of the pre-built Apple maps, which cover the commonly used Open Directory Server, Active Directory, and RFC2307 settings.

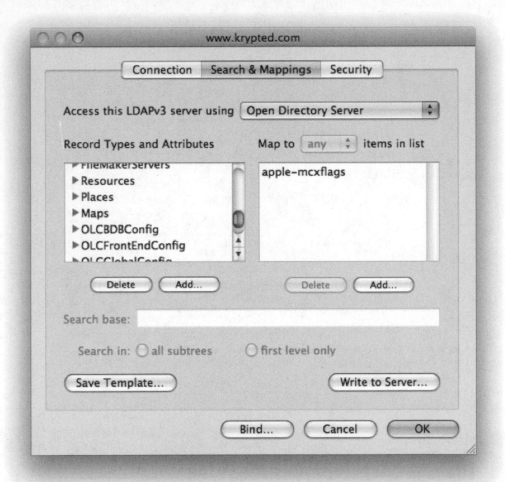

Figure 2-18. *Mapping LDAP Attributes*

RFC 2307 is a set of standards laid out for Unix-style operating systems to leverage LDAP as a centralized directory services solution. In fact, many of the attributes from Open Directory are taken directly from the standards laid out in RFC 2307. There is no manual mapping of fields for most aspects of LDAP if you are using an RFC 2307 compliant schema for LDAP, as those mappings are integrated for you out of the box.

`http://www.faqs.org/rfcs/rfc2307.html`

You can leverage otherwise unused fields with other Directory Services in order to provide required fields for Mac OS X, even if those fields do not exist in the foreign directory service. Once you are satisfied with your mappings, you can then save them as a template using the Save Template... button or write them back to the server, so other clients can use the mappings you may have painstakingly built. By leveraging the ability to write back into the cn=config container, you will save yourself from having to set mappings on each client, but instead set each client to From Server option using the Access this LDAPv3 server using the drop-down list shown in Figure 2-19.

NOTE: In order to use the Write to Server... button, you will need elevated (e.g., diradmin) privileges to the LDAP server.

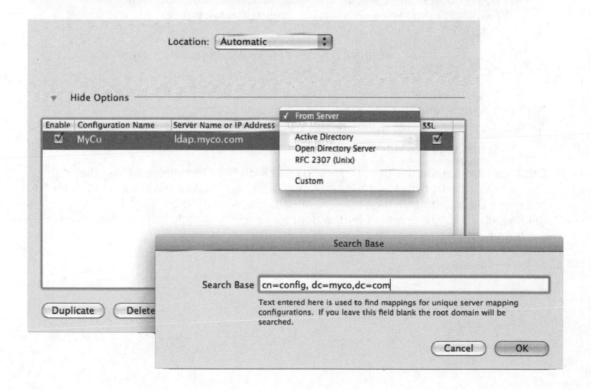

Figure 2-19. *Select From Server to read attribute mappings from the LDAP servers cn=config container*

Once you are finished editing mappings, click on the Security tab. Here, you can set user name (in the form of a Distinguished Name) and password as well as a few basic security policies to control access to the directory server and bound. Before you set these features, verify that your Open Directory servers also have them enabled and/or supported. The settings shown in Figure 2-20 are as follows:

- *Use authentication when connecting*: for unauthenticated static bind environments, forces client computers to use a username and password when connecting. This is where you can specify a distinguished name to utilize for directory authentication, allowing non-trusted binds to function when anonymous LDAP access is turned off.

- *Distinguished Name*: username of an account located in the LDAPv3 domain specified.

- *Password*: password for the Distinguished Name.

- *Disable clear text passwords*: sets the client to not establish a connection in the event that an authentication protocol cannot be found and password submission would otherwise revert to cleartext.

- *Digitally sign all packets (requires Kerberos)*: utilizes Kerberos for signing packets.

- *Encrypt all packets (requires SSL or Kerberos)*: encrypts all data, not just password, and requires SSL to function appropriately.

- *Block man-in-the-middle attacks (requires Kerberos)*: typically used in conjunction with Digitally sign all packets option.

Once you are satisfied with your settings, click on the OK button, or in order to go from an unauthenticated to a trusted static bind click on the Bind... button. If you do not see a Bind... button, then you are already using trusted binding. Finally, check the Search Policy and verify that the directory service is included, as described in the next section.

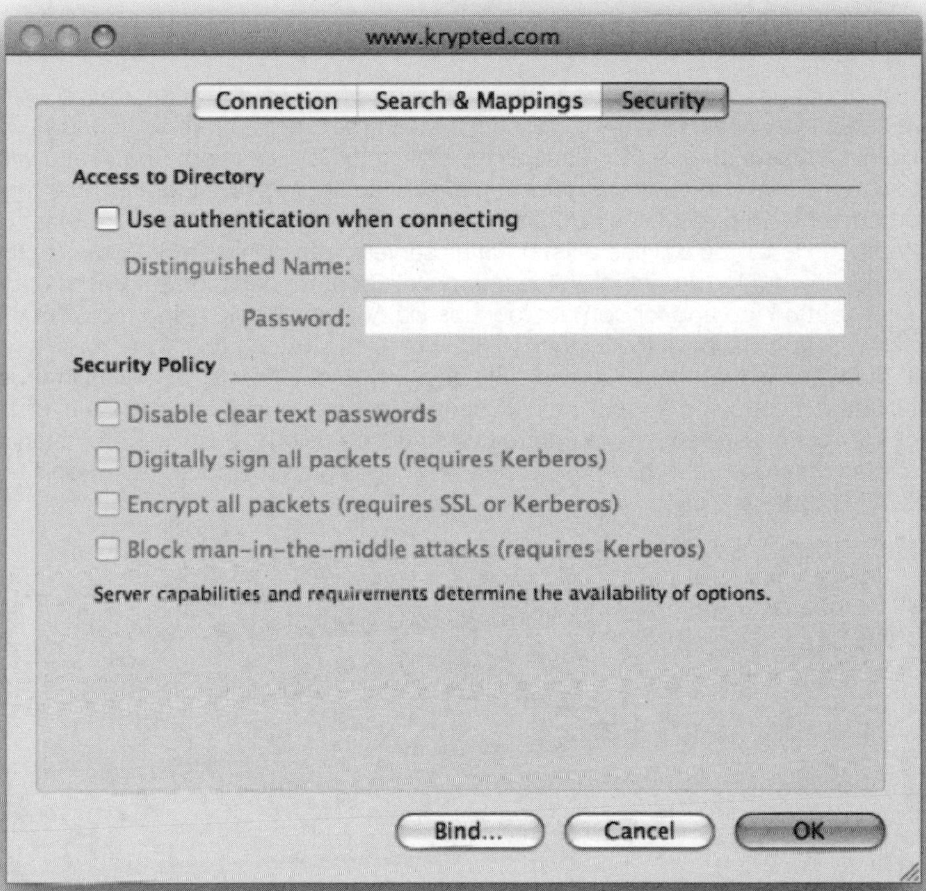

Figure 2-20. *LDAP bind security options*

Managing the Search Policy

You can bind to multiple directory services, and more specifically to multiple LDAP servers, by using the Search Policy settings to determine which takes priority over the others in the event that the username or computer name in one is duplicitous to another. By specifying the order of the various Directory Services, we can control the order in which they are queried for data. On all OS X machines, the local directory services database will always have precedence. That is, if my local database has a user 'jdoe', and the Open Directory System that I have bound to also has this user, when I login I will be authenticating against the computer's local user and will receive his information. This is very important to know about OS X. Thus, arranging the order in which Directories are listed is primarily useful for managing environments with multiple disparate Directory

Services. As I get into explaining Active Directory in more detail in Chapter 3, this will become a more fundamentally important concept to grasp as we move into taking a look at Mac OS X's Active Directory plug-in and leveraging dual directories.

The focus so far has been on using LDAPv3 as a means to establish centralized authentications services. However, the search policy also sets priority when using centralized Contacts. In order to manage the Directory Service search path, you will need to use the Directory Utility application. Once the utility is running, click the the lock and authenticate. Once authenticated, click on the Search Policy icon in the Directory Utility toolbar. Here, you will see a listing of all servers (called Directory Domains) that are currently in your local computers search policy for authentication purposes under the Authentication tab and for contact lookups via Address Book, using the Contacts tab. Each will typically have the Search pulldown menu set to "Local Directory" by default. This means that the server will only query the local Directory Service in order to process authentication and/or contacts. Change this setting to Custom Path in order to add network services to the search path. Once you are using a custom path, changing the priorities that a server is given is as easy as dragging each above the other in the list, as shown in Figure 2-21.

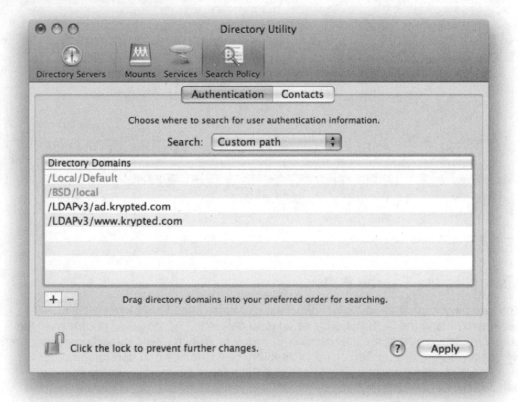

Figure 2-21. *The Directory Service search path*

According to how you bound to an environment, you may not see a directory server that you are bound to in the list of Directory Domains. If you do not see a server listed here, click on the plus sign (+) and you should see it in the list of Available Directory Domains. Click on the one you wish to add to your Search Policy, and then click on the Add button so it will be added to the list of Directory Domains and can be reordered as you see fit (see Figure 2-22).

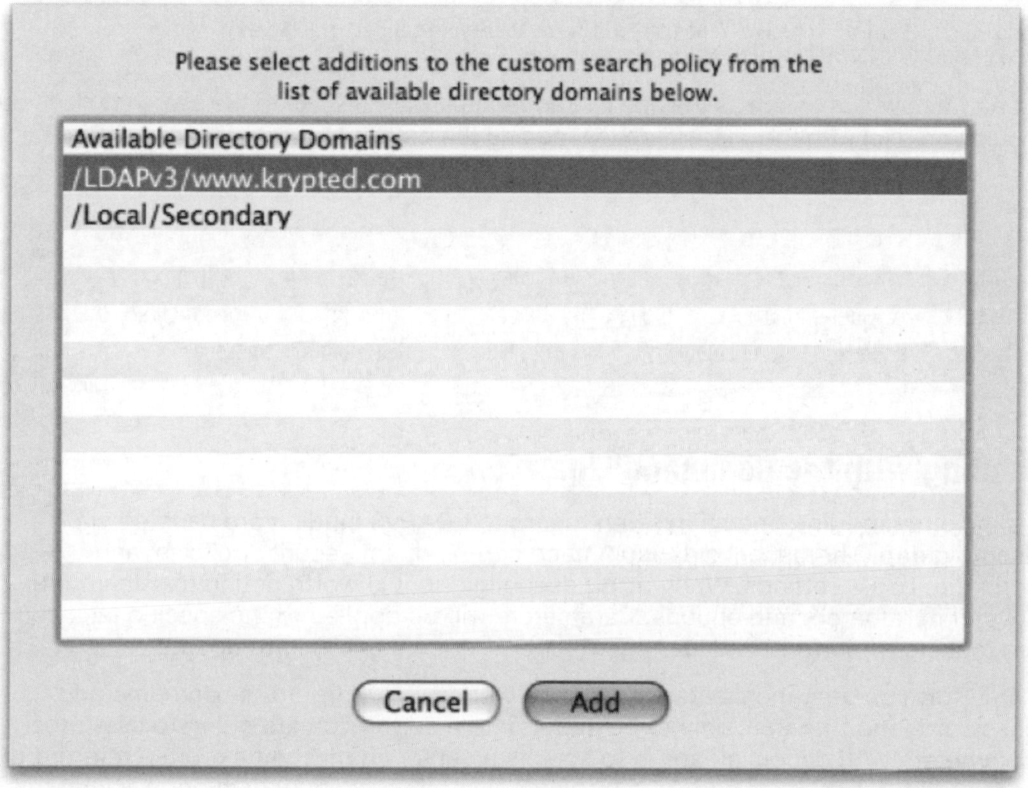

Please select additions to the custom search policy from the
list of available directory domains below.

Available Directory Domains
/LDAPv3/www.krypted.com
/Local/Secondary

Cancel   Add

Figure 2-22. *Add a Directory Domain*

As mentioned, you can perform all of the steps here from the command line. You will be using dscl not dsconfigldap, which you used for most other tasks in this chapter. This is because dsconfigldap is a command to specifically perform binding and manage certain aspects of the LDAPv3 plug-in itself, whereas the search policy is global across all directory services plug-ins.

You can also query and set search policy information from the command line. To see the current setting for the search path run the following command:

```
dscl -q localhost -read /Search
```

To change the search policy from a local search policy to a custom search policy, you would change the /Search dsAttrTypeStandard from LSPSearchPath (Local Search Policy) to CSPSearchPath(Custom Search Policy). To do so use dscl in conjunction with the –change option as follows:

```
sudo dscl /Search -change / SearchPolicy dsAttrTypeStandard:LSPSearchPath ⏎
dsAttrTypeStandard:CSPSearchPath
```

To add a new item (such as the one just added in dsconfigldap) to the search policy you would use dscl with the –append option, adding the path:

```
dscl /Search -append / CSPSearchPath /LDAPv3/seldon.foundation.com
```

> **NOTE:** A final aspect of search policies is that they can be used to control which directory server you query, the replica or the primary. Basically, you can bind to each and then use the Search Policy to switch between the two, controlling saturation points in the process.

Binding with the Command Line

Most command-line operations with regard to LDAPv3 binding are handled via dsconfigldap. The dsconfigldapcommand can bind, set security policies, and configure basic settings. When using dsconfigldap it is worth noting that there are several parameters and options. Parameters will be applied to the specific task you are looking to perform and identify which server configuration to update.

To perform an unauthenticated static bind without a prompt for a username and password (and therefore able to be added into a script) you are going to use three parameters with dsconfigldap: -a to specify a server (in this context often referred to as a configuration), -l to specify a local administrative account with permissions to perform such a task, and -q which supplies the password for said account. In the following example, these are set to seldon.foundation.com, admin, and daneel, respectively:

```
dsconfigldap -a seldon.foundation.com –l admin –q daneel
```

Alternatively, if you want to avoid passing passwords via stdin, and you are running from an admin account, you can perform an unauthenticated static bind without passing local credentials simply by running the tool as root:

```
sudo dsconfigldap -a seldon.foundation.com
```

While you previously used -a, -l and -q, the following parameters are also available and more common in trusted static bind environments:

- *-n <configname>*: configuration name for the server being added

- *-c <computerid>*: computer name to supply to the directory service

- *-u <username>*: LDAP administrative account for the server specified

- *-p <password>*: password for account previously specified

- *-r <servername>*: remove a server configuration

The following options are available regardless of the type of bind operation you are performing. These mostly include options for security and bind-time operations:

- *-x*: only allow communication if SSL is used

- *-s*: disable clear text passwords during authentication

- *-g*: force packet signing using Kerberos

- *-m*: block man-in-the-middle attacks using Kerberos.

- *-e*: if a server is capable of a security mechanism, then enforce it at the client as well and do so always

- *-f*: force the addition or removal of a configuration

- *-v*: process the command verbosely

- *-i*: run the command interactively, using passwords where needed

The following is an example of a command to perform a trusted static bind, using the additional parameters and commands that you've learned so far:

```
dsconfigldap -x -m -g -s -a seldon.foundation.com -n "Inner Rim" -u diradmin -p ↵
hindsightis4sight diradminpass -l admin -q daneel -c RD02100
```

You can also use dsconfigldap to unbind systems. Simply issue the dsconfigldap command followed by a -r and then the server name. In the following, we'll list the LDAPv3 servers and then loop through the list removing them one-by-one:

```
for dsrm in $(dscl localhost -list /LDAPv3)
do
  echo dsconfigldap -f -r "${dsrm}"
done
```

The preceding can be helpful if you are, for example, binding in an environment of pre-existing machines.

Scripting Binding

Throughout this chapter, you have provided a number of commands to programmatically bind to an Open Directory and/or LDAP environment. Now, we're going to put these into order to form a script that is capable of removing existing LDAPv3 servers and then perform a custom bind operation against the LDAPv3 environment, setting a computer name and then editing the search policy to include the newly bound directory service. You will be using the same domain name, username and password that you've been using throughout this chapter, as shown in the following:

```
#!/bin/bash
for dsrm in $(dscl localhost -list /LDAPv3)
do
  dsconfigldap -f -r "${dsrm}"
done
dsconfigldap –x -m -g -s -a seldon.krypted.com -n "Inner Rim" -u diradmin -p ↵
hindsightis4sight -l admin -q daneel -c RDO2100
dscl /Search -change / SearchPolicy dsAttrTypeStandard:LSPSearchPath ↵
dsAttrTypeStandard:CSPSearchPath
dscl /Search -append / CSPSearchPath /LDAPv3/seldon.krypted.com
```

Most scripts that you use will be similar to what you are using in the preceding code.

NIS

Network Information Service (NIS) was one of Sun's earlier attempts at providing directory services to clients. This isn't to say that all features of NIS are still supported, but basic support is there. Because Mac OS X maintains support for NIS and has a directory services plug-in dedicated to it, you can use Directory Utility to configure Mac OS X as a NIS client. If you need NIS, you know what it is. If you don't, then you will likely want to forget you mentioned it. If you need to set it up though, let's take a look at how to do it.

To set up your NIS client, open Directory Utility and click on the lock to authenticate (so you can make changes). Then click on the Services icon in the Directory Utility toolbar and check the box for BSD Flat File and NIS (checked by default in 10.6), as shown in Figure 2-23.

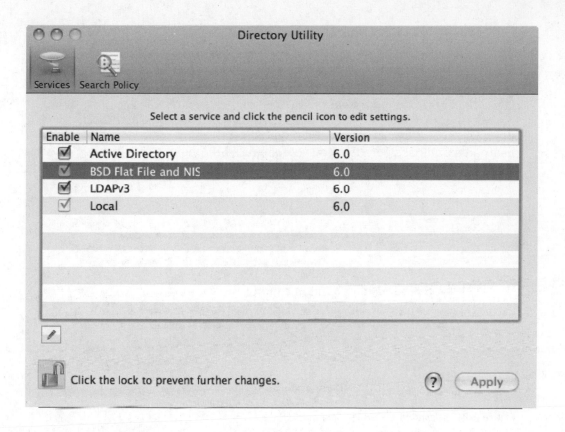

Figure 2-23. *Enabling NIS in Directory Utility*

Next, double-click BSD Flat File and NIS row. At the resulting screen shown in
Figure 2-24, check the box for Use User and Group records in BSD local node to
activate the plug-in. Next, enter the domain name of your NIS environment in the
Domain name: field and the IP address or hostname for your NIS servers in the Servers:
field. Because of the differences between NIS and LDAPv3, you will need to check the
Use NIS domain for authentication checkbox in order to populate the information for
your NIS environment into the search policy of your node. When you are satisfied with
your results, click on OK and then use dscl to test NIS functionality.

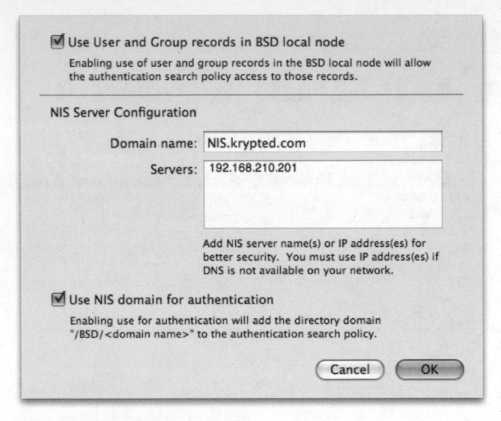

Figure 2-24. *Adding an NIS Server Configuration*

As you can imagine, there are commands you can use to manage NIS as well. These can be found in the /usr/sbin directory of your server and include the following:

- ypbind: perform binding operations
- ypxfr: obtains the map for a client from a directory server
- yppoll: query data from a directory server's map
- ypset: sets which directory server to use
- ypwhich: show hostname of yp server
- ypcat: show all of the available values in a NIS database
- ypmatch: show the value of a specified key in the NIS database

NIS was originally named Yellow Pages, which is why each command is prepended with the yp character set.

Mac OS X can act as a NIS server, although given the age you assume that you are either using NIS already or will not be implementing it. If you use NIS, you will want to manage the ypserv daemon, found in /usr/libexec. For more information on NIS, see the yp man page using the following command:

man yp

Kerberos

Kerberos is the preferred method for pretty much every directory service on the market to supplement LDAPv3, supplying enhanced password features, single sign-on, or both. Mac OS X is no different and the Kerberos client plays well either in its own Open Directory environments or in environments managed by other solutions. Mac OS X actually has a Kerberos Key Distribution Center (KDC) built into every single computer, used for securing peer-to-peer communications.

Managing Kerberos on a Mac OS X computer is mostly handled for you. There is very little to do in most environments. When you log into the first Kerberised service, be it an initial authentication into a Mac OS X client or via AFP to a SharePoint, at that initial authentication screen you will be authenticating into a Kerberos realm and will then not have to enter a password to access other services that are trusted by the realm. Beyond the basic realm configuration, most of the tools for Kerberos are often used for mass deployment of settings, manual configuration when those settings don't work correctly, and post deployment troubleshooting.

To control Kerberos using the GUI, you will use the Kerberos.app utility, which shipped with 10.5. Unfortunately, the Kerberos Ticket Viewer application was replaced in Snow Leopard with the "Ticket Viewer" Application, which is far more limited. The two can be seen side by side in Figure 2-25. Each respective utility is accessed through the Keychain Access menu of Keychain Access (which is located at /Applications/Utilities). You can also access each directly in the /System/Library/CoreServices/ directory. The 10.6 Ticket Viewer Application does not have any functionality to modify REALM configuration, and all edits must be made by hand, as discussed later in this section. Alternatively, you can copy the utility from a 10.5 install, and it will run in 10.6.

Once Kerberos.app has been opened, you can use it to browse the tickets (remember from Chapter 1 that a ticket is provided by the KDC based on the Ticket Granting Ticket). Using the toolbar, you can establish a connection to a new realm, renew tickets, Destroy tickets, get more information on tickets, and change the password associated with a ticket. In regard to per-user Kerberos ticket management, the Kerberos Ticket Viewer offers a one-stop shop.

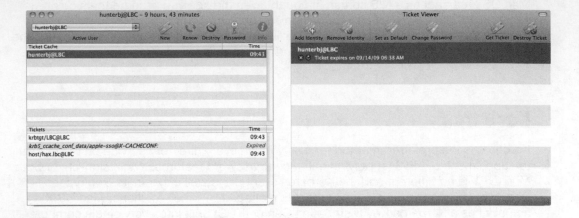

Figure 2-25. *10.5's Kerberos.app (left), 10.6's Ticket Viewer.app (right)*

In order to join a realm, click on the New button in the toolbar. As you can see in Figure 2-26, you'll now be prompted for an account name, a realm name, and a password. If the realm information is cached or has been supplied via DNS, then you will be able to select the realm from the Realm: drop-down menu.

Figure 2-26. *Authenticate to receive a Kerberos Ticket*

Kerberos.app and Ticket Viewer are fairly limited in what they can do. There is no interface for managing service principles and each option has very few parameters, whereas with the command line there are a plethora of options and parameters. For example, to list the tickets the current user has cached, you can use the klist command:

```
[helyx:~] hunterbj% klist
Kerberos 5 ticket cache: 'API:Initial default ccache'
Default principal: hunterbj@LBC

ValidStarting      Expires            Service           Principal
08/19/09 20:27:51  08/20/09 06:27:51  krbtgt/LBC@LBC
       renew until 08/26/09 20:27:51
08/19/09 20:27:54  08/20/09 06:27:51  host/hax.lbc@LBC
       renew until 08/26/09 20:27:51
08/19/09 20:28:23  08/20/09 06:27:51  vnc/mira.lbc@LBC
       renew until 08/26/09 20:27:51
```

As seen, the klist output is pretty basic and easy to read. You can see what I have by Ticket Granting ticket through the presence of the krbtgt/LBC@LBC service principal. You can also see that I have a host principal (used for ssh) and a vnc principal (used by OS X Screen Sharing).The klist command also has a variety of options as follows:

- -5: only display Kerberos 5-based tickets

- -4: only display Kerberos 4-based tickets

- -a: show a list of addresses

- -A: list all of the available tickets

- -c: show cached tickets

- -e: also display the encryption type of the session key

- -f: also list any flags for tickets, like -F for forwardable, -f for forwarded, -I for invalid, etc.)

- -k: list keys in the keytab file

- -K: show encryption keys from the keytab file

- -t: include timestamps in the output

- -n: show IP addresses

- -s: run silently, useful for a sanity check in a script to verify that the ticket cache is actually present

The kinit command can be used to initiate authentication into a realm, thereby generating and caching a ticket-granting ticket. In its most basic form, kinit can be called with no arguments, and will by default try to obtain a TGT for your current user in the machines default realm, as configured in the client's edu.mit.kerberos file. Alternatively, you can specify a specific username and realm to authenticate as:

```
[helyx:~] hunterbj% kinit -V hunterbj
Please enter the password for hunterbj@LBC:
Authenticated via Kerberos v5.  Placing tickets in cache 'API:Initial default ccache'
[helyx:~] hunterbj% klist
Kerberos 5 ticket cache: 'API:Initial default ccache'
Default principal: hunterbj@LBC

Valid Starting      Expires             Service Principal
08/19/09 22:01:29   08/20/09 08:01:29   krbtgt/LBC@LBC
        renew until 08/26/09 22:01:28
```

Additional options for the kinit command include the following:

- -V: verbose output

- -l: define the lifetime of the ticket when obtaining it

- -r: define how long a ticket is renewable

- -s: include a start time (and therefore caches a postdated ticket)

- -f : use forwardable tickets

- -F: do not use forwardable tickets

- -p: use proxiable tickets

- -P: do not use proxiable tickets

- -a: request a ticket with the host's address

- -A: request ticket without a defined address

- -v: validate a ticket in the keytab against the KDC

- -R: renew a ticket

- -k: obtain a key from a key in the local keytab file (cache) rather than from a live server

- -S: include the service name to use when obtaining ticket-granting tickets

The kdestroy command is fairly straightforward, with far fewer options than kinit—but then it has a specific task to delete tickets. The options are primarily in regard to defining which tickets to delete:

- -a or -A: destroy all tickets

- -c: name of cache to delete

- -p: name of principal to delete

- -q: run quietly (without feedback to the command line)

There are two other commands worth noting: kpasswd and kswitch. The kpasswd command can be used to change a principal's password. The kpasswd command prompts you for both your old and your new password. This can be useful, for example, if you are using an Active Directory environment or troubleshooting why users are unable to reset their own passwords. The kswitch command sets the cache for the default system.

There are also a number of files used to track various Kerberos statuses, caches, and settings. For example, the /Library/Preferences/DirectoryService/ DSLDAPv3PlugInConfig.plist property list file maintains a list of all of the service principles created when a user of the host authenticates into a realm.

The keytab file is perhaps the most critical file on an operating system to secure. Kerberos uses a keytab file to store pairs of Kerberos principals and their corresponding DES keys. In Mac OS X, the keytabfile is called krb5.keytab and is stored in the /etc directory. Much of the information in the keytab is barely readable to human eyes, much less editable. Therefore, much of the heavy lifting for the keytab will be handled using the kadmin and kadmin.local commands, and in some cases the ktutil command. The former two commands have the same options and features, with the one exception being that kadmin.local is meant to manage Kerberos on a KDC while kadmin is meant to manage Kerberos on all other hosts. The kadmin command supports in regard to utilized ciphers, password restrictions, ticket life, etc. For some example usage of the tool, see the "Troubleshooting Kerberised Services" section.

Earlier, it was mentioned that Mac OS X client acts as a KDC (it's actually an LKDC, to be more specific). The /etc/krb5.conf file can be used to show available realms. For the available realms, the krb5.conf file will show the supported encryption types of each realm along with the configuration options, mappings, rules, and location. An example of the krb5.conf file is shown in the following code:

```
[libdefaults]
  default_realm = KRYPTED.COM
  default_tgs_enctypes = RC4-HMAC DES-CBC-MD5 DES-CBC-CRC
  default_tkt_enctypes = RC4-HMAC DES-CBC-MD5 DES-CBC-CRC
  preferred_enctypes = RC4-HMAC DES-CBC-MD5 DES-CBC-CRC
  dns_lookup_kdc = true
[realms]
  KRYPTED.COM = {
  auth_to_local = RULE:[1:$0\$1](^KRYPTED\.COM\\.*)s/^KRYPTED\.COM/KRYPTED/
  auth_to_local = DEFAULT
  }
[appdefaults]
  pam = {
  mappings = KRYPTED\\(.*) $1@KRYPTED.COM
  forwardable = true
  validate = true
  }
  httpd = {
  mappings = KRYPTED\\(.*) $1@KRYPTED.COM
  reverse_mappings = (.*)@KRYPTED\.COM KRYPTED\$1
  }
```

The preceding file is split into three sections: [libdefaults], [realms], and [appdefaults], which respectively controls Kerberos behavior, information for a given realm, and settings per service. It is more than likely that you will not need to edit the kerb5.conf file with the exception of potentially disabling DNS utilization with Kerberos, which can help to reduce login times for domains using the .local namespace. This can be done by adding the following line into the [libdefaults] section of the configuration file:

```
dns_fallback = no
```

An OS X client utilizes a krb5.conf file, but stores it at the location: /Library/Preferences/edu.mit.Kerberos. In this file, you will also find the [realms] and [libdefaults] sections, but you will also find the [domain_realm] section, which deals with normalization and definitions of realms. The contents of a typical file are listed here:

```
[domain_realm]
        krypted.com = KRYPTED.COM

[libdefaults]
        default_keytab_name = /etc/opt/quest/vas/host.keytab
        default_realm = KRYPTED.COM
        default_tkt_enctypes = arcfour-hmac-md5 des-cbc-md5
        dns_fallback = yes
        dns_lookup_kdc = yes
        forwardable = true

[realms]
        KRYPTED.COM = {
                admin_server = seldon.krypted.com
                kdc = server.seldon.com:88
                kpasswd_server = seldon.krypted.com:464
        }
```

In the preceding, you will see another dns_fallback. If you first initiated a connection to the default_realm following setting the dns_fallback in krb5.conf, which I mentioned when discussing the krb5.conf file, this setting will be set to no; otherwise it will be set to yes, and will need to be changed if you want to disable reverse dnsenumeration. Again, only be concerned about the dns_fallback if you are seeing connectivity errors and think they are related to DNS issues (you cannot perform both a forward and reverse lookup on a realm's KDC or you are using a .local domain namespace).

You should also notice the kpasswd_server entry in the edu.mit.kerberos file, which defines what password to perform a reset against in the event of a failure. In large environments with services distributed across a number of hosts, you may find stale information here, which can also cause password change events to fail. If you do find yourself needing to make changes to this file, and the file was generated by a directory binding, know that your changes will be overridden. To prevent this, you will need to delete the lines containing the text:

```
# autogenerated from : /LDAPv3/myserver.com
# generation_id : 419733404
```

Any time you change information in your Kerberos files, you'll need to restart the Kerberos services. The Kerberos services that run on a Mac OS X client include [] edu.mit.Kerberos.KerberosApp, edu.mit.Kerberos.KerberosAgent, edu.mit.Kerberos.CCacheServer, and com.apple.KerberosHelper.LKDCHelper.

Each of the preceding services can be controlled using launchctl. For example, if you run the launchctl command followed by the list option, you should see the following line included somewhere in the output:

```
-       0       edu.mit.Kerberos.CCacheServer
```

In order to then stop the CCache Server, you could use the launchctl command with the stop option, followed by the name of the launchd item you would like to stop. In the case of CCache Server, it would be the following:

```
Launchctl -stop edu.mit.Kerberos.CCacheServer
```

Kerberising Services

After binding a client or server to a domain and joining it to a Kerberos Realm, it may be desirable to Kerberise the services that the node provides. That is to say you will configure the service in such a way that your OS X boxes will provide single-sign-on access to users with valid Ticket Granting Tickets (TGIs). The process to integrate your OS X server with your current SSO environment will vary based upon the Kerberos implementation that your company provides. For instance, in Open Directory environments, Apple provides several nifty tools which do much of the legwork for you: sso_util and krbservicesetup. For Active Directory, the dsconfigad tool can do all of the legwork as well. For other implementations, it may very well be possible to utilize some of Apple's tools. However, it might also be necessary to roll your own. In any scenario, it is necessary to have a proper edu.mit.kerberos file, as discussed in the previous section. During the Active Directory and Open Directory binding process, the Kerberos information in this file will be automatically generated for you. Until you can verify that you can obtain a ticket using kinit, or the Kerberos Ticket Viewer app, you don't want to mess around with Kerberising your services.

The easiest Directory Service SSO implementations to integrate are Apple's Open Directory and Microsoft's Active Directory. Neither are terribly difficult to pull off, but from the command line, the Active Directory tool is the most simplistic. You can use the

Server Admin utility to Kerberise services for a server by selecting the Open Directory Service and selecting the General tab. If the server is bound to a Directory and detects Kerberos, you will be presented with the ability to join a server to a Kerberos REALM, as seen in Figure 2-27. Click on the Join Kerberos button to generate service principals for all supported services, and then modify their configurations to utilize the new principals for authentication.

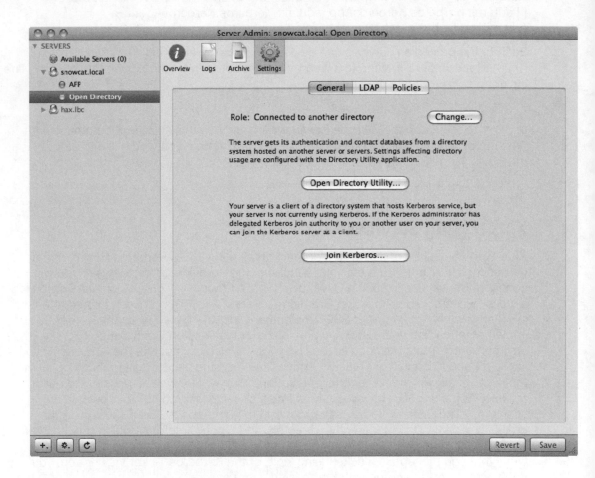

Figure 2-27. *Kerberising services using Server Admin*

To integrate with AD from the command line, once your OS X server has been bound you simply call dsconfigad with a single flag, -enableSSO:

```
sudo dsconfigad –enableSSO
```

For more information on Active Directory, see Chapter 3.

To integrate an OS X box with Open Directory from the command line, you can utilize the sso_util binary. This utility has a wide variety of uses, but first and foremost, it can be used to generate the appropriate service principals from the Kerberos Realm's KDC, place them in the node's local keytab, and even configure the node's services to use them. The syntax is rather basic as well and is as follows:

```
sudo sso_util configure -r REALM -a admin_name [-p password] service
```

We just feed it our REALM, a kerberos administrator's credentials, and we specify a service which will be generated. You can specify one or more of the following services afp, ftp, http, imap, pop, smtp, ssh, fcsvr, vnc, cifs, or all. When ran, the command will pretty much take care of everything for us. For example, to fully kerberise an OS X laptop to the Open Directory domain myco.com, the following syntax would be used:

```
sudo sso_util configure -r MYCO.COM -a diradmin all
```

With this syntax, you will be prompted to provide your password via secure text entry, which is preferable to potentially leaving your password in your shells history, or expose your password via ps. Alternatively, you can pass the password via the environmental variable $SSO_PASSWD_PATH.

> **NOTE:** To clear your shell's history in either the bash or tcsh shells, use the command history -c.

The sso_util binary has some other uses for larger OD environments as well. For example, it has the ability for a KDC administrator to generate Kerberose principals for a specific host, at which point a lesser privileged administrator can Kerberise the services on the host side. The process starts with the KDC admin first generating the record. In this case, we will be generating a record for host mail.myco.com in our OD domain myco.com:

```
sudo sso_util generateconfig -r MYCO.COM -R mail.myco.com -f /LDAPv3/odserver.myco.com
-U thatotheradmin -a diradmin all
```

The previous command will attach a secure record configuration to the computer LDAP object mail.myco.com found in the LDAP database at server odsrever.myco.com. This computer object will be found at the path /Computers/mail.myco.com. The LDAP dn for this in an OD environment is cn=mail.myco.com,cn=computers,dc=myco,dc=com. The secure record configuration is an encrypted data object stored in the computer's configData LDAP attribute. The data stored in this attribute is an encrypted string which contains the Kerberos host and service principals for the desired host. Because the service principals are very sensitive, it is recommended that you delete this entry after you have successfully kerberized a host using either Server Admin or the command that follows.

In the previous sso_util command, we specify the user that otheradmin as a delegate admin. That user can now run the sso_util command from the new server, and complete the Kerberisation process:

```
sudo sso_util useconfig -R mail.myco.com -f /LDAPv3/odserver.myco.com -a thatotheradmin
```

While the main pages of sso_util specify that the tool is specifically for Open Directory, it's most basic functions provided by the configure option will likely work with most vanilla Kerberos5 implementations. Even if you don't have Open Directory, this tool may still be able to automate pretty much all of the principal generation for you.

If the sso_util command doesn't work in your environment, Apple provides a lower level tool, krbservicesetup, which might work for your needs. The krbservicesetup command is actually called by sso_util and has a few downsides, but it is worth mentioning. The krbservicesetup tool can be used to configure a single service at a time, and handles Kerberos principal generation via kadmin and local service configuration. Secondly, you must specify the password as part of the command. For example, to generate a service principal for the imap service on mail.myco.com, I would use the following command:

```
sudo krbservicesetup -r MYCO.COM -a diradmin -p password imap
imap/mail.myco.com@MYCO.COM
```

Troubleshooting Kerberised Services

If you've gone through the previous section about setting up Kerberised services, and for whatever reason the previous tools do not accomplish the task, then you are not completely out of luck. However you may need to go through the grueling process of principal creation and service configuration. On top of this, each service has a different method for configuration, so it becomes a bit of a black art.

The first step in troubleshooting any kerberos error is to verify that your client and server's clocks are in sync. Kerberos is notorious for this, and it only allows for a skew of five minutes. Anything beyond this and the whole system breaks down. Next, ensure that the problem is truly server oriented and verify from multiple clients that Kerberised services are not being provided.

With that out of the way, it's time to troubleshoot the server. Consider for a moment that I am configuring my imap service to provide single sign-on. From your server, first ensure that the service has a respective service principal in the server's local keytab. To do this, use the klist command with the flags –kt, ran with root privileges via sudo:

```
%sudo klist -kte
Keytab name: FILE:/etc/krb5.keytab
KVNO Timestamp         Principal
---- ----------------- --------------------------------------------------------
9 08/19/09 21:15:56 imap/mail.myco.com@MYCO.COM (Triple DES cbc mode with HMAC/sha1)
9 08/19/09 21:15:56 imap/mail.myco.com@MYCO.COM (ArcFour with HMAC/md5)   3 08/19/09
9 08/19/09 21:15:56 imap/mail.myco.com@MYCO.COM (DES cbc mode with CRC-32)
9 08/19/09 21:15:56 vnc/mail.myco.com@MYCO.COM (Triple DES cbc mode with HMAC/sha1)
9 08/19/09 21:15:56 vnc/mail.myco.com@MYCO.COM (ArcFour with HMAC/md5)   3 08/19/09
9 08/19/09 21:15:56 vnc/mail.myco.com@MYCO.COM (DES cbc mode with CRC-32)

(output clipped)
```

Looking at this output, I can see that my local keytab (/etc/krb5.keytab) does indeed contain the imap service principal, three in fact. This illustrates the default nature of Open Directory's KDC behavior, it generates three principles for each service, encrypted via des, 3des, and md5, respectively. By supporting all three encryption algorithms, the service can provide maximum compatibility.

If the necessary Kerberos principals for your service don't exist, and sso_util isn't doing its job and creating them for you, then you can create your own principles. Principal generation is done via the kadmin or kadmin.local utility. The exact procedure may vary based upon your Kerberos toolset, but the following should work with most MIT based KDC's. First, we connect to our KDC via kadmin, preferably from our new mail server:

```
$ sudo kadmin -r MYCO.COM -p diradmin
Authenticating as principal diradmin with password.
Password for diradmin@MYCO.COM:
kadmin:
```

Next, we can run the listprincs command to see if our service principal already exists in the kdc:

```
>kadmin: listprincs
(output cut)
host/mail.myco.com@MYCO.COM
ldap/mail.myco.com@MYCO.COM
vnc/mail.myco.com@MYCO.COM
 (output cut)
```

We've cut the output of this command for brevity, but in large environments that command can return a long list of data. Alternatively, we can use the getprinc command to specifically query the principal we are interested in:

```
>kadmin:  getprinc imap/mail.myco.com@MYCO.COM
Principal: imap/mail.myco.com@MYCO.COM
Expiration date: [never]
Last password change: Wed Aug 19 21:15:56 PDT 2009
Password expiration date: [none]
Maximum ticket life: 0 days 10:00:00
Maximum renewable life: 7 days 00:00:00
Last modified: Wed Aug 19 21:15:56 PDT 2009 (diradmin@MYCO.COM)
Last successful authentication: [never]
Last failed authentication: [never]
Failed password attempts: 0
Number of keys: 3
Key: vno 9, Triple DES cbc mode with HMAC/sha1, no salt
Key: vno 9, ArcFour with HMAC/md5, no salt
Key: vno 9, DES cbc mode with CRC-32, no salt
```

Here we can see the principal does exist, and at the bottom, we can even see the three different encryption keys used by that principal. If this principal didn't yet exist, we could create it using kadmin's addprinc command. We specify the –randkey option to generate a random password for the principal:

```
>kadmin: addprinc -randkey imap/mail.myco.com
Principal "imap/mail.myco.com@MYCO.COM" created.
```

With the service principal created on the KDC, we now need to copy it to our local machines keytab file. If we ran kadmin from the local machine, this is very easy to do by using the ktadd and specifying our local keytab file at /etc/krb5.keytab:

```
>kadmin:  ktadd -k /etc/krb5.keytab imap/mail.myco.com
Entry for principal imap/mail.myco.com with kvno 3, encryption type Triple DES cbc mode
with HMAC/sha1 added to keytab WRFILE:/etc/krb5.keytab.
Entry for principal imap/mail.myco.com with kvno 3, encryption type ArcFour with
HMAC/md5 added to keytab WRFILE:/etc/krb5.keytab.
Entry for principal imap/mail.myco.com with kvno 3, encryption type DES cbc mode with
CRC-32 added to keytab WRFILE:/etc/krb5.keytab.
```

We can now run klist -kt as root on our machine and we should see the new principals listed in our local keytab file. If we ran kadmin from a different machine, we will need to write the principals to an arbitrary file, and transfer it to the server. Be careful with this methodology though, as if the keytab file is compromised, it can be used to hack into your server. If you find yourself needing to do this, run the ktadd command, but specify a different file to export to, say /Users/admin/mail.myco.com.keytab. From here, you will need to copy the file to the server, for simplicities sake we'll say you placed the file in the same path. From the new server, we will use the ktutil command to add this keytab to our existing krb5.keytab file. ktutil is not the friendliest of commands, but the basic operations are easy enough. First, fire up the utility, and read in our new keytab file with the rkt option:

```
$sudo ktutil
ktutil: rkt /Users/admin/mail.myco.com.keytab
```

Next, we'll read in our existing keytab file at /etc/krb5.keytab:

```
ktutil: rkt /etc/krb5.keytab
```

We now have loaded both our existing principals and our new principals into memory. The next step is to write out all of the loaded principals to our local file via the wkt option:

```
ktutil: wkt /etc/krb5.keytab2
ktutil: quit
```

We have now written our keytabs to a new file /etc/krb5.keytab2. At this point we need to make it our active keytab file:

```
mv /etc/krb5.keytab2 /etc/krb5.keytab
```

We have now merged the two keytab's entries, and you can now delete the transfer mail.mycoc.com.keytab file.

Once the service principals exist both on the KDC and in the server/client's local keytab file, the pieces are in place for a successful SSO setup, and all that is left is the configuration of individual service(s). The unfortunate reality of the situation is that each service is a little bit different in this respect. Some services, such as vnc and ssh, simply search for the principal appropriate for the connection hostname. For instance, from my client if I connect via ssh to mail.myco.com, it will search for the principal host/mail.myco.com@MYCO.COM. However, if I ssh to the same box via its bonjour address, mail.local, it will search for the principal host/mail.local@MYCO.COM, which will typically not exist. VNC works in a similar manner.

The AFP service utilizes a specific principle specified via its preference file found at /Library/Preferences/com.apple.AppleFileServer.plist. There are two specific keys that the AFP server uses for SSO: kerberosPrincipal and authenticationMode. The first attribute is simply the string text of the principal, afpserver/mail.myco.com@MYCO.COM. The second attribute defines the types of authentication. This attribute will contain one of three values: standard_and_kerberos, standard, or kerberos. The three values are fairly self explanatory. We recommend the first of the three, standard_and_kerberos. In this configuration, the AFP server will default to Kerberos, and if that fails for whatever reason, will revert to its standard authentication method: Diffie-Hellman Exchange (DHX).

The latter option can be configured for the AFP Service by using the Server Admin utility, as shown in Figure 2-28. Noticeably absent from that picture is a field to define the Kerberose principle. To set that, you can use the defaults command to modify the service's plist, and then restart the service to read in the new setting (active transfers will be interrupted):

```
sudo defaults write /Library/Preferences/com.apple.AppleFileServer kerberosPrincipal
'afpserver/mail.myco.com@MYCO.COM'
sudo killall AppleFileServer
```

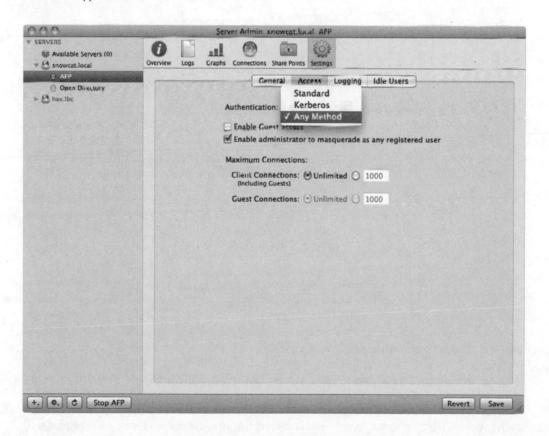

Figure 2-28. *Setting AFP Authentication methods in Server Admin*

Numerous other services have similar authentication selections to that shown in Figure 2-28: FTP, iCal, iChat, Web, and Xgrid. For each of these services, Kerberos authentication is enabled by default.

The mail service, like the ssh service, utilizes gssapi based authentication, which provides a more standardized interface over the Kerberos API for authentication services, but commonly utilizes Kerberos as it's actual authentication mechanism. The easiest way to enable Kerberos for mail services is via the Server Admin application. As shown in Figure 2-29, Kerberos authentication can be enabled individually for each protocol, SMTP, IMAP, and POP. Once again, it is recommended that you enable a non-Kerberos fallback authentication, unless security policies require it.

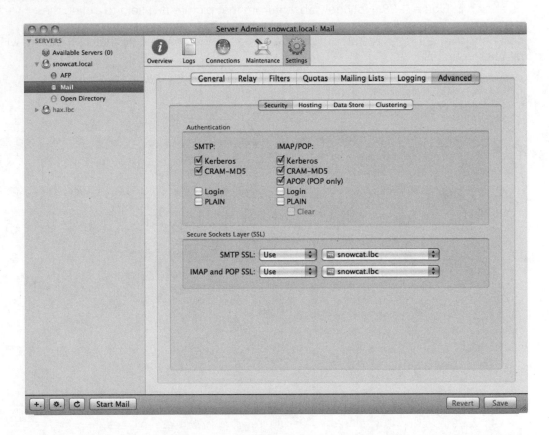

Figure 2-29. *Setting Mail Authentication methods in Server Admin*

After ensuring that your service is properly setup to use Kerberos, and the principals exist in the KDC and the local keytab, you should have a functional SSO-friendly service. If this still is not the case, then you'll have to resort to the logging facilities provided by each service. Keep in mind that the number one killer of Kerberos is its heavy reliance on synchronized clocks, so always check that your client and server's clocks are in sync.

Directory Services Preferences

Throughout this chapter we have focused on binding to LDAPv3 and therefore to some degree, LDAP. However, there are a number of settings for the directory services environment that we have not covered. As you can imagine, there are a number of preferences available for the directory services client framework, all of which can be assigned through the command line (and therefore from a script). You can also set a system as you would like the directory services preferences to be, and then deploy the actual plistfiles that make up many of these preferences.

In the /Library/Preferences/DirectoryService directory, you will find the following files:

- *ActiveDirectory.plist*: contains Active Directory Binding data including mappings, security levels, and computer credentials (discussed further in Chapter 3).

- *ActiveDirectoryDomainCache.plist*: Cache data related to bound Active Directory domains (discussed further in Chapter 3).

- *ActiveDirectoryDomainPolicies.plist*: Contains password policy data pertinent to bound Active Directory domains (discussed further in Chapter 3).

- *ActiveDirectoryDynamicData.plist*: Contains Active Directory Domain information, including available Domain Controllers (discussed further in Chapter 3).

- *ContactsNodeConfig.plist*: can be used do add Directory Domains to the contacts search policy (using Search Node Custom Path Array), show/reset DHCP LDAP information (DHCP LDAP), and configure the search policy by setting the Search Policy key to 1, 2, or 3 for Automatic, Local, or Custom respectively.

- *ContactsNodeConfigBackup.plist*: backup of the ContactsNodeConfig.plist.

- *DirectoryService.plist*: described in the preceding "Plug-ins" section, and can be used to enable and disable directory services plug-ins.

- *DirectoryServiceDebug.plist*: allows you to enable directory services debugging using the "Debug Logging" key, set the levels of verbosity for the debug log using the "Debug Logging Priority Level" key, and enable NetInfo (although NetInfo might not be too useful without nicl).

- *DSLDAPv3PlugInConfig.plist*: can be used to read, edit, and add server configurations and the timeout settings applied in the Custom LDAP Settings section of this chapter. Also maintains a key for "Service Principals to Create," defining which Kerberos service principles to create at bind time.

- *DSRecordTypeRestrictions.plist*: shows versioning information (not otherwise useful).

- *PasswordServerPluginPrefs.plist*: can be used to set or change the priority of encryption mechanisms.

- *SearchNodeConfig.plist*: can be used do add Directory Domains to the authentication search policy (using "Search Node Custom Path Array"), show/reset "DHCP LDAP" information (DHCP LDAP), and configure the search policy by setting the Search Policy key to 1, 2, or 3 for Automatic, Local, or Custom, respectively.

- *SearchNodeConfigBackup.plist*: backup of the SearchNodeConfig.plist.

Each of the keys in the previous files can be changed using the defaults command. While we've so far covered making settings change to actual files dedicated to the directory services property lists, there are also hooks into other services, such as the login window of Mac OS X. For example, the following command will edit the com.apple.loginwindow.plist file, setting the login window to display the status of the directory services daemon:

```
defaults write /Library/Preferences/com.apple.loginwindow AdminHostInfo DSStatus
```

Summary

In this chapter, we provide both a high- and low-level integration of OS X into several Directory Service systems such as Open Directory, NIS, and third-party LDAP implementations. We also covered integrating client and servers with Kerberos systems to function in an existing single sign-on environment.

In the next chapter, we will further explore directory services integration, with a specific focus on integrating OS X systems with Microsoft's Active Directory system.

## Chapter 3

Active Directory

Active Directory is a Directory Services solution developed by Microsoft. It is built using certain proprietary technologies, which only (currently) runs on the Microsoft Windows Server platform. Samba may soon turn out to be worthy of running in production as a Windows Active Directory replacement. While many of the back end components of Active Directory are designed for the windows client platform, Microsoft based much of the structure of Active Directory on open standards, such as the LDAP format known as RFC 2307 and the Kerberos v5 protocol defined in RFC 1510. Active Directory can be used to seamlessly integrate Windows systems en masse, but the real advantage of blending these technologies and open standards is that foreign operating systems can then be integrated with Active Directory as well.

Integrating Mac OS X and Mac OS X Server with Active Directory is very similar to integrating with the native directory services that a Mac OS X Server's Open Directory service can provide. The reason for this is Active Directory supports gaining access to information within its Jet Database by using the Light Weight Directory Access Protocol (LDAP). When thinking about directory services, it is sometimes best thought of as a large delimited document, such as something you would create in a spreadsheet program like Microsoft Excel. When a client attempts to use a directory for authentication and authorization it looks up an object such as a user account via the LDAP protocol much like searching for a field in a spreadsheet. This lookup entails finding the field in the directory that matches the requested information. For example, when a user types his or her username this information is stored as a key value pair in Active Directory.

If user zsmith logs in, then an LDAP query is started that attempts to find a user in the directory with that value. Once the user is found, the resultant set of keys that make up their user account can be accessed. For example, zsmith may have a home directory that is stored on a network server. This path name will be stored as a key (homeDirectory) in the Active Directory database. Apple has two default plug-ins for communicating with LDAP servers, the LDAPv3 plug-in and the Active Directory plug-in. These two plug-ins are very similar in terms of the back end communication they use. However, Apple developed the Active Directory plug-in to supplement missing LDAP attributes that are not normally available in a standard Active Directory Schema. The best example of this is the uidNumber attribute. This attribute is normally used to contain the numerical value associated with an account. On a native Open Directory Server, this value is mapped from the server's uidNumber attribute to the local clients UniqueID attribute. Without a UniqueID, users are not able to login, this is because of Mac OS X's UNUI underpinnings which require a UniqueID to track ownership on the file system.

If you use the LDAPv3 plug-in to authenticate to Active Directory (which is possible to do, though rarely implemented), the default RFC 2307 mappings would map a server attribute called uidNumber to a local plug-in mapping called UniqueID. When a user attempted to login they would then query the server attribute uidNumber, and because it was unavailable but required for login, they would be unable to authenticate to the login window. Apple saw this scenario and mitigated it in the design of the Active Directory plug-in. When a user logs into a workstation that is bound to Active Directory, the plug-in itself generates a numerical value based on other information in the native directory and maps it to the UniqueID attribute. You can think of this as a mask in front of the Active Directory server to make it seem more like a native Open Directory server.

Additionally, the Apple Active Directory plug-in will not only mask missing attributes but will also convert attributes that are in the wrong format for Mac OS X to being in the correct format. Go back to our example of a home directory that was hosted on a network volume. In Active Directory this network path is stored using Universal Naming Convention (UNC) or \\server\share. Despite its "universal" name, this format is not supported for connecting to URIs in Mac OS X. If you wanted to connect to \\server\share using the built in file-sharing clients, you would format the URI as smb://server/share. This simple format difference would mean the difference of being able to login or not using the LDAPv3 plug-in. In this instance, Apple again configures the Active Directory plug-in to read in the server homeDirectory attribute and then reformats and maps it to the local HomeDirectory attribute.

With all the supplements that are provided by Apple through the native Active Directory plug-in, it serves as an adequate tool for integration in many different environments. In the beginning of this chapter, we will cover the Apple-provided and supported tools that can be used to bind to Active Directory environments. However, depending on the needs of your environment you may need to take advantage of some Active Directory features which cannot be facilitated using just the Active Directory plug-in. The most common needs in an enterprise environment move beyond mere authentication and into the realm of ongoing client management. For this, Apple has a very robust set of management options known as "Managed Preferences" or MCX (covered extensively in Chapter 7). Though not natively supported by Active Directory, MCX can still be implemented alongside Active Directory via a few different methods. After reading this chapter, you will be familiar with the various options available, as well as the pros and cons of each.

On a native Open Directory server these management options are stored as keys within a given object. For instance, user zsmith (or more commonly a "workgroup" that he is a member of) may have a managed preference that configures his Dock to appear on the left-hand side. These management attributes cannot be natively stored in Active Directory without modifying the Active Directory schema, a modification that is global for all objects in an organization's directory. As such, from a political aspect, extending the schema can be difficult to push through in environments with a proportionally small number of Mac OS X workstations. For this reason, other options such as maintaining a separate supplemental Open Directory server or using a third-party active directory plug-in may best suit your needs. These options are covered in the following sections. Because the needs and business requirements of each environment are different, after explaining how to use the built-in Active Directory plug-in, the remainder of the chapter is dedicated to customizing the Active Directory plug-in and the common third party add-ons.

> **NOTE:** Apple has provided a video and a white paper on extending the Active Directory schema at http://seminars.apple.com/seminarsonline/modifying/apple/index.html?s=301

Binding to Active Directory

When binding to an Active Directory server, keep in mind that it is an individualized process; each workstation will need a computer account named for the machine created in the directory. While it is possible to pre-populate these accounts, the Apple Active Directory plug-in will create a computer account in Active Directory at the time of binding with the correct credentials if one does not already exist. As with Windows client account, each OS X computer account contains a unique pre-shared key used to authenticate that individual machine to the directory. This individualistic nature is an important aspect to consider when looking at automating the process. The process of binding a machine to Active Directory can be accomplished either through the use of a GUI interface or through a decently robust set of command-line tools. We will discuss the command-line components of this process (dscl and dsconfigad) later in this chapter. First, we will look at the manual GUI tools used to bind a Mac OS X machine into Active Directory.

Directory Utility

The Apple DirectoryService framework is a set of code allowing for modularized access to the different directory service plug-ins available (including third-party plug-ins). The graphical application for configuring the plug-ins is Directory Utility (Called Directory Access in 10.4). This application is bundled with all versions of Mac OS X, and in older versions can be found in /Applications/Utilities. With 10.6, Apple has migrated access functionality to the Login Options of the Accounts System Preference. The Directory Utility Application is not gone in 10.6; though, it has simply been relocated to /System/Library/CoreServices, a directory used by OS X to house internal support Applications. Once opened, you will need to authenticate as a local administrator to make changes to the directory services plug-in. If you are not automating this step, you will need to supply your on-site technicians with both local and directory administrator credentials to manually complete this process. You can customize the policies in your environment to supply desktop technicians with Active Directory accounts that only have access to bind computers into the domain; likewise, you can provide non-administrators with access to edit local configurations by modifying the file /etc/authorization. Specifically, directory service changes are defined by the authorization right 'system.services.directory.configure'. Through the modification of this right, you can grant access to change directory settings to your non-admin users.

To start the binding process, open the Accounts System Preference pane by clicking on the Apple menu in the top-left corner of your screen, selecting System Preferences and then clicking on Accounts. Next, click on the Login Options, as shown in Figure 3-1.

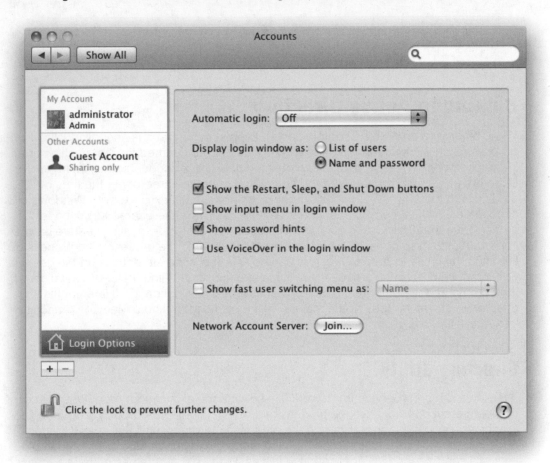

Figure 3-1. *Login options screen of accounts system preference pane*

To authorize your session to edit the System Preference, click on the lock in the lower-left corner of the screen. Then click on the button to Join… in the field for Network Account Server. This will bring up a pop-up screen that simply has a field for a server name or domain name. Type the name of your domain. After a time, the screen will expand so that you can enter the ID that the computer you are binding will have once it joins Active Directory, the user name of an account in your Active Directory that has credentials to bind to Active Directory, and the password for that account. Supply this information as seen in Figure 3-2 and then click on the OK button.

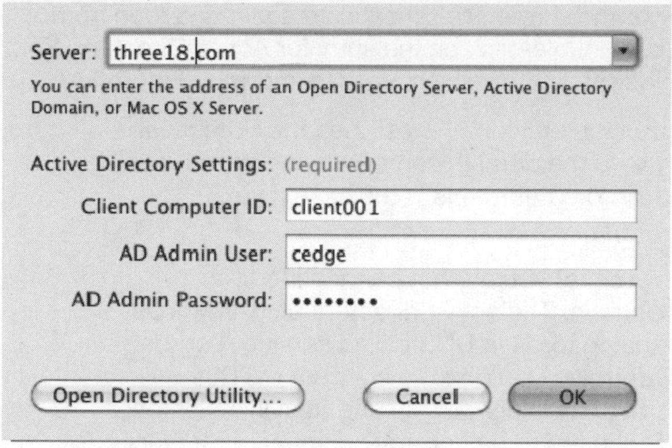

Figure 3-2. *Binding to Active Directory*

In an effort to simplify the binding process, Apple allows you to bind to both Open and Active Directory servers from this initial screen. Keep in mind that using this screen will only allow you to bind and not configure granular settings within either of the plug-ins, though this can be done at a later time, if necessary. To bind using a screen that allows you to configure more granular settings, click on Open Directory Utility... and then click on Services in the upper-left hand corner of the screen, as you can see in Figure 3-3.

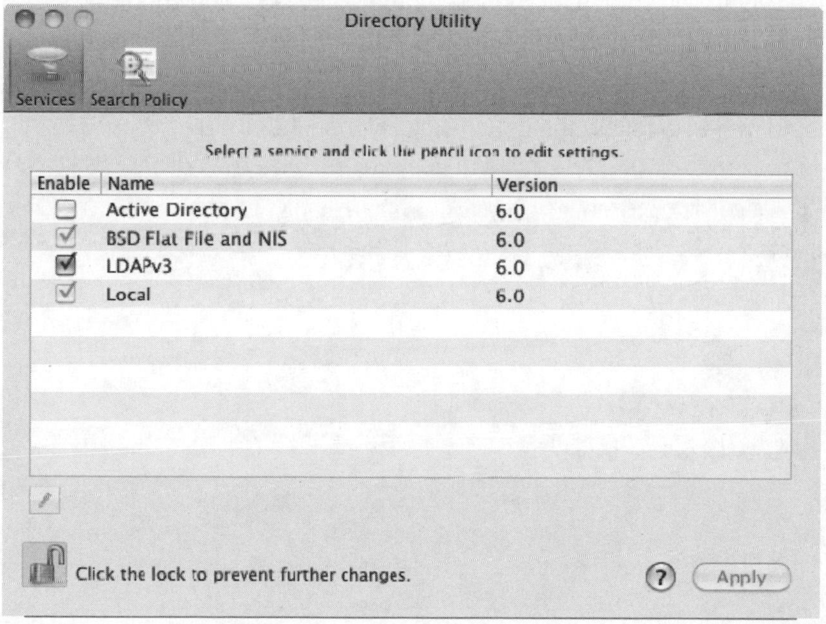

Figure 3-3. *Services in Directory Utility*

Use the lock in the lower-left corner of the screen to authenticate again and then from Services in the Directory Utility toolbar double-click on the entry for Active Directory. You will then be prompted with three fields by default, which are also shown in Figure 3-4:

- *Active Directory Forest*: If there is only one Forest then the Forest will invariably be the same name as the domain name, but check with an Active Directory administrator to confirm this is the case if you encounter binding issues.

- *Active Directory Domain:* Note that you are not connecting to a specific host, but rather a domain. The active directory plug-in will use this domain to look up special records in DNS called service records (SRV) to find the Domain Controller you need to connect to. This process is unique to the Active Directory plug-in and heavily relies on the client's configured DNS servers to be correctly pointing at servers that host these records or can facilitate communication to these servers; properly configured DNS is absolutely paramount for this process to succeed.

- *Computer ID:* This is the name of the computer account record as it will appear in the Active Directory domain. Note that this name also typically becomes a DNS name on the network, so if you are configuring a client named "wintermute" the Apple AD plug-in will dynamically request a DNS record be created for "wintermute.wallcity.org" if the Active Directory domain is wallcity.org and points to all the configured IP addresses (including virtual) for that client; the specified value should generally conform to DNS standards regarding A records, as defined in RFC 1035 accessible at http://www.ietf.org/rfc/rfc1035.txt. For best results, the length of this value should be a maximum 15 characters, and should generally follow the Letter Digit Hyphen (LDH) Rule.

> **NOTE:** For more information on Resource Records, see the following TechNet article: http://technet.microsoft.com/en-us/library/cc783389(WS.10).aspx.

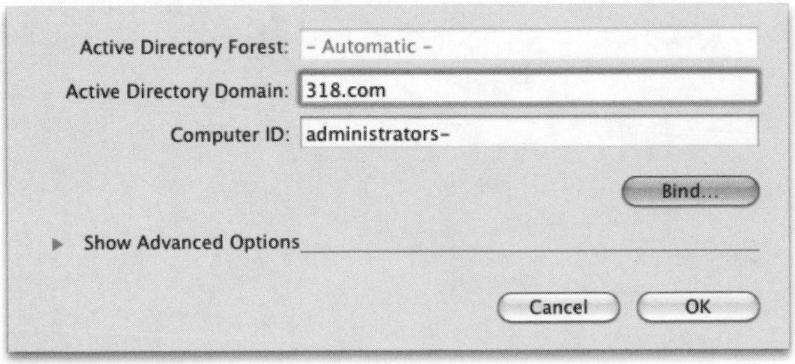

Active Directory Forest:	– Automatic –
Active Directory Domain:	318.com
Computer ID:	administrators–
	Bind...
▶ Show Advanced Options	
	Cancel OK

Figure 3-4. *Binding to Active Directory Using Directory Utility*

TIP: When naming OS X computers, you will generally want to follow what is referred to as the LDH rule. As defined, the LDH rule calls for the use of only ASCII alphabetic and numeric characters in addition the hyphen (-), no other punctuation or characters are allowed. Avoid all numeric names, and with any *nix system, avoid starting a hostname with a numeric character.

Next click on the Bind button and you will be asked to authenticate into the Active Directory domain using the following fields, as you can see in Figure 3-5:

- *Username*: Contains any valid user account that is capable of joining computers to the domain. Additionally, this user must have rights to create new objects in the container or organizational unit you are saving the computer into, access that can be delegated by the Active Directory administrator. If your Active Directory environment is strictly controlled, you may have to request a computer record be pre-populated rather than attempt to use the supplied credentials to create one.

- *Password:* The password for the above account.

- *Computer OU:* The search base for the Organizational Unit that clients will be added to. For example, if you create an Organizational Unit called Macs in a domain called pretendco.com then you would use CN=Macs,DC=pretendco,DC=com in this field.

- *Use for authentication:* Allows for authenticating into the client computer using a valid Active Directory username and password.

- *Use for contacts*: Allows for searching for contacts using Address Book.

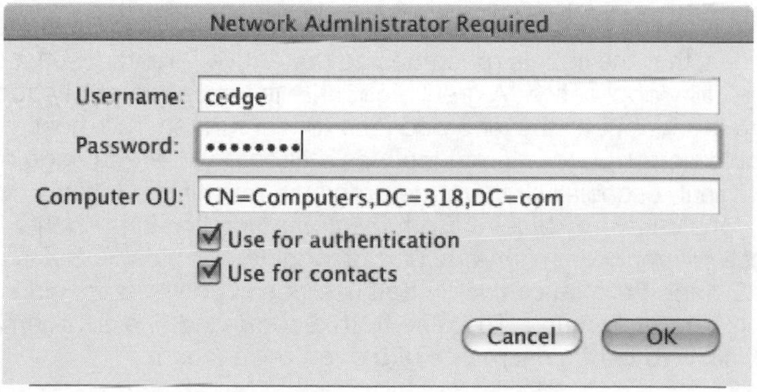

Figure 3-5. *Binding to Active Directory Using Directory Utility*

The most common binding problem with Active Directory environments is with the Active Directory domain's DNS having an incomplete set of service records. If we had a nickel for every time a Windows admin swore up and down there were no problems on their servers, only to have all problems resolved by a quick and dirty fix—an `ipconfig /rebuilddns` command runs from a domain controller hosting the Active Directory integrated DNS by rebuilding the required service records. Beyond DNS, a number of binding issues are caused between incompatible policies between Mac OS X and Active Directory. For example, LDAP signing as a requirement was not supported in 10.4.

> **NOTE:** As described in Chapter 1, you can use the directory services debug log and potentially tcpdump (which can be used to monitor port 389 to review traffic to and from your Active Directory Domain Controllers) to more granularly isolate binding issues.

Using the bind screen from the Accounts System Preference pane, you were not prompted for the organizational unit to place the computer record in whether you wanted to allow login or contact lookups. The computer record is automatically generated based on the host name of the computer you are using to bind and the authentication and contact lookups are assumed to be used. If you have not pre-populated the computer record, your computer account will be placed in the default container, computers. To continue with the previous pretendco.com example, Organizational Units are these containers, which are accessed using a convention whereas the container is a CN followed by a DC for each part of a fully qualified domain name. Therefore, if you were to enter the Computers container of mydomain.com instead of pretendco.com from our previous example, you would use cn=Computers,dc=domain,dc=com.

Testing Your Connection

Once you have successfully bound your computer to Active Directory, you should test the connection. First, verify that the light is green beside the Active Directory service as is listed in the Directory Utility application. A green light here is typically a pretty good indicator that everything is fine, but it's never a bad idea to test further. The most straightforward test would simply be to attempt login as a directory user, but logging out and then back is not efficient, especially if there are problems resulting in login window delays. More efficiently, you can verify binding from the command line (and should test it either way). As previously referenced, an integral part of logging in on Mac OS X is a user account's UniqueID attribute. You can verify that user resolution is happening and view the UniqueID using the id command. To do so from a command-line environment, enter the `id` command followed by the username of a directory account:

```
id zsmith
uid=1763670396(zsmith) gid=703907591(WALLCITY\domain users) groups=703907591
(WALLCITY\domain users),1842785604(WALLCITY\administrators)
```

The `id` command can indirectly display a local conflict. The Active Directory plug-in generates UniqueIDs, and with AD typically these numbers have 10 digits. In contrast, a standard local account, such as one that was configured using the Account System Preference pane and the setup assistant at first boot, has an id starting at 501, incrementing upwards. Open Directory users start at 1025. This makes it possible at first glance to determine the approximate origin of an account. For example, if you saw a unique id in the range of 600 to 1,000 then the account was likely initially created using the accounts system preference pane.

If the id command fails with id: jdoe: no such user check the account you are using for testing to see whether it exists and check that your computer is set to correctly try to "Search" for users in Active Directory. Typically this "Search Path" is filled in automatically for you by the Directory Utility application at the time of binding. However, if you are manually configuring or attempting to troubleshoot an automated binding you can verify this configuration in Directory Utility. Open the Directory Utility, choose Show Advanced Settings from the windows tool bar, select Search Policy, and verify the /Active Directory/... line item is displayed. Contrary to popular belief, the order listed is not typically relevant for user and group resolution, as you will see the local directory is always accessed first, then typically it should be the next network directory that contains users. If you are having problems that are resolved by moving /Active Directory up in the search order, you may have a configuration problem in your other directory servers or a conflict in the namespace that users occupy.

While id is probably the easiest, the best utility for testing your directory services is dscl. The utility provides an interface for programmatically interacting with the DirectoryServices Application Programming Interfaces (APIs). This program can be run via an interactive shell or from within scripts. After first binding to Active Directory, use dscl to test that the directory is available and that user resolution (the ability to resolve user accounts) is working. While you could just logout and log back in depending on any problems encountered, you can more easily see that binding is working from the command line. From a shell prompt, use the dscl command followed by the computer or path to connect to. In order to establish a connection to the currently running DirectoryService daemon, we'll use localhost:

```
dscl localhost
```

The syntax for moving through the configured directory services is much like navigating a filesystem or ftp server from the command line. Once you have initiated your session it will show an interactive prompt (>). Use the ls command to list the DirectoryService Plug-ins. If you do not see Active Directory listed, the plug-in itself is not enabled. Even if you are bound to an Active Directory domain, you will not be able to navigate to the directory node until this plug-in is enabled (by default only the LDAPv3 and local plug-ins are enabled), although when you use the Directory Utility to bind systems the Active Directory plug-in is enabled by default. Review the "Binding to Active Directory with a Script" section to see an example of how to enable this plug-in from the command line.

The ls command will show you the currently enabled plug-ins (including third party) in the list. In addition, you will be able to navigate into the Contacts and Search paths, which will show you the hierarchy of all configured and enabled plug-ins. You can then type cd followed by the name of any item in the list of current plug-ins.

```
Active Directory
BSD
Local
Search
Contact
```

In this case, type cd 'Active Directory'.

> **NOTE:** Standard command-line conventions apply here in regard to space. Be sure to use quotes around the path when using dscl as Active Directory is one of the few plug-ins that has a space in the name. Alternatively, you can use the built in tab auto-completion to automatically quote this path for you.

Once you have changed directories into the Active Directory plug-in, you will see the Active Directory domains and forests that were previously configured at bind time in the appropriate nesting order. The Apple Active Directory plug-in only allows you to configure one Active Directory forest at a time, the default behavior is to allow authentication from all domains within a forest on the local machine. This is an important note, as it means that depending on your organization's directory topology you may not be able to see the users if you are in a separate forest. If you would like to restrict access to this computer (or server) to only one domain, you will need to uncheck the Allow authentication from any domain in the forest button in the Directory Utility or run the command dsconfigad –all domains disable, depending on your configuration. You will see either All Domains or your domain name, wallcity.org when listing this value in dscl.

```
/Active Directory > ls
All Domains
```

To test that your binding worked correctly you can change directory into the respective value and do an ls. If you receive an error when changing directory, your Active Directory binding has most likely either failed or the current DirectoryService daemon has lost contact with your sites Domain Controller.

```
/Active Directory > cd 'All Domains'
/Active Directory/All Domains > ls
CertificateAuthorities
Computers
FileMakerServers
Groups
Mounts
People
Printers
Users
```

A common procedure used to verify connectivity is to use the dscl command along with the read verb to view the attributes associated with a given account. This will allow you to verify that user lookup is working within the Active Directory plug-in itself and look for any potential issues, such as a missing attribute. While you could ls Users, depending on the size of your organization you may not receive all of the information that you are looking for. By default, the LDAP server in Active Directory will return a maximum of 1,000 results. Although many more can be enumerated, this is just a limitation for how many are shown at once. Therefore, we will simply cd into the appropriate directory and then use read to view the attributes for a known good user account:

```
/Active Directory/All Domains > cd Users
/Active Directory/All Domains/Users > read zsmith

dsAttrTypeNative:accountExpires: 456878888655687
dsAttrTypeNative:ADDomain: wallcity.org
dsAttrTypeNative:badPasswordTime: 0
dsAttrTypeNative:badPwdCount: 0
dsAttrTypeNative:cn:
Charles Edge
dsAttrTypeNative:codePage: 0
dsAttrTypeNative:countryCode: 0
dsAttrTypeNative:displayName:
Zack Smith
dsAttrTypeNative:distinguishedName:
CN=Zack Smith,CN=Users,DC=wallcity,DC=org
continued...
```

> **CAUTION**: The LDAP server in Active Directory by default will return a maximum of 1,000 results. This limitation affects user, group, computer, and computer group listings in both dscl and Workgroup Manager, and therefore may negatively affect any scripting automations derived from this information. This is a hard limit in Windows 2000, but can be adjusted in later versions, as instructed in the Microsoft Knowledge base article found at:
>
> http://support.microsoft.com/kb/315071.

One thing to keep in mind is that while viewing data from the Active Directory plug-in directly (by changing directories into it), you can verify that you have a connection to your organization's directory services. However, simply being able to view the raw directory service data does not in fact mean that you can authenticate against it. As with dsconfigldap in Chapter 2, the final step is to use the information gathered about your test user and verify that you user matches in the /Search path as well.

```
/Active Directory/All Domains/Users > read /Search/Users/zsmith

dsAttrTypeNative:accountExpires: 456878097655687
dsAttrTypeNative:ADDomain: wallcity.org
dsAttrTypeNative:badPasswordTime: 0
dsAttrTypeNative:badPwdCount: 0
dsAttrTypeNative:cn:
Charles Edge
dsAttrTypeNative:codePage: 0
dsAttrTypeNative:countryCode: 0
dsAttrTypeNative:displayName:
Zack Smith
dsAttrTypeNative:distinguishedName:
CN=Zack Smith,CN=Users,DC=wallcity,DC=org
continued...
```

If the two read commands return different results you have namespace collision, which could possibly be resolved by altering your Search path (this was covered in much more detail in Chapter 2). In some cases, it may be necessary to simply delete the conflicting user account. You can view the current search path with dscl along with a read verb, the path, and the attribute to display (in this case, /Search SearchPath).

```
/Active Directory > read /Search SearchPath
SearchPath:
/Local/Default
/BSD/local
/Active Directory/All Domains
/Active Directory >
```

Once you have verified that user result ion is functional from the DirectoryService daemon, you can verify that Authentication is correctly happening (so far we have only verified that user resolution is possible). Type exit to end your interactive dscl session for the localhost.

```
/Active Directory/All Domains/Users > exit
Goodbye
```

Testing Authentication

Being able to look up user accounts in Active Directory allows you to apply them to local facilities, such as file system permissions, and to nest them in groups on other configured directory systems. Authentication is a corner stone of any modern Directory Service. Apple provides a command-line tool called dirt in Mac OS X 10.5 that you can leverage to access the DirectoryServices Application Programming Interface and perform authentication queries.

```
dirt -u zsmith -p 'bw4r3c3n1nj4s'
Call to dsGetRecordList returned count = 1 with Status : eDSNoErr : (0)

Call to checkpw(): Bad Password

path: /Local/Default
Username: zsmith
Password: bw4r3c3n1nj4s
Error : eDSAuthFailed : (-14090)
```

> **NOTE:** You can also run dirt interactively without supplying the -p flag. This is typically beneficial as passwords will be stored in the current users shell history when providing this parameter from the command line. If you use dirt with a password specified from the command line be sure to clear your history, history -c, and you may want to securely remove your history files as well, srm $HISTORY. Dirt is more thoroughly covered in Chapter 2.

As you can see from the example, the password specified was not correct, and the Directory Service request had an error with the numerical value of -14090. These error codes are documented as part of the DirectoryService API and can also be checked using the DirectoryServices main page.

> **NOTE:** While dirt was used to test authentication in Mac OS X 10.5, dscl is used to test authentication in Mac OS X 10.6.

Testing Authentication at the Login Window

Once you have tested user resolution with dscl and authentication with dirt, you are ready to begin a graphical login test. While you could have skipped to this step, it's normally best to test that "raw" authentication is working before trying to troubleshoot and isolate any issues encountered at a graphical prompt such as the login window, as seen in Figure 3-6.

Figure 3-6. *Login window*

Logout from the Apple menu and login as your test Active Directory user account, keeping in mind that many other factors will affect this type of login compared to the command-line tests you have previously performed. If all steps taken previously with id, dscl, and dirt succeed without issue, but you still cannot login then you likely have a home-directory specific problem. When you are logging in, you can use the text immediately below Mac OS X to click through various informational items about the system. One of these will indicate that Network Accounts Available, a useful troubleshooting step to verifying that you can authenticate.

Home Directories and the Apple Active Directory Plug-in

Home Directories can be one of the more complicated aspects of integrating Mac OS X with Active Directory. But it doesn't have to be. The Active Directory plug-in supplied by Apple by default creates a local home directory in the /Users/ directory. If you do not want to synchronize data to another location using Mobile homes or leverage network-based home directories then your work is made easier and you are basically done. However, depending on your required configuration you might have many tasks remaining. For example, a very common procedure on Microsoft Windows is to redirect folders to network share points. The most common folder to be redirected is My Documents. Redirection of My Documents via Group Policy object is not applicable to Mac OS X, and so the fun begins.

To configure the location of a home directory use Directory Utility from /Applications/Utilities folder (10.5) or /System/Library/CoreServices(10.6). Next, click on Services in the Directory Utility Toolbar and then check the box to enable Active Directory. If you are not already operating with elevated privileges, then you will be prompted for the credentials of an account with access to add data into Active Directory. Go ahead and type that in and then click on the Show Advanced Options disclosure triangle, as shown in Figure 3-7. Here, you will see a number of options to control the User Experience, Mappings, and Administrative options. The home directory options are in the beginning stored in the User Experience tab.

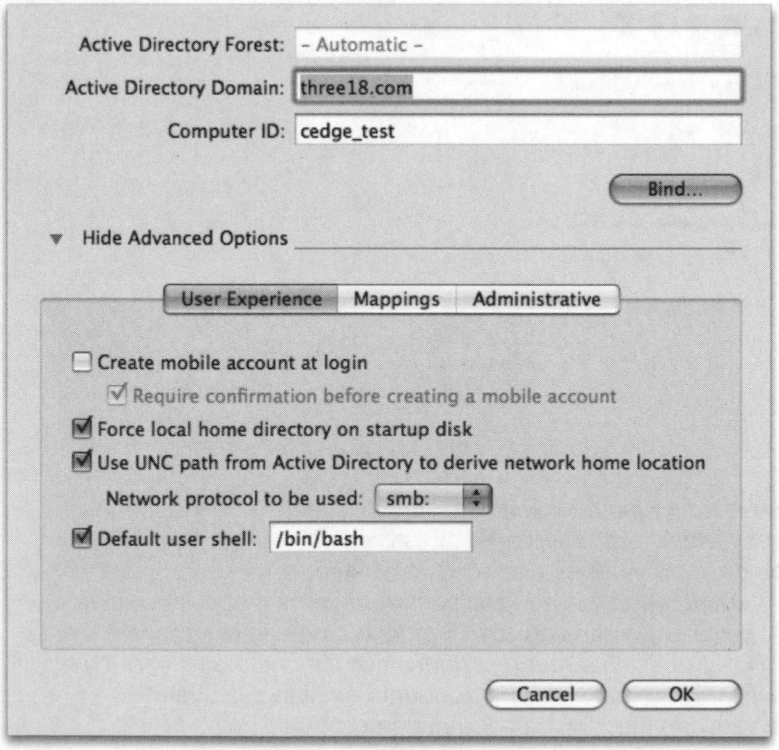

Figure 3-7. *User environment with Active Directory*

The very first option is to Create mobile account at login. By checking this box, you will cache an account locally, allowing login from the login window even when a system is not on your network. When a user logs in using an Active Directory account, they will now be prompted for whether the account will be a mobile account. Unchecking the box for Require confirmation before creating a mobile account will then suppress the dialog box and simply create the account automatically.

Next, choose whether to Use UNC path from Active Directory to derive network home location (which is a check-box to enable home folders that reside on a network path). Combined with mobile accounts and OS X's home folder syncing, this option allows data in the home folder to be available even when systems are not on the local network. This option is also preferable in order to keep the load minimized on your file servers that house home directories throughout the day.

> **TIP:** If you enable the Force Local Home on Startup Disk option, OS X will not attempt to resolve network home directories based on UNC paths. If this option is enabled, network home syncing will not properly function. The option Create Mobile Account at Login will have a similar affect of forcing a local home directory, but will also maintain UNC lookups, stored in the attribute OriginalHomeDirectory, which is necessary for home syncing.

If you have decided to leverage the Use UNC path from Active Directory option, then network home directories will be used. You will then have an option to specify the Network Protocol that will be used for home directories. Both AFP and SMB are supported. In Active Directory Users and Groups, when you set a users profile setting for the home folder location, the setting is provided via a UNC path; \\server\share\folder. The Active Directory plug-in converts the UNC path to a standard URL. So \\server\share\folder becomes afp://server/share/folder or smb://server/share/folder according to which protocol you have selected.

Once you have configured all of the options for home folders that are appropriate for your account, you can test your settings by logging in as an Active Directory username and password that has a profile location which has been configured. Then verify that login occurs as intended and the appropriate home directory is utilized given the paths and folders entered both into Active Directory and the plug-in. If you have any issues, attempt to mount paths manually and check the permissions on the destination directory structure.

DNS Concerns

Active Directory uses Sites to assign domain controllers to specific subnets on your network. The Apple Active Directory plug-in uses DNS to lookup a Global Catalog server for your domain and subsequently queries it to find the correct Domain controller to bind to. You can manually view these DNS records which use the SRV or "service" type to hold their information within an Active Directory integrated DNS network.

Open Terminal in /Applications/Utility, and enter in the following command to do a lookup on the service record to locate the global catalog:

```
dig -t SRV _gc._tcp.wallcity.org

; <<>> DiG 9.4.2-P2 <<>> -t SRV _gc._tcp.wallcity.org
;; global options: printcmd
;; Got answer:
;; ->>HEADER<<- opcode: QUERY, status: NOERROR, id: 50668
;; flags: qr aa rd ra; QUERY: 1, ANSWER: 1, AUTHORITY: 0, ADDITIONAL: 1

;; QUESTION SECTION:
;_gc._tcp.wallcity.org.          IN       SRV

;; ANSWER SECTION:
_gc._tcp.wallcity.org.  600     IN       SRV     0 100 3268 grodd.wallcity.org.

;; ADDITIONAL SECTION:
grodd.wallcity.org.     3600    IN       A       192.168.53.249

;; Query time: 59 msec
;; SERVER: 192.168.53.249#53(192.168.53.249)
;; WHEN: Sun Jun 7 21:52:50 2009
;; MSG SIZE rcvd: 93
```

The answer to the question that you are posing to dig is in the Answer Section. Here, it is shown as grodd.wallcity.org. If you do not receive the name of a domain controller, you will want to check that you are using the correct DNS servers for your site. A common error is related to using an external DNS server that has been manually configured at some previous time (e.g., 4.2.2.1). This forces your lookup to use your organization's external DNS provider, which may not match your internal DNS server, especially if you use an internal domain like .local.

Bind to AD

You will need two administrative usernames to bind to Active Directory, a local administrator and a domain administrator. The local administrator is used to write the configuration files to protected directories like /Library/Preferences/DirectoryService. This administrator can be replaced with the root user when running scripts to bind to Active Directory (e.g., a Package Installer that runs a post-flight script as root to bind to Active Directory). It's worth noting that the dsconfigad command does not need to run as root as it will use the directory service APIs to determine your admin membership based around rules stored in /etc/authorization. You could create a different group for administration in addition to the default "admin" group that would allow local administration of many components, such as binding. However, giving out admin access for the "right" that Active Directory uses would give them access to quite a bit of the systems authorization dialogs and so would effectively be overkill for just trying to delegate a non-standard admin to bind.

> **NOTE:** Instead, you could leverage system.services.directory.configure in /etc/authorization to achieve this goal for mass deployment scenarios where unprivileged accounts may be troubleshooting minimal network connectivity issues.

In addition to the local administrative credentials, you will need a domain administrator. This delegate administrator needs to have access to join computers to the domain and also write access to the organizational unit that you specify if you are using the "Services" binding section of Directory utility or the -ou option of dsconfigad. This domain administrator should be created with a very small amount of privileges other than domain addition, as you may need to give this username and password out to your onsite IT liaisons and embed it in scripts.

The following is an example of using the dsconfigad command. As you can see, we are specifying the domain administrator's password right on the line, and this would result in the password potentially being available in the shells history depending on how we run the command. We do not need to run sudo when running dsconfigad, as it will effectively do the privilege request on its own, and prompt for the password of the current user to escalate the privileges for the operation. Later, we will discuss using this command in a script.

```
dsconfigad -f -a mycomputername -u domainadmin -p domainadminspassword -domain
mydomain.com
```

Additionally, you can set the Active Directory plug-in settings one at a time using dsconfigad, while these options can also be set on the joining command. Keep in mind this ability to granularly set all plug-in options on the fly as you will be able to push out a change whether to create a mobile account on login using any tool capable of sending Unix style commands or scripts (such as Apple Remote Desktop). Like the previous command, sudo is never required as the dsconfigad command will determine admin rights on its own, though when calling the utility from a non-interactive tool, such as ARD, you will want to execute the commands with root privileges.

```
dsconfigad -mobile enable
```

One aspect common to many Active Directory deployments in imaging environments is the automation of binding. This is done because a bound system cannot be directly built into a "Gold Master" image, as the Computer ID of each imaged host will be different. For instance if one were to bind to Active Directory within a system that was to be cloned, the Active Directory preferences would be pushed out to all machines cloned from that image. These preferences contain the machine account name and password used for authenticating the joined computer to the Active Directory domain. While this configuration initially would allow authentication in most environments, once the computer password was cycled or once the machines were unbound, then all cloned systems would stop being able to authenticate. For this reason, joining or "binding" to the directory is then performed as a post flight operation on the cloned systems after first reboot. Imaging tools like Deploy Studio and the Casper suite include built-in scripts with graphical wrappers for accomplishing this purpose.

Naming Conventions and Scripting Automated Binding

One of the single most important decisions that will you make when determining the feasibility of a binding script will be your naming convention. This is because depending on your asset tag vendor you may have to work within a specified convention that does not correspond to anything that can be queried automatically on a fresh machine. If your asset tags were consecutive numerical values or a sequence of alphanumeric values set by the manufacturer, then you will have to match that value to a specified piece of hardware manually. Getting user input for specifics, such as asset tags, will mean that at least for your first boot, a live human being will have to be present at the time of binding to enter in this value. Most third-party imaging tools have the ability to show a dialog box that allows the imager to enter this information and have it pass to the script as a parameter. Two examples of this follow, one is Deploy Studios workflow step and the other is the Casper suites positional parameter configuration option. If you are using either one of these tools, it is suggested you consider using this functionality. However, if you are using another deployment methodology you may need to either have your script prompt the user for information, or provide this information via a pre-populated datastore, such as a csv file.

If you are ordering a large quantity of Mac OS X workstations from Apple directly, you consider asking your rep to provide you with a delimited list of Machine Access Control (MAC) addresses. Using this list, you can pre-assign hardware addresses to your organization's asset tag system or database. However, if you are dealing with existing inventory, you may still be required to prompt your imaging team for this information or at least collate it beforehand. If you are relegated to prompting your imaging team for this information a good technique is to store this custom name within a machine's firmware. Mac OS X provides a way of manipulating firmware variables using the /usr/sbin/nvram command. However, nvram cannot be assumed to be persistent, so it is best to maintain this data in a spreadsheet or database.

Binding to Active Directory can be autonomously accomplished using two main tools, dscl and dsconfigad. However, the Active Directory plug-in is not enabled by default and when looking at a binding script one major consideration is to enable this plug-in so that any bound forest will be available for use in the authentication search path for the system. You can do this by pre-populating this setting which is stored in the DirectoryServices.plist file /Library/Preferences/DirectoryService/DirectoryService.plist using the following command:

```
defaults write /Library/Preferences/DirectoryService/DirectoryService ↩
"Active Directory" Active
```

We often recommend to actually add this "enabled" copy of this file in your image prior to deployment. As if you programmatically have to enable the plug-in, you must restart the DirectoryService deamon to have it pick up on the changes. This process while only slightly intrusive can increase the time it takes a system to become usable when binding at startup or first boot automatically.

As shown earlier, using the Terminal application (found at /Applications/Utilities) can be leveraged to create a simple binding script using dsconfigad. However, this only allows you to bind to Active Directory and does not add the directory to the currently configured /Search or /Contact paths. This is an important difference when using the command line as it is an integrated step when using the graphical tools to add newly configured domains to the computers authentication search policies.

```
dsconfigad -f -a mycomputername -u domainadmin -p domainadminspassword -domain
mydomain.com
```

Once you have bound through the command line, the Active Directory domain will need to be added to your search path. To do so, you will use dsclfor testing binding. In this case, we will use it to change information in the /Search (where information regarding your search policy is stored). Therefore, first change the SearchPolicy attribute to custom by using the following command:

```
dscl /Search -change / SearchPolicy dsAttrTypeStandard:LSPSearchPath ↵
dsAttrTypeStandard:CSPSearchPath
```

```
dscl /Search -append / dsAttrTypeStandard:CSPSearchPath "/Active Directory/All Domains/"
```

As the previous code shows, you can also enable options in the active directory plug-in granularly. When specifying multiple advanced options, you can specify each with their own invocation of dsconfigad, or you can supply them all together via a single command. When specifying multiple options, the command can become a bit unruly, but the same result is achieved. Each option from the GUI translates to an option (or flag, if you will) at the command-line interface. There are a number of other options that are available, but each is likely not to be required for all cases.

Basic Options—Commonly Used:

- -a computerid: name of the computer to add to the domain (if none is specified then the default with be the hostname)

- -f: force the process (i.e., remove the existing entry from the Active Directory plug-in)

- -r: remove computer from domain (unbind)

- -luusername: username of an administrative local account

- -lppassword: password of the administrative local account defined with -lu

- -uusername: username of an Active Directory administrator

- -ppassword: password of the Active Directory administrator specified with -u

- -ou dn: fully qualified LDAP DN of container for the computer (defaults to CN=Computers)

- -domain fqdn: fully qualified DNS name of Active Directory Domain

- -show: show current configuration for Active Directory (this option doesn't make any modifications to the directory or the Active Directory plug-in)

Advanced Options—User Experience:

- `-mobile`: enable or disable mobile user accounts for offline use

- `-mobileconfirm`: enable or disable warning for mobile account creation

- `-localhome`: enable or disable force home directory to local drive

- `-useuncpath`: enable or disable use Windows UNC for network home

- `-protocol`: afp or smb change protocol used when mounting home

- `-shell`: none for no shell or specify a default shell `/bin/bash`

Advanced Options—Mappings:

- `-uidattribute`: name of attribute to be used for UNIX uid field

- `-nouid`: generate the UID from the Active Directory GUID

- `-gidattribute`: name of attribute to be used for UNIX gid field

- `-nogid`: generate the GID from the Active Directory information

- `-ggidattribute`: name of attribute to be used for UNIX group gid field

- `-noggid`: generate the group GID from the Active Directory GUID

Advanced Options —Administrative:

- `-preferredserver`: fully qualified domain name of the preferred Domain Controller

- `-nopreferred`: do not use a preferred server for queries

- `-groups` "1,2,...": list of groups that are granted Admin privileges on local workstation

- `-nogroups`: disable the use of groups that were specified in the – groups for granting Admin privileges

- `-alldomains`: enable or disable allows authentication from any domain in the forest

- `-packetsign`: disable, allow, or require to enable packet signing

- `-packetencrypt`: disable, allow, or require to enable packet encryption

- `-namespace`: forest or domain, where forest qualifies all usernames

- `-passinterval`: how often to change computer trust account password in days

If your environment requires customization of the Active Directory binding screens, the previous options can be used to granularly configure the options you would otherwise use in the screens in Directory Utility. You can also access a few that have not yet been added.

Map UID and GID

As previously mentioned, Mac OS X requires certain attributes to be able to login, such as primary group ID and Unique ID. As Active Directory does not contain the Unique ID by default, this value must be generated on the fly using some other kind of unique information. One important attribute of this generation is that it cannot be completely random; it is important that every system bound to Active Directory resolves the same UniqueID for any respective user. To accomplish this, Apple uses the first 32 bytes of the user's GUID to generate a numerical value used as a statically mapped value for the Mac OS X Unique ID.

> **NOTE:** Augmented Records can also be used to map information. In an augmented record environment, one would bind a Mac OS X Server as a member server to Active Directory and as an Open Directory master and then use Server Preferences to supplement missing records. While this is similar to a triangle (described later in this chapter), it is not widely adopted on a large scale and so not explored in detail in this chapter.

As the plug-in can run the same mathematical operation on the GUID on two different machines and received the same value, It acts as a practical substitute for manually configuring these values in your environment. Windows Server 2003 R2 and higher have a schema attribute called unixid, which could be used to store custom values in the directory. If your organization is already using unix clients that authenticate to Active Directory, then you may already have this information populated in the Directory. Mapping this information on the Mac OS X side is often only beneficial for consistency. However, it can play a vital authorization rule when using the NFS file sharing protocol, which uses the local systems UID to map privileges on remote server shares mounted on the clients system. If your organization does have these fields populated, it is incredibly important to make sure that these fields are populated automatically when you ingest new users. WindowsServer 2008 can do this using ADSI or Power Shell Active Directory command lets. Quest Software has some examples for manipulating large numbers of Active Directory fields in a programmatic fashion using this "new" language.

By default, UID and GID attributes are not mapped, but rather generated when you are using dsconfigad to bind a computer to Active Directory. To map the default fields referenced previously, open Directory Utility from /Applications/Utilities and then click on Services in the Directory Utility toolbar. From here, fill in the basic Active Directory binding information from earlier. Once you have done so, click on the disclosure triangle for Show Advanced Options and from the resultant screen, click on the Mappings tab.

From the Mappings tab, enter the information for the Active Directory attribute to map UID and GID information to. Alternatively, dsconfigad can be leveraged to map fields not included in the GUI. To do so you will use the -staticmap flag followed by the attribute type and then the value for the specified attribute.

Namespace Support Using dsconfigad

By default, dsconfigad assumes that your forest name is the same as your domain name, or authentication will only succeed to the domain that was specified when the system was bound. Some environments have multiple domains. Active Directory allows two accounts with the same username (although not the same GUID) to exist with a given forest, provided they are in separate domains. The Directory Utility allows you to specify either the forest or a specific domain, allowing you to control the scope in which a client system will authenticate against at bind time. When bound to a forest, the AD plug-in allows you to go a step further, providing the ability to authenticate to separate domains within a forest by adding the domain name to your login credentials.

But you don't want to have to unbind and rebind every time you'll log into a different domain, if you will be switching between domains often. To provide you with the option to login using multiple domains within one forest, you can use the -namespace flag followed by domain. The -namespace flag then prefixes the domain name to all accounts that are located in the forest. If you have conflicting accounts in separate domains then the computer should be bound into the domain with which your account resides. To enable namespace support you would use the following command:

```
dsconfigad -namespace forest
```

Once run, you will authenticate against the forest and will need to specify the domain name in front of the username every time a user authenticates to the system. If you would like to switch back to using domain namespace at a later date, you can specify the -namespace flag with domain as the setting and you will no longer have to enter this.

> **NOTE:** When run, the -namespace changes the primary ID for all accounts. Therefore, any user profiles for accounts from the Active Directory domain will need to be copied/moved into the new profile that is created, which will have a different naming convention.

Active Directory Packet Encryption Options

The Active Directory plug-in can be configured to enable the encryption options Apple has developed for communications between the Active Directory plug-in and Active Directory Domain Controllers. These include packet encryption, packet signing, and a timeout value for setting the computer account password rotation interval with your Active Directory domain controllers. These options are configured either post or during bind time using the dsconfigad command.

A number of Active Directory environments require packet signing in order to block man in the middle attacks and therefore to verify the authenticity of data being exchanged between the Active Directory plug-in and Active Directory, thus protecting both the domain and the client. From the Active Directory perspective, configuring packet signing requirements is a policy configured from an Active Directory domain controller. Active Directory password policies let you to allow or even require packet signing from the client for LDAP traffic, the protocol that data will be exchanged in this scenario. By default, packet signing is an allowed option for clients in Windows Server 2003 and Windows Server 2008, but is not required for client systems.

While not the default setting, it is a good practice. Therefore, many environments require packet signing for Active Directory clients. In Mac OS X if you want to require packet signing for the client to communicate the server then this would further validate that communication is signed (and therefore authentic), so you can set the packet signing setting to require as well for a more highly secure solution. If you require packet signing from either the server side or the client side, then you should verify signing is an allowed option, if not required on the other or you may run into incompatibility issues. To change packet signing options in Mac OS X, you would use the -packetsign flag with dsconfigad. Settings available with the -packetsignflag include: allow, disable, and require. Therefore, to configure dsconfigad to require packet signing use the following command:

```
dsconfigad -packetsign require
```

If the change is successful, then you will see the following output:

```
Settings changed successfully
```

Packet encryption is another option in Mac OS X and Active Directory. Packet encryption keeps the contents as secure as they are authentic by forcing data to be encrypted. To enable packet encryption, use the -packetencryption flag with the same settings available with the -packetsignflag (allow, disable, and require). As with packet signing, verify that both the server and client support encryption before setting the option to required, although for high security environments (or most environments these days) it is a good idea to set the client and the server to require both authentication and signing. To set encryption requirements for the client, use the following command:

```
dsconfigad -packetencrypt require
```

If the change is successful, then you will see the following output:

```
Settings changed successfully
```

Every computer that is bound to Active Directory has a computer account, and that computer account in turn has a password. Active Directory rotates these passwords routinely. The Active Directory plug-in supports the rotation by using the -passinterval flag with dsconfigad. The passinterval can be set and when set, defines how often, in terms of days between the password rotation intervals.

```
dsconfigad -passinterval 7
```

All of the settings in this section can be set or changed during bind time or following bind time, and can be independent of any other settings.

Dual Directory

As we've mentioned, you can use Active Directory and Open Directory together. To some, this is called a magic triangle, to others a golden triangle. We're going to use a term that has gained a bit more attention as of late, Dual Directory, to describe the setup. Most descriptions and walkthroughs are made more complicated than they need to be. Basically, you start out with a functional Active Directory environment and a functional Open Directory environment then bind your client machines to both directories, ensuring that both appear in the clients search path. From then on, the client will query each directory sequentially in the order defined by the search path until it receives a successful return.

You may be thinking that it probably isn't as easy as that, and certainly there are additional considerations, but at its heart that is the foundation of a triangle or dual directory configuration. The first such consideration is Single Sign On—both Active Directory and Open Directory utilize Kerberos for this functionality. In a dual directory setup, having two separate Kerberos realms can complicate matters, so it is often desirable to only utilize one Kerberos Realm. To integrate your Mac clients into an Active Directory environment, you will want to utilize the Active Directory Kerberos services, thus it will be desirable to tear down the Open Directory KDC.

> **TIP:** If an OS X server is bound to Active Directory prior to promotion to an Open Directory master, Active Directory Kerberos services will be utilized and Open Directory-based Kerberos services will not be set up.

For the purposes of this demonstration, we will use diradmin as the Open Directory administrative username and p@ssword as the password. If you have chosen to use an Open Directory administrative username other than diradmin then simply transpose as needed. Since your password is likely not p@ssword then please transpose that as well.

To destroy the shared Kerberos KDC on the Open Directory Master, you will use the sso_util command. As of Mac OS X 10.5, this is typically not required, so feel free to skip this step. The sso_util option we will use is the remove option, which will remove the KDC from the host on which it is run:

```
sudo sso_util remove -k a diradmin -p p@ssword
```
Next, we're going to use dscl to remove the Config options for the KDC (since this step is often not required it may fail):

```
dscl -u diradmin /LDAPv3/127.0.0.1 -delete /Config/KerberosKDC
dscl -u diradmin /LDAPv3/127.0.0.1 -delete /Config/KerberosClient
```

> **NOTE:** You can choose to leave the KDC intact. If you do and run into errors later on in this section, then you may want to return to this step and run these commands. They could resolve any potential issues.

Next, you will bind the Open Directory Master to Active Directory as you have been binding clients throughout this chapter. Because the directory services plug-ins can coexist with one another (for the most part, some third-party plug-ins cannot coexist with the Active Directory plug-in) you can do so without risking damage to other resources within your LDAP service on the Open Directory master.

Once you have bound your server to Active Directory, will want to enable the single sign on for all supported services by using the following command, which will create service principals for each respective shared service:

```
dsconfigad -enableSSO
```

Next, you're going to open Workgroup Manager and verify that you can view and authenticate to both your Active Directory and Open Directory domains. You can alternate between directories that you are bound to (or hosting) by clicking on the globe icon and then selecting other directories (including the local directory). Once you have switched between domains, if the settings are grayed out and will not allow you to alter them, then you can click on the icon of the lock to authenticate to each as an administrative account of that domain.

Next, bind a client to both Active Directory and Open Directory, using the same process outlined earlier in this chapter in the section "Bind to AD" and in Chapter 2. Once you have bound to both Active Directory and Open Directory from a client, click on the Search Policy tab in Directory Utility to verify that both your Active Directory and Open Directory DirectoryDomains are listed. Also, make sure that Active Directory is listed above the LDAPv3 domain for authentication purposes. It might not be likely that the LDAPv3 domain will contain any users that present a conflict with users in the Active Directory domain. However, keeping your Directory Domains with Active Directory listed above Open Directory may save you time in troubleshooting down the line and help to maintain optimal performance. In most dual-directory environments, Active Directory will contain the bulk of the data, and therefore should be the first target for lookups.

Next either log out and login to the client computer, or use dirt to verify that you can authenticate as an Active Directory user. Then, use dscl to browse both the Open Directory environment and the Active Directory environment to ensure that both directories are returning data. If you can, your client is now successfully configured for use in your Dual Directory environment.

Nesting

For many tasks, such as POSIX and ACL-based file system permissioning, you can directly utilize Active Directory groups, and OS X clients will properly recognize this resolution. However, other functionality, most notably MCX management, require special attributes provided by Open Directory and will not function when applied to Active Directory groups. To take advantage of Open Directory functionality, you will need to create Open Directory groups and apply the settings to these groups.

At first glance, this creates a bit of a management problem, as now we must maintain user membership for both Active Directory and Open Directory groups. Luckily, this problem is largely solved through support of nested groups, or more specifically, cross-directory network groups. That is, you can actually nest an Active Directory group inside of an Open Directory group and OS X clients will properly resolve the relation. This capability becomes pretty invaluable, as once you set up the initial OD group and AD membership, from then on, membership of the Open Directory group will be determined by that of the AD group. Administrators simply need to adjust user membership in Active Directory, and those changes will trickle down to the Mac side of the tree.

Nesting groups is a pretty simple endeavor. In this section, we will create a group called Support Users inside of Open Directory and nest an Active Directory group used for support users inside of the Support Users group.

To get started, open Workgroup Manager from the /Applications/Server folder on the Open Directory Master (or use Workgroup Manager on an administrative computer to connect to the address of the Open Directory Master). Next, click on the globe in the Directory Services bar and select /LDAPv3/127.0.0.1, which will display the contents of Open Directory. Click on the groups tab just below the bar and then click on the New Group icon in the toolbar. Enter the Name for the group. Due to the complexity of dealing with multiple like-named groups across multiple directories, it is recommended that you provide a designation for the directory under which the group resides. Thus, when creating an OD mirror group for the AD group "Support Users," we may want to name the correlating Open Directory group "OD Support Users" to easily discern between the two. As you assign a full name, a Short Name will automatically be generated, although you can customize this as desired. As with the full name, a directory specific identifier can prove very helpful. Thus, we'll name the group od_supportusers. When you are satisfied with the group name, click on the Save button.

Now click on the Members tab for the group and then click on the plus sign icon just to the right of the group list. This will bring out a sliding menu with the Open Directory users of your organization. Click on the globe icon at the top of the menu and select the Active Directory domain, then click on the Groups tab directly below it. Drag the desired group from the sliding menu to the list of members. When you are satisfied with your entry, click on the Save button and you should see a screen similar to the following.

At this point, you will be able to build permissions to files and folders and generate policies for the Open Directory user groups, which has the same effective membership as the nested Active Directory group. You can nest multiple Active Directory based users or groups inside of Open Directory groups in this manner in order to achieve a variety of results.

MCX via Dual Directory

If you have chosen to deploy a dual-directory environment, chances are you have done so to provide policy management for your OS X clients, and have chosen for whatever reason to not extend the primary directory's schema for such support. The primary benefit of deploying a dual directory environment is that it allows you to utilize the schema of one directory to supplement the other, through the use of nested group resolution, providing capabilities that otherwise would not be possible. Actual management of these policies is the same in a dual directory environment as it is in an Open Directory native environment—the majority of the work to generate policies is done in Workgroup Manager.

Managing the dock is one of the easiest settings to manage. It is also one of the easiest to demonstrate while being fairly unobtrusive to any users who it is applied to, in the event that issues arise from the managed preference and troubleshooting must occur. To manage the dock, go ahead and open Workgroup Manager from /Applications/Server, connecting to your Open Directory Master. Next, switch to the appropriate directory service (likely Open Directory) using the disclosure triangle in the Directory Service domain selection bar, and clicking on /LDAPv3/127.0.0.1 when you are complete.

To create a group, click on the lock icon to authenticate into the appropriate directory domain. Once authenticated, click on the group lists icon in the left part of the screen and then click the icon in the toolbar for New Group. Next enter a name for the group. The group name will be Dock Test with a shortname of testdock and then click on the Save button to create the test group for managed docks.

Next add the Active Directory user into an Open Directory group from Workgroup Manager. Start by clicking on the Members tab for the group in Workgroup Manager and then click on the plus sign (+), which opens a listing of users. In the list of users, click on the disclosure triangle for Directory, selecting the Active Directory domain. Then, drag the user you will be enforcing into the new group whose dock will be managed, saving settings to appear similar to what is seen in Figure 3-8.

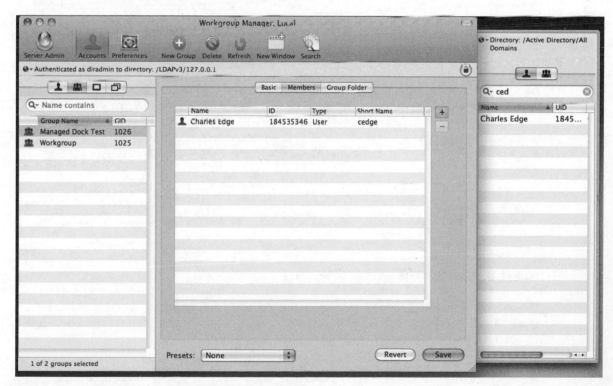

Figure 3-8. *Nesting Groups with a dual directory environment*

Once the users are created, it's time to set up the managed preference, similar to what was done in earlier sections. To get started, click on the Preferences button in the Workgroup Manager toolbar. At Preferences, click on Dock underneath the Overview tab and then click on the Dock Display tab, using the Always radio button. Click on the Right radio button and then click on Apply Now to commit those managed preferences. Then move the dock to the right side of the screen as you can see in Figure 3-9, a setting that is inherited by objects that are a member of the group.

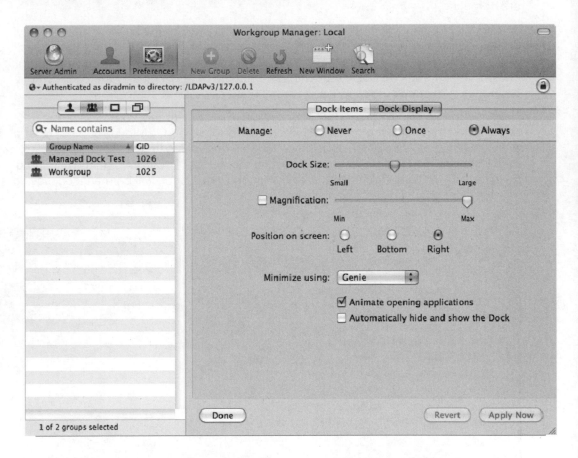

Figure 3-9. *Managing the Dock in dual directory*

Finally, log in as the user with managed preferences configured and you should see the dock displayed on the correct side of the screen, or whichever preference you decided to set if it wasn't the Dock locale.

In an AD/OD dual directory environment, there are some notable limitations that you should be aware of. First and foremost, Mac OS X cannot directly utilize an Active Directory Computer Record for policy management. In a managed computer environment, OS X clients associate to a specific computer record via the built-in ethernet interface's MAC address, designated by OS X as interface en0. As Active Directory Computer Records do not contain this information, OS X clients will not properly associate to their respective computer record when it is nested inside of an Open Directory computer group. In order to apply computer group-based management, you must create a computer record in Open Directory with the respective Mac address. This process is most easily accomplished by performing a trusted bind of your OS X clients to Open Directory, which will create the associated computer record. If you are already scripting your Directory Service binding, a trusted bind is a fairly trivial modification. Alternatively, you can pre-populate the Open Directory computer records, provided that you have documented the MAC address and computer name for your OS X nodes in the field.

MCX via Active Directory

If you can extend your Active Directory and you need to use managed preferences, then you should do so. If you can't then you would use dual directory or a third-party solution. If you extend your schema then you will be able to use Workgroup Manager to configure the managed preferences that you require. First, open Workgroup Manager and connect to an Active Directory. You can run Workgroup Manager from any Mac OS client that has previously been bound to Active Directory. In this case, we will connect to 127.0.0.1 initially and then click on /Active Directory/All Domains entry in the list of available directory services (the section with the globe and the disclosure triangle), clicking on the lock icon to authenticate as an administrator of your Active Directory domain when you are prompted to do so.

The Inspector allows you to view raw attribute data no matter the directory service that you are using. For the purposes of this example, we are going to enable the Inspector for Workgroup Manager so we can check that the managed preference has been applied and how the data appears once the record has been updated. From Workgroup Manager, click on the Workgroup Manager menu and click on Preferences. From Preferences check the box for Show All Records tab and inspector, clicking on OK when finished, as we covered in the previous section, MCX via Dual Directory.

Now highlight a user from Active Directory and click on the Inspector tab. You'll then see all of the attributes, as mentioned in Chapter 1. Whether or not your domain has been extended, you can now click on the Preferences icon in the Workgroup Manager toolbar. Using the pre-built managed preferences, you can then configure items in the list shown in Figure 3-10 (assuming your Active Directory schema has been extended).

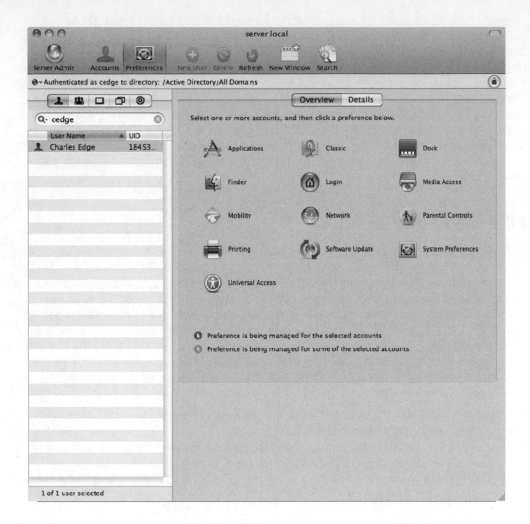

Figure 3-10. *Managed Preferences for Active Directory*

To continue on with the Dock managed preferences example, now click Dock and then click on Always, finally removing a couple of applications from the included list for testing purposes. Then click the Dock Display tab and set the Always option by checking the Always box. Finally, highlight the radio button for Right, as shown in Figure 3-11.

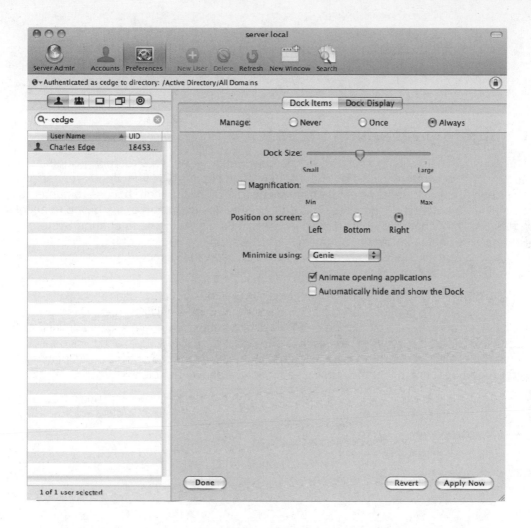

Figure 3-11. *Managing the Dock for active directory users*

When you're satisfied with your changes, click on the Apply button. If you do not get any errors, you can then authenticate to a client and the dock should appear with the items that were defined in the list and to the right of the computer, which indicates that the managed preferences manifest has been applied as intended. If you get any errors, review the items included in your schema extension from ADAM (or the ldif file used with ldifde). MCXFlags and MCXSettings (which is an array) are the most important items to check to make sure the Mac OS X managed preferences framework is going to be functioning as intended. Items that are not being configured properly can create errors in Workgroup Manager. If the MCXFlags and MCXSettings are present on the system, you can copy their entire contents into a separate document, pasting them into mapped fields from within Active Directory.

NOTE: When using an extended schema, similar limitations apply to Computer-group and computer-based management. It is necessary that computer records have a populated MAC address field so that they properly recognize applied management settings.

Configuring AD Admin Groups

The Active Directory plug-in allows for the designation of Active Directory group(s) to act as local administrators on the bound machine. This capability is very handy for assigning helpdesk groups to serve as local Mac administrators, giving them access to numerous administrative-specific resources. This setting provides members of the group to access rights similar to that of a local admin user. This includes the rights to change System Preferences, install software, modify system files, and run applications with root (admin) privileges. This also includes sudo access, which allows for execution of command-line executables with root access.

As with other Active Directory plug-in settings, administrative groups can be configured via Directory Utility. To configure administrative groups via Directory Utility, open Directory Utility. First, enable edits by clicking on the lock, and authenticate with a local administrative user. Next, using the Services tab, highlight the Active Directory Plug-in and click configure. If necessary, click on the disclosure triangle to show the advanced options. A list of admin groups can be found under the Administrative tab, as shown in Figure 3-12.

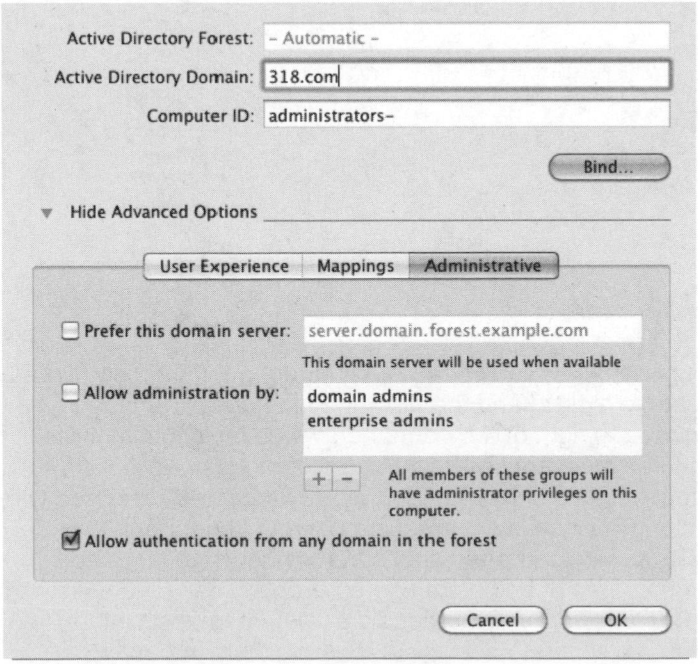

Figure 3-12. *Active directory administrative panel*

To assign an administrative group, check the box Allow Administration By and specify the name of the group that contains the desired admin users. In this case, we have created a special Active Directory group Mac Desktop Admins, which contains a nested group of our help desk team.

Nesting Administrators in the Local Admin Group

Many organizations provide centralized management in a decentralized environment. If you do not want to provide your support personnel access to local service accounts, and you want to specify people in your organization that can administer local systems, then you can give local administrators elevated privileges by nesting those users into admin groups. You can also accomplish this directly using the Active Directory plug-in at bind time.

To do so with nesting, though, use the *dseditgroup* command to nest a network group inside the local administrator group, which you can do using Workgroup Manager. However, we're going to look at doing so programmatically to ease mass deployment, especially when you are not using the stock Active Directory plug-in. To do so, use the *dseditgroup* command to resolve group membership:

```
dseditgroup  o read <active directory group name>
```

The -o option from followed by the read means to do a read operation on the specified group. If you were to run the following command, then you would read the mac_admins group.

```
dseditgroup -o read mac_admins
```

The output of the preceding read command would then give you the following output:

```
27 attribute(s) found
...
Attribute[5] is <dsAttrTypeNative:member>
        Value[1] is <CN=Charles Edge,CN=Users,DC-318,DC=com>
        Value[2] is <CN=Zack Smith,CN=Users,DC=318,DC=com>
        Value[2] is <CN=Beau Hunter,CN=Users,DC=318,DC=com>
...
```

The member section lists the group members. If you do not get any output then you should verify that there are actually members in the group by checking the domain or using the id command. Then verify that Mac OS X can resolve group memberships with id as well. You can also use the id command to see what groups a user is in. For example, to look up the groups that an account is a member of you could use a command similar to the following:

```
id cedge
```

Group memberships will then be output, along with the uid and gid:

```
uid=5678903(cedge) gid=45678(318\domain users) groups=45678 (318\domain users)
```

To nest the Active Directory group you can use dseditgroup with the -o option again, but this time leveraging the edit verb and add using the -a option to indicate a group manage; use the -t option for the type of the group with the -n option indicating the location. The following code is an example:

```
sudo dseditgroup -o edit -a mac_admins -t group -n /Local/Default admin
```

You can also add a network user to the admin group by using the same command but changing the type:

```
sudo dseditgroup -o edit -a <network username> -t user -n /Local/Default admin
```

If you combine this with mobile (cached) accounts, you can provide administrative rights to local machines, but then require password policies managed using server side preferences from Active Directory. To verify the nested user has localized elevated privileges, test a local process that requires local administrative access.

> **NOTE:** You can also use Workgroup Manager running on a local workstation to nest groups in this same fashion.

Third-Party Solutions

For the vast majority of environments, the functionality provided through Apple's native Active Directory plug-in will provide all that is needed for successful integration. However, there are numerous scenarios where functionality is needed outside of that provided through Apple's solution. Apple considers these edge cases for the most part, but if you need a feature such as multiple-Forest support (rather than simply multiple-Domain support, which is part of the Active Directory plug-in), or DFS, Microsoft's Distributed File System, then you may need to turn to a third-party solution.

Centrify's DirectControl

Centrify is a third party directory solution which includes server-side software to augment Active Directory, and for OS X clients includes a custom Directory Service plug-in. From an OS X perspective, Centrify is a rather elegant solution, as the software directly utilizes the Directory Services API. As such, the Centrify client plug-in is a first class citizen next to Apple's native LDAP and Active Directory plug-ins. From an Active Directory perspective, Centrify allows for extended functionality without the need for schema extensions. This extended functionality is then used to distribute policies to clients through what Centrify identifies as Zones.

DirectControl Installation

To get started with DirectControl, first download the installation iso file from Centrify, mounting the iso on a valid Windows Domain Controller, preferably one in a test or lab environment for your initial installation and testing. For many environments, you may choose to have Centrify perform an on-site jump-start for your organization. But for the purposes of this chapter we're going to have you perform a basic initial installation and testing, assuming that you are doing so in a laboratory environment. Before you get started though, make sure the server you are installing the Suite on is part of the Active Directory environment and that it is running IIS.

Let's go ahead and start the installation. To begin, run the installation msi file that is included in the iso file on a Domain Controller. You will first see the Suite Type screen, where you select the Suite of applications that will be installed, based to some degree on the licensing that you paid for. Since we're testing, use the Enterprise Administrator Suite so you have the full complement of applications and then click on Next. Optionally select the components of the Enterprise Administrator Suite to install. When you are satisfied with your selections, click on Next, as you can see in Figure 3-13.

NOTE: For most cases, you will need the AD property page extension, the Zone generator, and the Global Policy Editor. Other packages are optional for the most part.

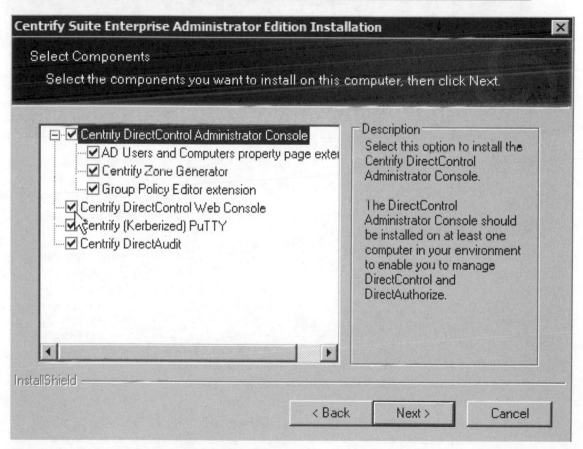

Figure 3-13. *Choosing Centrify components for installation*

You will now get a chance to check out the settings for the installers and then the actual installation will begin. At the Confirm Installation Settings screen, review the settings you will be using and then click on the Next button. If you are installing the Web Console, .Net will install first, and here you are likely best using the default options. DirectControl will then install. Click Next to run the installation steps.

Licensing is always fun. Writing about licensing sometimes seems silly, but it's better than skipping over it. At the Review License Agreement screen, read the license agreement and if you accept it, click on the I agree to these terms radio button. Then, click on the Next button to continue. The User Registration screen needs a username and an organization name, so type those in and then click Next, as shown in Figure 3-14.

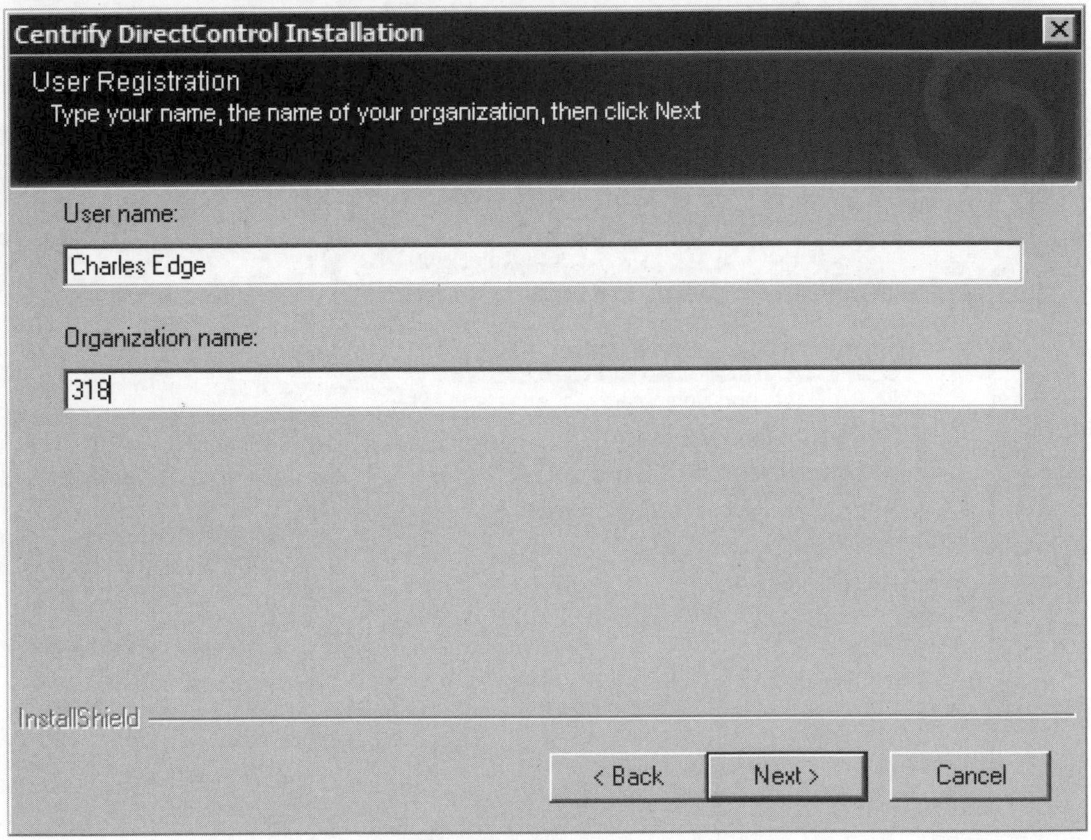

Figure 3-14. *Assigning a username and organization in Centrify*

Next, choose a location for DirectControl to be installed. At the Choose Destination Folder screen, customize the target directory or allow the installation to occur in the default directory. If you would like for the Centrify folder to be created in C:\Program Files then click on Next. Otherwise, click on the Browse button, browse to the required folder, and then click on the Next button.

Earlier you selected which applications in the suite to install. Now we're going to select the specific parts of DirectControl to install. At the Select Components screen, you will define which portions of DirectControl to be installed. Earlier we selected the Centrify applications, but now you are going to configure the components of each to be installed. Because this is a testing environment we're going to look to get our full complement of options except for the Extension for NIS maps, since for most environments there will not be any NIS clients. Having said this, the NIS option isn't just for administrators stuck in the 1990s. It can be practical when DirectControl is being used so that Unix and Mac clients can authenticate through NIS into Active Directory. Either way, click Next to continue.

The web console uses .Net, which has the ability to use Publisher Evidence Verification, useful in high security environments. If installing the web console then you will be prompted to Disable Publisher evidence verification. Click Next to see the screen that is used to confirm the components of Centrify DirectControl to be installed. If the Confirm Installations Settings screen matches the options you wish to have installed then click on the Next button, or use Back to go back to previous screens and alter the options. Clicking Next will install the DirectControl components. When it is done, click Finish and then you can start the setup. Once you are done, reboot the host in order to move on to configuring DirectControl.

Configuring DirectControl

When the installation is complete you will need to set up DirectControl to connect to the Active Directory forest that the computer objects will be connecting to. The process starts with the Connect to Forest dialog. Before you do anything, double-check that your DNS is set appropriately and that you know the address for a system that is a domain controller for the forest. Once you have the appropriate information, enter the address of the appropriate domain controller and the appropriate credentials and click on OK to begin the Setup Wizard, as shown in Figure 3-15.

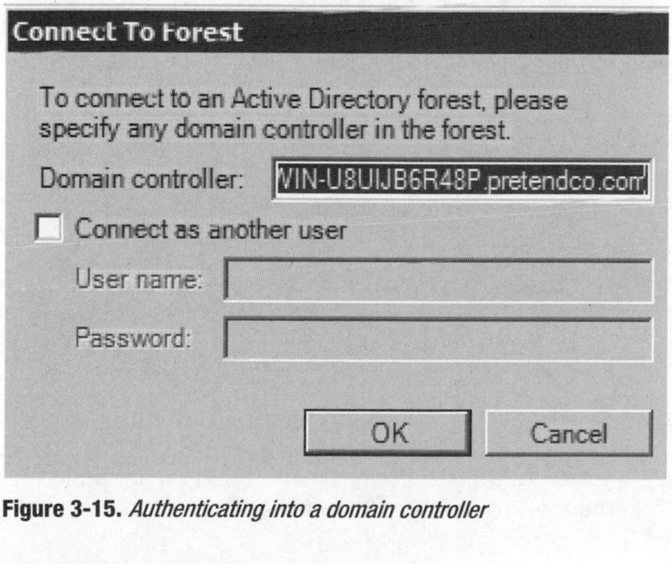

Connect To Forest

To connect to an Active Directory forest, please specify any domain controller in the forest.

Domain controller: VIN-U8UIJB6R48P.pretendco.com

☐ Connect as another user

User name:

Password:

[OK]   [Cancel]

Figure 3-15. *Authenticating into a domain controller*

The first few screens of the setup are innocuous. You will see the Welcome screen where you will click on Next. At the User Credentials screen, enter a valid username and password for an Administrative account and then click on Next.

Licensing is a necessary evil. At the subsequent Install Licenses screen, select a location for your License Keys. The default location is likely best, unless you have a good reason to change this location. At the Install License Keys screen, configure the keys that are populated into the default location from the Install Licenses screen. Enter the licensing key provided by Centrify and then click on the Next button.

To Centrify a Zone is similar to an Organizational Unit. A Zone has member objects, but also allows for delegated access over the objects within the Zone. Next, provide a location for your Zones within Active Directory. You do not need to customize this information, so you can go ahead and click on Next unless you need to do so.

In a standard Active Directory environment, when you bind to the directory your system is stored in cn=Computers. Similarly, all objects have a default Zone membership. At the Create Default Zone screen you will supply the default Zone, although most will simply leave the default setting and click on the Next button, as shown in Figure 3-16.

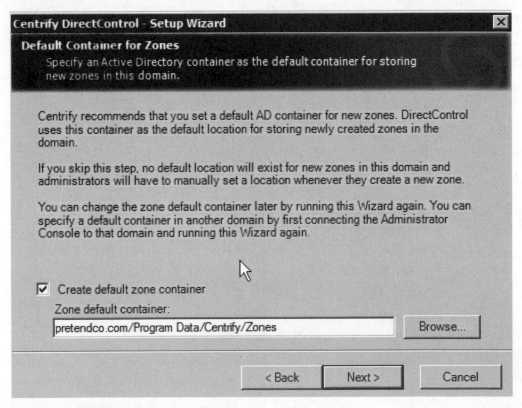

Figure 3-16. *Defining a default zone container*

While zones are similar to an OU, they are not an OU. In fact, a zone can be linked to an OU or a container. The Default Zone then will require you to enter a domain controller that has the OU or container accessible. If you did not customize the previous screen then chances are you will not need to customize this screen either. For more on Zones, Centrify has provided a write-up at http://www.centrify.com/directcontrol/zones.asp.

When you are importing data into Open Directory one of the fields available is the first UID to use. This is similar in Centrify. At the next screen you will enter a starting UID number that will be assigned to objects. User IDs by default start at 10,000, but feel free to customize this setting. Unique identification isn't just required for users, groups need unique IDs as well. Next, provide a starting GID (GroupID) space for groups to occupy (for the most part, the same rules apply as for users).

> **TIP:** It is generally recommended that you choose a range outside that provided by Apple's native solutions to easily differentiate the source of a record.

Next, set the Default home directory that will be used for accounts in your Zone as it would appear in the local system. The Default home directory is set to /home/${user} as can be seen in Figure 3-17. For the Mac OS X clients, you're going to change this to /Users/${user}, so when a user logs in the local folder /Users/USERNAME will be created on each computer, where USERNAME is the user logging in. The next screen (Default Shells) allows you to configure the default shell by using the full path to the shell. For example, if you wanted the default shell to be bash you would use /bin/bash. When you are Satisfied with your shell setting, click on Next.

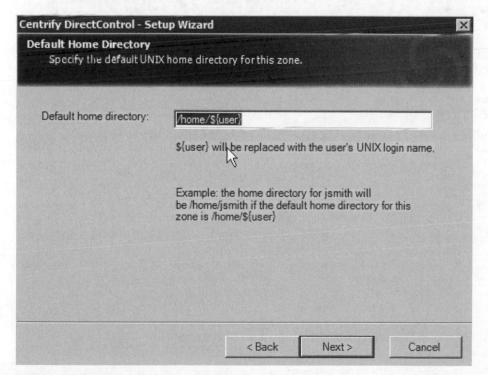

Figure 3-17. *Providing default home directories*

In Mac OS X, each user needs a default group assigned to it. At the Select and Set the Default Normal Group dialog, you will be setting the Active Directory group that will be used for a UNIX GID for that group. Here you can use the Browse button to find an existing group. You can also use the Create... button to create a new group. You will need to use the UNIX GID: field if you wish to use a unique identifying number for the AD group provided. While the unique number can be fairly arbitrary, do use your standard numbering scheme and organizational standards. Click Next to commit your changes, and if there are any issues with them Centrify will bring up a screen telling you to fix the issue.

If you are using NIS, then Centrify will act as the NIS server. The Agentless Client Support screen is where you will configure the NIS Server settings, which is the essence of what Agentless Client means to Centrify. Next, provide a password hash type and a NIS domain that NIS clients will use when connecting to the server. Once set, use the NIS domain listed in this field as the domain in Directory Utility. When you complete your NIS settings, click on Next.

You will now see the Delegate Permissions screen, where you can set the server to be able to control settings on the workstation. By checking the field seen in Figure 3-18, to Grant computer accounts in the Computers container permission to update their own account information you allow Centrify to alter settings of the local computer once it has been joined to Active Directory.

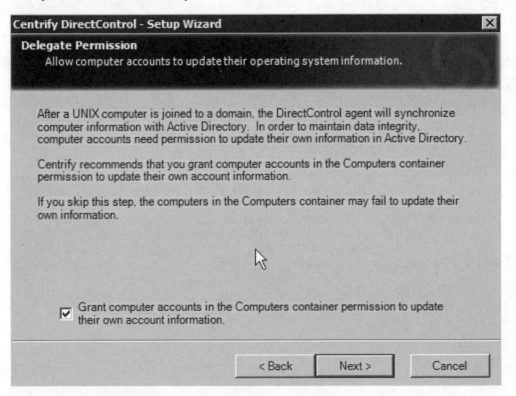

Figure 3-18. *Allowing computers to update information in Active Directory*

Next you will configure how informational data is exchanged with Active Directory. The Register the AD Administrative Notification Handler verifies the Active Directory information from the Centrify database. It is recommended to check the Register administrative notification handler for Microsoft Active Directory Users and Computers snap-in field and then click on the Next button. At the Setup Property Pages screen, configure whether property pages are used when opening Active Directory Users and Computers are updated by Centrify. Unless you have other tools that hook into Active Directory to ease administration, check this box and then click on the Next button.

When the Setup Wizard is complete you will see the Setup Wizard Summary page, where you will review the settings and then select Next or Cancel, if the setup does not match your vision of what is being installed. Finally, at the Centrify DirectControl Setup Wizard screen, click on the Finish button to complete the setup wizard.

Using DirectControl

Once installed, it's time to get comfortable with the DirectControl interface. To do so, open Active Directory Users and Computers from Administrative Tools and then open an account. Then click on the newly added Centrify tab. The Domain: field contains the Active Directory domain that an account belongs to, which should be populated by default with the domain name that you are using. The field for User has a UNIX profile in these zones and is where you configure an account's Zone so that it will be managed (by default all accounts will be placed in the default Zone that was specified during installation). The UID:, Login name:, Shell:, Home directory:, and Primary group: fields all provide settings that are then expanded and applied by the Centrify Active Directory plug-in. If you click on the Add button and select the default zone created earlier then you will populate the remainder of the fields based on the settings previously used.

Next, look at how you can add accounts into zones from within DirectControl. To do so, open Centrify DirectControl from Start ➤ Programs ➤ Centrify, as shown in Figure 3-19. When Centrify DirectControl window opens, click on the disclosure dialog for Centrify, then Zones and Users to bring up a screen showing the account just added to the default zone. From this screen, you will not typically manage memberships—these are usually managed by Active Directory Users and Computers. Instead, you will more than likely use the DirectControl application itself to run reports.

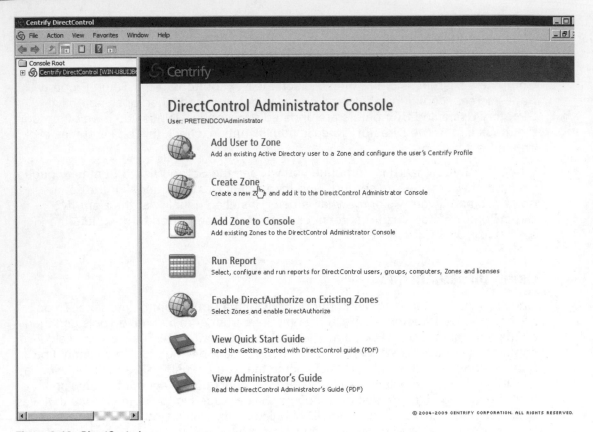

Figure 3-19. *DirectControl*

You are now ready to set up policies. To get started, select an Organizational Unit and open the Group Policy Object Editor (GPOE). Then click on the Action menu, selecting Add/Remove Templates... You can then right-click on an object and then click on Add/Remove Templates... At the resulting screen, click on centrify_mac_settings.xml and then click on the Open button. You will now see Mac OS X Settings for Users and Computers. You can then browse policies and configure policies for users and computers, just as you would configure group policy objects for Windows.

Let's look at setting up a specific policy: the Dock position preference that we've been using throughout this chapter. To do so, browse to the centrify_mac_settings.xml from within GPOE and click on User Configuration, Centrify Settings, and then Mac OS X Settings. From here, click on Dock Settings, then double-click on the Adjust the Dock's position on the screen Policy to open a dialog box that allows you to set the Dock's position. Set it to the right side (or the left if you are in the mood to not follow along) of the screen and then click on the OK button.

Once you have finished setting up the server, install the client and bind it to the server. The Centrify client allows you to bind to the server and log in as the user, verifying that the dock appears at the correct location. You can now configure other policies in the same manner that you configure policies for Windows users. Correlate those that you use with your organization's security policy.

Likewise

Likewise has two products to assist with the integration of Mac OS X within Active Directory. The first is Likewise Open, which is open source software and acts as a replacement for the Active Directory plug-in. Likewise Open provides support for multiple forest environments, credential caching and integrates SSH on Mac OS X with Active Directory. The second is Likewise Enterprise, which is a server-side solution rather than a client-side solution. Neither product requires changes to the Active Directory schema.

To integrate Likewise Open on a Mac, first download and open the package installer. At the Introduction screen, click on the Continue button. At the Read Me screen, read the information provided and then click on Continue. Next, at the License screen, read the license information and provided you accept the licensing agreement, click on the Continue button. When prompted to Agree, click on the Agree button. At the Installation Type screen, click on the Install button in order to install the files into the default location.

The installer will complete installing the plug-in, and provided the installer is successful you will be greeted with the Install Succeeded screen. Here, click Close and you will be ready to bind to Active Directory using the Likewise plug-in.

To bind to Active Directory using the plug-in, open Directory Utility from /Applications/Utilities. Next, if you click on the Services icon in the Directory Utility toolbar, you will notice the new Likewise–Active Directory entry. Click here and then click on the pencil icon to begin the GUI aspect of the Active Directory binding process.

You will now see the Join Active Directory wizard. Here, the Computer name: field will automatically be populated with the hostname of your computer. You can customize the name or enter the name of the Active Directory domain in the Domain to join: field. If you would like to leave the system in the default Computers Organizational Unit (OU) then you can now click on the Join button. Otherwise, you can click on the OU Path and enter the path of the OU you would like the system to join.

You will now be prompted for the username and password of a user with rights to join the Active Directory domain. Provide the appropriate information as seen here and click on the OK button. When the wizard is complete you should see a screen as follows indicating a successful bind to Active Directory.

If you click on Likewise–Active Directory in Directory Utility you will now see a screen indicating that you have joined the appropriate domain as follows. Finally, you can also use the command line to join Active Directory by leveraging the /opt/likewise/bin/ domainjoin-clicommand. There are other commands located in the /opt/likewise/bin directory as well, which can be used to perform other operations as required by Active Directory, including of course, mass deployment.

Likewise Enterprise

To integrate Likewise Enterprise into your heterogeneous environment, Likewise, similar to Centrify, first requires you to install the Likewise Console on a domain controller. Once done, you will be able to join Mac OS X computers into your Active Directory environment and obtain additional options than what is allowed with the standard Active Directory plug-in, included with Mac OS X and Mac OS X Server.

What's the difference between the two? There are many, but they are likely to change in releases that will follow shortly after the publication of this book. Therefore, if you are in need of a solution to bridge the gaps left by the built-in Active Directory plug-in for Mac OS X, I recommend that you bring in both vendors and let them explain their value proposition. Compile a list of requirements beforehand and then test each solution to see which most closely conforms to the needs and mentality of your organization.

Thursby ADmitMac

ADmitMac provides features that aren't available with the default Active Directory plug-in, such as Distributed File System (DFS) support, support for home directories on DFS based volumes, Active Directory based cross-realm trusts, and more caching options. There is also an ADmitMac deployment tool, which reduces your reliance on manually scripting Active Directory binding and offers more options that can be used to protect your Active Directory administrative password.

> **NOTE:** The AD Commander can be used to authenticate and manage Active Directory objects from a Mac OS X client.

Before you look at trying to mass deploy ADmitMac, you obviously need to figure out what it can do for you and which options you will use. Then you will programmatically figure out how to deploy it. To get started with your testing, you will first want to download the installer from Thursby and then run the ADmitMac installation package. Clicking Continue at the Introductions screen, Read Me screen, and after reading the developer's notes.

The next step in the installer package is to deal with licensing. At the Software License Agreement screen, read the agreement and click on Continue. If you accept the agreement, click on the Agree button at the dialog. At the License Code Entry screen, enter your username, the organization name, and the license code you were supplied with by Thursby. Then, click on the Continue button.

At the Installation Type screen, click on Change Install Location to select a different location to install ADmitMac or click on the Install button to complete the installation process. When the installation process is complete the ADmitMacSetup Assistant will automatically start. Here, click on Continue to start the wizard.

Next, you will be prompted to setup WINS on the client computer. Most Active Directory environments no longer rely heavily on WINS support. Additionally, WINS is available using the Apple Active Directory plug-in. However, if you would like to enable WINS support you can do so by choosing to do so through DHCP or Manually. When you are satisfied with your settings, click on the Continue button.

Next, configure the Security Policy Settings, similar to the PacketSign option in dsconfigad. Here, select whether digital signing is required and select the bullet that most applies to your environment in terms of hashing and then click on the Continue button.

You will now be prompted to enter the name of the domain for your Active Directory environment. Enter the domain in the Domain: field and click on the Continue button as seen here.

Next enter the name that the computer record should be generated with into the Computer Name: field and the Organizational Unit (OU) that the computer should reside in using the Computer OU: field. Also enter the username and password of a user who has permission to create an object in Active Directory and click on the OK button.

The computer will now bind to Active Directory. When it is finished you will have the option to use the assistant to move local accounts into Active Directory accounts. This is only for systems with existing users that need to be migrated to Active Directory users. However, if you would like to invoke the application later you can do so using the Home Mover program that is located in /Library/Application Support/ADmitMac.

Now that your client is bound into Active Directory, you can use the Directory Utility application from /Applications/Utilities to alter any of the settings that have been previously configured and to configure shared folders on the local client using Active Directory credentials. The Directory Utility plug-in can also be used in dual directory environments to specify exactly where to look for managed preferences.

> **NOTE:** At the time of release for this book, ADmitMac does not yet support Snow Leopard. However, we have been assured that by the time the book is printed that it will be supported. Therefore, given the historical importance of the ADmitMac solution and the prevalence in the marketplace we have left this section in place, written based on Leopard rather than Snow Leopard.

Quest

Quest, as with Centrify and Likewise, is used to leverage an existing Active Directory infrastructure for providing policies for Mac OS X. Quest is based on the VintelaAuthentication Services (VAS). Quest will give you a new mmc snap-in for Windows Server's Group Policy Object Editor (GPOE) that will allow you to configure preference manifests and custom properly list (.plist) files similar to how you would do so from with Workgroup Manager. The screens look almost identical to Workgroup Manager except that policy items are formatted to fit within a GPOE screen.

Quest adheres to the RFC 2307 standards. In Windows Server 2003 R2 and Windows Server 2008 domains, LDAP attributes are already part of the 2307 standard, so there is no extension of the Active Directory schema required. However, data from 2307 will need to be translated so the client is required, which leverages the Microsoft CSE (Client Side Extensions). More information on CSE can be found using TechNet: http://technet.microsoft.com/en-us/library/cc736967.aspx.

To configure the VAS plug-in on a Microsoft Windows Domain Controller, set up a client to connect to Active Directory so that policies configured within the VAS GPOE snap-in will be applied to the client computer.

To configure VAS for Mac OS X, you will start off by logging into an Active Directory Domain Controller, unzip the VAS installer by double-clicking on the VAS-3.x.x.x.msi pack, then clicking Next at the Welcome screen. At the subsequent License Agreement screen, read the licensing agreement and then click on the I accept the terms in the license agreement option, assuming the terms are palpable to you. At the Destination Folder screen, click on the Next button. Alternatively, you could click on the Change button to install Quest VAS into a folder other than C:\Program Files\Quest Software\Vintela Authentication Services directory. At the Setup Type screen, click on Complete. At the Ready to Install the Program screen, click on the Install button. When the installer has finished its tasks click on the Finish button.

Once the VAS installation is complete open a GPOE screen to create your first domain policy. To do so open the Windows Start Menu, click Run, enter mmc into the Open: field, and click on the OK button. At the Console screen click on the File menu and select Add/Remove Snap-In and then at the Add Standalone Snap-in screen, highlight Group Policy Object Editor and click on the Add button.

At the Welcome to the Group Policy Wizard screen, click on Browse and then select Default Domain Policy. Once you see the Finish button then all is complete and you can move on to the next step: editing policies for Mac OS X. Use Default Domain Policy to browse to Mac OS X Settings and select Workgroup Manager. If you have built policies for Open Directory using Workgroup Manager then the items in the resulting list will seem familiar to you. This is because the developers of VAS have gone through and copied the policies available in Workgroup Manager.

A common managed preference is to limit removable media options for clients. The terminology that Quest uses to do so is a Media Access policy object. From the Domain Policy screen, double-click on any feature (in this case Media Access) to bring up the Properties screen. Here, you can elect to enforce the policy using Never, Once, and Always, mirroring the options available in Mac OS X Server's Workgroup Manager yet again. The Never option disables the policy, which is the configured preference by default. The Once option enforces it for the first logon event once it has been enabled, but then leaves the option to allow the end user to alter a setting. The Always option enforces the policy at each logon and while a session is active. For the purpose of this example, click on Always to enforce the policy and then uncheck the Allow button, clicking on the Apply button when you are done.

Once you have saved the option, verify that it has been enforced by navigating to the GPOE Console again and checking that the policies are set to Yes under the column for Configured preferences. Custom policies are available in Quest, just as they are an option in Workgroup Manager on Mac OS X Server. Policies for software that is not included by default does rely on the software developer (including Apple) to create preference manifests to make their application's preference keys available for management through managed preferences. If a developer has not done so, you can also use standard property list files (.plist) to configure policies for many applications, but it is less granular in nature. Quest provides a few common plistfiles into their Preference Manifests section, including a manifest for Microsoft Office that you can use with other solutions as well. A common example of a manifest often used but not included by default is the ManagedClient options for Dashboard and iWork.

Once the policies on the server match your organizations policies, you'll more than likely want to install the VAS for Mac OS X client software and start testing the configuration. To do so, open the installation tools folder, the client folder, and then the osx folder where you will find the dmgcalled installation. Copy this to a client and open the VAS.mpkg file to begin the client-side installation, clicking on Continue at the Welcome sorcen.

At the following screen read the License Agreement, (we realize these are kinda' dull, but they do occasionally contain really good information to know) and click on the Continue button. Assuming that you accept the licensing agreement, go ahead and click on the Agree button to continue. The Installation Type screen is next, where you can change the location that Quest will be installed to by using the Change Install Location... button or the Customize... button to choose which components to install (as you can probably guess there is little purpose to doing). Go ahead and click on the Install button to have the software complete the installation.

You can also simply use the installer command to deploy the package in a more silent manner (using ARD). Here, you will use the following installer command, specifying the vasclnt package, to complete the installation:

```
/usr/sbin/installer -pkg Packages/vasclnt.pkg \ -target /
```

Next open the Directory Utility to join the client computer to Active Directory. Click on the Services icon in the toolbar to bring up the available plug-ins. Make sure that there are no other Active Directory plug-ins enabled for this machine and then double-click on the Active Directory (Quest VAS) entry.

Next, you will be asked to enter a Domain Name for your Active Directory environment (see Figure 3-20). Type the pertinent domain name, clicking the Join Domain button (or the Enter key if you will) when you are complete.

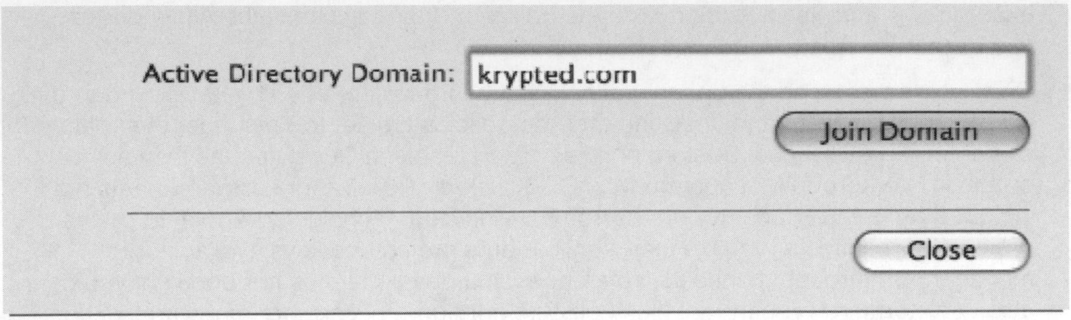

Active Directory Domain: krypted.com

Join Domain

Close

Figure 3-20. *Binding with Quest*

When you are requested to type in a valid username and password with the appropriate permissions to join the Active Directory domain type in the appropriate information, clicking on OK when you are satisfied with your entry. You can also click on the disclosure triangle to enter other pertinent information, such as a preferred domain controller, like with the Mac OS X Active Directory plug-in. Assuming the binding occurs successfully the domain binding process is then complete. Your client will now be able to authenticate against Active Directory using the Quest VAS plug-in and policies applied to computer and user objects through GPOE will be applied as intended. Make sure that the Active Directory plug-in supplied by Apple is not also enabled.

Quest also provides a command-line interface for automating binding once you have deployed the installation package. In order to use the command-line interface, cd into the /opt/quest/bin directory, where you will find the klist, ldapmodify, preflight, vastool, vgptool, ktutil, ldapsearch, uptool and vgpmod tools, each custom tools for searching, checking bindng, and managing settings for the Quest client.

The /opt/quest/libexec/vas/scripts/vasjoin.sh script can be used as follows, (assuming your working directory to be /opt/quest/libexec/vas/scripts):

```
./vasjoin.sh -u Administrator join -f mydomain.com
```

Summary

The default Active Directory plug-in should work to provide centralized authentication services for most, but not all. In addition to centralized authentication, an enterprise needs its directory service to provide policies. Extending an Active Directory schema is an option for most environments looking to provide policies for Mac OS X clients. For those where extending the schema will not be possible, a Dual Directory environment should be your first thought, and, provided you fully test the environment, you should also consider augmented records.

Why? Purely due to total cost of ownership. You will not be able to justify the platform if you have to bolt too many pay-for features on. The more third-party solutions that are introduced also dilutes ownership for troubleshooting and lateral support options.

Overall, your life will be easier on a lot of different levels if you will be able to minimize the third-party solutions.

If you do bring in a third-party solution, then it should have its own total cost of ownership justification. For example, if you estimate that the cost of managing and maintaining a secondary directory service (including training, equipment, setup) for a Dual Directory is more than licensing Centrify for 10,000 users, especially considering that an Active Directory administrator who knows little to nothing about a Mac can manage it, then you have a clear decision in front of you at the tail end of year one, if not sooner.

Overall, the most cost effective method of producing managed preferences is going to be extending your Active Directory schema. But there are still a number of cases where third-party solutions will need to be leveraged—try to use these as ways to drive down the total cost of ownership by leveraging advanced features of each solution to enable more automation for your environment. Make sure that the business cost here is known by all, especially those responsible for making these types of budgeting decisions.

## Chapter 4

Storage

Storage can be an extensive topic, but the storage paradigm for the Mac platform is unique—there are far fewer options than with other environments, which helps to constrain the conversation. It's not that you can't use most enterprise-class storage systems, it's just that you won't find the proliferation of storage types, file systems, and storage-access protocols that you will with, say, Windows. Still, OS X supports iSCSI and Fibre Channel (FC, which we'll discuss when we get to Xsan SAN systems) as well as numerous network access protocols—client and server—that run over Ethernet: Apple Filing Protocol (AFP), Network File System (NFS), and Server Message Block/Common Internet File System (SMB/CIFS).

For the purpose of this chapter, we're going to divide storage into two types. The first, client storage, we'll define as data repositories accessed via the AFP, SMB/CIFS, NFS, or Dfs (Microsoft's Distributed file system) network protocols. Though you may be using others, these are the major players. We'll assume your organization already has a solution in place to supply one of the four, and the Mac will simply be fitting into an existing paradigm. The second type of storage we'll cover is SAN (Storage Area Network) systems—specifically, drive networks accessed through FC or iSCSI protocols. The benefits of a SAN lie primarily in the centralization of data and storage resources, true block-level access to storage, and much better performance.

In addition to client storage and SANs, this chapter looks at ExtremeZ-IP, a software package that allows Windows Server to share existing data to Mac clients using their native protocol, AFP.

Client Storage

The first and most visible type of client storage holds your users' shared files and folders; the second is used to synchronize or store users' home directories (which are similar to profiles in Microsoft Windows). For the purpose of this chapter, we'll call the former *file storage* and the latter *home-folder* or h*ome-directory storage*.

Whichever you're dealing with, for file sharing, AFP is the Mac's native language and will perform the best from the client perspective. Though other protocols also enjoy wide adoption in enterprises, for the most part, if you can provide your Mac clients with storage over AFP, they'll get the best performance and you'll have the fewest issues to troubleshoot on the client side. That said, if you already have a NetApp, EMC, or Isilon Systems setup providing storage over SMB or NFS, then you can definitely use it. You can also reshare existing SAN or NFS solutions using Mac OS X Server, ExtremeZ-IP, or Helios. In the next few sections we'll cover manually connecting to storage over these three main protocols (AFP, SMB and NFS).

AFP

As we mentioned, AFP is the native file sharing protocol for Mac OS X. It's important to note that AFP is not AppleTalk and is based on the TCP/IP stack. Mac clients can connect to AFP volumes easily using the Finder or the mount_afp command. If an AFP server has Bonjour enabled and exists on the same subnet as the client, the node will automatically discover the running service and appear in the Finder's sidebar. In this chapter, though, we'll assume that your environment is too large to locate services reliably over Bonjour or that you have a centralized Bonjour service, so we'll only look at using AFP to manually mount volumes.

To do so from Mac OS X, click on the Go menu in the Finder, and select Connect to Server. In the Server Address field of the resulting dialog box, you'd normally enter <protocol name>:// followed by the address of your server—for example, smb://seldom.kryped.com. (Note that the OS defaults to AFP, so although we enter the protocol name in Figure 4-1, we could have just typed in the server address.) Now click the Connect button.

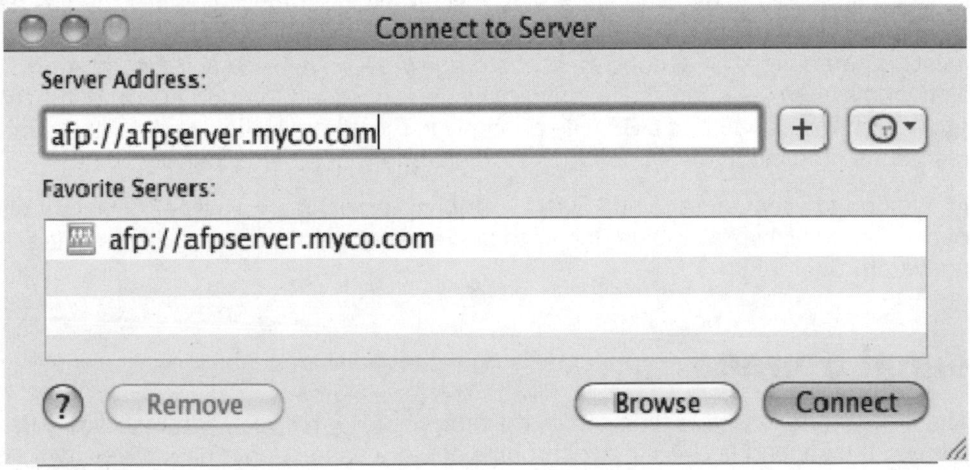

Figure 4-1. *Connecting to an AFP server*

TIP: You can also click the plus sign (+) to save this server to your Favorite Servers list. Additionally, you can select the clock icon to see recent connection history. Clicking one of the shares in the resulting list will connect you to it.

If your system has already obtained a single sign-on ticket from Kerberos (discussed in Chapter 1), you won't be prompted for a user name or a password, you'll just see a dialog box in which you can choose the share points to connect to. In Microsoft Windows you can do the same by using the run dialog box and entering the address of a server, but the Mac dialog lets you select multiple servers using the Shift or Command keys. Once you're satisfied with what you've selected, click OK. You'll see the appropriate shares available under the Shared section in the Finder sidebar. You can also find mounted shares by selecting Computer in the Finder's Go menu (Command+Shift+C) as shown in Figure 4-2.

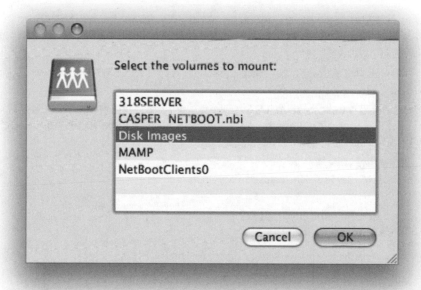

Figure 4-2. *Mounted shares. To make multiple selections, hold down the Shift or Command key while choosing.*

If you use the `mount_afp` command to connect to file-sharing volumes, you must provide the command with a lengthy string that contains a number of items embedded in the URL. The `afp://` URI, like others, allows you to specify authentication credentials directly in the URL, which you do via standard conventions following the format:

```
afp://username:password@server/mount
```

This format extends to numerous protocols including HTTP, FTP, and SMB. For example, afp://admin:daneel@seldon.krypted.com/outerrim will connect to the share point *outerrim* that's hosted on the server seldon.krypted.com using the user name *admin* and the password *daneel*. You can optionally specify a path on the local system that the volume will be mounted to, rather than using /Volumes as is the default. Therefore, the syntax to mount the AFP volume from the command line (assuming you were to mount it in the standard directory, which is /Volumes) would be:

```
mkdir /Volumes/outerrim
mount_afp afp://admin:daneel@seldon.krypted.com/outerrim /Volumes/outerrim
```

Notice that we must first create the destination folder, otherwise mount_afp will fail. In addition to specifying a password on the command line, you can instruct the mount_afp command to use an existing single sign-on ticket:

```
mount_afp "afp://;AUTH=Client%20Krb%20v2@seldon.krypted.com/outerrim" ↵
/Volumes/outerrim
```

You may want to specify an alternative user in some cases—for instance, if you'll be logging in using an administrative account. This is handy for certain operations. You can do so with a statement such as:

```
mount_afp "afp://username;AUTH=Client%20Krb%20v2@seldon.krypted.com/outerrim" ↵
/Volumes/outerrim
```

For this to work, you need a valid, active TGT (Ticket Granting Ticket) (which will be recognized via klist). This won't always be available, but it's possible to use an active TGT obtained by another local user. To do so, run sudo from root as follows:

```
sudo -u username mount_afp ↵
"afp://;AUTH=Client%20Krb%20v2@seldon.krypted.com/outerrim" ↵
/Volumes/outerrim
```

In this case, you don't need to specify the user name in the afp:// URL, because the sudo command will execute as *user name*.

You can also perform an automount with guest access, as in this example:

```
mount_afp "afp://;AUTH=No%20User%20Authent@seldon.krypted.com/outerrim" ↵
/Volumes/outerrim
```

In addition to mount_afp, you can use the mnthome command to mount an AFP home folder from a command-line session. However, this requires the configuration of a home directory automount, as described in Chapter 7.

SMB

To manually connect to an SMB volume from Mac OS X, select the Go menu from the Finder, and choose Connect to Server. In the dialog box that appears, enter smb://

followed by the address of your server, then click the Connect button and submit your user name and password in the resulting prompt dialog. Just as when you follow this process using AFP, you'll get a list of share points you can access.

You can also mount SMB shares with the mount_smbfs command, using pretty much the same syntax as you would with mount_afp. Follow the command itself with the options (if any—the example below shows none) and the path. You won't need to prepend the protocol name to the URL, though. So, for example, to mount the same volume as shown in the AFP section, you'd type this:

```
mount_smbfs //admin:daneel@seldon.krypted.com/outerrim ⏎
/Volumes/outerrim
```

> **NOTE:** There is also an SMB client, appropriately named smb_client that's similar to the ftp client, if you wish to use SMB interactively from the command line.

NFS

As with the previous protocols, you can manually connect to an NFS volume from Mac OS X by selecting the Go menu in the Finder and picking Connect to Server. In the resulting dialog box, enter nfs:// followed by the address of your server, a slash, and then the full path of the export. Click the Connect button.

If you're unsure about what should follow the slash, you can get the information from the exports file found in the /etc folder on the NFS server. The sample exports file that follows was built in the Mac OS X Server Admin tool. To match your environment, yours may have been created manually, so it may not look exactly the same, but it should be similar to this:

```
### [ Begin Server Admin managed exports. Do Not Edit.
/Volumes/SharedData/Mule -maproot=nobody -sec=sys 192.168.210.201
### ] End Server Admin managed exports.
```

In the previous example we're exporting a share point of the folder Mule to the IP address 192.168.210.201. Volumes/SharedData/Mule, the full path of the export, is the information you're looking for. The Mule directory, in our installation, is hosted on seldon.krypted.com and we can access the directory (but only from 192.168.210.201) using nfs://seldon.krypted.com/Volumes/SharedData/Mule. This is what you enter into the Server Address text box of the Connect to Server dialog, as shown in Figure 4-3.

Provided you're using the system at this IP address, when you click the Connect button you'll instantly connect to the volume. Notice the lack of a password. This is because NFS relies on IP addresses rather than user-namepassword combinations to determine who can access data stored on the shares it provides.

NOTE: You can leverage Netgroups through YP/NIS (discussed further in Chapter 2). If you're more confident with using local BSD files to manage users and groups, you can also enable the BSD local node entry in Directory Utility as described in Chapter 2.

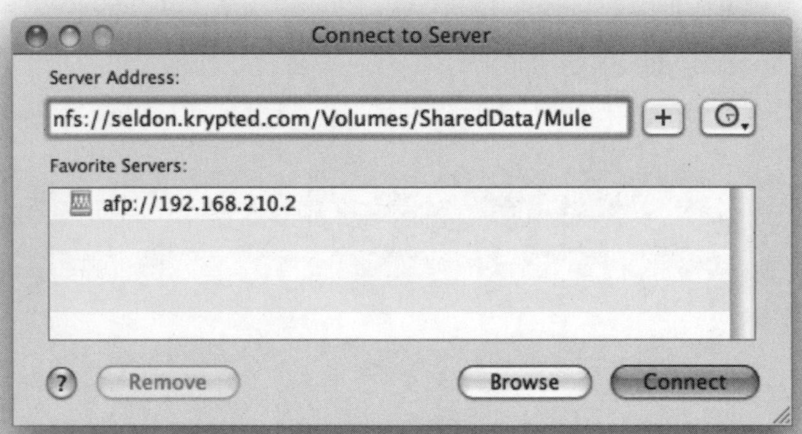

Figure 4-3. *Mounting an NFS share through the Finder*

You can also use `mount_nfs` to make remote NFS volumes available locally. To do so, follow the command with the name of the server, the characters `:/` (a colon followed by a slash), and the path to the mount point, as in this example:

```
mount_nfs seldon.krypted.com:/innerrim /innerrim
```

The `mount_nfs` command has a number of options, which you can view using the `man mount_nfs` command. You can see all of the mounted NFS volumes for the host with `showmount`.

Automounts

To avoid issuing a command every time a client system needs access to remote storage, you can set up *automounts.* OS X lets you configure them either globally, through directory services, or on individual hosts. The latter requires you to use NFS. Before you create an automount, we recommend using the procedure in the NFS section just covered to connect to the volume manually and verify that you know the correct settings.

The process to set up a local automount depends upon the system that you are running. In 10.4 and 10.5, automounts are configured using Directory Utility (found in /Applications/Utilities). Once the app is opened, click the lock to authenticate to allow changes. Next, click on the button "Show Advanced Settings." From here, click on the Mounts Tab, and press the plus icon (+) at the bottom-left side of the Remote NFS URL list to create a new mount, as shown in Figure 4-4.

NOTE: For more information about managing mounts en masse, see Chapter 7.

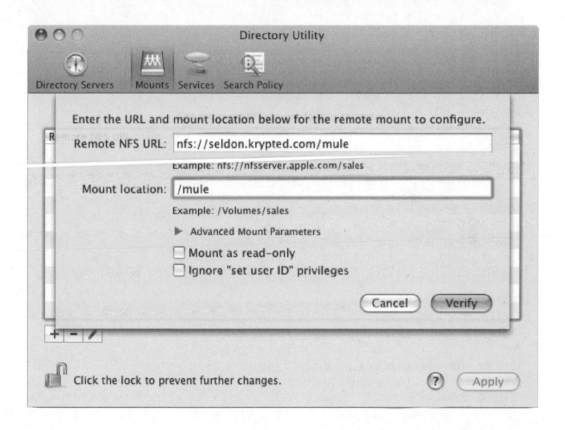

Figure 4-4. *Creating a Remote Mount with Disk Utility*

In that dialog, enter the parameters you used to establish a manual connection, then click Verify. Back at Directory Utility (Figure 4-5), click the Apply button, then test to insure you can browse to the directory-mount location as configured; in this case, our NFS mount can be found locally in the /mule directory.

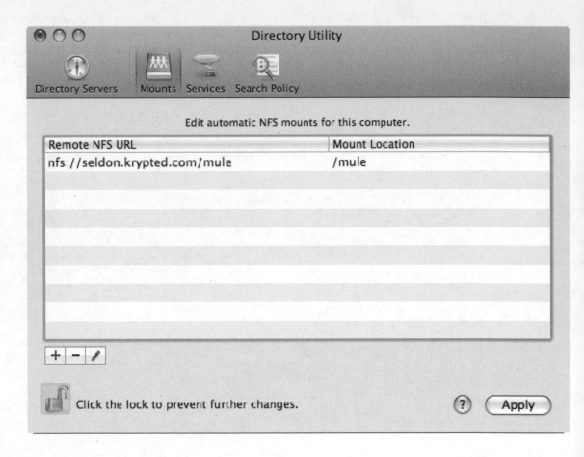

Figure 4-5. *Directory Utility NFS Mount List (10.4 and 10.5)*

In 10.6, the process is extremely similar; however, the automount GUI is now hidden inside of the Disk Utility application, found in /Applications/Utilities. Once opened, access the automount GUI by selecting NFS mounts under the File menu. From here, the interface is pretty much identical to that found in Directory Utility, as can be seen in Figure 4-6.

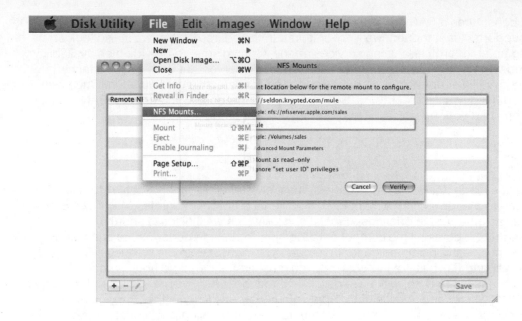

Figure 4-0. Configuring NFS Mounts using Disk Utility in 10.6

Home-Directory Storage Provisioning

Automounts can serve a purpose beyond what the name implies—they can provide storage for the home directory given to Mac OS X clients. When located on a server, the home directory is known as a Network Home Directory. When stored on a client and synchronized to a server, it's called a Mobile Home Folder (also referred to as a portable home directory). We'll cover home directory implementation more exhaustively in Chapter 7.

SAN Storage

Centralizing your storage for multiple hosts can have a number of positive effects for many environments. Many centralized storage environments are SANs. Proper planning will have long-lasting positive effects on your installation. And in the planning stage, one of the most critical considerations is what your SAN will be doing. That determines the requirements for performance, total capacity, concurrent access, uptime—even future expansion (another area where thinking in advance is imperative). Once you've completed planning, you need to gather the necessary equipment, software, and documentation for the installation. Whatever form your SAN takes, it'll be a bit of an investment, but a decent one if you plan appropriately for your environment. Fail to do that, though, and you may end up with a large bill and a system that doesn't work for you.

What constitutes a SAN can be different to different people. Because Apple distributes and supports Xsan, though, we'll cover it first. In the course of this, we'll also look at setting up standard file-sharing services on the Xsan volume, to provide high availability beyond what is capable when using a traditional file server that uses direct-attached storage. We'll set up multiple server heads in an active/active configuration. Once we've covered Xsan, we'll look at using iSCSI initiators to interface with common SAN solutions that your organization may already have in production.

Xsan

Apple has made Xsan one of the easiest, most cost-effective and versatile storage area networking platforms on the market. This powerful software integrates Mac OS X Server (as well as other Apple offerings), *Fibre Channel* (which we'll discuss shortly), and RAID architecture. It binds all the components together to provide performance and flexibility that pushes centralized storage for heterogeneous networks to the next level. To grasp the power and flexibility of this solution, you must first understand how it organizes and provides access to data, which we describe throughout this chapter. The combination of Mac OS X Server and various other Apple offerings provides multiple computers concurrent access to large amounts of media, organized using pools of storage and interconnected using Fibre Channel, providing fast and virtualized connectivity to the target storage.

SAN installations are as diverse as the businesses they serve. And although Xsan was developed primarily for professional video, admins can leverage it to provide storage for a wide array of uses including file sharing, mail clustering, and calendar-server clustering. In an Xsan installation you'll find a variety of components. These typically include Apple Xserve RAID or Promise RAID storage, client systems with Fibre Channel cards, transceivers, Xsan software, fiber cabling, an FC switch, a dedicated Ethernet network for management, and one or more systems (known as metadata controllers or MDCs) devoted to running the Xsan. Each node must also run either Xsan for client connectivity and administration or, on Windows and Linux PCs, Quantum StorNext (which you can purchase at www.quantum.com).

Fibre Channel is an extension to SCSI that allows connections to a wide variety of devices and multiple petabytes of data via copper and optical cabling. Client nodes must be connected via FC to access an Xsan installation. Fibre-attached servers can reshare data over various file- or Web-sharing protocols, but the exclusive direct access to storage through Fibre Channel provides security and much better performance. Each file or Web server added to the SAN will make it faster provided you haven't saturated the back-end storage.

Cabling and Transceivers

Apple FC cards that come with two SFP (small form-factor pluggable) ports (most do) also include two, 2.9-meter copper cables with SFP connections on each end. You shouldn't use longer copper cables.

For connecting systems that are further than 2.9 meters from the SAN, Apple advocates converting from standard copper cables to LC (Lucent Connector) or SC (Subscriber Connector) optical cabling and highly recommends that it be multimode, which, throughout this chapter, we'll assume to be in use. Because most devices added into an FC network use LC adapters, going that route typically offers the path of least resistance when installing your SAN. LC multimode cables are typically orange, indicating a maximum throughput of 4gbps, or light blue (for 10gbps) and contain two optical cables per sheath, making them easy to identify. To use LC cabling, the SFP connection built into systems must be adapted from SFP to LC using a transceiver.

Not all LC cabling can support the maximum speeds, so it's important to ensure you're using the proper type. The maximum length of an optical cable is determined by its diameter. You can run cables that are 9µm in diameter up to 10km. This is typically referred to as *long haul.* The only long-haul transceiver supported by Apple for the Xsan is the Finisar FTRJ-1319-P1BTL. Short-haul cables are 50µm and can run 500 meters; 62.5µm cables can span 300 meters.

If you'll be using transceivers, Apple recommends sticking with the same manufacturer and model for all devices connected to your *fabric* (an interconnection of FC host ports). It's also worth noting that the online Apple Store sells Finisar transceivers.

Storage

We refer to a single device chassis containing a number of drives as a *shelf* of storage. You can combine the disks on a shelf of storage into a logical RAID that, depending on its type, offers a variety of features such as redundancy or faster access times. The most common RAID products used in an Xsan environment are the Apple Xserve RAID in legacy installations and the Promise Vtrak in newer setups. (You can use other Fibre Channel RAID devices, including those from EMC and Active Storage, but they will likely not be supported by Apple.) Each RAID unit, or shelf, will typically have multiple controllers.

Each RAID can provide a number of LUNs (Logical Unit Numbers). A LUN is a logical partition of the storage that resides on a given shelf. On an Xserve RAID device, a LUN is restricted to drives managed by a given controller. With a Promise RAID product, a controller can provide LUN failover between controllers as long as they're within the same shelf or in a connected expansion chassis. Each controller is then plugged into the Fibre Channel switch.

> **NOTE:** While there are many hardware vendors that supply components you can use in an Xsan, the devices must all be approved by Apple if you want support from Apple.

Virtualized Storage

As you add more RAID devices to your environment, you aggregate the storage. Xsan can combine a set of LUNs into a *storage pool.* A storage pool can span multiple shelves or be on a single unit but should typically contain at most four LUNs. Because the storage pool will reduce the capacity of all its LUNs to that of the smallest one, LUNs you choose to pool should be of similar capacity.

Combining multiple storage pools creates volumes, and with Xsan you can mount and unmount these on client systems. For most purposes, such a collection will present as any other local hard drive despite running the Apple clustered file system (ACFS) rather than the default OS X file system, HFS+. Servers treat Xsan volumes much as they would direct-attached external storage despite the significantly more-complex back-end infrastructure.

Once configured, Fibre Channel is the network that interconnects all of the clients, servers, and storage. In FC jargon, the first two are referred to as FC *initiators.* Storage devices such as disk-based raids, tape libraries, or other storage media are referred to as *targets.* Built on top of this storage and communications infrastructure, the Xsan software provides the virtualized, logical constructs used to provide maximum speed, redundancy, and concurrent access.

> **NOTE:** Although not strictly considered a component of an Xsan, a UPS capable of powering the equipment is absolutely necessary. This one item can save an administrator some painful headaches. If your entire data center is powered by a UPS, you're probably covered; if not, you should certainly invest in one and set up the automated shutdown software to unmount clients, stop volumes, and gracefully shut down the computers that manage the SAN.

Initiators

Now that we've covered the physical components of an Xsan, it's important to understand those that reside on Mac OS X. For the purposes of this chapter, Xsan clients are systems that log into an Xsan and mount volumes. Metadata controllers are systems that manage those same volumes. The Xsan software installs and runs a number of services on the computer that manages the actual Xsan.

All of the computers that act as Xsan *initiators* (non-storage devices, such as clients and controllers) run the Xsan software and have a host bus adapter (HBA). Apple sells rebranded LSI Logic HBAs for use with Xsan or for connecting directly to an Xserve RAID or Promise RAID component. Each FC port on these cards has a factory-assigned WWPN (WorldWide Port Name) and WWN (WorldWide Name), the equivalent of an Ethernet adapter's MAC address. In a standard setup you probably won't need to customize any of the card's settings. If necessary, though, you can do so using the FC System Preference pane. Configuration choices are: Automatic, Point-to-Point, and Arbitrated Loop. With Xsan initiators you, use Automatic or Point-to-Point. Each of the host adapters gets plugged into the Fibre Channel switch.

NOTE: The release tab on the cable is very close to the chassis when the Apple FC PCI card is installed in the upper PCI slot of the dual PCI riser card. The limited space can make it difficult to press the tab on the connector to release the cable. In this case, use a flat object such as a screwdriver or knife to depress the tab before pulling on the cable. Do not force the connectors.

You can use Quantum StorNext to set up non-Apple clients on the Xsan. The software supports AIX, IRIX, Linux, Solaris, and Windows clients. Many of these non-Apple machines can connect to the switch with Fibre Channel cards manufactured by ATTO Technology, LSI, Qlogic, and other suppliers (ATTO and Qlogic both have drivers for Mac OS X as well).

Switches

For a SAN to be considered a fabric, it must have an FC switch. With Xsan, we strongly recommended that you use one supported by Apple. Such devices include the Brocade Silkworm 200E, 4100, and 4900, the Cisco MDS 9000 Series, and the QLogic SANbox 2-64, 1400, 5200, 5600, 9100, and 9200 series. If, for an earlier Xsan release, Apple certified a switch that you're using, the company will likely continue its support even if the device isn't in the current list of qualified switches (which you'll find at www.apple.com/xsan/specs.html).

Whatever the brand of switch, in an Xsan deployment, some parts of the configuration process are identical. Before anything else, you should upgrade the firmware (which you should do with most any device). Even after setup, continually updating firmware is important. (Of course, in many cases, you don't want to do so at the expense of bringing a SAN down unless there's a compelling reason for the upgrade.) Once your switches are running the latest firmware, you can administer most through a Web-based interface.

You also want to prevent any interruption in communications with your targets. This includes Registered State Change Notifications (RSCNs), which should be suppressed on initiator ports for all switches. Typically, a client sends an RSCN when connecting to a fabric, and that can cause communications interrupts. Because client workstations tend to reboot often, suppressing RSCN on initiator ports ensures that communication between initiators and targets remains uninterrupted.

You should also make sure that communications occur at the appropriate speed. If a switch and a target or a switch and a LUN are both capable of running at 4Gbps, you should verify that the link appears as 4Gbps on both ends. Switches, targets, and initiators assign speeds automatically (in much the way most Ethernet cards and switches auto-sense), so you don't usually have to statically set a port's speed. But as you add new devices to your fabric, verify that they communicate at the proper rate. When a SAN client displays poor performance or high latency, statically assigning link type and speed can sometimes address the issue. Also, Promise support advises that you statically configure controllers with these settings to reduce latency.

When dealing with FC link negotiation, having some basic knowledge about various port topologies is important. These are broken down according to type and use. The FC spec calls for several initiator port topologies:

- *N_port (node port):* Specifies a point-to-point topology.

- *NL_port (node-loop port):* Refers to a client port that will negotiate as an arbitrated loop device. Generally, you should avoid this configuration, but many tape drives support NL_port topologies only.

On the fabric-switch side, you'll find these topologies include:

- *E_port (expansion port):* Used to connect two switches together via an ISL (Inter-Switch Link) connection.

- *F_port (fabric port):* Negotiates a point-to-point connection with an N_port device.

- *FL_port (fabric loop port):* Can operate as an F port but can also connect via arbitrated loop to NL_port devices.

- *G_port (generic port):* Can operate either as an N_port or E_port, as needed.

- *GL_port (generic loop port):* This is a generic port that can act as a G_port or an FL_port. This is the topology used by Qlogic switches out of the box.

When setting up FC switches and storage, also set the NTP (Network Time Protocol) service, and when possible, centralize logging and set e-mail alerts. Each of these steps can help down the road if you ever need to troubleshoot your Xsan or have issues that you need to be alerted about.

> **NOTE:** Xsan environments do not support switching hubs. When added (and sometimes on rebooting), a device sends out a loop initialization primitive (LIP) to request an address. All activity on the loop can cease as each device establishes a connection within the newly enumerated fabric. A hub-based SAN consists of one loop and therefore must be entirely rebuilt every time any device is added or removed. This wreaks havoc on an Xsan, and can even cause a LIP storm, which can cause endless streams of initialization requests. FC switches can also respond poorly to LIP requests, which are sent when a computer with an improperly set startup disk reboots. The FC port will be queried for a startup disk and a LIP will occur. Because of this, for all clients that are Xsan initiators (yes, that includes your metadata controllers) you should go to the Startup Disk System Preference pane and set the startup disk. We also recommended that you statically set your FC connections to point-to-point (N port) using the FC System Preference (In 10.4, this is found in /Applications/Servers).

Brocade Switches

You administer Brocade Switches through a Web portal (at the IP address 10.77.77.77) using *admin* for the user name and *password* for the password. The first time you use the Web Tools you'll have to enter a license.

Emulex Switches

Some older Emulex SAN switches—the 12-port 355, the 375, and the 9200—maintain legacy support for Xsan. Emulex switches require that you set the host machine ports to *Initiator with Stealth* and the storage-device ports are as Target with Stealth. You can access Emulex switches at the IP address 169.254.10.10. They require no user name and the default password is *password*.

QLogic Switches

The latest QLogic firmware supports administration through a Web portal only. With devices using old versions of the firmware, install the included configuration application on a workstation attached to the switch and go to the IP address 10.0.0.1. The company has updated and enhanced the software, which it now calls the Qlogic Fabric Suite. To authenticate with the switch for the first time, use *admin* for the user name and *password* for the password.

In the past, Apple supported the QLogic SANbox 2-8 and 2-16. As noted previously, the company currently certifies the newer SANbox 2-64, 5000 series (which offers devices with 4 10-gigabit stacking ports and 16 2-gigabit device ports), Qlogic 9000 series. Qlogic switches are a common in Xsan environments.

Cisco Switches

The most recent brand added to the line of supported switches with Xsan is Cisco. The Cisco MDS 9000 family supports 16- and 32-port modules. The Cisco FC switch is the most highly configurable and feature-rich of the FC switches supported by Xsan. The tradeoff of flexibility is that the Cisco switch is the most complicated of the bunch. While there is a Web-based utility for the system, it is only for monitoring. Initial setup of the switch is performed through the serial port on the system.

Zones

You can control access to the SAN using either LUN masking or switch zoning. All of the switches we've mentioned so far support FC zoning. Zoning is similar to creating a VLAN on an Ethernet switch. With LUN masking, you slice the physical storage into partitions (LUNs), and establish filters based on the LUNs' World Wide Names to ensure that only the intended servers have access. When using LUN Masking, you can use the switch to designate a LUN as accessible to one system only or to put both target and initiator ports in a larger zone with other devices, then use the software on a target to restrict access to an initiator.

Admins who decide to use zones can go about it a few different ways. With the first, you build a zone based on whichever device is in the physical port you include. You can find this *port zoning* helpful in environments where administrators simply need a map of which ports are in which zones but don't need access to make changes. Note, though, that if you add new targets, they may appear to be formatted on a number of clients, and could be formatted accidentally by an unwitting user. The second zoning method does so by the address of devices. Across brands, you'll find different terms associated with these approaches.

Opinions about zone management of clients also differ, as do methods. Some people create a new zone for every initiator, restricting what targets each can access. Others leave all their initiators and targets in one big zone and simply let initiators access each target as needed. Still others choose to create two zones, one for metadata controllers and one for client initiators. Each approach has merits, but given that these methods will have similar effects, in most cases your choice boils down to doing whatever filts the security policy and the logic of your environment.

In general, zoning based on Fibre Channel WWNs provides the most resilient setup, eliminating port-lock in and providing a generally less-ambiguous management environment, provided you properly nickname. If your switch supports aliases, grouping target WWNs into a single alias container can greatly simplify deploying a large number of targets across multiple zones. If storage is grouped/aliased in logical divisions, adding new storage is a much more efficient process, as you need only upgrade the group to have the addition applied across all zones that reference the alias.

> **TIP:** Generally, when using a tape library that's directly attached to the FC fabric, you'll need to zone the tape drive to be accessible by only a single host port (basically, the backup server). This is often necessary to ensure consistent functionality and to prevent the backup software from producing odd errors.

Configuring Storage

Whether you're configuring switches or storage, the basic precept is pretty much the same: Don't impede the ability of the initiator to write data to the target. Do everything you can to maximize the likelihood that data will be efficiently delivered to the appropriate location.

Whichever vendor you choose, when setting up storage you'll have these options, or some combination of these options for configuring logical RAID constructs:

RAID 0: Offers no redundancy. Gives the fastest data access speeds and is the most inexpensive option but can't guarantee data availability, since it offers no fault tolerance.

RAID 1: Provides data mirroring. Highest-cost option with regard to data capacity. A RAID 1 mirror set typically provides significantly better read speeds than a single member, though write speeds will be roughly equivalent.

RAID 3: Utilizes data striping with one drive dedicated to parity. RAID 3 sets can suffer a single drive loss without data loss.

RAID 5: Stripes both userland and parity data across all of the drives, yet produces a relatively small diminishment in capacity (generally the equivalent of a single drive or less). Provides redundancy at the lowest cost in drive space. RAID 5 sets can suffer the loss of a single drive without loss of data.

RAID 6: Similar to RAID 5 but with a second parity drive so that if two drives go down concurrently, the RAID setup isn't compromised.

Promise Vtrak

Promise ships two types of RAID devices that Apple has certified to work with Xsan: the E-class, which has RAID controllers and the J-class, which is an expansion chassis that has a SAS (Serial-Attached SCSI) interconnect and that you can hook up to an E-class unit. For approved Promise storage, Apple provides a collection of scripts that configure the Vtrak automatically. They include the following, along with the Web pages where you'll find them:

Metadata and Data on one E-class: http://support.apple.com/kb/HT1160

Data Only on one E-class: http://support.apple.com/kb/HT1161

Metadata and Data on an E-class and J-class (with SAS interconnect): http://support.apple.com/kb/HT1162

Data only on an E-class and J-class (with SAS interconnect): http://support.apple.com/kb/HT1163

Data only on one J-class: http://support.apple.com/kb/HT1121

The scripts provided by Apple are meant to offer a starting point. You can easily tweak the settings according to the Xsan-specifc configuration parameters and by following the instructions published at the http://support.apple.com/kb/HT1200 Web page. If you use Apple's scripts to configure Promise RAID systems, make sure that the metadata LUN has a Read Policy of ReadCache, and a write policy of WriteThru. This ensures that any pending writes to a metadata LUN get written to disk immediately. Data storage LUNs, on the other hand, should have a Read Policy of ReadAhead, and a Write Policy of WriteBack. These settings ensure data that buffering during read operations is more aggressive, and that write buffers have filled before they're written to disk.

Promise RAID hardware that has the latest firmware ships with Bonjour enabled. When you plug the device into your Ethernet network, it pulls an IP from DHCP and becomes accessible through Safari using Bonjour (from the Safari History, click the Bonjour entry under COLLECTIONS). Once you've connected, you'll be able to upload the Vtrak scripts you've downloaded from the Apple site. Click the Administrative Tools icon and select Import. Change the drop-down list for Type: to Configuration Script and then click the Browse button and choose the script you want to upload, clicking on Submit when you're ready. When the RAID system finishes formatting, you can label the LUNs (a process we'll get to later in this chapter).

Xserve RAID

To set up the Xserve RAID (a legacy device employed prior to the Apple-Promise relationship), you use the RAID Admin utility, which lets you configure Multiple LUNs or RAIDs in each RAID device. Use the program when specifying the drives to put in each array as well as RAID levels and also when configuring RAID settings and notifications.

Before you can do anything, you have to add a RAID to administer, so select Applications, click on Server, open RAID Admin, and you'll see the dialog box shown in Figure 4-7. Click the Add System button, and from the list of available Xserve RAIDS, choose the one you'd like to configure. Enter the password (the default is *public*) to view the RAID system's setting, then click Add and you should see your choice appear in the utility's RAID list.

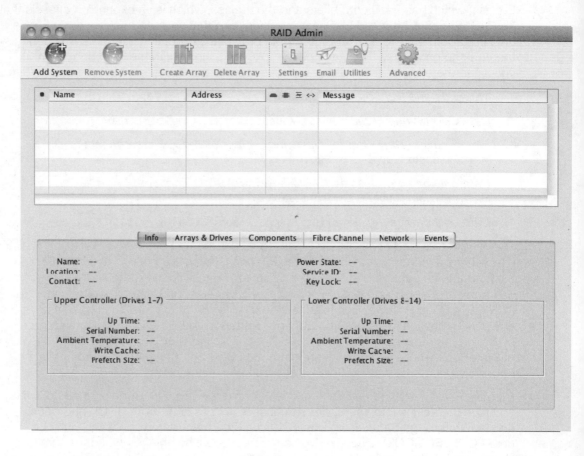

Figure 4-7. *The Raid Admin utility*

Once you've added all of the Xserve RAIDs, you'll want to make the settings of each conform to the Apple standards. To do that, click Settings in the Raid Admin utility toolbar, enter the management password for the Xserve RAID you're customizing, and then, under the System tab, make the following adjustments to the settings:

- Enter the Name for the Xserve RAID in the System Name field.

- Select a Time Synchronization Method (hopefully you'll just be able to use an NTP server), and if appropriate, enter an NTP server to use for clock synchronization.

- Use the Change button in the Passwords section to change the monitoring password, the management password, (or both) for the Xserve RAID to something other than the default settings. The monitoring password allows for access to the main window UI to view stats, configurations, and logs. The management password lets you access the advanced configuration options presented in the toolbar.

- Check the box for *Restart automatically after a power failure* to have the Xserve RAID reboot on its own after a loss of power.

Each controller on the Xserve RAID has its own network controller. By default these receive DHCP addresses. We suggest that you give each network controller a static IP address or use Static Mappings in your DHCP pool to give controllers IP addresses. If the addresses change, controllers become unavailable in RAID Admin, and you must re-add them, which generally isn't a good idea. Xserve RAIDs do support Bonjour discovery in case you forget the configured IP address. You can modify network settings from the Network Tab.

You'll find the FC settings under the Fibre Channel tab. This is where you can view the WWN, create hard loops, set speeds to static, and define the topology. Generally you can leave the default settings unless you'll be using arbitrated loops in your FC topology (see Figure 4-8). These settings will be detected automatically, for the most part, but sometimes you may need to assign them manually. For example, if you use an FC switch that doesn't detect the speed of the FC on the Xserve RAID automatically, you may need to set this value by hand.

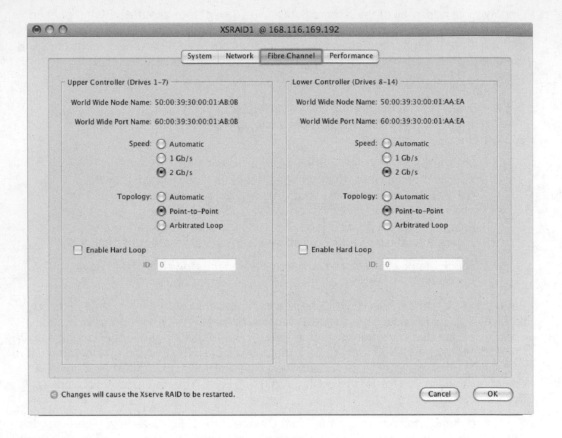

Figure 4-8. *Xserve RAID Fibre Channel Configuration*

Under the Performance tab you can customize certain features to enhance the performance of the Xserve RAID (see Figure 4-9) in an Xsan environment. You can:

- Enable Controller Write Cache (recommended for performance only if a UPS provides power protection to the unit)

- Enable Host Cache Flushing (recommended to have disabled for best performance)

- Enable or disable the drive write cache (recommended for performance only if a UPS provides power protection to the unit)

- Set read prefetch to 1, 8 or 128 stripes for each controller

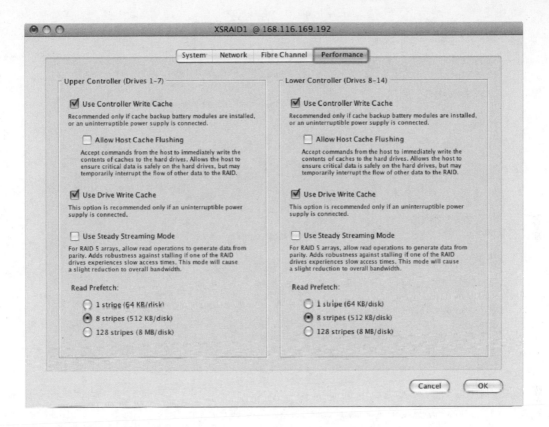

Figure 4-9. *Xserve RAID Performance Settings*

Now you'll want to set up the RAID system's LUNs. The admin utility refers to these logical portions of an Xserve RAID as *arrays*. You assign each a RAID level according to your requirements. The Xserve supports levels 0, 1, 3, 5, and 0+1. With Xsan you should use level 1 for your metadata LUN and 5 for data LUNs. In the admin utility, select the Xserve RAID on which you'll be creating a LUN and click the Create Array button in the utility's toolbar. When prompted, enter the management password for the Xserve RAID and click OK, then select the RAID level, as shown in Figure 4-10.

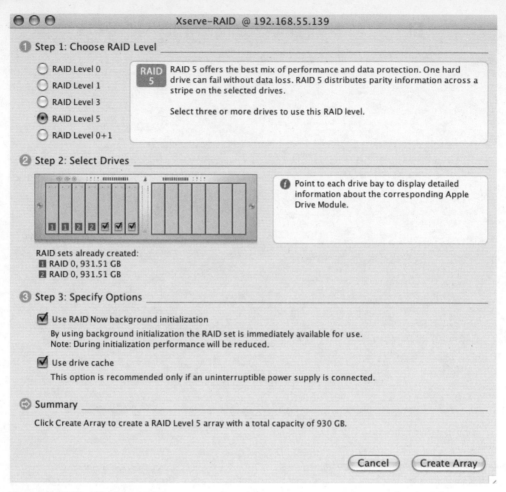

Figure 4-10. *Creating a new LUN*

Next, select the drives you want included in the LUN—simply click in the box that represents each drive in the Step 2 diagram of Figure 4-10. If you wish to begin writing data onto the Xsan during the drives' initialization period, leave the background initialization option enabled. With drives used in an Xsan environment, we prefer to leave the *Use drive cache* option enabled. Check this box and then click the Create Array button.

TIP: With most Xserve RAIDs, fully formatting the drives takes 36 to 72 hours. If you'll be working on the Xsan during its first day and a half of deployment, you might want to consider using the background initialization option. The performance of the Xsan won't be optimal during the initialization process, but that's the only issue with the feature.

Configuring Ethernet

Yes, we said it, Ethernet. But why do you need to worry about a bunch of category 5e or 6 cables if you have fiber now? Because in an Xsan environment, we use the Fibre Channel environment only for streaming actual data. We need a dedicated network for command and control. This means that most Xsan clients will have two Ethernet networks. The first is the standard corporate LAN, which allows for managing network and storage devices, directory services data, and network volumes. It also provides general IP connectivity.

The second Ethernet network is dedicated to metadata. An Xsan client uses this network to communicate with an Xsan metadata controller to request access to an existing asset or ask for access to write data. The MDC is responsible for informing the Xsan client about where data will be streamed to a drive. Whenever a SAN client wants to access a SAN resource, it must first request that resource from the SAN's active MDC. This prevents conflicts with other clients on the SAN. The metadata controller is responsible for ensuring the data integrity of the volume and the filesystem objects on it.

Because a lot of IO requests may be occurring concurrently, it's critical that the metadata network be very fast and have minimal latency. Nearly every operation performed on an Xsan requires filesystem queries, so any latency introduced between the Xsan clients and MDCs will result in perceivable performance degradation on the volume. This can become particularly problematic if you use your SAN for basic file-server storage and it contains mostly smaller files.

This means you need a good switch. Most often you'll use a managed switch with the management features disabled (especially spanning-tree PortFast). The switch and cabling should be Gigabit and there should be very little latency.

You also want very little traffic on the metadata network to help reduce collisions. This means there should be no DHCP server. Also, you shouldn't do management of SAN-connected devices using the metadata network. You need no router/default gateway, and DNS shouldn't be running. In addition, make the subnet mask as small as possible, with class C being about the largest.

The configuration on the client systems will also be stripped down. You need only an IP address and a subnet mask. List the metadata network second in the Ethernet stack with your organization's main network listed first.

Lastly, though not officially required, we recommend you always set up forward and reverse DNS specifically for the metadata network, and when possible, make that data available over it. Creating a new top-level domain, such as metadata.xsan, for this purpose is one common practice. So a primary metadata controller may have a public hostname mdc.myco.com that resolves to the corporate 10.0.2.10 IP address, and its secondary Xsan interface has an IP address of 192.168.2.10, which resolves to mdc.metadata.xsan. As an alternative, you can simply create another subdomain, such as xsan.myco.com, in your organization. In this case the metadata controller would have resolution on its secondary interface point to mdc.xsan.myco.com.

If possible, each client's secondary interface should have DNS entries configured for a DNS server local to the Xsan subnet, such as a backup metadata controller. Having DNS services configured on the metadata networks can help prevent DNS-related timeouts should the primary interface fail. These failures can be particularly detrimental on OS X metadata controllers, causing extremely laggy performance and possibly complete SAN downtime. With Xsan 2, this is less of an issue, but Xsan 1 is fairly sensitive to DNS problems.

Setting up the Xsan

When building an Xsan, the installation of the Xsan software is typically one of the last tasks. It's important to verify DNS operation, TCP/IP connectivity, and connectivity to FC LUNs, prior to configuring the software.

To verify DNS functionality, first use `changeip`, as covered in Chapter 1, to check that the forward and reverse DNS of the primary interfaces on your future metadata controllers resolve properly. Next, use `dig` to test DNS for the metadata network as well. For example, the following will look up the hostname for the IP address 192.168.210.2:

```
dig +short -x 192.168.210.2.
```

To test forward lookups, the syntax is:

```
dig +short myhost.myco.com
```

Alternatively, you can use the `host` command to perform both forward and reverse lookups. The command requires no additional flags for either type of lookup:

```
host 192.168.210.2
host myhost.myco.com
```

You'll also find other utilities that accomplish the same purpose. Windows users will be familiar with `nslookup` utility, which Apple has deprecated as of OS X 10.4. Another command, `changeip_ds` (the full command path is `/usr/libexec/changeip/changeip_ds`) can perform reverse DNS lookups, when used with the `–nameforaddress` flag. Additionally, you can simply ping the hostname, in which case the host will use internal facilities to resolve and display the appropriate address.

Once you have all of your storage, hosts, and switches in place and have cabled them and verified connectivity, you're finally ready for Xsan software installation and configuration. You'll want to start with the metadata controllers, the aforementioned traffic cops of the SAN. Make one final check to ensure that you're satisfied with the DNS naming and have a good working installation of Mac OS X on the proposed metadata controller before proceeding (we recommend redundant storage for the host OS in the form of a RAID 1 internal volume).

Installation

The first step in setting up Xsan is to install the package file that comes with the software, keeping the default settings. Next, run the update to ensure that the Xsan software and admin tools are the latest versions.

Once you've completed those steps, you'll find the Admin tool in the /Applications/Server directory (which you can remove when doing a custom installation). The bin, config, debug, examples, man, and ras folders will appear in the /Library/FileSystems/Xsan folder. The bin folder will contain the Xsan command-line binary files, which allow you to do everything you can do within Xsan Admin and more. The config folder, at first, will have only a uuid (Universally Unique Identifier) file, but will collect more once you set up the SAN.

Now you're ready to place the Xsan Admin application in your dock and open it. The first time, you'll see the SAN Setup dialog, which will show an introduction screen. Click Continue to go to the Initial SAN Setup dialog, where you can choose from two options. If this isn't the first MDC you're installing (we assume it is), select Connect to Existing SAN. Otherwise, pick Configure new SAN and click Continue.

At the next screen, name the SAN (see Figure 4-11). What you decide on can be somewhat arbitrary and isn't the same as a volume name. In this screen you can also enter the administrator's name and e-mail address. (This is purely to provide administrator contact information to Xsan users.) Click Continue.

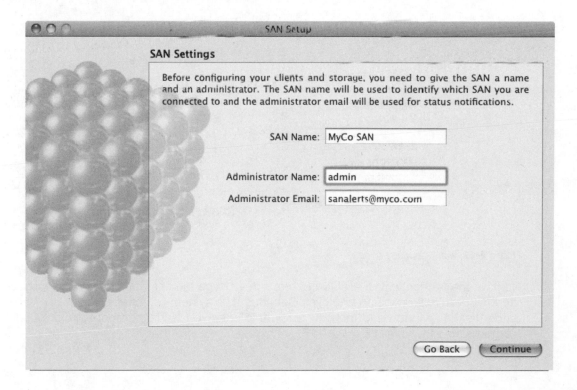

Figure 4-11. *SAN Settings*

You're now at the Add Computers screen, where you'll see a list of client systems that already have Xsan software installed (see Figure 4-12). We can easily add these later, so click the Select None button to clear all the check boxes for the computers on the subnet, unselecting them. For now, check only the box for the MDC you're currently establishing, then click Continue.

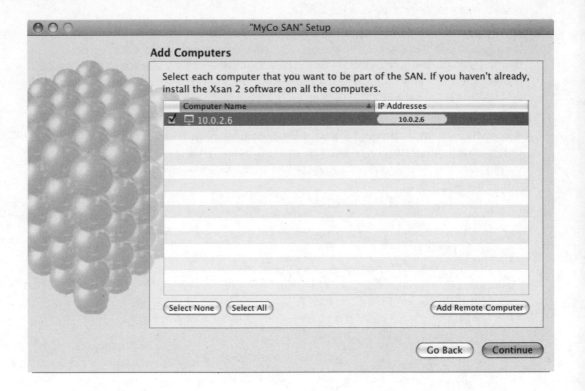

Figure 4-12. *Add Computers screen*

Next, at the Authenticate SAN Computers screen, type the username and password for the MDC you're working on and click Continue. The system will briefly present an authenticating window and then will ask you to enter your serial numbers into the Serial Numbers screen, seen in Figure 4-13.

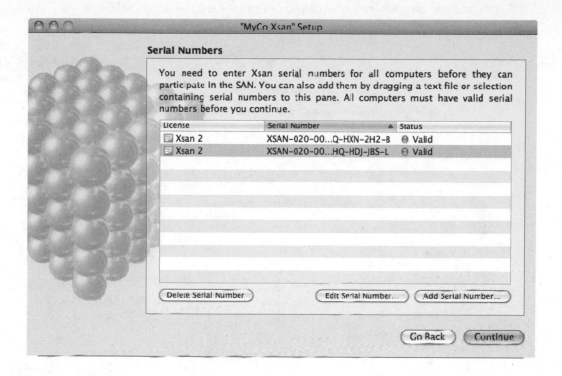

Figure 4-13. *Enter Xsan 2 Serial Numbers into a global pool*

As of Xsan 2, you no longer need to associate a serial number with a specific client. Rather, you build a pool of serial numbers which Xsan provisions to clients automatically as they join the SAN. (Each client needs a unique serial number to be able to mount the volume). When you purchase Xsan, Apple will often distribute serial numbers via e-mail. In this case, you can simply lasso them and drag them into the License area of this screen. Otherwise you can use the Add Serial Number screen to type each one in manually. In either case, Xsan 2 will then dynamically allocate licenses to clients when needed.

Hit Continue to go to the SAN metadata network screen. Per best-practice guidelines, the metadata network should be dedicated—in other words, solely for Xsan traffic with no other devices attached. To keep dropped packets and collisions to a minimum, it should have a good switch (no D-Link, LinkSys, or the like) and shouldn't be a VLAN from a bigger switch or have any managed switching services (such as link aggregation or spanning tree protocol) enabled.

Also per best practices, each client should have two connected network interfaces. One is for your standard network and must be able to provide directory services, Internet access, file server access, and so forth. The second, the metadata interface, should be dedicated to Xsan traffic and need not be routable or running any DHCP services. As a result, clients on this interface will need static IP addresses. In the SAN metadata network screen, choose the network your metadata will run on and click on the Continue button, as seen in Figure 4-14.

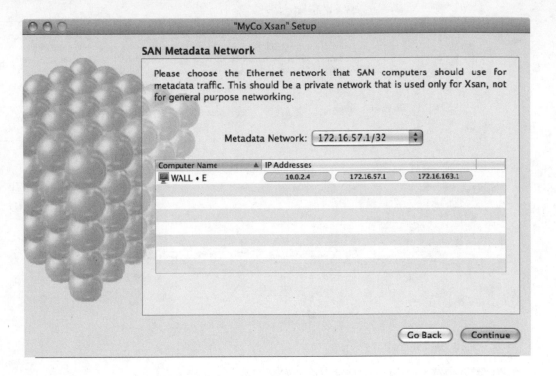

Figure 4-14. *Xsan Choose Metadata Network*

This brings you to the Summary screen. Review the settings carefully, and if they're correct, click on the Continue button. You'll then be brought to the Create Volume screen, where you can make one or more volumes. First, let's take a brief detour. For now, choose to bypass the process (we'll go through it momentarily), which will send you to the main Xsan Admin Screen. At this point, if you look in your config folder, you'll see these files in the /Library/FileSystems/Xsan/Config directory:

- Config.plist: This XML file contains licenses, the SAN name, controller settings, and the like.

- Fsnameservers: You'll find a listing of metadata controllers here.

- Notifications.plist: This file holds XML data used for e-mail notifications.

Later, as you create volumes, Xsan will add other files (each volume will have its own CFG file and an accompanying FSM (Finite State Machine) process spawned by Xsan). Now let's create a Volume.

Creating a Volume

Once you've created your SAN set up, you need to build a volume. This is the logical entity end users see, and you can configure it to mount for them automatically when they log into their Xsan clients. Once you understand the different components that make up a volume, creating one is straightforward.

To begin, open Xsan Admin and click on the Volumes section in your SAN Assets sidebar. At this point, you should have a blank listing of Volumes. In the bottom right-hand corner of the screen, click on the plus sign (+) to begin the volume-creation wizard, which will open to the SAN Setup screen, seen in Figure 4-15.

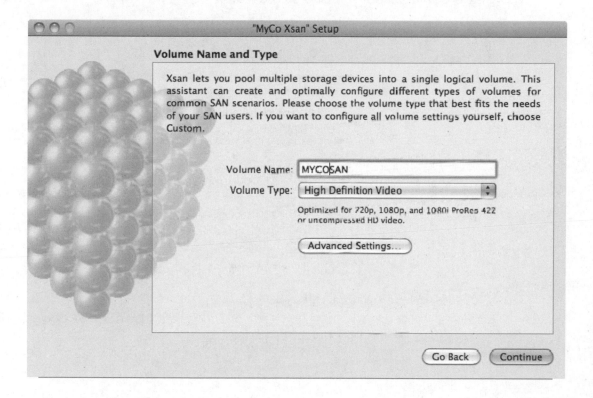

Figure 4-15. *SAN Setup screen*

In this screen, type the volume name and choose what type of data will reside on the volume. Note that you can't use spaces or special characters in the name, nor can you change it, so ensure that whatever you specify will last through the ages. Other than the name, the options you choose during volume creation will directly impact the performance of the SAN in a variety of ways. To see and adjust the settings that the wizard applied (based on your selection of data types), click on the *Advanced Settings...* button, which pops up the window shown in Figure 4-16.

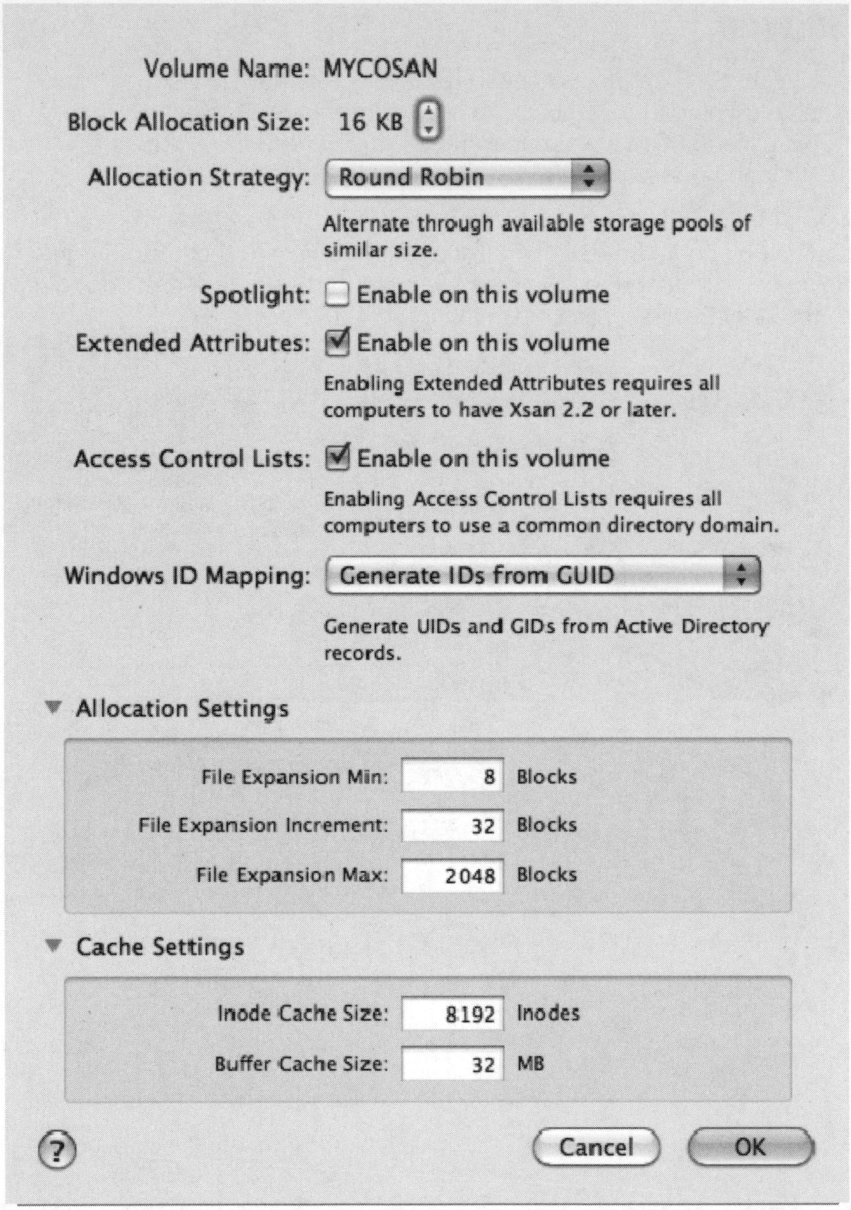

Volume Name: MYCOSAN

Block Allocation Size: 16 KB ⬍

Allocation Strategy: Round Robin ⬍

Alternate through available storage pools of
similar size.

Spotlight: ☐ Enable on this volume

Extended Attributes: ☑ Enable on this volume

Enabling Extended Attributes requires all
computers to have Xsan 2.2 or later.

Access Control Lists: ☑ Enable on this volume

Enabling Access Control Lists requires all
computers to use a common directory domain.

Windows ID Mapping: Generate IDs from GUID ⬍

Generate UIDs and GIDs from Active Directory
records.

▼ Allocation Settings

File Expansion Min:	8	Blocks
File Expansion Increment:	32	Blocks
File Expansion Max:	2048	Blocks

▼ Cache Settings

Inode Cache Size:	8192	Inodes
Buffer Cache Size:	32	MB

(?)   (Cancel)   (OK)

Figure 4-16. *Advanced SAN settings*

The most import setting here is the block allocation size. Xsan uses the storage-pool stripe
breadth and volume block-allocation size to decide how to write data to a volume. Writes
typically impact performance more than reads, so it's important to match these in a
manner that makes sense given the type of data the SAN will be storing. As of the time of
this writing, Apple hasn't released a tuning guide for Xsan 2.x, but you can find the one for

Xsan 1.*x* at http://images.apple.com/my/server/docs/20050901_Xsan_Tuning_Guide.pdf. Per the *Apple Xsan Deployment and Tuning Guide*:

> *In general, smaller file system block sizes are best in cases where there are many small, random reads and writes, as when a volume is used for home directories or general file sharing. In cases such as these, the default 4KB block size is best. If, however, the workflow supported by the volume consists mostly of sequential reads or writes, as is the case for audio or video streaming or capture, you can get better performance with a larger block size. Try a 64KB block size in such cases.*

There are other options for this portion of the volume setup. Here is a bit of information about them:

- *Allocation Strategy:* This determines how data is written to the *affinity tags* (a collection of storage pools—we'll cover them shortly). Round robin is the default strategy and the recommended one in most cases. It works by simply iterating through storage pools during writes. For instance, when writing file1, round robin will go to storage pool1; when writing file2, it will go to storage pool2. If you want to ensure that your data gets evenly distributed across pools, you can use another approach: balance allocation. This configuration uses the pool that has the most available capacity. Fill allocation, on the other hand, loads storage pools to capacity in sequence; it won't use storagepool2 until storagepool1 runs out of room. The two options, though, can degrade performance, as it's possible for a single LUN to bear a higher percentage of the load over time.

- *Spotlight:* This option lets you enable and disable the OS X system search tool (Spotlight) for volumes. Given that it doesn't currently work effectively in Xsan 2.x, you should disable it.

- *Access Control Lists:* You can enable and disable ACLs on the volume using this setting, but typically you should leave it enabled, as ACLs provide for extensible permissions management.

- *Windows ID Mapping:* If Windows machines will participate in the SAN, leave this option at its default—enabled.

Allocation Settings: Always check with a technical project manager before customizing any of the following three settings in this section of the dialog box.

- *File Expansion Min:* This value determines the minimum number of blocks written to a SAN file for the first expansion request. Increasing it speeds up writes for large files; decreasing it speeds them up for a large number of smaller files.

- *File Expansion Increment:* To change the number of blocks used for each expansion request after the first, adjust this number.

- *File Expansion Max:* The maximum number of blocks used for the file. Can help to reduce fragmentation on your volume.

Cache Settings: Always check with a technical project manager before customizing the two settings (listed below) in this section of the dialog box.

- *iNode Cache Size:* In Unix, data structures called iNodes hold information about files. A file—which always has an iNode—is uniquely identified by the file system it's on and its iNode number on that system. To track the data that resides on it, Xsan (which is just a file system)— uses iNodes. This setting specifies that maximum number of these data structures that a metadata controller can cache on a volume.

- *Buffer Cache Size:* Altering the size of the buffer cache changes the amount of memory the metadata controller can use for storing a volume's metadata. The cache is useful when you have a system with high latency—buffers act to mitigate latency issues.

When you've finished with the advanced settings, click OK to return to the listing of volumes. At this point, if the software detects any unlabeled LUNs, it will give you the option to label them—unless a LUN has a unique identifier, you can't integrate it into an Xsan volume. We recommend using a labeling practice that indicates the specific shelf the LUN is in as well as its controller. For example, *PROM_03J_C1* would specify the Promise Jclass expansion unit and controller affinity 1. Having good labels helps to easily identify storage in the event that troubleshooting is needed.

Once you click Continue, the wizard will take you to the Configure Volume Affinities pane, where you can start setting up affinity tags (the collection of storage pools mentioned earlier). The tags, which allow Xsan to share bandwidth, are best used to group storage pools that have similar characteristics. For instance, you might want to create a tag called *Video* that contains LUNs optimized for sustained high throughput. Alternatively, you might have a *Files* tag containing LUNs tuned for efficiently handling random I/O rather than for delivering raw sustained throughput. (If they'll receive heavy use, it's often better to keep items like these in separate volumes).

When building an affinity tag, it's important that the LUNs which it contains are of similar capacity—as mentioned earlier, the storage pool will reduce the capacity of all its LUNs to that of the smallest. With Xsan 2, building tags is complicated a bit, as the GUI does configuration by Affinity Tags rather than storage pools. When adding LUNs to a tag, Xsan 2 automatically groups LUNs into storage pools. It determines the composition of the pools based on the usage pattern you defined when creating the volume. If you chose any of the media usage types, then an affinity tag will contain storage pools consisting of four LUNs each. If you selected the File Server option, pools will consist of two LUNs.

As such, when building an Xsan primarily for video, the best approach is to add LUNs in numbers divisible by four. To see why, suppose you add nine LUNs to an affinity tag. The system will create three storage pools, two composed of four LUNs. But the third, with just a single LUN, will have performance drastically inferior to that of the other two. As a result, you'll have intermittent bandwidth problems on your SAN. If you can't add LUNs in groups of four, at least try to avoid adding an odd number to a storage pool. If you think you'll be creating an unbalanced setup, please consult a technical project manager first.

Once configured, you can view the volume's composition by consulting the XML file located at `/Library/FileSystems/Xsan/config/`*VolumeName*`-auxdata.plist` (replacing *VolumeName,* of course, with the volume's actual name). The Xsan Admin software uses this file during volume expansion. Specifically the software employs the values specified at StoragePoolIdealLUNCount and StoragePoolStripeBreadth, which it applies to any newly added pools.

The metadata affinity tag is a special beast and has a unique makeup. Optimally, the tag will sit on its own RAID controller to prevent congestion that could negatively affect performance across the entire volume.

The affinity tag options are:

- *Any data:* Selecting this lets the Affinity Tag house metadata or user data.

- *Journaling and metadata only:* This limits tags exclusively to use for the information that tracks where the pieces of the user data reside on the SAN and to use for metadata.

- *User data only:* Choose this, and writing data to the volume will be the only use allowed for the tag.

- *Only data with affinity:* This forces data written to the affinity tag to a specified folder.

- *Stripe Breadth:* Use this option to set the size of each data stripe (in blocks) written to one LUN in a storage pool before moving on to the next.

Setting the proper stripe breadth requires a bit of consideration, and is dependent upon the volume's make-up. Specifically, we need to know the volume's storage-pool block-allocation size, which we defined earlier.

This setting is applied specifically to the storage pools that make up the affinity tag. Its purpose is to properly tune the transfer sizes to best coincide with I/O characteristics of the host OS. OS X transfers data in 1MB chunks, referred to as the transfer size. Apple explains that the goal is to configure the stripe breadth such that each transaction with a storage pool is equal to your transfer size.

Thus, in a the default Xsan, the block size of 16KB uses a 4-LUN storage pool. To ensure a 1MB stripe across all 4 LUNs, Apple recommends a 16-block breadth (consisting of 16KB) to each LUN. For example, if you increase the block size to 64 KB (say, to suit data streaming), set the stripe breadth to 4 blocks, so that each LUN again receives a 256KB write. If you choose the File-Server purpose when creating your Xsan volume, the standard storage pool size is 2 LUNs; as such, you'd use a default setting of 32 blocks.

Apple's Xsan 2 Admin guide recommends using the formula:

`stripe breadth = (transfer size / number of LUNs) / block allocation size`
where stripe breadth is expressed in blocks, and transfer size and block-allocation size in bytes. But this formula differs from our recommendations (and the recommendations Apple provides in its Xsan 1.4 tuning guide). In our findings, the best approach is to configure transfer settings such that the OS X transfer size directly correlates to each transaction with a LUN (rather than a storage pool).

Given that, we suggest setting this value so that the stripe breadth itself is equal to 1MB (rather than the aggregate across all LUNs). So in our previous example, where the File System block size is 16KB, we'd use a stripe breadth of 64 blocks, resulting in a 1MB transfer to each LUN before moving on to the next. In this case, we don't really care how many LUNs are in a storage pool. From Apple's *Xsan Deployment and Tuning Guide*:

> *The Mac OS X (or Mac OS X Server) operating system, which handles file data transfers for Xsan, performs 1 megabyte (MB) data transfers. As a result, Xsan gets maximum efficiency from the operating system when it transfers blocks of data that are a multiple of 1 MB.*
>
> *At the other end of the transfer, the LUN also works well when it receives 1 MB of data at a time. So, when data is written to a storage pool, you get the best performance if 1 MB of data is written to each LUN in the storage pool The amount of data Xsan writes to a LUN is determined by the product of two values you specify when you set up a volume:*

- The volume's block allocation size (in kilobytes)
- The stripe breadth of the storage pools that make up the volume (in number of allocation blocks)

transfer size = block size x stripe breadth

It's worth noting that fundamentally, not much changed between Xsan1 and Xsan2. Certainly, Apple made great improvements to its GUI admin tools, but the underlying functionality of LUNs, storage pools, and data allocation did not drastically change. As such, we feel that many of the tuning principals prescribed by Apple for Xsan 1.4 still fundamentally apply to Xsan 2.

The Apple tuning guide says little about metadata stripe breadths. The default breadth on a metadata storage pool is 256 blocks. But according to Quantum, this is too high. The company recommends a 16- or 64-block stripe breadth for metadata storage pools. Therefore, if you have a relatively small volume with a small number of files, consider using 16. If you have a larger environment with big files, think about trying 64, rather than the default of 16.

The calculation to make the stripe breadth times the storage pool equal 1MB is more important for your data storage pool than for your metadata pool. As with many things Xsan, you'll get the biggest bang for your buck from tuning stripe breadths and block sizes to match the environment is where you will get the biggest bang for your buck. This is just a starting place, though. You should plan on tearing down and rebuilding your volume a few times to maximize speed (after all, doing so usually takes less than five minutes.

After setting up volume affinities, you can configure your volume's metadata controllers. The wizard will show you each system that's set as a metadata controller. Generally two such controllers should suffice for any given volume or set of volumes. Once configured, metadata controllers run an instance of the FSM process. You can track performance, in terms of memory and processing required, as you do with any other service using tools such as Activity Monitor or the Unix top command.

To start setting up the metadata controllers, when you're done with the Configure Volume Affinities pane, click on Continue. In the Volume Failover Priority pane that appears, you can customize the priority assigned to a controller. Simply drag items higher or lower in the list to raise or lower priority. The top item, which has the highest priority, should always be the default MDC. Also, more than three MDCs can cause unneeded latency on the volume, so feel free to deactivate any that aren't needed.

When you click Continue, you'll now see your new Volume, as illustrated in Figure 4-17 be seen below). The Affinity Tags and the percentage of each that is consumed with data will also appear along with the capacity of each (in the Size column), the available disk space (under the Available column) and the active MDC (in the Hosted By column). You can also see the structure of the volume in terms of affinity tags and LUNs.

Figure 4-17. *Xsan Volume overview*

Click on the volume name and then the gear, as shown in Figure 4-18. Here, you'll see a number of available options.

Figure 4-18. *Volume options*

Use the Edit Notification Settings to configure Xsan to send SAN administrators e-mail updates (we recommend triggering alerts when the volume reaches 75 percent of capacity). Use Edit Failover Priority to add or remove MDCs or just change their priority. Use the Force Failover to test failover between MDCs and use Start and Stop to Start and Stop the volume.

When you created the volume, Xsan automatically started and mounted it on the metadata controller. You've now completed the volume set up and can move on to adding computers that can see the volume.

Adding a Computer

Now that you've created your volume, it's time to add clients that can access it. This is one place where Xsan 2 is very different from Xsan 1.*x*. To add a computer that has access to your volume, click on Computers in your SAN Assets list and then on the plus (+) sign in the lower right-hand corner of the screen.

This invokes a list of computers that have the Xsan software installed and have been discovered via Bonjour (as seen previously in Figure 4-12). You can add clients running version 1.4.2 or 2.*x* to your SAN. You can also add clients using 10.5.0 through 10.5.2, but you'll receive an amber warning indicator for system with software that preceded 10.5.3.

If the client you're trying to add doesn't appear in the list, you can click on the Remote Computer button and enter the machine's DNS name or IP address. If the DNS name won't resolve, you'll receive an error saying that the information is invalid.

If you use the Select All button on this screen to select all the clients, when you click on Continue and enter the proper authentication credentials, you'll be able to enter a user name and password for all clients at once or each individually.

Authenticate into all of your clients and click on Continue. You've now added them all and can click on the Mount icon to mount the volume for each (if it hasn't mounted already). If you've been following along with this walk-through then you now have an Xsan with a mounted volume and clients.

> **NOTE:** In order to add a new controller, promote an existing client to a controller, or demote a controller to a client, all clients on the SAN must be online and reachable via the Xsan Admin Application.

Resharing the Volume

To view the shared folders on a system, open Server Admin and click on the name of the system you want in the Servers list. Now click the File Sharing button in the Server Admin toolbar and you'll get a list of the logical volumes that your server can see along with a handy disk space image that shows how full the various volumes are. At this point, you can select Share Points to see which folders are currently being shared over SMB, AFP, NFS or FTP. If you click on Volumes and then the Browse button, you'll be able to configure new folders that you want others to access as share points. Browse to the folder you want shared, then click on the Share button in the upper right-hand corner below the tool bar.

With the Xsan volume selected, three tabs appear along the bottom of the screen: Share Point, Permissions, and Quotas. Click on Share Point to review and modify these settings:

- *Enable AutoMount:* This gives you choices for setting up an Open Directory automount for the share.

- *Enable Spotlight Searching:* Selecting this allows the volume to be searchable using the OS X system search tool.

- *Enable as Time Machine Backup Destination:* Turn on this setting if you want to let client computers use the OS X utility for safely storing copies of their data.

- *Protocol Options:* This brings up the screen that allows you to configure SMB, AFP, NFS, and FTP settings (looks very much like the old screen in Workgroup Manager)

Once you've set the options for your share point, click over to the Permissions tab, where you can determine who has access to shared data. From this point, access to share points is controlled by file system permissions. You'll see ACLs listed above POSIX permissions, and when you drag a user or group into the window, a blue line will appear, indicating that the object will stay if you drop it on the window.

Finally, if you click on the Quotas tab and enable quotas, you'll find that you can't drag users and groups into the window. Using Server Admin, you can't configure users that don't have a home folder on the volume. You can, however, configure quotas at the command line.

Xsan Block Sizes

Xsan can act as the back-end storage to provide front-end network file-sharing services for a Mac OS X environment. This isn't to say that it'll work like a charm without some fine-tuning, though. In tuning any Xsan volume, one of your most important tools is the block size. As mentioned previously, the stripe breadth multiplied by the block size should come to about 1MB. You'll have to customize the stripe breadth on the storage pools whenever you change the block sizes for the volume.

If you're using Xsan as a repository for data to be shared over clustered file storage, then it's important to maintain a small block size. How small? That depends on your data. If it's in large files, you may be able to stick with the default settings for clustered file storage in the volume setup wizard. If it's in small files, though, consider going even lower.

AFP Tuning

When an AFP client gets disconnected from a share point, it attempts to look for a token in order to reconnect automatically. If the server doesn't have the token, the client can't reconnect because it's comparing the presented token with its own cache (stored, by default, in /etc/AFP.conf). However, if you're using an Xsan, you'll want your servers to share a token location.

The token store is the reconnectKeyLocation key in the /Library/Preferences/ com.apple.AppleFileServer.plist property list. You can use the defaults command to move the tokens to an Xsan volume. Follow the command with the appropriate option switch (in this case, *write* to put data into the property list), followed by the name of the property list and then the key that we'll be writing into. We want to write text into the key, with the text string being a path. If the volume name is bighonkinvolume, the command will be:

```
defaults write com.apple.AppleFileServer reconnectKeyLocation ↵
/Volumes/bighonkinvolume/AFP.conf
```

Additionally, you'll want to customize file-locking mechanisms in some cases. AFP locks files at the application layer by default. With Xsan, where multiple file-server heads are involved, it's best to use locks at the file-system level. Therefore, you can use the AFP settings for the daemon to prevent AFP from locking files itself. The command is:

```
serveradmin settings afp:lock_manager = no
```

Tickle Times

In Windows, when you've connected to a share using, say, a mapped drive letter, that share shows as active. At some point, if the client can't communicate to an SMB/CIFS server with the open session, the drive will appear offline to the Windows client. AFP does something similar, but the result is what, as perceived from the Finder, appears to be constant communication with the AFP server. Actually, it's verified by the server every 30 seconds. With the AFP client, if no poll is sent from the server, the client will also attempt to reach out to the server to verify that the connection is available. This process is known as *tickling*.

AFP uses the tickle to verify that clients are still connected to a server. This communication causes a small amount of network congestion, but in some environments you want to keep even that to a minimum. This is similar to the concept of disabling protocols in a network stack that aren't being used. Such protocols aren't likely to cause issues on one machine, but when employed by thousands of hosts, they can effectively cause a denial of service on the server.

Provided that you use AFP, you're just not going to want to disable the tickle. By default, it happens every 30 seconds with no user intervention (other than connecting to a share point and having a session greater than 30 seconds). But while you might not want to disable it, you can reduce traffic by increasing the number of seconds between updates. For example, the following command will up the time between tickles to 60 seconds:

```
serveradmin settings afp:tickleTime = 60
```

In order to set the tickleTime value back to 30 seconds, you would simply issue the following command:

```
serveradmin settings afp:tickleTime = 30
```

Setting a tickle time isn't for everyone. In fact, you'll rarely need to take this kind of step. But if your Mac servers are causing a lot of collisions on the network, and using packet analysis you determine the traffic comes from DSI/AFP (Data Service Information/AFP) packets, that's a fine time to test out tickleTime as a solution. If it doesn't resolve your issue, you can always move it back to 30 seconds. While increasing the tickleTime variable can cause beach balls to spin for a fair amount of time when you lose a server connection, doing so can also reduce the amount of traffic slightly, which scales into larger environments.

Even to a seasoned Windows admin, the concept of a constant communication channel for file services may be foreign, it's just a reality of playing in the Apple sandbox.

Using Third-Party Clients

With the Quantum StorNext client, you can connect systems running other OSes to Xsan. StorNext also provides controllers that Mac Xsan clients can connect to. Not all versions of Xsan are compatible with all versions of StorNext. Apple provides a compatibility page at http://support.apple.com/kb/HT1517. When adding third-party clients to an Xsan, you should still follow the usual best practices for infrastructure, such as using a dedicated metadata connection with a static IP assignment and, ideally, DNS forward and resolution.

Installing Linux Clients

Linux running Helios can make for a good alternative to running AFP or SMB shares off of an Xsan using Mac OS X Server. A Linux system can run Quantum StorNext software and mount a Mac OS X-based Xsan, then share data out. Currently only RedHat Enterprise Linux (versions 4 and 5) and SUSE Linux Enterprise Server (version 10) support the product.

Once you've bought and registered Quantum's software, make sure your StorNext client can ping the metadata controller over the metadata network by whatever IP address is used for metadata. With that done, you can get underway.

For starters, go to your metadata controller and backup metadata controller, run the cvfsid command, copy the text string it produces, go to http://Prodreg.quantum.treehousei.com/login.aspx, and complete the form there using the string. Once you get the necessary information back from Quantum, add it to the /Library/FileSystems/Xsan/config/license.dat file on each metadata controller and reboot them. Now you're ready to set up your clients.

To do so you'll need the auth_secret and fsnameservers files from one of the metadata controllers (an Xsan's metadata controllers will have identical auth_secret files) and the StorNext rpm client installer.

From each client, first verify that you can ping the metadata controllers. Then, extract the rpm with the command:

```
tar xf sn_dsm_linuxRedHat40AS_x86_64_client.tar.gz
```
or use gunzip to extract it. Next, install the rpm by issuing the command:

```
rpm -ivh sn_dsm_linuxRedHat40AS_x86_64_client.tar
```

Now copy the auth_secret and fsnameservers files to the /usr/cvfs/config directory created by the installer, then use the cvlabel -l command to verify that you can see all of the LUNs that make up the volume. And for good measure, make sure you can ping each of the metadata controllers by IP address one more time. Finally, add cvfs to the list of file systems in the PRUNEFS field of the /etc/updatedb.conf file.

With those tasks finished, you're ready to mount the volume. In the /mnt directory, create a folder with the same as your volume (for this example we'll use myXsan). Next, open /etc/fstab and add this line:

```
Xsan          /mnt/myXsan         cvfs      verbose=yes 0 0
```

Now try to mount the volume using the command:

```
mount -t cvfs Xsan /mnt/myXsan
```

Provided it works, you can reboot and proceed with setting up Helios.

> **NOTE:** All metadata controllers need to have that license DAT file. If they don't, your clients won't fail over properly. When you're finished with the integration, we recommend backing up the entire /Library/FileSystems/Xsan/config directory and running a cvgather to make a tar file of your Xsan configuration.

Windows Clients

As with Linux, Windows can access Xsan via StorNext. This allows you to install and configure Microsoft UAM-based volumes, standard SMB/CIFS, shares and even ExtremeZ-IP using an Xsan volume—the same back-end storage can serve a number of different platforms. To install Xsan on a Windows client you'll actually be installing StorNext and you'll need a version of appropriate for your version of Windows.

The first step in setting up StorNext is to register the software with Quantum. To do so, go to http://prodreg.quantum.treehousei.com/Login.aspx. Now wait to get the registration information back in an e-mail, which usually takes about an hour but can take up to 24. While waiting, you need to get some other information before you can get your actual license: unique identifiers for each Xsan metadata controller. To get them, you must run cvfsid on each of the metadata controllers (but not on any other systems). Go to the primary MDC, cd into the /Library/FileSystems/Xsan/bin directory and then run the ./cvfsid command. The output you get will look something like:

```
C1A1B97A11 MAC 0 mdc.domain.com
```

Copy the text string, and repeat the process on your backup MDC for volumes accessible by StorNext clients, then go to www.quantum.com/swlicense. In the form you see, enter both the serial number for each host that will run StorNext as well as the output of the cvfsid commands from earlier.

Quantum usually responds to these requests in about the same time frame as with the initial request. Once you receive the e-mail response, open the license.dat file from /Library/FileSystems/Xsan/config and paste the message content that is indicated as being required into the file using pico or vi. After the files are updated, reboot the metadata controllers. Each will then create a file called .auth_secret in its

/Library/FileSystems/Xsan/config directory. This file is hidden, so to access it through finder, you need to cp it to removable storage or copy it to another location that's not hidden.

Now you can install your Fiber Channel card into your Windows system. If you've patched the StorNext client into your network environment, you'll see a prompt to install the Promise drivers. If you're installing a Vtrak from Apple on Microsoft Windows, you can download the Promise drivers from http://www.promise.com/support/download/download_eng.asp.

You can also use the drivers (or generic ones) if the Promise is serving as a target and connecting to those LUNs (managed by Xsan) via StorNext. But although you can use generic drivers because StorNext is managing the LUNs, most Windows administrators won't want to (nor should they). To see the LUNs, check Windows Device Manager.

Now install the StorNext software on the client, following the defaults and rebooting when the installation completes. Then copy the .auth_secret file to the c:\Program Files\Stornext\config folder and reboot the StorNext computer. When you log back in, go to Start ➤ All Programs ➤File System Services, a new entry added by the base StorNext installation.

The main application you'll use here is Client Configuration, which allows you to interact with an Xsan as a client. In many cases we'll remove most of the other applications from the Start menu so that users don't accidentally do more to the SAN than we'd like, which, regrettably, is an option otherwise.

From the Client Configuration application, click on the *fsnameservers* tab, and type the IP address of each metadata controller. The hostname in .auth_secret tells the StorNext client which MDC it can talk to and which hosts can communicate with it, based on a pre-shared shared key. Now click on the *Drive Mapping* tab. This is where you set the way in which Microsoft Windows interprets the Volume seen by StorNext. Doing so allows the Windows client software to be aware of which volumes reside on the server and can mount them as needed. The Drive Map option simply allows you to specify which Windows drive letter will be mapped to each volume. When you've finished the mapping, you should be able to browse as needed.

If you create a folder called debug in c:\Program Files\StorNext, after you restart, the StorNext FSS (File System Service) will create a file called c:\Program Files\StorNext\debug\nssdebug.out, which contains very verbose logs from the perspective of the StorNext system. These can be useful, for example, in debugging connectivity issues with other StorNext systems, Xsan, or both.

StorNext for Windows includes many of the commands available with Xsan on Mac OS X. The default location for the commands is c:\Program Files\StorNext\bin. You can use the cv-based commands (explained further later in this chapter) in much the same way as on a Mac, which can help with troubleshooting.

For example, if you're having problems getting a volume to mount even though it shows up when you go to map the drive in Client Configuration, you can use cvlabel -l (assuming your working directory is the StorNext bin directory) to see the LUNs you host can access. If you can't see the LUNs, you also can't map a drive to them (you can in the Client Configuration utility, but you won't be able to see the volumes in Windows Explorer or from a command prompt). Once you confirm that you can see Xsan LUNs from StorNext and that you can communicate with the metadata controller, stop and start the FSS to see if the volume then appears in Windows Explorer.

If you're using StorNext systems as actual metadata controllers, you'll find a number of other commands you can leverage; again, in much the way you would with Xsan. For example, to start a volume, you can use the `cvadmin` command followed by `start` and then the name of the volume. For example, if your volume is *bighonkinvolume* you'd use:

```
cvadmin start bighonkinvolume
```

Xsan Management

If set up properly, Xsan is typically very stable and healthy when first installed. As with any system, though, over time various maintenance and troubleshooting tasks will need attending to. Volumes fill, frames start dropping, response times slow, files corrupt, and many more problems occur with increasing frequency. The purpose of this section is to help you figure out what's going on and how you can nurse your Xsan back to health.

Reinstalling the Software

A number of client-configuration issues seem to call for uninstalling and reinstalling the Xsan software. But do you actually have to uninstall the software, reinstall it, run Software Update, reboot, re-add the client to Xsan Admin on the MDC, and then attempt to mount when, for example, a single client isn't mounting a volume? No. That's a lot of crap when one step will reset a client back to the way it was before it ever joined its first Xsan. Just delete the contents of the `/Library/Filesystems/Xsan/config` folder (but not the folder itself) and then reboot.

On reboot, the Xsan process is waiting to be controlled by a metadata controller, so use Xsan Admin to add the client—it should receive the same serial number it had before and mount the SAN volumes automatically. This will fix a few different client-specific issues. Don't, however, try this with a metadata controller unless you know what you're doing!

Upgrades to your Xsan

Once your Xsan is installed and working perfectly, chances are you won't want to do anything to it. But eventually you'll have to perform software updates, volume expansion, the occasional (and regrettable) changing of IP addresses, and other maintenance. Also, make sure the Metadata Controllers are running the most recent version of the operating system in use in your environment.

Operating System Upgrades

All MDCs should run the same version of Mac OS X. When upgrading one to a new version, you should upgrade all the others to the same version. During upgrades, do not make any modifications to the Xsan using Xsan Admin or the command-line utilities. Upgrade all MDCs before you make any configuration changes. When performing a clean installation of Mac OS X, all of the Volume configuration data and SAN contents could be lost.

If you can take Xsan volumes down during the upgrades, you should—you'll greatly reduce the possibility of problems. But if the volumes must be up, is possible to upgrade while they're accessible to client systems. When doing this, run the upgrades on the metadata controller and restart, then run the upgrades on the backup metadata controller and restart. If you have no backup metadata controller, promote a client system to become a backup metadata controller, fail the volume over to it and then upgrade the metadata controller. By following this procedure, you prevent data loss due to a single point of failure during an upgrade.

If you choose to upgrade the Xsan without interrupting the availability of the Volumes and you have 2 Metadata Controllers then it is also a good idea to temporarily upgrade a client system into the role of a Backup Metadata Controller to mitigate the risk of having a single point of failure during the upgrade of each metadata Controller.

Upgrading the Volume

The process of adding storage to an Xsan volume, *volume expansion,* not only provides the benefit of increased capacity, it also can increase bandwidth. On an Xsan 2.0 volume you can perform two types of volume expansion: Storage Expansion and Bandwidth Expansion.

With the latter, you add LUNs to an existing storage pool. This is relatively intrusive, though, and you can only do it on volumes built with the Custom data type. You may have to do this when a storage pool isn't configured in a manner consistent with others on the volume, and performance is paramount.

This type of expansion will result in a misbalance of information across the storage pool's LUNS, and you'll have to defragment to avoid severe performance degradation. As such, you should always defrag shortly after performing the expansion. Remember, though, because you're modifying existing datastores that the volume uses, bandwidth expansion is inherently risky, and you should avoid it if possible.

With storage expansion, you add new LUNs to a an existing affinity tag, which in turn creates a new storage-pool member. Because you're simply introducing elements, this type of expansion isn't as intrusive as a bandwidth expansion, and is less prone to problems.

When performing volume expansion, generally you want to add storage in increments equivalent to existing storage pools (typically four LUNs per pool). Xsan 2 will do its best to determine existing pool utilization based on values set in the volume's auxdata.plist file, and you can carry out more granular edits of these as needed.

Prior to running the expansion, we recommend you follow a few procedures. First, ensure that all new LUNs consist of RAID sets that are consistent with the designated affinity tag's current LUNs.

> **TIP:** You can determine your volume's ideal LUN count by consulting its respective auxdata.plist file, found at /Library/Filesystems.

Next, verify recent backups of the volume by performing a test restore. Now stop the volume, and perform a repair on it using the command:

```
cvfsck -wv VolumeName
```

When that completes, back up the metadata by issuing the command:

```
snmetadump -d VolumeName
```

Also, perform a cvgather on the volume (which, among other procedures, backs up the volume's configuration files) by entering this at the command line:

```
cvgather -f volumeName
```

After these steps, you're ready to perform the expansion, which you can do using Xsan Admin by dragging your new, labeled LUN into the desired affinity tag. As mentioned, it's best to add LUNs in numbers compatible with existing settings. So if the volume uses 4 LUN storage pools, the number of LUNs you add during expansion should be divisible by 4. If you have a custom volume, you'll need to manually create the storage pools and assign 4 LUNs to each. After dragging all desired LUNs into the proper affinity tag or storage pools, click Save. The expansion will proceed, generally taking 20 to 30 minutes.

Following the actual expansion, it's a good idea to carry out additional maintenance on the volume to ensure proper health. In particular, to ensure that data is properly re-striped across the pool, an snfsdefrag is an absolute requirement. Running the command

```
snfsdefrag -dr /Volumes/VolumeName
```
will rebalance the data.

Even after performing a volume expansion, it may be desirable to rebalance the data onto the newly added storage. By spreading it across the storage more evenly, you not only help prevent slowdowns, you actually get a net gain in speed. That might not be the case if you don't rebalance. In Xsan 1.4, this was usually a straightforward task, because each storage pool had a different affinity name, so you could balance data using, for example:

```
snfsdefrag -r -k newstoragepoolaffinitykey -m 1 /Volumes/VolumeName
```

This command would relocate any files with more than one extent to the new pool's affinity key. Unfortunately, this technique gives you no clean way to completely balance out data, because it relocates all fragmented data, a process that could easily exceed the capacity of the pool. So when using this method, it's important to monitor the process and ensure that pools don't over-balance, so to speak.

There's a better alternative: Change the volume's allocation strategy to Balance and then defragment the volume (the options are Fill, Balance, and Round). This relocated fragmented files to the lowest-capacity pool, an extremely effective method for balancing data. In Xsan 2.*x*, you can change a volume's allocation strategy at the GUI level, which results in a quick restart of the volume.

In our experience, the quick restart does *not* result in Xsan client service interruption to the volume, and active transfers proceed with no disruption. Even so, it's best to perform the switch at a time when there's minimal activity (preferably none) on the volume and no active transfers in progress.

Xsan 1.4 doesn't officially support changing allocation strategies on a volume. To do so, you must completely stop the volume, then change its strategy to Balance in its configuration file before restarting. Once you've converted the volume to the new strategy, you can proceed with the optimization, which is a fairly straightforward defrag performed with the command

```
snfsdefrag -r /Volumes/VolumeName
```

This will defragment any files with more than one extent, re-provisioning the optimized files to the next LUN in the allocation strategy. And because we're now using the Balance strategy, the next LUN will always be the one with the lowest capacity—our new LUNs, in this case. If, however, you had a healthy Xsan volume, this command may not properly balance data, because fragmented files will be rare. In such an event, run the command

```
snfsdefrag -r -m 0 /Volumes/VolumeName
```

This will defragment files with more than 0 extents, which is every file on the system, letting you rest assured that the volume will be nicely balanced at the end of the operation. Given that using the -m 0 flag with snfsdefrag can avert improper balancing, you may want to use it from the get-to, rather than excluding it.

The main trade off here is that doing so reprovisions all files on the volume, which can be a very time consuming task. If the volume has standard levels of fragmentation, running the command without the flag should do a decent job of balancing without having to operate against non-fragmented files as well. The second problem caused by using the -m 0 switch is that the operation will flag files it affects for backup. Thus any following incremental backups will essentially be a full backups. Save yourself the trouble and set your backup system to perform a new full backup after the migration.

Changing IP Addresses

Because Xsan retrieves the locations of files and the status of information on the SAN using the metadata network, it's important to keep this network as free from interference as possible. File-sharing, backup operations, and other bandwidth-intensive tasks should occur on your organization's standard network.

Using DHCP servers on an Xsan metadata network is not a good idea because it can make clients fail to not respond to the administrative commands sent from the Xsan Admin utility. In general, DHCP is inappropriate for Xsan metadata Controllers and Xsan clients. Certain environments sometimes require DHCP-supplied static IP addresses, though. Provided those addresses don't change, DHCP is acceptable in an Xsan installation—but on the production network only, not on the metadata network.

If you ever need to change the metadata controller's metadata IP address, the best option is to first demote the metadata controller to a standard Xsan client, then remove it from the SAN. After you change the IP address of the former metadatacontroller, re-add it to the SAN, specifying it as a metadata controller.

Common Xsan Repair and Troubleshooting Procedures

Proactive maintenance is essential, but despite your best efforts, problems will crop up. Certain types occur more frequently than others, though, so you'll often find yourself repeating the same repair procedures. Here are some of the more common ones.

Resetting Xsan Client settings

As mentioned earlier, when remedying Xsan issues, you should rarely have to uninstall and reinstall the software. Often, simply returning it to its default settings will do the trick. All you need do is delete the contents of the /Library/Filesystems/Xsan/config folder (but not the folder itself), and then reboot. If this doesn't resolve a client-specific issue, read on for additional measures to try.

Rebuilding an Array on an Xserve RAID

Sometimes a drive fails or a controller for a RAID setup with redundant drives (RAID 5 or RAID 3, for example) goes down, and you have to rebuild the parity drive. You should do so as quickly as possible , but it can result in data loss. And if a second drive in the array fails, you could lose most of the data. Although the failure has caused parity problems, the data itself may be safe, so you should back it up first, and as soon as you can. With that precaution in place, you can carry out the parity rebuild.

Start the process by opening RAID Admin from /Applications/Server, then selecting the RAID containing the damaged array, and clicking on the Advanced button in the toolbar. Enter the management password for the Xserve RAID device in question, click on the button to Verify or Rebuild Parity, then on Continue, selecting the array. Select Rebuild Array and the process will start. In a few hours, when it completes, perform a Verify Array. Finally, verify the data on the volumes.

If the rebuild doesn't go well and you lose the array, you'll likely need to delete and re-add it. In many cases, this will cause you to lose the data stored on that array and, therefore, on the volume—one of the many good reasons to have a backup.

Rebuilding an Array on a Promise RAID

Promise RAID setups, like those of Xserve (or any other) will eventually suffer a drive failure. But the Promise products contain a few features that differentiate them Xserve's.

One feature, Media Patrol, is a failure-detection routine that watches for bad blocks. A feature called Predictive Data Migration (PDM) will preemptively rebuild a RAID set on a global hot-spare drive. If a drive does fail, this significantly accelerates the parity rebuild.

However, under certain circumstances, these features can be detrimental to performance. For instance, PDM will kick in if it detects even a minor drive malfunction. In certain instances, this results in a data parity rebuild, but never activates the global hot spare as a replacement. And with the default notification settings, none of this activity will result in an e-mail notification. During the rebuild performance is degraded.

If you experience poor performance with an Xsan that uses Promise hardware, you can look for clues to the source in a few places. First and foremost, make sure to check the event logs on all your Promise RAID sets. If you see a lot of Media Patrol or PDM events, you likely have a failing drive. PDM, as noted earlier, attempts to intelligently detect drive failures and will begin to build a hot-spare drive into the array. But while this means that when the drive ultimately fails, the overall rebuild process will take a very short time, in the meantime the process can seriously degrade performance.

If you continue to experience performance problems on Promise equipment, consider disabling Forced Read Ahead on your Promise controllers. Apple's publicly available configuration scripts turn this option on by default, but it's truly needed only in high-throughput environments, such as those that process uncompressed HD. In the majority of scenarios, you can greatly increase Xsan read performance by disabling Forced Read Ahead.

Latency

In Xsan, the `PIO HiPriWr` value in logs (specifically the `sysavg` value) shows you how latent the connection to your metadata LUNs is. `HiPriWr` values are written on an hourly basis to a volume's cvlog file found at `/Library/Filesystems/Xsan/data/volume/log/cvlog`. Alternatively, you can summon these values as needed by using the tool cvadmin:

```
cvadmin
>select MyVolume
(MyVolume)>debug 0x01000000
```

For a metadata LUN on an Xserver RAID set, the average latency, shown by `sysavg`, is usually 500ms or less. Promise RAID's active/active controllers result in additional latency, and will result in values between 800ms and 2,000ms.

If the physical fiber connection to a system's LUNs is too slow (or latent), it can cause instability and worse, volume-integrity issues. If you run into issues with latency on the fabric then it probably comes from problems with the fabric . To address the issue, look into statically assigning FC port configurations on targets and initiators. Specifically, ensure that connections are of type N_Port, often referred to as PTP (point-to-point). On its boxes, Promise support recommends always statically configuring Fibre interfaces to N_Port 4GB static settings to help reduce latency. After ensuring you have static settings, assign an ALPA ID of 255 to prevent Fibre Channel LIPs from being sent.

In situations where latency is excessive, you can deal with it programmatically by increasing the buffer cache size. This will allow Xsan to cache more data, helping mitigate the effect of latent LUNs on the overall performance, health, and viability of the SAN. Additionally, you should increase the iNode Cache allowing Xsan to write iNodes more effectively if you have latency on your Metadata LUNs. You define these settings in the volume setup wizard, but can update them in your SAN volume's volumename.cfg file in /Library/Preferences/FileSystems/Xsan/config.

Schedules

3:15 a.m. Most of us may be asleep, but plenty of people are hard at work and need data access. Unfortunately, those attempting to get it from an Xsan may end up a little frustrated—Mac OS X system software runs its weekly or daily scripts at 3:15 a.m. To reduce user irritation, you can disable the periodic scripts by editing their *launchd* calls, which you'll find in the following files:

- /System/Library/LaunchDaemons/com.apple.periodic-daily.plist

- /System/Library/LaunchDaemons/com.apple.periodic-monthly.plist

- /System/Library/LaunchDaemons/com.apple.periodic-weekly.plist

If you disable these scripts, though, you should still let them run every once in a while. Chances are that, with a little planning, you'll be able to run the process at regular intervals.

Fragmentation

You'll find the snfsdefrag tool, which is part of Xsan, in the /Library/Filesystems/Xsan/ bin directory. You can use the utility to look up fragmentation statistics as well as to perform defragmentation operations. If you're using Xsan as back-end storage, you may need to perform defragmentation operations routinely.

> **NOTE:** When you're defragmenting a volume we recommend that you always use the -v switch to enable verbose mode.

The snfsdefrag utility can defrag individual files or recurse directories or volumes. Before you initiate the actual operation, though, you should run it with the -c switch to perform an extent count so you can see how many each fragmented file has. To do so on bighonkinvolume, type

```
snfsdefrag -c -r /Volumes/bighonkinvolume
```

The -r option causes the utility to recursively search through the volume. Additionally, you can specify a single directory (likely one deeper in the hierarchy). You can also select files based on their number of extents by using the -m option followed by the desired maximum number allowed. For instance, to output a summary of all fragmented files with 2 or more extents, you'd use

```
snfsdefrag -c -r -m 2 /Volumes/bighonkinvolume
```

There's also a –p option, which you can use to free up blocks that were allocated (according to the way you configured the File Expansion Min value during volume setup) but not used.

The –k option is one of the most useful for environments in the midst of migrating. You can use it to specify an affinity to which you'll move a file following the defragmentation process. That lets you move data between affinities and allows for the safe (or as safe as possible) removal of storage pools during migrations.

Backup

An Xsan has a special file system—it's case sensitive, accept characters that some backup tools don't recognize, and allows data sets of over 100TB at times. All of these factors make for a fairly complicated backup paradigm. You can't use just any application. But there are a number of third-party tools on the market that have been developed to do the job. Here are some, along with the URLs for their web sites:

Archiware's PresSTORE: www.archiware.com

Atempo Time Navigator: www.atempo.com

BakBone's NetVault: Backup: www.bakbone.com

TOLIS Group's BRU Server Backup & Restore Software: www.tolisgroup.com

Maintaining regular backups of an Xsan volume is an absolute must. A cluster file system performs a delicate dance with many members, and badness can occur in a variety of scenarios. The file system itself is completely reliant on the back-end as a whole. If you run your business on an Xsan, not having protection is a huge mistake.

The Xsan Command Line

A number of command-line utilities let you perform Xsan management. You'll find these in the /Library/Filesystems/Xsan/bin folder. We recommend adding this to the search path of your shell of preference so you can use the commands without having to type in the full path or to the Xsan bin directory every time.

> **NOTE:** Whether or not you make substantial use of the Xsan command line, having a fundamental understanding of it will increase the depth of your Xsan knowledge. If you'll be putting an Xsan into production, we highly recommend that you read this section.

Fibreconfig

Although not a part of Xsan, you'll use `fibreconfig` often because it mirrors the functionality of the Fibre Channel System Preference pane, but it's faster, very verbose, and has more options for configuring Apple-branded FC cards. To get started, use the -l option to query `fibreconfig` for all information about your FC environment by in typing in `fibreconfig -l`, which will produce this output:

```
Controllers

    PortWWN 10:00:00:05:1C:B2:90:1A
      Port Status: Link Established
         Speed: Automatic (2 Gigabit)
       Topology: Automatic (N_Port)
          Slot: Slot-2
          Port: 1

    PortWWN 10:00:00: 05:1C:B2:90:1B
  Port Status: Link Established
         Speed: Automatic (2 Gigabit)
       Topology: Automatic (N_Port)
          Slot: Slot-2
          Port: 0

Targets

    NodeWWN 20:05:00:B0:A1:19:9B:14
        Status: Connected
          LUNs: 0, 1, 2, 3

    NodeWWN 20:05:00:B0:A1:20:2A:1A
        Status: Connected
          LUNs: 0, 1, 2, 3

    NodeWWN 20:05:00:B0:A1:13:9B:14
        Status: Connected
          LUNs: 0, 1, 2, 3

    NodeWWN 13:05:00:B0:A1:19:2A:1A
        Status: Connected
          LUNs: 0, 1, 2, 3
```

Notice that the PortWWN of the controller is listed as well as an indication as to whether the port is connected.

Immediately below that, you'll see the card's speed and topology—the only two controller settings you can customize. When you alter them, you need to use the -c option followed by the controller's PortWNN to identify the card on which you're making the change. This means that to change both of the controller's ports, you have to run the command twice.

Available topologies for the card include nport, nlport, and auto (the default). Occasionally you'll have an issue that requires you to set the topology manually. You can automate the process for a number of hosts by sending them the `fibreconfig` command using the -t option followed by the topology to set. For most Xsan environments, you'll want to use N Port. To customize the topology you can use the following two commands (one per controller) as part of a script (or more likely, convert the address to a variable and use the variable instead):

```
fibreconfig -c 10:00:00:05:1C:B2:90:1A -t nport
fibreconfig -c 10:00:00:05:1C:B2:90:1B -t nport
```

You can statically assign speed from the command line as well. To do so, use the –s option followed by one of four speed choices: 1 Gb, 2 Gb, 4 Gb, or auto. To customize the speed you can use the following two commands (one per Controller, and again, using a variable in the place of the address if you're doing so programmatically):

```
fibreconfig -c 10:00:00:05:1C:B2:90:1A -s 4gigabit
fibreconfig -c 10:00:00:05:1C:B2:90:1A -s 4gigabit
```

The other setting you can customize from the command line is the Loop Arbitration Physical Address (the AL_PA). If you use this setting with an Xsan, however, it can cause some serious issues, long term, but if you must, to set the AL_PA with fibreconfig, use the –a option followed by an address.

> **NOTE:** To implement changes you make to any of these settings, you must do a reboot.

The fibreconfig command is very useful for automating reporting with Xsan, especially when used en masse through Apple Remote Desktop (ARD). You can use it to display which targets are available to metadata controllers and clients by focusing on the NodeWWN information. This can be incredibly useful in triangulating zoning and RAID-controller issues quickly and effectively. For example, you can obtain a listing from fibreconfig but constrain the output to NodeWWN items with grep as follows:

```
fibreconfig -l | grep NodeWWN
```

You can also obtain the unique address information from all of your clients concurrently without touching each system, again using a combination of fibreconfig and ARD. This can be a very useful way to get a list of addresses by node name so that you can label your FC switch ports, allow access if you're LUN-masking on Promise device, or just documenting settings. To grab the PortWWN, simply send the following command through ARD:

```
fibreconfig -l | grep PortWWN
```

Overall, there aren't a lot of settings available with the fibreconfig command. Of those settings, most that are useful in an Xsan environment are also available from the GUI. But when managing many Xsan clients, fibreconfig can help speed up the process of narrowing down issues, reporting, setting up RAIDs, and FC switch configuration.

Labeling LUNs

You can label LUNs using the cvlabel command rather than doing so within Xsan Admin. If you want to list all your available LUNs first, simply type cvlabel -l. The command cvlabel -c >labels will dump your label information out to a standard text file called *labels.*

Next, open the file in your favorite text editor, and change the very first text field to the name that you want for your LUN within Xsan Admin. Edit any other lines you'd like to be labeled, and save the file. Now run the command `cvlabel labels`, which will read the file you just edited and label the LUN for use with ACFS using the name you just provided, making it appear in Xsan admin.

> **TIP:** Xsan Admin (2.*x*) will show you only the LUNs from the Fibre Channel controller, but you can use cvlabel to label LUNs on local hard drives and even removable media. Though you should use this for testing only, it does give you the ability to test Xsan commands that you otherwise might not be able to run in a lab environment.

cvadmin

The `cvadmin` command allows an administrator to view and change volume and storage-pool settings. Options include -H, which specifies a host to run against (if you don't indicate a host, the command attempts to run on the localhost) and -F, which sets a volume name to run against. There are also -f and -e, options, which load commands from a file and from stdin respectively. Or you can run `cvadmin` interactively by simply typing `sudo cvadmin` at the command prompt, which will provide output similar to the following:

```
Enter command(s)
For command help, enter "help" or "?".
```

In the following example, we have one volume and two metadata controllers. When we first invoke `cvadmin`, it displays all of the valid file-system services (which in this context means volumes per metadata controller) and selects our only volume. Notice that, in the output shown below, MyVolume has two entries. This is completely normal, because you should see one entry per volume per MDC. In this case, we have one volume and two metadata controllers, so we have two entries. The asterisk denotes the active FSS (or active metadata controller), 192.168.56.5.

```
List FSS

File System Services (* indicates service is in control of FS):
1>*MyVolume[0] located on 192.168.56.5:51520 (pid 512)
2> MyVolume[1] located on 192.168.56.6:51520 (pid 509)
```

To perform any worthwhile tasks using these tools, you need to select a volume. In this particular instance, there's only one volume, so `cvadmin` selected the active one and displayed the statistics for it. But when there are multiple volumes, you must select one before you use `cvadmin`. For example:

```
Select FSM "MyVolume"

Created :       Tue Jan 13 15:33:57 2009
Active Connections:     1
Fs Block Size : 16K
Msg Buffer Size :       4K
```

```
Disk Devices :  2
Stripe Groups :  2
Fs Blocks :     61277616 (935.02 GB)
Fs Blocks Free :        61006893 (930.89 GB) (99%)
```

So there's no confusion as to which volume you're administering, the cvadmin prompt always displays the active volume—MyVolume, in our case, as you can see here:

```
Xsanadmin (MyVolume) >
```

To get a full list of available commands you can look in the cvadmin man pages type *help* in an interactive cvadmin session. Below we've listed the most frequently used commands and what they do.

>*fail VolumeName:* Entering fail and the volume name starts failover of the volume by initiating an FSS vote among your metadata controllers. The MDC that provides services for this volume and has the highest failover priority should win the election. If no failover is available, the volume will fail back to its original host.

>*fsmlist:* This command outputs a list of FSM processes on the machine that's selected, which is useful when determining which volumes the machine is capable of hosting as a metadata controller.

>*repof:* If you need an open file report, repof will generate one, saving it to /Library/Filesystems/Xsan/data/MyVolume/open_file_report.txt. The output contains a slew of information, but the actual file name is noticeably absent. Argh! You do get an inode number for the file in question though, so you can use a command such as find /Volumes/MyVolume -inum X to determine the actual file from the published inode number. The repof command can be very useful when attempting to determine why a client will not unmount a volume.

>*start:* The start command is equivalent to starting the volume in Xsan. However, by specifying a hostname/ip, you can start file system services on just that particular MDC, which can be handy for maintenance purposes.

>*stats:* Issuing this command produces volume statistics.

>*stop:* The stop command is equivalent to stopping the volume in Xsan. But by supplying a hostname/ip, you can stop file system services on just that particular MDC, which can be handy for maintenance purposes.

>*who:* You can list all metadata controllers, client, and administration sessions open relating to this volume using who. Nodes with the volume mounted will be indicated with a [CLI] entry.

If you need help with more-complex troubleshooting, you can try these commands:

>*activate VolumeName* xxx.xxx.xxx.xxx: This command activates FSS services for the specified hostname and IP you put in place of *VolumeName xxx.xxx.xxx.xxx.* Alternatively you can leave off the IP and you'll activate the local server (if applicable). You can also run activate on an MDC if it's not showing appropriate FSS services available. If you see errors to the effect that an MDC is on standby, activating the volume on the respective server will often address this issue.

>*debug 0x01000000:* Entering this debug command will immediately generate I/O latency numbers and save them in /Library/Filesystems/Xsan/data/MyVolume/log/cvlog immediately (a process that normally occurs only hourly). The key figure in the output is the sysavg number for PIO HiPriWr SUMMARY. If your metadata is hosted on an Xserve RAID volume, this number should be below 500ms. If you're using storage systems from Promise, the active/active controller setup introduces additional latency, so the numbers should be in the 805 to 1,000ms range.

>*latency-test:* Run latency tests between the FSM and clients. It can be used to isolate problematic clients on the SAN.

>*paths:* Output a list of LUNs visible to the node and the corresponding HBA port used to communicate with that LUN. This option can be helpful when you are getting those pesky "stripe group not found" errors.

>*show:* This will output information about the stripe groups/storage pools used by this volume. It is useful for cross referencing index numbers outputted in system.log to human readable storage pool names. It also provides various statistics and configuration, such as stripe group role, corresponding LUNs, affinity tags, multipath method, and other useful bits of information.

Overall, the cvadmin tool is very useful when troubleshooting metadata controller behavior. But you don't use it when you want to perform Xsan setup or client-management operations. To label LUNs, use cvlabel. To mount and unmount volumes, you'd likely use the new xsanctl tool or mount -t acfs. To perform defrag operations and volume maintenance, use the snfsdefrag and cvfsck tools, respectively. And while you can add serial numbers and create volumes from the command line, you'll probably find it much easier to continue performing these operations through the Xsan Admin GUI tool.

Repairing Volumes

When checking for volume-integrity and repair issues on Xsan volumes, don't use the standard fsck command; use its replacement, cvfsck. And if you're going to repair a volume, check the Apple Knowledge Base article at http://support.apple.com/kb/HT1081.

Other Commands

You can also leverage other Xsan commands for use in Xsan management. Here are some, along with descriptions of what they do:

cvcp: To copy files or directories in and out of an acfs volume (one managed by Xsan) use cvcp. It has Xsan specific options and runs faster than the standard cp command. During the initial migration of data into the Xsan, we recommend using this command rather than copying with the finder.

cvmkdir: This command lets you create a new directory on an Xsan volume with an affinity.

cvmkfile: You can use `cvmkfile` to make a file on an Xsan volume, a procedure that's useful for testing speed.

cvmkfs: If you need to create a new Xsan volume, `cvmkfs` will do it.

cvupdatefs: You use `cvupdatefs` during some upgrades of Xsan software (for example, from 1.*x* to 2.*x*)

fsm and fsmpm: These are the Xsan processes that you invoke from `launchd` instead of running manually.

Additionally, you'll find a number of useful files. This list describes some of the types and where to look for them.

Logs for Volumes: `/Library/Filesystems/Xsan/data/volume name/log/cvlog`

Configuration Files for volumes: `/Library/FileSystems/Xsan/config/VOLUME.cfg` directory.

Configuration files for the Volume auto-start list: `/Library/Filesystems/Xsan/config/fsmlist`.

Configuration files for the Controller list: `/Library/FileSystems/Xsan/Config/fsnameservers`

Default Volume Configuration File: Located in `/Library/Filesystems/Xsan/config`, each volume has a corresponding CFG file.

iSCSI

The iSCSI network storage protocol allows sending and receiving of SCSI commands over a TCP/IP network. This allows you to leverage the low-cost Ethernet medium to get SAN performance and network-based storage. While you can use pretty much any Ethernet switch, we recommend that if you use iSCSI, you either dedicate a switch to it or use quality switches and build a dedicated VLAN for iSCSI traffic.

> **NOTE:** Small Tree (`http://www.small-tree.com`) makes a 10-gigabit Ethernet adapter and software with support for Mac OS X as well as a number of multi-port Ethernet cards that can supplement the two built into most modern Mac OS X desktop machines.

You can use iSCSI storage with Mac OS X. As with Xsan, to get started with iSCSI you'll need an initiator and a target (or in many cases, lots of targets). Studio Network Solutions (SNS) provides a software-based iSCSI initiator called globalSAN that you can download from its site and use for free. Alternatively, you can look into the ATTO Xtend SAN, which runs about $200 for one user, which drops to about $90 per seat for 100 users. ATTO supports Xtend whether or not you use any of their other products.

Software-based initiators will use the CPU of your system and a built-in or third-party standard Ethernet port, but you can also buy a dedicated card that will off-load the processing to itself. In some cases, for various performance reasons, you'll need to do this. The examples in this section, though, use the Studio Network Solutions (SNS) globalSAN software. SNS provides its software-based iSCSI initiator free of charge, and it can be downloaded from the web site: `http://www.studionetworksolutions.com`.

> **NOTE:** At the time of this writing the globalSAN iSCSI initiator is not compatable with 10.6, though Studio Network Solutions has commited to publishing a compatible version.

To get started, first download and install the software. GlobalSAN uses a fairly standard package installer that can be installed with a simple double-click. Once installed, you will see the globalSAN iSCSI System Preference Pane, as seen in Figure 4-19.

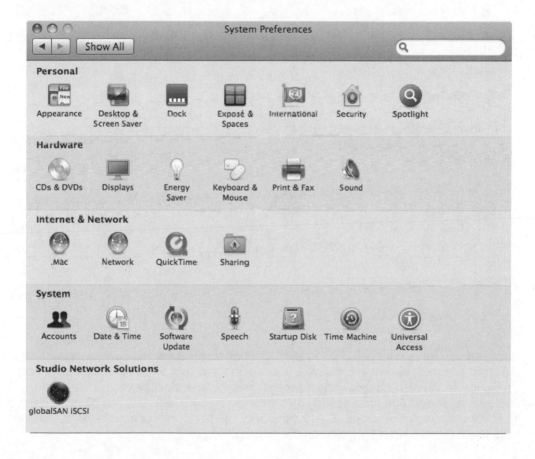

Figure 4-19. *System Preferences with globalSAN iSCSI Preference Pane*

If you click on the globalSAN System Preference you'll be able to add your first portal. Each iSCSI share will have a unique IP and be referenced as a portal. Click on the add icon (+) to add your first portal, as seen in Figure 4-20.

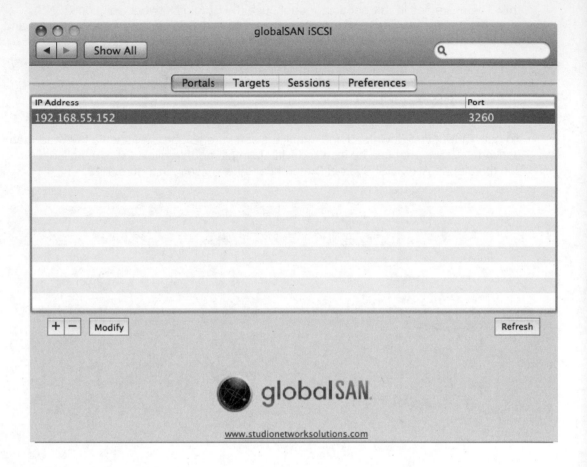

Figure 4-20. *globalSAN portals*

Now that you have your portal populated, click on the Targets tab and you should see the storage listed, shown in Figure 4-21. Click on the target and then click on the Log On button to initiate your session into the storage. At this point, it will mount on the Desktop (provided you have already given it a file system), and you will be able to use it as you would any other storage. You can check the box for Peristent if you would like to have the volume always mounted on the system.

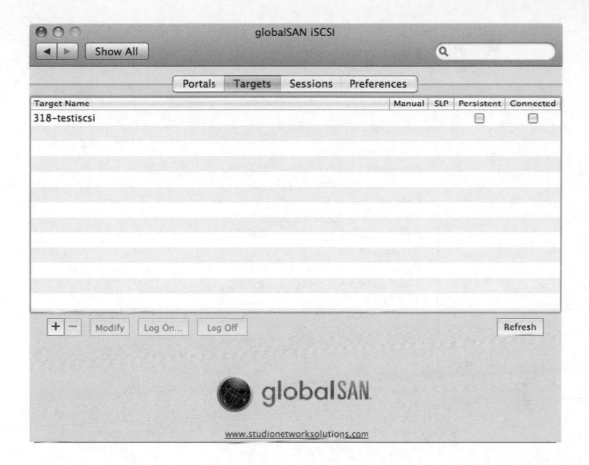

Figure 4-21. *globalSAN Targets*

If you click on the Sessions tab, then you will be able to look at various statistics about your storage including the LUN identifier and disk name, as seen in Figure 4-22.

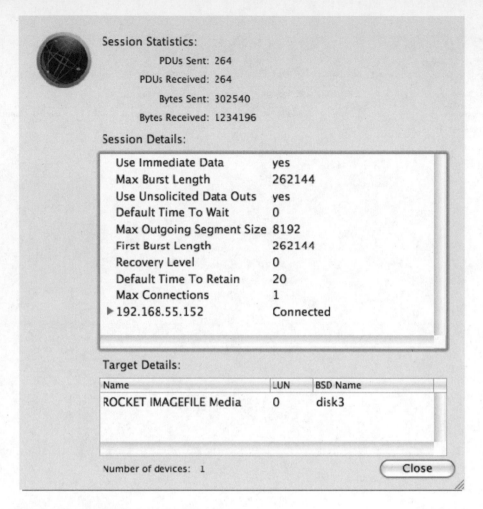

Figure 4-22. *globalSAN Session Statistics sheet*

If you don't yet have a file system on the storage, then you can open Disk Utility (shown in Figure 4-23) and you will see the storage listed there, click on it, click on the Partition tab and you will then be able to give it a file system.

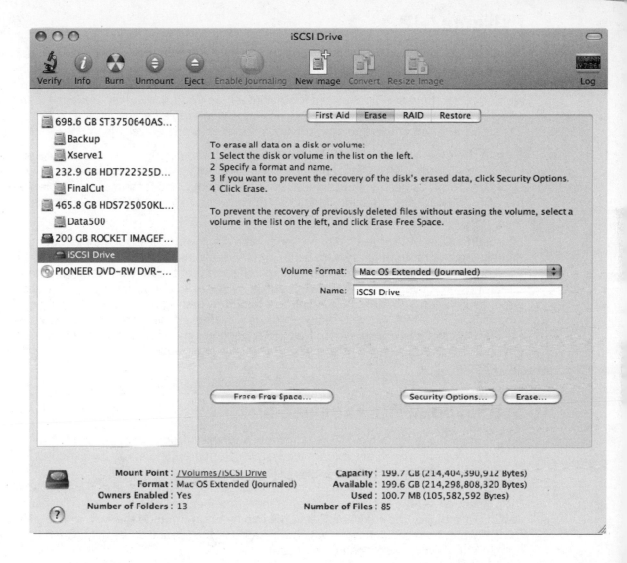

Figure 4-23. *Formatting iSCSI disks using Disk Utility*

Once the disk has been formatted, it will then mount on the system and interact just like any other local volume. Thus, integrating Mac OS X clients into existing iSCSI infrastructures is neither difficult nor expensive, thanks to the kind folks at SNS, who offer the globalSAN iSCSI initiator for free (as in beer).

ExtremeZ-IP

Microsoft has pulled UAM support from the latest Windows Server release. Given that Microsoft is focused on SMB/CIFS and Dfs, and that the set-up and clustering features of the File Sharing service on Windows Server are well documented, in this chapter we won't cover setting up File Services for Macintosh on Windows Server. Because many organizations would rather host AFP services on Windows rather than Mac OS X, ExtremeZ-IP often enters into conversations about enterprise-level integrations.

ExtremeZ-IP lets you provide AFP access to client computers using Windows Server. It also allows for the integration of print services for clients, integrates seamlessly in Active Directory, requires no client to be installed, is clusterable, and is far more scalable than the AFP services integrated into Mac OS X Server. And ExtremeZ-IP Enterprise has integrated Dfs support

Microsoft's Distributed file system presents, as a single virtualized location, what may actually be a number of file servers being used to replicate data among multiple hosts. Enterprises often use Dfs to host home directories so that the network can replicate the directories effectively, which results in flexibility, scalability and redundancy. This allows large environments to move home directory locations among hosts without changing locations in the users' Active Directory profiles. Given the prolific stature that DFS has attained the lack of DFS support in Mac OS X becomes a common pain point for many environments and leveraging ExtremeZ-IP can help to smooth enterprise-class integration.

Setting up AFP in ExtremeZ-IP

To get started with ExtremeZ-IP, download the software from http://www.grouplogic.com, extract the installer from the ZIP file, run the executable, and select Next at the Welcome screen. Heed the warning to close all open applications—including Windows Explorer (explorer.exe)—and Services, then click on the OK button. At the licensing screen, indicate whether you'll be installing a licensed version or a trial of the software. Select the choice appropriate to the way you obtained the software, then click on Next, which will produce the license agreement. Read the agreement, then choose whether to accept.

At the Registration screen enter the name of the person that the software is licensed to in the Name: field and the company that the software is licensed to in the Company: field. Finally, enter the license number. (You won't see this screen if you're using a trial copy.)

Now you'll see a Choose Destination Location screen. If you're installing the software in the C:\Program Files\Group Logic\ExtremeZ-IP directory, you can simply click on Next; otherwise, click on the Browse button, select your installation location, and hit the Next button once again. At the Select Program Folder screen, click on Next if you want the program name to show up in the Start menu under All Programs, or click on another subdirectory if you'd like to customize where the item will appear, then click Next when you're satisfied.

At the following Choose Destination Location screen, select where to install the ExtremeZ-IP Print Support files and then click on Next (or simply click Next if you're OK with it being installed in the c:\ExtremeZ-IP Print Support) directory. In the ExtremeZ-IP Installation pop-up screen that appears, choose whether the ExtremeZ-IP services should start automatically when Windows boots (which will set the services to Automatic rather than Manual). The installer will then run and you'll see another pop-up screen asking if you want to share out your Print Support files. If you'll be using ExtremeZ-IP as a print spooler for Mac OS X clients, you'll likely want to answer affirmatively.

Finally, at the Post-Install Actions screen, leave the Launch ExtremeZ-IP Administrator box checked so that, on completion of the install, the administrative application (shown in Figure 4-24.) will open. Click Next to finish the installation. If you uncheck the Launch Admin box, you can still start the utility by going to Start ➤ All Programs ➤ ExtremeZ-IP ➤ ExtremeZ-IP Administrator.

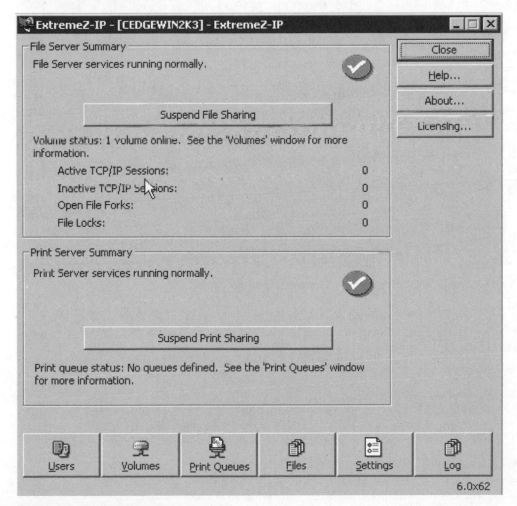

Figure 4-24. *ExtremeZ-IP Administrator*

Configuring ExtremeZ-IP

The ExtremeZ-IP Administrator tool lets you create shares and assign them the appropriate permissions as well as configure the AFP service. Usually, the first task you want to undertake is dealing with the AFP global settings, so click the Settings button at the bottom of the Administrator screen (Figure 4-25), which brings up the Settings dialog shown in Figure 4-25 with the File Server tab active. In it, you can create a log-in greeting, similar to the one available in Server Admin for Mac OS X Server, and you can set the TCP port over which AFP will run (548 by default). You can also choose whether the server will be able to warehouse home directories, and you can define the log-in types to (many environments will disable guest access and cleartext log-ons).

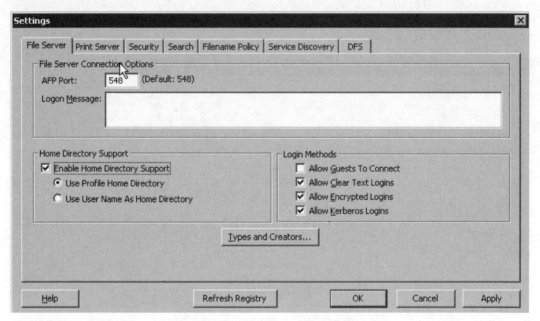

Figure 4-25. *Settings Dialog of ExtremeZ-IP Administrator Tool, File Servers tab*

Once you've applied the settings for the AFP functionality, click on the Security tab, where you'll be presented with the options, divided into three sections, shown in Figure 4-26 and listed here:

Permissions

■ *Allow Mac clients to change folder permissions:* Mark this check box so Mac OS X users can alter rights on files and folders, giving those users some security over their data. Disable the option to use only inherited permissions already set on the Windows server.

■ *Reset permissions on move (global):* Turn this on if you want target permissions to match those of the ACLs when data moves into the directory structure controlled by ExtremeZ-IP. Folder and file permissions will change to those of their new parent folder.

- *Support UNIX permissions and ACLs:* Put a check in this box so that ExtremZ-IP will support ACL in addition to POSIX. Windows manages security exclusively via ACLs; OS X can also use Unix permissions and Mac-type folder permissions.

- *Support ACLs on all volumes (global):* Enabling this will extend ACL support enabled with the previous option to volumes shared out over AFP

- *Show only accessible volumes:* With this option turned on, users that don't have access to volumes on the server will not see them (even grayed out).

Other Options

- *Allow remote administration of server:* Enable this option if Windows users with administrator privileges need to use the ExtremeZ-IP remote-management features to configure the server from offsite.

- *Allow workstations to save password (OS 9 only):* With this setting checked, Mac OS 9 workstations can cache passwords to volumes Users authenticating from Mac OS 9 clients will see the Remember Password in Keychain dialog.

- *Notify Mac clients of password expiration in xxx days:* Select the check box, and you can fill in the number of days before password expiration that users will receive warnings. When the feature triggers, users will receive password-change prompts each time they log in and select a volume.

- *Enable IPv6:* If you select this option, which lets AFP use IPv6, you may have to install the protocol manually on some Windows systems where it has not yet been utilized before they can serve ExtremeZ-IP.

Directory Services: This section of the security tab is where you configure LDAPv3 and Active Directory integration.

- *Use Global Catalog:* Removing the mark from this check box will cause ExtremeZ-IP to search only the domain specified.

- *Account:* In the text box to the right of this label, enter the administrative user name for the directory service.

- *Password:* Type the administrative password for the directory service into the provided text box.

- *Domain:* Fill in this field with the domain name for the directory service.

- *Additional directory search criteria:* Here you can set a custom search path for the directory service.

- *Validate Account:* Click this button to verify that the LDAPv3 service is accessible.

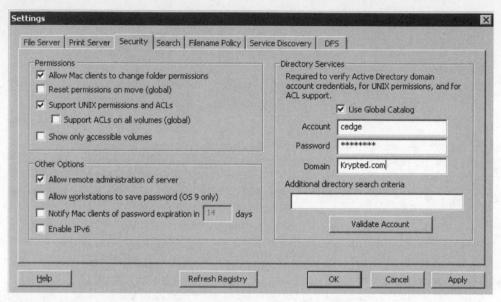

Figure 4-26. *Settings Dialog of ExtremeZ-IP Administrator Tool, File Servers tab*

When you've applied your settings, select the Search tab if you wish to enable Spotlight support, then choose the Filename Policy tab if you want to customize file names that ExtremeZ-IP will allow for files and directories on the server. Now click on the Service Discovery tab. You'll be looking at the screen shown in Figure 4-27. Here, you can adjust the settings for Bonjour, AppleTalk (likely not needed unless you have Mac OS 9 clients) and Zidget/HTTP support, which configures the client to access the wide-area Bonjour implementation on ExtremeZ-IP.

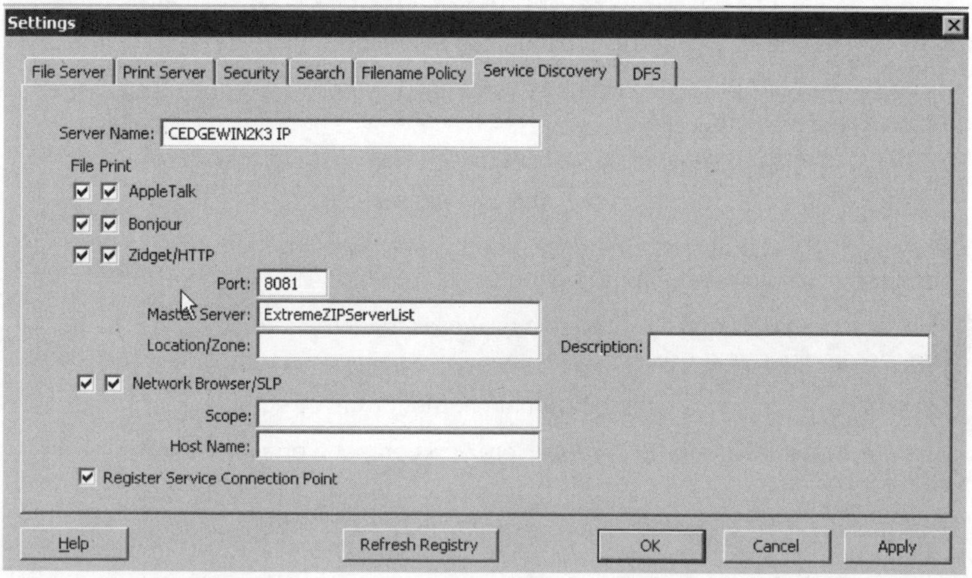

Figure 4-27. *Settings Dialog of ExtremeZ-IP Administrator Tool, Service Discovery tab*

Setting up DFS in ExtremeZ-IP

GroupLogic has a great explanation of how you get a Mac client to use ExtremeZ-IP. You'll find it in a technical whitepaper that documents the installation and configuration process. To get the paper, go to http://www.grouplogic.com/resource-center/pdfs/How-Microsoft-DFS-Home-Directories-Work-w-ExtremeZ-IP-60-A-Technical-White-Paper.pdf.

Managing Filesystem Permissions in OS X

There's a lot of misinformation and confusion surrounding the proper management of permissions in OS X. Discussion of the topic have been fairly heated since the migration from OS 9, which had very loose capabilities for delegating, assigning, and managing rights. OS X, in contrast was a native multiuser OS, and as such, it had permission-based restrictions in its heart and soul.

Admins doing migrations "panic'd," mass chaos ensued, and suddenly all you heard were complaints about permissions problems. Granted, in the early days, dealing with rights in OS X was a bit of a nightmare, but the situation is much better now. There's no reason why a modern-day environment running 10.5 or 10.6 should continue to be plagued by permissions problems. Grasping the two main OS X discretionary access control (DAC) systems is paramount to a proper understanding of OS X permissions.

POSIX-Based Permissions

OS X inherited its POSIX-compliant permissioning from its Unix progenitors. POSIX is a long-standing system, in both Unix and Linux, for defining the owner, group, and mode of a file. The mode, presented through a series of numeric values, represents the permissions of the file. Using POSIX, you can apply access restrictions at three different levels: that of the owner, of the group, and of everyone else. Each levels has three possible access capabilities, represented by three different modes: *read, write,* and *execute.* Each level has a numerical mode value, which determines its respective access rights.

POSIX uses three-bit flags to represent modes, thus a numerical value denotes each mode. In most-significant to least-significant bit order, a 1 in each position gives read, write, and execute permission. Put another way, read's binary and decimal values are 100 and 4, write's are 010 and 2, and execute's are 001 and 1. Thus, a user with full access has a mode of 111 binary and 7 (4+2+1) decimal. Numbering by sets of 3 bits (which can represent the 8 decimal digits 0 through 7) is called *octal notation*.

You don't really need to know the binary system, but knowing the numeric values of each mode is important. Each level: user, group, and everyone, has a mode represented by an integer value based on these three bits.

For example, consider the list of files and directories in the /Users folder that the command ls -al /Users produces:

```
helyx:~ hunterbj$ ls -al /Users
total 0
drwxr-xr-x 10 root     admin  340 Jul 1 20:22 .
drwxrwxr-t@ 51 root     admin 1802 Jul 7 00:58 ..

drwxrwxrwt 13 root     wheel  442 Jun 29 23:54 Shared
drwxrwxr-x+ 20 demo     admin  680 May 29 18:15 demo
drwxr-xr-x+ 55 hunterbj staff 1870 Jul 8 00:57 hunterbj
```

In every line of the output, the first field (the one containing combinations of dashes and the letters d, r, t, w, and x) reports the POSIX permissions, as laid out in a bitmap. Rather than using 1's or 0's though, it displays identifiers (the dashes and some of the letters) for each permission attribute. Let's look at the line that contains the word *demo* twice:

```
drwxrwxr-x+ 20 demo     admin  680 May 29 18:15 demo
```

Here, the string "drwxrwxr-x" holds the POSIX permissions. In an ls output, the first digit, *d,* specifies the file system type, in this case a directory. The next three digits, *rwx* (read, write, and execute), represent the mode for the owner, who in this example is demo in the admin group. Thus, user demo has read, write, and execute privileges for this folder. The next three digits represent group privileges, and the final three represent everyone privileges. For the vast majority of POSIX privilege management, you'll be using these three basic access rights: read, write, and execute.

To an extent, these privileges are fairly self explanatory: If you have read permission for a file, you can open it and view its contents. If you have the permission for a directory, you can list its contents. The write privilege, when applied to a file, allows for both modification and deletion. But—a user without write privileges for both a file and its parent directory can't delete the file. Thus, removing the write privilege from a directory is a handy way of establishing an append-only or drop-box privilege scheme.

The execute bit, when enabled for a file, allows execution of it. This is not the same as opening a file. The former implies that the file contains executable binary data or uncompiled code which references an interpreter via a hash-bang (#!) statement (for which you'll find more detail in chapter 8). The executable bit also plays a very important role with directories: It controls whether users are allowed to traverse a directory's path.

A person who lacks the privileges—via ownership, group membership, or public permissions—won't be able to list the contents of the directory. Nor will that individual be able to access any file-system elements the directory contains. Because of this, denying execute privileges is a good way to completely block users from accessing data at the perimeter of a directory structure, thus allowing you to continue to use owner, group, and everyone management. In contrast, denying users read privileges on a directory will not prevent them from traversing into its subdirectories, where they'll have any access granted at the everyone level (which may include read access to sensitive data).

For day-to-day management of POSIX permissions, these three modes will be your primary weapons against those pesky users. But you have a few more options. In the previous ls output we showed, you may have noticed some special permissions on the directory /Users/Shared. Here's the line again:

```
drwxrwxrwt 13 root    wheel  442 Jun 29 23:54 Shared
```

Under the everyone digits (the letters in **bold**), instead of the expected *x* (execute), we have a *t*. This is referred to as the sticky bit. When enabled on a directory, it prevents deletion of a file inside of that directory by anyone other than the file's owner. Thus, if Jimbob creates a file, then gives everyone read and write privileges, Geraldine will be able to edit its content, but not delete it. Only Jimbob can delete the file. It's worth noting, though, that with write privileges, nothing stops Gerry from simply deleting all of the file's contents.

To assign the sticky bit to a directory, you simply use a forth octal number, which has a value of 001. Thus, the Shared folder in the example line above has a mode of 1777, with the 1 (001 binary) being the "sticky" directory. To actually apply this mode to a file, use the chmod command, run as root if you're the owner of the targeted directory:

```
chmod 1777 /Users/Shared
chmod -R 777 /Users/Shared/*
```

The second line specifies the –R flag, which will actually apply the mode 777 to all items inside of the /Users/Shared/ directory. Thus, all files in the directory will be editable by anyone, but because of the first command that was run, only the owner can delete a file.

The fourth octal has two modes in addition to sticky: *set-group-ID-on-execution,* which has a value of 010, and *set-user-ID-on-execution bit,* which has a value of 100. In OS X, these two operate solely on executable files that contain binary executable data (no #! scripts). If either of these modes is set on an executable, whenever that file runs, it will do so in the context of the owner and group assigned to it. Thus, if a program is owned by root and has setuid on, whoever runs that program will have root access (within the confines of that program). This is a bit of a scary thought, so use this capability with great care. Many a local privileged-escalation exploit has been born from the setuid bit.

You should understand one final aspect of POSIX permissioning in OS X: How the system deals with group assignment on newly created files and directories. Historically in OS X, when a user creates a file, that file will assume group ownership based on the creating user's primary group id. But with OS X 10.5, Apple introduced compliance with SUS3 (Single Unix Standard, version 3), which dictates that the group established to the new file will be inherited based on group ownership of the parent directory. This is a *much* better system, and produces a lot less frustration.

With this change, you can now use group permissions on directories to establish group-specific collaboration areas. There's just one small wrinkle in this plan. By default, OS X ships with a umask value of 022. When you create a file, the default mode is full privileges, 777, filtered by the 022 umask. To determine ultimate privileges, you simply subtract the number representing the umask from that of the privileges. So in this case, newly created filesystem objects will have a mode of 755 (777 minus 022), or rwxr-xr-x.

The main problem here is that middle octal, the group octal, which assigns read (r) and execute (e), but not write (w) rights. By default in OS X, newly created files are *not* group writeable. Failing to recognize this leads to serious permissions problems in a collaborative environment. Luckily, you can change the umask. To do so in OS X 10.5, simply run the umask command with the desired mode. In this case, we want rwxrwxr-x, so we use a umask of 002. The command for this is (brace yourself): umask 002.

Unfortunately, executing umask may not affect all running processes, and the result won't persist across reboots. To remedy the situation, we recommend using the launchd launchd-user.conf file found in /private/etc. To set this, simply run echo "umask 002" >> /private/etc/launchd-user.conf as root. That's it. Reboot and you're done.

You may also want to set this on your file servers as well. But depending on your environment and usage, though, this can have security implications, so proceed with caution. A better solution, at least with AFP, is to use either AFP inheritance or ACLs, as described in the next section.

If you're running OS X 10.4 or earlier, the process for changing the umask is slightly different. We recommend installing the program Umask Doctor and setting it to launch at login if you do not wish to do this programatically. This utility specifically performs this duty, and it works out pretty well. Alternatively, you can simply make the change via the defaults command run with root/sudo privileges:

defaults write /Library/Preferences/.GlobalPreferences NSUmask 2

Note, however, that the NSUmask value is actually a decimal representation of the octal umask, so you'll have to do a conversion. One approach is to revert to the binary representation of the umask and convert that to decimal. For example, in binary, the three octets of the umask 022 are 000, 010, and 010. Concatenated, they make the binary number 000010010, which is 18 decimal ($0 \times 2^0 + 1 \times 2^1 + 0 \times 2^2 + 0 \times 2^3 + 1 \times 2^4 = 18$) and that's the number to substitute for the NSUmask value. There's one other note: The programs that honor the NSUmask value always seem to run under GUIs. Not all third-party programs support this value, but generally the major players do.

So that my friends, is POSIX permissions in a nutshell. The system may seem somewhat limited, but really, you're limited only by your own ingenuity and the speed at which your fingers type. In a POSIX environment, groups and nested hierarchies are your friend.

Access Control Lists

Mac OS X 10.4 saw the introduction of ACLs, which have been continually refined. For a traditional Windows system administrator, ACLs are likely easier to work with than POSIX—ACLs match the permission options almost identically. In fact the OS X NFSv4 ACL format, is compatible with Windows ACLs.

An ACL is extensible, which allows you to assign very granular permissions to specific users and groups. It frees you from the constraints of the POSIX user/group/everyone paradigm and greatly simplifies permissions management. On top of their extensibility, ACLs also define numerous different access levels and inheritance capabilities, which allow for especially effective permissions hierarchies. The easiest way to manage ACLs on a file system is via the Server Admin application (Workgroup Manager in OS X 10.4). Figure 4-28 is showing the File Sharing tab.

Figure 4-28. *OS X Server Admin Screen, File Sharing tab*

You get to the File Sharing interface by highlighting the server container in the Server Admin List, then clicking on File Sharing. Here, you can browse your file systems or share points and assign both POSIX and ACL permissions. Server Admin is a great tool for modifying POSIX, but it groups read and execute privileges under a single Read selection.

You can modify POSIX owners and groups by dragging them into the respective slots and then choosing the appropriate level of permission for each. To create ACLs for users and groups, drag them into the ACL list and apply appropriate permissions. Apple has several basic presets for you to use: *Full Control*, *Read & Write*, *Read Only*, *Write Only*, and *Custom*. The company also provides numerous fine-grained access writes in four main categories: *Administration*, *Read*, *Write*, and *Inheritance*. To modify granular permissions, highlight the ACL, then click on the pencil below. Here are breakdowns of the categories:

Administration

The Administration section includes two permissions capabilities:

Change Permissions: Users who have this right can manage privileges on a file via POSIX or ACLs. They may also delete any ACLs on the file or folder, so assign this permission with caution. When using chmod to manage ACL's (discussed later), you grant the change permissions with the writesecurity privilege.

Change Ownership: Enabling this for a user lets that individual assume ownership of a file. However, that person can't transfer ownership to anyone else. To do so, a user must have root access. You grant the change ownership privilege with the chown permission when using the chmod utility.

Read Permissions

By checking the global read box, you ensure that users have the ability to traverse and list folders, as well as read file data and metadata stored via extended attributes. The Read section contains five specific permissions:

Read: The read privilege, when applied via ACLs, behaves similarly on both files and directories, letting users view the content of both. If you're working with ACLs from the command line, you grant this right using read for files and list for directories.

Execute: As with read, when applied using ACLs, execute acts similarly on both files and directories. From the command line, you grant this privilege using the execute permission for files and the search permission for folders.

Read Attribute: You grant this permission, using the readattr privilege, to let a user to view the data describing a file's characteristics, such as its permissions. You enable this permission with the readattr privilege.

Read Ext Attribute: This permission allows a user to read a file's extended-attribute data—file attributes not understood by the OS, such as information about the OS X quarantine system and disk-image checksums. Third-party software for metadata purposes. Extended attributes are also responsible for the data found under the More Info tab when you get information on a file. Use the readextattr permission to grant this right.

Read Permissions: Given this privilege, a user can view security information, such as ACLs or POSIX permissions, about a file or folder. To assign this right, use the readsecurity privilege.

Write Permissions

By checking the Global Write box in the ACL, you ensure that users have the ability to alter file data, however. But this is rarely useful without the ability to read the data as well. While write-only access on a directory can certainly be handy for creating a private drop box, we recommend that you do this via the POSIX everyone permission—its interface deals with the task better by displaying a custom drop box icon (if you've granted write access via an ACL without read, then the folder will show up with the red access-denied icon). The write-permissions category also allows users to create and modify file data, including file metadata stored via extended attributes. There are six specific write permissions, as shown here:

Write Attributes: This permission allows a user to change a file's attribute data.

Write Ext Attributes: Granting this right lets a user edit files' and folders' extended attribute data (extra information about a file's traits) as well as create new entries in that data. You'll rarely want to make such data user accessible, though. Software behind the scenes usually manipulates this data.

Write/Add Files: The write privilege, when applied via ACLs, behaves similarly on both files and directories. The permission no longer grants the ability to delete a file or create a new directory. These abilities are now bestowed by delete and append, respectively. When applying ACLs via the command line, you can use write on both directories and files, but on directories, it's ultimately interpreted as the add_file permission.

Delete: As noted in the information above about Write/Add Files, you now give users the right to eliminate files using the delete flag rather than write.

Append/Add Directories: This capability is a subset of the POSIX write capability. It allows users to create new directories and edit existing files. Note that to create new files, a user must have write privileges. Using chmod, from the command line, you assign the append/add directories privilege using append. The flag is interpreted as add_subdirectory.

Delete Child: This permission, which applies solely to directories, lets a user to delete sub items (provided the user has delete privileges for those items). The delete_child flag assigns the right.

Inheritance

This section applies solely to directories. You use inheritance to customize how permissions are inherited by a directory's children. For instance, if you apply ACL inheritance to just the first level of subfolders and files, new folders users create will inherit their parents' permissions, but items created inside the new folders will not. Likewise, by using the inheret_only flag, you can assign ACLs specifically for inheritance, but not have them apply to the parent object, which can be very useful. You control inheritance with the four separate rights in the following list:

Apply to this folder: When selected, the ACL will apply to this folder. Otherwise, the folder will have only_inherit permission, and the ACL will be active only on children that inherit the ACL.

Apply to Child Folders: When you activate this option, newly created child folders of the directory will inherit the ACL. Use the directory_inherit permission to grant this privilege.

Apply to Child Files: When enabled, this privilege will cause new files created in the directory to inherit the ACL. You use the file_inherit permission to grant this right.

Apply to All Descendants: If you activate this option, the inheritance properties of the directory will pass on to newly created directories; allowing for automated propagation of ACLs as users create additional directories and files. Otherwise, the directory you're currently attending to will have the limit_inherit privilege.

Knowing these basics allow you to better grasp Apple's presets: *Full Control* assigns read, write, and administration capabilities; *Read & Write* contains the permissions from each respective category. Likewise *Read Only* and *Write Only* are limited to their respective categories. When using Apple's presets, full inheritance applies to the folder and its children (both file and directory), as well as to inheritance of inheritance data.

Using chown and chmod to manage permissions

To change POSIX ownership of a file or folder, you use the chown utility. Its syntax is fairly straightforward:

chown *owner[:group] /path to file*

If all you're doing is changing ownership, you can omit the *:group* [the colon followed by the actual value for *group*]. Alternatively, you can use the chgrp command, which has similar syntax, if you merely want to change group ownership. To change ownership, you must either have granted the chown ACL right, or you must be running as root.

You can use chmod to manage both POSIX and ACL permissions. Realize, however, that managing ACL's from the command line can be a bit hairy—it's not for the faint of heart. In any case, first though, the basics. As demonstrated earlier, you can use chmod to modify POSIX permissions. The syntax is:

chmod [-R] mode */path to file*

As discussed in this chapter's section on fragmentation, the –R option, if used on a directory, applies the mode recursively to all descendents. To modify or create an Access Control Entry (an entry in an access control list) or ACE using chmod, you use the +a, and –a flags. For instance, to grant full control of file test.txt to the user hunterbj, run the command

```
chmod +a "hunterbj allow read,write,execute,delete,append,readattr,writeattr,↵
readextattr,writeextattr,readsecurity,writesecurity,chown" test.txt
```

Subsequently, you can view the ACLs on that file by passing the –e flag to ls as follows:

```
ls -ael test.txt
-rw-r--r--+ 1 hunterbj staff 0 Jul 9 00:56 test.txt
0: user:hunterbj allow read,write,execute,delete,append,readattr,writeattr,↵
readextattr,writeextattr,readsecurity,writesecurity,chown
```

Likewise, if you want to grant full control for a directory, run:

```
chmod +a "hunterbj allow list,add_file,search,delete,add_subdirectory,delete_child,↵
readattr,writeattr,readextattr,writeextattr,readsecurity,writesecurity,chown,↵
limit_inherit,only_inherit" testfolder
```

To remove an entire ACE, you can use the –a# flag followed by an index number, as shown in the first example below, which. Or, if you wish, you can remove only specific attributes as shown in the second command, which removes only delete privileges, leaving the others in place.

```
chmod –a# 0 test.txt
chmod –a "hunterbj allow delete"
```

When first applying ACLs or when making changes, you'll likely want to propagate what you've done to existing files and folders, since inheritance rules apply only at file- or folder-creation time. You can apply permissions recursively via the chmod –R +a command, but we'd recommended that you do this in Server Admin via its Propagate Permissions menu item, which you can find by clicking on the widget, shown previously in Figure 4-28, directly to the right of the pencil icon a bit above the bottom of the screen. With this method, descendant file-system objects will receive inherited, rather than explicit permissions.

When a large portion of your file system contains explicit permissions, management becomes harder. In addition, explicit permissions override inherited permissions, so you might end up with unexpected results. You can create inherited ACEs with chmod as well, though. You do so by using the +ai flag instead of the +a flag. For example, the following commands will set a non-inherited ACE on /MyAwesomeFolder, but will then recursively copy inherited ACE's to all descendants:

```
chmod +a "hunterbj allow read,write,execute,delete,append,readattr,writeattr,↵
readextattr,writeextattr,readsecurity,writesecurity,chown" /MyAwesomeFolder
chmod –R +ai "hunterbj allow read,write,execute,delete,append,readattr,writeattr,↵
readextattr,writeextattr,readsecurity,writesecurity,chown" /MyAwesomeFolder/*
```

> **TIP:** Due to the way that the chmod utility parses the ACE, using the documented syntax for chmod does not work correctly when used with user or group names that contain spaces in the shortname. This creates issues with many Active Directory groups. Fortunately, to get around this issue, you can use the colon as a delimiter. So, to assign an ACL for the group "MYCO\Mac Server Admins," the following syntax can be used: chmod +a 'MYCO\Mac Server Admins:allow:read,write,execute' /MyAwesomeFolder

You can also remove ACLs via the chmod's –N argument. Combined with –R, you can use chmod to recurse through directories and remove all ACLs. The command syntax is `chmod –RN /MyAwesomeFolder`

.DS_Store Files

In a number of environments that use SMB, AFP, and other file-sharing protocols with Mac OS X, Windows, and Linux clients, OS X leave a number of hidden files behind. If you've managed such environments, you've likely noticed the .DS_Store files and possibly even tried eliminating them. Try as you might, though, always seem to come back. Well, you don't have to live with them.

You can tell your Windows clients not to show hidden files. From Windows XP, open Windows Explorer from the Start menu, an icon, or via the command line (explorer.exe is the executable). Select the Tools menu, then *Folder Options...*, click on the View tab, then mark the *Do not show hidden files and folders* radio button. For Vista and up, open the Folder Options control panel, choose the View tab, and then select *Do not show hidden files and folders.*

If this proves unwieldy, though, you can prevent each Mac OS X user account from making the .DS_Store files. This isn't to say you should —OS X uses the files to track the view and icon placements of a folder. But if you need to get rid of the files, you need to get rid of them.... To do so, create a file called com.apple.desktopservices.plist in the ~/Library/Preferences folder of each user account. Its contents should be:

```
{
DSDontWriteNetworkStores = true;
}
```

The easiest way to go about this is on a single system is simple to run the following command for each user:

```
defaults write com.apple.desktopservices DSDontWriteNetworkStores true
```

If, however, you have a large number of clients and use Open Directory, you'll want to push out the com.apple.desktopservices.plist as a managed preference—or, for future users, you can drop the file into /System/Library/User Template/English.lproj/Library/Preferences. Now the file is part of the user template. We discuss managed preferences extensively in Chapter 7: Client Management. Note that after following this procedure, you should probably reboot. Also, though setting this option will keep new .DS_Store files from being generated on network volumes (aka network stores), it won't do so for local volumes, including those on an Xsan (since Xsan volumes are basically interpreted by the finder as local volumes, in this context).

Once you've disabled the creation of new .DS_Store files, you'll probably want to eliminate those already on the volume. Use the find command in conjunction with the -name and -exec flags followed by rm as (replacing *path to share* with the path to your actual share). Here's the syntax:

```
find /path to share -name .DS_Store -exec rm {} \;
```

For the command to process correctly, the account under which it's running must be able to access files in all folders of the tree where .DS_Store files may exist. If you find new .DS_Store files appearing after you've followed all these procedures, look at the owner of the new files. Typically you'll find that your procedure skipped that user's account.

Summary

In this chapter, we discussed how to implement storage solutions on your OS X clients using network protocols such as AFP, NFS, and SMB. This includes the traditional members of the Mac OS X storage ecosystem. We also covered Fibre Channel and connecting to iSCSI targets, but didn't delve deeply into providing non-Apple LUNs for either—attempting to show how to build a LUN for hundreds of products—those from EMC, HP, Hitachi, NetApp, Sun and a slew of other vendors isn't an effective use of anyone's time. Each vendor (and open-source project provider, if you prefer) will offer extensive documentation. The important knowledge to convey was how to deploy the solutions that can run on Apple iron.

The chapter heavily focused on SAN-based storage for a reason: Storage centralization and virtualization—made possible through SAN technologies—benefits IT departments by delivering immense flexibility and increased data management capabilities. Concurrent simultaneous access to data opens up a world of possibilities—clustered services, live backups over FC without saturating public networks or servers, and a cornucopia of other options. Additionally, storage virtualization allows for growth and expansion, adding performance or storage-based nodes as needed. SAN technology is at the center of the virtualization movement, and it's here to stay.

In the next chapter, we'll discuss various groupware options available to your OS X clients. We'll cover topics such as integrating with Exchange, Groupware, and Lotus Notes, as well as some Apple-hosted products such as iCal Server and Address Book Server. Where appropriate, we'll also discuss how to store back-end assets (if they're running on Mac OS X) on Xsan or other clustered Mac OS X file-storage offerings.

## Chapter 5

Messaging and Groupware

Groupware is one of the most important communication vehicles in the modern enterprise. Tracking what people are doing in shared calendars, whom your organization does business with in shared contacts, and communicating with them all with email are requirements today for any large organization. In fact, It goes a step further in that you need to extend the same functionallty you have at the desktop onto mobile devices, including, of course, the iPhone and iPod Touch.

For the purpose of this chapter, we will include messaging solutions as part of the overall groupware ecosystem. We do so because every conversation about shared contacts and calendars includes e-mail. Some even include instant messaging frameworks. Over the course of this chapter, we will cover the various solutions that have become common on the Mac OS X platform, starting with Microsoft Exchange.

There are a number of groupware platforms, each with varying degrees of compatibility with the Mac. Microsoft Exchange is clearly the most prevalent, so we'll spend more time in this chapter covering Exchange than any other solution. However, Exchange isn't the only solution out there. Lotus Notes, GroupWise, and a few others have become fairly common in enterprise organizations and so these are included as well.

But what if you want to be in a purely Mac OS X environment? Well, you can. We're not going to say that this will come with the same level of scalability, application functionality, cross-pollination among applications, and maturity that some of the other solutions (especially Microsoft Exchange) can provide, because it can't. The pure Mac solution is just not there yet. However, Snow Leopard does introduce some new features on the groupware front that certainly bring a first-party solution much closer to reality. Moreover, the Mac solution is worth exploring on a service-by-service basis, considering that licensing and complexity can cause many of the other solutions to come in at a much higher total cost of ownership for Mac clients than for their Windows counterparts.

Exchange Integration

Mac OS X can communicate with Microsoft Exchange in a variety of ways; most notable is its support for Outlook Web Access (OWA) from a web browser. But if you use Microsoft Exchange 2003 or earlier, you need to consider Entourage, an e-mail client and personal information manager from Microsoft. You can use POP or IMAP mail accounts with other solutions, or you can use Mail.app, iCal, and Address Book in an Exchange 2007 environment that you may already be leveraging. While not the only option, Entourage is a mature product for Exchange integration and the most widely adopted for such environments.

Exchange 2007 consists of a number of roles, each controlling the functionality that a server is able to offer to clients and to other Exchange servers. Most of the integration that will be done with Exchange will be done through the Client Access Server (CAS) role. For the most part, the technologies included in the CAS role existed in Exchange 2003 and earlier, but the idea of breaking Exchange into predefined roles, and the CAS role specifically, is new in Exchange Server 2007. One component of Exchange 2007 that does not exist in previous versions is the Exchange Web Services (EWS) API, which opens up a number of options, including Entourage for Exchange EWS (an Exchange 2007/EWS-optimized Entourage app), or using Mail.app to interface with Exchange. However, as yet adoption of Exchange 2007 has been relatively limited. In an Exchange 2003 environment, in many cases you will be able to leverage WebDAV, an extension to the http protocol, when connecting from an OS X client.

Entourage

Microsoft Entourage is a part of the Microsoft Office family of products that most environments have already deployed. Microsoft Entourage client licensing is not necessarily bundled with Exchange. Exchange 2003 and earlier do provide a license for a standalone Microsoft Entourage client; however, Exchange 2007 does not and so will require additional licensing.

If licensing is not an issue (for example, you already own Microsoft Office for your Mac clients), then Entourage should be considered as an option for your clients to connect to Exchange. Entourage has a look and feel that is fairly similar to Microsoft Outlook, and it has much of the same features (although not all), so a user coming to a Mac from a PC will find it easier. While Entourage 2004 supports Exchange, 2008 is highly recommended. It is worth noting that Microsoft has officially announced the death of Entourage and will be releasing Outlook for Mac (release date unknown).

NOTE: Microsoft Office 2008 for Mac Home, Student, and Teacher Editions do not contain Exchange support. You must connect over IMAP (and thus lose most groupware functionality).

Paths

One of the very first tasks to undertake when integrating Mac OS X into Microsoft Exchange is to log into Outlook Web Access. If you can log into OWA without issue, you should also be able to set up Entourage integration or even configure an iPhone or iPod Touch (as we describe further in Chapter 10).

In order to authenticate into WebDAV, you should be able to access the server over http or https. These are the same general paths (often dubbed virtual paths) you will use with Entourage. In Exchange 2003, the /exchange path handles mailbox access for both OWA and WebDAV, so it may appear as though they're the same protocol stack (they're not). In Exchange 2003, there are two other paths to consider: the /public path handles requests for public folders; the /exchweb path has resources that are used by OWA and WebDAV (and so still need to be accessible even if you don't typically type them in). You can also follow the paths with usernames in the form of the fully qualified e-mail addresses if you're receiving errors that you can't authenticate when you haven't yet been prompted for a password. The following are paths you may need to use to access OWA (which, in an Exchange 2003 environment, typically means you can also access WebDAV). In this example, we are accessing an Exchange server at the address exchange.krypted.com:

Mailbox access:

- https://exchange.krypted.com/exchange/username@domain.com
- https://exchange.krypted.com/owa
- https://exchange.krypted.com/exchweb
- https://exchange.krypted.com

Public Folder Access:

- https://exchange.krypted.com/public
- https://exchange.krypted.com/public/username@domain.com

In Exchange 2007 there can be even more paths, because Exchange 2007 has a lot more features. This is not to say that the paths mentioned above have been deprecated; in most cases they have not. Exchange provides support for these using legacy virtual directories (made possible by davex.dll) that should be able to handle Exchange WebDAV requests. However, the following are the mailbox-access URLs you may run into:

- https://exchange.krypted.com
- https://exchange.krypted.com/owa
- https://exchange.krypted.com/exchange
- https://exchange.krypted.com/exchweb

Overall, WebDAV integration is a safe bet, but there is a newer and better way: EWS. EWS leverages SOAP (Simple Object Access Protocol) to exchange data through XML, allowing for more developers to interact with Exchange. EWS is faster and chews through less bandwidth, adding synchronization support for categories and tasks (not otherwise provided by WebDAV). If you will be using Entourage for EWS or Mail.app, you will instead want to check for EWS connectivity, which is different from the paths previously mentioned. Possible URLs that you will see include:

- `https://exchange.krypted.com` (more than likely an administrator used a virtual directory to help shorten the path)
- `https://exchange.krypted.com/ews` (Exchange should throw a Directory Listing Denied error)
- `https://exchange.krypted.com/ews/Exchange.asmx` (the default setting)
- `https://exchange.krypted.com/ews/Serivces.wsdl` (a redirect to a blank page)

Once you have confirmed your paths you can move on to setting up the client application.

> **TIP:** Paths may also be followed by a colon and then the port number that the service is running on if a custom port has been used (`https://exchange.krypted.com:8443/ews`).

Troubleshooting Exchange 2007 Virtual Directories

In a number of deployments Entourage simply will not work, even though Outlook Web Access will authenticate users. To resolve this, we often use a series of Windows PowerShell commands. PowerShell is the command-line scripting language used for Windows Server 2008 and Exchange Server 2007 environments. To start off, we'll get a list of all of the virtual directories using the Get-OwaVirtualDirectory cmdlet without any operators:

```
Get-OwaVirtualDirectory
```

If you are having an issue with a specific virtual directory, you can delete it using this command:

```
Remove-OwaVirtualDirectory "owa (Default Web Site)"
```

The preceding command uses the owa virtual directory, but it could have used Exchange, Public, Exchweb or Exadmin as well. To re-create the directory, use the following command (again replacing owa in the quoted portion of the command with the specified virtual directory you are re-creating:

```
New-OwaVirtualDirectory -OwaVersion "Exchange2007• -Name "owa (Default Web Site)"
```

Because a virtual directory is just that, virtual, you will not encounter any problems from deleting it, except that while it is offline your clients who use it will not be able to connect to the server. Note that when you re-create the virtual directory, you will need to go into IIS and customize the permissions as defined by your organization's security policy before using the virtual directory again. The ability to delete virtual directories or, more importantly, to create new ones is a great help when troubleshooting connectivity issues. After you've created a new virtual directory, before you customize permissions, test Entourage. Then, after you customize the permissions, test Entourage again. Or, you may want to create an entirely new virtual directory without deleting the existing one during testing.

Because Exchange, Public, Exchweb and Exadmin are not native to Exchange 2007, you would actually replace Exchange2007 with Exchange2003or2000 for those directories. So if you wanted to re-create Exadmin, for example, you would use the following command

```
New-OwaVirtualDirectory -OwaVersion "Exchange2003or2000" -Name "Exadmin (Default Web Site)"
```

Entourage Setup

First, install Entourage, and feel free to accept the default values during installation. Once the application has been fully installed, proceed to updates, an option available through the Entourage Help menu, until the software is running the latest revision. If you will be automating the installation, read further for more information on doing so.

With the software installed, you can set up your first account. Though there is an account setup wizard that launches when you first open Entourage, we will walk through configuring an account manually (without having Entourage "locate" the server). If you do run the Entourage wizard, you will have to provide your domain. Note that Entourage does not automatically supply all of the different settings. Microsoft can attempt to autopopulate all the data it wants, but the fact is that in real world environments, very few DNS servers have the perfect records to do this. It's nothing that Microsoft has done wrong, just that some Active Directory environments have years of cruft hiding in their bowels. In some cases, you might see no other symptoms in your environment, except that Entourage would not automatically complete setup. That is, until you go to prep your domain for 2010 server.

To manually setup an account, click on the Tools menu and select Accounts to bring up the Accounts window, shown in Figure 5-1. Now click on the disclosure triangle to the right of the New icon and click on Exchange... You will see the Account Setup Assistant. Click on the *Configure Account Manually* button.

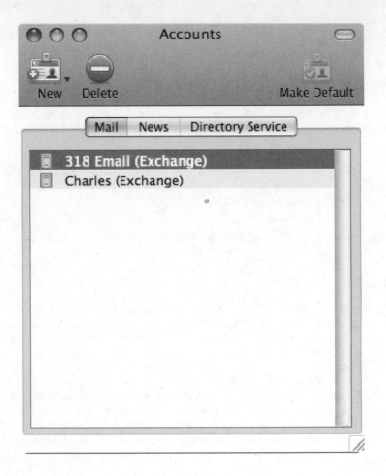

Figure 5-1. *The Entourage Accounts pane*

You should now see the Edit Account screen shown in Figure 5-2. Here, you can provide the most important Exchange account settings, which configure basic access to the server, as follows:

- *Account Name:* A name displayed within Entourage for keeping track of different accounts you install on the system.

- *Name:* The name displayed on outgoing messages.

- *E-mail Address:* The "reply-to" email address used in the message headers.

- *Use my account information:* Configure account settings for an account on the Exchange Server using information entered into Entourage.

  - *Account ID:* The unique username from Active Directory, used to, for example, authenticate into Outlook Web Access.

  - *Domain:* The Active Directory domain for your organization.

  - *Password:* The Active Directory password for the Account ID that resides on the domain.

  - *Save My Password in My Mac OS Keychain:* Saves the password to the Mac OS X keychain so the user doesn't have to enter it each time she initiates a session to the server.

- *Use Kerberos authentication:* Uses a Kerberos service principal to the Exchange Server to track account information. (Because it leverages single-sign on, it does not require a username and password.) Be careful using this type of authentication if your users travel and will not have VPN access; unless your key distribution center (KDC) is publicly accessible, clients will not be able to authenticate from remote networks.

  - *Kerberos ID:* Allows the user to select a previously joined Kerberos realm (which should be present if the node is bound to Active Directory and the user is authenticated into the local host as an Active Directory account) or to authenticate into a new realm.

- *Exchange Server:* The IP address or FQDN (fully qualified domain name) of the Exchange Server that houses the OWA role (that is, the front-end server in Exchange 2003 or the server with the CAS Role installed in Exchange 2007).

  - *This DAV service requires a secure connection (SSL):* This option forces an SSL connection. It is important to note that Entourage 2008 still uses the now deprecated X509Anchors keychain found at /Library/Keychains. Any custom CA certificates you add will need to be added to that keychain for Entourage to properly resolve the CA chain.

  - *Override default DAV port:* Use a port other than the defaults (which are 80 for standard http and 443 for https).

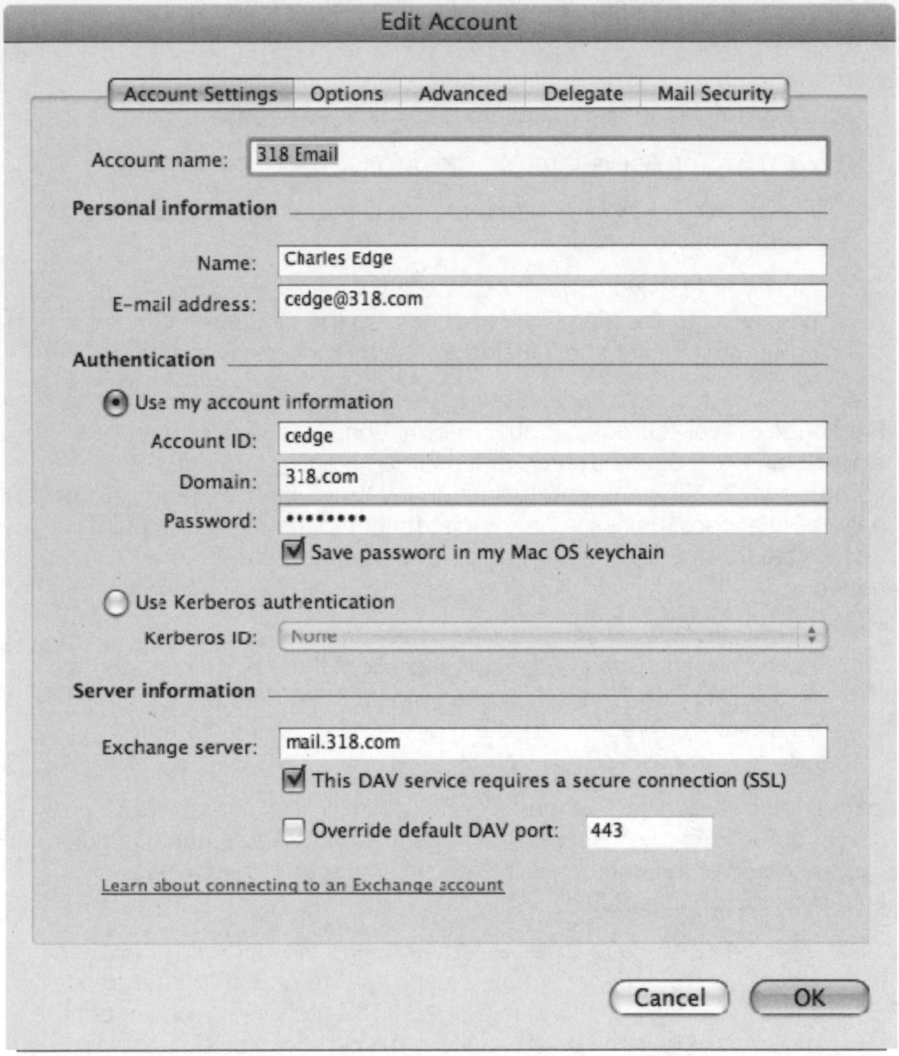

Figure 5-2. *Entourage Exchange account settings*

Once you are satisfied with your entries, click on the Advanced tab where you can configure access to public folders, directory services, such as the global address book, and certificates (see Figure 5-3).

Public Folder settings:

- *Public Folders server*: The IP address or host name of the server, sometimes followed by the path to the public virtual directory.

- *This DAV service requires a secure connection (SSL):* The public folder virtual directory requires SSL for access.

- *Override default DAV port:* Use a custom port number (if you had to append a : at the end of a URL to log into the web portal).

Directory Settings

- *LDAP server:* The IP address or host name of the server. LDAP is used for Global Address List (GAL) lookups. In some cases the Exchange server can be used, although you may need to use a domain controller instead. If lookups are slow for branch offices, consider using a localized global catalog server for that office.

- *This server requires me to log on:* If checked, Entourage will authenticate to the LDAP servers when performing lookups against the LDAP database.

- *This LDAP server requires a secure connection (SSL):* The server requires communication over an SSL port.

- *Override default LDAP Port:* Use a custom port number for LDAP access.

- *Maximum number of results to return:* The maximum number of results for a given LDAP query. This is similar to how the Active Directory plug-in returns a maximum number of objects, as described in Chapter 3. If you increase this number, lookups for addresses in the GAL could take longer, but you may need to increase it in large organizations if users have search issues.

- *Search base:* The search base of the domain. For most environments, this is not required. If the search base is needed, you should be able to obtain it from Active Directory. You can usually determine this value by performing an ldap search against one of your global catalogs:

```
ldapsearch -h myglobalcatalog.myco.com -x -a never -s base namingContexts
```

Client Certificate-based Authentication

- *Selecting a client certificate:* Pressing the select button opens a dialog box to choose an installed SSL certificate to use for authentication. If an appropriate certificate is not listed, you will need to add one into the keychain.

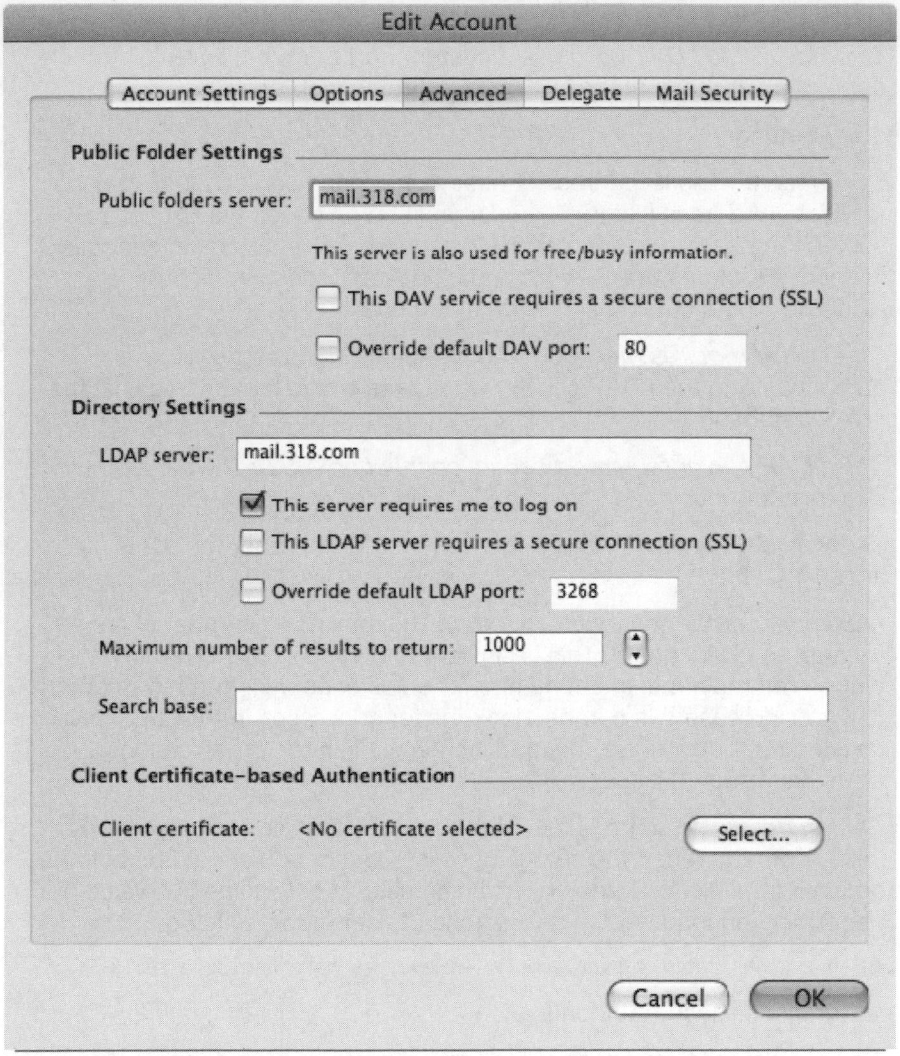

Figure 5-3. *Entourage Exchange account advanced settings*

One of the great features of Exchange is that users can configure who has access to
their information and rights to perform actions on their behalf. This is called delegation,
which Entourage supports. Once you have configured the initial account settings, as
required by your organization, you can go ahead and configure delegation. This is
where you can configure Entourage to allow you to send email as another user of the
organization or provide other users with access to send mail as the account being
configured. To configure access, as shown in Figure 5-4, select the Add button and then

select each user for whom access should be provided (or added to your send as options).

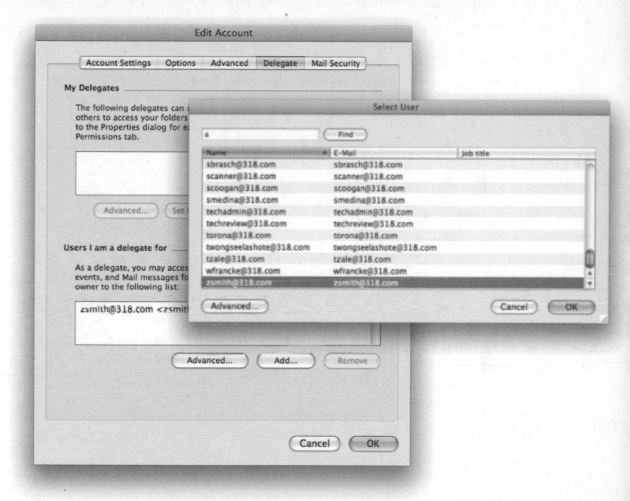

Figure 5-4. *Entourage account delegation user selection*

Finally click on the Mail Security tab to configure the digital signing and encryption options of Entourage (see Figure 5-5). Be sure to have any digital signatures you need (whether supplied by a public CA or by your own signing environment). Digitally signing objects allows for non-repudiation (the objects definitely came from you because only you have your private key). Encryption lets you encrypt all mail, so users who receive your mail will need a predefined web of trust with your e-mail in order to be able to view the contents of the message.

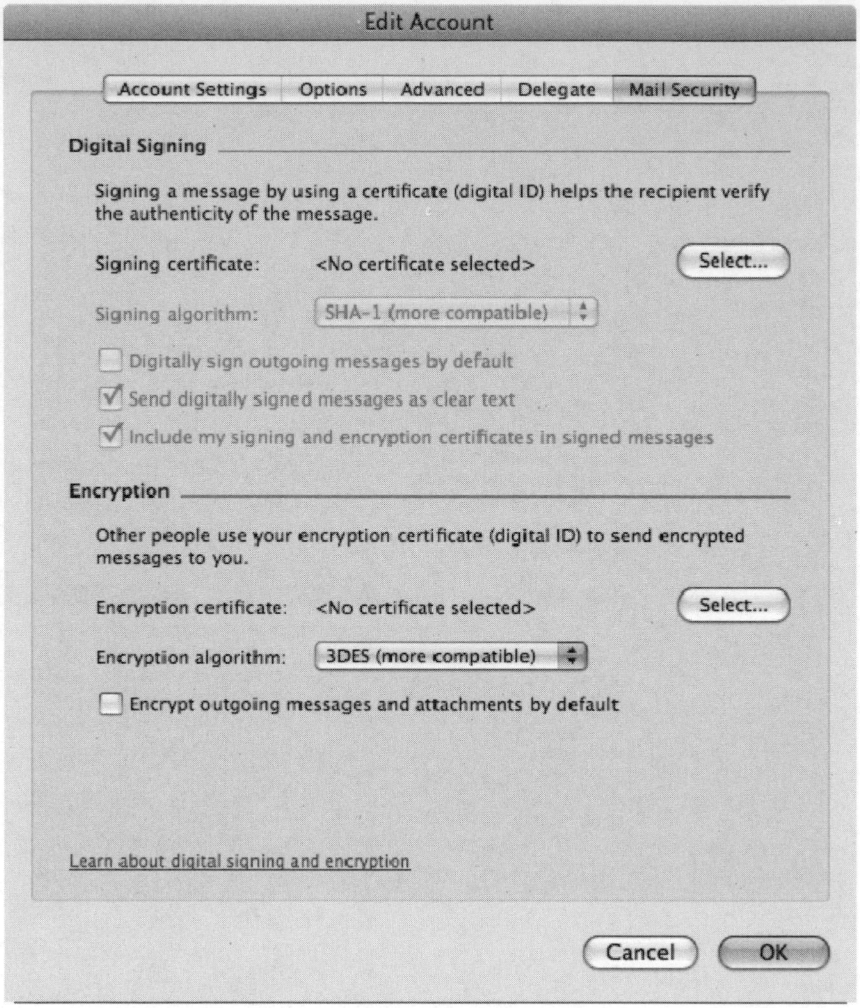

Figure 5-5. *Entourage Exchange account security options*

Automatic Client Configuration

In a large organization, you need to automate as much of the installation process as possible. Part of this automation might involve deploying the actual software, another part might be to customize the settings for the software, and finally, you may want to automate the account configuration for a user. These three tasks need to be viewed as three separate automations.

Deploying the Package

Microsoft Office comes with a built-in package installer. The installer is actually a metapackage (a collection of multiple packages bundled together) that can be installed automatically using the following command (assuming that the package is stored in a directory called /installers/ on your computer):

```
installer -applyChoiceChangesXML /installers/scripts/officeanswer -package ↵
"/installers/Office Installer.mpkg" -target /
```

If you have a volume license, the media should contain the serial numbers for your organization and you will need to do nothing more in regard to licensing. After installation, you no longer see the serial numbers but they do update a file called SetupInfo.plist that is stored in the /Applications/Microsoft Office 2008/Office directory. The contents of this file are as follows (substituting the character *1* to obfuscate my serial information):

```
<?xml version="1.0" encoding="UTF-8"?>
<!DOCTYPE plist PUBLIC "-//Apple Computer//DTD PLIST 1.0//EN" ↵
"http://www.apple.com/DTDs/PropertyList-1.0.dtd">
<plist version="1.0">
<dict>
        <key>SetupInfo</key>
        <array>
                <string>11111</string>
                <string>111-11111</string>
                <string></string>
                <string>Office 2008 for Mac</string>
                <string>111111</string>
                <string>0</string>
                <string></string>
                <string>1</string>
        </array>
</dict>
</plist>
```

You can take this file and add it to a target desktop as a postflight task, even on systems not installed with the original volume-keyed media, thus separating your Microsoft Office installation into two automations (one to deploy the package and another to establish the serial number). Alternatively, you could embed the serial number into the Office Installer package (.mpkg) file. To do so, you would place it into the Contents/PlugIns/ProductKey.bundle/Contents/Resources/Office/ subdirectory of the metapackage in the form of a file called SetupInfo.plist.

Custom Package Installation

While all of the components of the Microsoft Office package are installed by default, it doesn't have to be that way. You can deploy Microsoft Office using a custom set of items to be installed.

Microsoft Office has a number of choices you select from when you are going through the graphical installation process. These include the applications to install, the language packs, fonts, automator actions, and the Dock items that get placed into the Dock on installation.

To remove various options, you can use the installer command as before, only this time the –applyChoiceChangesXML option is followed by an answer file. The answer file contains a number of keys that, when included, will tell the Office package what *not* to install. The contents of the answer file can contain the following keys (although you don't want to use them all):

```
<array>
        <string>word</string>
        <string>excel</string>
        <string>powerpoint</string>
        <string>entourage</string>
        <string>messenger</string>
        <string>proofing-tools</string>
                <string>danish</string>
                <string>dutch</string>
                <string>finnish</string>
                <string>french</string>
                <string>german</string>
                <string>italian</string>
                <string>japanese</string>
                <string>norwegian</string>
                <string>portuguese</string>
                <string>brazilian</string>
                <string>spanish</string>
                <string>swedish</string>
        <string>fonts</string>
        <string>automator</string>
        <string>dock</string>
</array>
```

Running the Microsoft Office installer package with all of the items disabled (as would the above file would do, would be a fairly pointless venture. Therefore, we'll disable only the non-English options in proofing tools and Microsoft Messenger. To do this, you would first build an appropriate XML file containing each of the items you wish to deactivate from the preceding list. Disabling the non-English proofing tools and Messenger would mean a file with the following contents:

```
<array>
        <string>messenger</string>
        <string>proofing-tools</string>
                <string>danish</string>
                <string>dutch</string>
                <string>finnish</string>
                <string>french</string>
                <string>german</string>
                <string>italian</string>
                <string>japanese</string>
                <string>norwegian</string>
                <string>portuguese</string>
                <string>brazilian</string>
                <string>spanish</string>
                <string>swedish</string>
</array>
```

Once the file is built you can save it. (For this example, the file was saved as /installers/scripts/officeanswer.) You can then use the following command to run the installer, taking into account the "choices" defined earlier:

```
installer -package "/installers/Office Installer.mpkg" -target /
```

Account Setup

You can also automate the setup of the actual Exchange account by leveraging AppleScript. To do so, you could have a login item that checks whether the AppleScript has been run and runs it if it has not, or you could add that logic into the script. However you choose to push out the AppleScript, it is worth noting that you can control Entourage to a large degree using AppleScript events. To get started, open the AppleScript editor of your preference and enter the following:

```
tell application "Microsoft Entourage"
        make new Exchange account with properties {name:"My Exchange Account", Exchange ↩
ID:"jdoe", domain:"myco.com", full name:"John Doe", email address:"jdoe@myco.com", search ↩
base:"dc=myco,dc=com", Exchange server
settings:{address:"https://mail.myco.com/exchange", ↩
requires SSL:true, port:443}, public folder server settings:{address:" ↩
https://mail.myco.com/public", requires SSL:true, port:443}, LDAP server ↩
settings:{address:"ldap.myco.com", LDAP requires authentication:true, requires SSL:true, ↩
port:636, maximum entries:1000}}
end tell
```

This AppleScript could be set up to launch when a user logs in and then to self-destruct. You can even add some code to pull data from the environment using the shell command whoami, or continue with AppleScript using the following:

```
tell application "System Events"
        set shortName to name of current user
        set fullName to full name of current user
end tell
```

Using these values, you can then properly set the display name for the account, the user's short name (used for authentication), as well as populate the user's Full Name record, which is used for displaying a friendly From: name when sending emails (such as John Doe rather than jdoe@myco.com). Instead of a login item, you can also call the AppleScript using the osascript command. However, because this AppleScript is configuring a userland application, it requires an active user session to run. Because of this, a login item is generally the best avenue for this type of deployment. Alternatively, a LaunchAgent could be used (discussed in Chapter 8).

Postflight Tasks

Assuming the serial number was deployed with the initial package, there should be only a few things remaining to complete your Office for Mac deployment and allow you to use Entourage effectively. The first is to suppress the Microsoft First Run dialog box, present by default following an installation (and usually causing a great number of calls to support teams unless suppressed).

The Office Setup Assistant will present you with a number of questions as part of the Microsoft First Run process. In order to suppress this you will need to add a key to the com.microsoft.office property list stored in ~/Library/Preferences/com.microsoft.office.plist. Here, we'll provide a key of 2008\FirstRun\SetupAssistCompleted with an integer of 1 as the value for the key, which indicates that the Setup Assistant has been completed. To do so, we'll use the defaults command and write the key information into the com.microsoft.office defaults domain as follows:

```
defaults write com.microsoft.office "2008\\FirstRun\\SetupAssistCompleted" -int 1
```

We could also have added the com.microsoft.office.plist into the Managed Client environment in Workgroup Manager, as we describe doing in Chapter 7. Once done, keys can be pushed out to these property lists quickly and easily from the centralized directory service. In addition to managing the FirstRun process with com.microsoft.office.plist, you can also use preference files com.microsoft.Excel.plist, com.microsoft.Powerpoint.plist, com.Microsoft.Word.plist and com.microsoft.autoupdate2.plist to customize various settings for Microsoft Office, including autoupdates, toolbars, default file formats, and providing a means for users to have their unique information placed into the file by default.

Once you have deployed Microsoft Entourage, there will likely be times when you need to alter the settings for the client. For example, you might want to supply a Name to the registration information. For this, you can deploy a custom plist file to all of your users. To do this, you need to set up your admin client with the configuration you'd like to push out. Click on the plus (+) sign in Workgroup Manager and browse to a configured user's Library folder. From here, navigate into Preferences, folder, Microsoft, and then finally Office 2008. Inside of this folder resides the Microsoft Office 2008 Settings.plist file. Once you've imported this file, change *Manage import preferences* to *Often*, double-clicking on Microsoft Office 2008 Settings. Open the disclosure triangle for Often and then change the string for the 1000 value to what you want the 'Registered To' name to be. Then save and test, logging in as the user to see if the managed setting was applied. See Chapter 7, Client Management, for more information on deploying preference files.

> **TIP:** You can also set the 1600 field in the same file to match the company name from the registration dialog.

AutoUpdate

Microsoft Office includes Office AutoUpdate, which runs independently of Software Update. Many environments will control patch deployment to users, in order to proactively keep help desk calls from rolling in as patches are applied (user questions about why Office is asking for update, plus potential support issues arising from a deployed update can be lethal). Additionally, all Microsoft patches for Office for Mac are now bundled with previous patches, so many of the updates are fairly substantial in size, which can chew through your bandwidth.

If you have another vehicle to deploy the Microsoft patches (like Jamf or ARD), you can disable AutoUpdate using the defaults command to write the *HowToCheck* key into the com.microsoft.autoupdate.plist file as follows:

```
defaults write com.microsoft.autoupdate HowToCheck -string "Manual"
```

Similarly, you can push out the com.microsoft.autoupdate domain prefs through MCX, Apple's built in client management system (discussed further in Chapter 7). You'll find this preference file at ~/Library/Preferences/com.microsoft.autoupdate.plist

Disable Sync Services

Microsoft Entourage's Sync feature can be a bit problematic for certain environments. While administrators can disable the feature, users often simply turn it back on. But you can turn it off programmatically if you wish. The settings are stored in ~/Library/Preferences/com.microsoft.entourage.syncservices.plist. To read the contents of the com.microsoft.entourage.syncservices domain, use the following command:

```
defaults read com.microsoft.entourage.syncservices
```

Your results will be similar to the following:

```
{
"sync calendar" = 1;
"sync contacts" = 1;
"sync notes" = 1;
"sync tasks" = 1;
}
```

The above is an array with boolean values for each item. Changing the 1's to 0's will disable syncservices. To do this, you would use the following command:

```
defaults write com.microsoft.entourage.syncservices '{"sync calendar" = 0;"sync ↵
contacts" = 0;"sync notes" = 0;"sync tasks" = 0;}'
```

> **TIP:** You can then resend the array using a 1 in place of a 0 to enable each item individually.

Archiving Mail

Microsoft Entourage does not provide a built-in mechanism for archiving mail. Microsoft Exchange does and one of the best ways to effectively implement mail archiving for users is to leverage the built-in Exchange functionality. However, for one reason or another, a number of sites are unwilling or unable to do so.

In a Microsoft Outlook environment, you may have automated archival to .pst files and possibly saved those .pst files onto a network share where they could be backed up. In Entourage, you can move mail to the local database, but this can be problematic as the database can't be backed up while open, it becomes bloated over time, and the file is not readable by non-Apple-based client computers. If you want to archive within Entourage but not on the server-side, look into the shareware application Entourage Email Archive X, found at http://www.softhing.com/eeax.html. Alternatively, Apple provides a mirror of the software:

http://www.apple.com/downloads/macosx/email_chat/entourageemailarchivex.html.

Native Groupware Support

OS X traditionally has not had a strong first-party groupware presence. Traditionally groupware inherent-apps, such as Address Book, iCal, and Mail, were largely consumer-oriented and, as such, did not participate well in groupware-oriented environments. This statement holds a little less true for Apple's Mail app, which does support prominent email protocols. With 10.5, Apple began to show its intention to address the issue with the introduction of iCal server and iCal's support of the CalDAV standard.

Let's face it though, when talking groupware the 800 lb. Gorilla in the room is Microsoft Exchange, and in 10.5, more often than not, that will mean you will be using Entourage to leverage these services. 10.5's native toolset just didn't cut it when Exchange was in the picture. With the introduction of 10.6, Apple has made some significant strides toward addressing this issue. Native Exchange support in 10.6 includes full support for Exchange email, calendaring, contact, and GAL access. Each respective function in 10.6 is provided via a dedicated app: Mail, iCal, and Address Book. Each application leverages Exchange Web Service (EWS) for integration, which provides excellent feature compatibility, but it also comes burdened with a very significant gotcha: EWS is a relatively new technology, one which is only supported in Exchange 2007 or later. If Exchange 2003 or earlier powers your environment's groupware presence, have your Entourage installers handy as you will likely find OS X's native support lacking even in 10.6. When Exchange 2007 is in the picture however, Apple's solutions are certainly worth a look.

Manual Setup

Mail.app includes support for, well, email, and does the job adequately, though it does lack support for some fringe features, such as setting out-of-the-office status. For these, users will regrettably need to take a trip to webmail. Notably, it includes support for separate internal and external servers, with the ability to specify custom paths for each, a boon for any environments that utilize a private internal domain namespace.

To configure Mail.app to connect to an Exchange Server, startup the app and open its Preferences, found under the Mail menu. With the preferences window open, select the accounts tab and click the plus button in the bottom-left corner to create a new account. As shown in Figure 5-6, in the resulting window, enter the full name, email address, and password for the desired account. In the next window, also shown in Figure 5-6, specify the account description, the incoming mail server, and the account credentials. This dialog also includes two checkboxes, allowing you to also set up

Address Book and iCal. Because of this capability, it is desirable to configure Exchange accounts from Mail.app, unless you are looking to implement only a particular service.

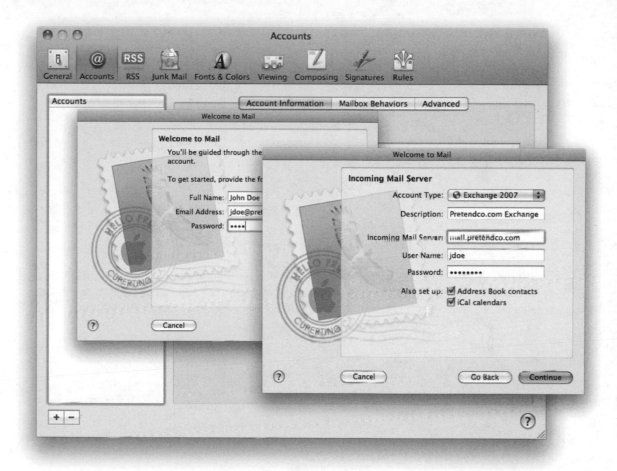

Figure 5-6. *Configure Exchange in Mail.app*

Once the account has been set up, it will be listed in the Mail accounts list. From here, you can highlight the account and edit further details, such as configure a separate server and path for internal vs external access, as shown in Figure 5-7.

TIP: Though Exchange contact and GAL access is provided via Address Book, Mail will search both when entering email recipients.

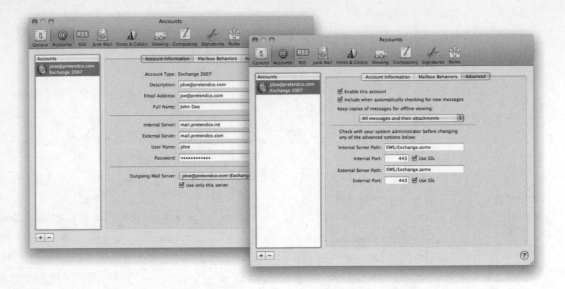

Figure 5-7. *Configure Separate Internal and External Servers in Mail.app*

As previously mentioned, new to iCal in 10.6 is Exchange support (see Figure 5-8), and the app sports decent capabilities, including support for free/busy schedules, to-dos, invitations, file attachments, and delegation.

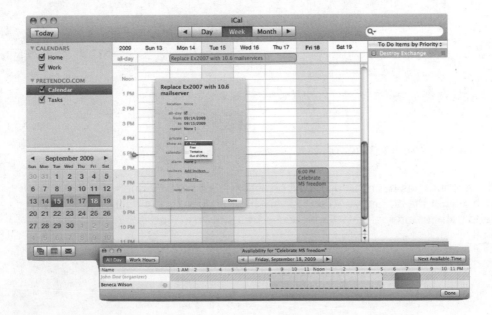

Figure 5-8. *Exchange Support in iCal*

Address Book provides support for Exchange contacts and allows for searching of the Exchange GAL. When an Exchange account is configured in Address Book, the account will be listed in the left-hand pane. Additionally, the configured account will have a new entry placed under the "Directory" group, which allows for searching of the GAL, as shown in Figure 5-9.

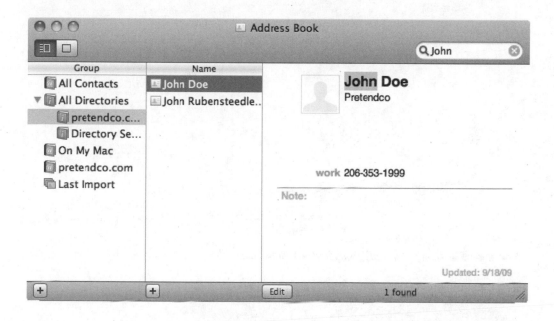

Figure 5-9. *Searching the GAL in Address Book*

As mentioned, it is possible to configure Exchange accounts both in iCal or Address Book without configuring a mail account. To perform this operation in either program, open up Preferences from the application's menu (the iCal and Address Book menu) and select the accounts tab. Similar to the procedure show in Figure 5-6 for mail, click on the plus button in each respective app's accounts pane to add a new account. In each case, select Exchange 2007 as the account type and enter the appropriate settings. Similar to the account setup in Mail.app, when configuring Exchange accounts in Address Book or iCal you have the option to automatically configure the Exchange account for all groupware apps, similar to how the Mail.app process can set up Address Book and iCal. Figures 5-10 and 5-11 show configured accounts in both apps, respectively. Similar to Mail.app's support, both Address Book and iCal support separate entries for internal and external servers. In Figure 5-11, shown also is the delegation tab, which is where users can configure delegate calendars to display or can also control which users can see their own.

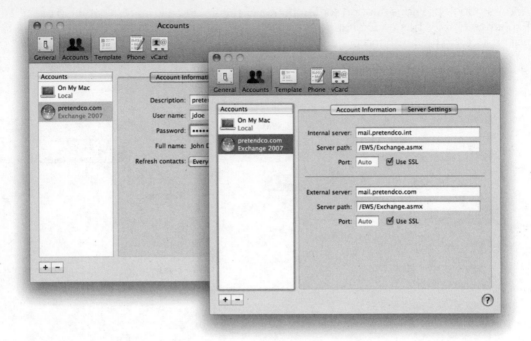

Figure 5-10. *Exchange Accounts configured in Address Book*

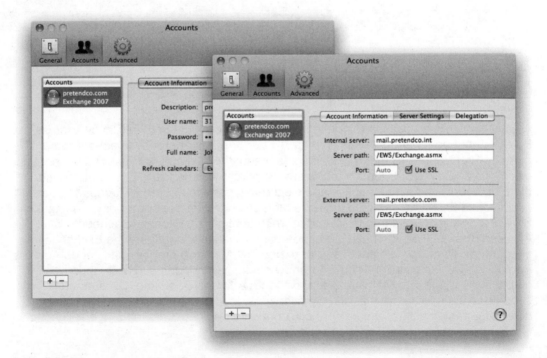

Figure 5-11. *Exchange Accounts Configured in iCal*

GroupWise and Lotus Notes

Novell's GroupWise has a client for Mac OS X, which can be obtained from `http://download.novell.com/index.jsp`. While Novell does continue to make the GroupWise client for Mac, at the time of this writing, official support is limited to OS X v.10.4. Based on our testing, it will need an update to be a viable solution in a 10.6 environment.

> **TIP:** Lotus Notes also has a client for Mac OS X. It can be obtained from `http://www.ibm.com/developerworks/downloads/`.

Both Lotus Notes and GroupWise are considered edge cases. However, they both continue to support the Mac OS X platform. This isn't to say that their clients will support each new operating system and that patches will not occasionally cause the software to stop working. But that's why you should always run patches in a lab first and perform the necessary regression testing.

iCal Server

So far in this chapter we have focused on using Mac OS X as a client to other solutions. Now we're going to shift gears a little and talk about using an entirely Apple-based groupware solution. The first step on this journey is using iCal Server to supply shared calendars to users. To do this, you will need an Open Directory environment, or at a minimum, augment records to another directory service. The augments will be created automatically if you first set up your OS X server in WorkGroup mode, bind to your directory service, and then use the Server Preferences tool rather than Server Admin to perform the setup.

iCal Server uses CalDAV, an extension of the WebDAV protocol that Microsoft Entourage can use to interface with Exchange. CalDAV is a well-defined open standard and so developing around it is in no way a black box. However, it is not as widely dispersed as Microsoft Exchange and so there are fewer tools that integrate with it. Still, nothing is likely to work better with iCal Server than the iCal client itself, included by default with all Mac OS X installations. Alternative clients include open source programs Mozilla Sunbird and the Mulberry email and calendaring application. Additionally, there are several third-party Outlook plug-ins available, though they tend to perform as second-class citizens.

Setting up iCal Server

To get started with iCal Server, first install the service. On a freshly installed Mac OS X Server that is either running as a directory server or already bound to one, open the Server Preferences application. Server Preferences can be found at /Applications/Server and when opened looks far less intimidating than Server Admin (see Figure 5-12). This is because Server Preferences is a fairly dummied down version of Server Admin.

To enable the iCal service, click on the orb just to the left of the iCal icon. Then, as shown in Figure 5-13, click on the *Limit each calendar event's size to:* field and provide a number (in megabytes for the maximum size of a calendar event, keeping in mind that calendar events can contain attachments). Next, click on *the Limit each user's total calendar size to:* field and provide a maximum per user. If you will not be using attachments, you can use a number around one megabyte or smaller, at which point storage becomes a minimal issue. Next, move the slider to the *On* position and the service will start up.

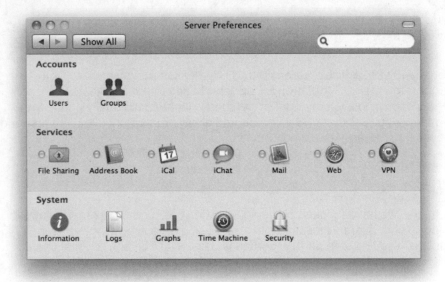

Figure 5-12. *The Server Preferences application*

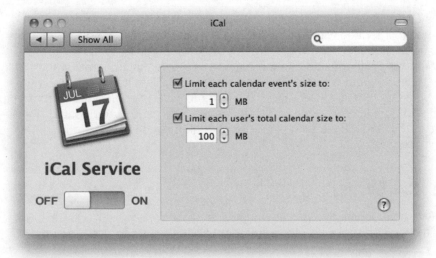

Figure 5-13. *Enabling iCal service using Server Preferences*

At this point you might be saying to yourself, "that can't be all there is." Well, you're right. You can use the iCal service in Server Admin in order to more granularly configure settings, as shown in Figure 5-14. To set up the iCal service from the Server Admin tool, click on the name of the server in the SERVERS list and then on the Settings icon. Next, click on the check box next to the iCal entry and you should see the iCal service appear in the SERVERS list underneath the name of the servers when you click on the Save button.

Now click on the iCal server entry and you will see a number of options, including:

- *Data Store:* The location on the server's file system for the iCal database.

- *Maximum Attachment Size:* The maximum size of a given attachment (and therefore the maximum size of a given event).

- *User Quota:* The maximum size of a user's calendar.

- *Authentication:* The authentication method used—Digest, Kerberos or Any Method. (Forcing to Kerberos or Digest can be useful in troubleshooting or to enforce encryption policies.)

- *Host Name:* The DNS name of the server (or service if you have multiple records pointing to the host).

- *SSL:* Allows you to select a certificate that has been installed on the host. Even if you are using a self-assigned certificate on the Mac OS X Server, you should use SSL when possible.

- *HTTP Port Number:* The port number that the HTTP iCal Service's listener uses.

- *SSL Port Number:* The port number that the SSL iCal Service's listener uses.

- *Log Level:* The verbosity with which you want the iCal server to trap event logs.

- *Push Notification Server:* By default this will list the current server, but it can be used to select another host in high-volume environments. The Push Notification Server enables the most seamless interaction between iPhone and Mac OS X Server's groupware services offerings. More on Push Notification later in this chapter.

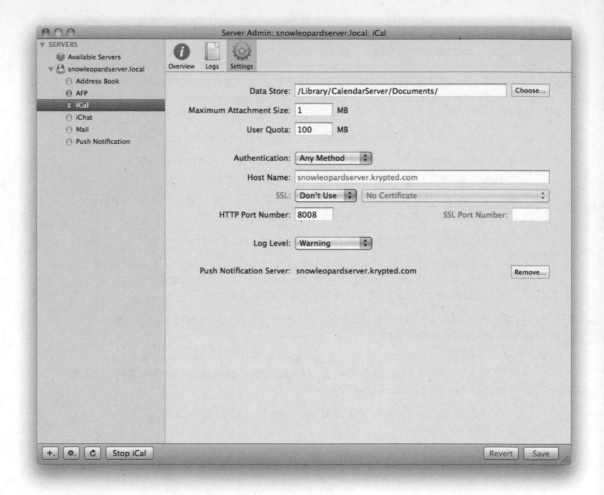

Figure 5-14. *Configuring the iCal service using Server Admin*

Once you are satisfied with your settings, click on the Save button to start up the service. Again, you may be thinking, "that can't be all the options, can it?" Again, you'd be correct. In addition to the two GUI panels developed by Apple, there are a host of other options that can be accessed using the `serveradmin` command. To see the available settings, use this:

```
serveradmin settings calendar
```

You will then see the following items:

```
calendar:SudoersFile = "/etc/caldavd/sudoers.plist"
calendar:DirectoryService:params:restrictEnabledRecords = no
calendar:DirectoryService:params:restrictToGroup = ""
calendar:DirectoryService:params:cacheTimeout = 30
calendar:DirectoryService:params:node = "/Search"
calendar:DirectoryService:type = "twistedcaldav.directory.appleopendirectory.↵
```

```
OpenDirectoryService"
calendar:Aliases = _empty_dictionary
calendar:BindSSLPorts = _empty_array
calendar:EnablePrincipalListings = no
calendar:DocumentRoot = "/Library/CalendarServer/Documents/"
calendar:EnableDropBox = yes
calendar:SSLPrivateKey = ""
calendar:ServerStatsFile = "/var/run/caldavd/stats.plist"
calendar:ProcessType = "Combined"
calendar:UserName = "calendar"
calendar:BindHTTPPorts = _empty_array
calendar:EnableAnonymousReadRoot = yes
calendar:HTTPPort = 8008
calendar:ServerHostName = ""
calendar:PIDFile = "/var/run/caldavd.pid"
calendar:Authentication:Digest:Algorithm = "md5"
calendar:Authentication:Digest:Qop = ""
calendar:Authentication:Digest:Enabled = yes
calendar:Authentication:Kerberos:ServicePrincipal = ""
calendar:Authentication:Kerberos:Enabled = yes
calendar:Authentication:Wiki:Enabled = yes
calendar:Authentication:Basic:Enabled = no
calendar:ReadPrincipals = _empty_array
calendar:EnableTimezoneService = yes
calendar:FreeBusyURL:AnonymousAccess = no
calendar:FreeBusyURL:Enabled = yes
calendar:FreeBusyURL:TimePeriod = 14
calendar:UserQuota = 104857600
calendar:MaximumAttachmentSize = 1048576
calendar:MultiProcess:ProcessCount = 0
calendar:EnableProxyPrincipals = yes
calendar:DefaultLogLevel = "warn"
calendar:EnableMonolithicCalendars = yes
calendar:ErrorLogFile = "/var/log/caldavd/error.log"
calendar:SSLCertificate = ""
calendar:EnableSACLs = no
calendar:Notifications:CoalesceSeconds = 10
calendar:Notifications:Services:XMPPNotifier:Host = "snowleopardserver.krypted.com"
calendar:Notifications:Services:XMPPNotifier:JID = "com.apple.notificationuser@↵
snowleopardserver.krypted.com"
calendar:Notifications:Services:XMPPNotifier:Enabled = yes
calendar:Notifications:Services:XMPPNotifier:Service = "twistedcaldav.notify.↵
XMPPNotifierService"
calendar:Notifications:Services:XMPPNotifier:Port = 5222
calendar:Notifications:Services:XMPPNotifier:ServiceAddress = "pubsub.↵
snowleopardserver.krypted.com"
calendar:EnableAnonymousReadNav = no
calendar:DataRoot = "/Library/CalendarServer/Data/"
calendar:BindAddresses = _empty_array
calendar:AdminPrincipals = _empty_array
calendar:RedirectHTTPToHTTPS = no
calendar:RotateAccessLog = no
calendar:GroupName = "calendar"
calendar:EnablePrivateEvents = yes
calendar:AccessLogFile = "/var/log/caldavd/access.log"
```

```
calendar:Scheduling:CalDAV:EmailDomain = ""
calendar:Scheduling:CalDAV:HTTPDomain = ""
calendar:Scheduling:CalDAV:AddressPatterns = _empty_array
calendar:Scheduling:iSchedule:Servers = "/etc/caldavd/servertoserver.xml"
calendar:Scheduling:iSchedule:Enabled = no
calendar:Scheduling:iSchedule:AddressPatterns = _empty_array
calendar:Scheduling:iMIP:Receiving:Server = ""
calendar:Scheduling:iMIP:Receiving:UseSSL = yes
calendar:Scheduling:iMIP:Receiving:PollingSeconds = 30
calendar:Scheduling:iMIP:Receiving:Username = ""
calendar:Scheduling:iMIP:Receiving:Type = ""
calendar:Scheduling:iMIP:Receiving:Password = ""
calendar:Scheduling:iMIP:Receiving:Port = 995
calendar:Scheduling:iMIP:MailGatewayServer = "localhost"
calendar:Scheduling:iMIP:Enabled = no
calendar:Scheduling:iMIP:MailGatewayPort = 62310
calendar:Scheduling:iMIP:AddressPatterns = _empty_array
calendar:Scheduling:iMIP:Sending:Server = ""
calendar:Scheduling:iMIP:Sending:Username = ""
calendar:Scheduling:iMIP:Sending:Address = ""
calendar:Scheduling:iMIP:Sending:UseSSL = yes
calendar:Scheduling:iMIP:Sending:Password = ""
calendar:Scheduling:iMIP:Sending:Port = 587
```

Many of these settings appear fairly cryptic, but you'll find they allow for very granular configuration of the service. You can customize these items by using the same command and but pasting the particular setting on to the end of it, along with the desired value. For example, if you want to force all users who can authenticate into the iCal service to have an account in the directory services, you would use the following command:

```
serveradmin settings calendar:DirectoryService:params:restrictEnabledRecords = yes
```

> **TIP:** You can further reduce the maximum attachment size to the bytes level using the `calendar:MaximumAttachmentSize` setting.

Managing Calendars

Once you have enabled the iCal service, you will want to provide access to calendars for your users. To do so, you can enable the service for an account, again using the Server Preferences tool. Simply open Server Preferences and click on the name of a user you'd like to configure and you'll see a listing of services the user can access on the right side of the screen as in Figure 5-15.

Figure 5-15. *Enabling services for users*

The next step is to set up iCal on the user's workstation. To get started, open iCal from the /Application directory, then click on the iCal menu, selecting the preference option (or use the Command+comma keystroke). Next, click on the Accounts icon in the application preferences toolbar and then on the plus (+) sign. You will see the Add an Account screen where you can fill in the name, e-mail address, and password of the user whose account you are setting up (see Figure 5-16). Click on the Create button when you are finished.

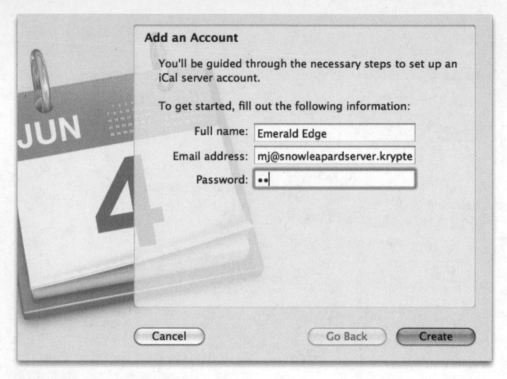

Figure 5-16. *Creating an iCal account*

The server will now look up the account type and automatically fill it in for you (see Figure 5-17). If it can't find an account type, it will automatically select CalDAV. (iCal supports both Exchange 2007 and CalDAV.) Next, fill in the Description field with a name that will appear in iCal for the calendar and then fill in the Account URL, which should generally be http:// or https:// followed by the name of the server and then the calendar in question, (for example, `http://myserver.com/calendarname`). Next, supply the username and password for the user whose calendar was just enabled, clicking on the Create button when you are ready to move to the next screen. If you are in a Kerberized environment, you can click on the *Use Kerberos v5 for authentication* check box to enable Kerberos access (standard Kerberos considerations apply).

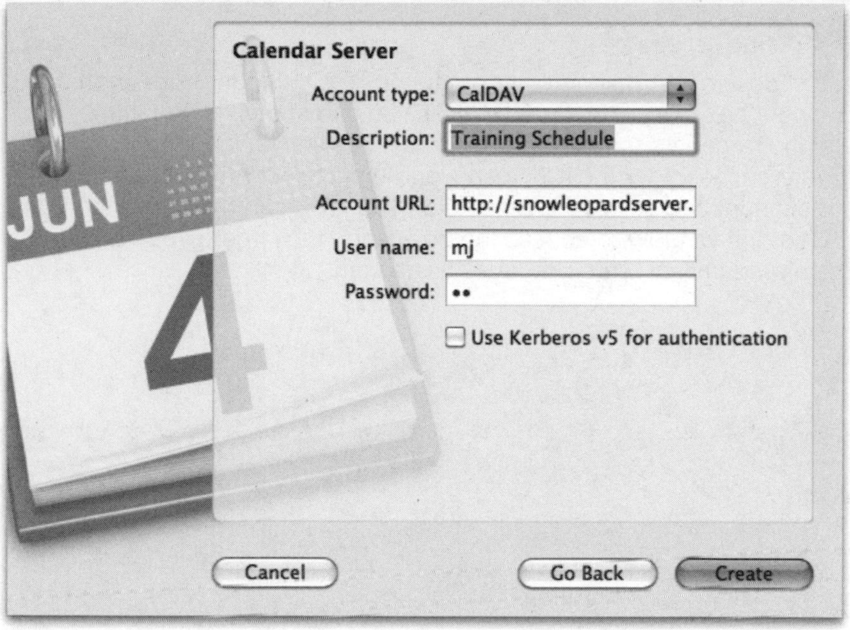

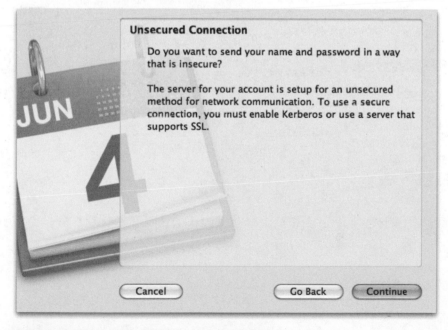

Figure 5-17. *iCal account creation connection information*

If you don't enable Kerberos or SSL, you will be prompted as to whether you want to use an unsecured connection. Now you can click on the Continue button to complete the setup of your server as seen in Figure 5-18.

Figure 5-18. *iCal account creation security confirmation.*

Delegating Access

Using iCal Server, it is possible to delegate access to a user's calendar from another user. Once your account has been configured in iCal, you can access delegation capabilities through the Accounts tab of iCal preferences, as shown in Figure 5-19. With iCal open, select Preferences under the iCal menu, and then select Accounts. From here, highlight your account and select the Delegation Tab. You can then click the Edit button at the bottom of the window to access the delegation tab, where you can add users and grant them read only or write privileges as desired.

Figure 5-19. *Delegating calendar access*

Backing up Calendars

The calendar file itself is located by default in the /Library/CalendarServer/Documents directory. You can customize this folder, so when you're going to back it up, be careful that no one has changed the default location. Simply backing up the contents of this directory with standard software will provide an archive of the data. You can verify the directory used by your Calendar store by running the command:

```
serveradmin settings calendar:DocumentRoot
```

However, you may choose to back up the settings for the service as well. To do so, you can use the serveradmin command and list all of the settings as shown earlier in this chapter. But this time we will push the contents into a file by adding the greater-than symbol > at the end of the command, followed by the file name. For example, the following will back up the service settings to a file called icalbak in the /backups directory:

```
serveradmin settings calendar > /backups/icalbak
```

Clustering CalDAV

In Chapter 4 we covered storage options for Mac OS X. Assuming you are using a storage medium capable of supporting multiple writes on the same volume, you can use the iCal service in a clustered fashion. Clustering iCal Server can provide an Active-Active solution, giving users a performance boost if the connections on your server are saturated, and also providing high availability.

To cluster the iCal service, you configure two iCal servers in an identical manner. To do this, you can configure the settings as you just did when backing up the iCal server to the /backups/icalbak file. To configure the same settings on the second host, use the same serveradmin command but swap the > for a <, assuming that the icalbak file has been copied to the same location on the second server:

```
serveradmin settings calendar < /backups/icalbak
```

After running this, update the SSL settings on the second host to ensure a proper SSL cert is specified. Next, we'll move the calendar files to the server in a shared directory location. In this case, we'll copy the /Library/CalendarServer directory to the /volumes/Xsan/ volume we previously created. Then we'll point the directories for the calendar server at our shared storage:

```
serveradmin settings calendar:DocumentRoot = "/Volumes/Xsan/CalendarServer/Documents/"
serveradmin settings calendar:DataRoot = "/Volumes/Xsan/CalendarServer/Data/"
```

When you are comfortable with the settings, stop and start the iCal service:

```
serveradmin stop calendar
serveradmin start calendar
```

The part that is up to you is how to distribute the load across the two servers. Load balancers are the most obvious choice in many environments, but operating in a shared namespace and using round robin DNS will work as well, likely incurring no additional hardware costs for your setup (beyond, of course, having two or more copies of the Mac OS X Server software).

Wiki Integration

Users are also able to view and manage calendars through the OS X server's web services, provided it is enabled. To do so, simply turn on Calendar Services through the web pane of Server Preferences, as seen in Figure 5-20. The web interface, also shown in Figure 5-20, allows users full read and write access to their calendars, and enables them to create new calendars, schedule events and send invites, and view free/busy schedules. Notable limitations include the inability to access delegated calendars, to-dos do not register, nor can you attach files to events.

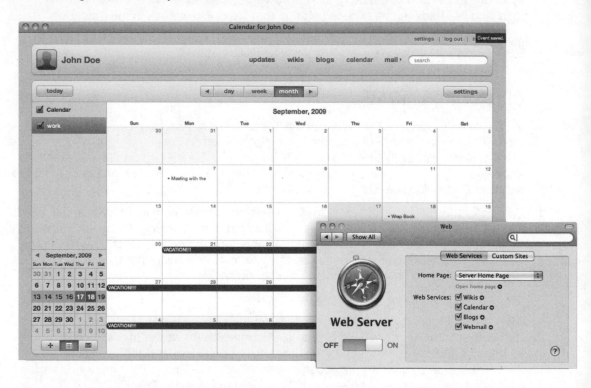

Figure 5-20. *Configuring calender web services in server preferences (front), web calender interface (back)*

Troubleshooting

So you installed your new server and you're having a few problems. Let's look at the common issues and a few simple fixes for them.

If you find yourself in a situation where iCal will not start, there are a few things you can try. As always, consult the log entries. In many cases where the service simply won't start, your log entries may indicate that the service is unable to create a virtual host. This is typically a DNS related problem so check your host name. iCal needs the host name to be correct in order to start. Use `scutil -get HostName` or `changeip -checkhostname` to verify DNS resolution. Next, make sure that the host name listed in the iCal Server settings is identical to this value. If you prefer to use the `serveradmin` CLI to control your services, you can also use the command:

```
serveradmin settings calendar:ServerHostName
```

And then configure the setting using:

```
serveradmin settings calendar:ServerHostName  = "SomeHostName"
```

You can also use the `calendar:HTTPPort` to change the port number you are using for connectivity.

If the service is reportedly running, but you still don't have connectivity, you can verify that your iCal server is running by visiting it in a web browser at `http://icalserver.myco.com:8008/`

If the server is up and running, you should be presented with a generic web page that lists various XML configuration settings used by the Python-based `twistd` engine that iCal server is based on. If the service is not running, verify proper settings of the service, paying close attention to the Document Root. Verify that there is a data store at this location, which will be nested inside of two folders: Data and Documents. Verify that the calendar user _calendar is the owner of these directories and has full read/write/execute access.

Here's another common problem with the iCal server: you set up a user, check the box in Workgroup Manager to Enable Calendaring, and then save your settings—but you get the following error in your logs:

```
Jul10 10:21:56 cedge Workgroup Manager[2282]: +[WPUser userWithGUID::] returned nil!
```

In this case, you are probably enabling a calendar for a local user. Make sure you are using an OD-based user and see if you get the same error. Likewise, you can navigate to the user calendar URI in a web browser:

```
http://icalserver.myco.com:8008/principals/users/snowcat
```

If you receive a 404 when browsing to this address, the calendar server is not properly resolving the user record.

Another issue you may run across occurs when everything is configured and the account has been created for the user, but when you add the account in iCal it fails to connect. If you find yourself in this situation, verify that the port specified at the end of the hostname in the `http://` URL is correct. Verify that you can connect to the remote server port via telnet if necessary, or by using a web browser as previously discussed. When you connect to the server this way, you will be prompted to authenticate. If you can authenticate as the user whose calendar you are trying to set up, you can use the information in this screen to determine ACL information and other security settings that could be keeping the calendars from working. Pay attention as well to the authentication method you are using. If you have selected Kerberos authentication only, your client will need to be able to directly contact the KDC to receive the proper service principal. Also keep in mind that while your default port might be 8008, if you are using SSL your default port is actually 8443.

Once you get this far, you should be able to create an event and see data listed in the Overview tab for iCal. If so, you should be able to find out about anything you want in the iCal server.

Address Book Server

The Address Book service is new in Mac OS X Server 10.6 and is based on the emerging CardDAV standard, a specification that defines the exchange of vCard information via the WebDAV protocol. Also based on the `twistedcaldav` engine, the Address Book Server setup and configuration will be much the same as with iCal: you can use Server Preferences to get the job done easily; you can use Server Admin if you require more options; or you can use the command line for optimal granularity. The Address Book Server maintains its own data store, but also allows the option to search Open Directory for User or Contact information.

Setting up Address Book Server

To set up the Address Book service on Mac OS X Server, open the Server Preferences application from /Applications/Utilities , then click on the button for Address Book. When it opens, uncheck the option to limit each user's total book size if you'd like to disable user Address Book quotas, as shown in Figure 5-21. Next, move the slider from the OFF to the ON positions and wait for the service to complete installation and fire up.

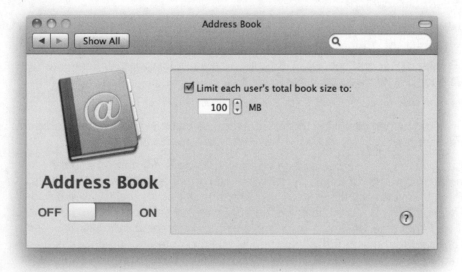

Figure 5-21. *Server Preferences Address Book pane*

Once the service has started, click on the Show All button (see Figure 5-22) to get back to the main Server Preferences screen. Click on Users and then check the box for the Address Book service per user who you would like to enable the service.

Figure 5-22. *Server Preferences Users pane*

As with the iCal Server service, you can also use Server Admin, located in /Applications/Server to more granularly configure the Address Book Server service. When you click on the Address Book entry for your Address Book Server in Server Admin, you'll see the screen in Figure 5-23.

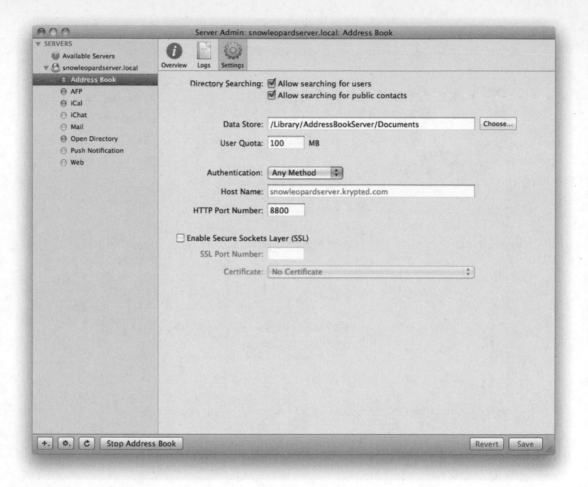

Figure 5-23. *Configuring Address Book Server in Server Admin*

Here, you have the following options:

- *Directory Searching:–* Allows for searches against the address book server to optionally query Open Directory for LDAP-based users (cn=users,dc=myco,dc=com) and/or public contacts (cn=people,dc=myco,dc=com).

- *Data Store:* The path to the Address Book database.

- *User Quotas:* Maximum size per user for the Address Book database in megabytes.

- *Authentication:* Allows you to choose Digest or Kerberos authentication (or both).

- *Host Name:* By default, this value is dynamically generated based on the determined host name of the server; it can also be overridden.

- *HTTP Port Number:* The port that the HTTP service will listen on for Address Book traffic.

- *Enable Secure Sockets Layer (SSL):* Enables SSL (requires a certificate to be accepted).

- *SSL Port Number:* If SSL is enabled this option allows for the customization of the port that the listener will run on.

- *Certificate:* Allows you to choose an SSL certificate that will be used when serving out SSL encrypted traffic.

With all services, if SSL is an option, it is strongly recommended that you use it. The stock configuration of Mac OS X Server comes with a self-assigned SSL certificate and it is a fairly straightforward task to use it to secure your services. Alternatively, you can obtain a certificate from a third party as those are often easier to deploy. If your organization has an internal certificate authority, you can use its services to sign certificates for your OS X host.

Once you are satisfied with your settings, click on the Save button in the lower right hand corner of the screen and then restart the service using the Server Admin utility or from the command line. To restart the service from the command line, you can use the following two commands in sequence:

```
serveradmin stop addressbook
serveradmin start addressbook
```

If you need more granularity for your Address Book Server configuration, you can also use the serveradmin command with the settings option to view all of the settings that can be changed:

```
serveradmin settings addressbook
```

This would result in the following list:

```
addressbook:SudoersFile = ""
addressbook:DirectoryService:params:restrictEnabledRecords = no
addressbook:DirectoryService:params:cacheTimeout = 30
addressbook:DirectoryService:params:restrictToGroup = ""
addressbook:DirectoryService:params:node = "/Search"
addressbook:DirectoryService:type = "twistedcaldav.directory.↵
appleopendirectory.OpenDirectoryService"
addressbook:BindSSLPorts = _empty_array
addressbook:EnablePrincipalListings = no
addressbook:DocumentRoot = "/Library/AddressBookServer/Documents"
addressbook:SSLPrivateKey = ""
addressbook:ServerStatsFile = "/var/run/carddavd/stats.plist"
addressbook:ProcessType = "Combined"
addressbook:UserName = "_calendar"
addressbook:BindHTTPPorts = _empty_array
addressbook:EnableAnonymousReadRoot = no
addressbook:DefaultLogLevel = "info"
addressbook:HTTPPort = 8800
addressbook:ServerHostName = ""
addressbook:PIDFile = "/var/run/carddavd.pid"
addressbook:ReadPrincipals = _empty_array
```

```
addressbook:UserQuota = 104857600
addressbook:MultiProcess:ProcessCount = 0
addressbook:EnableProxyPrincipals = no
addressbook:Authentication:Digest:Algorithm = "md5"
addressbook:Authentication:Digest:Qop = ""
addressbook:Authentication:Digest:Enabled = yes
addressbook:Authentication:Kerberos:ServicePrincipal = ""
addressbook:Authentication:Kerberos:Enabled = yes
addressbook:Authentication:Basic:Enabled = no
addressbook:MaxAddressBookMultigetHrefs = 5000
addressbook:ErrorLogFile = "/var/log/carddavd/error.log"
addressbook:SSLCertificate = ""
addressbook:EnableSACLs = yes
addressbook:AB_EnabledGroups = _empty_array
addressbook:EnableAnonymousReadNav = no
addressbook:DataRoot = "/var/run/carddavd"
addressbook:BindAddresses = _empty_array
addressbook:AdminPrincipals = _empty_array
addressbook:MaxAddressBookQueryResults = 1000
addressbook:RedirectHTTPToHTTPS = no
addressbook:EnableSearchAddressBook = yes
addressbook:DirectoryAddressBook:params:queryUserRecords = yes
addressbook:DirectoryAddressBook:params:liveQuery = yes
addressbook:DirectoryAddressBook:params:cacheQuery = no
addressbook:DirectoryAddressBook:params:peopleNode = "/Search/Contacts"
addressbook:DirectoryAddressBook:params:fakeETag = yes
addressbook:DirectoryAddressBook:params:ignoreSystemRecords = yes
addressbook:DirectoryAddressBook:params:queryPeopleRecords = yes
addressbook:DirectoryAddressBook:params:dsLocalCacheTimeout = 30
addressbook:DirectoryAddressBook:params:queryAllAttributes = no
addressbook:DirectoryAddressBook:params:userNode = "/Search"
addressbook:DirectoryAddressBook:params:cacheTimeout = 30
addressbook:DirectoryAddressBook:params:maxDSQueryRecords = 150
addressbook:DirectoryAddressBook:type = "twistedcaldav.directory.↵
opendirectorybacker.OpenDirectoryBackingService"
addressbook:RotateAccessLog = no
addressbook:AnonymousDirectoryAddressBookAccess = no
addressbook:GroupName = "_calendar"
addressbook:AccessLogFile = "/var/log/carddavd/access.log"
addressbook:ResponseCompression = yes
```

Connecting to the Address Book Server

Once your server has been configured optimally for your environment, it's time to configure your clients to connect to it. To do so, open the Address Book application from /Applications, click on the Address Book menu, and then click on Preferences. Click on the Accounts icon in the Preferences screen, shown in Figure 5-24.

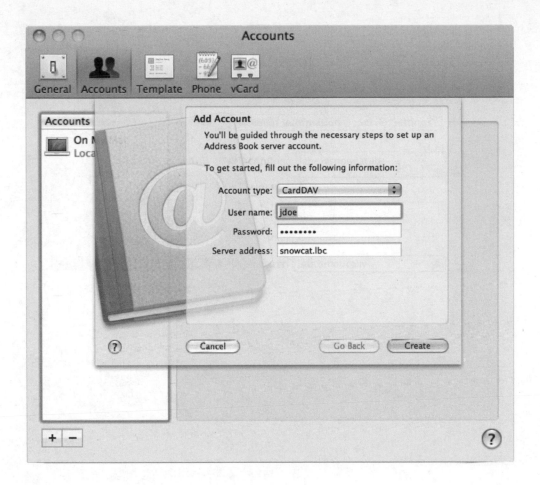

Figure 5-24. *Adding an address book account*

Click on the + icon in the lower-left corner of the screen to bring up the Add Account screen, also shown in Figure 5-24. Enter the type of account (CardDAV), the username from the directory service, and the password for the account. Click on Create when you are finished.

Once you are back at the Accounts screen, you can set the refresh rate for contacts (see Figure 5-25). This is the interval that synchronization will occur for the account whose setup was just completed.

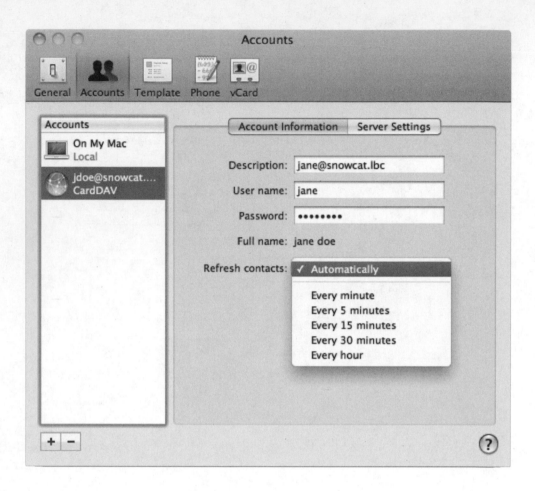

Figure 5-25. *Setting the refresh rate for contacts*

TIP: Mac OS X 10.5 users will use the Directory application in the /Applications/ Utilities directory to view and edit directory-based Contacts in the Address Book. However, CardDAV and therefore 10.6 Address Book Server is only supported by Address Book in 10.6. For 10.5 support, a third party client will be needed.

Backing up Address Books

Backing up the Address Book Server data store is similar to backing up the iCal Server information store. The path to the database can be found through Server Admin or using the following command:

```
serveradmin settings addressbook:DocumentRoot
```

Once you know the path, you can back up the data store as you would most other directory structures. The service runs with the _calendar username as the default owner, although the root account will provide access as well. The default location to the information store is /Library/AddressBook/.

Instant Messaging

Solutions

Mac OS X comes bundled with iChat, which can use AOL Instant Messenger (AIM), Jabber, or a .Mac/MobileMe account for standard instant messaging. The Mac OS X Server iChat solution is actually a pretty interface for managing the popular Jabber open-source instant messaging server. Most other applications have support for Mac OS X as well, including Microsoft Messenger.

Microsoft Messenger

Microsoft Messenger is installed as part of the Microsoft Office 2008 suite, which ties in well to the Office Communication Server environment at most enterprise environments. Mac clients are available for most other third-party messaging solutions, and if they are not, a Jabber server environment can often be propped up to allow for federation between services.

If desired, Microsoft Messenger can tie into the Mac OS X Kerberos libraries and be configured using the current Kerberos REALM. During setup, the Microsoft Messenger application will prompt to *Use my network ID and password*, which triggers the IM client to request a Service Ticket to use for authentication to the Messaging services (see Figure 5-26).

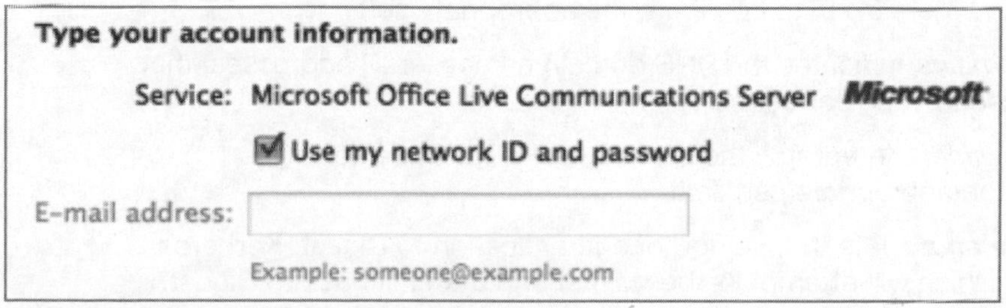

Figure 5-26. *Microsoft Messenger Kerberos authentication*

iChat Server

The iChat application in Mac OS X is a fantastic tool for instant messaging. It supports video, conferencing video, file transfer, and even sharing screens over an iChat session. These capabilities make it a great support tool for the service desk, as well as an excellent communication platform that can enhance an organization's intra-company communications. If you like, iChat can also be leveraged to extend internal communication externally (though it is primarily intended for internal communications).

To set up the iChat Server, the steps you perform are roughly the same as those for other services. For a simple server setup, use the Server Preferences tool (shown in Figure 5-27), which allows you to configure server-wide logging and archiving of chat transcripts, and to enable server-to-server communication, which allows XMPP (Extensible Messaging and Presence Protocol) federation between hosts.

Figure 5-27. *Server Preference iChat pane*

Once you have a functional iChat service, chances are you'll be interested in pushing the boundaries of what it can do beyond the default two options in Server Preferences. Just as with iCal and Address Book, you can also access the service from within Server Admin. To do so, click on the iChat service under the SERVERS list, then under the General tab (as in Figure 5-28) to configure the appropriate settings:

- *Host Domains:* Indicates the DNS domain names (or IP addresses) that will be used by the Jabber server.

- *SSL Certificate:* Integrates the service with SSL. Once selected, choose the appropriate certificate.

- *Authentication:* Sets the method of authentication to Digest, Kerberos or both, which will attempt Kerberos first and then fail back to Digest.

- *Enable XMPP server-to-server federation:* Allows you to federate the server with other servers, which means that users of one host can establish chat sessions with users from another host. This can be useful if you have multiple servers in multiple locations, or if you want to extend your server to communicate with third-party hosts.

- Require secure server-to-server federation: Forces XMPP federation to use SSL.

- *Allow federation with all domains:* Allows all other XMPP-compliant servers to communicate with yours.

- *Allow federation with the following domains:* Configures other servers (by IP or DNS) that are federated to this server.

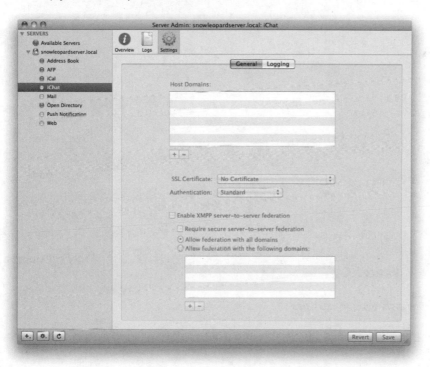

Figure 5-28. *Configuring iChat settings in Server Admin*

Transcripts

You can also configure message archival (transcript storage) options using Server Admin. To do so, click on the Settings tab as shown in Figure 5-29. Enable the *Automatically save chat messages* features, which will store a centralized copy of all of the instant messaging chat sessions for each user on the server. Next, click the *Choose* button to select a location and then use the *Archive saved messages every* field to configure how long messages are kept before they are moved into a compressed archive file. Unfortunately, this function is limited to text-based transcripts. Audio and Video chats, once initiated, are peer-to-peer and, as such, the server never sees the data..

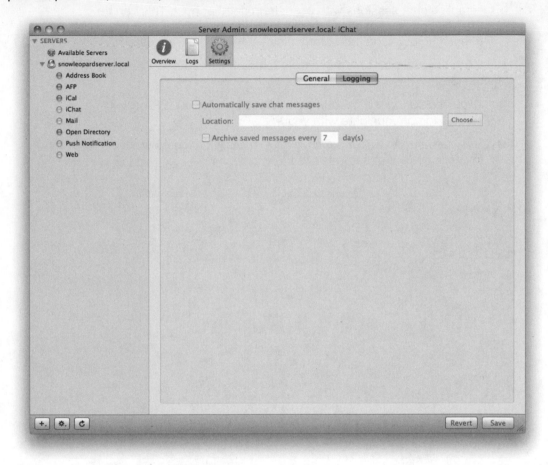

Figure 5-29. *Saving and archiving chat messages*

The serveradmin command can again be used to list additional configuration settings for the service:

```
hax.lbc:~ hunterbj$ sudo serveradmin settings jabber
jabber:enableAutoBuddy = no
jabber:s2sAllowedDomains = _empty_array
jabber:requireSecureS2S = no
jabber:sslCAFile = "/etc/certificates/hax.lbc.chcrt"
jabber:sslKeyFile = "/etc/certificates/hax.lbc.crtkey"
jabber:hosts:_array_index:0 = "hax.lbc"
jabber:authLevel = "ANYMETHOD"
jabber:s2sRestrictDomains = no
jabber:savedChatsArchiveInterval = 7
jabber:eventLogArchiveInterval = 7
jabber:savedChatsLocation = "/var/jabberd/message_archives"
jabber:enableSavedChats = yes
```

```
jabber:enableXMPP = no
jabber:logLevel = "ALL"
```

Archiving Transcripts via iChat

If you do not host your own iChat server and still want to save chat transcripts, the iChat application can fulfill that role. To manually configure transcripts per user in iChat, select Preferences from the iChat menu. Click on the messages tab to access the functionality to save chat, shown in Figure 5-30.

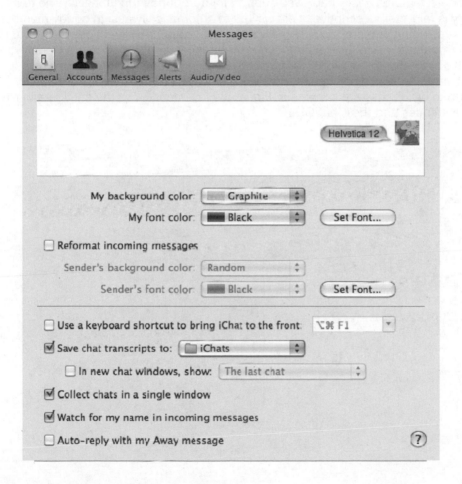

Figure 5-30. *Configuring iChat to save chat transcripts*

More pragmatically, you can deploy these settings via MCX, as discussed in chapter 7, or you can script the preference chain to your fleet through with the `defaults` command:

```
defaults write com.apple.iChat AutosaveChats -int 1
```

Rerun the command with –int 0 to turn the feature off. When enabled, iChat will save all chat transcripts to the logged-in user's Documents/iChats directory and stores all chats in daily date and time stamped sub folders. The location for this storage can also be changed through the `defaults` command:

`defaults write com.apple.iChat SavedChatsFolder -string "~/Library/Backups/iChats"`

Autobuddy

Snow Leopard features vastly improved support for autobuddy functionality. The term autobuddy is fairly self descriptive; it allows you to automatically assign buddy members to your users, letting you prepopulate their buddy list. Autobuddy functionality in 10.6 is accessed through the Groups Pane of Server Preferences application and provides you with the ability to assign autobuddy population based on group membership, which works out very well. Once configured, user's will automatically see Buddy Groups for each group to which they are a member. Figure 5-31 demonstrates the configuration in Server Preferences and the iChat GUI.

Figure 5-31. *Configuring iChat Autobuddy Lists in Server Preferences (back) and the resulting iChat buddy list (front)*

Mac OS X Mail Server

While most enterprises will already have a stable messaging and groupware infrastructure, Mac OS X Server can also be leveraged for much of the same type of functionality. We have already extolled the virtues of the Address Book, iCal, and iChat; Mail rounds out the groupware offerings quite nicely and also enables Push Notification to handheld devices. In environments where an incumbent solution exists for mail, the Mac OS X mail service can provide ancillary messaging services, such as supplemental or archival mail storage, listserv functionality, virus and spam filtering before mail goes into a separate solution, or act as a relay.

While the Mac OS X Server's mail service doesn't provide as many services for other platforms as it could, it's not because the services that make up the Mac OS X Server mail service are immature. Mac OS X Server uses *Dovecot* for the message database (POP and IMAP), *Mailman* for listservs, and *Postfix* for mail services (SMTP). These tools, deeply rooted in Unix, go back sometimes decades and are as stable, when used for the appropriate environments, as Microsoft Exchange.

Setting up a Mail Server

Setting up Mac OS X Server to be a mail server is much like setting up the other services that have been described. To enable the service, you can use the Server Preferences application. Click on the Mail icon and you will see some simple settings that can be configured for the Mail service (see Figure 5-32). Use the check boxes to enable a few features and then move the slider to the ON position to fire up the service:

- *Relay outgoing mail through ISP.* Enables all mail being sent from or through the server to be routed through the organization's ISP, which, among other benefits, eliminates the need for reverse DNS.

- *Reject email from blacklisted servers: Use spam blacklist server (DNSBLs):* Enables spamhaus blacklist servers (default is zen.spamhaus.org).

- *Enable junk mail and virus filtering:* Enables ClamAv for virus filtering and SpamAssassin for antispam and allows you to set how aggressively it filters email.

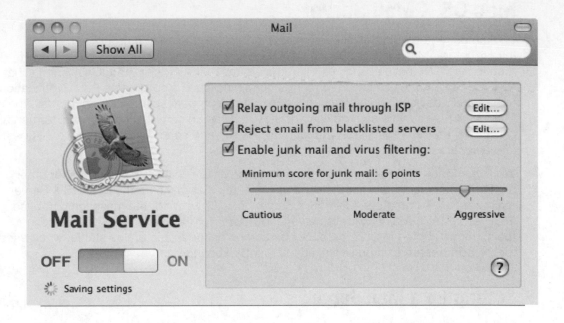

Figure 5-32. *Mail Service Server Preferences settings*

The features available in Server Preferences are minimal and it is highly likely that any substantial user base will require far more configuration. As usual, you can also use Server Admin to configure the Mail Server, with much more granularity.

Configuring Mail with ServerAdmin

To configure mail services with the Server Admin tool, you must first enable the service in the server overview pane, as described with other services. You can then configure numerous details, as shown in Figure 5-33. Here are the general global settings you can configure:

- *Domain name:* The domain name of the primary mail domain.

- *Host name:* The host name of the mail server (defaults to the name entered at the time the server was setup if it has not since been altered).

- *Push Notification Server:* Allows the server to be used with the push notification service to provide iPhone compatibility.

- *Enable SMTP:* Enables the SMTP service and daemon.

- *Allow incoming mail:* Enables inbound mail acceptance for configured users.

- *Hold outgoing mail:* Do not send outgoing mail until it is manually released.

- *Relay outgoing mail through host:* Relays all mail not destined for local storage through specified server. This option enables an OS X mail server to operate as an intermediate Mail Transfer Agent (MTA), which can be used to route local email to a centralized company SMTP server or to an ISP's SMTP server. The extensibility of the postfix MTA engine means you can use it to provide customized e-mail filtering, which can ultimately be integrated into existing business systems.

- *Authenticate to relay with user name:* The username for the SMTP server specified in the previous field.

- *Password:* The password for the SMTP server.

- *Copy undeliverable mail to:* If an e-mail address is specified, it will be copied on all non-delivery reports (NDRs), a good measure for proactive admins.

- *Copy all mail to:* Allows for a backup account to store a copy of each incoming and outgoing e-mail that routes through the SMTP daemon. A good measure for the guy who has the "I read your e-mail" bumper sticker, and means it.

- *Enable IMAP with maximum of:* Enables the IMAP service and allows you to limit the maximum number of connections to it.

- *Enable POP:* Enables the POP service but does not allow you to throttle the number of connections.

- *Deliver to "/var/mail" when IMAP & POP are disabled:* stores messages as flat files in the /var/mail directory If no services have been enabled to route mail to.

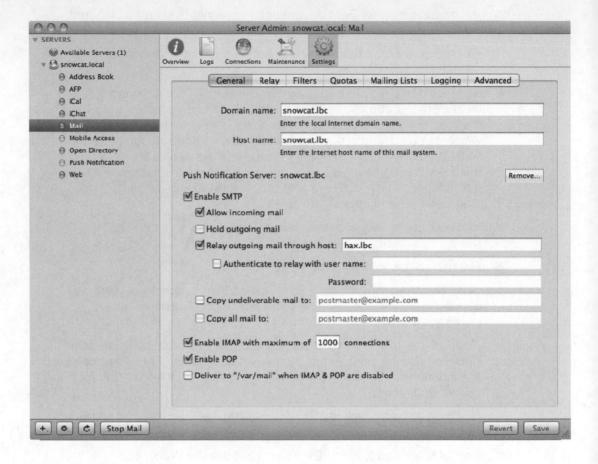

Figure 5-33. *Configuring Mail in Server Admin*

You can also configure the supported authentication mechanisms. To do so, click on the *Advanced* tab, where you will be able to configure authentication options for SMTP and for POP/IMAP services, as shown in Figure 5-34. Of these options, login, PLAIN, and Clear all actually utilize cleartext passwords, so you should think twice about enabling them without SSL configured. CRAM-MD5 is the preferred authentication method and all popular mail clients support it. However, there will be times when your best (or only) option is SSL + cleartext authentication. Notably, if you are using an Active Directory back end for authentication, you will likely need to use this option. Additionally, if you plan to enable webmail, the backend squirrelmail process will require cleartext authentication to be enabled in its default configuration.

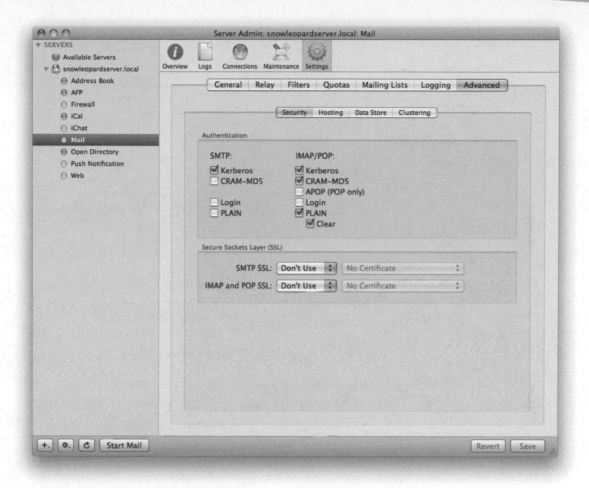

Figure 5-34. *Mail Service authentication settings*

Protecting the Mail Servers

Once the settings are configured, click on the Relay tab, shown in Figure 5-35. Here you can configure how the server manages attempts to relay SMTP traffic through it. Using the *Accept SMTP relays only from these hosts and networks* option, you can configure which IP addresses (and ranges) are able to relay mail through the SMTP service. With *Refuse all messages from these hosts and networks,* you can also configure a blacklist of IP addresses that you will never accept mail from (for example, those you feel are abusive). Finally, you can configure the *Use these junk mail rejection servers (real-time blacklist)* option to indicate multiple RBL servers that your SMTP server will use when checking the source server that is attempting to relay or deliver mail.

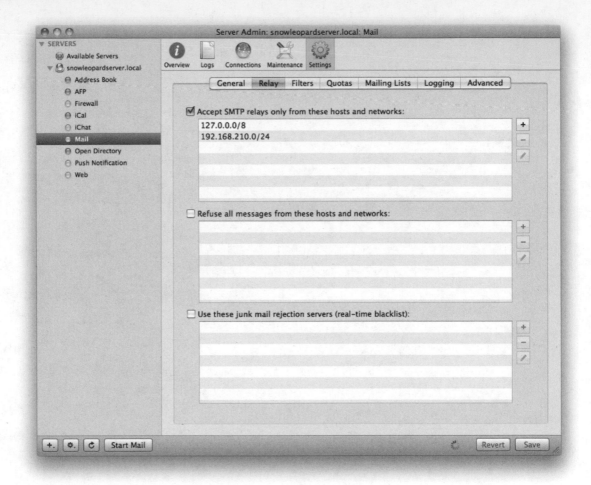

Figure 5-35. *Mail Service relay configuration*

It is worth noting that in the *Accept SMTP relays...* option, the networks and IP addresses listed specify *unauthenticated* external relay only. Relay in the context of SMTP means that the mail is destined for a different mail exchanger. Messages destined for a mail user stored locally on the mail server are not messages requiring relay, but rather delivery. E-mails bound for local users will be accepted from hosts that are not explicitly listed in the *Refuse all messages* list, or designated as a spammer by a specified RBL. Be particularly careful when configuring IP address relays, as a poorly planned relay configuration can result in your email server being flagged as an "Open Relay," meaning that your server has been determined to be delivering SPAM. For this reason, it is recommended that you leave the allowed relay list relatively sparse and instead require your users to authenticate in order to relay mail.

You can also configure junk mail and spam filters by clicking on the Filters tab (see Figure 5-36. Here are options you can set:

- *Enable junk mail filtering:* enables the spam filter, which is based on the open source spam filter SpamAssassin

- *Minimum junk mail score:* When junk mail filtering is enabled, each message is assigned a score that identifies the likelihood the message is spam. You can use this field to identify the score that a message would need to exceed before it is flagged as spam and the appropriate action (defined in the *Junk mail messages should be* field) to be taken.

- *Accepted languages:* Allows you to configure acceptable languages for incoming mail. All mail determined to be not on the list will be marked as junk and the appropriate action will be taken.

- *Accepted locales:* Defines acceptable geographical regions that mail will be accepted from.

- *Junk mail messages should be:* Defines the appropriate action that will be taken with regard to mail identified as being junk mail.

- *Attach subject tag:* Can be used to augment the subject line of incoming mail flagged as spam.

- *Encapsulate junk mail as MIME attachment:* Moves mail flagged as spam into an attachment, which requires user interaction before the mail client will attempt to parse and present the message.

- *Enable virus filtering:* Enables ClamAv scanning for incoming messages.

- *Infected messages should be:* Defines the appropriate action to be taken on e-mail identified as containing a virus.

- *Send notification to:* Allows infected mail to be sent to a specified mailbox.

- *Notify recipients:* Sends an email advising the receiver of an infected message without sending the message itself.

- *Update the virus database:* Updates the virus database on a timed interval, defined in number of times per day.

- *Enable server side mail rules:* Enables preprocessing of rules for all mail coming into the server.

NOTE: If you choose that what happens to junk mail messages is anything other than Delivered, the recipient will never see them and the sender will never know they were deleted. Only the e-mail address you specify will be notified, which means that you, the admin, will have to deal with the message. You may be distressed by the lack of an option to inform a sender that their message was rejected due to spam, but keep in mind that from: addresses are almost always spoofed on actual spam messages, and you could end up flooding legitimate email addresses with delivery notices.

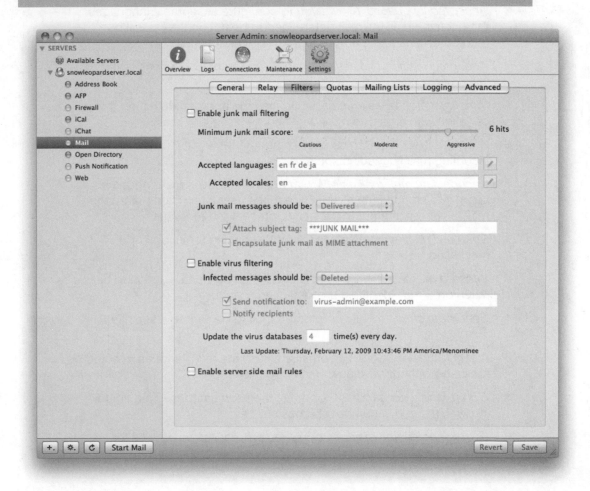

Figure 5-36. *Mail service filtering options*

Another way to protect the mail server is to keep users from abusing resources. Not that anyone will do so on purpose, but storage in many environments is a finite resource while consumption typically is not. Therefore, you can configure how mailbox quotas are handled globally using the Quotas tab, shown in Figure 5-37 (quotas themselves are set per mailbox using the Quotas tab on a per-account basis in Workgroup Manager). Here, you specify settings that match your organization's business logic:

- *Refuse messages larger than:* Identifies the maximum attachment size for incoming mail to the organization.

- *Enable quota warnings:* Warns users when their mailbox exceeds a specified size.

- Disable a user's incoming mail when they exceed 100% of quota: Blocks a user's mail if his mailbox is full.

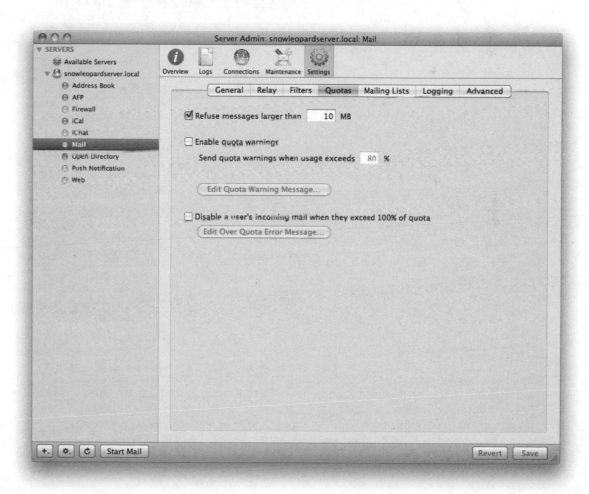

Figure 5-37. *Configuring Mail service quotas*

Mailing Lists

Mac OS X Server comes with a fully functional listserv. To configure it, click on the Mailing Lists tab in Server Admin and check the box for *Enable server group mailing lists* (see Figure 5-38). You can then use the *Enable mailman mailing lists* check box to enable actual lists. Use the plus Icon (+) to create mailing lists, and then the Users & Groups button to drag users to the list.

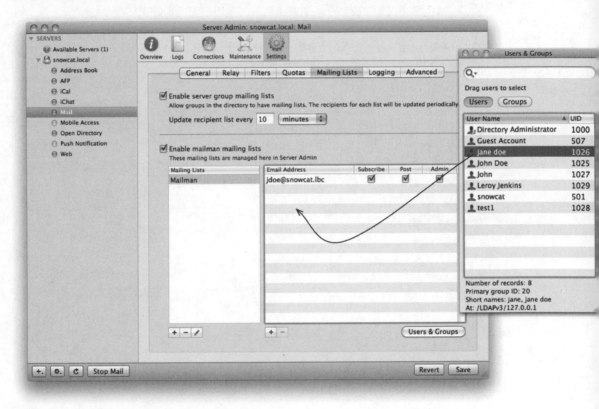

Figure 5-38. *Enabling mailing lists in Server Admin*

Mailman is a far more complex solution than this simple screen seems to imply. The configuration files provide an abundance of further options that can be used to tailor the system to your liking, including full support for automated subscription and unsubscription via e-mail. Mailman is a tried and true solution and is pretty much the same beast on OS X as in other environments.

Logging

Mac OS X Server by defaults logs events from the mail server. You can customize these events on the Logging tab. Here you can customize the log levels for SMTP and IMAP/POP, as well as for junk mail and viruses (Figure 5-39). Additionally you can set logs to be compressed on a timed schedule by using the *Archive logs every* field, which specifies the number of days logs are stored before they are compressed.

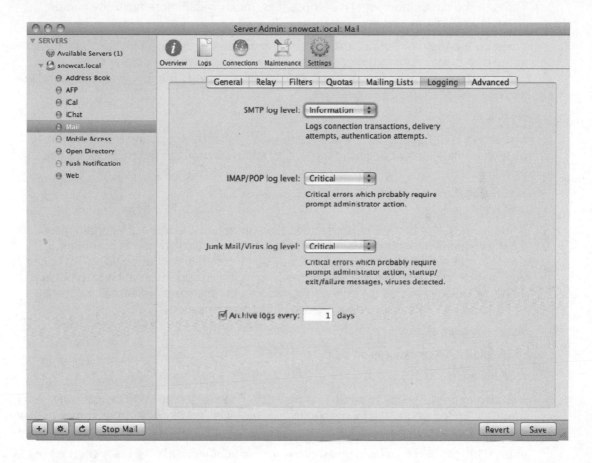

Figure 5-39. *Mail service logging options*

The Command Line

The Mac OS X Mail Service is one of the most feature-rich, with pages of options that can be configured using serveradmin, as described in previous sections. The following command will display a list of settings:

```
serveradmin settings mail
```

You can also leverage the various configuration options provided by each of the OS X mail servers' underlying packages. Postfix, for instance, is robust and highly extensible and can be made to work with many plug-ins. For instance, you may wish to inject your own filtering code into the MTA process to watch for emails with particular criteria. To inject your own filter into the MTA pipeline, you would modify the postfix master process config file found at /etc/postfix/master.cf. The main.cf file is another file that controls the overall behavior of Postfix. While the administration GUI in Server Admin provides a decent amount of configurability, it exposes only a small subset of Postfix's capabilities. Through the direct modification of these files, much, much more flexibility can be wrangled out of the system.

While on the topic of Postfix, there are numerous command line-binaries that can assist in the day-to-day management of your mail server. For instance, the postqueue command can be used to manage basic delivery queuing. The following command will output a list of all queued massages:

```
postqueue -p
```

Messages in the queue can be flushed (re-sent) either by specifying the -f flag to flush all queued mail, or by specifying the -i flag and a queueid to resubmit just a single email:

```
postqueue -f
postqueue -i B8EB9C6BDBD
```

If you have queue problems, sometimes the only solution is to delete certain messages from the queue altogether. Malformed messages can certainly cause problems. To delete a message from the queue, the postsuper command must be used. Postsuper is very similar to postqueue, but it includes (and requires) superuser access to utilize it. Postsuper also provides the only supported way to delete particular mail messages from the queue. For instance, to delete a specific queued message:

```
sudo postsuper -d 308AE53AF9
```

or to release all messages on hold:

```
sudo postsuper -r hold
```

It is also extremely easy to send an e-mail using postfix's sendmail compatibility features. For example, the following single line of shell code will send an e-mail to user jdoe@myco.com:

```
printf "To:jdoe@myco.com\nFrom:myserver@myco.com\nSubject:This is the subject\n\n⏎
This is the message body.\n"  | sendmail -t
```

Choosing Mailbox Locations

The internal storage of a Mac OS X Server is often not where you'll want to store the database of the mail service. Instead, if you have spacious and fast external storage, you will often use that (obviously, number of users and intensity of use would define the storage requirements). If you want to move the mail database, click on the Advanced tab of the Mail Settings and then on the Data Store subtab, where you will see the location of the default mail store, as shown in Figure 5-40. The default store can stay here, or it can move to external storage by using the Choose button to select an alternate location. The key point, however, is that you can create multiple mail stores at multiple locations, allowing you to use different storage for different tiers of users depending on speed, department, or other requirements you put in place to determine whose mail goes where.

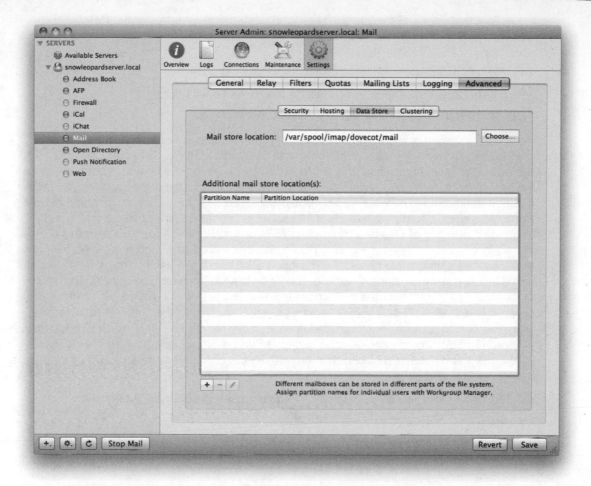

Figure 5-40. *Advanced mail service settings*

If you are satisfied with your settings, click on the Save button and then restart the Mail service. Once you have created additional mail partitions, you assign individual users to each in Workgroup Manager, under the user's mail tab.

The Dovecot Mailstore

Starting with Snow Leopard, Mac OS X Server uses the Dovecot mailstore as the storage mechanism for mail. The Dovecot mailstore by default exists at /var/spool/imap/dovecot. This folder contains two subdirectories, *sieve-scripts,* which holds third-party sieve scripts, and *mail*, which contains subdirectories with user data, named after the respective user's GeneratedUID value. To determine a particular user's GeneratedUID, you can use the `dscl` command

```
dscl /Search read /Users/jdoe GeneratedUID | awk '{print $2}'
```

which generates the output, which will be the name of our folder:

```
C3C4E3BB-1FE8-4A6E-B445-5474CC4E3223
```

Each user folder is owned by the respective user and contains index and cache files, mailboxes, and e-mail messages. For e-mail message storage, dovecot uses a flat-file system. That is, every message is represented by an associated file that contains the e-mail's contents, including any attachments in a standard mime-encoded format. Each of a user's mailboxes is represented by dot-prepended directories. Thus, for the mailbox *Sent Messages*, a folder called *.Sent Messages* is created. Each of these mailboxes contains a number of files and directories for storage. For each mailbox, e-mails are stored in a subdirectory named *cur*. These files are stored with a standardized file name that includes a unique identifier, the message size, and the message flags. The user's IMAP Inbox is represented by her root folder on the file system. Specifically, for user jdoe, his inbox is represented by e-mails existing in the folder /var/spool/imap/dovecot/C3C4E3BB-1FE8-4A6E-B445-5474CC4E3223/cur, using the GeneratedUID value found earlier. In order to optimize mail listings, dovecot creates per-mailbox index files that are used to provide accelerated access to commonly queried data, though the index files themselves do not contain any otherwise unrecoverable data. Dovecot utilizes the following cache files:

- *dovecot.index:* Main index file, contains mailbox summary information, including number of messages and size of and pointer to message cache file

- *dovecot.index.cache:* Cached mailbox data, including message headers, sent date, and other message information.

- *dovecot.index.log:* Transaction log file. Used to improve performance in situations where there are multiple concurrent connections.

- *dovecot.index.log.2:* Rotated transactional log file.

Rebuilding a mailbox in Dovecot is pretty straightforward. To rebuild the index for any Dovecot user's mailbox, you can simply remove the cache and index files mentioned above. The index file will be automatically re-created, and the cache file will begin to repopulate with data as it is requested. If you want to rebuild all index files for a user, the command is fairly simple:

```
find /var/spool/imap/dovecot/mail/C3C4E3BB-1FE8-4A6E-B445-5474CC4E3223 -name ↵
"dovecot.index*" -exec rm {} \;
```

This command will delete all index files for the user, which will subsequently be rebuilt. While this can be done on a live system, you are deleting files that contain synchronization data, so it's probably a good idea to ensure there are no active connections to the user's mailstore. Upon reconnecting to the server, there may be slight delays for the user as the index files are rebuilt.

Setting up Public folders

Public folders in dovecot can be configured a few different ways. The easiest way is to simply use symlinks. A dot prefixed symbolic link to external directories will be properly resolved by Dovecot and will be presented to the user as a standard mailbox. When setting up such a public share, it is important to note that Dovecot operates within the user context. Thus each user who is granted access to the public folder via symlinks must also have the appropriate file system permissions, designated via either standard POSIX or ACL management. To set up a shared folder in this manner, you can run the following commands:

```
## cd into the mail store so we can use relative paths
cd /var/spool/imap/dovecot/mail

## create our shared folder and mailbox
mkdir -p Shared/.MySharedFolder

## setup POSIX and ACL privileges on the mailmox for our users
chgrp -R staff  Shared/.MySharedFolder
chmod -R g+rwx Shared/.MySharedFolder
chmod +a "staff allow ⏎
list,add_file,search,delete,add_subdirectory,delete_child,readattr,writeattr,readextattr,⏎
writeextattr,readsecurity,file_inherit,directory_inherit" Shared/.MySharedFolder

## create our symlinks for our users. We first cd into our user's folder so that we can
## use relative paths on our links
cd C3C4E3BB-1FE8 4A6E-B445-5474CC4E3223
ln -s ../Shared/.MySharedFolder .MySharedFolder
```

> **NOTE:** The ../ portion of the above path references the parent directory. Thus, inside of user jdoe's email folder, we are creating a link to the "Shared" folder in the parent folder. Using a relative symlink like this allows us to move the entire mail store to a different directory or volume without the paths breaking.

At this point, user jdoe will have full access to the mailbox *MySharedFolder*. We could then symlink the same directory to another user, say janedoe. The beauty of file-system-level permissioning here is that you can do all kinds of cool stuff with ACLs. For instance, you could prevent janedoe from deleting items, leaving her only with the ability to add new items to the store.

Backing up Mail

With the introduction of Dovecot in 10.6, backing up mail got quite a bit easier. In 10.5, the cyrus database risked potential for corruption when backed up live. Though this was far less of an issue than with earlier versions of OS X, the reality was that it was still recommended to take the system offline to back it up. No longer! Now, mail can be backed up by your standard backup program, be it Netvault, TiNa, or rsync, or even Time Machine. Because each message is stored as its own file system entity, granular message-level or mailbox-level restores are possible.

To perform a restore, just replace the appropriate e-mails or directories into the user's mail root. You can restore entire mailboxes simply by placing the respective dot-prefixed folder there or: alternatively, you can create your own "restore" mailbox, using the following command (here we use 'jdoe' in the mail paths for brevity, it is necessary to use the user's GeneratedUID, as discussed above):

```
## create the new Mailbox Restored, and it's cur subdirectory, which holds the mail files
mkdir -p /var/spool/imap/dovecot/mail/jdoe/.Restored/cur

## copy our backed up email files into our restore mailbox's cur/ directory.
rsync -avu /path/to/my/backupemaildir/ /var/spool/imap/dovecot/mail/jdoe/.Restored/cur/
## make sure the new user is the owner
chown -R jdoe /var/spool/imap/dovecot/mail/jdoe/.Restored
## Delete our index file, forcing them to be rebuilt
rm /var/spool/imap/dovecot/mail/jdoe/.Restored/dovecot.index*
```

You can also copy individual e-mail messages into pre-existing mailboxes without much fanfare, though it is once again recommended that you remove the index file.

There are other notable mail-related configurations and database files that you may want to backup, though it's not strictly required:

- /var/amavis: Contains filtering information, including the SpamAssassin Bayes database (all learned junkmail)

- /var/clamav: Contains the latest virus definitions

- /etc/freshclam.conf: ClamAv configuration file

- /etc/amavisd.conf: Amavisd configuration file.

- /etc/mail/spamassassin: SpamAssassin configuration files.

If you are running a 10.5-based mail server, it is recommended to backup its Cyrus database without the service running. An excellent tool named mailbfr can be found at http://osx.topicdesk.com. It is a free utility and manages the backups of the 10.5 database, including stopping and starting the services as necessary.

Clustering Mail Services

As mentioned previously, the Mail Service provided by Mac OS X Server can be clustered, provided you have shared storage with file-level locking. Currently, the only supported means to implement mail clustering is through Xsan.

To set up a cluster, you must first run the Service Configuration Assistant, found by clicking the *Change* button on the Mail services Clustering tab. Once the assistant fires, you will be presented with the option to create a new cluster or join an existing one, provided that the system detects an available Xsan volume, as shown in Figure 5-41.

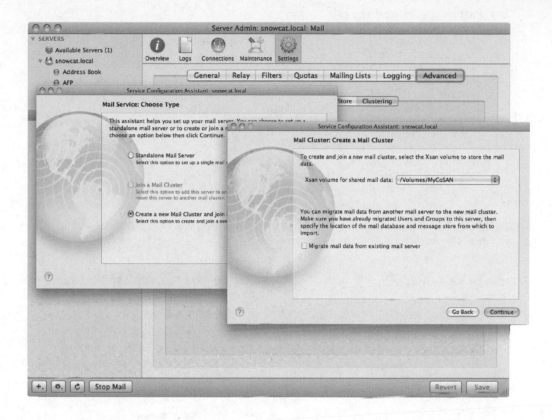

Figure 5-41. *Changing the Mail clustering setting*

Once a cluster is established, it will be stored in a hidden directory, .MailCluster, at the root of the volume. The Mail Service Cluster will be managed by the first host that is added to it. Inside of the .MailCluster folder, you will find a directory named after the name of the Xsan volume, and inside of it reside both configuration files and the mail datastore:

```
bash-3.2# ls /Volumes/MyCoSAN/.MailCluster/MyCoSAN/
MailClusterConf.plist    config                data                    lock_files
```

Inside of the config folder you will find both standard dovecot and postfix configuration files. The data folder contains the mail store, smtp spool, mailman datastore, and serverside email rules (vacation messages, serverside filters, and sievescripts). Worth mentioning in this folder is the MailClusterConf.plist file, which contains data relevant to the configuration of the mail cluster, including a list of member servers:

```
<?xml version="1.0" encoding="UTF-8"?>
<!DOCTYPE plist PUBLIC "-//Apple//DTD PLIST 1.0//EN"
"http://www.apple.com/DTDs/PropertyList-1.0.dtd">
<plist version="1.0">
<dict>
        <key>cluster_name</key>
```

```
          <string>MyCoSAN</string>
          <key>cluster_path</key>
          <string>/Volumes/MyCoSAN</string>
          <key>cluster_type</key>
          <string>combined</string>
          <key>members</key>
          <array>
                <string>snowcat.lbc</string>
          </array>
          <key>name</key>
          <string>MyCoSAN</string>
          <key>path</key>
          <string>/Volumes/MyCoSAN</string>
</dict>
</plist>
```

Once the cluster is configured, you can verify in the Mail Service's overview that clustering is enabled, as seen in Figure 5-42.

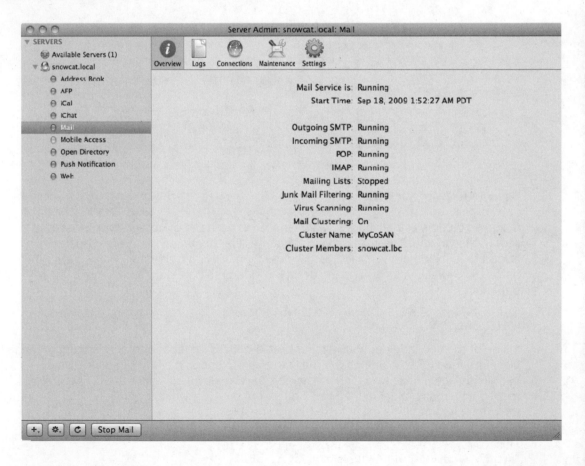

Figure 5-42. *Mail service overview with cluster*

Leveraging Push Notification

New to 10.6 is Apple's Push Notification service. The push notification requires minimal configuration and can be started through Server Admin. In order to take advantage of the push notification services provided by OS X Server, services must be configured to utilize the server. The Mail and iCal services are the only services shipping with 10.6 that can be configured to use the push notification service, shown in Figure 5-43. To enable Push notifications for one of these services, configure it in the desired services configuration screen.

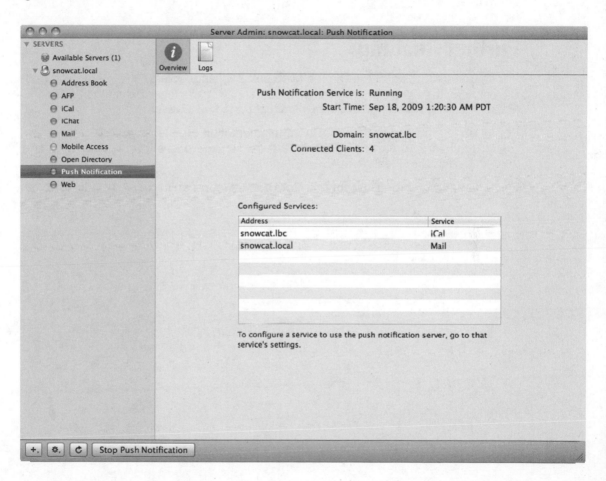

Figure 5-43. *Push notification service*

Summary

In this chapter, we learned how OS X clients can interact with various groupware solutions, most notably Microsoft Exchange. We also discussed heavily the new groupware options provided by Apple's latest Server OS release, 10.6 Snow Leopard, including Address Book Server, iCal Server 2, iChat Server, and the OS X mail server.

In the next chapter, Mass Deployment, we discuss the various technologies and tools involved with efficiently deploying software and operating systems en masse to your entire fleet.

Further Reading

For an understanding of the various Microsoft Exchange roles, their interaction, and the services they provide, see the Microsoft TechNet article on Exchange 2007 at http://technet.microsoft.com/en-us/library/bb124937.aspx

For an understanding of the WebDAV implementation on Exchange 2003 and below, see the MSExchange.org article at http://www.msexchange.org/articles/Access-Exchange-2000-2003-Mailbox-WebDAV.html

Documentation for the Dovecot mailstore can be found at: http://wiki.dovecot.org/

## Chapter 6

Mass Deployment

Chances are that if you deal with enterprise-level systems management you'll need to deploy systems en masse from time to time. If you have a hardware refresh rate of, say, 25 percent per year and a total of 10,000 computers, you'll have to deploy 2,500 machines every year. The tasks involved in the process are usually repetitive, lending themselves to batch processing. As a result, you can—and should—put solutions in place that let you automate deployment of systems on an ongoing basis.

If planned properly, you can extend the file sets and tools you develop, using them to provide everyday troubleshooting capabilities. For example, suppose a problem is resident on only one computer, but the symptoms present themselves across multiple users. Many IT departments have a policy of simply reimaging such systems, on the assumption that the computer in question has somehow varied from an approved image. This may seem counter intuitive, and an entry-level troubleshooting technique, however while it may technically satisfying to isolate an issue on a machine, doing so may be take much more time than simply reimaging a system. In this way, the user has less down time because you have cloned the same configuration on to all machines, so if an issue only presents on one, the chances of it being systemic are low. In most organizations, reimaging as part of a troubleshooting paradigm can sharply reduce the Total Cost of Ownership (TCO) while simultaneously serving to keep the environment as homogenous as possible (which further reduces TCO).

To reduce the time spent reimaging, it's a good idea to keep user data in sync with or stored on another host or segmented from the system in some fashion, such as a dedicated partition for user data, or utilizing Apple's external account technology. In Microsoft Windows, this would commonly be accomplished using roaming profiles. In the Apple enterprise vernacular, there are two similarly common options for user data storage, Portable Home Directories and Network Home Folders. This helps save your support personnel from either having to back up each user folder or computer prior to reimaging or replacing a system. One of the goals of implementing an imaging solution should be to reduce the amount of time spent fixing problems. Commoditizing computers will help you to achieve that goal. In Chapter 7, we'll cover portable and network home folders.

Planning Your Mass Deployment

The first step in preparing to roll out a large number of systems (after you read this chapter, of course) is to sit down and make a checklist or matrix in the form of a spreadsheet. Include every task required to set up a new computer, listing each in the order your personnel must perform it. The items should be: binding to the directory service, creating local administrative accounts, setting preferences, locking down permissions, installing software, installing updates, and whatever other specific procedures apply to your environment. Remember that mass deployment is sometimes one big hack, and therefore needs to be documented for your predecessor and yourself six months from now.

Remember to solicit content for this deployment matrix from your end users. After all, your institutions primary purpose for having computers is to serve your end users and not your IT staff. This list should be ever growing and should be linked in some way to your trouble ticket tracking system. If you consider imaging not to simply be a one-time process, but to be an integral workflow in supporting machines, you can use it to track problems that can be circumvented or mitigated simply by added preflight stages to your imaging process. For instance, if you see that 20 percent of your helpdesk tickets relate to improper mail client configuration, perhaps your image should include one of the many automatic setup scripts available for common mail clients such as Microsoft Entourage (Outlook).

The tasks that systems require may depend on factors, such as the department they're in and what they're used for. Next, you need to determine which tasks you'll carry out on which systems. If the steps are the same for all machines, then following these two steps will likely be the easiest approach: Initially, simply deploy a large, monolithic image to every system. A monolithic image is simply an image of an entire system, including applications, operating, and other requirements. Follow that with other tasks (carried out by scripts, package installers, or both) that you couldn't include in the image—for example, Active Directory binding, which must run at first boot. While granularity is normally an IT person's best friend, keeping things as simple as possible can also be an important mantra with mass deployment. Much like lawyers are coached never to ask a question they don't know the answer to, never include an imaging step either pre- or post flight that you cannot guarantee through testing will work with all the variables of your infrastructure. Imaging should serve to simplify your IT infrastructure, not complicate it. A good example of this was a deployment performed at a large institution. The on-site IT staff pushed out a non-universal copy of their antivirus software, which caused startup issues on older PowerPC machines. If their imaging testing would have been performed on both architectures this would have been caught. The technician in charge of this deployment used a newer Intel machine for testing. Due to this, it's extremely important you have a cross section of hardware to test with what matches your organization's current computer inventory.

If procedures must differ for different parts of your organization, make sure to account for the specific differences in your matrix. Split your tasks (like preferences to be set, bindings, and software to be installed) into two categories as you can see in Table 6-1. The first should be the lowest-common-denominator tasks (and software, if required) that pertain to every single computer. Examples include operating-system installation, binding the OS into Active Directory (or other directory service), and other global tasks. This is sometimes best framed as a timeline, from start to finish. This timeline would separate the takes that you would perform manually if you were asked to setup a new employee's workstation.

Tasks to put in the second category are those that involve taking the groups of computers and users in your checklist and making them correspond to constructed users and groups in your global directory service. Based on this checklist, you now have an object-oriented model for who gets what items in your environment. This will serve as the blueprint for your deployment system.

Table 6-1. *Object-Oriented Tasks*

Global Tasks	Packages
Enable FileVault Master Password	Install Adobe Suite
Install Mac OS X	Setup for VPN Access
Install Microsoft Office	Fill Bookmarks for HR Dept.
Setup 802.1x	Add Server Admin Tools
Add Hidden Local Admin Account	Add Citrix Client
Bind to Active Directory	Install iWork
Bind to Open Directory	Setup IChat

If you are an ITIL-based IT shop, then you likely already have a repository of all "supported" applications in the form of a Definitive Software Library (DSL). In this case, you will take the supported applications from your DSL and place them into one of the two columns.

NOTE: Once you know who gets what software, try to get volume-license keys from every vendor. Sometimes the cost can be prohibitive, but you really want to try even if your automation choices become very limited or if you have to install a unique key for even a single software package. Also, be aware that smaller software packages may still require activation even with volume license keys. Every vendor is different. Software that is not as widely deployed may have serious design considerations if the vendor does not officially support mass deployment. Always test your images and processes on at least two systems to see how your software will handle being moved between different machines, and if necessary in your environment, hardware platforms. Some software registration systems utilize machine specific data, such as Mac address or other hardware information. In the event that software registration cannot be so easily baked into your image or package, you may need to utilize post-flight scripting to accomplish your task.

Monolithic vs. Package-Based Imaging

Mac OS X mass deployment is sometimes the subject of much debate. One of the leading topics in this debate is whether monolithic or package-based installations are the preferred methodology. This set of authors would like to put this to rest and say both are preferred in all environments time permitting. The question then becomes more of a matter of workflow order rather than the headlining technology. Monolithic installations can simply be the end result of package-based installs, where package-based installs are just the steps of monolithic installs split up into different file sets. That said, the preferred methodology is typically to always start with packages and then build monolithic images from the resultant packages depending on their size. In this way, you can add and remove items as needed, without the same rebuild time that starting anew would require. If your end result is a large monolithic image, then larger datasets can be deployed as one stream of multicast data rather than independent package installs via unicast. An example would be a package installer in excess of 50GBs, such as one of Apple's Pro Applications. While a single package installer would allow you to easily remove or update this in your image, including this much data in your "base" monolithic will increase deployments speeds for a number of reasons. If your network supports multicast, you would be able to push the image to an arbitrary number of computers via a single stream of data. If you have an image in excess of 50GBs to be deployed to more than a dozen computers, this can mean big savings in network bandwidth and deployment speed. Multicast deployment of packages is not a capability available to any of the most popular deployment systems. In this regard, creating a large base image can result in a significant yet more efficient deployment, rather than have post-flight installers run on each system independently. Each technique has its own merits, but when it comes right down to it nearly every deployment will benefit from a mixture of the two.

While it can seem contradictory given the ease of creating an initial monolithic image, after a few years of imaging, it seems like everyone ends up learning that pushing out images monolithically is typically more time-consuming than breaking that same image up into parts. In package-based imaging, you put down a very sparse "base" image, which could even be a bare-metal image containing nothing except for a Mac OS X install which has never been booted (such as what is configured from the factory on a new machine), then perform post-flight tasks to add the rest of the software and do the configuration.

With the purely monolithic technique, each time you go to build a new image, you may have to start from a clean OS installation then perform a certain series of tasks on the system before making the image of it. If you have multiple architectures in a deployment (like, PowerPC and Intel), you could find yourself carrying out the procedure once for every architecture. This redundant work compounds if you have different departments that receive different software, thus causing you to create more and more images. With each equipment refresh or major update to push to clients, you might need to create a new image. Additionally, due to what is typically lack of documentation, if your original image builder leaves, you often have no idea which changes, scripts, and software was originally included in your image without back tracking forensics.

Why would anyone use a single large image? Well, for one, it's pretty easy to do. In fact, for most simple environments, it's far easier than breaking that image into parts in relation to preparation time. For example, if you want all the computers you deploy to have the same configuration; you can embed that into the computer from which you'll create an image. For example, click a button which creates a preference, rather than create an installer which installs that preference. Then, when you push that image out, the setting is there. Later, if you want to change the setting, you can send a script to do so, either through Apple Remote Desktop (ARD) or as an imaging task for subsequent sets of imaged computers. At that point, however, you're going to have to figure out which files were created by that change or, better yet, how to do this programmatically (through a script) so you don't mess up other settings along the way.

As you get more granular with your packages and scripts, you may end up using an automation of some sort to alter each system-preference pane, configuration file, application, serial number, and anything else you can think of that you do to each new machine. That automation may consist of a managed-preference procedure (discussed in Chapter 7), a script, or a package. It's not uncommon to have 100 tasks to perform on a system, post-imaging, but getting to that point can be time consuming. In the long run, a truly package-based imaging system offers the most systems-management flexibility.

> **NOTE:** While it may end up more work for some environments to build a number of scripts or packages to automate your deployment, it's a great learning experience if you have time and will aid in the ongoing imaging process as you have new machines and new operating systems (and builds) to redeploy under.

The monolithic image approach for an imaging environment as described in Table 6-1 would then result in a solution similar to Figure 6-1, with packages deployed post installation.

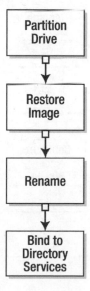

Figure 6-1. *Workflow for monolithic imaging*

Taking the imaging workflow to a more package based approach would then result in a workflow more similar to Figure 6-2, where we take things into more of the object-oriented realm.

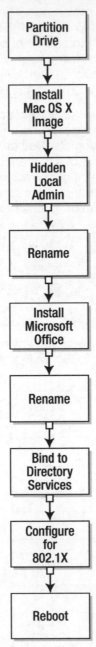

Figure 6-2. *Package-based imaging*

As we've indicated, on the outside, Figure 6-2 will seem like more work. However, when you introduce change into your environment then the larger the environment the less work this will inevitably be.

Automation

The more computers you deploy, the more you'll want to automate the setup process. If you have to bind 25 machines into Active Directory and each takes roughly 5 minutes, you'll dedicate about 2 hours—not too bad. But if you have 1,000 systems, we're talking about 83 hours. In that case, though writing a script to automate the process may consume 5 hours, you've saved 78 hours. On the other hand, for just 25 computers, writing a script wouldn't seem to make sense, since you'd spend an extra 3 hours. Except, if those 25 systems ever need reimaging, the work you did to automate the process will have paid off. An often overlooked component of this type of work is the massive amount of scripts that are already currently available. Like many other IT professionals, the authors of this book often publish their scripts online in publicly accessible forums. With this said, when estimating time to create a script such as one used for Active Directory binding, always research to see if one is already available freely from some other source. This small amount of forethought may even mitigate all development time if the script does exactly what you need it to do, and if not It may be easier to start with an example then from scratch.

Refer to your checklist to decide which tasks you'll automate. Generally, you perform automation one of two ways: using packages (thus the term package-based imaging) or scripts. Packages are installers; scripts can also "install" items, but most often, you use them in the deployment process simply to augment or transform existing data. This line gets blurred a bit in the regard that packages can be "payload" free, meaning that they can be created with the express purpose of running scripts. Wrapping your final scripts in a package installer has huge advantages, as Apples package installer infrastructure includes many different components, such as pre- and post flight scripts, sanity checks for memory, system version, as well as graphical installer bundles ,which mean you can even put a basic user interface "on top" of your script to help with the uninitiated.

Later in the section "InstallEase and Iceberg" of this chapter, we'll cover package-creation more thoroughly. But for now, take a good look at your checklist. Some software comes in the form of a package installer that you can use for deploying the software. If you do use existing package installers, budget a couple of hours for testing each. If you can't use an existing package, then you can either create a new one or you can write a script to place all of the files, or even parts of files, in their appropriate locations.

> **NOTE:** As experienced scripters (and managers of those who script), take our word for this: When you get a budget estimate for writing a particular script, just double it. This will save you a lot of grief down the road.

Image Delivery

Monolithic images can be pretty easy to deploy, especially on an ad hoc basis. The general outline of the process is this: Reboot a target system (often referred to as an *imaging* or *base* system) into target disk mode, connect it to a master-control computer, and then use Carbon Copy Cloner (http://www.bombich.com/software/ccc.html), Super Duper! (http://www.shirt-pocket.com/SuperDuper), or Apple's Disk Utility (in /Applications/Utilities on Mac OS X) to clone the master system to an attached system or an image file. You can also deploy images over a network, using Apple Software Restore (ASR) or NetRestore, which is a graphical interface to asr running on Mac OS X Server, NetInstall, which leverages NetBoot for imaging, or a variety of third-party products.

Most of the complexity of an imaging solution arises from the automation that you put in place, so whether to automate becomes an issue of economy of scale. As noted earlier, the more systems you have, the more you'll want to automate, starting with the delivery of an image, but then moving into renaming systems, binding to directory services, installing software and making operating system or application configuration changes.

Through this section, we'll trace the emergence of an image-delivery environment from childhood toward maturity. We'll start with one of the simplest solutions—Disk Utility—to deliver an image directly to a computer, then move toward using the default solutions from Apple, and finally explore third-party solutions that can automate even the smallest of details.

If you actually try each of the options we lay out, you'll spend a number of hours simply waiting for images to be created—transferring what is typically a 5 to 10GB file system into a file and reordering isn't exactly the fastest operation. So feel free to follow along with the screens and commands, but don't feel you must wait for each step to complete unless you see a compelling reason to do so (for example, you're considering using that solution as a mass-deployment strategy).

Creating an Image

The ability to create a hard-drive image and copy it to another hard drive is a basic, longtime feature of the Mac OS. We'll begin by illustrating the process using the tried-and-true Disk Utility, included with Mac OS X. This tool can produce an image of the computer, which, by default, it does in the form of a disk image (DMG) file.

We'll start by building the base system that will act as the template. First, install OS X on a computer and go through the checklist of settings and procedures you normally follow. Don't, however, perform any trusted binding of the system into a directory service. (Creating this binding is the default with Active Directory, which we covered in Chapters 2 and 3, so don't do any Active Directory binding prior to making the image.)

Next, install the applications you normally run (using, one hopes, the volume licensing keys), populate them with your usual files, and reboot the system into FireWire target-disk mode. You can do so by selecting Target Disk Mode in the startup-disk preference panel before you reboot or by holding down the T key at boot-up. When the system has restarted, it will display a gray screen and a masquerading FireWire logo. At this point, connect the base system to the admin computer to create the image file on the latter.

One aside: If you don't have volume licensing for your software, you may be better off by *not* licensing the base-image applications, depending on how draconian the software's serial number mechanism is. On the other hand, there may be no such checks, and the maker may even bless using the same license on all machines as long as you've purchased it. Your mileage will vary heavily by application and vendor.

> **NOTE:** An arbitrary version of Mac OS X will usually support all hardware that was available at the time of its release. However, Apple will sometimes release a newer build of the operating system for a new hardware model that just shipped. This new build may have the same operating system version, but may also contain additional components that were added for that specific hardware (i.e., new track pad driver) which incremented the build identifier of the system. When presented with this scenario, you should typically make your base or monolithic image from that newest operating system build. However, the next OS point release should contain all additions in this "build train" specific operating system (and more). You can determine a system's build number by running the terminal command sw_vers. If you must deploy your image before Apple releases their next point update, such as a lull between 10.6.1, and your deployment date, be aware that "build train" specific operating systems are not officially supported by Apple on anything other than the original hardware. While they often work, this is a consideration to be aware of if you phone in for support.

Next, as with Microsoft Windows, you'll want to remove those pesky unique cache files from that computer. If you don't, they may be re-created in the image file. The following are the files to delete:

- `.DS_Store` files (using the `find /Volumes/volumename -name .DS_Store -exec rm {} \;` command)
- `.Trashes` files (using the `find /Volumes/volumename -name .Trash -exec rm {} \;` command)
- `/System/Library/Extensions.kextcache`
- `/System/Library/Extensions.mkext`
- `/Library/Preferences/SystemConfiguration/NetworkInterfaces.plist`
- `/var/db/BootCache.playlist`
- `/var/db/volinfo.database`
- Contents of `/var/vm/`
- Contents of `/Library/Caches/`
- Contents of `/System/Library/Caches/`
- `/var/vm/sleepimage`
- Contents of `/Users/Shared/`

- `/var/log/secure.log`

- `/var/db/krb5kdc`

- `/var/db/volinfo.database`

- `/var/root/Library/Preferences/com.apple.recentitems.plist`

- Contents of `/var/root/Library/Preferences/ByHost/`

> **NOTE:** This step is similar in functionality to removing the files that are unique to a computer by using `sysprep` in Windows environments, but the procedure does not carry out some other tasks that `sysprep` does.

Once you've deleted the unique information, don't restart the clone. Instead, on the system connected to the target-disk-mode computer, open Disk Utility (*Applications* → *Utilities*), which will produce the screen shown in Figure 6-3. Click on New Image in the application toolbar.

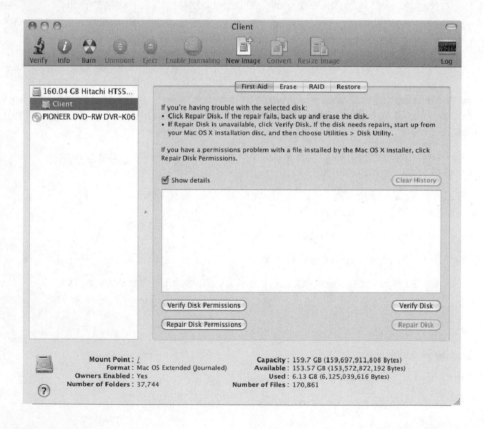

Figure 6-3. *Apple's Disk Utility*

In the resulting window, click on the FireWire disk's volume name (listed along the left side of the screen), then select New Image from the tool bar or go the File menu located in the Mac OS X toolbar, choose Folder, and select New Disk Image from Folder. Either way, you'll get options you can apply to the new image, as you can see in Figure 6-4. Configure the Image Format setting to Read Only and verify that the Encryption: option is set to none. Click Save when you're done.

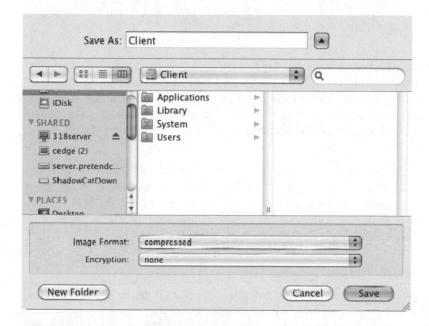

Figure 6-4. *Choosing where to save the disk image*

Disk Utility will now image the drive. The process can take a while, so this is a great time to check out hdiutil by reading the next section, and maybe even using the section as a guide while you try out the command.

> **NOTE:** If you'd selected the actual drive device rather than the volume, the disk's partition and size information would have been embedded in the image. By choosing the volume itself, as shown in Figure 6-4, you prevent the utility from recording the size and makeup of the disk. This is extremely important, as it allows you to deploy the volume to other systems that have different capacities.

Creating an Image from the Command Line

Mac OS X comes stocked with a number of tools to manage compressed files. Some, such as gunzip and tar, are standard tools found on most Unix variants. But hdiutil is specific to the Mac and a pretty powerful implement for creating and managing disk images.

Use hdiutil to create an image, called MacBook.dmg, in your working directory by entering this at the command line:

```
hdiutil create MacBook.dmg -size 10g –fs HFS+ -type SPARSE
```

Note that, in this case, you don't need to include the file's path. But if you want the freedom to summon the file from wherever you've decided to put it, you can simply prepend the path.

The sample command, which leverages the create verb, simply tells hdiutil to produce a disk image, give it a maximum capacity of 10GB, and format it for the HFS+ file system. (But if you'd like, you can use the -fs option to specify an alternative format.) By default, the file's volume name will be the same as that of the file, minus the *.dmg* suffix. The command creates an imaged volume name of MacBook, but you can specify a different one using the -volname flag.

The -type SPARSE option causes the command to generate a file that takes up only as much room as the data it contains, rather than consuming the same amount of space as the entire disk. But with a sparse image, as you add data, the file can expand to accommodate the extra up to the limit you set—10GB, in this case. If that's too little capacity, you can change the maximum size of your DMGs, making MacBook.dmg bigger. To do so, use the resize verb with the size flag, as in the following code:

```
hdiutil resize -size 50g MacBook.dmg
```

If you want, instead of creating a new image from scratch, you can do so from an existing volume using hdiutil. The steps you performed earlier, graphically, were fairly straightforward, but you could have carried them out from the command line much more quickly. To do so, use the create verb along with an option to define the source folder (-srcfolder) of your imaging station. (This time, the example gives the path to the DMG file.)

```
hdiutil create -srcfolder /Volumes/MacHD /asr/MacBook.dmg
```

Notice that the command line specifies the –srcfolder option rather than –srcdevice. This is for the same reason that you select the volume, rather than the disk, in the graphical interface. At this point, you have a MacBook.dmg image file, so you can mount it. For that, you call on the attach verb and specify the DMG file you'd like to mount as follows:

```
hdiutil attach MacBook.dmg
```

> **NOTE:** You could also have used the -attach flag with the create verb, which would have created the DMG file and mounted it in one command.

You can now copy data into and out of your DMG file as you would with a standard volume. This is useful for adding startup scripts, for example, binding to your directory service, then running the sanitization process (removing files unique to the computer that created the image) defined in the "Creating an Image" section earlier in this chapter, just in case you forgot to do so before making the image. Once you're done, you can unmount the DMG using detach:

```
hdiutil detach MacBook.dmg
```

The detach verb has one very useful flag, -force, which (obviously) you use only when you have to force a disk image to unmount.

The attach verb, on the other hand, has a variety of options. The -readonly flag will mount the volume strictly for viewing. The -nomount flag, as you might guess, doesn't actually mount the volume, which can be useful if, for example, you want to run disk utilities against it. If you want to mount the disk image at a path other than the default /Volumes directory, you can use the -mountroot flag followed by the directory path you prefer.

Another commonly used flag, -owners, (followed by on or off) comes in handy. Set to off, this causes the drive to act much like one plugged into a system when you've checked the box to ignore permissions. We highly recommend that you always mount the disk image with ownership off; otherwise it's very easy to corrupt permissions—not good when you intend to duplicate this image to hundreds of computers in your fleet. Obviously, you'd prefer that the original permissions persist. There are other flags, but these are the ones we find ourselves using most often.

> **CAUTION:** Whenever you work on a base-image volume or disk image, ensure that the volume is mounted with permissions enforced, otherwise you may corrupt permissions on your base model. This means that if you make changes you would need to do so with elevated privileges on your own system so as not to take ownership of files and then make sure to chmod based on the UID of the user(s) on the target system rather than your own.

Next, let's say you want to burn that DMG file to optical media. Accomplishing the task is simple using the burn verb and referencing the image file, as you can see in the following:

```
hdiutil burn /asr/MacBook.dmg
```

The hdiutil command will prompt for a blank disk to burn.

Alternatively, you may want to convert the image file to a more compatible format, perhaps to facilitate mass duplication of the optical media on non-Macintosh systems. Because the ISO format provides a burnable, platform-agnostic image file, it's a commonly used choice for this type of task. To take the MacBook.dmg file from the current working directory and convert it into an ISO image, use the convert verb and specify the -format flag along with an output destination.

```
hdiutil convert MacBook.dmg -format UDTO -o MacBook.iso
```

You can also use convert to make the MacBook.dmg file read-only. Simply specify -format followed by the code for read-only and the file name for the converted file, as shown in the following code:

```
hdiutil convert MacBook.dmg -format UDRO -o MacBook_ro.dmg
```

To make the mynew.dmg file read-write, save it as mynewreadwrite.dmg, then enter the command:

```
hdiutil convert MacBook_ro.dmg -format UDRW -o MacBook_rw.dmg
```

The full listing of conversion options and what they produce (from the main page of hdiutil) is:

- *UDRW:* UDIF read/write image
- *UDRO:* UDIF read-only image
- *UDCO:* UDIF ADC-compressed image
- *UDZO:* UDIF zlib-compressed image
- *UDBZ:* UDIF bzip2-compressed image (OS X 10.4+ only)
- *UFBI:* UDIF entire image with MD5 checksum
- *UDRo:* UDIF read-only (obsolete format)
- *UDCo:* UDIF compressed (obsolete format)
- *UDTO:* DVD/CD-R master for export
- *UDxx:* UDIF stub image
- *UDSP:* SPARSE (grows with content)
- *UDSB:* SPARSEBUNDLE (grows with content; bundle-backed)
- *RdWr:* NDIF read/write image (deprecated)
- *Rdxx:* NDIF read-only image (Disk Copy 6.3.3 format)
- *ROCo:* NDIF compressed image (deprecated)
- *Rken:* NDIF compressed (obsolete format)
- *DC42:* Disk Copy 4.2 image

With hdiutil you can also burn an ISO file as well as perform a checksum and segment an image file by using the verbs burn, verify, and segment, respectively. As you convert your disk image (if you do so), keep in mind that ultimately you'll need it to be in read-only format if you want it to be deployable via ASR or other methods.

Though hdiutil has a number of other great options (for example, the ability to use shadow files), we'll review just one more, encryption, because it's more relevant to our topic. When you execute hdiutil using the -encryption flag with create, the command asks you to supply a password. (And naturally, to mount the disk image, you'll have to enter whatever password you assigned.)

You can also pipe the password into hdiutil by using echo along with the flags -encryption and -stdinpass. But because this puts the password into your shell's history—which you don't want—you'll need a second command. The two look like the following:

```
echo -n "MyPassword" | hdiutil create -encryption -stdinpass -size 1g secret.dmg
clear history
```

The first line creates a 1GB disk image called `secret.dmg` that you can open using MyPassword. The second wipes out the history, including the saved password. This command pair can be useful for storing sensitive information created as part of preflight or post-flight imaging or used for deploying sensitive information with a predefined password

Operating System Packaging with Composer

Composer, a utility from JAMF software (`www.jamfsoftware.com`), creates package and image files. To make the latter, the drive you're cloning must be connected to your computer and can't be acting as a boot volume. With those conditions met, you can create an image quickly and easily. Open Composer and click on the New Package button in the Application toolbar. Now click on these three selections: Create OS Package, the icon for the drive you're cloning, and Choose (see Figure 6-5).

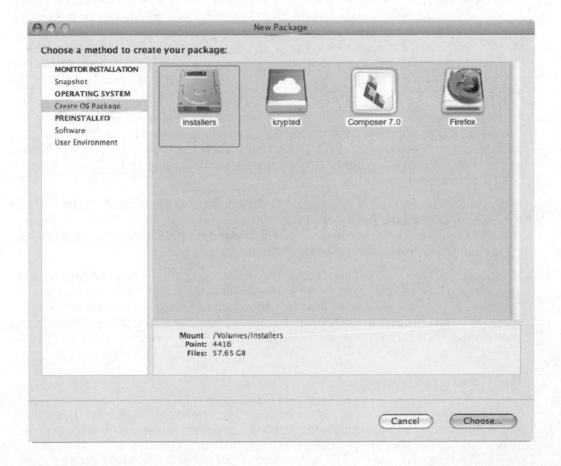

Figure 6-5. *JAMF's Composer*

The program will prompt you for the location where you want to save the DMG file. When you click Save, not only will Composer produce the image, it will create a complete ASR image of the drive and even do all of the machine-specific cleanup we discussed earlier in the section called "Creating an Image."

Bare-Metal Images

The steps we've just outlined are very common when creating standard monolithic images. But there are a number of opinions about what constitutes a bare-metal image. Some consider it a base install of Mac OS X. Others consider it to be the actual Mac OS X installation media. Basically though, for a solution that's more package-based than monolithic, the base image should have as little as possible in it—the more configuration that post-imaging packages and scripts handle, the more granular you can be with your imaging.

The difference between the two ways of creating a bare-metal image is this: When using the OS installation disk as your bare-metal image, once you've installed the base Mac OS X disk image, you customize every single action as a task (*including* the operating system installation) at image-delivery time. As a result, you won't need to sanitize the system. When you use an installed system, you set up a base OS install, do nothing else to the system, and then create the image, so you need to sanitize out the unique information.

When should you employ one method of making a bare-metal image over the other? Create the image with the installation media when you're worried about having to sanitize, or when you're concerned about incompatible hardware variations in machines you're deploying, so you'd rather just image a disk than install a new OS every time you need a new base image.

This mostly becomes an issue because new machines shipped by Apple often require a disk with an OS version at or above the one that comes on the installation disk. While Mac OS X tends to be fairly inclusive of all hardware drivers in retrospect for modern systems, the developers can't plan for all future systems as well.

That being said, there are circumstances when certain options are best configured in the base image. For instance, if you want all of your client machines to connect to a non-enterprise but internal company WPA Wi-Fi network, but don't want to disclose the pre-shared key, then it's best to configure this option into the base image. The circumstances in which you'll need a modified base image are rare, but will occasionally occur.

Deploying Images

Deploying base images to hundreds of machines can be extremely hard on bandwidth and on the server hosting images. Multicasting can relieve the stress by offloading the heavy lifting to the switching infrastructure, and there are a number of solutions you can use for this type of image deployment, including DeployStudio and NetRestore (both use asr as a back end protocol). With multicasting, the server provides a single stream of imaging data to which client machines can subscribe and then read. In such a scenario, the server constantly streams the block data of the image over the network. On reaching the end of the image, the server starts re-streaming from the beginning. After subscribing to the stream, clients begin laying down data to their internal drives according to the current progress of the stream. A client will continue to write data until it has completed a full loop of the stream.

A multicast deployment becomes essential as deployment numbers scale; even a Gigabit Ethernet connection will become fully saturated after about 20 concurrent unicast restore streams. Solutions capable of multicast deployment in OS X include the Apple-provided ASR and NetInstall tools, two solutions that have been available for a long time. Over the past few years, a number of third-party solutions to help deal with imaging for Mac OS X have also emerged. These range from free alternatives, such as NetRestore (for 10.4 and below) and DeployStudio, to proprietary solutions that come at a cost, such as the Casper Suite and LANRev. There are also a number of solutions that you can use to extend features of Windows- or Linux-based imaging solutions, such as Altiris and KACE.

Which is the best mass-deployment package? Whichever best automates the aspects of a deployment that your organization considers most important (and, as a result, provides the best return on investment in by cutting hours involved in repetitious pre- and post-flight imaging tasks). For example, the Casper Suite is very popular in environments implementing ITIL (Information Technology Infrastructure Library) because it takes into account a number of ITIL best practices, allowing for both deployment and long-term management of approved fixes and software. But many environments less-complex needs that an admin can satisfy simply by laying down an image, often opting to use very cost-effective tools such as NetRestore, ASR, and DeployStudio.

Most of these solutions support both unicast and multicast image deployment. While multicasting definitely is preferable in large environments, implementation isn't always possible due to increased network management complexity, particularly in larger, highly segmented networks. If this is an issue, either for technical or political reasons, unicast deployment may be the reality you face. In such cases, deploying site-, building-, or subnet-specific image servers may be desirable to more evenly distribute network load. Likewise, you'll want to perform deployments strictly during off-hours to prevent them from saturating your network backbone.

Restoring with Disk Utility

Earlier in this chapter, we described how to create an image. If you followed the instructions in the previous section, that was a monolithic image—likely one with no automation in it except for maybe a quick script to sanitize the system. Every computer that gets the image will have a unique computer name and should be named prior to being put into production. We'll be deploying the image over FireWire, which is a unicast method and limited to one computer at a time.

To roll out this image, you can again use Disk Utility, located in /Applications/Utilities. Simply click on the destination volume for your image and then click on the Restore tab, as shown in Figure 6-6. Here you'll see two fields, Source: and Destination:. Click on the *Image...* button to select the DMG file you created in the last section, then drag the target volume into the Destination: field to restore the image. When you're ready, click on the Restore button.

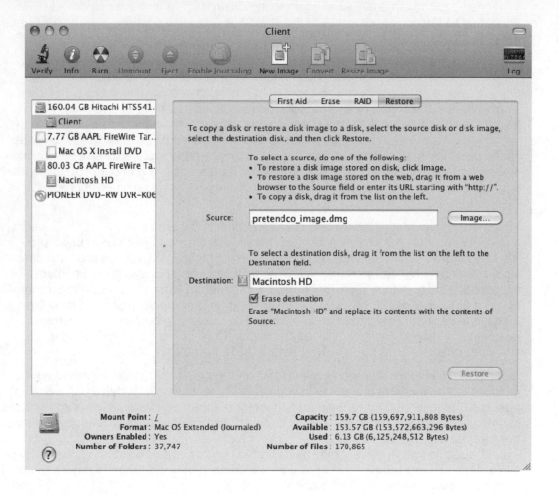

Figure 6-6. *Restoring an image in Disk Utility*

When the restore process completes, you can boot the computer with the destination drive and see if everything is as it should be. This system should be identical to the source machine, with the exception that any settings unique to a computer (MAC address, and so forth) would have changed. Conveniently, Apple stores these settings together in the ByHost directory.

You can also perform the image restore from the command line using hdiutil, as we did to create the image in the first place. The more experienced you become with imaging, the more likely you are to use the command line—or even just a quick shell script—to do much of your imaging.

At this point, you've completed imaging in its most basic form. For some environments, this process will work; others will require a multicast deployment model, or one that lets you simultaneously deploy to a large number of computers. Other environments might also require more granularity in the DMG as well as the pre- and post-flight imaging tasks. In the next section, we'll review a few options for multicasting your image so you can go fishing, play some Halo, or do whatever you like while the systems configure themselves. Or better yet, learn about ASR in the next section so you image 50 (or 500) systems at a time and take a vacation instead.

Using Apple Software Restore

Every copy of Mac OS X has included the command-line utility `asr`, so you can perform multicast imaging right out of the box without installing a thing. You can then use `asr` to perform a unicast or multicast restore (the command can be used to create images, restore images and server images). When the utility runs in multicast mode, it loops an image on the network as described earlier. The advantage of this is that whether you have 100 or 1,000 clients, they'll all image using the same stream of data without bogging down the imaging server by making disparate requests for different sections of the image.

The disadvantage is that if a client misses some data, which will happen eventually, that system will have to wait for the loop to come full circle to where the data was not properly delivered. With a unicast restore, in contrast, every client begins at byte 0 on the source image and requires its own dedicated stream of data from the server.

No matter which restore you use, you'll need to take an image and scan it first. To do so, you use the `asr` command along with `imagescan` to calculate checksums of the image file's contents and store it in the image. When you run `imagescan` on a disk image, the tool creates a number of checksums that are used to ensure successful restores. Additionally, the utility scans the image file and hints it for multicast restore, making sure the data arrangement on the image is optimized for block transfers. The command you issue will look like the following:

```
asr imagescan --source '/asr/MyImageName.dmg'
```

> **NOTE:** You can use the `--filechecksum` and `--nostream` options with the `imagescan` verb. The flags will, respectively, calculate checksums on a per-file basis and bypass reordering of the files for multicast. 10.5 and later require images to be scanned to be restored using Disk Utility, however asr can disable the check using the "-noverify" option from the command line. This is obviously never a best practice but will save time if you are testing.

To perform a unicast restore, run the `asr` command along with the `restore` verb from a host with access to both the DMG file from which you're restoring and the hard disk to which you're restoring. You can define the `-source` and `--target` as paths to files (tab autocomplete might just be your best friend if there as many spaces in your paths as in ours). You can also perform the erase and therefore have a proper restore as shown in the following code:

```
asr restore --source "/Users/$USER/Desktop/Mac OS X 10.5.4 Image.dmg" --target
/Volumes/ClientMachineHD/ -erase
```

For a multicast restore, you must first create a property list for the ASR process, specifying the settings that the network service will use. For this example, we've created a folder called /asr and placed in it a plist called config.plist. To function, asr requires two settings: data rate and multicast address. The data rate is the maximum speed in bytes that asr can write data, which we'll set conservatively at 8000000 (8Mbps).

The multicast address is the address for the data stream. To write these settings into the file, use the defaults command followed by a write, the file path/name, the key you're writing into the file, a flag to indicate the type of key (if required), and the contents of the key. You then specify a multicast IP address where you announce your datastream.

The Internet Assigned Numbers Authority (IANA) defines multicast address ranges from 224.0.0.1 through 239.255.255.255, with 224.0.0.1 through 224.0.0.255 reserved for special purposes. Many common solutions, such as Norton Ghost, use addresses in the 224.77.0.0/16. Following this example, use the multicast address 224.77.2.2. It's very important that you discuss the appropriate address to use for your specific network with your network administrators as multicast IP conflicts can arise if you do not. With that in mind, set the data rate and multicast address as follows:

```
defaults write ~/asr/config "Data Rate" -int 8000000
defaults write ~/asr/config "Multicast Address" 224.77.2.2
```

After you've written the data, read it and verify that it's correct using the defaults read command:

```
defaults read ~/asr/config.plist
{
    "Data Rate" = 8000000;
    "Multicast Address" = "224.77.2.2";
}
```

Now that you've scanned the image for restoration, load up the ASR server. To do so, use the asr command with the server option:

```
asr server --source ~/asr/MacBook.dmg --config /asr/config.plist
```

> **NOTE:** When configuring the data rate, you must consider both your network connection speed and the speeds of your clients. The Data Rate value specifies not the speed of the actual network transmission, but rather the speed at which your clients can write data to disk. This difference is particularly crucial in the case of compressed disk images. With these, data sent is compressed but will be uncompressed to disk. Modern-day SATA hard drives can typically sustain much higher transfer rates than the older 2.5-inch PATA drives in iBooks. Decompression of data can also be a processor-intensive task. When deploying images to slower computers, using compressed images may actually result in longer restore times.

Once you've started the ASR server, you'll need to restore the ASR image onto a target computer. To do so, boot your clients to a system such as a NetBoot server or a boot disk that has network access to the ASR server and the asr command available to it. From there you can run the following command, which is similar to our previous restores, but with asr://path to denote the multicast address of the ASR stream (in this example the server will be 239.255.100.100):

```
asr restore -source asr:// 239.255.100.100-target /MacHD
```

NetInstall

Every copy of Mac OS X Server includes NetBoot and its children NetRestore and NetInstall. As we showcase in the next sections, NetBoot can boot a Mac OS X computer to an image created specifically for the purpose of booting off the NetBoot server (even in some high security facilities without an internal drive present). A computer booted to a NetBoot image still provides a fully functional and interactive OS X experience, but any changes made to the system will revert to the standard configuration on reboot (Network home directories, which are discussed in Chapter 7, can mitigate this behavior.) That makes NetBoot a fairly popular solution in lab environments and kiosks, where the operating system loaded on each system is fairly static. Netboot typically works best if your environment supports DHCP assigned IP addresses and either does not block or forwards broadcast traffic between your network segments.

Netinstall uses netboot, but rather than boot a fully configured system, it typically starts an Apple installer program. This pre-installation environment is similar to Windows PE as it does not always include all the same components as normal operating system (such as the Quicktime framework or the python and ruby programming support files), NetInstall is used to image Mac OS X computers on a netbooted computer. NetInstall boots a Mac using NetBoot. It then copies the operating system locally to the target computer acting much like the stock installation DVD, but with the added benefits that it can be used to install multiple hosts concurrently over the network and that additional installation tasks can be configured. NetBoot and NetInstall are functionally the same, with the latter simply being a single-purpose NetBoot image created specifically for the deployment of software.

Both NetBoot and NetRestore can leverage HTTP, AFP, NFS to copy your image across the network. Additionally, aside from a one to one "unicast" using NFS or HTTP, ASR can image client systems using one continuous stream of data, known as "multicast." Whether you use Netinstall or NetRestore the NetBoot server itself sees all the images are all the same, but the client will interpret what to do with them differently based on the operating system stored inside the image. In the "NetRestore" section, we cover using NetRestore for deploying a fully populated image and in this section we will look at deploying an image installation media because at this time NetInstall is to be used strictly to push out installers and provide pre- and post-flight tasks. However, it is worth noting that historically NetInstall could be used for both the bare metal operating system found on installation media and for deploying a fully populated installation with the software (a monolithic image) and may eventually come back to that in a subsequent patch release down the road of Mac OS X 10.6 or later.

The first step in using NetInstall is creating what Apple refers to as a *Workflow,* using System Image Utility. The Workflow is, at its most basic, simply a single task that images a computer. However, you can also use workflows for many other purposes, such as reformatting a hard drive or running preflight or post-flight scripts and packages (which run, respectively, before or after delivery of the package's payload, as you might guess). Later in the chapter, we'll discuss ordering packages appropriately in further detail.

To get started with your first Workflow, first insert the operating system installation media into the system you will be running System Image Utility. Then open System Image Utility (located by default in the /Applications/Server folder of the Mac OS X Server (or client computer with the Server Tools installed). For this example, use the System Image Utility on the Mac OS X Server computer that will run the NetInstall service. Provided that the installation media is installed you'll see the Create a Network Disk Image screen as can be seen in Figure 6-7.

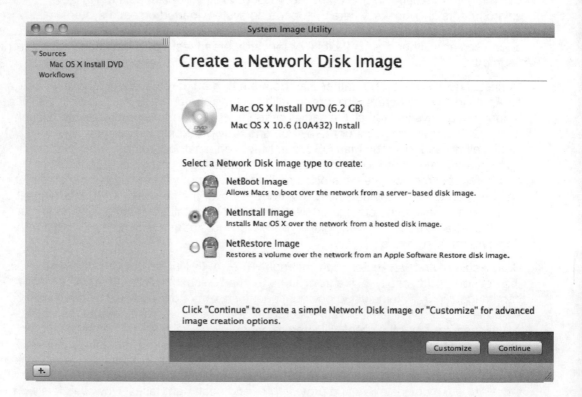

Figure 6-7. *Creating a Disk Image in NetInstall*

Go ahead and click on the radio button for NetInstall Image and then click on Continue. You will then be prompted to supply a Network Disk name (as you can see in Figure 6-8), which will be the name of the volume that the disk image is mounted as and a Description, which can be used to provide more detail about the image that you are creating. Populate these fields as is appropriate for your environment and then choose whether to allow the image to be served from multiple servers using the Image. When you are satisfied with your settings, click on the Create button and you will be asked to agree to the licensing agreement (since the installation on the client is automated and no licensing agreement will be presented there).

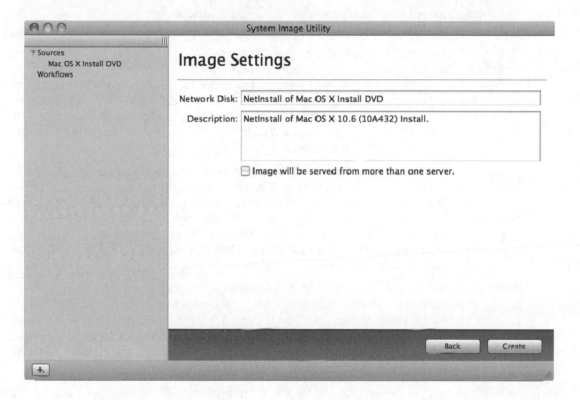

Figure 6-8. *NetInstall Image Settings*

Finally, provide an administrative user name and password when prompted in order for the image to be generated. At this point, System Image Utility will create a folder, with an NBI extension, that contains the resulting NetInstall image as well as a configuration file named `NBImageInfo.plist`, which defines the NetBoot image's environment. When added to a server's `NetBoot` folder, ServerAdmin will use this file to both read initial settings as well as modify them based on configuration changes. You'll also find the folders: `i386` and `ppc` in a NetBoot image's `.nbi` directory. These contain kernel-specific files: `booter`, an EFI binary file needed for initial boot;

mach.macosx, our kernel; and mach.macosx.mkext, a NetBoot-optimized kernel-extension cache.

> **NOTE:** By default NetBoot will use the /Library/NetBoot/NetBootSP0 folder as the first image to serve, so you can list the folder in the In: field. You can also copy the image elsewhere and then share it manually through NetBoot at a later time. Mac OS X Server will recognize that the image in Server Admin automatically, however you may need to enable the image before it is visible on the network. Keep in mind that you may want to create your image on a model of your target host as it may have a newer build then what your server has currently installed.

Now that you've created your image, open /Applications/Utilities/Server Admin.app, and in the SERVERS list, click on the server you're going to configure NetBoot for. To administer the NetBoot service, you first need to add it to the list of services displayed in Server Admin. So with the server selected, click on Settings in the Server Admin toolbar and then on the Services tab. Locate NetBoot in the list of available services, check the box to enable its display, and click Save. You'll now see the service displayed underneath the server name in the server list.

Next, you need to configure, then start the NetBoot service. Click on NetBoot in the list of available services, then click on the Settings icon in the Server Admin toolbar. By default, NetBoot isn't enabled for any of the network adapters on your server. Check the boxes in Enable NetBoot on at least one port for the network interfaces you'd like to use to serve NetBoot. A port dedicated purely for NetBoot is never a bad idea. Next, select the hard drive you want to house your NetBoot/NetInstall images, check its box under the Images column, and click Save.

When you enable a volume for NetBoot, a few things happen. First, the system will create a supporting folder structure at the root of the selected volume, usually Library/NetBoot/, which will contain two folders. The first, NetBootClients0, is shared out over AFP and used for NetBoot shadow files. Diskless NetBoot clients use the share for temporary file storage. The second folder, NetBootSP0, houses the server's NetBoot NBI bundle. Both folders are configured as NFS global exports.

NFS is a key player in NetBoot and so is another protocol, TFTP. NetBoot loads both the kernel and the booter over TFTP. The protocol's root folder exists in OS X Server at /private/tftpboot/. Inside is NetBoot folder, which contains symbolic links to each of the server's NetBoot sharepoints. Typically, this is only NetBootSP0, but some servers will have more than one. (Later in this chapter, we'll discuss referencing these protocols to statically set remote-boot capabilities.)

With the server setup done, you need to copy your image's NBI bundle into the previously selected volume's new /Library/NetBoot/NetBootSP0 directory. After you've copied (or moved) the image's .nbi folder, click on the Refresh button in Server Admin. You should now see the image listed under the Images tab of the NetBoot Settings screen. Check the box to enable the image, click on the Save button, and finally, click on Start NetBoot to bring up the actual NetBoot service.

Once you've configured the service and have it running, you should be able to boot your client computers from it by pressing the N modifier key at boot, which instructs a client to attempt a network-based boot.

Boot Modifier Keys

Mac OS X can boot from sources other than your default internal start-up disk through the use of modifier keys. When you power a system on, using these keystrokes will send commands to the system to perform the following:

- *C:* Boot from optical media.

- *D (with restore disk in optical slot):* Boot from hardware test mode.

- *Command-Option-O-F:* Boot from OpenFirmware (if you have open firmware).

- *Command-Option-P-R:* Reset Parameter RAM.

- *Command-Option-P-R (until you hear two tones:* Reset non-volatile RAM.

- *Command-Option-N-V:* Reset non-volatile RAM (similar to above according to hardware).

- *Command-Option-Shift Delete:* Bypass the default startup volume and look for another blessed volume.

- *Command-Option-T-V:* Boot that Quadra you hax0r'd OS X onto to use a TV for a monitor.

- *Command-S:* Boot from single-user mode, a command-line only environment where you need to mount disks manually.

- *Command-V:* Boot in verbose mode, which shows what's loading in a command-line-like environment as it loads. I boot my machines in this manner 100 percent of the time, using the nvram boot-args="-v" command.

- *Eject:* Ejects media from the optical slot/tray.

- *F12:* Ejects media from the optical slot/tray.

- *Mouse button:* Ejects media from the optical slot/tray.

- *N:* Boot from a NetBoot volume.

- *Option:* Boot from the startup manager, a list of available startup volumes that lets you select a startup volume.

- *Option-N:* Boot from a default boot image on a NetBoot volume.

- *Shift:* Disables nonessential kernel extensions (drivers).

- *Shift (if held after submitting login credentials):* Disables user startup items, launch daemons, and launch agents.

- *Shift (left shift key at the OS progress menu):* Bypass automatic login.

- *T:* Boot from Target Disk Mode, turning a system into a glorified FireWire drive (including access to optical drives).

- *Trackpad button:* Ejects media from the optical slot/tray.

- *X:* Forces the system to boot into Mac OS X (used only with systems that can run OS 9).

You can also boot an Xserve to a NetBoot server, using the start-up modifier keys without a keyboard. To do so, boot the system holding down the system-identifier button until the top row of lights blink in succession, Knight Rider style. At this point, let go of the system identifier button, then press it again, and you'll notice that the bottom light will change positions. The position number, from right to left, indicates the following:

1: Boot from an optical drive (similar to using the C modifier)

2: Boot from a NetBoot server (similar to using the N modifier)

3: Startup from the first blessed system found on an internal drive (useful if going from NetBoot or optical)

4: Look for another blessed system on another internal drive (similar to Command-Option-Shift-Delete modifier)

5: Boot from Target Disk Mode (similar to using the T modifier)

6: Reset NVRAM (similar to using Command-Option-N-V modifier)

8: Diagnostic mode

Once you've selected the desired boot option, press and hold the identifier button until all status indicators light sequentially. Release the button, and the system will finish booting. If you want to select the optical drive, you need to press the identifier an additional time once you've inserted the disk.

Bless

You can use the bless command to define boot options in a more granular fashion programmatically. It can define where a Mac OS X computer will boot from. The –folder option defines a directory to boot from, while you can use the –file option to choose a specific booter file (such as bootx).

To boot from a second volume, use the –folder option with the path to a volume's /System/Library/CoreServices directory:

```
bless –folder /Volumes/mySecondHD/System/Library/CoreServices –setBoot –nextonly
```

The command in this example calls bless with the –setBoot option, which tells EFI to use this device as its primary boot device. The –nextonly option is particularly helpful, as it allows booting to a device just once, after which it resumes operation from the previous start-up disk. This option has great utility: rebooting to maintenance partitions or NetBoot images, rebooting for complete reimaging, and rebooting into Boot Camp. Make this option your friend; take it out, wine it, and dine it. Your life will be dreary without it.

Speaking of Boot Camp, bless has dominion here too. To properly bless a Boot Camp partition, first figure out which partition, or slice, contains the foreign OS. Use Disk Utility on the drive with the Boot Camp partition you want to boot from as shown in the following code:

```
$diskutil list /
/dev/disk0
```

which will produce output similar to this:

```
#:                       TYPE NAME                 SIZE            IDENTIFIER
0:     GUID_partition_scheme         *149.1 Gi         disk0
1:     EFI                            200.0 Mi         disk0s1
2:     Apple_HFS helyx                122.9 Gi         disk0s2
3:     Microsoft Basic Data            25.9 Gi         disk0s3
```

For Windows, specifically, look for the "Microsoft Basic Data" slice. From the output above, you can see that we want to use disk0s3. To use Windows, you must specify the device and the –legacy option, which indicates BIOS support. Running the following command will tell your machine to reboot into Windows:

```
bless -device /dev/disk0s3 -setBoot -legacy -nextonly && shutdown -r now
```

The bless command also lets you specify a NetBoot location via the –NetBoot option. You define a specific server to NetBoot from by using the –server option. For example, you'd tell the Mac OS X computer to boot from the NetBoot instance running on server 192.168.210.99 with the command

```
bless -NetBoot -server bsdp://192.168.210.99
```

By default, NetBoot doesn't function across subnets because the Boot Service Discovery Protocol (BSDP) is non-routable. Specifying the –server option alone won't allow you to NetBoot across subnets. To boot an EFI-based Mac from a NetBoot server on a different subnet, you must also define the .nbi file, the mach.macosx file, and the .dmg file of the NetInstall file you created earlier. The following will perform the same command as above but assumes you're actually booting from a NetBoot image on a different subnet:

```
sudo bless -NetBoot -booter
tftp://192.168.210.99.edu/NetBoot/NetBootSP0/NetInstall.nbi/i386/booter kernel
tftp://192.168.210.99/NetBoot/NetBootSP0/NetInstall.nbi/i386/mach.macosx options
"rp=nfs:192.168.210.99:/private/tftpboot/NetBoot/NetBootSP0:MacBook.nbi/NetBoot.dmg"
```

Using what we learned in the earlier command, the underlying technology of the NetBoot service might become a little clearer. The TFTP and NFS services do the heavy lifting, so it's actually entirely possible to provide NetBoot services, even if you don't have any Mac OS X Servers available. You can use the bless command for a wide variety of other common tasks. Issue the man bless command to check the man page for more information and features.

Apple's NetRestore

NetRestore is a graphical front-end to the asr command line tool, which we covered in the "Using Apple Software Restore" section of this chapter. Using System Image Utility on a Mac OS X Server it is possible to create a NetBoot disk image that automatically boots a client and runs the asr commands that we referenced above for both uni-cast and multi-cast (mASR) restores. Once a client is booted into the NetBoot environment they can select a location (in the form of an image) to restore to their system and then start the restore using a standard looking installer interface.

System Image Utility can also be used to create the image itself, providing another tool in the arsenal for image creation. To create an image for restoration using NetRestore, open System Image Utility from /Applications/Server with installation media inserted or with a volume mounted that will serve as the source for your NetRestore disk image. Provided that System Image Utility is able to read the media, the Create a Network Disk Image screen should then appear. Here, click on the NetRestore Image radio button as seen in Figure 6-9 and then click on the Continue button. For the purpose of our example, we will be imaging using a monolithic Mac OS X client that has been booted into Firewire Target Mode and connected to our imaging station.

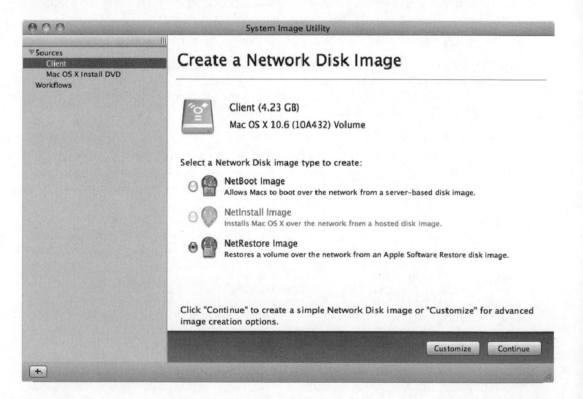

Figure 6-9. *Creating a Network Disk Image*

At the Image Settings screen, first provide a name that the mounted disk image will have in the Network Disk field as you can see in Figure 6-10. Then provide an explanation of what the image is for in the Description field. If the image will be hosted from multiple NetBoot or NetRestore servers, next click on the check box for Image will be served from more than one server. Finally, provide the particulars for creating a new local administrative account for the restored computer, including a name, short name and password. When you're satisfied with your settings, click on the Create button.

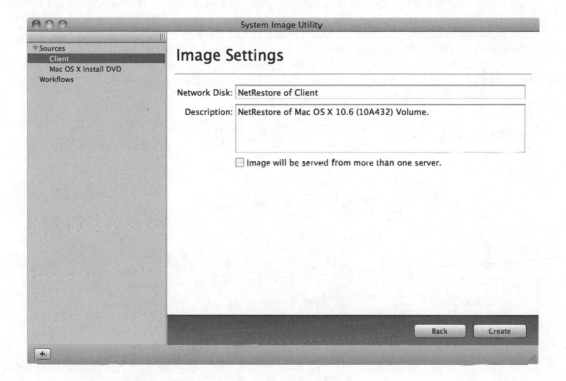

Figure 6-10. *NetRestore Image Settings*

Because your image will install an operating system you will next need to accept Apple's licensing agreement. Click on Agree if you do and then provide an administrative password in order to generate the image. According to the speed of your connection, wait for the client system and the size of the volume that you are creating an image from.

While waiting, ponder the fact that you could also have installed an operating system and a number of software titles, configured settings as you would like them to be and then booted that system into Firewire Target Disk Mode and made a NetRestore set from the populated system. This would in effect have the same result as running the image and then any subsequent post-flight actions. However, as your environment moves into a more mature imaging framework it would inevitably become too cumbersome. You can continue to push out large images though, generated on the fly using InstaDMG.

Once the image has been created, you'll then want to use the steps described in the "Using ASR" section earlier in this chapter to configure an ASR stream. Alternatively, you can place the resultant image onto a share point or even on an HTTP server. Document the path that you'll then use for accessing the image, and now it's time to setup that NetBoot image so that you can provide access to restore the disk image.

To create the NetBoot image, open System Image Utility again. Then click on the plus sign in the lower-left corner of the screen and select Create New Workflow. You will then be presented with two screens: the Automator Library and a populated workflow in the System Image Utility screen. Remove each of the pre-populated workflow items by clicking on the X in the upper right hand corner of that screen. Here you can drag items from the Automator Library to the workflow. First, drag Define NetRestore Source, then drag Create Image, as you can see in Figure 6-11.

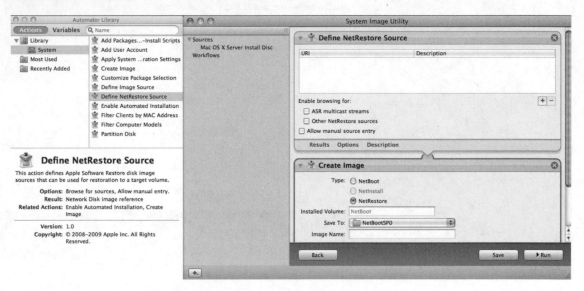

Figure 6-11. *Creating a NetRestore Workflow*

Once you have populated the tasks that comprise the workflow you can move on to configuring the settings for each task. For the Define NetRestore Source, first click on the plus sign and then provide the path to the location that you have hosted the image. If you are creating the path for multicast asr then check the box for ASR multicast streams. If you would like to list other disk images that can be restored, check the box for Other NetRestore Sources, and if you would like for the user to be able to type in a path to restore, click on the box for Allow manual source entry. (This final option is useful for new environments where you are testing, to check the path and potentially type in other paths if you need to.)

For the Create Image task, select a Type of image that you will be creating, which should be NetRestore. Then provide a name for the image in the Image Name field and finally a location to save the image to, which if NetBoot has previously been used will default to the /Library/NetBoot/NetBootSP0 directory that the NetBoot service looks to by default for which images to host. From Server Admin you can now use the enable checkbox for your NetBoot service for the newly generated image and test booting a client to the image.

To boot a client to the image, simply boot holding down the N key (note that at this point that client system will more than likely be erased, so make sure that it does not have data that you need on it prior to doing so). There are a number of things that can cause NetBoot not to work in your environment, as we'll describe in further detail in the "Bless" section later in this chapter. However, if NetBoot can function in the environment then the client should boot to a list of images that you can restore from based on the paths that you entered in the Define NetRestore Source action from the Automator Library. Select the location to restore to and then test the system when it is finished imaging.

While the system is imaging, it's time to ponder something else. If you look on the server in the Automator Library, you'll see a number of other tasks that could have been performed, including Add Packages, Add User Account, and Enable Automated Installation. The Add Packages option can be used to deploy a package. This could include any installer, custom-made packages and even payload free packages, which are typically used as vehicles for scripts; you can also use a package to perform automated binding on deployed client systems. You could also use the Add User Account option to create multiple accounts. The real power of this system though comes from the Enable Automated Installation, which can take your 3 or 4 touch deployment down to a one touch deployment, meaning boot the client holding down the N key and it will be completely imaged from start to finish, without having to "touch" the system again.

DeployStudio

DeployStudio is similar to the now-retired NetRestore, a commonly used free application that leveraged NetBoot and ASR to create a nicely automated mass-deployment system, if perhaps a rather utilitarian interface. NetRestore's killer feature was the ability to pack everything into a decent Graphical Interface and its ability to be extended on the fly with user contributed scripts and packages, combined with the ability to deploy software packages and scripts easily. Luckily, while bombich's netrestore was widely deployed, Deploy studio is more the fully featured effective replacement. In fact, DeployStudio far surpasses even Netrestores ease of use for entry level admins. Additionally, DeployStudio is written in a much more capable language known as Cocoa, which allows DeployStudio to look and feel like a rival to even some Apple tools.

DeployStudio, like all modern imaging tools for Mac OS X, automates the setup of ASR and a number of other technologies described previously. It uses a series of automations, called Workflows (similar to those in System Image Utility, but without the raw Automator-style interface), to set up an automation routine. Example workflows include partitioning a disk, deploying a master image, installing numerous post-imaging packages, and perhaps, to end the process, performing a Directory Service Binding script interface. DeployStudio presents all of this functionality via a simple, easy-to-understand graphical interface which is constantly being improved. Best of all, it's free. So why didn't we lead off with this tool? Because whether you use the graphical tool or the command line, it's vital you understand both as they all use the same basic set of technologies for all the tools we cover.

You can also use DeployStudio to roll out Windows for Apple Boot Camp environments using winclone. This isn't to say that it's going to sysprep the OS, but it will format the drive appropriately and lay the OS down on it which itself may then contain a sysprep file ready for the mouse trap to spring. Further automation is up to you (see Chapter 9).

To get started with DeployStudio, download the latest stable installer at http://www.deploystudio.com, extract the installation files, and start the actual install. In the Welcome to the DeployStudio Server Installer screen, click Continue, then click Continue again at the Important Information page, reading each along the way. Next, read the Software License Agreement, clicking on Continue if you're okay with having no major strings on your free software. Then click on the Agree button. Now you'll see the Standard Install portion. Select where on your hard drive you want to install DeployStudio (by default it's placed in the /Applications/Utilities directory). You can also select the applications you want to install. Note that the setup program will install DeployStudio's Admin, Server, Runtime, and Assistant components as well as a tool called Startup Disk, which provides access to the Startup Disk control panel. Available options include:

- *DeployStudio Admin:* Used to configure workflows in an interface similar to the one used by NetInstall.

- *DeployStudio Assistant:* Setup tool for performing initial configuration, creating NetBoot sets and USB/Firewire disk images for booting clients.

- *DeployStudio Runtime:* Used to manually run DeployStudio workflows from machines not booted to the DeployStudio disks (NetBoot or USB/Firewire). The runtime is pretty useful in seeing both what the environment for a station being imaged looks like and creating Masters (or images).

Once you're satisfied with your selections, click Install and wait for the setup to complete, then click on the Close button and go to /Applications/Utilities (or wherever you placed your application bundles), and verify that you see them. Next, open the DeployStudio Assistant, which will guide you through the configuration of DeployStudio.

> **NOTE:** DeployStudio Runtimes can now be run on live volumes. Therefore, you can now run the DeployStudio Runtime as a package installer and release packages to users or groups as a means of a self installation solution, allowing for a more zero-tier support mechanism with regard to package installers.

When you first open the software, you'll be prompted to start the services. For the purpose of this walk-through, start the service immediately. At the first Assistant screen, choose one of the following:

- *Set up a DeployStudio Server:* Configures the DeployStudio Server and the DeployStudio repository (all of the following options will require a DeployStudio Server to be set up in your organization).

- *Set up DeployStudio PC on this computer:* Set up server to accept PXE booted clients and image hosts based on information from the DeployStudio Server.

- *Create a DeployStudio NetBoot set:* Similar to the previous choice for NetInstall option, but pulls the automations from a DeployStudio Server.

- *Create a DeployStudio bootable external drive (USB & Firewire):* Similar to the previous option for unicast deployment over Firewire but pulls the image from a server (http) running DeployStudio.

NOTE: As you toggle through the DeployStudio options, you'll notice that the choices on the left side of the screen will change, providing you with a general idea of which tasks remain to be completed in your specific configuration.

Assuming this is the first DeployStudio Server, select the Set up a DeployStudio Server option, and click on Continue. At the Welcome screen, read the instructions, then click on the Continue button to bring up the Server connection screen. As requested in this window, enter the server address, user name, and password. For the address, fill in the IP or DNS information for the server, prepended with https:// and followed with the port number :60443. In the next field, enter the user name of the local system, and in the last text box, type in the password of the local system.

If you're accessing the server from the host on which you initially installed DeployStudio, you should be able to click on the drop-down list for the Server address: field to populate it with the information for the address itself. In our experience, if you're running Assistant directly from the DeployStudio Server and you don't see the server populated in the drop-down list, more than likely you chose to not start the services earlier. You can do so now using launchctl, as illustrated in the following code:

```
Launchctl load -w /Library/LaunchDaemons/com.deploystudio.server.plist
```

NOTE: If you start the services and then later decide that you don't want to use DeployStudio, it has an uninstalled included in its installation disk image. You can also stop and unload the deamon services to temporarily free up the typically minor amount of resources its database components use. The command to disable is:

```
launchctl unload -w
/LibraryLaunchDaemons/com.deploystudio.server.plist
```

When you've completed the server-connection information, click on the Continue button. At the Repository Type screen, enter the repository location you'll use. The repository contains the DeployStudio database, software packages, master images, scripts, and logs. It can become pretty big, so plan accordingly. If you'll be deploying systems using a USB or Firewire drive, you can choose to have a local repository.

Most likely, though, you're setting this up to do mass deployment, in which case you want to specify a Network sharepoint, assuming you'll be using a server. Click on Continue, and at the Repository Settings screen, select the local folder that will host the repository if you chose local in the previous screen (see Figure 6-12). If you chose a remote destination, fill in the URL to an AFP or SMB sharepoint. For instance, to use the sharepoint DeployStudio on the deployment server deploy1, issue this command:

```
afp://deploy1.myco.com/DeployStudio
```

Enter a username and password for the share, and if desired, a subfolder and mount options. Always manually attempt to mount a remote client, read information from it, and write to it before filling it in here. When you're ready, click on the Continue button again, and you'll be prompted to set up email notifications, a fairly straightforward step.

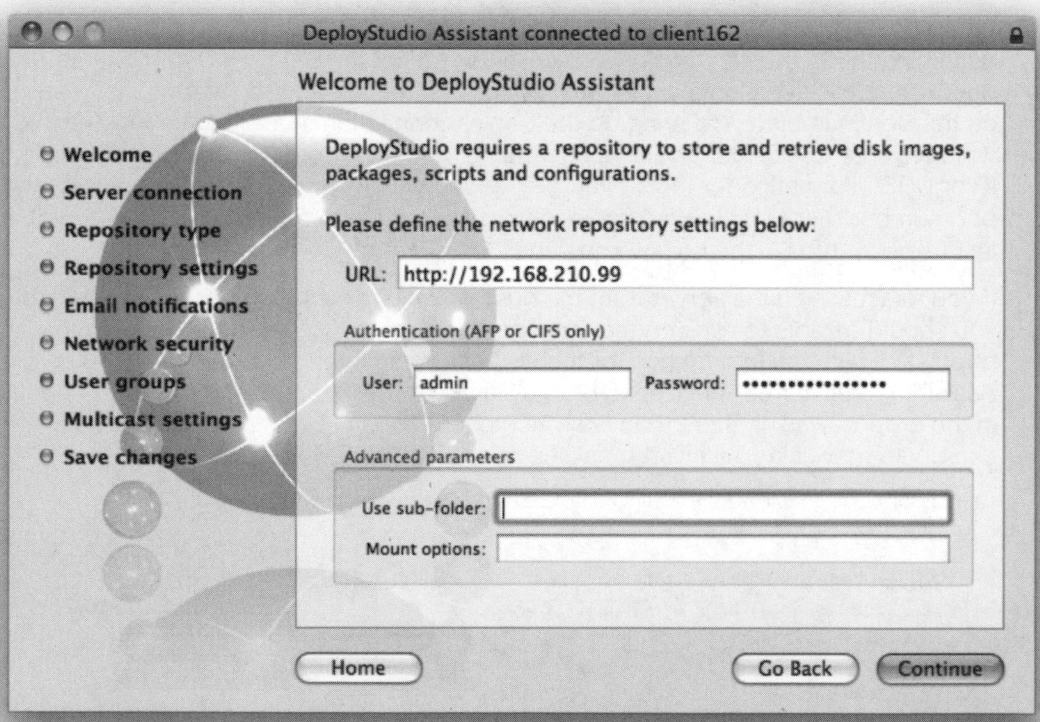

Figure 6-12. *Welcome to DeployStudio Assistant*

By default, these alerts go out to an administrator only when an error occurs. You can, however, change this so that a notice will go out when the imaging process completes. (Reminders are nice, aren't they?) Optionally, you can check the box for Include log file in mail body to see a granular report of the imaging options you've applied. When you're satisfied with your email settings, click on the Continue button to move on to the Network Security screen (see Figure 6-13).

Here you can choose whether to use HTTPS during your imaging. If you choose HTTP, the default port will be 60080. With HTTPS, it will be 60443. You can also customize the TCP/IP port that DeployStudio will use by typing a different integer into the Port: field. When you've finished this, click on Continue to move to the next step.

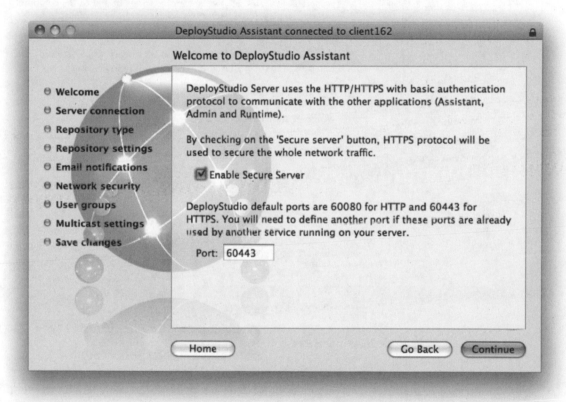

Figure 6-13. *DeployStudio Assistant – Network Security.*

Now you've arrived at the *User groups* screen (Figure 6-14). Here, you can define who can perform various tasks on the server and which groups have access to which features. The groups can exist either in the local directory, or in remote directories such as Open Directory or Active directory. We generally like to create a local group on our DeployStudio using the Accounts System Preference pane for DSAssistant, DSAdmin, and DSRuntime. That makes adding members with local accounts pretty simple. In larger environments, you may want to use only directory groups.

In any case, you can specify three different privilege groups: Assistant setup, which can run the setup assistant tool; Admin, which can run the DeployStudio Administrator tool; and Runtime, whose members can use the runtime application. Once you've appropriately configured permissions to the DeployStudio toolset, click on the Continue button.

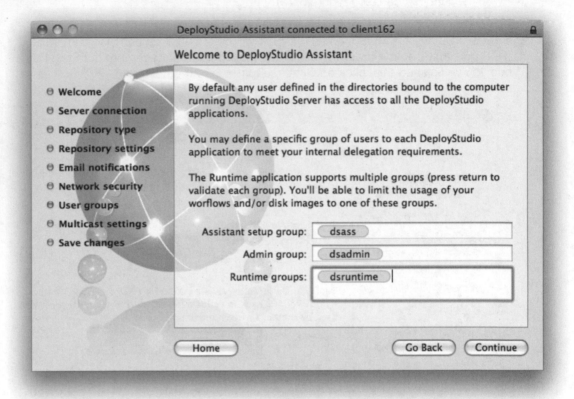

Figure 6-14. *DeployStudio Assistant–User Groups*

Next, you're presented with a screen in which you can set DeployStudio's multicast functionality (Figure 6-15). The values applied here are going to be fairly similar to those in the file you generated earlier for ASR. Select the network interface, type the multicast address for the listener to bind to, and customize the first port that you'll use to stream. Now set the maximum number of streams and the data rate and provide a TTL, which defines the maximum number of hops a multicast stream will traverse (provided you've configured your routers for multicast support). Of the final three options, in most environments you customize only the maximum number of streams and the speed per stream. With your ASR settings taken care of, click on Continue to bring up the Save changes screen, and there click on Continue to write the settings to disk.

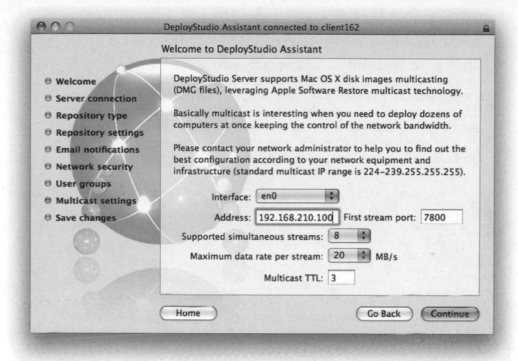

Figure 6-15. *DeployStudio Assistant–Multicast Settings*

Tip Don't worry too much about these settings, you can always go through and enter them again, if you wish, by simply rerunning the DeployStudio Assistant and connecting to the DeployStudio Server!

Now that you've completed the setup, it's time to actually use your server. Enter DeployStudio Admin, which you'll find with its brethren in /Applications/Utilities. When you open the admin tool, it prompts you for a valid server, user name, and password. Log in as one of the users in the DSadmin group and enter the address, followed by the port number just specified in the DeployStudio Assistant. By default, the connection information should be available in the drop-down menu. Once you've connected, along the left side of the screen (Figure 6-16), you'll see the five options described on the following:

- *Activity:* Allows you to view events.

- *Computers:* Lists the computers, by MAC Address, that you will be imaging (or have imaged). You can import information into Computers using ARD or CSV files.

- *Workflows:* Similar to the Automator-style interface of NetInstall and allows you to configure the steps for an installation.

- *Masters:* List of all images located in the repository. To populate the Masters list (the base or bare metal images you will use in your workflows), you will need to use the DeployStudio Runtime.

- *Scripts:* Central repository for scripts to be run as part of workflows on compulers specified (the existing scripts are mostly for Mac OS X 10.4 and should not be used to image computers wlth later versions of the OS). You can pull most scripts from your NetRestore deployment and use them on a DeployStudio deployment. You'll also find other scripts, more compatible with 10.5 and later, located in subfolders of the DeployStudio root directory defined during installation.

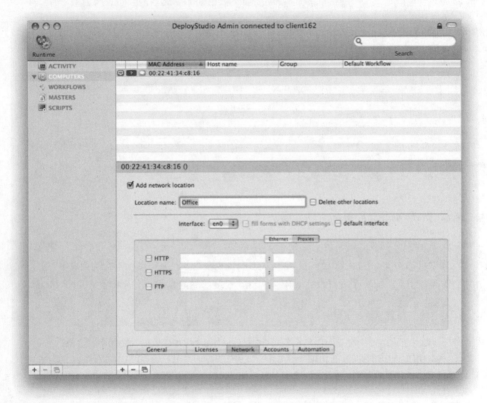

Figure 6-16. *DeployStudio Admin Computers*

NOTE: If you're migrating to DeployStudio from NetRestore, you'll be happy to learn that both store data in the same format. The format of the CSV file should be (per line with no colons in the MAC address):

MACAddress,computername,hostname

You use the DeployStudio runtime to play workflows, including those for capturing an image or putting one onto your desktops, which you'd typically want to do for mass deployment. You can run DeployStudio Runtime manually from Mac OS X as well, so you can test your workflows by playing images onto a local Firewire or USB drive. We'll use the runtime to create a master (base image) from a source volume. Open DeployStudio Runtime and authenticate to the server you set up earlier in this section, then select *Create a master from a volume* and click on the Play button, as shown in Figure 6-17.

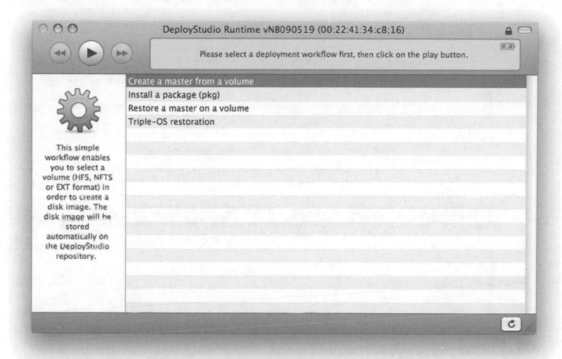

Figure 6-17. *DeployStudio Runtime*

Next, provide the specifics for creating the image (see Figure 6-18). Select a source hard drive to base the image on, then enter the desired name of the image into the *Image Name:* field. In the *Keywords:* field, enter some text to help you find the image later (for example, Office 2008, Firefox, MacBookPro June, or whatever will help differentiate this image from others you may set up). Software package lists can become extremely well-populated, so the better you tag your software, the happier you'll be when you can easily find whatever you need. Also, set *Type:* to Read Only for now—this is the most reliable, albeit the slowest. Next, enter the format for the image's file system—for OS X machines, this will pretty much always be HFS+. The tasks in this process are very similar to those you performed earlier when you used `hdiutil` to create an image with a given format from a specified source, then cleaned up the machine-specific files. When you're ready, click on the play–button icon (near the upper-right-hand corner of the window) to begin building an image of the hard drive.

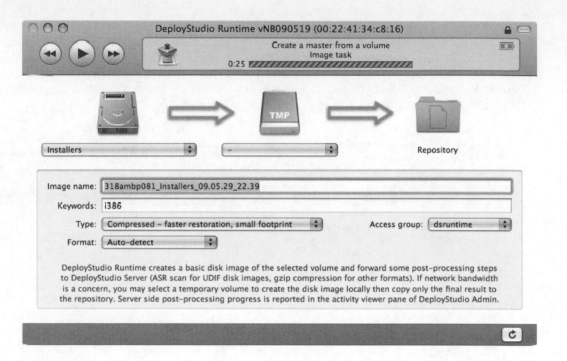

Figure 6-18. *Creating a master*

You should be able to see your initial master (image), now that it's in the repository (if you were patient enough to let the imaging process complete). Click on MASTERS from the DeployStudio Admin program and you should see it listed. Next, upload any packages you've built into the Packages directory in the DeployStudio root folder. Once you've added them, you can install them using a workflow. To create one, click on WORKFLOWS (see Figure 6-19) and then on the plus sign at the bottom of the screen. Give your new workflow a name, such as *Marketing Dept MacBook Deploy,* which we used in our example.

Next, click on the plus sign on the gray bar in the center of the screen and you'll see a slider appear with a number of task options. For our workflow, we'll choose Partition Disk, followed by Restore a Disk Image. And, finally, we'll install any custom packages and scripts pertinent to our build. You may not want to install all of the packages in your system, but you certainly could. The fact that you're performing imaging in an almost object-oriented fashion means you can pull any supported applications from your entire library with a package and copy the package to the repository. (If you need to embed serial numbers and the like, you may want to wait until we cover packages in more detail in a few pages.) You can also use scripts to implement the various settings and configurations each client needs. The workflow concept will be a recurring theme through just about any imaging application.

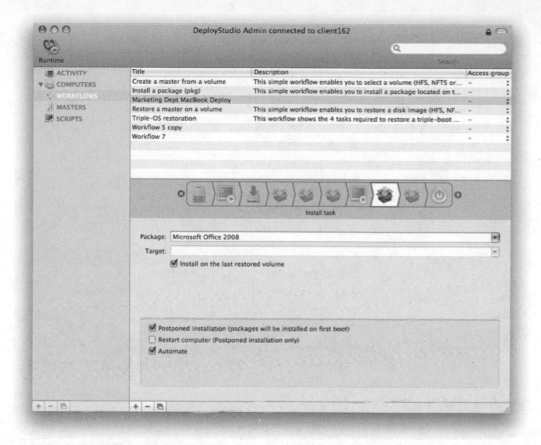

Figure 6-19. *Configuring workflows*

Once you have a functional workflow you'd like to test, you can use DeployStudio Assistant to create a DeployStudio bootable external USB or FireWire drive. For instance, you can make a USB jump drive that you use to boot a machine and load the runtime to image over a network. To set this up, select the appropriate option from the DeployStudio Assistant screen and click through the various dialog boxes until you get to the Available volumes: field. Select the drive to use as an external boot drive or the option to make the drive into a single partition if you'd like to erase multiple partitions on it currently. In the next pane, specify the remote server connection that the new volume's Runtime application will connect to.

Next, enter a username and password to allow communication between the DeployStudio Runtime and the DeployStudio Server, and optionally, type in a Virtual Network Computing (VNC) password, which lets you control hosts booted from the runtime through VNC (see Figure 6-20). The remaining options let you specify whether to display the log window by default, when to put the host display to sleep (to save energy while it's imaging), and how long the runtime will remain open yet inactive (for example, if imaging were to finish or fail to complete). When you're ready, click Continue.

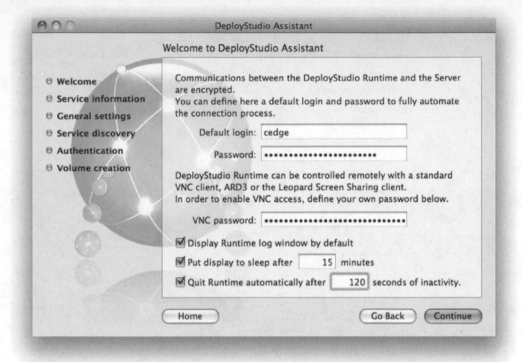

Figure 6-20. *Creating a DeployStudio NetBoot Set*

You can also configure a NetBoot set that will achieve much the same goals of the USB drive, but rather than booting to removable media, you boot to a NetBoot server. The resulting NetBoot system is a very small installation capable of running only the Runtime and giving you VNC access to control the host. The steps are similar to those described above, except that rather than erase the target drive, you create a NetBoot set, which you can copy into your /Library/NetBoot/NetBootSP0 directory and enable in Server Admin. After this, you can boot clients by holding down the N key (if it's the default image) or by selecting the volume in Startup Disk.

If you use your DeployStudio Server for other tasks, you may want to turn DeployStudio off to avoid consuming resources. To do so, open System Preferences, select the DeployStudio Preference Panel, then click on/off or use the command-line method covered previously in this chapter.

> **TIP:** You can upgrade DeployStudio by installing the package for the most recent version, which simply updates the application bundles and leaves the database itself untouched. While generally updates have been fairly stable consider backing up the Deploy Studio repository folder prior to any major upgrades.

Other Third-Party Solutions

There are a number of solutions for mass deployment and patch management in addition to those we cover from a technical point of view in this Chapter. These include LANrev, Puppet, Radmind, and even Deep Freeze by Faronics. Deep Freeze can be used to place a computer into a frozen state. The system can then be thawed for changes and rebooted to place it back into a frozen state. This is typically reserved for lab environments. LANrev is a popular product that supports Mac, Windows, and Linux.

Radmind is a suite of command-line tools you can use to manage the software installation and configuration state across a group of computers. It provides a very complex toolset for ensuring consistent deployments across an arbitrary number of clients. Radmind can detect and manage changes to systems via a *loadset*, a predefined list of contents that you can compare to what's resident on clients and then use to replace, add, or remove client files. Using loadsets and overloads (listings of files, directories, and items associated with them), administrators can install, customize, and update software. Radmind is very good at keeping a collection of systems synchronized with a master environment—a capability you might need in a lab, for example.

Radmind is slowly being uprooted by products like Casper and Package-based imaging solutions. The original developers have moved on from this tool. However, it still has a religious user base.

Puppet is an open-source administration and policy framework, written in Ruby and used for numerous types of system automations. Radmind and Puppet take a similar approach to synchronizing systems with a master—both alter a remote set of files, but they use different methods. Radmind looks at file systems; Puppet uses *facters*, which are similar to the loadsets defined in Ruby, but far more granular. Puppet then employs a *client library*, which houses instructions for reaching predefined states. Because Radmind is great at maintaining file systems and Puppet is great at, and highly configurable for managing finely grained states, you'll find both useful.

For example, you can use Radmind to manage certain directories you want to remain static, such as those involved in deployments of the Developer Tools from Mac OS X. Then you could put Puppet to work to let users change settings in a non-managed client environment while still allowing you to maintain some control. Or you might choose to manage servers with Puppet and workstations with Radmind.

Both offer highly customizable environments for managing Mac OS X (and other operating systems). They are, however, far more difficult than GUI-centric tools, such as Casper Suite, LANrev, and DeployStudio. For that reason, Puppet and Radmind often get lumped together as very similar competing technologies. In fact, though, they're not that similar.

If you're interested in exploring the capabilities of Puppet, consider the book *Pulling Strings with Puppet: Configuration Management Made Easy* by James Turnbull, published by Apress.

Casper Suite

Earlier, we looked at using Composer to create monolithic images. Though you can purchase the product by itself, it's actually part of the Casper Suite of tools for Mac OS X mass deployment—and the rest of the bundle is pretty darn useful. Its server-side component, JSS, or Jamf Server Software, integrates with Active Directory and Open Directory. JSS determines which computers and groups receive which packages in an object-oriented fashion. Casper Admin manages the process of selecting who gets what, but JSS can also do so.

One strong feature of the suite, *policies*, puts packages, scripts, and other maintenance tasks into groups configured to run at certain times. A highly customizable scheduler lets you activate policies during specific time windows. You can have policies apply to computers based on a number of criteria, such as IP subnet, computer group membership, or even membership in *Smart Groups.* The last are similar to iTunes smart playlists in that they're dynamically generated based on pre-specified criteria.

For instance, I could create such a group for all computers running OS X versions prior to 10.5.7. I might then design a policy that's active from 7:00p.m. to 7:00a.m. and add the 10.5.7 combo updater package. Thus every night, any machines not running 10.5.7 would execute the update. Policies are very dynamic and powerful tools for managing software deployments across a large number of systems.

The Casper Suite also comes with a self-servicing solution that allows users to install their own packages. Letting users select from a list of acceptable tools—installing and removing them without contacting system administrators—can greatly reduce support requirements.

Casper Suite can do a lot for you, including asset tracking, network reconnaissance, and more, but the server-side component, Casper Admin, and Composer provide the biggest productivity boost.

Automation

Once you've built your base image for deployment, it's time to consider the other tasks from the checklist you created at the beginning of this chapter. These chores may include items such as create an admin user, customize default user template, bind to Open Directory, bind to Active Directory, or install third-party software—Microsoft Office, for example, or Adobe Acrobat. Chances are that nearly everyone reading this chapter will want to perform at least one of these tasks, so let's step through an example.

Types of Automations

Preflight automations run before imaging and post-flight automations (whether packages, scripts, or image copies) run after. Thus, you can apply automations in the order that will most logically supply the necessary software or configurations to a desktop. You can also nest automations by including one script in another or by using different scripts as functions within larger scripts. Generally though, the more granularity you have, the better, and so it's often best to leave each as a standalone script unless you need to transfer data from one automation to another. If you do so, you can then set your certain automations to execute either before or after others.

Packages, images, and scripts are the major elements of deployment automations in Mac OS X. The easiest of these to create and use is probably the image, which houses files that you can copy (or drop) into the file system of a computer as a post-flight task. Scripts are useful primarily when you have an extremely small but focused payload—one, for example, that simply want enables a service or performs a regex operation on a configuration file. Deployment scripts generally are AppleScripts or shell scripts; the former are useful mostly for configuring userland GUI apps that have no command-line interaction. Packages can be the most complicated deployment elements but also the most powerful.

Delivering file-system payloads is the primary purpose of packages, but you can also use them to fire scripts prior to and after performing an installation. You can also create packages that, rather than containing a file-system payload, exist solely for the purpose of running pre- or post-action scripts. For this reason, packages represent the most feature-rich option. Using tools such as Composer or PackageMaker, you can build your own packages, but the easiest implementation method is likely to be reusing the one distributed with the original software installer.

At first, determining which type of automation to use for each task can be daunting. But as a rule of thumb, if you just need to put some files into a location, you're best off using an image or a package. If you need to run a command to rename a computer or perhaps to perform a trusted bind to a Directory Service, you'll likely want to use a script (though you might use a package to actually deploy that script). Additionally, the software that you use can play a big part in determining whether to use packages, scripts, or images—and in what order.

When people are getting started with automating tasks for images, they typically use snapshots to capture changes and create packages. Over time, though, you realize that a snapshot replaces the entire file, which may not be appropriate for preferences files, given that they often store information for a number of different functions. Most experienced imaging aficionados move away from snapshots and use shell scripts to automate the setting of preferences on imaged computers.

TIP: You can also create a DMG file based on the contents of, say, a scripts directory—useful if you'd like to keep a directory with a number of scripts in a folder called Scripts on the root of your hard drive. To do so, you'd use hdiutil with the create verb, followed by the name of the DMG file and finally the -srcfolder flag, which requires the actual source directory. As an example, if we wanted to turn this folder into a DMG called myscripts.dmg we could use the command:

```
hdiutil create myscripts.dmg -srcfolder /Scripts
```

User Templates

New users on Macs have a certain set of default settings that are copied into their user profiles the first time they log in. If a home directory for a user doesn't exist when that person first logs in, the system will create a new one using the contents of the directory /System/Library/User Template/English.lproj as a template (for English users). You can modify the contents of this directory, copying new files or editing existing ones. When someone creates a new account, the system will copy these files into it. This customizes the look and feel, default documents, fonts, and other aspects of user accounts without you having to do so each time you create a new user or whenever someone logs in for the first time.

This can be incredibly useful when you're not using network or mobile accounts, you have a number of different people logging into computers, and you want to provide specific settings or files. It goes without saying that you could set many policies more easily through MCX (Managed Client for OS X), but this won't always cover settings you want, and using templates can be easier in many circumstances.

For example, let's say you want to provide all users with a default set of stock fonts. By simply copying fonts into the /System/Library/User Template/English.lproj/Library/Fonts directory, you'll provide the fonts to users when they log in. We could just install the fonts in /Library/Fonts and be done with it, but a user who has the fonts in the home directory can remove them, if needed, rather than being stuck with them. The same would be true for any items stored in the home directory, including Microsoft Office preferences, many of which you can't modify via MCX.

You can also employ user templates to perform scripts the first time a new employee logs in. For example, if you have a Microsoft Exchange environment, you can have Entourage automatically set up a user account on the person's initial log-in by having a self-destructing LaunchAgent in the user's home folder (~/Library/LaunchAgents). This would create LaunchAgents, a script, and the agent itself in the user template, but if you have a large number of users it would save a lot of time in setup.

Of course, if you're using Open Directory, Active Directory, or some other directory service, there are better ways to accomplish much of what you can do with user templates. Still, templates are great tools to keep in your batbelt.

Migrating from Monolithic Images

A number of organizations currently use monolithic images. Moving to a package-based solution may seem like a time-consuming and complicated task, but you can take small steps towards accomplishing it. Composer 7 gives you one of the quickest and easiest ways to get to a package-based imaging solution. And the product has a great new feature that will scan your hard drive for installed packages, letting you create one package per installed software product. This allows you to, for example, take a monolithic image, generate a package for individual pieces of software installed on the image, then create a package for each. You can download Composer 7 from http://www.jamfsoftware.com.

After the installation, when you first open the software, you'll see a screen asking you to choose a method for creating your package (see Figure 6-21). Select PREINSTALLED on the left-hand side of the screen and you'll see a listing of each software package installed on the computer. Select the appropriate titles (or use Command-A to select them all) and click on the Choose button.

Figure 6-21. *Creating a New Package with Composer*

Composer will begin generating the packages, and it will use the original software you installed as the source. Once Composer has finished, you'll also add your custom bindings and then create any scripts and other automations to complete the items on your checklist. But even if you don't do that, Composer can perform a number of the tasks for your migration.

Custom Packages with Composer

You can also use Composer to generate other types of packages. One of the product's powerful features is its tool for taking system-state snapshots. To put the feature to use, build an original file-system state list (by performing a software installation or configuration change) and have Composer record it. Then build another and record that.

Comparing the before and after snapshots lets you create a list of modified files, which (for the most part) will be representative of the software you installed.

To start the process, from the main screen of Composer, click on the New Package icon in the toolbar. In the left-hand pane of the dialog that appears (Figure 6-22), choose the Snapshot option. In the main part of the window, you should see three options: Normal Snapshot, New & Modified Snapshot, and Monitor File System Changes. For the sake of speed, pick the last.

This option does its monitoring using FSEvents, which is the primary system behind Spotlight and Time Machine and provides the ability for an application to track file system changes. You could use Composer's Normal Snapshot, which creates before and after picture but records only enough data to detect new (rather than modified) files. Unfortunately, this method, though faster (creating a snapshot is a fairly slow process) will miss any file modifications.

That, potentially, is a large problem, and it's the reason for the New & Modified option— which, sadly, takes even longer than Normal Snapshot. However, it has benefits. One of the main advantages to using snapshots instead of FSEvents is that change-tracking persists through reboots and is generally more stable when there are large numbers of data changes.

Figure 6-22. *Making Snapshot Packages with Composer*

Once you've chosen Monitor File System Changes, at the resulting screen, type a name for the software package and then click on the Begin button to initiate filesystem activity-monitoring. Now, just install the software as you would normally. You can minimize Composer 7 if needed, but make sure to leave the application running. When you complete the software installation and configuration, come back to the Composer 7 window and click on the Build Package button (Figure 6-23).

Figure 6-23. *Capturing a Snapshot Package*

Under SOURCES in Figure 6-24, you'll see a new item bearing the name you provided in the previous step. You can now select the source list and browse the contents of the package. Be especially careful to note any files that shouldn't be members. For example, we installed Firefox and are creating a snapshot package of Firefox. But we ended up with data from /var/servermgrd and /var/vm. To remove the extraneous files, you click on /var in the package and then on the Delete button in the Composer 7 toolbar.

When first building packages from snapshots or monitoring, including unnecessary and potentially harmful files is a very common mistake. So again, take extra care to check thoroughly for unwanted items. You should be especially vigilant about getting rid of unnecessary items in /System, /Library, /private, /var, and /etc.

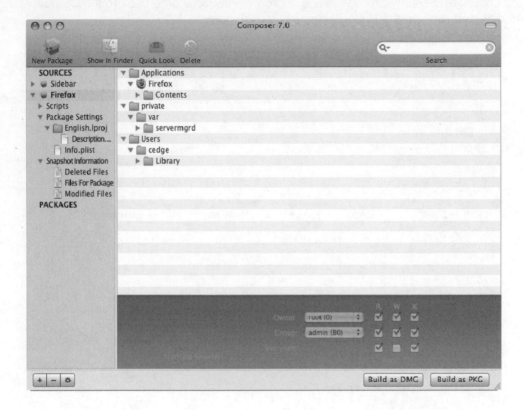

Figure 6-24. *Browsing Package Contents and assigning permissions with Composer*

Once you've whittled the package down appropriately, navigate to Package Settings in the left pane of the dialog and type the information for the package into the Description.plist file. Finish by checking the other content that will go into the package as well as by verifying the permissions for the files that will be installed, and finally, click on Build as PKG.

If, instead, you click on Build as DMG, the same data that would otherwise be in the package will go into your DMG file. But as mentioned previously, packages give you the ability to deploy scripts and ensure version control, making them the preferred choice, in general. So choose Build as PKG, select a valid location for saving your package (you'll get a prompt to do so), and finally, test the package.

But once you've gone to the trouble of creating a package and have been using it for a while, expect to encounter expect to encounter one of the more annoying aspects of being on a deployment team: Vendors continue to update their offerings. Now you have to change the package. Luckily, this is a place where Composer shines. From your imaging workstation, just install the update for the version of the given package that's currently on the machine. From the File menu, select Download Latest Diffs and you'll be able to create a package based solely on the delta between the original package and the new one.

> **TIP:** Snapshots are incredibly useful when you just want to figure out what data changed—for example, if you need to determine which property-list file to deploy a setting to. If there's only one setting in a property list, then you can make a package out of it. But if a preference file has a number of items, you may be better off simply creating a script to augment the file. That way you don't risk changing other settings by accident—or worse yet, rendering systems unbootable because you change a file in a way that's inconsistent with what the operating system demands.

InstallEase and Iceberg

InstallEase is a free package-creation tool from LANrev. Its feature set is similar to that of Composer, allowing administrators to either create packages based on before and after snapshots, or to select specific files and directories manually. Once you've taken a snapshot with InstallEase, you use the straightforward GUI to fine-tune the package's payload. InstallEase has several advanced features as well, such as the ability to generate uninstall packages, or—when used in conjunction with LANrev's client-management suite—to install user-centric files triggered on log-in. The product lets you generate Apple PKG files, disk images, and Iceberg projects.

Iceberg, a third-party package- and metapackage-creation tool provided under the BSD license, is very similar to Apple's PackageMaker, discussed in the next section. Functionally, though, it doesn't have a whole lot to offer that you can't accomplish using the most recent versions of PackageMaker. It does, though, provide a handy interface for the implementation of pre- and post-flight scripts.

FileWave

FileWave is another mass deployment and patch management solution. FileWave is different from most other third-party solutions in that it does not natively create and leverage packages. Instead, FileWave uses File Sets. These are portable between operating systems and can be deployed at imaging time or post-imaging using the native installers to FileWave.

FileWave has the additional feature that it can deploy a file set to a desktop and then leave it there inactive for a period of time. This allows you to push all of your software to client computers and then activate it or inactivate it on the fly as needed.

FileWave can also be used as a managed client solution, license management solution, and inventory management solution, much the same way as LANrev and the Casper Suite can be used. Because this chapter really focuses on packages and standard Apple deployment technologies, FileWave is not more prominent, but the lack of page count is not a direct correlation to the feelings that the authors have on the product. It is a solid solution, and if a third-party solution is being looked at then it should be on the list along with others that we cover more thoroughly.

PackageMaker

As with Composer, you can use PackageMaker from OS X to create packages from snapshots. But PackageMaker lets you define a lot more information for a package, including information that gives more granular control over scripts. Composer can add scripts to a package but can't provide as much control over how they're handled.

Apple provides package installers as an installation solution with every copy of Mac OS X (using Installer.app). PackageMaker, though, is set up with the Developer Tools (also known as Xcode) and is also an optional installation distributed with the Server Admin Tools. While you can find the developer tools on the setup media that came with your client system, the most up-to-date resource for the tools is http://developer.apple.com. As a sidenote, you can download Mac OS X Server Admin tools at http://www.apple.com/support.

Once you've installed the Developer Tools, you can find PackageMaker inside the /Developer/Applications/Utilities folder. If the Developer Tools aren't installed, you can do so by downloading the Server Admin tools and dragging the PackageMaker application from the disk image's Utilities folder onto your local drive, as you can see in Figure 6-25.

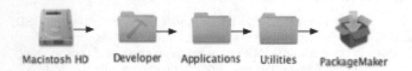

Figure 6-25. *Location of PackageMaker*

When you run PackageMaker for the first time, you'll immediately be prompted for the name of the organization and the Minimum Target. For the first, type the inverse of your organization's domain name (which is a pretty standard naming convention for packages in the Mac OS X community, following Apple's lead of com.apple.applicationname). For example, if your organization is named *Apress.com,* you can simply enter *com.apress.* The Minimum Target refers to the minimum version of Mac OS X on which you'll be installing packages created in PackageMaker. If the software is exclusive to 10.6, then select 10.6 in the drop-down menu.

Next, create a faux root directory to represent the destination Volume of the computers you'll be installing on. You can create this folder anywhere, but we recommend that you keep it in a standard location. At the time of this writing, the location for all PackageMaker project files is an external FireWire hard drive.

Figure 6-26 shows the Corporate Fonts Installer folder on the currently logged-in user's desktop. The sub-folders Company Fonts and Resources are, respectively, the faux root directory of the installation files and the location of the final package-installer's support files, such as the ReadMe documentation , pre- and post-flight scripts, and configuration files used during installation (for example, postflight.conf).

Now that you've built the package-project directory structure, you can save the untitled package-maker project on the same level as the faux root (Company Fonts) and the Resources folders, but take care not to save the project in one of the two sub-folders. The name of the PackageMaker project can differ from the final package name. This example uses the same name as the faux root folder (Company Fonts) for consistency.

Now that you've saved the PackageMaker project file in the package-project directory, you can associate the project file with the Faux root Directory. The easy way is to drag the faux root directory and drop it into the Contents section of the PackageMaker project file, as shown in Figure 6-26.

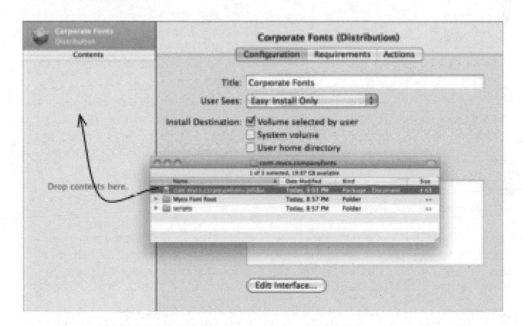

Figure 6-26. *Dragging Items into PackageMaker*

Once you've established the association, you'll want to update the PackageMaker project file to use relative path names, as illustrated in Figure 6-27. This will allow you to move the package-project directory without breaking the path to the faux root directory. In other words, after you've enabled this setting, you can freely move the parent directory, Corporate Fonts Installer, without needing to reassociate the project files with the sub-folders (such as the faux root and Resources directories). You can find this setting in the Action Menu, next to the faux-root path name.

You'll need to repeat this operation for the Resources folder you created in the package-project directory. When using the Relative to Project setting, the graphical interface will not notify you if the program detects a post-flight script in the Resources directory. We recommend that you select each script you've created, such as those for pre-flight and post-flight, using the same methodology as previously (including choosing Relative to Project) for the script specification.

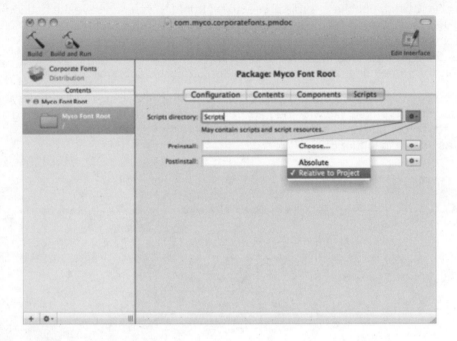

Figure 6-27. *Adding scripts in PackageMaker*

Now that you have your PackageMaker project files in order, you can copy the items you'd like to install and put them into the specified PackageMaker project's faux root directory. This example creates a font-installation package. The installer will copy the CustomCorporateFont.ttf font file into the destination volume's /Library/Fonts/ directory.

You don't need to worry about creating a folder structure that already exists on the system—in other words, if you create an /Applications folder in your faux root, it will act as a place holder for the same folder on the destination volume. At installation time, the installer will see that /Applications already exists and merge your installer's faux-root contents with the existing file set. If you create a directory structure that doesn't already exist, then as you'd logically expect, the installer will create it so the child files you're installing will be placed into the correct directory structure, relative to how they originally were created in the faux root.

When you're satisfied with your installation file set, you can build an initial package (Figure 6-28) to begin testing with. PackageMaker installation packages should always be tested on a clean system that mimics a majority or cross-section of your client computers. Keep in mind that using the same system over and over again may skew results, because the file sets installed may not be completely clean between each iteration of the build process. For this reason, we recommend you always start tests on freshly restored systems.

We also highly recommend that you establish a click matrix—a set of operations you'll perform after a package installation to verify that the newly installed files haven't adversely affected any mission-critical functionality. This is crucial for preventing efficient snapshot-based systems, such as package installers, from creating problems in your end users' workflow. We mention an example of this behavior in the "Snapshot" section of this chapter.

Once it has built the package, the software will begin the installation automatically. Even if you're not installing on this system, you may still want to choose Build and Run, just to verify that the Installer.app application can appropriately open the newly created package installer. When you've verified that the package installer opens correctly, you can simply quit if you don't want to test the installation. The name of the package installer doesn't have to match any of the previously defined values. In this case, a Corporate Fonts.pkg file will be created on the currently logged-in user's desktop.

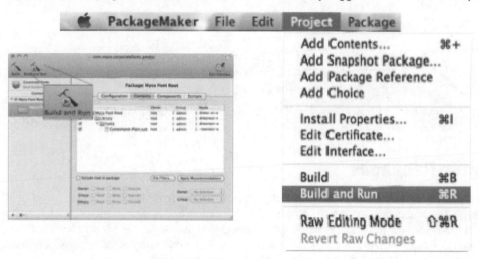

Figure 6-28. *Build and run packages to test*

After you've run the package through the click-matrix test suggested earlier and you've installed all files and package scripts, verifying that they ran correctly, you're ready to use the package to deploy (Figure 6-29). Keep in mind that when testing, you always want to mimic your final installation environment as closely as possible. This may require that instead of actively installing with Apple Remote Desktop, you run the package installer on a volume other than the current startup disk, so you can mimic how a network installer would passively install files.

The best way to carry out the simulation, other than testing with the final deployment medium, is to mount a machine in Firewire Target Disk mode (hold down the T key at startup, or enable the mode in the Startup Disk System Preference Pane). Once the target volume is mounted, choose the appropriate volume while running through the installation steps. This type of testing will often reveal installations that work correctly with tools such as Apple Remote Desktop but fail when using network installers such as NetInstall or DeployStudio.

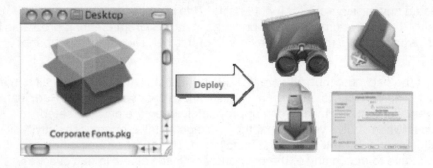

Figure 6-29. *Ways To deploy packages*

> **NOTE:** We strongly endorse picking the right tool for each job. Composer is very easy to learn, making it well worth the minimal investment to purchase it. However, when you reach the limits of what it can do, chances are good you'll look to PackageMaker to move to the next step.

Negative Packages

Negative packages are those you use to remove (rather than add) applications. The easiest way to remove an application is with an uninstaller that the application vendor provides. If you don't have that (or if it doesn't work, which happens), more than likely you'll want to use a negative package. You can also use it at install time to remove any applications bundled with the operating system if they were in a standard- or bare-metal image.

Suppose you're attempting to remove Norton AntiVirus for the Mac in an automated fashion and the uninstaller distributed by Symantec isn't doing the trick. To start, look at the package contents to determine what was added to the system. You can find the contents from the Bill of Materials (BOM) for the package, which resides in the `Contents` directory in the initial installation package. Then you can simply build a shell script to remove all the files added during the installation. Note, however, that this often fails to remove all items that were installed or moved, and it can also leave settings in various locations.

But there's another method to determine what files are in a package: Perform a snapshot before installation and another following. You can do this easily using the package-snapshot feature of PackageMaker, Composer, or another snapshot-based packaging utility. Rather than create a package, you use the tool to look at what was actually installed—which might include items not in the BOM.

When you've determined what was added to the system, you can remove it all. The following script will, to continue the example, remove Symantec's Norton Antivirus from Mac OS X.

```
#! /bin/bash
launchctl stop `launchctl list | grep com.symantec.SymSecondaryLaunch | awk '{print
$3}'`
launchctl stop `launchctl list | grep com.symantec.scanNotification | awk '{print $3}'`
launchctl stop `launchctl list | grep com.symantec.diskMountNotify | awk '{print $3}'`
launchctl stop `launchctl list | grep com.symantec.quickmenu | awk '{print $3}'`
kextunload -b com.Symantec.SymEvent.kext
kextunload -b com.Symantec.SymOSXKernelUtilities.kext
kextunload -b com.Symantec.kext.KTUM
rm /etc/liveupdate.conf
rm /etc/Symantec.conf
rm /usr/bin/symsched
rm /usr/bin/navx
rm ~/Library/Preferences/com.Symantec.Scheduler.plist
rm /Users/Shared/snorosx
rm -rfd /Library/Contextual\ Menu\ Items/NAVCMPlugin.plugin
rm -rfd /Applications/Symantec\ Solutions
rm -rfd /Applications/Norton\ AntiVirus
rm -rfd /Library/Receipts/NAVContextualMenu.pkg
rm -rfd /Library/Receipts/NAVEngine.pkg
rm -rfd /Library/Receipts/Norton\ AntiVirus.pkg
rm -rfd /Library/Receipts/SymEvent.pkg
rm -rfd /Library/Receipts/SymOSXKernelUtilities.pkg
rm -rfd /Library/Receipts/NortonQuickMenu.pkg
rm -rfd /Library/Receipts/SymSharedFrameworks.pkg
rm -rfd /Library/Receipts/Norton\ AutoProtect.pkg
rm -rfd /Library/Recepits/Symantec\ Scheduled\ Scans.pkg
rm -rfd /Library/Recepits/Symantec\ Scheduled\ Scans.pkg
rm -rfd /Library/Receipts/Symantec\ Scheduled\ Scans.pkg
rm -rfd /Library/Receipts/navx.pkg
rm -rfd /Library/Receipts/LiveUpdate.pkg
rm -rfd /Library/Receipts/Symantec\ Scheduler.pkg
rm -rfd /Library/Receipts/Stuffit.pkg
rm -rfd /Library/Receipts/SymInstallExtras.pkg
rm -rfd /Library/Receipts/SymHelpScripts.pkg
rm -rfd /Library/Receipts/SymantecUninstaller.pkg
rm -rfd /Library/Receipts/Symantec\ Alerts.pkg
rm -rfd /Library/Application\ Support/Norton\ Solutions\ Support
rm /Library/Application\ Support/NAV.history
rm -rfd /Library/Application\ Support/Symantec
rm -rfd /Library/PreferencePanes/SymantecQuickMenu.prefPane
rm -rfd /Library/PreferencePanes/APPrefPane.prefPane
rm -rfd /Library/PrivateFrameworks/SymAppKitAdditions.framework
rm -rfd /Library/PrivateFrameworks/SymBase.framework
rm -rfd /Library/PrivateFrameworks/SymNetworking.framework
rm -rfd /Library/PrivateFrameworks/SymSystem.framework
rm -rfd /Library/PrivateFrameworks/SymScheduler.framework
rm -rfd /Library/StartupItems/NortonAutoProtect
rm -rfd /Library/StartupItems/NortonMissedTasks
rm -rfd /Library/Documentation/Help/Norton\ Help\ Scripts
rm -rfd /Library/Widgets/Symantec\ Alerts.wdgt
```

```
rm -rfd /System/Library/Extensions/SymEvent.kext
rm -rfd /System/Library/Extensions/SymOSXKernelUtilities.kext
rm -rfd /System/Library/Extensions/KTUM.kext
rm /System/Library/Extensions.mkext.NxdE
```

A package with just that script in it and no files to place into the file system is a payload-free (given the lack of files) negative package and would remove data rather than adding it.

Installing a Package

You can install a package by double-clicking on it and following the prompts until the process completes. You can also use the `installer` command to install a package.

The installer command also has an option, `-applyChoiceChangesXML`, which allows you to build an answer file for any options that can come up during a package. The answer file is used to toggle options in a package on or off in XML format. The most notable use of the –applyChoiceChangesXML option is to choose which component of Microsoft Office is deployed during installation, which we explored further in Chapter 5, Messaging and Groupware.

Package Scripts

As mentioned previously, a package file can contain a number of scripts that execute at various points in the installation process. There are a number of choices of predefined script designations that you might find in a package's resources folder. We've listed their names here, along with their functions:

- *InstallationCheck:* Runs at the beginning of the installation process, prior to authentication. Typically used for basic sanity checks.

- *VolumeCheck:* Fires when a user is given the option to choose a destination. Runs against each attached volume to determine eligibility.

- *preflight:* Runs prior to installation.

- *preinstall:* Executes prior to installation, but requires that the current package has never been installed on this machine.

- *preupgrade:* Identical to preinstall, but is triggered only in upgrade situations, when it finds a receipt, in /Library/Receipts, with a previous version.

- *postinstall:* Activates after the successful first installation of a software package.

- *postupgrade:* Fires after a successful upgrade installation.

- *postflight:* Runs at the end of an installation, regardless of the success of the installation.

Each script typically gets three variables as arguments—Package Path, Target Location, and Target Volume. The exception here is VolumeCheck, which receives only the path to a volume. In every case, an exit code of 0 signifies success, and you should make sure your scripts exit cleanly. A script failure reports to end users as an installation failure.

Customizing Prebuilt Packages

As noted, a number of application vendors support customization of their packages to further automate a deployment. As an example, we'll look at CheckPoint's VPN-1 SecureClient, which lets users connect to a company's VPN servers. When you install the package, the process runs, as a manual post-flight task, in the /Library/Application Support/Installers/ directory.

The application bundle of each installer contains a userc.C configuration file that the installation routine copies to the correct location for the CheckPoint VPN software. You can take advantage of this when rolling out a new version of the CheckPoint client. Add the userc.C file which you've customized for a particular deployment area (such as Corporate) and place the file within the package installer package. Now Control-click on the client and choose Show Package Contents, which will produce the screen shown in Figure 6-30.

Figure 6-30. *Placing a file into a package bundle*

Next, place the `user.C` file in the `Resources` folder, as shown in Figure 6-30. This customized `userc.C` file will be copied automatically to the correct directory on the destination volume by a vendor script such as the following:

```
#package customization - check for added userc.C
USERCEXISTS=`ls -l $PACKAGE_PATH/Contents/Resources/userc.C |
wc -l | awk '{print $1}'`
if [ "$USERCEXISTS" -gt "0" ]; then
    if [ "$INST_DEBUG_LEVEL" -gt "0" ]; then
        $ECHO Replacing userc.C file.
    fi
    cp $PACKAGE_PATH/Contents/Resources/userc.C $SRDIR/database/userc.C
fi
```

This is a very useful method for enhancing a package installer to deploy environment-specific configurations without re-creating the package's payload. In this case, the vendor already supplied the post-flight script. But you can also modify a non-flat-file install package by right-clicking on the package, selecting Show Package Contents, and then editing an existing script or dropping your own post-flight script file into the package's Resources directory.

Customizing OS X Preferences

Often, in the course of a mass deployment system, you'll want to customize OS X system or application preference files on a machine-specific basis. With the advent of OS X, the standardized format for many of these files is that of the property list (plist). These files contain serialized data organized in a key/value format capable of storing common data types: strings, numbers, dates, booleans, arrays, dictionaries, and raw binary data. Using these data elements, applications can store complex data structures for a wide variety of uses.

The plist format isn't the most efficient for large data sets, though, so the information stored rarely exceeds a few hundred kilobytes. Still, that's ideal for application-preference storage.

Prior to OS X 10.2, plist files could exist in XML format only. But while XML files are convenient for human perusal and hand editing, they're not the most efficient for runtime processing. So in an effort to optimize performance, Apple introduced the plist binary format for more efficient access by running processes.

You can edit plist files in numerous ways. With those in XML, you can use the text editor of your choice. But generally, when a running process accesses the file, the OS convert the format into the more efficient binary, after which your favorite text editor is all but useless. Thus, before opening the file, you may want to verify the format using the `file` command-line tool:

```
$ file /Library/Preferences/com.apple.AppleFileServer.plist
/Library/Preferences/com.apple.AppleFileServer.plist: Apple binary property list
```

In this instance, the preference file com.apple.AppleFileServer.plist is in binary format, and were I to attempt to open it in a text editor, I'd be greeted with a nice display of gobbledygook. All is not lost, though. If you want to explore the raw XML, you can use the plutil executable, which can convert between XML and binary formats as well as run syntax checks on the file. To convert the above example into hand-editable format, you can call plutil with the -convert argument with a statement like:

```
$ plutil -convert xml1 /Library/Preferences/com.apple.AppleFileServer.plist
```

Now, you can run file against the plist again to verify that the conversion worked properly:

```
$ file /Library/Preferences/com.apple.AppleFileServer.plist
/Library/Preferences/com.apple.AppleFileServer.plist: XML 1.0 document text
```

Sure enough, the plist file is now in XML format, and you can view it with any text-capable editor. To convert it back to binary format, run plutil again, substituting binary1 for xml1 (though, as noted, the OS will usually handle the conversion for you).

Converting a plist file to XML is all well and good, but hand-editing files is of limited value in a mass-deployment scenario. Certainly you can use perl, sed, or awk in combination with extended regular expressions to modify an XML plist, but that's a fairly ugly endeavor and not for the faint of heart. Luckily, a number of tools exist to help edit plist files programmatically, most notably are defaults and plistbuddy, described in the next few sections of this chapter.

Defaults

When you need to deal with the contents of a property-list file, you can call on the defaults command, which lets you read, write, and delete data in the plist format. You can also use defaults to list the contents of a preference domain. In OS X, each application has its own preference, often referred to as *defaults*. To prevent configuration collisions, each application must belong to a different domain, which is structured based on a dictionary of keys and values that can be strings, numbers, or even another dictionary or array.

Each key in a preference domain represents the configuration of a particular setting or a behavior within the application that the domain represents. For example, the command defaults read com.apple.mail will read all preferences used by Apple's mail application. On the file-system level, each domain has a .plist file to store these settings.

All applications and services built into Mac OS X have their own domains. There is also the NSGlobal Domain, which contains CoreServices preference items. Most third party programs will also leverage the property list format to store their own preference files as well, considering that Apple has made it clear in developer documentation that this is the preferred method to store preference settings. At first, the defaults framework within Mac OS X may seem fairly complicated. If you're familiar with the Microsoft Windows Registry, using that as an analog might help. The Registry has a number of keys, each specifying a number of settings available either from the operating system or third party applications (whether available through the GUI or not). The OS X defaults system is a feature-rich and easily integrated method of changing application and operating-systems settings.

Showing hidden files in the Finder provides another example of using `defaults`. To see the contents of a property list, you can use `defaults` along with the `read` verb. To look at the contents of the `com.apple.finder` domain, which controls the Finder, you simply type the command:

```
defaults read com.apple.finder
```

Though this will display the contents of `com.apple.finder`, by default, the contents include no key for showing hidden files or for hiding files. With a little research, however, you'll discover that you can use the `AppleShowAllFiles` key, which is Boolean value. So to see hidden files, enter the command

```
defaults write com.apple.finder AppleShowAllFiles -boolean true
killall Finder
```

But there's a problem with viewing hidden files: You may well see a lot of stuff you really don't want to see. To return to a state where you don't have to view all the invisible files, just delete the `AppleShowAllFiles` attribute:

```
defaults delete com.apple.finder AppleShowAllFiles
killall Finder
```

Alternatively, you could simply set the opposite value:

```
defaults write com.apple.finder AppleShowAllFiles -boolean false
```

In addition to working with the `defaults` command to edit standard string and Boolean values in a key, you can also bring information in from other sources using a script. For example, here's a script that pulls a URL from a random list of servers:

```
#!/bin/bash

Sus="http://swupd.krypted.com:8088
http://sus.krypted.com:8088
http://sus1.krypted.com:8088
http://sus2.krypted.com:8088
http://sus3.krypted.com:8088
http://sus4.krypted.com:8088
http://sus5.krypted.com:8088
http://sus6.krypted.com:8088
http://sus7.krypted.com:8088
http://sus8.krypted.com:8088
http://sus9.krypted.com:8088
http://sus10.krypted.com:8088"
sus=($Sus)
num_sus=${#sus[*]}
```

```
echo -n ${sus[$((RANDOM%num_sus))]}
exit 0
```

This simply creates an array of the supplied software update servers (the items that start with http:// and located between the quote marks) and then chooses a random item from the list, writing the output to the screen of the chosen item. In this case, the array has been called sus, and the randomization performed using the $RANDOM function. If you have a number of software update servers you could replace the servers in this array with your own, and the script would simply write the server chosen from the array to the screen. Then to have it actually specify the server, remove the line that begins with echo -n and substitute

```
defaults write /Library/Preferences/com.apple.SoftwareUpdate CatalogURL
${sus[$((RANDOM%num_sus))]}
```

For deployment, we've handled updates two different ways. With the first, we run this script at startup as a log-in hook (it's really quick since it doesn't do much) and let the OS run software updates based on whatever schedule we've employed. The second method sets execution of software updates to occur strictly manually, but adds a line at the end of the script to run the updates, allowing you to schedule the task using launchd or to run it manually over ARD. To configure software updates to run manually, issue this command on the target system one time (it will persist):

```
softwareupdate –schedule off
```

Now, after it randomly chooses a software-update server, the script will encounter an instruction telling it that each time it runs, it should install all available software updates from that server. Here's that instruction, which we put at the end of the script:

```
softwareupdate -i -a
```

You could build a lot more logic into this process, but this shows you the basics of assigning a random software update server using a shell script, highlighting the defaults command in; for example, a non-MCX-managed environment. (We'll more on MCX and software-update scripts in Chapter 7.)

When Not to Use Defaults

Mac OS X comes with a variety of commands for managing settings without having to edit a configuration file or, in some cases, making it so you actually don't want to edit a property-list file. For example, you can get and set the computer name far more easily than with defaults by using scutil. This command returns the computer name:

```
scutil –get ComputerName
```

If you want to change the name, you use –set. So to make the computer name kryptedmacbook, you use the command

```
scutil –set ComputerName kryptedmacbook
```

Now, let's say you're writing a shell script and you want to put the computer name in a variable called computernm). At the command line, type:

```
computernm=$(scutil –get ComputerName)
```

Network settings are another aspect of client and server configuration that you can deal with more easily using a tool other than `defaults`. (We'll have more on network setup in Chapter 8.)

PlistBuddy

`PlistBuddy` is another tool for modifying property list files. In many ways, the functionality of the `defaults` command and `PlistBuddy` overlap. But PlistBuddy is better-suited for more complex structures. The `defaults` command is great for modifying simple data types, such as numbers, strings, dates, and to an extent, arrays. Once you start dealing with more complex structures, though, such as nested dictionaries, you can quickly find yourself in a headache-inducing maze of nested braces. For these complex files, PlistBuddy can help.

You'll find the tool in the `/usr/libexec` directory and you can invoke it either interactively or non-interactively. For the purposes of deployment, we'll focus on the latter. `PlistBuddy` has many options, but for most scenarios you'll use the following arguments:

- *Print key:* Prints the value of the specified key or the entire file if none is provided.

- *Set key value:* Sets the value at entry.

- *Add key type value:* Adds a key with specified type and value. Types include string, array, dict, bool, real, integer, date, and data.

- *Delete key:* Deletes the specified key from the plist.

These four options can handle the majority of your interactions, and you can learn about handling others by examining the PlistBuddy man page (type `man PlistBuddy` from any 10.5 machine).

As mentioned, while the `defaults` command is very useful for basic plist interaction, PlistBuddy is absolutely essential for more-complex interactions. An excellent example of this involves modifying an OS X machine's `SystemConfiguration` preferences file. The file, which resides in `/Library/Preferences/SystemConfiguration/preferences.plist`, contains extensive data about a computer's configuration including the `ComputerName` value, as noted in the previous section where we discussed `defaults`. In that context, we recommended that you not use `defaults`, opting to use the `scutil` instead. But `scutil` can only modify `ComputerName` for an active running system. What if you want to change the computer name on a non-running system, as in a mass-deployment imaging situation?

While most such systems we discuss in this chapter contain some sort of automated naming systems, if you decide to roll your own using ASR, you may want to modify the system configuration on a non-active system after deploying an image. For this scenario, `PlistBuddy` is the perfect utility. First, though, you need a database of computer names to poll. The easiest structure to use for the data set is a flat-file CSV arrangement. For instance, consider the following data in a file:

```
00:1f:f3:d1:d5:c7,Macbook-1234
00:1f:f3:d1:55:77,Macbook-1234
```

Here we have a very basic comma-delimited list consisting of computer MAC addresses and computer names. This CSV file could be stored on a remote server and provided via Web services. By using `curl` to fetch this remote CSV file and then `PlistBuddy` to modify the preferences `.plist` file on the newly imaged system, you can create a fairly basic post-imaging script that can dynamically rename a machine.

Say the data is stored in the file `machinedata.csv` on the Web server `NetBoot.myco.com`, and we've just finished laying down an image to our volume mounted at `/Volumes/MacbookHD`. Here's a script to update this newly imaged system with the appropriate ComputerName automatically:

```
#!/bin/bash

## setup a variable for our offline system's system configuration file
preferencesfile="/Volumes/MacBookHD/Library/Preferences/SystemConfiguration/preferences.
plist"

## fetch the csv file
curl http://NetBoot.myco.com/machinedata.csv -o /tmp/machinedata.csv

## get our primary ethernet MAC address
## this assumes we are booted off our target computer as opposed to imaging
## an external system over firewire
ethernetAddress=$(ifconfig en0 | awk '/ether/ {print $2}')

## search our machinedata.csv file for the appropriate ComputerName
computername=$(grep "$ethernetAddress" /tmp/machinedata.csv | awk -F, '{print$2}')

## make sure we have a computername value, if not, use the ethernet address
if [ -z "$computername" ]; then
        computername="Mac-$ethernetAddress"
fi

## set the computer name on our offline volume's system configuration
/usr/libexec/PlistBuddy -c "Set:System:System:ComputerName $computername"
"$preferencesfile"

## also update the bonjour name
/usr/libexec/PlistBuddy -c "Set:System:Network:HostNames:LocalHostName $comutername"
"$preferencesfile"
```

This is an optimal scenario for `PlistBuddy`, and its advantages become immediately apparent if you attempt to replicate this functionality using `defaults`. (Hint: it's not worth your time.) The `PlistBuddy` commands are actually referencing multiple nested dictionaries, specified by the hierarchy `System:System:ComputerName` or `System:Network:HostNames:LocalHostName`. Here, each colon-separated item up to the final key represents a nested dictionary. In each instance, the last key, `ComputerName` and `LocalHostName`, is a string element containing the respective values.

You can use `PlistBuddy` to read out these values by simply substituting `Print` for `Set`:

```
/usr/libexec/PlistBuddy -c "Print:System:Network:HostNames:LocalHostName"
"$preferencesfile"
```

When Not to Use PlistBuddy

While PlistBuddy is a great utility for dealing with more-complex plist data structures, it's important to note that the utility is simply modifying the contents of a file. But you should avoid modifying preference files of an actively running process—doing so can cause problems with the running state of the process. In less-extreme cases, the process could simply overwrite your changes with active runtime values.

Image Regression Testing

When you're creating a large number of images, testing each one can be critical to verifying a successful deployment. Here are the types of testing you might undertake.

The most straightforward form of image testing is going through the process manually and seeing what happens when you try to do a number of predefined tasks. Doing so requires having a testing system that you can re-image as needed. But manually testing images may give only a fraction of what can be done in the same amount of time if the process is automated. If you have a well-regimented image- and software-deployment environment, the results of testing against specific known configurations typically provide an early warning sign of problems in the image or a specific build of a package.

There are a few different solutions for Mac OS X that can be used for regression testing. Eggplant is primarily used to test software applications during development, but can also be used for this purpose. Regression testing is mostly useful in larger environments, with a large number of builds. Not only can it be used to qualify images, but regression testing can also be leveraged to qualify updates. By automating various testing tasks you can often quickly reduce the change and release management times for new software and operating systems. Eggplant can be obtained from Redstone Software at http://www.testplant.com.

Much of this may seem to be in the ether a bit, so let's look at how to automate some post-flight imaging checks you may do on images prior to deployment. Eggplant uses VNC to run checks on the remote systems and then recognizes events based on known, predefined patterns. If the pattern is a match then the test is a pass, if not it is a fail. Because Eggplant uses VNC it comes with VINE server, although you can use ARD as well if you've enabled VNC in your ARD configuration.

The System-Under-Test (SUT), is the client that you are testing. Install Vine Server on the SUT from the System-Under-Test-Utilities folder located on the Eggplant installer. Copy the Vine Server to the SUT and open it, providing provide a VNC password that your eggplant instance will use. Then install Eggplant (Starter Edition is fine for our testing purposes) by dragging the Eggplant application bundle into the /Applications directory on your Eggplant station. Open it and provide the license key to be placed at a blank workflow where you can build new scripts and images (images in the sense that they are actual image files as opposed to disk images).

To get started, create a new, empty script by clicking on the File menu and selecting New Script. In the New Script dialog, provide a name for the script (we're going to call ours Test Office). Then add the client or clients to test by choosing *Add Connection...*

from the Connection menu. When asked, provide an IP address, port number, and password for VNC. In the display name field, provide a name for Eggplant to reference the client moving forward and click on the Save button.

Next we're going to capture our first image. Now that you have a client configured, click on the Connect button with the client highlighted to open a VNC session into the client. Click on *Enter Capture Mode* from the application toolbar to capture images and define actions to be carried out on the STU. When in Capture Mode the screen is dimmed except for a box used to capture an image to a file, which is integral to creating actions. Resize the box by mousing over the corners and move the box over the Microsoft Word icon in the dock, resizing the screen to match the icon. Then, from the Eggplant toolbar click on Capture Image. You will then see a dialog box to associate a task with the image you are capturing and name it. Enter a name for the image into the *Image Name:* field. For the purposes of this example, we'll call the image *Word_Dock*. In the Where: field create a folder called Test Office (or another name that helps you to remember what the items for this script should be called). Then choose *Capture Image* to *Click.* Other actions we could have selected include *Double-Click on an item*, *Move an Item,* and *Wait for Item to appear.*

When you click on Microsoft Word, the Microsoft Project Gallery will, by default, open. Assuming Microsoft Office, and the Project Gallery open properly, you'll then open Word by creating a new document. Therefore, the next scripted action will be to highlight the Word icon for Word Document in the Gallery, and create an image, selecting the action to double-click on it. From the Window menu you can then select Current Script to bring up the script.

> **NOTE:** Eggplant is image-dependent. Changing the location of a file or directory can cause your tests to fail.

Now quit Word on your SUT and then click on the Run Script button of the Current Script window in Eggplant on the testing system to verify that the test was completed whether Microsoft Word opens properly. If it does, your script has run successfully.

While this example looked at Word, a common application that requires testing, it is worth noting that Eggplant can be used for testing any application in this manner. We also picked a very simplistic test in order to showcase how to get up and running. As your skills with scripting against Eggplant increase, you will be able to automate any number of tasks.

Summary

Imaging environments often reflect the maturity level of your infrastructure. In the beginning, you may be creating a large image with all of your software and automations included in the image. Over time you'll likely create an image and then move into more of a package-based deployment to supplement the image, perhaps going so far as to move to a bare metal image with full package management layered on top.

In this chapter we looked at creating and deploying images and then creating and deploying packages. We covered the Apple solutions, and we also covered a number of third-party solutions. The amount of page space provided to each solution is not worthy of any single solution, but if your interest was piqued by any solution, we strongly recommend that you get an evaluation or an engineer from the vendor onsite to your organization to fill in the gaps. Additionally, some solutions (namely the Apple solutions and those from JAMF Software) have dedicated training courses with substantially more information than is possible to include in this chapter.

## Chapter 7

Client Management

Put simply, no environment is too small to preclude evaluating your client management strategy. Whether you have two desktops or 100,000, there are tools and practices that can make both your life and your users' lives easier. A properly managed environment can save endless administration hours, and in many cases thousands of phone calls to an organization's support center. Long gone are the days of shuffling from computer to computer meticulously duplicating settings. Numerous tools now abound to save you from this monotonous nightmare—tools which provide you with the ability to affect tens, hundreds, or thousands of computers from a central point quickly and effectively. These tools empower you to effectively manage a computing environment with minimal staff cost.

What exactly is entailed in a good client management system? The answer will certainly vary depending upon whom you ask. If you ask a Windows system administrator, you're likely to hear talk of proper Active Directory Organizational Unit (OU) structure and elaborate Group Policy Object (GPO) inheritance trees, or you might hear of third party solutions and deploying .msi installers for settings, as described in Chapter 6. From a help desk perspective, the focus will largely be on finding, connecting to, and controlling client desktops (both the screen and the policies). Policy enforcement to ensure consistent environments across a multitude of desktops is also an invaluable way to ease the burden of remote support.

Mass deployment and imaging, along with package management systems, will often be lumped into the client management category because they intertwine. However, there is a distinction to be made. The latter is utilized to ensure a consistent, specially tailored software environment that is preconfigured to utilize your management systems. It is primarily focused on the deployment of a particular system's software environment. In contrast, controlling the user desktop experience is one of the main focal points of client management, providing facilities for automated setup of supported userland applications. These include dock, desktop and Finder customization, login items, network mounts, application preferences, media access, and any application that writes data into the user's home folder, such as Entourage. For the purposes of this book, client management picks up right where mass deployment ends—once the systems are deployed client management can be used to push default settings out and then lock certain features of the system down.

This chapter will attempt to provide insight into the important considerations that are needed to ensure that your post deployment environment is planned in a manner that will not only ensure its initial success, but will also be easily adaptable as technical needs or policies change. A successfully planned and managed client implementation is predicated by numerous metrics:

1. The existence of a tiered management hierarchy, structured appropriately for the environment to ensure granularity and scalability.

2. The chosen policy implementation properly addresses the technical needs of the managed node's workflow, as well as the managed user's workflow.

3. The chosen policy implementation adheres to global MIS policies.

4. Management restrictions are as unobtrusive to end users as possible.

5. Policy implementation is performed centrally, is dynamic, and can be easily changed across both a small and large scope of machines or users.

After reading this chapter, you will become familiar with numerous management principals to effect these goals: managing Open Directory's managed preferences system, user data planning, implementation and management, software update management, account and password policy management, and last but not least, live interactive management of your computer fleet using Apple Remote Desktop.

Managed Preferences

Managed preferences in Mac OS X provide administrators with a valuable tool set for managing many aspects of the Mac OS X computing environment. Their capabilities run a wide berth, providing many functions, such as managing individual userland application settings, applying user restrictions to inserted or removable media, controlling application access, and deploying network proxy settings. And they can also provide for managing computer hardware energy saver settings, including the ability to centrally deploy computer shutdown and reboot schedules.

Managed preferences in OS X are based off of Apple's MCX system, so the terms are often used interchangeably. Short for Managed Client OS X, MCX is a piece of Apple's solution to the user and computer management equation. MCX settings utilize LDAP for their application. This is typically Apple's Open Directory, but it is certainly possible to extend the schema of alternative LDAP servers to provide full functionality (such as Active Directory or eDirectory).

Managed preferences are configured through the Preferences interface of the Workgroup Manager Application, as shown in Figure 7-1. On a macro level, preference management can be applied at four different levels, each represented by a tab in the top-left region of Workgroup Manager. These levels include individual users, groups, individual computers, and groups of computers. Standard groups, once managed, are referred to as workgroups. The other levels are simply referred to as managed users, managed computers, and managed computer groups.

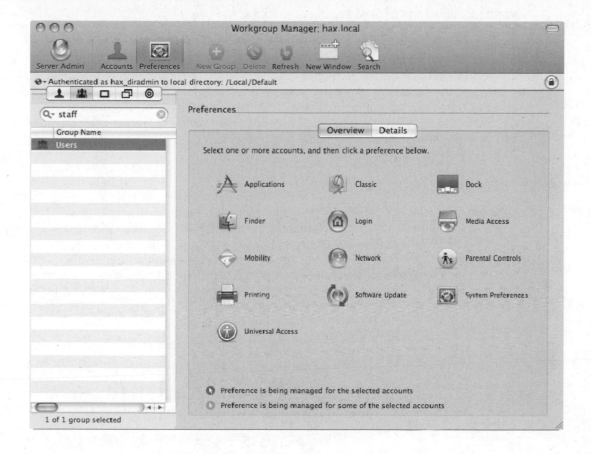

Figure 7-1. *Managed preferences overview*

In Mac OS X 10.4, computer groups were nonexistent. Preceding them were computer lists, now deprecated except for basic policy management and otherwise functionally equivalent. Computer lists are limited in two crucial ways. They cannot be nested and computers could only be a member of a single list, a limitation particularly cumbersome in larger environments. One noteworthy computer list-based feature of 10.4 was the guest computer list. The guest computer list was used to manage any computer, which was configured with an untrusted bind to an LDAP domain and didn't have a unique computer record with the appropriate Ethernet address. This is a fairly common occurrence in loosely managed environments, and the presence of this catchall computer-level management list was very useful. This functionality still exists in 10.5 and 10.6, but is implemented as a single computer record, the guest computer. The guest computer can be found under the computers tab of WGM, but is not available until explicitly created. To do so, there is a nifty Create Guest Computer menu item found under the Server menu in Workgroup manager.

Certain management settings are not available at the user and workgroup levels. These management levels apply to active user sessions, so settings outside of this purview, such as login scripts, energy saver settings, and login window preferences are only managed on the computer and computer group levels. Time Machine settings are another noteworthy management capability only applicable on the computer level. On the flip side, the computer-oriented management levels do not share the same deficit—they have access to the entire purview of applicable management. Because of this, having a well structured and populated managed preferences paradigm that includes users, groups, and computers is highly recommended.

Preference Interactions

One key feature of MCX behavior to understand is the way that managed preferences are determined when managed on multiple levels. Apple defines three different managed preference behaviors, referred to as preference interactions, which determine the resultant policy from multiple levels of management. Overriding preference interactions refer scenarios where two different levels manage the same domain, each explicitly providing conflicting settings. In these cases, OS X prioritizes management levels, as shown in Figure 7-2.

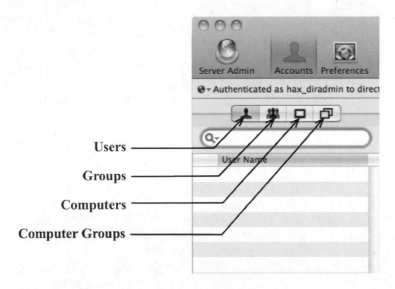

Figure 7-2. *Account types election in Workgroup Manager*

This works out well for the most part, although there are a few ramifications to discuss. Most important, managed preferences applied at the user level will be the dominant preference, persisting for that user in any environment that they log in to, despite any computer or computer list managed preferences that are applied. After this, you have computer and computer groups taking precedence over workgroups. This proves to be beneficial in lab or kiosk environments where the nodes are typically special usage and may need specific configurations. Workgroups, though the lowest on the totem pole, will be your primary application point. The granularity of user-based management is both a blessing and a curse. While it's great to ensure VIP status for certain users and implement further managed preferences for problem users, it also becomes a management nightmare in medium-to-large environments where a number of policies overlap on a given object due to a combination of users, groups, computers, and computer groups.

Another form of interaction is referred to as combined interactions. Some examples of these include printers, login items, and dock items. In a combined interaction scenario, preferences from all of the different levels are aggregate. Therefore, if you have a login item deployed for a specific user and a login item deployed for a group the user is in, then both login items will take effect when the user logs in.

Inherited interactions are the third type of preference interaction, and simply refer to a managed preference that is only managed at a single level.

> **NOTE:** Introduced with 10.5 was the ability to combine preferences across groups. In 10.4, users would be prompted to select a workgroup upon login, and solely that workgroup's preferences would be applied. With 10.5 and later, you can define settings across multiple workgroups. When a user logs in, and is a member of multiple workgroups, they can be configured to receive the combined policies of those two groups. This was a big boon, as it simplified the management of complex hierarchies, particularly opening up the ability to apply management across nested workgroups. The ability still remains to mimic the 10.4 behavior, if needed.

For the most part, standard preference interactions apply when combining workgroup management. However, an obvious conflict presents itself: When an overriding preference interaction occurs between two groups how is precedence determined? In the case of nested groups, where one of the conflicting groups is a member of the other, the child-most group will override its parents. That is, if GroupA is nested inside of GroupB, GroupB's managed preferences will be applied. If the conflicting groups are independent, the unfortunate answer is that there is no way to explicitly set precedence in such an event—the resulting preference will be determined from the first group sorted alphabetically. This typically shouldn't be a problem, as a properly structured system should avoid conflicting group settings. If the situation is absolutely unavoidable, one option available is to utilize computer access lists, which serve as a handy filter for workgroup-based management.

At this point, you may wonder how it is possible to determine the type of interaction that will be applied to a managed preference. The answer is actually a little more straightforward than may be expected. In fact, the answer will be fairly obvious. Any preference, which has a single definitive setting, will result in an override scenario. There can be only one after all. Combined interactions are utilized in list-based management panes, such as dock items, login items, home sync items, printers, system preferences, and applications. In each of these cases, the user will be presented with the aggregate of explicitly allowed items.

Utilizing Tiered Management

Once mastered, the system provides for very flexible and granular management. In order to truly utilize the system to its potential, you must first have a good understanding of the environment where it is being deployed. This is typically best accomplished by tailoring the system to the organizational structure of the business that it serves. Take note of the various delineations in your workforce, and consider categories such as tenure, job roles and duties, departments, and locations, if applicable. Perhaps some of these categories transcend others, but the goal is to tailor the specific groups that you would want to target for management; the more specific, the more adaptable the system will be for your needs.

Picture a fairly large media organization, like Mediaco. Mediaco has two different campuses, each with fully staffed departments. Mediaco has numerous editors at both locations that need access to the global company media repository. Each campus also has a file server hosting data for multiple departments. A flexible group management structure for this is outlined in Figure 7-3.

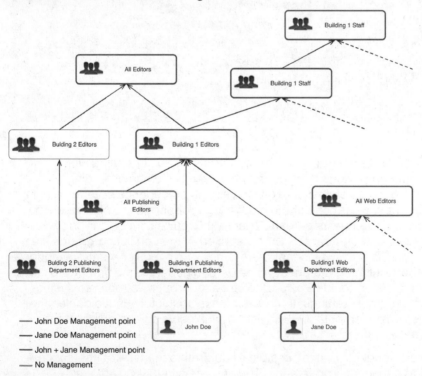

Figure 7-3. *Tiered management*

In this example, you have created numerous groups to represent your structure. The user, John Doe, has been added to the group, Building1 Publishing Department Editors. This group is in turn members of both the All Publishing Editors group, but also the Building1 Editors group, which is once again nested into multiple groups. In this example, even though the user is only a direct member of one group, you can still apply management at six different workgroup tiers. Through the root All Editors group, you may add a login item for the company media repository file share. You can then specify your departmental file server login item on the group, Building1 Publishing Department Editors. Now, when John Doe logs in, he has both his department's SharePoint and the global SharePoint mounted and ready for access.

Computer groups can be similarly tiered, though there is a strong case to be made for the ability to provide logistical-based management. For instance, Mediaco wants to turn off desktop computers at night to save energy costs. Immediately, the need to distinguish between laptop and desktop machines is apparent. Further delineation may be advisable in your organization to account for backup/maintenance schedules, usage patterns, and so forth.

There really isn't a wrong way to deploy groups provided your methodology meets your needs. There certainly are methods to improve efficiency and security. The more specific and tiered your group structure, the happier you will be whenever a policy change is needed. Likewise, the more controlled and consistent your structure is, the easier it will become to avoid membership mistakes. These mistakes can be particularly costly. Workgroup structure is also utilized for file system access controls via POSIX/ACL permissions as well as service access control lists (SACLs). Having a fine-tuned workgroup and computer group structure will provide you with a clean, consistent system that has the ability to adapt quickly, securely, and (hopefully) with consistency. Having a decent structure from the start cannot be overstated because responding to the latest need by simply creating another ad hoc group will ultimately lead to an incomprehensible mess.

Managed Preferences in Action

Here's where you get to the core of Managed Preferences: applying it to workstations. Over the next few pages, we will detail the more notable capabilities in the Managed Preferences system and the steps required for their implementation.

Preference Manifests and Custom Preferences

As mentioned in the "Managed Preferences" section earlier in this chapter, managed preferences are applied via the preference pane of workgroup manager. Through this tool, Apple provides a nice, clean, and simple graphical interface for managing the most common applications. However, this is not a definitive list of what can and cannot be managed through MCX. After all, third party programs can be constructed in such a way to fully support MCX management. Apple's system provides support in two different ways. Preferably, Application will support management via Apple's Preference Manifest system. Preference manifests allow a third party application to provide an interface that can be utilized by system administrators to apply management settings to the application. In Workgroup Manager, preference manifest support is accessed via the Details tab of the managed preference interface. In this interface, you can click the plus button and navigate to the application on the file system that you want to manage. Upon selecting the desired app, the interface presents the option to import current settings (see Figure 7-4).

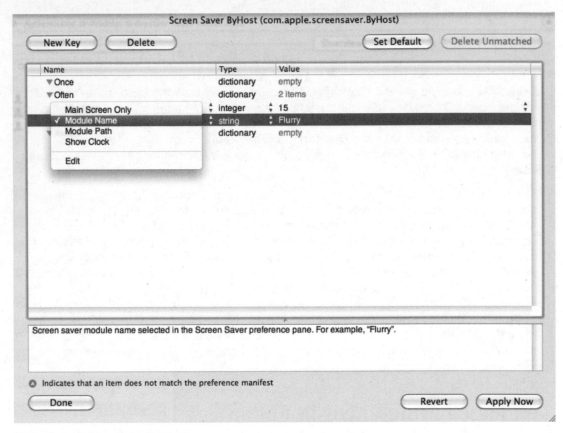

Figure 7-4. *Preference manifest keys*

To determine if an application supports preference manifests, uncheck this option. If the application has no manifest, you will immediately be presented with an error stating this. Once a manifest has been added to Workgroup Manager, it will be presented permanently for that user. Each manifest is stored in the directory at ~/Library/Preferences/com.apple.mcx.manifests and in the file ~/Library/Preferences/com.apple.mcx.plist. If desired, you can clear them out by deleting these files.

If the application does have preference manifest support, then upon importing the application into the system (without importing your personal settings), the details pane in Workgroup Manager will have an entry for the applications preference domain, such as com.myco.myapp. The new management functionality isn't apparent until you try to add a new key under the Once, Often, or Always sections in that domain. When you create a new key, you will be presented with a menu selection of supported attributes. Each attribute will often have associated applicable values presented via a selection menu. However, often custom values can be entered in and properly utilized. It all depends upon the application.

If an application does not support manifests, you're not completely out of luck. If this is the case, you must resort to the second method that Apple provides to manage an app: you can push out just about any defaults-based setting to an app. That is, any application that properly utilizes Apple's provided preference system and results in preferences being stored in a file found at ~/Library/Preferences/com.myco.myapp.plist. By selecting the option to import settings, regardless of manifest support, it will copy settings for the application in question from your current operating environment and apply them to the managed machines. Alternatively, in WGM you can add the preference file itself. Be careful when doing so as there is often junk that will be in the file. If you push out your starting window position, other users might not be too happy with your choice.

> **NOTE:** One big limitation to this method is that the %@ string substitution (discussed further in Chapter 8) used for preference manifests is not supported. This means that preferences with user-specific settings are not well suited to be deployed from an existing preference file. If you really must cross that road, some heavy scripting would be needed to parse the settings file and then deploy the customized MCXSettings attribute additions to each individual user object. As always, test thoroughly before unleashing on the masses.

The most comprehensive preference manifests is provided by Apple in the ManagedClient MCX. To utilize this manifest, under the details tab of Workgroup Manager preference management add the ManagedClient.app application found on any OS X system at the path /System/Library/CoreServices/ManagedClient.app. The ManagedClient app contains a manifest which exposes a great deal of various settings for management. This includes the ability to manage Screen Saver preferences, Login Redirections, Menu Items, VPN Settings, and Finder Sidebar Items to name a few. It is definitely worth consulting this manifest if the management setting you wish to deploy cannot be found in the provided GUI.

Setting MCX from the Command Line

It is certainly possible to set MCX settings from the command line. To access this functionality, the dscl tool is used. dscl has numerous commands, such as mcxread, mcxset, mcxedit, mcxexport, and mcximport. Using these commands you can fully manipulate mcx settings programmatically. For example, you can use mcxset to set a very basic value:

```
dscl -u mydiradmin /LDAPv3/dirserv.myco.com mcxset /Groups/coolpeople com.apple.dock no-glass always -boolean true
```

The previous command will set the appearance of the dock (key no-glass) to display without the 3D-background for all members of the group coolpeople, applied always.

Likewise, if you wanted to push out a setting to enable the Debug menu in Safari to aid in troubleshooting a user issue you could use the same method:

```
dscl -u diradmin /LDAPv3/dirserv.myco.com mcxset /Groups/coolpeople com.apple.Safari
IncludeDebugMenu always 1
```

This tool can be very handy for duplicating settings, like duplicating some home directory syncing values from one group to another. To do this, first export the good group's com.apple.homeSync settings:

```
dscl -u mydiradmin /LDAPv3/dirserv.myco.com mcxexport /Groups/syncpeeps -o
/tmp/syncpeeps_homesync.plist com.apple.homeSync
```

Next, import those settings into your new group:

```
dscl -u mydiradmin /LDAPv3/dirserv.myco.com mcximport /Groups/newsyncgroup
/tmp/syncpeeps_homesync.plist
```

This is by far the easiest way to duplicate a group's synchronization settings across a domain, but the tool is not limited there. For example, if you wanted to simply duplicate ALL MCX settings the same mcxexport/mcximport process can be run, omitting the com.apple.homeSync domain to capture all managed preference domains for that group.

The man page for dscl is unfortunately light on details regarding the various mcx interaction devices. However, the file located at /System/Library/DirectoryServices/dscl/mcxcl.dsclext/Contents/Resources/mcxdsclhelp.txt provides much information about using dscl to manipulate MCX.

Automated Client Setup

In this section, I will discuss various MCX configurations that can be deployed to assist with configuration of the user environment: managing application preferences and configuration, network proxy configuration, and printer deployment.

Mail

MCX has the ability to automatically configure mail account for your users. It is fairly basic in nature and provides the ability to populate a single email account. Unfortunately, preference interactions for Mail result in an override, so it is not possible at this time to deploy both a personal mail account at one tier, and a departmental or group account at a different tier. The single account that you do deploy can be either a POP or IMAP account.

In order to deploy mail accounts, first get com.apple.mail.managed and com.apple.mail (aka Mail-10.6) into your Details screen following the steps covered in the "Preference Manifests and Custom Preferences" section earlier in this chapter. Once this has been added into Workgroup Manager, you can automatically deploy email accounts for clients by using the com.apple.mail.managed domain in 10.5 and the com.apple.mail domain in 10.6. In either domain, you will have a number of keys that allow you to manage client settings for Mail.app, as shown in Figure 7-5.

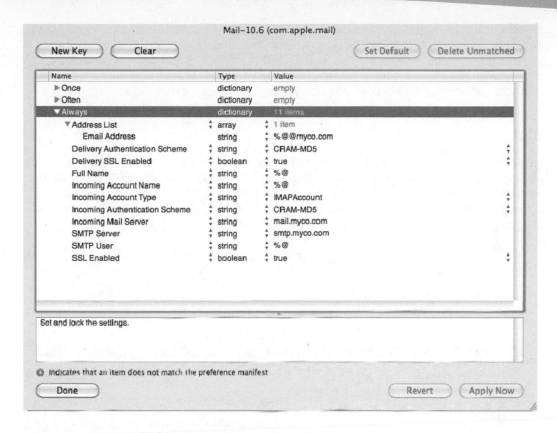

Figure 7-5. *Deploying managed preferences for Mail.app*

Figure 7-5 represents a recommended configuration for a mail account (mileage may vary according to the setup of each organization). Notice the variable substitution being used here as well, the string %@ is substituted for the user's short name.

> **NOTE:** In Mac OS X 10.5, the com.apple.mail.managed manifest would be used rather than com.apple.mail, which is for Mac OS X 10.6. The com.apple.mail.managed domain only provides Mac OS X 10.5 and doesn't have as much functionality as the 10.6 implementation. For instance, the com.apple.mail.managed also does not support deploying SSL settings.

In this example, you are setting up an IMAP account with CRAM-MD5 authentication. To deploy a POP account, you specify a Mail Account Type of POP Account. Attempting to deploy account types ExchangeAccount or iToolsAccount (Mobile Me) will fail because they are not supported. Supported authentication schemes in the manifest is limited to GSSAPI, however, you can successfully utilize values CRAM-MD5 and NTLM. With the latter option, there is no provided way to deploy the domain setting, so it is of limited use.

Overall, the mail preference manifest is rather limited. For example, it is not possible to deploy authenticated SMTP settings, nor Exchange accounts at the time this book is written. If you want to deploy these, you'll need to use a scripted solution, which is described further in Chapter 5. Hopefully, in the future, these features will be added so that you will not need a scripted solution for deployments requiring more custom setups.

iCal

Deploying CalDAV accounts for iCal is pretty straightforward. Also accessed through the ManagedClient manifest (as with Mail before it), iCal is only possible to leverage managed preferences to deploy a single account. It allows for specifying account name, server address, and SSL, as well as a few lesser used settings. Figure 7-6 is a screenshot of a configured iCal preference manifest, deployed at the "Often" level.

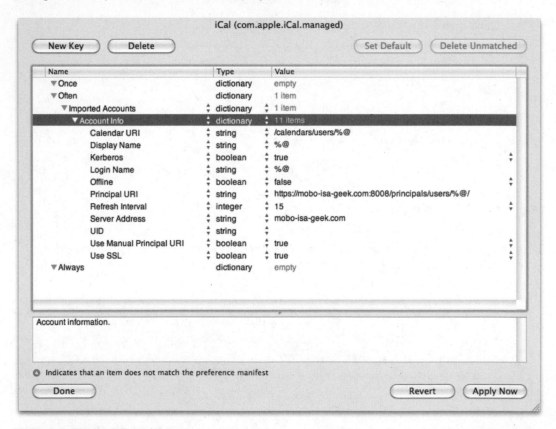

Figure 7-6. *Managed iCal preferences*

Here, you have configured the server address, the URI to the calendars themselves, which is relative to the server address and enabled SSL authentication. Again, we have chosen to make use of the %@ to push out settings specific to each user connecting to the iCal solution.

NOTE: While Managed Preferences can be used when setting up automatic iCal configuration, you are better off using DNS as described in the iCal Server Administration document at http://www.apple.com/server/macosx/resources/documentation.html.

Address Book

Strictly speaking, there is no preference manifest support for Address Book even in 10.6. However, it is still possible to deploy a custom LDAP server for inclusion in Mail.app lookups. Because there is no preference manifest support for Address Book, you will need to begin by importing a current preference file. The easiest way to do this is simply to configure the LDAP server in Address Book on your admin station. Next, add the preference file located at ~/Library/Preferences/com.apple.addressbook.plist and specify the "Once" for management. Next, you will want to edit the preference domain and par down all of the unwanted garbage in the file. Specifically, you only need to save the key AB3LDAPServers, and its children, as shown in Figure 7-7.

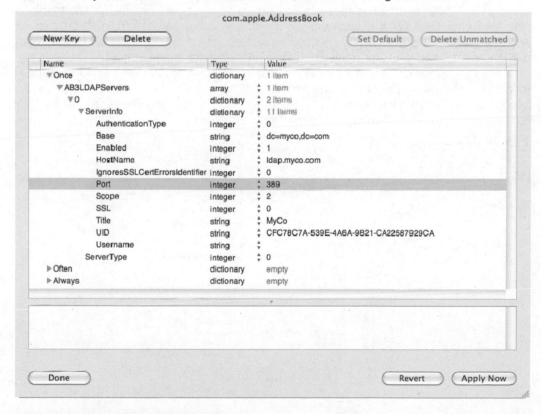

Figure 7-7. *Deploying LDAP accounts via MCX*

Application Preferences

Many users will want to customize a particular application's preferences or behavior that isn't otherwise included in the stock ManagedClient bundle. This may be something as simple as pre-populating registration information for Microsoft Office, possibly for deploying LDAP server connections utilized for lookups with Address Book and Mail. If you're security conscious, you may want to deploy a preference for Safari to disable its infamous Open safe files after download option.

As discussed earlier, in order for MCX to manage an application, that application needs to utilize Apple's **defaults** preference system. While the majority of native OS X applications fall into this realm, a good chunk of third party vendors don't yet support managed client preferences. The largest offenders here are educational software, as well as large cross-platform packages, such as Adobe's Creative Suite and Firefox. MS Office has a mixed history with MCX, though Office 2008 is much better in this regard, short of Entourage, which still relies primarily on its database for configuration.

The easiest way to deploy application settings is to first configure the application in a clean environment, specifically with your settings. Once done, you can utilize Workgroup Manager to import your preferences, and then whittle them down to a clean, deployable set. In this case, Word has been installed and configured with the desired settings. To deploy these settings, open up Workgroup Manager and select the preference management layout. Next, highlight the desired group for deployment, then in the far right pane select the Details tab. Click the plus button at the bottom, navigate to and select Microsoft Word, make sure the option to Import my Preferences is checked, and click add (see Figure 7-8). Because the settings are pulled from the active environment, you must be running Workgroup Manager from the computer which configured Office with your settings.

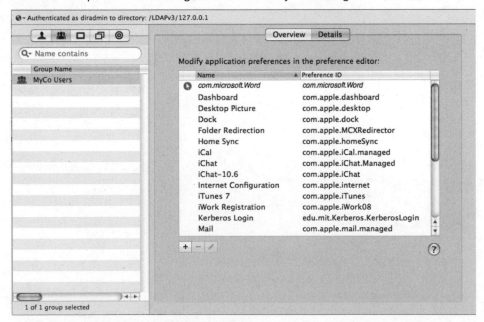

Figure 7-8. *Adding the Office preferences manifest*

Alternatively, you can copy the preference file from the configured user's ~/Library/Preferences folder to your admin machine, and then add the preference file rather than the MS Word app in Workgroup Manager. After performing either of these actions, there will be a new entry in the list, labeled com.microsoft.word in italics. The italic text signifies that this is an imported preference which does not match a known preference manifest. Nonetheless, MS Word will honor the settings.

If you edit the new managed settings for com.microsoft.word, you see there are several dozen various preferences that are now managed, not all of which are pertinent to your purposes. In order to ensure as clean an environment as possible for your users, you will want to narrow this list down to only the specific preferences that you want to deploy. Figure 7-9 shows a managed preference on the com.microsoft.office domain, added by adding the preference file found at ~/Library/Preferences/com.microsoft.office.plist. The managed preferences for this domain have been reduced to the keys 2008\FirstRun\ SetupAssistantCompleted, and 2008\Toolbars\ShowWysiwyg, which prevent the setup assistant from launching, and enable Fonts in the toolbar to be displayed in their appropriate typeset.

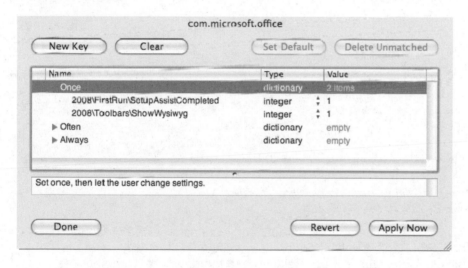

Figure 7-9. *Configuring the office preference manifest*

Figure 7-10 shows the Word specific management settings. Notice that several options have been moved from Once to Often. Background save, for example, is managed in the Often category to ensure that user's don't permanently shoot themselves in the foot by disabling autosave. Next, you'll enable auto grammar and spell checks, but allow the user the option to turn those off on their own. Moving items between categories Once and Often can be accomplished through copy and paste. Try to avoid deploying third party preferences in the Always category—support for this in third party apps is fairly rare and may not be honored by the application.

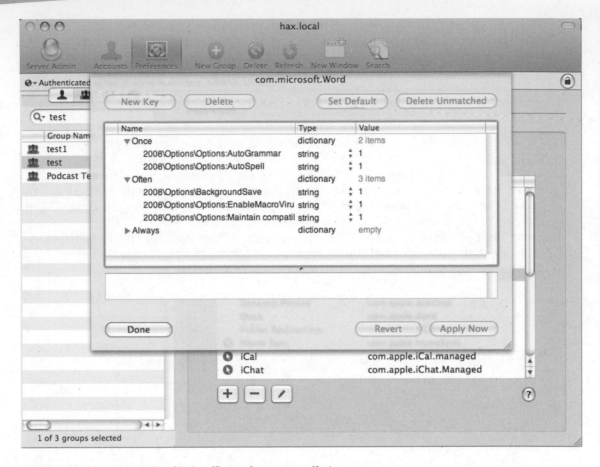

Figure 7-10. *More granularity with the office preferences manifest*

This general workflow can be applied to most applications provided the developer includes support for Apple's default preferences system. If there is a preference manifest available for the application, make sure to thoroughly test whether the managed preferences are actually honored. If the application that you add supports preference manifests, then the details list will display the domain in non-italic text, and will provide key validation to affirm proper management settings are applied for that application. To determine whether an application supports the defaults command to manage preferences, look for a property list (plist) that stores the preferences for the application.

> **NOTE:** You can also use the `defaults read` command to see all registered property lists and then pipe output into the grep command to limit the output. However, this can be a difficult way to try and isolate preferences.

Deploying Proxy Settings via a PAC File

A PAC file is a Proxy Auto Configuration file. PAC files automation configure proxy settings for users and are commonly utilized in large organizations with complicated network architectures. Support for configuring network proxy settings is provided via Workgroup Manager's managed preference GUI, shown in Figure 7-11. Found under the Network section, it is possible to deploy a multitude of various proxy settings. Closely resembling the proxy configuration found in every OS X client's Network Preference Pane, it is possible to deploy application specific proxy settings for http, https, gopher, ftp, or rtsp. SOCKS layer 5 tunneling is also supported here. Additionally, .pac automatic proxy configuration files can be deployed to your clients via MCX as well.

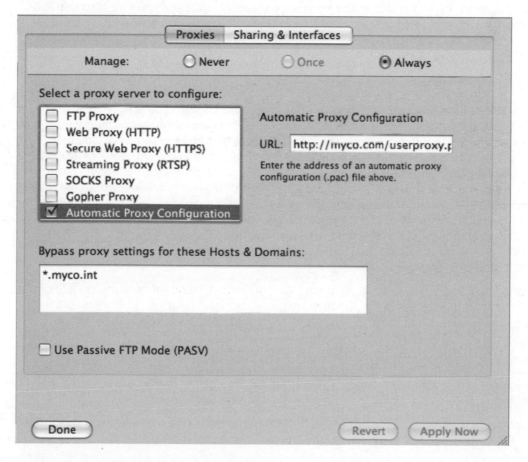

Figure 7-11. *Proxy managed preferences configuration*

Proxy configuration is available at all MCX levels. However, it is important to note that not all applications will utilize these settings. Firefox is by far the most notorious offender here. It has its own internal proxy configuration and ignores the global system setting. Indeed, Firefox generally snuffs Apple's defaults system and is immune to the reach of MCX. Likewise, command-line apps will often require either their own internal proxy configuration or will require the configuration of environmental variables for the purpose. The exact configuration will vary from application to application, but if needed environmental variables can be deployed via MCX as well.

To configure the proxy auto config option, open Workgroup Manager and then click on Preferences. Click on the computer or computer list to manage, click on Network, and then the Proxies tab. Figure 7-11 represents the deployment of a .pac proxy configuration file located at `http://myco.com/userproxy.pac`. You can also use the Bypass proxy settings for these Hosts and Domains field. In the previous example, you are also deploying an exception for internal myco.int domain.

Network Printing

The ability to easily deploy printers to your user base can be a huge time saver—managing printers across multiple locations and hundreds of users by hand would take enormous amounts of time. The good news is that MCX works very well for managing which network printers are available to users, allowing an administrator to remotely assign printers at all of the typical MCX management layers. From an end user's perspective, they will simply see all of their deployed printers from the available printer list in any printer dialog box. Beyond this, MCX provides numerous facilities: setting default printers (useful for deploying at the computer and computer group levels); forcing a footer on the printout which includes the user's name, date, and optionally the printing computer's MAC address; and restricting access to a printer by requiring administrative access.

In order to deploy a network printer via MCX, you must first configure the printer on your administrative computer. Once configured and tested, open up Workgroup Manager, select the object that you wish to manage, and then select the Printing preferences pane, as shown in Figure 7-12. There is no right answer here for deploying printers. In some cases, it may make sense to deploy the occasional printer to an individual user. In lab or kiosk environments, it makes more sense to deploy at the computer group and set a default printer. This way, when a user logs into that computer, their default printer will be the closest one to the computer.

In large environments, it may even be desirable to create and utilize groups specifically for printer management to provide better visibility and scalability.

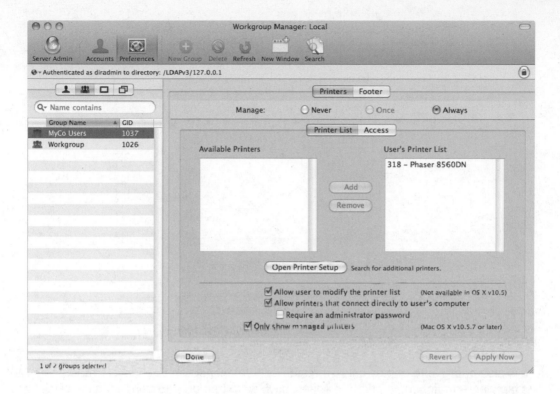

Figure 7-12. *Managed printers*

The one major "gotcha" to MCX printer management is that it has somewhat limited support. Its support lies primarily in network printers, which support the postscript protocol and ppd files. Printers, which require specialized binary drivers, are not going to function properly with this system. If you desperately need to support such a printer through MCX, your best bet is to utilize an OS X print server, which can re-share the printer and provide an abstraction layer. To pull this off, configure the print server to print to the printer, and share out the printer using the Printer's service in Server Admin. Next, configure your admin client to print to the server's shared printer, and then deploy it via MCX.

In Mac OS X 10.4, it was possible to use MCX to enable an option to display only managed printers. This was a very handy option to ensure that only the printers that are managed are displayed in the list. This was a handy feature to ensure that any other printers which had been set up at one point or another will no longer be accessible. Fortunately, the option is still available in 10.5, it's just hidden a bit. To access the functionality, first deploy the desired printer preferences to your desired target. Next, select the Details tab of managed preferences, and edit the preference domain com.apple.mcxprinting. Under the always domain, add a new key named ShowOnlyManagedPrinters. Set the value type to boolean, and specify a value of true, as shown in Figure 7-13. From here on, the printers you specify in MCX will be the only printers listed in a user's print dialog box.

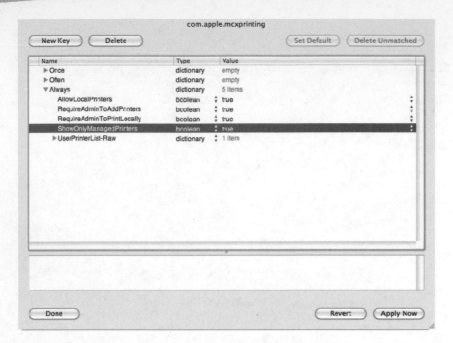

Figure 7-13. *com.apple.mcxprinting managed preference manifest*

It is also possible to deploy printer presets using managed preferences. Printer presets are simply pre-configuring a printer's values, such as to turn on duplexing for a supported printer or to turn on grayscale output for another. Though there is no GUI facility for it, the process is pretty straightforward. You'll want to start off with a user environment that has a clean preset list. Configure the printers and the specific presets that you want to deploy. Once perfected, snag the preference file stored in the user's preference folder, specifically ~/Library/Preferences/com.apple.print.custompresets.plist. In Workgroup Manager, select the object where you want to deploy the presets, and select the Preferences interface. Once here, click on Details, and click the plus button to add a preference file. Navigate to the com.apple.print.custompresets.plist file and add it in. When adding the plist, you'll likely want to manage import as an Once only setting. Otherwise, you will prevent users from creating their own presets.

Managed Printers deployed across multiple groups will result in a combined MCX interaction. That is, a user will have access to all printers deployed from all applicable workgroups, computer groups, etc. Other settings, such as custom presets, or the default printer will result in an override, following the standard MCX pecking order.

TIP: There is an option available which allows users to add their own printers. This functionality was limited to admin users until 10.5.7. In environments where administrators needed users to be able to add their own printers, there were workarounds involving editing the /etc/authorization and /etc/cupsd/cupsd.conf files. If these files have been edited, then you will need to undo the edits in order for this feature to start working again.

Restricting Applications

MCX application restrictions have been a bit of a moving target.10.4 had a fairly configurable setup, allowing the option to explicitly allow applications or to specifically deny applications. Unfortunately, the system wasn't terribly resilient and was pretty easy to bypass. With 10.5, a new take on application restrictions were put In place. For this context, you will be referring primarlly to the system introduced with 10.5 and carried forward to 10.6.

In 10.5 and later, restricting applications with MCX is done on an explicit allow basis. That is, once you choose to restrict applications for a user, an implicit deny will be applied to all applications that are not in the allowed applications list. Because of this, it is important to have a good understanding of the applications that will be utilized in the managed environment prior to embarking on this endeavor. If not properly planned, you will be flooded with support requests from users, claiming that they can't access their applications. However, when implemented using application signing, the system proves to be extremely resilient to various hacks that might be used to subvert it.

When restricting applications with MCX, you have two primary options, both accessible from the Applications pane of Workgroup Managers Preference interface, as shown in Figure 7-14.

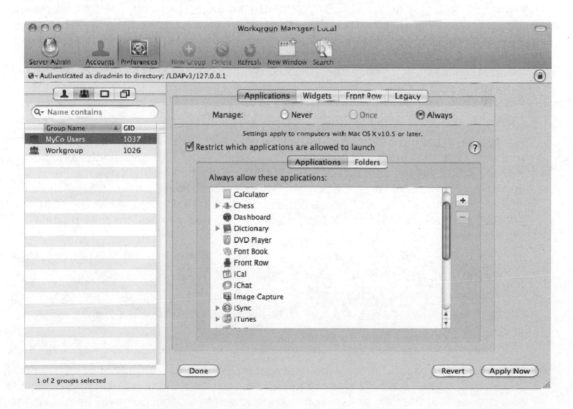

Figure 7-14. *Configuring application whitelisting*

Using this interface, you can allow a specific application, or you can specify a whitelisted folder wherein any application resides is always trusted. The latter, if setup improperly, can be easily exploited. However, if you ensure that you specify only directories, which are not writeable by the user, then it can be an acceptable measure. However, local file system permissions can be easily bypassed through single user mode, so it may be desirable to configure a firmware password to prevent this easy avenue.

There are a few general whitelist folders, which will make life a bit easier. Specifically, enabling all applications located in the folder locate at /System/Library/CoreServices will allow numerous support applications to run. Whitelisting the /Library/Quicktime folder is needed to prevent numerous QuickTime plug-ins from malfunctioning and whitelisting /Library/Printers is necessary for certain printer drivers. Each of these folders is immutable to non-admin users, so they are generally fine for whitelist exclusions. /Library/Application Support is another directory, which can contain binary support files needed by various applications.

For the most part though, you will want to allow specific applications. This allows for fine-grained targeting without the need to worry whether file system restrictions have been bypassed. Combined with application signing, the system is a very secure way to ensure that the only applications which launch are the intended applications. Application signing is a feature introduced with Leopard, and allows for an application to be signed by a trusted certificate, similar to a standard SSL environment. Application signing is without a doubt the way of the future. The Mach-O binary format is a bit notorious for being an easy target for code injection, exposing a potential avenue for viral infection. By signing an application, you can ensure that the code present in the executable is in the state shipped by the manufacturer. If it is modified, it will no longer match your signature, and will thereby be treated as a foreign entity.

Application signing is utilized very heavily by the iPhone and iPod Touch (described further in Chapter 10), as well as in Mac OS X, which as of 10.5 ships with all Apple apps signed. In 10.5, it is utilized primarily in my MCX application restrictions and the application firewall. When an OS X client has an active application firewall that specifies which applications have access, it utilizes code signing to ensure the identity of the application. If an unsigned application is added to the list, the system will sign the application for you behind the scenes.

> **NOTE:** When adding an application to an allowed applications list, you must first specify the application from the client machine running Workgroup Manager. If the application that you wish to allow is not resident on this computer, you will not be able to select it from the list, and thereby will not be able to provision access to the app.

Likewise, when you add an unsigned application to the allowed applications list, you will be greeted with an option to sign the application, or add it to the list without signing it. If you choose the latter, the application will be allowed to launch, but it will be possible to utilize this inclusion for exploitative purposes. Because the application is not signed, it is possible to alter any arbitrary application to impersonate the application, and thereby bypass any restrictions that would otherwise be applied. As such, if any allowed application is unsigned, it represents the ability for the user to launch any application, provided they have the skills to do so. When an allowed application is not signed, it will appear with a yellow triangle next to its entry, as seen for Firefox in Figure 7-15.

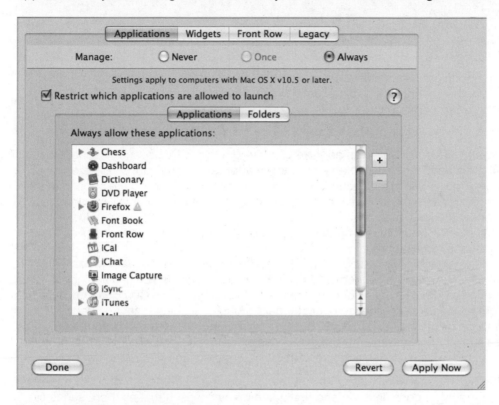

Figure 7-15. *Adding an unsigned applications*

There are some ramifications for signing an application when adding via Workgroup Manager as well. Most notably, when you sign the application with Workgroup Manager, you are signing only the local copy of that application. As such, all those hundreds of copies of that application in the field remain unsigned, and therefore restricted from launching. In order to fulfill a securely restricted environment, it will be necessary to deploy the signed applications to all of your clients. Alternatively, Apple has provided the command-line utility codesign which allows for the signing of applications from the command line. The syntax to sign an application is as follows:

```
codesign -s identity /Path/to/Application.app
```

For most environments, the identity in the previous command will be the name of the certificate as you see it listed in the keychain in which it is stored. Whereas the identity is determined by searching the keychain search path for a certificate whose subject matches the provided string, using this utility and a self-signed certificate you can sign any applications client-side through automation. As long as you have deployed your

RootCA to all of your clients as outlined in Chapter 2, then you can ensure proper validation of your applications.

> **NOTE:** You cannot use an invalid certificate to sign applications. If you see a red "x" on the certificate In Keychain Access this will have to be resolved prior to using the certificate to accomplish a successful codesign.

Using the codesign command, you can sign the Microsoft Word application using a certificate in the keychain. For this example, you will call the certificate mycert. Simply use the following command:

```
codesign -s mycert /Applications/Microsoft\ Office\ 2008/Microsoft\ Word.app
```

Deployed applications result in an additive process. If a user's management surface has application restrictions applied at any level, those application restrictions will be applied everywhere. This is particularly noticeable when application restrictions are applied at the computer level. When this occurs, all managed users on that computer will have application restrictions. If an administrator opts to not disable management globally, the admin will also inherit the computer's application restrictions. While the application preference pane does indeed allow an option to uncheck "Restrict which applications are allowed to launch," this setting will be overridden based upon standard MCX search policy. Thus, if you apply management to an admin group, and deploy this setting unchecked, it will be overridden because of the MCX search policy. Computer and computer groups take precedence over standard groups, meaning that you need to deploy this option at the user object to override your computer settings. Unfortunately, this becomes a pretty big hassle, and isn't even possible in some environments, such as an AD/OD triangle, where user objects are stored in AD and outside of the purview of MCX.

Thus, deploying application restrictions at the computer and computer group demands a decent amount of consideration and testing. In many cases, it makes more sense to create separate user groups for computer-specific application classes, and then using computer access filters to grant access to that specific application-based group.

Computer Access Filters

In larger environments, the likelihood of having groups, which have conflicting settings, is increased. In many cases, it may be desirable to filter out which group settings are applied to specific levels. Alternatively, it may be desirable to control which users actually have access to login to a particular computer. Both of these features are provided in Workgroup Manager preferences management, under the access tab of the login managed preference pane (see Figure 7-16). Because computer access is a computer-specific task, the access tab is only accessible under the computer and computer group sections.

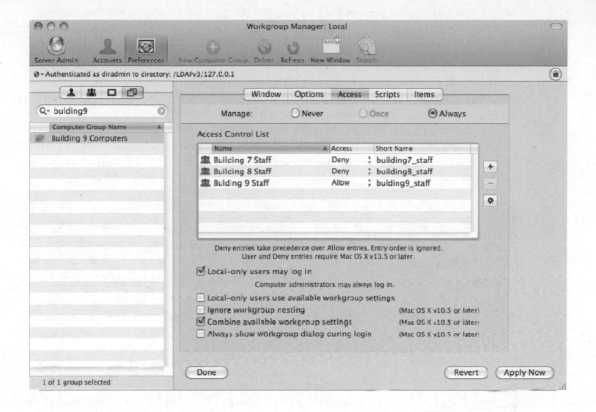

Figure 7-16. *Computer access control lists*

This interface allows for control of which groups have access to login to specific computers. This has the additional effect of filtering out which groups apply MCX. As with Application management, once you define access restrictions, an implicit deny is applied to any user or group not in the list.

For example, consider a scenario where a user is a member of two groups Mobile Home Users and Network Home Users. Perhaps the former group has mobility configured for the user, such that a mobile account is created for the user of this group on login. It may be desirable to suppress this behavior on certain computers, therefore you would simply create an allow rule on these computers for the group "Network Home Users." When the user logs in, they will not inherit any of the management settings defined for Mobile Home Users, due to the implicit deny nature of login restrictions. This in turn becomes a very handy tool for you to filter group MCX application. The down side of this is that you must now explicitly allow all groups, including the entire nested hierarchy, if you want all of these tiers' management settings to be applied. Suddenly, you now have allowed entries for numerous groups, including some potentially very broad groups (such as an All Staff).

If you want to use a tiered management hierarchy along with actual computer access restrictions, you have a rather large conundrum. On one hand, you want to apply the management settings applied to the All Staff group, but the unintended consequence is that you now have granted login window access to all members of the All Staff group. From here, you must use explicit denies to deny access to the desired users and groups. Using explicit denies isn't a bad idea anyway, but this means that your computer access list may easily reach 20 to 30 entries in larger environments.

> **NOTE:** Implementing an explicit deny entry on a group will always take precedent over any explicit allow entries. An explicit deny on a group will prevent all members of that group access, regardless of whether they have membership to a different group that is allowed access. This means that deny entries should only be utilized where login access to all members of a group must be unconditionally prohibited.

Common Tasks

There are many other common Managed Preferences management tasks which are worthy of a mention, but not an extensive write-up. Notably, one of the most common Managed Preferences to apply is automated login items, which specify applications, documents, or SharePoints that launch upon login to a computer. Login items are very handy for initiating user environments, such as firing up support applications or by auto mounting a network share.

To add a login item, simply add it to the Items section found under the Login Workgroup Manager preferences pane. This item can be an application, a document, or a network share. For the former two, the added asset will need to be accessible at the same path on the target client. To deploy a network share login item, simply connect to the SharePoint from your admin station. Once the SharePoint is mounted on the desktop, simply drag it into the login items list. With the network share highlighted, make sure to check the box Mount share point with user's name and password, shown in Figure 7-17. This will ensure that proper access to the share is provided to the user.

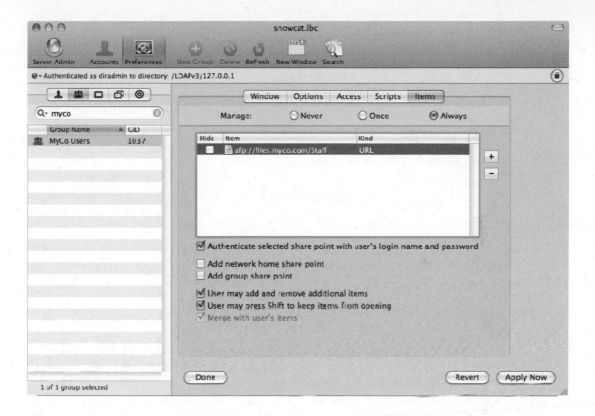

Figure 7-17. *Adding login items*

This list is additive, so login items across all of a user's managed groups will be applied. It is worth noting the options for users to be able to add their own items. This can be handy if you want a few things to launch, but you want the user to be able to customize their own environment as well.

At some point, you may also want to modify a user's dock, perhaps adding in a reference to a company SharePoint or a business application (to some end user's after all, an application does not exist unless it's in the Dock). Apple has a nifty GUI both for adding items to the dock, and for organizing the order in which they appear. Like login items, managed dock items are additive across management groups. The option Merge with User's Dock allows users to modify the dock, outside of the management preferences that you want. This is probably preferable in none-kiosk environments, as the Dock is a powerful, important part of the OS X experience.

To add in a network SharePoint, first mount it on your administrative workstation then drag it into the Documents and Folders list. This will create an .afploc file with the information used to mount the SharePoint initially. Alternatively, you can construct your own .afploc file and drag that in. This is definitely useful if you do not want to, or simply can't connect to, the SharePoint at the time of management. Constructing your own .afploc. file can only be done from the command line:

```
## defaults requires absolute paths to the file!
defaults write /Users/myuser/Desktop/myhost URL "afp://myhost.myco.com/MyCoShare"
mv ~/Desktop/myhost.plist ~/Desktop/MyCoShare.afploc
```

```
The contents of the .afploc are as follows:
<?xml version="1.0" encoding="UTF-8"?>
<!DOCTYPE plist PUBLIC "-//Apple//DTD PLIST 1.0//EN"
"http://www.apple.com/DTDs/PropertyList-1.0.dtd">
<plist version="1.0">
<dict>
        <key>URL</key>
        <string>afp://192.168.210.2</string>
</dict>
</plist>
```

You can replace the URL information (in this case, afp://192.168.210.2) with the FQDN for your server, allowing you to create new .afploc property lists on the fly. From here, you can simply drag the location file into the Documents and Folders section. These files can also be utilized by the login items pane, and they can be double-clicked upon from the Finder. When added to the Dock, the resulting dock item will utilize the file name for the mouse-over display text.

Other Options in the Dock preference management pane are options to add a My Applications folder to the dock, which is a dynamically generated list of allowed apps for a user to use. This is a handy folder in heavily managed environments. If you plan to deploy these apps, make sure to test it thoroughly, as you may be presenting applications to the user that you weren't aware you have granted them privileges to. Outside of this, you can add links to the User's documents folder or to mount their network home. (This is useful if you configure users with local home directories, but want them to have easily accessible personal storage space on a server.)

> **Note:** Apple utilizes another popular location file, the .webloc file for numerous other purposes. For instance, you can embed vnc://, smb://, cifs://, and http:// URLs in a .webloc file, utilizing the same procedure specified here.

Another common MCX management setting involves the deployment of a Software Update Server. Configuration for this is provided via a very basic Software Update Workgroup Manager Preference pane, which allows you to specify a Software update server to query.

Many other management settings are available through the GUI, preference manifests, and custom .plist files. Worthy of another mention is the Apple provided Managed Client Preference manifest, which exposes a great deal of various settings for management. This includes the ability to manage Screen Saver preferences, Home directory redirections (discussed later in the section titled User Home Folders), Menu Bar Items,

VPN Settings, and Finder Sidebar Items to name a few. It is definitely worth your time to add in this manifest and peruse its offerings.

Troubleshooting and Testing

In elaborate environments, it can become difficult to track all of the different groups and tiers where specific preferences are managed. On top of that, accurately predicting how all of the various preference interactions will unfold obviously becomes more difficult as more elements are included. Luckily, Apple provides several tools with the ability to review the resultant policy in a particular environment. The first method to determine the final applied management settings for an environment is to take a look at System Profiler from the managed desktop. Under the Managed Client heading of the Software section of System Profiler.app can be found a breakdown of each active managed preference by domain, including the source of each applied setting. Alternatively, the command line equivalent can be used by querying the datatype: SPManagedClientDataType:

```
%system_profiler SPManagedClientDataType
```

The primary limitation to both of these tools is that they must be run from the actual environment. That environment may even have application restrictions to prevent the running of these tools, which naturally makes troubleshooting a fun endeavor. In this case, there are a few options. On option is to temporarily enable access to System Profiler.app, so that it can be opened and managed client settings can be reviewed and tweaked. This is a bit of a pain and care has to be taken to ensure the restrictions are put in place when done. Another option is to invoke the system_profiler command-line binary remotely via an Apple Remote Desktop (ARD) admin station. This works fine, but the main limitation here is that the output can be a bit difficult to parse.

Apple provides another command line tool, mcxquery, which can be used to query the resulting MCX settings from arbitrarily passed data. It is possible to specify user, group, and a computer, and view the resulting MCX data. For instance, to query the MCX for user johndoe, logging into computer 'johndoe-macbook', I would use the syntax:

```
mcxquery -user johndoe -computer 'johndoe-macbook$'
```

Note the $ at the end of the computer name. This character will be suffixed to the names of computers when they perform a trusted bind to Open Directory. In the previous example, 'johndoe-macbook$' should be the corresponding name for the computer when viewed in Workgroup Manager. Because the character $ is a bash special character, you must wrap the computer name in single quotes. Alternatively, a MAC address can be specified:

```
mcxquery -user johndoe -computer 00:1f:f3:d1:d5:c7
```

Or the guest computer:

```
mcxquery -user johndoe -computer guest
```

This command becomes very handy for testing new policy changes, but it of course has caveats. The most important mcxquery limitation lies in the fact that the tool does not do automatic user membership lookups. That is, if you don't explicitly specify a group with the –group option, then NO workgroup management settings will be output, regardless of group membership of the specified user. This limitation becomes a larger issue when logging into a computer involves combining several workgroup settings. Outside of nested groups, determining combined workgroup settings isn't possible with this tool at this time. Oddly, computer group resolution is fully supported. When specifying a computer, you will see all the applicable computer group settings that are in play.

Compared to this, the second caveat is really more of a quibble. Output isn't the cleanest. There isn't a great way to query specific preference domains, so you just have to sort through all of the settings until you find what you're looking for. The tool supports outputting to XML, but that isn't really pleasant to read either. Luckily, you can take advantage of the powerful tools in OS X to make your life easier. One key tool is the Apple application Property List Editor, which is installed as part of Apple's development tools. With this app installed, you can pretty easily send it output from mcxquery, giving a pretty decent way of traversing through the MCX domain. This can be done with the syntax:

```
mcxquery -user johndoe -group editors -computer \
'johndoe-macbook$' | open -f -a \
/Developer/Applications/Utilities/Property\ List\ Editor.app
```

Once this command is run, Property List Editor will open up and display the mcxquery data in a nice presentable fashion. If you're like me, and will be constantly testing settings like this, you may even want to create an alias for this command.

To accomplish this in the bash shell, open your ~/.bash_profile file and add the following text, all on a single line:

```
function gmcxquery() { /usr/bin/mcxquery -format xml $@ | open -f -a
/Developer/Applications/Utilities/Property\ List\ Editor.app ;}
```

If you use tcsh shell, then edit ~/.tcshrc and add the following text as a single line:

```
alias gmcxquery='/usr/bin/mcxquery -format xml \!:* | open -f -a
/Developer/Applications/Utilities/Property\ List\ Editor.app'
```

After completing the edits, save the file and reload your shell (most easily accomplished by quitting Terminal and reopening Terminal). Now, type the command:

```
gmcxquery -user johndoe -group editors -computer guest
```

If all went well, the output will be nicely displayed in Property List Editor. With identical syntax to the original mcxquery executable, you now have a very easy way to test managed preferences on a machine without actually logging into the machine. Believe me, this can be a significant time saver.

At some point after changing an applications managed preferences via the GUI, you may find remnants of management settings. This symptom most often occurs when you switch management settings from Once or Always to Never. Every once in a while, MCX gremlins can rear their ugly little heads and have you pulling your hair out. Never fret. Use gmcxquery to determine the source of the errant management setting, and then follow it up with a dscl mcxdelete command. For instance, I recently had an issue where a lab decided to remove applications restrictions for the summer, but despite the GUI claiming the application restriction were set to never, users still could not open up supposedly allowed applications. Using gmcxquery, this is an easy problem to solve. After a quick untrusted bind of my machine to the domain:

```
gmcxquery -user myUser -group lab -computer 'lab2-par145$'
```

From here, I look for application of the com.apple.applicationaccess.new, which I am quickly able to spot. However, I also easily spot some legacy settings in the com.apple.application domain, which is used for legacy 10.3 and 10.4 support. In each case, the source of the settings was the 'lab' computer group. Resolving the issue is easy enough, harnessing the power of dscl's mcx capabilities:

```
dscl -u hunterbj /LDAPv3/mydirserv mcxdelete /Groups/lab com.apple.applicationaccess
dscl -u hunterbj /LDAPv3/mydirserv mcxdelete /Groups/lab com.apple.applicationaccess.new
```

Upon next login, users proceed to successfully open previously restricted applications. Between System Profiler, its command-line equivalent system_profiler, and mcxquery, you have some decent tools to troubleshoot an MCX environment. Each tool has their own benefits: mcxquery is highly accessible and can be utilized to test basic policy application changes, but will not always give the whole picture due to its failure to perform group lookups on specified users. System Profiler on the other hand displays the final absolute settings, but must be run from within the managed environment, limiting its usefulness outside of a troubleshooting environment.

User Home Folders

In a standard desktop computing environment, in order for a user to be able to do anything useful and have the merits of their work persist, they must have a non-volatile place to store that work. Most modern day multi-user operating systems provision a specific directory, typically called a home folder, on the file system for this purpose.

In OS X, there are two different types of home directory storage. A Local home folder is the most common type, and simply means that a user's home folder resides on a local disk of the machine that they are using. A Network home folder, on the other hand, resides directly on remote storage accessed via a network file system while data appears to reside on local disk. In actuality, all activity results in file system activity on a remote server.

The following sections will explain the differences between these different storage types, provide explanation on how to determine which scheme is right for your users, and provide you with the necessary information to implement an efficient, effective home directory strategy.

Local Home Folders

In OS X the default store location for user's home directories is on the root volume at the path /Users. Every user created using the Accounts Preference Pane of System Preferences will be automatically provisioned a folder inside this directory, named after the user's short name. For instance, if you were to create a user and specify a shortname of "bob," that user would be provisioned a local home folder at path

/Users/bob. If you were to inspect this folder, you would see a default OS X user directory containing the following folders:

- *Desktop*: This folder serves as the user's desktop folder. Any item residing in this folder will be displayed on the user's desktop.

- *Documents*: This folder is used primarily for user-generated documents. Occasionally, applications will store support files in this folder, but this is considered poor form. One infamous offender here is Microsoft Office, which stores numerous files, including the entire Entourage email database, inside of this directory in the folder Microsoft User Data.

- *Downloads*: This folder is used for content downloaded via Safari, iChat, or other supporting Cocoa-based apps. This folder typically only contains transitional or low priority items. Users should be encouraged to properly organize items in this folder into more appropriate folders in their home directory.

- *Library*: The user Library folder is a user-specific version of the main library folder at /Library. This is where the behind-the-scenes data resides that can be edited by applications. Data in this folder is typically not fit for direct user interaction or presentation. Its uses include, but are not limited to, application databases, preferences, plug-ins, fonts, and cache files.

- *Movies*: This folder is pretty self-explanatory, and is intended for the storage of videos. This folder in an average user's home directory is typically pretty barren. This folder isn't heavily utilized by applications. The most notable app to make use of this folder is iMovie.

- *Music*: Like Movies, this folder doesn't leave much ambiguity. The most notable app to make heavy use of this directory is iTunes, which stores all of its music, movies, podcasts, and iPhone/iTouch applications. It is not uncommon for users to sneak in 10–15 gigabytes of data into this folder.

- *Pictures*: This folder is utilized for picture storage. iPhoto maintains its database in this folder, as do other third-party photo organizers.

- *Public*: This folder serves as a public store for other users. This folder is readable by all users on the machine, and serves as a place for a user to save work and allow other user's access to it. This folder also contains a Drop Box, where other users can leave work, only to be viewed by the home folder's owner.

- *Sites*: This is a per-user web folder utilized by the OS X's web server. Users can implement their own html sites here and access them at http://servername/~username.

A user's home folder is their own private repository, meaning there are access restrictions in place to prevent other users from violating this privacy. However, there are a few limitations to these restrictions that are important to know about, both as a user and as an administrator. The most notable characteristic is that the root of the user's home directory is world-readable. That is, every user on the computer can read and open any item placed in this directory. This is primarily notable in that many users have absolutely no qualms saving items in the top level of their home directory, unwillingly exposing these items to any user on the system. You do not want your users to fall into this habit, especially if you are dealing with sensitive data. It is important that you train your users to properly utilize the folder structure in place. If you have a user base that is particularly unwilling to learn, in some cases it may be desirable to simply restrict users from saving directly into this folder, forcing them to save to an existing subdirectory. Read on to the "User Templates" section to learn how to do this.

Another notable characteristic of the default restrictions in a user's home folder is the use of ACL's to maintain the in-place folder structure. Specifically, all of the default folders contain an 'everyone deny delete' ACL to prevent their removal.

```
[helyx:/Users/hunterbj] hunterbj% ls -el
total 0
drwx------+  9 hunterbj  staff    306 Jan  9 12:37 Desktop
 0: group:everyone deny delete
drwx------+  4 hunterbj  staff    136 Jan  9 00:46 Documents
 0: group:everyone deny delete
drwx------+  4 hunterbj  staff    136 Jan  9 01:24 Downloads
 0: group:everyone deny delete
drwx------+ 30 hunterbj  staff   1020 Jan  9 12:18 Library
 0: group:everyone deny delete
drwx------+  3 hunterbj  staff    102 Jan  9 00:46 Movies
 0: group:everyone deny delete
drwx------+  3 hunterbj  staff    102 Jan  9 00:46 Music
 0: group:everyone deny delete
drwx------+  4 hunterbj  staff    136 Jan  9 00:46 Pictures
 0: group:everyone deny delete
drwxr-xr-x+  6 hunterbj  staff    204 Jan  9 01:23 Public
 0: group:everyone deny delete
drwxr-xr-x+  5 hunterbj  staff    170 Jan  9 00:46 Sites
 0: group:everyone deny delete
```

These ACLs ensure that a default baseline is maintained across all user directories on the system.

The standard home folder also provides a means for users to privately exchange files with other users. This is implemented through the 'Public' and 'Sites' directories. As can be seen the previous output, these folders are the only folders inside a default home folder that are world-readable. The Public folder is meant for file exchange. A user can place an item inside of their public folder and it will be then accessible to all users, but only with read access. They will not be able to make changes to any files. However, they do have the ability to upload new files. Inside of every users Public folder, there is a directory named Drop Box. This drop box folder is world-writeable, but not world-readable. This means that user's can place items into this folder, but they cannot see any of the items inside (including their own). The Drop Box folder is, of course, accessible to the home folders owner, so only they can see items left for them in this directory. Though everyone has write access to this folder, a user will not be able to overwrite an existing file with the same name created by a different user, only their own.

The Sites directory is a unique directory, and requires that Web Services be enabled for it to be utilized as intended. When web services are available, users can place items in this directory and they will be accessible for public consumption via a standard web browser. For instance, a user could place a PDF file, like presentation.pdf, into their sites folder. Other users would then be able to download and review this document in a web browser through the url `http://clientip_or_dnsname/~username/presentation.pdf`.

In large environments, the functionality of the Public and Sites folders can be less attractive when used with local home folders, and in such environments these folders are typically barren. Each workstation must have file and/or web services enabled, each with their own data stores. Other users must remember both the node to connect to as well as the user's short name. In small workgroups, bonjour discovery largely combats this problem, so all workstations on the same subnet with File Sharing enabled will be automatically listed under the Shared group in the Finder sidebar. Conversely, Safari's bonjour network discovery feature makes it easy to discover local machines running http services via Web Sharing. In a Windows environment, a Mac OS X workstation with SMB sharing services enabled will behave much like a native Windows machine.

In environments such as heavy media where workstation performance is paramount, behind the scenes file server activity may be an unwelcome resource drain. Network home folders, are better suited for use here. Data is centralized and can be served out from fewer points (if not a single point), so resource utilization can be better tracked, managed, and scaled. From an end user's perspective, a user only need remember the server's address and their coworker's short name to find the resource that they want.

Local home folders have their advantages and disadvantages. Their primary advantage lies in their minimal reliance on infrastructure. You need not have super robust network or storage systems to maintain a good user experience. All user resources are stored locally on a user's desktop internal storage, storage which will typically provide the fastest, lowest latency access to data. For this reason, local home folders are often desirable whenever performance and user experience is paramount.

The disadvantage in local home folders lies in the decentralization of data that is inherent in such a model. All data maintenance routines become more complex as you now have to deal with each individual node to gain access to data. This is particularly true for the deployment of file-system security auditing and policy enforcement. For instance, if data retention requirements require that all user data be backed up, then support requirements to manage and maintain the backup system to provide coverage for all of your nodes will increase. This isn't a big deal for a few dozen nodes, but scalability is definitely a consideration that needs to be made. Luckily, there are tools available to aid in this type of management, such as Apple Remote Desktop.

Local Home Folder Configuration

The process of configuring a user with a local home directory depends mainly on the directory services model that you are working with.

No Directory Services

If you have forgone the option of a centralized directory service, then your primary interface will be the Accounts pane of the System Preferences Application. The System Preferences Application can be accessed under the Apple Menu, in the Dock (by default), or by opening the application located in the Applications folder. As mentioned previously, any account created using this tool will receive a home directory in the default directory of /Users. However, introduced in this tool with Mac OS X 10.5 was the ability to specify an alternate directory as well as make additional modifications. This interface can be found by right-clicking (or control + click) on any account listed and selecting Advanced Options. As shown in Figure 7-18, you have the ability to change numerous attributes including User ID, Group ID, shortname, shell, and home directory. Additionally, you can change the user's GUID or assign aliases to the account.

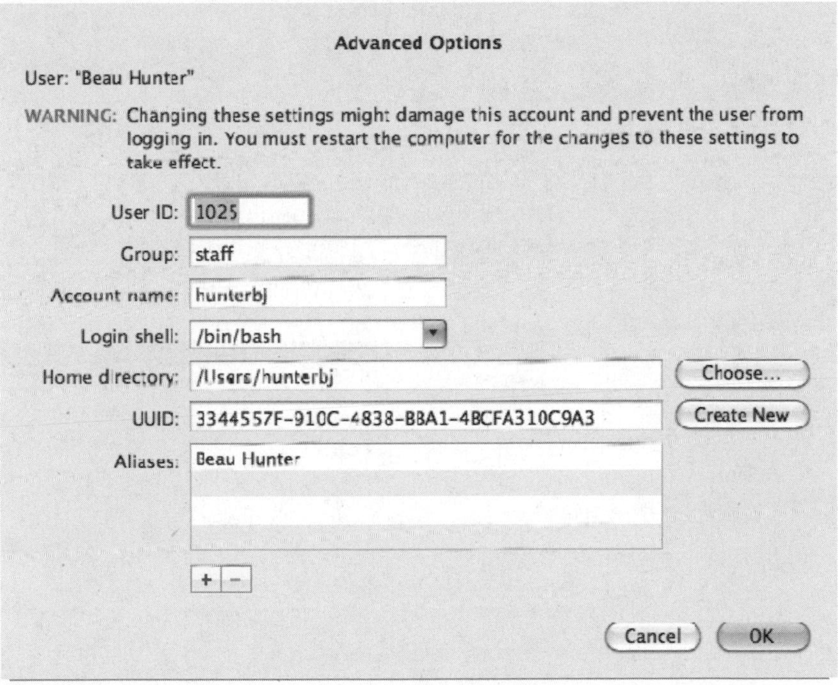

Advanced Options

User: "Beau Hunter"

WARNING: Changing these settings might damage this account and prevent the user from logging in. You must restart the computer for the changes to these settings to take effect.

User ID:	1025
Group:	staff
Account name:	hunterbj
Login shell:	/bin/bash
Home directory:	/Users/hunterbj Choose...
UUID:	3344557F-910C-4838-B8A1-48CFA310C9A3 Create New
Aliases:	Beau Hunter

Cancel   OK

Figure 7-18. *Changing a User's GGUID in System Preferences*

Open Directory

If you are utilizing Open Directory for your directory system, you'll define your home directory for your users by utilizing the application Workgroup Manager.app found on any server in the folder /Applications/Server. This utility can also be installed on any OS X client machine by downloading and installing the Server Admin Tools package available on Apple's support site (http://support.apple.com/downloads/#server%20admin%20tools).

Once installed, open the application and connect to your server. To assign a user a local home directory, go to the Home tab with the appropriate user selected. Listed in this tab will be any predefined home directory paths as well as any configured automounts. As shown in Figure 7-19, /Users is the default home directory location and will typically be a predefined option. If this is not the case, you can manually specify the path. Once a path has been defined for any user, it will be listed as a predefined option. To manually specify a new local path, first note the user's short name, found under the basic tab then click the plus button. In the "Full Path" field, enter in the local path for that user. For instance, if I want to utilize the standard /Users directory for user with short name bob, then I would enter the value /Users/bob. From then on, the /Users path will be listed as an option in the list. You can also mass select users and assign them the homedirectory path with a few clicks.

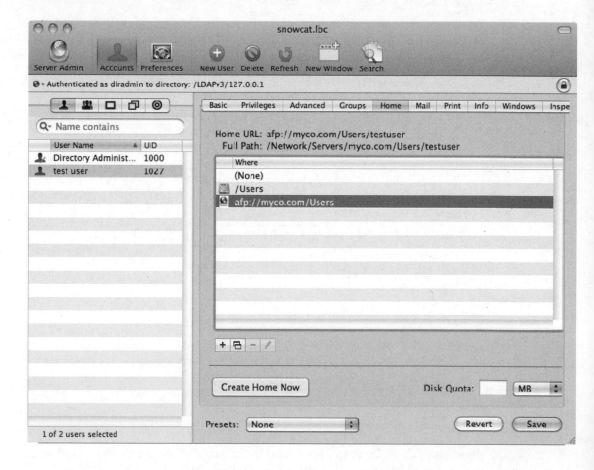

Figure 7-19. *Selecting a home directory in Workgroup Manager*

Active Directory

Configuring Active Directory users to utilize local home directories can be done in a few different ways. If all Active Directory users on the machine are going to have local home directories, then the most straightforward way to do this is by utilizing the Force Local Home on Startup Disk option in the Active Directory plug-in. Alternatively, the Create mobile account at login option will provide the same effect, with a few differences. When used, the latter option will create a mobile account, caching all user information locally for any user that logs in. For more information on Active Directory see Chapter 3.

Third Party LDAP Directory

Configuring LDAP users to utilize local home directories can be done in a few different ways, depending on your user implementation. If your LDAP schema already contains the homeDirectory attribute it is typically utilized for this purpose. You just need to map the NFSHomeDirectory attribute in Directory Utility. Each user will need the value of this attribute set to /Users/*shortname* in your LDAP database. Upon login, they will be assigned a home directory in the /Users folder. If your LDAP schema does not support this attribute, you have a few options. The cleanest way to implement this without altering your schema is by mapping the RecordType NFSHomeDirectory to value #/Users/uid, where uid is the attribute that is utilized for the user's short name. This sets all users home directory to the path /Users/*shortname*. The big limitation here is that all users on this machine will have their home directory in /Users, which may not always be desirable. To maintain granularity, you would either have to extend your schema to support the homeDirectory attribute, or you can utilize an existing, unused LDAP attribute. To perform the mapping, use Directory Utility to map the NFSHomeDirectory record to the appropriate value, and ensure that home path values are pre-populated for all of your users. See Chapter 2 for more information on attribute mapping with LDAP.

Network Home Folders

Network home folders are structured identically to local home folders. They contain the same subdirectories that perform the exact same function. The difference between the two lies in where a user's data is stored. When a user with a local home directory logs into a computer, that user's home directory will be stored on that computer's hard drive. Any new files that the user creates will be stored locally to that drive. When that user later logs into a different computer, they will not have access to any files created on a different computer. If your users move from computer to computer, this creates a problem. It's certainly possible to enable file sharing on all of the workstations, so users could connect to the other computer and access their data, but this quickly turns into an unmanageable nightmare. Users need to remember which computer has which document. Those documents will get duplicated and version tracking will go out the window. Your users will be miserable, and you, in turn, will be miserable. Most often, a centralized file server comes into play, offering users the ability to upload their files and then they will be able to access them from different nodes by connecting to that server. The central flaw here is that it promotes the *illusion* that data is centralized. Often times in these scenarios, desktop resident data is completely forgotten. If it's not on the server, it doesn't exist, and doesn't require protection. This mind-set can lead to expensive mistakes because your data is only as protected as your users are regimented.

Enter network home folders. Network home folders store data on a network file server. (It's not just a clever name.) When a user logs into a computer, the user's home directory is never stored on that local machine, but rather directly referenced from a remote network file server. When a user creates or edits documents, those documents are actually updated on a remote server. This all happens transparently, unbeknownst to the user. The main benefit provided by this is mobility. By freeing user data from the embrace of each individual workstation, users are capable of freely moving from node to node, traveling with them their entire computing experience. If your organization does not use assigned workstations, with network home directories, your users will enjoy a single experience wherever they login. The benefits of this experience are reaped by IT as well. The advantage of having all user data centralized on the home directory server(s) is not small. Indeed, the ability to mass deploy software, settings, files, audit security, and provide data protection are all greatly increased when data is consolidated.

OS X currently supports home directories over a handful of network file protocols, such as AFP, SMB, as well as NFS. AFP is your native protocol and will typically be your first choice when available. SMB support has greatly improved in OS X over the years, and can be utilized for an acceptable experience as well, though it will typically be relegated to environments with Windows-based file servers. NFS flaws are traditional to the protocol, security being the primary barrier. However, the introduction of Kerberized NFS in 10.5 provides improvement here, trusting your environment globally supports it.

The network home folder model is not without its flaws. The largest barrier to entry is the necessary server-side resources needed to provide an acceptable computing experience, let alone approach the performance provided by fast local storage used by local homes. Robust server, network, and storage infrastructure are needed. Gigabit Ethernet to the desktop will help and to the server is also highly recommended. A dedicated Intel Xserve with fast external RAID storage and gigabit Ethernet can acceptably host 40–50 simultaneous light to moderate users when implemented properly. This is not a hard limit or a guarantee because the qualification for "acceptable performance" will vary greatly from workflow to workflow and from user to user. If performance is paramount in your environment, or if you are unfortunate enough to host particularly feisty users, then the decision to migrate to network home folders should not be taken lightly.

Special consideration must be paid to your user's workflow to identify data usage patterns, which can be detrimental to a file server. Economies of scale play a large role here. If all of your users run applications that are IO heavy, then all of those transactions hit the wire, and your server will begin to lag. Likewise, if your users are in the habit of dealing with large data sets, then even a gigabit pipe on a server can be easily saturated. Luckily, Mac OS X supports 802.3ad link aggregation, also referred to as NIC bonding. This is the process of taking two network interfaces on a server, and presenting them to the network as a single unified connection. This provides benefits both in redundancy and in throughput. It doesn't offer perfect 50/50 load balancing, because your switch must support it and it will disable Lights Out Management (LOM) capabilities on your Xserves. LOM is a big advantage for server management, so it is recommended to utilize a PCIe-based NIC if you plan to go this route. This is a good way to provide a larger pipe into a server and combat saturation in data heavy environments.

Redirection

As previously mentioned, network home directories are both a blessing and a curse. On one hand, they provide a very valuable service to any environment where users do not have pre-assigned computers and may move about from node to node at will. However, if you take into account all of the various activities that can occur inside a user's home directory, it quickly becomes apparent that the overhead necessary for deploying the storage infrastructure to handle the burden imposed by such activities is not insignificant. An IMAP account of even a moderately sized user mailbox can easily contain tens of thousands of files. A user logging into a computer results in a flurry of activity as numerous components load their support files. There is the occasional application in which file system needs are particularly burdensome on a file server. iPhoto and other media management applications involve not only high levels of I/O requests, but they can also be throughput intensive when used with higher quality or uncompressed media. Another class of horrible offenders are video editors, as they require a consistent, uninterrupted data stream. While most high-end applications of this variety rarely use the home directory for media storage, the nearly ubiquitous iMovie does. Even at its lowest quality, DV media played in iMovie requires a 5MBps stream, and things get worse with HD formats. The main thing to understand is that if your user's standard usage patterns involve high I/O or high bandwidth activities, the viability of network-based storage deteriorates. However, their exclusion shouldn't be a forgone conclusion.

Redirection is the process of utilizing symbolic links in a network home directory to redirect traffic to a local disk. For instance, if your users utilize IMAP mail (you're not using POP, right?) then there's no reason to let that traffic burden your server. Through redirection, you establish a symbolic link at ~/Library/Mail which redirects traffic to a local path of your choosing, say /Users/theUser/Library/Mail. This way, whenever you start up mail, all of your data will be accessed off of your local disk. When a user migrates to another machine and opens up mail, it will need to re-download any messages, but this will be of minor consequence compared to the alternative. The typical candidate for redirection is ~/Library/Caches, which contains a decent amount of application cache data that has no business burdening your server. The use of this folder was slightly mitigated with the introduction of 10.5 and the /var/tmp/folders caching structure, but it is still used and redirection will definitely lighten the load on your server. If your users have large numbers of fonts, redirection of the ~/Library/Fonts folder can help to reduce login times. However, this can often present its own management problems. For this reason, it is encouraged to install Fonts at the machine level in /Library/Fonts, or to utilize Font management software, such as Extensis' Universal Type Server.

Implementation of redirection can be deployed with two distinct methods. The first method is new to 10.5 and involves the use of MCX and the preference manifest provided by /System/Library/CoreServices/ManagedClient.app. Specifically, you will be editing the preference manifest for domain com.apple.MCXRedirector. When you create a new key, the Always target provides three different keys to choose from:

- *Login redirections*: These are redirections which are fired upon login.

- *Logout redirections*: These are redirections which are fired upon logout.

- *Other redirections*: These are fired periodically whenever policies are set. After a network change, login, logout, or reboot.

The former two are primarily the ones we're interested in. You can have a login hook that creates your symbolic links at login, but then destroys them at logout.

Once you have created your MCXRedirector key under the always target, you want to set the key Login Redirections. With the new Login Redirections key highlighted, you create yet another key, which is used to define your redirect actions and paths. The redirection system provides you with four actions to choose from:

- *deleteAndCreateSymLink*: This action deletes the network folder and creates a symbolic link to the specified local path.

- *renameAndCreateSymLink*: This action renames the existing network folder, prepending "Network" to the name of the directory. After renaming, it creates a symbolic link to the specified local path. Unfortunately, due to the lack of consistent logout cleanup, I recommend avoiding this option and instead utilizing a login hook, which gives you much more flexability. However, this option can be used instead of deleteAndCreateSymLink to ensure that you avoid deleting user data.

- *deletePath*: This action simply deletes any item at the specified path.

- *deleteSymLinkAndRestore*: This action is the counterpart to renameAndCreateSymLink. Essentially, it will delete the existing symbolic link and restore the previously renamed directory. Unfortunately, this option does not function reliably. For this type of functionality, I recommend implementing a login hook.

For these purposes, you are going to choose the second option. This allows you to maintain a network version of the redirected folder, but promotes local storage for the primary folder itself. Thus, if you were to perform redirection of the Movies folder because your users utilize iMovie, then they will have the ability to access their network movies folder at ~/Movies (Network). This provides your users with the ability to manually copy files to the network folder to facilitate migration to a different machine. At the same time, it relieves the burden of iMovie's heavy data usage from your server. While a user's movie media may not seamlessly transfer with them like the rest of their homefolder, it is an acceptable compromise in many environments.

To finish the policy creation, you will specify your Folder Path, which is ~/Library/Movies. You also want to specify the Destination Folder Path key, which signifies the local path that will house your data. For this, you enter in a value of /Users/%@/Movies. As discussed in Chapter 8, %@ is a variable for your user's shortname. Thus, when bob logs in, his home directory movies folder actually references /Users/bob/Movies.

To ensure a clean environment, you might also want to deploy a logout redirection, which deletes all of the redirections that you created at login. To do this, you will create a new Logout Redirections key under your Always target, and create a new "deletePath" action key. The key Destination Folder Path is ignored by this action and can be removed. The path specified by Folder Path is used to determine the alias to remove. If you specify the value ~/Movies, the action will delete the symbolic link at ~/Movies, but will leave the data on the local disk untouched. It will also rename your Movies (Network) folder back to just Movies and order is restored to the universe (see Figure 7-20).Unfortunately, at the time of this writing, this functionality is only partially functional.

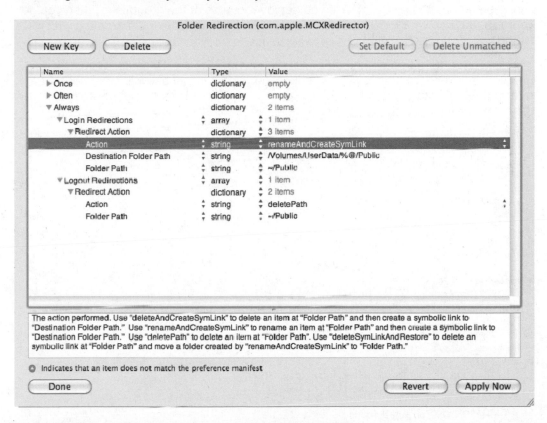

Figure 7-20. *Setting MCX login and logout redirects in Workgroup Manager*

Basic redirections deployed through MCX are quick and easy, and they work. However, there are a few implications that will determine their usefulness in your environment. The biggest gotcha is that they require 10.5. 10.4 clients will pretend they don't exist. The second consideration is in regard to MCX itself. MCXRedirector can be deployed at any level, user, group, computer, or computer group. For reasons previously discussed, I discourage the use of user-level management, though it's important to recognize that the granularity that they provide can be useful. If you only have a couple of network home users, this may be a good option, but utilizing a group for this still scales better. It is also recommended to avoid deploying these at the computer or computer group level.

The main reason for this is that these redirections are user agnostic. That is, when they're deployed at the computer level they will redirect the folders of all users who login, even those with local homes. This isn't a terribly big deal, but it's unnecessary and unsightly. If you use /Users/%@/… as your redirection store, or if you utilize portable home directories (discussed in the section "Home Directory Syncing" later in this chapter) then you will definitely have problems. Therefore, this really leaves you to deploying at the group level. This works for the most part, but what if certain users should have network homes on some computers (wired nodes), but should also have local homes on others (laptops)? If you deploy redirects at the group level, then you get your redirects on your local homes. This example illustrates the main problem with MCX-based redirections. There is no way to introduce them with logic.

This leads you to the other method of redirection: loginhooks. Because of the unparalleled freedom that you have, redirecting folders is just a few lines of code away, or not. Login hook scripts, when done properly, require a decent amount of logic. A very basic login script is pretty easy to assemble.

```sh
#!/bin/sh
PATH="/bin:/usr/bin:/usr/sbin"

# simple login redirection script

# get our user
theUser=$1

# get our home
eval theHome=~$1

# if we are a local user, exit
if [ -x "/usr/bin/nicl" ]; then
# 10.3 & 10.4 test
[ $(nicl . -read /users/"$theUser" &> /dev/null) == 0 ] &&
echo "User is a local user, aborting! " && exit 1
elif [ -x "/usr/bin/dscl" ]; then
#  10.5 test
[ $(dscl . -read /users/"$theUser" &> /dev/null) == 0 ] &&
echo "User is a local user, aborting! " && exit 1
else
        echo "DS Tool not found. " && exit 1
fi

# specify our redirect folder, make sure it exists,
# set ownership and permissions
redirectDir=/Users/Local/"$theUser"
mkdir -p "$redirectDir" &> /dev/null
chown "$theUser" "$redirectDir"
chmod 700 "$redirectDir"

# redirect ~/Library/Caches. For 10.3 compatability,
# operations on the home directory must be performed as
```

```
# the user. root does have write access to AFP shares.
mkdir -p "$redirectDir"/Library/Caches
sudo -u "$theUser" rm -rf "$theHome"/Library/Caches
sudo -u "$theUser" ln -s "$redirectDir"/Library/Caches \
"$theHome"/Library/Caches
chown "$theUser" "$redirectDir/Library/Caches"
echo "Redirected $theHome/Library/Caches to \
$redirectDir/Library/Caches"

exit 0
```

Then the requisite logout hook (don't blink).

```
#!/bin/sh
PATH="/bin"

# simple logout redirection script

# get our user
theUser=$1

# get our home
eval theHome=~$1

# if there's a symlink, break it down
[ -L "$theHome"/Library/Caches ] &&
rm "$theHome"/Library/Caches &&
echo "Removing symlink at $theHome/Library/Caches"

exit 0
```

For the logouthook, you don't need to test for a local user. If the users are local they won't have a symlink to begin with. If they do, it shouldn't be there, so you may as well delete it.

This is a pretty bare-bones login redirection script, and it doesn't have a ton of sanity checks. What if the destructive redirect destroys valuable data, and you need to move it rather than delete it? What if a user is logged into two sessions at once? When one instance is logged out, the other's symbolic links will be torn down, leading to an unstable environment. Therein lies the strength in loginhook based redirections, you can pretty much add any functionality that you're willing to invest time into scripting. Luckily, we've invested that time so you don't have to. For a more feature packed login script, see the package 07_loginhooks.zip in the book's resources. You can find the code samples for this chapter in the Source Code/Download area of the Apress web site, www.apress.com. This zip file contains two shell scripts, loginhook, and logouthook, which are used to create and tear down redirection environments. See the loginhook scripts inline comments for more details on configuration and usage.

Unfortunately, in reality network home directories just aren't well suited for certain uses. Apple discourages their use in Final Cut Studio workflows. Color in particular seems to have the most issues, it simply doesn't launch. Miscellaneous apps that are poorly coded may simply not behave properly. Sometimes these apps can be fooled into operating through redirections or preference modification, but not always. Make sure to take care to thoroughly test your productivity apps before deploying network home directories on a wide scale.

Network Home Folder Configuration

Depending on your directory service model, you will utilize either Workgroup Manager or Directory Utility to configure Network Home Directories. While it is possible to implement network home directories in environments without centralized directory services, their presence is highly recommended.

Open Directory

In order to assign a user a network home directory in an Open Directory environment, you must first configure the home directory SharePoint and automount, specifying the automount as your user's home directory. When logging in as a network home user, the bound client will utilize values stored in the user's record as well as the configured automount information in order to properly mount the user's home.

To configure the SharePoint and automount, you utilize the Server Admin application, located in /Applications/Server. Once open, ensure that your file server appears in the list, and add it if necessary. With the main server entry selected, highlight the File Sharing section and then the Share Points subsection. For this example, you will utilize the existing Users SharePoint, though it doesn't have to be. The big gotcha here is that spaces were not allowed prior to 10.5, so the SharePoint User Homes won't work out so well. With the Users SharePoint selected, check the box to enable automount. Once checked, you will be presented with a sheet to specify automount configuration, as shown in Figure 7-21.

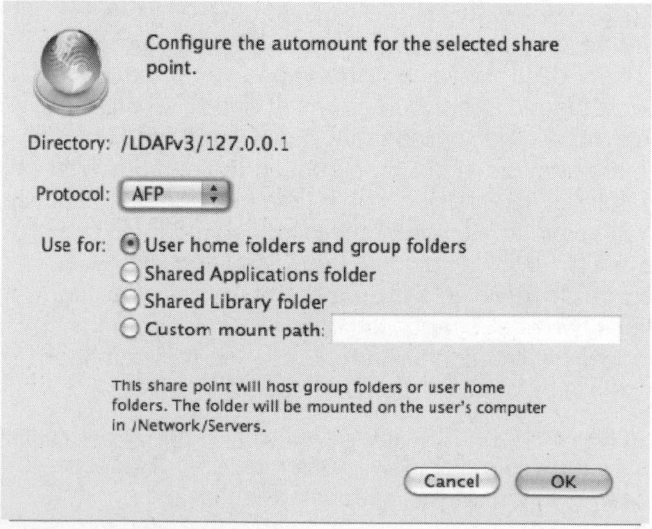

Figure 7-21. *Server Admin: SharePoint automount options*

Here you can select your protocols and your mount point. As this SharePoint will be utilized for user home folders, you select that option and save. This SharePoint has now been configured to be utilized for network home directories. You can verify this by observing your Open Directory Mounts container with Workgroup Manager's Inspector or with dscl.

```
[myserver:~] hunterbj% dscl /LDAPv3/127.0.0.1/ read \
/Mounts/myserver.com:/networkHomes RecordName VFSLinkDir VFSOpts \
VFSType

RecordName: myserver.com:/networkHomes
VFSLinkDir: /Network/Servers/
VFSOpts: net url==afp://;AUTH=NO%20USER%20AUTHENT@myserver.com/networkHomes
VFSType: url
```

An automount record contains four essential attributes in your directory. The RecordName attribute follows typical NFS mount syntax; the server's IP or DNS name, a colon, and then the path to the share. In this case, it will be the full file system path of the share from root of your server's file system. Therefore, if your "Users" SharePoint resides on a secondary volume (as it always should), then your mount RecordName might be myserver.com:/Volumes/dataVolume/networkHomes. The path portion of value is utilized clientside as the file system mount point for the automount. The VFSLinkDir attribute specifies the base path, which is prepended to the path provided by RecordName. In the previous scenario, a client machine would mount the user's home directory at /Network/Servers/hax.lbc/dataVolume/networkUsers.

One important limitation to know about here is that there is a character limit to an automount pathname when use specifically with network homes—the entire path, including /Network/Servers, cannot contain more than 89 characters. This leaves 72 total characters at your disposal. In 10.3.5–10.4.11, the automount path was at /private/Network/Servers/ which allowed only 64 usable characters. Prior to this, there was a slew of rubbish leaving you with only 39 characters. 72 characters is actually ample for most environments, but if you find yourself running against this limitation, you do have a couple of options.

The first recommended option is the cleanest, and it cuts out a decent amount of fat depending on your environment. In fact, it's so clean that I often deploy it even when the limitation is not a concern. The basic concept is that you map the top level of your share's path to the root of your file system. To understand this, consider the previous example, where the automount mount point for the "Users" SharePoint was at /Network/Servers/myserver.com/Volumes/dataVolume/networkHomes. This path contains over 19 characters which only apply to a single machine, the server itself. Your remote clients only know about the server name (myserver.com) and SharePoint (Users). Why can't you cut out all this excess, like /Volumes/dataVolume/networkHomes? In fact, you can confidently bypass this once you realize a few things about automount behavior. First, every OS X machine has a symbolic link at /Network/Servers/*fqdn*. On myserver, the command ls –l /Network/Servers/myserver.com/networkHomes yields the same results as ls –l /networkHomes.

Thus, by placing a symbolic link of the sharepath to its basename on the root of the file system, you can simulate this on the server:

```
$ln -s /Volumes/dataVolume/networkHomes /networkHomes
```

Once run, /Network/Servers/myserver.com/networkHomes is a fully functional path to your data. All that's left to do is modify the automount data, replacing the old path with your modified version.

The VFSOpts attribute specifies that this is a dynamic AFP automount. The ;AUTH=NO%20USER%20AUTHENT string specifies that the machine will first attempt to mount the automount as guest. Once a user logs in, it will reconnect to the SharePoint with the user's access levels. However, there is an important ramification here. If you have a limited license server, each connected home directory user will utilize two connections. This value can be changed to ;AUTH=Client%20Krb%20v2 to utilize Kerberos authentication on the automount. Alternatively, an authentication string can be dropped all together. Loginwindow will dynamically authenticate and mount the share.

```
VFSOpts: net url==afp://;AUTH=Client%20Krb%20v2/hax.lbc/networkHomes
```

Though SMB based home directories are supported, there is no GUI to perform this configuration in an OD-based environment. However, you can modify your automount's uri to specify the smb or cifs protocol:

```
VFSOpts: net url==smb://hax.lbc/networkHomes
```

To create an automount from the command line, you would perform the following:

```
dscl -u mydiradmin /LDAPv3/mydirsirv.myco.com
> delete Mounts/hax.lbc:\\/Users VFSLinkDir /Network/Servers
 > create Mounts/hax.lbc:\\/Users VFSLinkDir /Network/Servers/
 > delete Mounts/hax.lbc:\\/Users
 > create Mounts/hax.lbc:\\/Users VFSType url
 > create Mounts/hax.lbc:\\/Users VFSOpts net
 > append Mounts/hax.lbc:\\/Users VFSOpts
url==afp;AUTH=NO%20USER%20AUTHENT@hax.lbc/Users
 > append Mounts/hax.lbc:\\/Users VFSLinkDir /Network/Servers/
 > read Mounts/hax.lbc:\/Users
```

Open the application and connect to your server. To assign a user to a local home directory, go to the Home tab with the appropriate user selected. Listed in this tab will be any predefined home directory paths, as well as any configured automounts. /Users is the default home directory location and will typically be a predefined option in the list. If this is not the case, you can manually specify the path. Once a path has been defined for any user, it will be listed as a predefined option. To manually specify a new local path, first note the user's shortname, found under the basic tab, then click the plus button. In the Full Path field, enter in the local path for that user. For instance, if I want to utilize the standard /Users directory for user with shortname bob, then I would enter the value /Users/bob. From then on, the /Users path will be listed as an option in your list. You can then mass select users and assign them the home directory path with a few clicks.

Home Directory Syncing

Also referred to as Portable Home Directories, Home Directory syncing provides the ability to allow a user to use a local home directory, but also periodically synchronize files with a network home directory. This type of setup is great for users who utilize both a personal laptop and a wired desktop machine. In such cases, the wired desktop machine could utilize either network home directories, or it could be configured to utilize a local home, and then sync the content with a network home directory as well. In either case, you can configure settings which manage these preferences, specifying specific folders to include in the sync, and the interface also provides a very capable filtering system to easily ignore cache files and other machine-specific files.

Home directory syncing is broken up into two different sync types: Login/Logout syncs and background syncs. As the name suggests, Login and Logout synchronizations fire upon the beginning and end of a user session. The best utilization of login/logout syncing is probably best described by the setting's preference keys: syncedPrefsFolders. That is, this option is best used for application preference files, or any file, which during a user session is constantly in use and therefore not a good candidate for background syncing. By default, Apple specifies two folders to sync at login/logout: ~/Library, and ~/Documents/Microsoft User Data. The former option includes Application preference and support files, Safari and Firefox bookmarks, and User Fonts. The latter folder contains many Microsoft Office settings, most notably the Entourage database.

Background synchronization, as its name implies, synchronizes files and folders in the background during an active user session, by default every 20 minutes. As mentioned, not all files are good candidates for this. For the most part, background synchronization should be configured for user-generated content, such as the Desktop and Documents folders.

One thing to consider is that Login and Logout syncing can cause significant delays in the login and logout process as the user must wait for the synchronization to finish before they can begin to use the computer or close the laptop's lid for the day. Because of this, users may be very prone to simply hitting the cancel button. Essentially, if you do not build a very specific login item sync list, then the entire login syncing process will likely be compromised due to user intervention. The entourage database is a great example of this. Entourage databases can reach gigabytes in size, and even a wired computer will take a good chunk of time to send this data to the server. Most users will not find a 30 minute login time to be acceptable. So, keep this list slim. If you need to synchronize Firefox bookmarks, explicitly specify the folder ~/Library/Application Support/ Firefox. Use ~/Library/Safari for Safari but use ~/Library/Preferences for all user application preferences. Avoid directories with deeply nested hierarchies, as these will cause syncing delays as the system scans through everything. For the grunt of the work, background syncing is your go-to player. 10.6 has some good improvements here, does a better job in general of informing you of when a particular set of items will sync, and gives you better control over the process.

One other noteworthy aspect of login/logout synchronizing is that the system has detection routines to determine if another computer has synchronized changes. If, upon logging in, the FileSyncAgent, which is responsible for synchronization, detects that the user has had an active session on another machine, it will present the user with a dialog stating that another login session was detected. The dialog will ask the user if they would like to delay syncing. Upon the next sync the system will require the user to choose a default conflict resolution source, presenting the option of local files versus network files. This setting is then applied to all items for that synchronization. This differs significantly from conflict resolution on background synchronizations, which allows you to specify the preferred source of each conflict individually.

If you have sync settings applied to a user account, upon first creation of the account, a complete sync of both login items and background items is required in order for the login process to complete. If the initial synchronization is cancelled, then the login will fail and the user will be returned to the login window. Make sure that if your user's have large home directories that you set this expectation when you deploy the change. Subsequent login syncs will attempt to perform a synchronization of background items as well, but they can be cancelled without detriment to the login; the sync will simply pickup where it left off during the next scheduled scan. Alternatively, if you are running 10.6, you can specify better control preference syncing vs. background syncing, and specify that background syncing items do not sync at login or logout.

To configure a user to utilize a portable home directory, you use a process that is a bit of a hybrid between a network home directory user and a mobile user with a local home directory, often referred to as a Portable Home Directory. In Workgroup Manager, the desired user must have their home directory specified to a configured automount SharePoint, exactly as you would configure a user with a network home directory. Once this is configured, you must specify mobility management for the user, such as you would do when setting up a user with a local home directory. Once you have done this, you must use managed preference to define the user as a mobile user. For the purposes of this exercise, you are going to utilize a computer group named "Mobile".

First, open up Workgroup Manager and connect to the Open Directory Master. Next, find the desired management object to apply the managed settings to. Once selected, open up the Mobility pane in the preference management section. In the default Account Creation Tab, under the creation section, select the option to create a mobile account at login, but do not require confirmation, as shown in Figure 7-22. Click Apply.

After this change, when the user logs into a computer that is a member of this group, a mobile account will be created—a copy of the user Open Directory record is copied into the local directory services store. This record contains the user's password, and enables the machine to permit a user to login to the computer even when the machine cannot contact the Open Directory server. Creating mobile accounts is an absolute must on laptops that will routinely leave the company campus and thereby lose access to company internal servers. In fact, in many wired-desktop environments, it may be desirable to force mobile accounts for users. This creates a more robust desktop setup that will more gracefully deal with any Open Directory outages. There are not many benefits management-wise to not create a mobile account for any user who will utilize a local home directory.

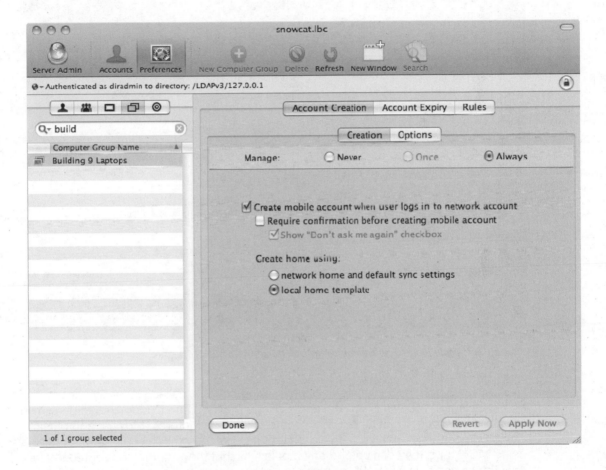

Figure 7-22. *Force mobile account creation on login using Workgroup Manager*

Now that you have configured mobility, you must also configure the actual syncing settings. You will first configure the login syncing, called preference syncing in 10.6. In this particular instance, you will be syncing the user's preference folder, their personal applications folder, and their Firefox and Safari bookmarks. Respective GUIs are shown for 10.5 and 10.6. Notice that the 10.6 GUI on the right has specific checkboxes allowing for granular control of when certain items sync (see Figure 7-23).

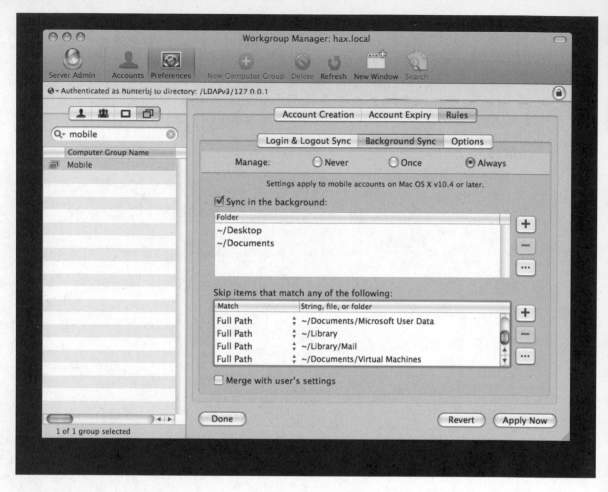

Figure 7-23. *Configuring Login/Preference Syncing using Workgroup Manager*

Next, you will configure the background syncing options, called Home Syncing in 10.6. In this instance, you will synchronize the User's Desktop and Documents folders. You are not concerned about other media content, such as Pictures, Movies, and Music. Users can certainly connect to their home folder manually (or you can mount it for them using MCX), and they can upload any media files that they deem important (perhaps only the server-side home directories are backed up). In this case, you want to make sure you exclude some potentially sync-busters, such as the Entourage database at ~/Documents/Microsoft User Data, or potential Virtual Machines at ~/Documents/Virtual Machines (or ~/Documents/Parallels if you are using parallels instead of VMware), as shown in Figure 7-24.

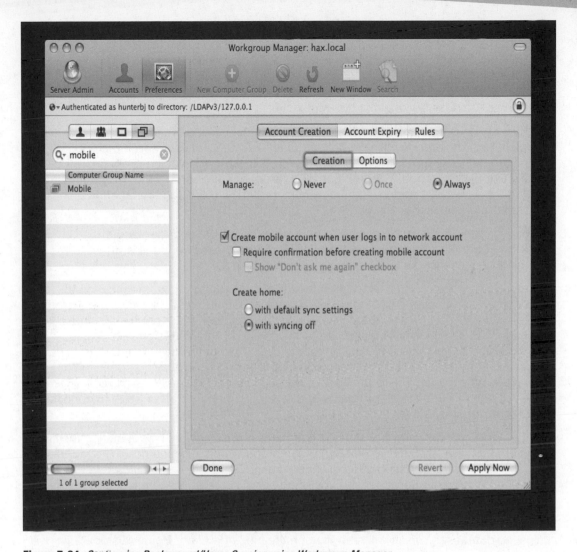

Figure 7-24. *Configuring Background/Home Syncing using Workgroup Manager*

In order to reduce syncing times, Mac OS X 10.5 server introduced a new feature that would track server-side modifications to files. This adds additional logic to help a client and a server determine which files need to be synced and to help with conflict resolution. To disable server-side syncing, simply enable the option in server admin. With the main server entry selected, choose the settings tab. Under the general settings tab, you will be presented with the option to enable several OS X services, such as NTP serving, as well as Server Side File tracing for home directory syncing. When this option is enabled, clients will connect to the server via an ssh connection over port 2336. This connection is used to converse with the server to build an accurate change manifest. Once this is created, syncing is done per usual over AFP. If you do not enable this option, all change detection will be performed over AFP.

Troubleshooting Syncing Issues

Troubleshooting Home Directory syncing issues is something that you will inevitably have to deal with when you deploy them at a large scale. In the following few paragraphs, you will try to present a summary of the players involved to help you to determine the possible origin of different issues.

When syncing issues arrive, the first thing to determine is the breadth of the issue: Is the problem only occurring with a single user or is it affecting all user's with the applied management settings? One of the most common causes of syncing problems is due to conflicting sync settings. Your ~/Library/Preferences folder isn't going to sync if you exclude the ~/Library folder. Use the system_profiler and gmcxquery function discussed earlier to verify applied settings.

After this, consult the log file found at : ~/Library/Logs/FileSyncAgent.log and ~/Library/Logs/FileSyncAgent-verbose.log. Between these two log files, there will typically be evidence as to the nature of your problem.

If server-side tracking is enabled, then the client uses public key authentication to contact the server over port 2336. For this authentication, preshared keys are stored at ~/Library/FileSync/FileSyncAgent_key_dir. In this directory, there contains a public key and a private key used to authenticate to the server. In earlier versions of 10.5, if permissions of this folder were such that the user was not the owner, and did not have exclusive access to the keys, then authentication would fail. This would result in a complete sync failure. This issue was addressed in a point-release patch. The system now will detect permissions problems and repair them prior to attempting to connect to the home directory server.

If interested, you can view the ssh configurations for this service by consulting the files /System/Library/CoreServices/FileSyncAgent.app/Contents/Resources/FileSyncAgent_s shd_config and the corresponding client configuration at /System/Library/CoreServices/FileSyncAgent.app/Contents/Resources/FileSyncAgent_s sh_config.

If syncing problems persist despite your efforts, you can simply delete all of the user's Filesync databases, which will rebuild upon the next operation. Doing this operation will delete file history, it is possible that files present at one location will be deleted during the process. Because of this, and when working with syncing issues in general, it is never a bad idea to have a full backup of the user's data on both sides: server and client. If you are reasonably sure that all pertinent data exists at only one location, do yourself a favor and back it up prior to proceeding. With that out of the way, to delete the user's sync database, run the following commands from *both* the server and the client, replacing with the user's short name.

```
sudo rm -r ~theuser/.FileSync
sudo rm -r ~theuser/Library/FileSync
```

In the majority of scenarios, assuming the client is getting good MCX sync data, the previous action will resolve the syncing issues. If the problem still isn't resolved, you could try resetting ownership on the user's home directory, which may or may not be an issue:

```
sudo chown -R theuser ~theuser
sudo chmod -R o+rw ~theuser
```

Password Policies

When you have large groups of people, and confidential information to disseminate to them, then special precautions must be made to ensure that the information doesn't become available to those who may do harm with it. The most common access restriction utilized in IT today is the standard username plus password paradigm. Adoption of two factor and token-based authentication certainly is worth a look, but for this context I will discuss primarily how to best constrain global and per-user password policies to maximize the security that they can provide. When left to their own devices, end users will choose the shortest, easiest, and most guessable password as possible. Strong passwords to them are nothing more than an inconvenience, and in many cases, a barrier to work.

Unless you have the infrastructure to implement tokens or smart cards, your users are stuck in a password world. The unfortunate reality is that the burden to ensure data confidentiality ultimately falls on you, the system administrator. Luckily, Mac OS X Server includes a set of tools for implementing password strength requirements and implementing required, scheduled rotations. These tools are presented to you via the familiar Workgroup Manager application (for managing per-user settings), and in Server Admin (for managing system-global settings). Additionally, in typical fashion Apple provides a command-line tool pw policy for more advanced uses.

To access global password policy settings, first open up the Server Admin application found in /Applications/Server and connect to your Open Directory server. Once connected, view the settings section of the Open Directory service and select the Policy tab. Under this tab, settings can be found for global user authentication requirements (the Password tab), computer binding requirements (the binding tab), and supported hashes, which will be utilized by the OS X password server (the authentication tab). Figure 7-25 demonstrates the user's password tab, providing options to force password strength, such as minimum length, numeric digit, special character, and uppercase character requirements, and even allows for preventing user's to reuse previously used passwords. In this tab, you can also force global rotation requirements, designating an arbitrary timeframe between password changes.

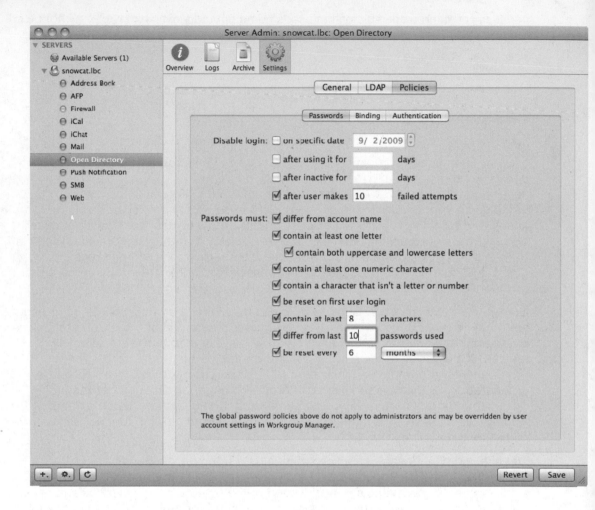

Figure 7-25. *Configuring Global Password Policies in Server Admin.*

The command-line equivalent to these global settings is found using the pwpolicy command. Specifically, the -getglobalpolicy and -setglobalpolicy flags. To require a minimum of 8 characters, you should use an alphanumeric password with at least one special character for all users. The following is the syntax:

```
sudo pwpolicy -a hunterbj -setglobalpolicy "requiresNumeric=1 minChars=8 requiresAlpha=1
requiresSymbol=1"
```

In this example, you are specifying an Open Directory administrator user name with the -a flag, and then using -setglobalpolicy to set your specific items. To both ensure your settings took, and to get a list of possible settings, you rerun the command with the -getglobalpolicy flag:

```
sudo pwpolicy -a hunterbj -getglobalpolicy
Password:
usingHistory=0 canModifyPasswordforSelf=1 usingExpirationDate=0
usingHardExpirationDate=0 requiresAlpha=1 requiresNumeric=1 expirationDateGMT=12/31/69
hardExpireDateGMT=12/31/69 maxMinutesUntilChangePassword=0 maxMinutesUntilDisabled=0
maxMinutesOfNonUse=0 maxFailedLoginAttempts=0 minChars=8 maxChars=0
passwordCannotBeName=1 requiresMixedCase=0 requiresSymbol=1 newPasswordRequired=0
minutesUntilFailedLoginReset=0 notGuessablePattern=0
```

After reading this output, you can definitely see the options that you just set. Likewise, you can verify that the settings have properly updated in Server Admin.

> **Note:** Global and per-user password policies do not apply to Open Directory Administrator accounts.

Password Changes at Loginwindow

When first deploying systems to hundreds of users, it is likely that you will first utilize a standard password or password pattern so that users can successfully login for the first time. However, as you will likely often need to disseminate this information in an unsafe manner (such as email), it is important that you ensure that users reset their passwords to a personal value as soon as possible. To do this, you can modify the global password policy to force a password change upon first login. To accomplish this, you can simply check the option for the password to "Be reset at first login." Alternatively, you can set this option using pwpolicy:

```
sudo pwpolicy -a hunterbj -setglobalpolicy "newPasswordRequired=1"
```

When troubleshooting user desktop issues, it may be necessary to reset the password. When doing so, you will usually want to force the user to change his or her password as soon as you're done with your work. The best way to do this is to force a password change at next login for that specific user. To do this, open Workgroup Manager and connect to your Open Directory server, finding the user account in question. With the user selected, password policies can be found by clicking on the Options button under the Advanced tab for the user. Here, you can set numerous per-user password policies. As mentioned in Figure 7-26's warning, settings set here can override global policies.

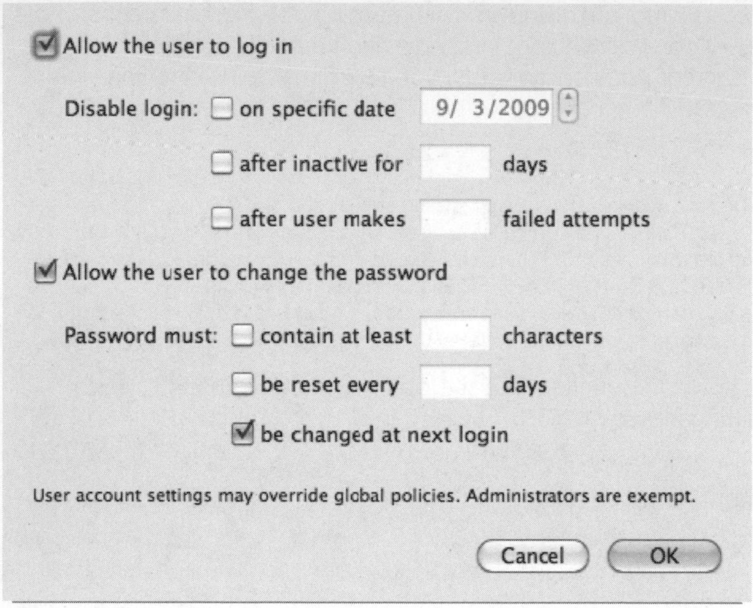

☑ Allow the user to log in

Disable login: ☐ on specific date   9/ 3/2009 ⬍

☐ after inactive for   ____ days

☐ after user makes   ____ failed attempts

☑ Allow the user to change the password

Password must: ☐ contain at least   ____ characters

☐ be reset every   ____ days

☑ be changed at next login

User account settings may override global policies. Administrators are exempt.

(Cancel)   (OK)

Figure 7-26. *Configuring per-user password policies using Workgroup Manager*

There are a few caveats to forcing a user to change their password this setting. First and foremost, not all network services in OS X support the ability to force a password change. Notably, the services that do support this are limited in 10.5 and 10.6 to loginwindow, the account system preference pane, an AFP authentication, Kerberos, and the web password change portal introduced in 10.6. For other unsupported services, such as ssh, iCal, mail, and wiki services, when a user has a forced password change active, then these services will simply fail authentication. As such, it is important that you properly communicate with your users both that you reset their password, as well as make sure that they are familiar with the procedure to reset it. If your email system utilizes Open Directory for authentication, setting this will lock them out of their email and constrain your ability to communicate with them.

Managing Keychains

Managing keychains will become a clear and present issue in the life of a Mac administrator. Keychains in OS X are encrypted files, which are used to store various sensitive information. Keychains are a system-wide framework that allows applications to utilize, providing a single universal method for password management. Each user has a default "login" keychain, which is automatically unlocked at login, provided the password provided at login is the same as that configured for the keychain. The login keychain is used by numerous applications such as Safari, Finder, Mail, and Entourage to store credentials. If a user opens these applications, and the keychain is locked, they will be presented with a dialog box to enter their keychain. If the user's login password and keychain are mismatched, it will be very confusing to the end user, and will force a level of frustration when they never know which password to use at any given moment.

As you may know already, the main issue is that when a user changes their password via any means other than the system preferences account pane, then their keychain password will not get updated. This creates a challenging issue for end users, as remembering a single password for them is hard enough. Combine this with the fact that in order to address the issue, users need to be taught about the Keychain Access application, this may or may not be plausible in your environment. Luckily, the Macintosh community springs into response. The folks at www.afp548.com have provided a handy utility, called Keychain Minder, which can be installed on client machines, and set to autostart. When configured like this, Keychain Minder will start at user login, and ensure that the login keychain has successfully unlocked. If not, the application will present the user with a dialog box, asking them to enter in their former password as well as their new password. After verifying the new password is the same as the login keychain, it updates the password. If the user cannot remember the old password, the application provides an easy interface to start over with a new one.

Keychain Minder can be found for download at http://www.afp548.com/article.php?story=20080828125103334.

Apple Remote Desktop

Apple Remote Desktop is a desktop management suite sold as a separate product from OS X Server. Commonly called ARD, the client for this application is installed by default on every OS X machine. Prior to management availability, a client machine must have the service turned on and access levels configured for users. This can be done by visiting the Remote Management service found in the Sharing Preference pane. The Sharing pane can be accessed by visiting System Preferences under the Apple menu. Under the Remote Management service UI, you will find options to configure the service for all users or for specific users. From here, you can add individual users, and configure levels of remote access, though typically, the only local user that would need remote access would be the 501 user. This user will typically have full access to the machine, and may or may not present visible queues to the end user when they are being observed or controlled. You can also configure this application via the command line and the kickstart command, found at /System/Library/CoreServices/RemoteManagement/ARDAgent.app/Contents/Resources/kickstart. For example, to configure access to your machine for your 501 user, myAdmin, runs the following command as root:

```
/System/Library/CoreServices/RemoteManagement/ARDAgent.app/Contents/Resources/kickstart
-configure -access -on -users myAdmin -privs -all -restart -agent -menu
```

From here on out, the machine will accept login connections for that user, regardless of whether or not you enabled the service in System Preferences or from kickstart.

Scanning Networks with ARD

Apple Remote Desktop possesses a network scanner that can detect machines via bonjour, by a specific IP address or by a range of IP addresses. Multiple Scanners can be set up, making it easy to rediscover DHCP machines on remote subnets.

To create a network scanner, simply select New Scanner from the File menu. Name the scanner appropriately, and in the right hand pane, configure the scanner's settings. Options are Bonjour, Local Network, Network Range, Network Address, or File Import. These are mostly self-explanatory. Local Network searches subnets local to all interfaces on the machine. Network Range allows you to specify a starting and ending IP address, which is handy for scanning remote subnets. File Import allows you to import a file that has newline delimited subnet ranges. This is handy if you have rather intricate subnet configurations and want to capture multiple ranges in a single scan:

```
10.0.1.2-10.0.2.50
10.0.3.100-10.0.3.102
```

> **TIP:** To list or to scan? ARD has both static lists and dynamic scanners. If you find yourself coming and going from a network a lot, you will be much happier with a scan. If you are managing static IP addresses only, or have only a single subnet for all machines then lists are probably better suited. Lists are also better suited if you need to repeatedly target specific machines.

Controlling machines

Controlling machines is pretty straightforward. First, you must add client machines to your local database. To do so, use a scanner that you previously configured. The scanner will display found machines with a blue icon. Simply drag them to the All Computers container on the left. Once you have performed this action, computers listed in the scanner will have a blue icon next to them, as shown in Figure 7-27.

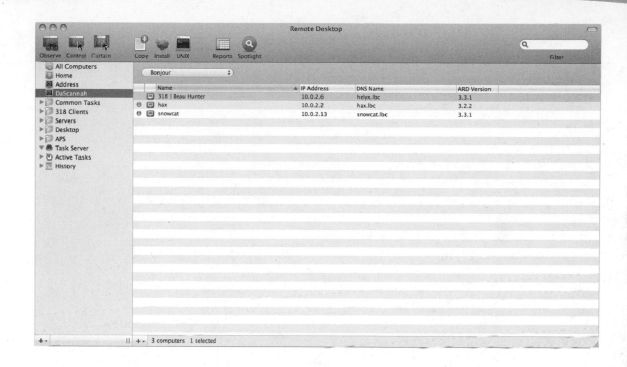

Figure 7-27. *Discovering machines with the Scanner in Apple Remote Desktop*

Once added, you can control a machine by selecting it in the list and selecting the Control button. Now you will have remote control of the remote client's console session, assuming (or sharing) control of it's keyboard and mouse. It is important to note that all ARD sessions and loginwindow sessions share the same console. This is the equivalent to /console connections in Windows Terminal Services.

Sending Commands, Packages, and Scripts

One extremely powerful feature of ARD lies in its ability to distribute package installers, send remote unix shell commands, and even copy files to machines. When copying files, ARD will attempt to utilize multicast for distribution, making distribution of files and packages to machines on the same subnet extremely efficient. To push installation of a package to multiple machines, simply select them in your scanner or list and select "Install Packages." Here, you can install standard mkpg and pkg-based applications. You can deploy multiple packages at one time, they will execute in the order that they appear in the list. This makes it especially happy for pushing software installs and then subsequent updates all in one swoop. Figure 7-28 shows the GUI for remotely executing UNIX shell scripts via ARD's Send Unix Command.

Figure 7-28. *Deploy packages in Apple Remote Desktop*

Unix shell commands are an equally invaluable utility for remote machines. For example, you may need to temporarily enable ssh access on a group of machines for remote management. Using ARD, you can easily push out the command to do this. First, select the desired target computers from a scanner or list and select the Send Unix Command option from the Manage menu. Alternatively, you can click on the Unix button in the toolbar. Regardless of your choice, you will be presented with the window shown in Figure 7-29. In the top field of the window, enter the command:

```
launchctl load -w /System/Library/LaunchDaemons/ssh.plist
```

This command loads a system daemon, and because of that needs to run with root privileges. To do this, select the option Run as User: and enter a value of root.

Figure 7-29. *Remotely execute shell scripts in Apple Remote Desktop*

When you're done with your SSH work, you can disable it by simply redeploying the command with the 'unload' parameter.

Enabling Directory Service groups

With ARD, it is possible to configure authentication for a user existing in a network directory service. There are a couple of different approaches for this. First, you must enable directory authentication client side. This can be done graphically in the ARD application. Next, you will want to be able to manage the target clients in ARD with a local user. Once this is setup, select the target clients in a list or scanner and select the menu item Change Client Settings, found under the Manage menu. From here, you will be presented with a list of configuration options. This will ask you a series of configuration questions. On the fourth pane of the assistant, you are presented with the option to enable directory based-administration. This option will enable directory users found in specific groups: ard_admin, ard_interact, ard_manage, and ard_reports. From there, it will use membership in these groups to grant respective rights to the members. The ard_admin group represents full access and is the most common. The ard_interact group limits interaction to screen control. Alternatively, you can configure these options through the kickstart command:

```
kickstart -activate -configure -clientopts -setdirlogins -dirlogins yes -setdirgroups -
dirgroups ard_admin, ard_interact, ard_manage, ard_reports -restart -agent
```

If you find that you need to deploy specific administrators to specific computers, the use of a single global ard_admin group isn't going to help you much. Instead, you can deploy MCX configurations that tell the application to utilize specific groups. The easiest way to deploy this setting is via the dscl. Specifically, you will be deploying a setting which will tell ARD to consult a group (or groups) of your choosing in place of the standard ard_admin, ard_interact, ard_manage, and ard_reports groups. You can subplant one or any of your groups. For example, if you want to have two administrative groups applied to your "lab2" computer group, you would use the following syntax:

```
dscl -u hunterbj /LDAPv3/hax.lbc mcxset /ComputerGroups/local com.apple.remotedesktop
ard_admin always "(admingroup1,admingroup2)"
```

Once you have deployed the MCX settings, you just need to restart the machine and you should then be able to manage your machine. Unfortunately, this functionality was broken around the time of the introduction of Remote Desktop 3.2.2 and OS X 10.5.3 and the issue persists as of 10.5.7. This is the only official way to deploy ARD management capabilities to specific groups. However, you can use a workaround. This workaround involves creating an ard_admin group in the local directory node. From here, you can nest Open Directory groups inside of these local groups, thereby granting them ard_admin capabilities. To do this, you use the following syntax, locally on the client (as root):

```
dseditgroup -o create ard_admin
dseditgroup -o edit -a myadmingroup1 -t group ard_admin
```

By running these two commands, you create the local group and then nest your DS group inside of it. It isn't quite as clean as pure directory groups, but it gets the job done.

Enabling Directory-Based Administrator Groups

It is also possible to enable a directory service group to possess local administrative access to workstations. This procedure is essentially identical to nesting ard_admin groups. However, instead of nesting your groups inside of ard_admin, you'll do it into the standard admin group. To set up administrative OD groups, you utilize similar syntax:

```
dseditgroup -o edit -a myadmingroup1 -t group admin
```

If you are using AD, then the AD plug-in actually provides you with a nice GUI to do this. Surprisingly, there is no equivalent UI for OD groups. See Chapter 3 for more details on the AD plug-in.

To help deploy these configurations in one fell swoop, I have provided a script for you to use. This script, labeled setNetworkAdminRights, will nest specified OD groups inside of the local admin and ard_admin groups.

Quota Management

Quota support in OS X allows you to set per-user quotas on a per-user level under the Homes tab of Workgroup Manager. Once user-specific quotas have been assigned here, you must then enable quota enforcement on the volume(s) hosting the home directory. To do this, connect to the home directory server using the Server Admin application. With the server connected, select the main server entry and select the File Sharing tab. With the Volumes section selected, highlight the home directory volume and select the Quotas tab. Check the box to enable quotas. After a brief wait, the list should populate with data that is on the drives, and will show current quota limits and utilization (see Figure 7-30).

Figure 7-30. *Enabling Quotas in Server Admin*

Login Hooks

As discussed earlier, login and logout hooks provide the means to run scripts prior to and after a user's login session. Here, the term "hook" is synonymous with "script." The term hook is used simply as a colloquialism referring to the manner in which the script is caught by the login or logout processes. Login and logout hooks are functionally identical, so you will use the term login hook going forward. Unless otherwise indicated, information is similarly applicable to logout hooks.

Login hooks are executed under uid 0. That is, they run with root privileges. In order to properly identify the user environment in which they are running, the system passes the logging-in-user's short name as the first argument to a login script. Login hooks can be utilized to perform custom folder redirections, custom mounts, and file system modifications. The real beauty of login hooks is that you have access to the same tools that you would have in an OS X shell environment. You can use it to deploy Perl, Python, and bash scripts, which can pretty much do your bidding.

Login hooks in OS X are deployable only at the computer and computer group level. However, out of the box, OS X clients are not configured to trust loginhook settings deployed from a directory server. To enable this trust, you must modify loginwindow's root domain preference to enable login scripts:

```
defaults write /var/root/Library/preferences/com.apple.loginwindow EnableMCXLoginScripts
-bool true
```

Next, you have to establish your acceptable trust level, represented by your MCXScriptTrust attribute. Following are a number of trust levels (ordered from most to least strict):

- *FullTrust*: The client will only trust loginscripts specified by Directory Servers to which the client has performed a trusted bind to. A FullTrust relationship also requires that the options to block man in the middle attacks, and Digitally sign every packet are checked.

- *Authenticated*: The client will trust a server only if it has successfully authenticated via a trusted bind.

- *PartialTrust:* Like a full trust, a partial trust requires a trusted bind. Packets here must also be Digitally signed. Active Directory bindings typically occur at this level.

- *Encryption*: The client will trust only servers supporting ldaps:// connections, and for whom root CA file is defined in /etc/openldap/ldap.conf. (See Chapter 1 for more details on SSL and Directory Services.)

- *DHCP*. The client will trust only servers specified in Option 95 of their active DHCP packet, as discussed in Chapter 1.

- *Anonymous*:The client will trust loginscripts configured in any configured directory server.

If you are unsure of which option to set, you can run a query from a client to determine the possible levels:

```
dscl localhost read /LDAPv3/dirserv.myco.com dsAttrTypeStandard:TrustInformation
TrustInformation: Authenticated Encryption
```

You can now use this information to configure your client. When setting your MCXScriptTrust value, the value that you set will determine the trust level such that if your client trust connection is at least as secure as the value specified, then the login script will be trusted. For the preceding example, you could set either Authenticated or Encrypted. If you are confident that all other Macs in your fleet will have a similar trust level, then you can pick the strongest of the values—in this case, Authenticated. To establish this MCXScriptTrust, you run the command (as root on every client):

```
defaults write /var/root/Library/preferences/com.apple.loginwindow MCXScriptTrust -
string Authenticated
```

At this point, you have now laid the groundwork for deploying login scripts. Obviously, life will be much easier if you build the previous measures into your standard configuration at imaging time. Now, it's time to actually deploy your loginhook script. In order to deploy a script, a little prework needs to be done. First, the script needs to have a pound-bang statement (like #!/bin/bash) as its first line. Second, it cannot have a file extension. Lastly, the script must be marked as executable on the file system. To make a script executable, use chmod:

```
chmod +x /path/to/scriptfile
```

With this prework done, all you need to do is deploy the actual loginhook managed preference. To do this, open up Workgroup Manager and login to the Open Directory Master as a directory administrator. Once connected, find and select the computer(s) or computer group(s) where you wish to deploy the loginhook. With the desired object(s) selected, navigate to the Login Preference management pane. In this pane, shown in Figure 7-31, under the scripts tab you will find the ability to specify login scripts. Additionally, you can specify whether login hooks configured in the machines local loginwindow.plist file will be allowed to run. Be careful, if you have any client management systems, such as jamf, disabling this option can interfere with its function.

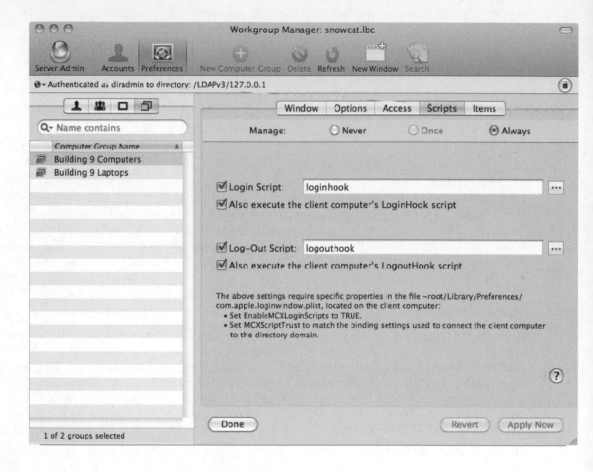

Figure 7-31. *Deploying loginhooks via Workgroup Manager*

To set local loginhooks, run the following command as root on the local client:

```
sudo defaults write com.apple.loginwindow LoginHook /path/to/loginhook.sh
```

Software Update Server

With Mac OS X server, Apple provides the Software Update Server service, which allows you to host your own local software update repository. Referred to as swupd, and built on top of the Apache web server, this service can provide updates to all client computers on your local LAN. This not only saves potential gigabytes of data from hitting your WAN connection, but it also allows you to funnel updates to your clients, releasing them only after your IT organization has had the ability to vet their compatibility with business critical applications.

To Configure a Software Update Server, use the Server Admin application to start the service and enable the appropriate updates. You have a few options in regard to how the service handles new updates. For instance, you can choose to automatically copy all updates or only new updates from Apple's centralized server. By choosing to copy, but not autoenable the updates, you ensure that the updates are local to your LAN, and available for immediate deployment when you are ready finally able to enable. If you choose not to auto enable updates, then you must manually specify which updates will be enabled for deployment. The process swupd_sync is responsible for syncing enabled updates from Apple, and presenting any new updates in the interface.

> **TIP:** Enabling Software Update services on a server can result in a significant amount of data to the folder located at /usr/share/swupd. Make sure the system has adequate space on its disk drive prior to enabling this service. If necessary, you can move the software update store. Moving the directory to a separate volume and then setting up a symlink can do so. The second option is to modify the apache.conf file utilzed by swupd, located at /etc/swupd/swupd.conf.

To configure software update services on the client side, you can do so locally on each by running defaults (as root):

```
defaults write /Library/Preferences/com.apple.SoftwareUpdate CatalogURL
http://myserver.myco.com:8088/
```

Alternatively, you will probably prefer to deploy these settings via MCX. To do so, Workgroup Manager provides a managed preference pane (called Software Update). This preference can be deployed at all tiers of management.

In addition to the graphical Software Update, it is possible to run Software Updates in the background, without the user's knowledge. To do so, you will want to utilize the software update binary, located at /usr/sbin. This command has a few common uses. If you run your own update, you'll probably want to automate the following command with launchd or cron:

```
softwareupdate -i -a; shutdown -r now
```

With this syntax, the command will install any available updates and then restart. However, this command would restart whether updates were installed or not. For operations like this, a more advanced script is required. Luckily, I've got one of those for you. The following script, runallswupdates.sh, can be copied to /etc/rc.local on newly imaged machines. Upon boot, they will run all applicable updates and reboot. This process will continue until all updates are run, at which point the script will self destruct. Alternatively, it can be pushed out in full via ARD's run unix command:

```
#!/bin/bash
PATH=/bin:/sbin:/usr/bin:/usr/sbin
    declare -x swupdServer="hax.lbc"
    #if set to 1, we will reboot when updates recommend it
    declare -i restartOnRecommended=1
    ## Binary vars
    declare -x defaults="/usr/bin/defaults"
    declare -x softwareupdate="/usr/sbin/softwareupdate"
```

```
        declare -x grep="/usr/bin/grep"
        declare -x shutdown="/sbin/shutdown"
        declare -x rm="/bin/rm"
        [ ! "$(whoami)" == "root" ] && printf "Must be run as root! Exiting!\n" && exit 99
            ## set our swupd server
            "$defaults" write /Library/Preferences/com.apple.SoftwareUpdate CatalogURL
"http://$swupdServer:8088/" 2> /dev/null 1>&2
            ## run software update, redirect output so we can actually get useful info
            declare -x swupdateText="$("$softwareupdate" -i -a 2>&1)"

            ## check for text indicating no updates were avail (sloppy but necessary)
            declare -i noUpdates="$(printf "$swupdateText" | "$grep" -c "No updates are
available.")"
        if [   "$noUpdates" -eq 0 ]; then
                ## Here if software update was just run with updates applied
            declare -i recRestart="$(printf "$swupdateText" | "$grep" -c '\[recommended\]')"
            declare -i reqRestart="$(printf "$swupdateText" | "$grep" -c '\[restart\]')"
            declare -i numUpdates="$(printf "$swupdateText" | "$grep" -c '\*')"
            if ( [ "$reqRestart" -eq 1 ] || [ "$recRestart" -eq 1 ] && [
"$restartOnRecommended" -eq 1 ] ); then
                printf "$numUpdates Update(s) installed. We will reboot!\n"
                #"$shutdown" -r now
            else
                printf "$numUpdates Update(s) installed, but no restart is required.\n"
                #printf "recRestart:$recRestart reqRestart:$reqRestart
restartOnRecommended:$restartOnRecommended\n"
            fi
        else
                ## Here if no updates were available, selfdestruct if we're located at
/etc/rc.local
                if [ $0 == "/etc/rc.local" ]; then
                    "$rm" /etc/rc.local
                fi
                ## reset swupd server to standard
                "$defaults" delete /Library/Preferences/com.apple.SoftwareUpdate
CatalogURL
                exit 0
        fi
```

Further Reading

One of the perennial favorites with regard to centrally managing Mac OS X is John,
which is found at the following URL: http://web.me.com/johnd/JohnDs_Site/
Tips_%26_Tricks/Tips_%26_Tricks.html.

Chapter 8

Automating Administrative Tasks

One of the greatest strengths of Mac OS X and Mac OS X Server is the abundance of scripting languages it supports out of the box. Many of these scripting languages are interpreted by a host program rather than run directly as lower-level machine code, and thus they are text files with human-readable syntax. Because such languages are translated into machine code at run time, interpreted programs are sometimes much slower than their compiled equivalents. However, because you can edit these programs and then run them immediately, they are common tools used by system administrators to automate tasks.

Some interpreters are specifically made to run code such as Python, Perl, or Ruby, while others are more interactive and are meant for day-to-day use, facilitating most of the command-line administration tasks covered in this book. Typically, this interactive interpreter component is referred to as a *shell*. The primary purpose of a shell is to translate commands typed at a terminal into some kind of system action. In other words, the shell is a program through which other programs are invoked.

There are several different Unix shells, including the C shell (csh), the Bourne shell (sh), and their more modern equivalents, tcsh and bash. In the most recent versions of Mac OS X, new users are assigned the bash shell as the default shell. In early versions of OS X the default user shell was tcsh, perhaps due to the presence of Wilfredo Sanchez on Apple's team. The former lead engineer for Mac OS X was also a developer of the tcsh shell. However, bash has proliferated through the various Linux distributions and has become one of the most prominent shell programs in use today. Perhaps recognizing this, Apple switched the default shell to bash in Mac OS X v.10.3, and it remains as such today in 10.6.

While the choice of a shell and its resultant scripting language can sometimes be difficult, we recommend you learn at least the basics of the bash shell before moving onto any other shell and language that may be better suited to your higher-level tasks. This is because, unlike with languages such as python or Perl that are more strictly used for scripting, you will typically use the bash shell every time you open up a terminal to run any command. The more comfortable you become with bash scripting, the more you may find yourself writing one-line scripts that allow you to automate even basic operations. For instance, every principle discussed in the "Scripting the Bash Shell" section of this chapter applies to the interactive environment presented when you fire up Terminal.

In this chapter, we present some basic building blocks you need to build your own complex automations. In the process, we attempt to show you some real world syntax examples of scripting in action. Hopefully by the end of this chapter, you'll be armed with enough knowledge to tackle the problems you face in your environment. We'd like to make a strong point at the outset: while you do not have to use the command line to be a good system administrator, most good system administrators do. This is because a simple operation, such as creating a series of folders, can be done using basic scripts, and in using these scripts you will find your administration becomes not only more efficient but also (and importantly in large environments) more consistent.

This chapter is not intended to provide in-depth coverage of all shells; that could be a book unto itself. This chapter will introduce you to scripting with bash and then supply some information on Perl for those who begin to outgrow the bash environment. We will walk through the basic constructs and control statements, providing a decent foundation for you to build on. Due to its default support in the latter iterations of Mac OS X, we will focus primarily on the bash shell syntax, but we will also include fully constructed examples of scripts using PHP, Perl, and python.

The Basics

Every shell has some built-in functions that it performs directly, but most commands you enter cause the shell to execute programs that are external to the shell. This sets the shell apart from other command interpreters, as its primary mechanism for invoking functionality is largely dependent upon other programs. That's not to say that shells don't have built-in capabilities. They do; they can read, create, and append files, manipulate data through globbing and variable mangling and, they can utilize looping constructs. However, the ability to parse and extend that data will more often than not require external calls. This chapter seeks to arm you with the ability to fully utilize the Bash shell's internal functions, as well as introduce pertinent external functions that will help you to fully employ the power of the command line.

The first step toward learning the shell is actually firing it up and getting your feet wet, preferably on a non-production box. In OS X, this is done simply by opening up the Terminal application on your system. When the application opens, provided your user account has the default shell assigned, you will be presented with a bash prompt, something like:

```
helyx:~ hunterbj$
```

The default prompt consists of the following template:

```
computername:current directory username$
```

In this example, the current directory is ~. The tilde represents a user's home directory. Thus for any respective user, ~ expands to /Users/username. The tilde can be used when specifying paths for commands. You can always reference your own home directory via ~, and you can even reference other users' home directories as well:

```
helyx:~ hunterbj$ cd ~monica
helyx:monica hunterbj$ pwd
/Users/monica
```

In this text, we are issuing the cd command to change directories and passing ~monica as an argument. We can see at the shell prompt that our new directory is monica. We then issue the pwd command, which outputs our current path. In this case, it's Monica's home directory at /Users/monica.

> **NOTE:** Pathnames can be passed to commands in two different forms. An absolute path contains every folder and element relative to the root (/) of the drive. A relative path contains items relative to the current directory. For instance, if I run the command cd /Users, I have provided cd with an absolute path to the Users directory. Next I run the command ls monica, providing a path monica, relative to my current directory, /Users. Alternatively, I can run the command using an absolute path ls /Users/monica and net the same results regardless of my current directory.

You'll want to become familiar with the basic commands that are normally used for administration. Here's a list of some of the most common ones:

- cd: Change directory. This command takes a single argument—a path to a directory. You can use cd to change to the parent directory.

- pwd: List current directory. Pwd accepts no arguments.

- ls: List the contents of the current directory. Ls has numerous options. A common set of arguments -alh will show all items in list form (by default, any file beginning with a period is invisible). Optionally, a directory or file can be provided, and ls will output either the file's information or a directory list. For instance, ls -alh /Users will output a detailed list of files and folders present in the directory /Users.

- rm: Delete a file or directory. Rm offers several options. It can be passed a file or directory for deletion. If a directory is passed, the -r flag must be used to recursively delete all children. For instance, the command rm -r /Users would delete the entire /Users folder (probably best to avoid that one).

- nano: A very basic text editor for editing files from the command line. Nano uses emacs-style keyboard shortcuts, supports arrow keys for navigation, and is pretty basic. It accepts a path to a file as an argument. When you're finished editing, type Ctrl+x to save the document. (Another common text editor is vi, but that utility, though rewarding, is much more difficult to learn.)

- **sudo**: Execute a command with root privileges. By default, this command can only be run by administrators. It has numerous options, but in its most basic form, it can simply be prefixed to any command to execute that command with root privileges. For instance, to edit a system configuration file, such as an OS X machines Software Update server settings, I could run the following, which invokes the defaults process with root privileges:

```
sudo defaults write /Library/Preferences/com.apple.SoftwareUpdate CatalogURL↵
http://swupdate.myco.com
```

- **history**: Shows the last commands completed from a command line. The history command requires no other parameters or options.

- **whatis**: Searches the whatis database, handy for determining the appropriate command to run. For instance, by using the command whatis "change owner", you can determine that the chown command may be what you're looking for. You can then use the man command, discussed next, to determine the capabilities of the chown command.

- **man**: Used to access manual pages for the hundreds of command-line programs that come with your computer, so it may well be the most important command to know. For instance, you can type man hier to see information on OS X's directory structure, while man chown brings up the manual page for the chown command, giving you the syntax and functionality of that command.

- **find**: Lets you search for a file or directory by name. find is a fairly complex command and has a lot of utility. In its most basic form, it can be used for a simple directory search. For example, if you were trying to hunt down .DS_Store files on a network share mounted at /Volumes/MyCoolNetworkFolder, you could run the command find /Volumes/MyCoolNetworkFolder -name ".DS_Store". Pretty nifty. Even better, find lets you take the output that it's matching and use this as input for another command. Say you want to delete all .DS_Store files. To do this, run the command: find /Volumes/MyCoolNetworkFolder -name ".DS_Store" -exec rm {} \; In this implementation, we use find's -exec option, and call the external program rm. The braces {} represent a matched item by the utility, and the \; characters terminate our -exec call.

- **echo**: Used to output text to the stdout data stream (discussed later in the section "Standard Streams and Pipes"). When writing scripts, the echo command is a great way to ensure that your script gives proper feedback to the user.

- grep: Used in combination with piping to filter a command's output (piping is discussed later in the section Standard Streams and Pipelines). For instance, the command ls /Users | grep -i admin would filter the output of ls /Users, outputting only user home folders that match the admin criteria, using a substring match so that user home "admin" would match, as would "mycoadmin". The -i flag means that grep will ignore capitalization. In another form, grep can be used to search files for strings. The command sudo grep -r http://www2.myco.com /etc/apache2 would search the directory /etc/apache2 and output the filenames containing the string http://www2.myco.com. The -r flag tells grep to recursively search through a directory. You can omit the -r flag and search across a single file if necessary. You can prefix the sudo command to ensure that the grep search has access to all necessary files.

- ps: List running processes. This command has numerous arguments. One common iteration is ps auxww. The flags auxww result in the output of all running processes across all users on the system. You can use piping to filter this list: the command ps auxww | grep httpd will determine if the Apache daemon (httpd) is running. If httpd is found, the command will display the processes running id (the PID column), as well as CPU and memory utilization.

- chmod, chown: Can be used respectively to change permissions and ownership on a file or group of files. Both commands utilize the -R flag to recurse across all children of a directory. In the following example, chown changes the owner of the folder /Users/hunterbj to hunterbj and changes the group to admin. We then utilize chmod to ensure that the owner (o) has both read and write (rw) access:

```
chown -R hunterbj:admin /Users/hunterbj
chmod -R o+rw /Users/hunterbj
```

- kill: Terminate a running process. This command has a few optional arguments, but in its most basic form, it is simply given the process id of a running process to terminate. A process's id can be determined through the ps output, as discussed above. The kill command must be run with root privileges via sudo in order to terminate a process running as root. Other common flags include -HUP, which can be used to restart a process. Alternatively, the infamous -9 argument, equivalent to -KILL, can be used to forcibly terminate a process without prejudice regardless of state or any pending activity.

These are merely a selection of the available commands. If you know a few commands that, when executed, will complete a larger overall task, you can then combine them to make a program, which we'll call a script. This is how most people start to learn shell scripting.

NOTE: The bash shell has the ability to search back through your history file. Press Ctrl+r to do a "reverse" search through the history file by typing some or all of the original command or its arguments. Continue to press Ctrl+r to cycle through previous incarnations.

To switch between shells, you need only type the name of the shell you desire to use. As you alternate between shells, you'll notice that the appearance of the screen and the area where you input text appears slightly different.

Scripting the Bash Shell

The makings of a typical script includes a hash-bang line `"!/bin/bash"`, variable declarations `"declare FOO=BAR"` , and optionally command variable declarations, This is all we need to create a static script. We will cover these terms more in-depth in the following section, as well as explore the logical constructs that make a script such a powerful wrapper for the command-line tools Mac OS X provides.

The bash shell is based on the Bourne shell (sh), and is syntactically backward-compatible. In fact, the b and a in BASH stand for Bourne Again, a tribute to sh and its author Stephen Bourne. The bash shell is very capable, and has support for numerous control statements. This includes support for standard control statements: if/elif/else constructs, case statements, as well as for, while, and until loop statements.

A control statement in a programming or scripting environment provides ways for a coder to control the execution of code. These statements provide the means to perform basic tests on data, which will then define the flow of execution, all based upon the criteria we design. Through the use of if/else and case control statements, we can control whether or not code gets executed at all. These functions are referred to as branching statements, as they control specific paths of code execution. Looping statements, such as for, while, and until are control statements that allow for reuse of code through iteration. Bash provides looping statements in the form of "for", "until", and "while" loops. Each of these looping statements provides capabilities to help you manage highly repetitive tasks. Control statements serve as the fundamental tools for logical execution of your code.

The bash shell also includes some internal data manipulation routines, provided via globing and variable mangling, though for any advanced parsing, such as regular expressions, you'll be much better off with an external program that is suited for the purpose. That being said, we'll walk you through some of the commonly used bash constructs, which will bestow upon you the building blocks towards implementing your own automations.

> **NOTE:** On many systems, /bin/sh is linked to the bash installation. However, be aware that with bash built upon the basic sh constructs, language like "declare" will not work when called from an sh script. We will show you how to set the hash or sh bang to specify that your script runs in bash; you can add the code at the top of your script [-z "$BASH"] && exit 1 to check for this as well.

Declaring Variables

Variables are the single most important concept of scripting in relation to automating administrative tasks. As we mentioned, while other languages have relative benefits, most admins typically end up using bash for basic day-to-day administration, where many tasks can be accomplished by very simple scripts, or even a single line of chained commands ("one liners"). A one-line script could look something like this:

```
systemsetup -setnetworktimeserver my.server.com
```

This code is straight to the point, but perhaps you are in a Windows Active Directory environment and the server you use for time is also your authentication server. Your script may have "my.server.com" listed 10-20 times by the time you are finished. Now imagine you need to change that code later on. You could cut and paste all 20 lines, but if you use variables you can declare the server once and then retrieve this value over and over again in your script. You can even then use it to echo output as well. Even for your one-liner scripts, using variables will allow them to grow over time and cut down on the number of typos, as you have just one line rather than 20 to check when you have a problem.

```
declare TIME_SERVER="my.server.com"
systemsetup -setnetworktimeserver "$TIME_SERVER"
echo "Time Server: $TIME_SERVER has been set"
```

> **NOTE:** When a variable is used in a script, the script "expands" the variable to its respective value (in this case $TIME_SERVER becomes "my.server.com"). However, a variable may not always contain string data, which is why you can have a dynamic error message using the simple echo command. Because of this, it is important to always double quote variables. Expansion works within double quotation marks, not single quotes. Double quotes also help when working with file-system paths that have spaces, often the cause of issues with novice users. When in doubt, quote. If you want to see variable expansion as it occurs (often helpful for debugging a script) add -x to the hash bang , like this: "#!/bin/bash -x".

Each variable has a name that uniquely identifies it within scope. Variable names need to begin with an alphabetic character and cannot contain a period. In other words, if you work for a company called 318, you'd often need to declare variables called, for example, "THREE18" to avoid starting with a number. Variables can't be longer than 255 characters.

In traditional programming languages you must declare a variable and the kind of information that will go into it before using the variable (in other words, you tell the script what going into variable before you actually "put" something in it). In modern scripting languages, this is usually considered good practice (and great for readability), but it's not required. In the bash shell, the command to declare a variable is declare. When you declare a variable, you can then call it multiple times, adding and removing data from it, augmenting it, or just reading it for reference.

For example, in bash, the two following statements will both work:

```
#!/bin/bash
declare -i CUSTOM_PORT=8088

echo "My software update server is running on port $CUSTOM_PORT "

# Example script 2
CUSTOM_PORT="8088"

echo "My software update server is running on port $CUSTOM_PORT "
```

In the first example, we are explicitly defining the variable CUSTOM_PORT as an integer, and setting it to 8088. In the second, typecasting in bash automatically determines the type of data that a variable contains. Typecasting occurs when a variable is set to a certain type (such as an integer) and then used to store a different data type (say the string "Hello World"). In this case, there is a type conversion from integer to string. While both of the preceding examples work, relying on automatic typecasting can present problems in certain circumstances; if your script logic is expecting an numeric (integer) value and is passed a string instead, your script will die with a fatal error. The following script shows how this works:

```
#!/bin/bash
# A simple script that checks if a console user is active
# We will cover the "who | grep 'console' -c" portion later
# for now just know that this test will return "1" if a user
# is logged in and nothing if no one is logged in

declare -i CONSOLE_USERS="`who | grep 'console' -c`"

# The command above returns nothing if no users are logged in.
# However, when declared as an integer, if this variable is
# set to a null / nothing string, it will convert that to the
# number zero; that way the result of the command doesn't matter.
# We can always rely of the result being a numerical value,
# which we can then numerically test against, using the greater
# than or equal to syntax -ge. This type of test expects
# CONSOLE_USERS to expand to a numerical value
# If we did not use -i, then any numeric tests on $CONSOLE_USERS
# would fail if there were no users logged in. The script would
# expand CONSOLE_USERS to nothing instead of 0

# You can test this by changing the declare line above to
# declare CONSOLE_USERS=
# which will simulate the command returning nothing
# and without the use of the -i, it will stay just that: nothing
```

```
# which will cause the test below to fail with the error:
# "line 17: [: -ge: unary operator expected"

if [ $CONSOLE_USERS -ge 1 ] ; then
        echo "Console user logged in, exiting…"
        exit 1

else
        echo "No console users, we can go to town..."
        # Your code goes here
fi
```

This script uses comments to explain the flow of the script; these are covered later in this chapter. For now, be aware that any line that starts with a # (except for line 1) is a comment and the script will not "run" that text. This is a best practice and you should always comment all of your code, adding notes to explain your script's logic and activity. The more complicated a script gets, the more important that commenting becomes. If you do not comment the script effectively, you will not be able to trace your own steps at some point, much less have anyone else be able to take over your work when you, say, get a promotion to Senior Deity of Computer Operations for integrating 10,000 Macs into your enterprise in a week.

Variable Mangling

The bash shell has several facilities for internally altering data in variables. This is referred to as "variable mangling," and bash allows for numerous string operators to be applied to a variable that will filter its value. Mangling in bash uses curly brackets {} that enclose the variable name prepended to a number of possible special operator characters.

One common use of variable mangling is to perform pattern matching on a variable, both left to right (specified by the hash (#) character), and right to left (specified by the percent (%) character):

```
MY_VAR="the value of a variable"
echo ${MY_VAR#the}
        returns:  "value of a variable"
echo ${MY_VAR%a *}
        returns: "the value of"
```

This can be handy for grabbing filenames, or extensions explicitly:

```
MY_FILE=songname.mp3
echo "Filename: ${MY_FILE%.*} extension: ${MY_FILE##*.}"

returns: Filename: songname extension: mp3
```

Notice the use of the greedy string operator (##); this ensures that even if the file has additional periods in its name, the only one we consider the extension (and thereby exclude from our filter), is everything past the last dot. The ability to remove file extensions this way is very handy. For instance, the Apple defaults command requires you pass in the filename without the .plist extension. In the following script, we utilize this method to isolate the file extension when needed, allowing us to perform our operations. The commands here are not as important as the concept—that now we can use the same variable for both operations and have the extension automatically removed for commands that require it.

```
#!/bin/bash

declare -i TIME_OUT=5
# This sets the timeout of the AD plug-in in 10.5+

declare PLIST_FILE=\
"/Library/Preferences/DirectoryService/ActiveDirectory.plist"

# The path of the plist \ is used to continue the command on the next line
# Note that the path has a .plist extension, which normally would cause
# The defaults command to fail. However, with variable mangling we can
# remove the .plist extension of the PLIST_FILE value when we use it
# with defaults and then call it normally when we use a command that
# requires a more standard path with file extensions like plutil.

if [ -w "$PLIST_FILE" ] ; then

        defaults write "${PLIST_FILE%.plist}" 'LDAP Connection Timeout' $TIME_OUT

        plutil -convert xml1 "$PLIST_FILE"

else

        echo "File is not writable try sudo $0"
fi
```

> **NOTE:** We use a variable that is automatically set by the shell, $0 here. This is the full path to the script and it's good for making dynamic usage error messages match your script path and name automatically.

Another form of variable mangling provided by bash is substitution, which uses four operators, :-, :=, :+, and :?. Suppose I use the command echo ${MY_VAR:-hello}. If the variable MY_VAR exists and isn't null, the command will output its value. If MY_VAR doesn't exist or has a null value, the string "hello" will not print out. The := operator is very similar. The main distinction is that when := is used, it will set the variable $MY_VAR to the value specified, in this case "hello." The :+ operator is essentially the inverse of the :- operator. In the command echo ${MY_VAR:+hello}, if $MY_VAR exists and is not null, then we return "hello." If it doesn't exist or is null, it will return a blank value. Lastly, the :? operator can be used to perform sanity checks. For instance, when used with the syntax echo ${MY_VAR:?my error}, if the variable $MY_VAR is not set, the script will immediately terminate, printing the error message "my error." If no error is specified, a generic "parameter null or not set" error is output, along with the variable name. Use of the :? operator is a great way to ensure that critical variables are set.

NOTE: Scripts can be very damaging if certain operations are called with malformed data, so be extra diligent in using these string operators to verify that appropriate values are set.

The bash shell also provides further capabilities for data substitution via the / and // operators. For instance, if MY_VAR has a value of Hello World, the command echo ${MY_VAR//Hello/Hi} would output the text Hi World. The use of // vs. / simply denotes how greedy the matching is: echo #{MY_VAR/o/a} would output Hella World, while the command: echo #{MY_VAR//o/a} outputs Hella Warld. A real-world example of this follows. Excuse our rather hacky use of Apple script via osascript to get this MAC address value, but it's a simple way to get only your MAC address returned.

```
#!/bin/bash
declare MAC_ADDRESS=`osascript -e 'primary Ethernet address of (system info)'`
echo "Address with colons: $MAC_ADDRESS"
echo "Address without colons: ${MAC_ADDRESS//:/}"
```

Standard Streams and Pipelines

In any *nix terminal environment, numerous information channels exist that control the flow of information between a process and its console session. The three primary data channels from a scripting perspective are standard input (stdin), standard output (stdout), and standard error (stderr). These data streams can be captured, evaluated, and redirected through scripting.

- Standard input, or stdin, represents data resulting from a read operation. This can be text input via keyboard or text that has been programmatically redirected.

- Standard output, or stdout, represents any data output by a program. The output will typically go to the current console session but can also be redirected to other programs or files.

- Standard error, or stderr, is a data channel that represents textual error information. For instance, if a program detects an error in one of its subroutines, it will typically spit the details of this error out to stderr. Understanding the use of these channels by any program you intend to script will help you to more efficiently write your code.

As mentioned, we can use pipelines or redirects to control the flow of data between separate programs. The most common use of pipelines is the practice of piping stdout from one script to stdin of another. Take the previous until loop example. In this instance, we call the command:

```
ps auxww | grep -v "grep" | grep -c "Finder"
```

If you were to look up the man page for grep (man grep), you would find that the program takes optional flags and two arguments, a string pattern and a path to a file. However, in this context, we are simply calling grep with only one argument. How does that work? Well, the answer is due to our implementation of command pipes |. As mentioned, the pipe is used explicitly for passing data between programs. In this case, we are passing data from the ps command out to grep. The grep command recognizes that it is being passed data over stdin and utilizes this data as its second argument. After filtering this data and removing any occurrences of the term grep, it outputs the modified data to stdout, which is piped to yet another instance of grep. This program is responsible for outputting a numeric count for the number of times the term Finder appeared in data passed to it through stdout. In a command pipeline, the resulting text output will be that parsed by the final command in the chain.

In many cases, you may want to redirect the flow of data to a file. To do this, you use data stream redirectors. In bash, the most common implementation of redirectors is through the >> and > operators:

```
ps auxww > ~/process_list.txt
```

In this example, we are redirecting stdout of the ps program to the file located at ~/process_list.txt. The use of the > operator means it will overwrite any data that previously existed with the file. Thus, every time the above command is run, the file will contain only data from the most recent operation. The >> operator in contrast is an append operation; any data previously will simply have our latest data added to it. This is a less destructive redirect, and is desirable in many scenarios.

It is also possible to redirect the data streams themselves. For instance, perhaps we want to set a variable to the output of the ls command:

```
lsTxt=$(ls /Applications)
```

This syntax will capture the output of the ls program's stdout as a single string. However, if ls is passed a nonexistent path, it will output its text to stderr, which will never be passed to our lsTxt variable. To address this issue, we can use data stream redirects once again. To pull this off, we want to redirect the stderr channel (in *nix systems channel 2) to stdout channel, channel 1:

```
lsTxt=$(ls /Applications 2>&1)
```

This way, lsTxt will contain either the file listing or any subsequent errors. With bash, it is also possible to perform two redirects:

```
ls /Applications >> /lsLog.txt 2>&1
```

In this context, we are redirecting stdout to append our file found at /lsLog.txt. However, we are also redirecting stderr to stdout. This command will output the results of both data streams into the file. This becomes a handy way to log all activity reported by a process, rather than just merely relying on stdout.

If and Case Statements

If/else and case statements in bash serve primarily as traffic routers. Both of these facilities are specifically referred to as branching statements; their purpose is to directly affect the flow of code. For instance, perhaps there is a VIP user on the network who needs VIP treatment. If this particular user logs into a computer, we need to ensure he has a "Deep Thoughts" folder on his desktop, and then perhaps we need to prune this folder for old files, sweeping them away into a "Stale Thoughts" folder. In the end, the specific task doesn't really matter, it is only important that we recognize that all of this activity represents a "branch" of code; a full path of activity initiated by the evaluation of an initial `if` statement. That `if` statement represents a test—is this user my VIP? If he is, the next step is a flurry of activity. Otherwise (`else`) skip the code and proceed as usual.

> **NOTE:** When coding or scripting in any language, the general rule of thumb when implementing branching statements is to organize your code so that the most commonly executed branch is in the first block.

For basic string comparison, both if/else and case statements are pretty similar, though lengthy case statements tend to be easier to read than lengthy if/else statements. Here is the syntax to implement each in bash (Note: the USER variable is set automatically by the bash shell and expands to the username of the user running the script):

```
# Check to see if our user is "jdoe"
if [ "$USER" = "jdoe" ]; then
        echo "My name is John"
        exit 0
elif [ "$USER" = "janedoe" ]; then
        echo "My name is Jane"
        exit 1
elif [ "$USER" = "jsmith" ] ; then
        echo "My name is jsmith"
        exit 1

else
        echo "Failed over to catch all…"
        exit 192
fi

# While the above works, it's rather ugly, so a case statement normally is much more
readable

## case statement
case $USER in
r"jdoe")
                echo "My name is John";
                exit 0;;

        "jsmith" )
                echo "My name is jsmith" ;
                exit 1;;

        "janedoe")
                echo "My name is Jane";
                exit 1;;
         *)
        echo "Failed over to catch all…";
        exit 192 ;;
esac
```

We have introduced a few new concepts here. First, the test brackets [ ]. The use of brackets represents a conditional expression, which will ultimately evaluate to true or false. In bash, test brackets are used with conditional operators to form tests. One example of this is in the previous example's if statement:

```
if [ $CONSOLE_USERS -ge 1 ] ; then
\
```

This logic in English would translate as: if the string variable $USER is equal to the string "jdoe", execute the following code. In this case, "is equal to" is syntactically denoted by a string comparison operator, =, which compares two arguments (referred to as a binary operator) and returns true if they have equal string values. It's antithesis, != will return true if the two given arguments are not the same. In our case statement, the variable $USER is tested in a similar fashion (=) against each of our possible matches, each denoted by the values specified prior to the closing parenthesis. When a match occurs, the respective code block is executed until it reaches the break specifier ;;. In the case statement, the last line *) represents a wild card, and is the equivalent to an else block in an if statement; its execution is dependent on all prior matches failing.

In addition to these two binary operators (= and !=), bash provides several arithmetic-based binary operators:

- -eq: arg1 equals arg2

- -ne: arg1 does not equal arg2

- -lt: arg1 is less than arg2

- -le: arg1 is less than or equal to arg2

- -gt: arg1 is greater than arg2

- -ge: arg1 is greater than or equal to arg2

Beside binary operators, the test facility provides us with many valuable unary operators (to test against a single argument). Unary operators more often than not are used to perform tests against filesystem objects. Two of the most common unary operators are -f and -d, which respectively test for the presence of a file or directory.

```
if [ -d /System/Library/CoreServices/Finder.app ]; then
        echo 'Finder was Found!'
fi
```

This code will print the text "Finder was found!" if a directory exists at the path /System/Library/CoreServices/Finder.app (which is true in any OS X system because the Application bundle "Finder" is in fact a directory like almost all modern apps). There are numerous unary operators, most easily found by consulting the man page for test, using man test. Here are some that are notable:

-f string: true if string is the path to a regular file

-d string: true if string is the path to a directory

-r/-w/-x string: true if string is a file that is readable, writeable, or executable (respectively)

-L string: true if string is a path to a symbolic link

-z/-n string: true if string is zero or non-zero length (respectively)

NOTE: You can also run these checks directly using the test command (although you might have to wrap the test condition into quotes or double parenthesis depending on exactly what you're attempting to test), like so:

```
test -d /Users/ && echo "directory exists"
```

```
#!/bin/bash
if ( [ "$USER" == "janedoe" ] || [ "$USER" ="jsmith" ] ); then
echo "User is jane or john"
else
        echo "User is not jane or john"
fi
```

In the if/elif example, we also demonstrate the use of the logical OR operator ||:

```
if ( [ "$USER" ="janedoe" ] || [ "$USER" ="jsmith" ] ); then
```

The logical OR operator and its partner the logical AND operator (&&), often referred to as Boolean operators, are used to test against multiple expressions. In the implementation above, we are using the logical OR operator to test against two possible usernames, janedoe and jsmith. We want to know if a user is *either* of these usernames, so we need to be able to run both tests. In this example, if we used && instead of ||, the end result would always evaluate to false, as the $USER variable will never be equal to both values. When using logical operators && and || to combine expressions, execution of the control statement will terminate immediately after it evaluates to false or true, respectively. Thus, in the above example, if the username is janedoe, the test will never be executed against "jsmith". In similar spirit, if we used && in that statement, the test against "jsmith" will only ever get tested if the first expression is true (the username is "janedoe"). Understanding this becomes very important to writing clean, effective code. Recognizing this, we can take previous example:

```
if [ -d /System/Library/CoreServices/Finder.app ]; then
        echo 'Finder Found!'
fi
```

and then slim it down to a single "one-liner":

```
[ -d /System/Library/CoreServices/Finder.app ] && echo 'Finder found!'
```

As we learned earlier, if our expression returns false (in this case because the Finder.app directory could not be found), then the test will abort and the `printf` statement will never fire. In this iteration, we are also omitting our `if` control statement, as our branching code (`printf "Finder found!\n"`) can easily fit onto a single line.

In our previous example, the case statement as you may have deduced, also uses a logical OR operator, implemented by supplying multiple matches in a single test block:

```
case "$USER" in
"jdoe")
        echo "My name is John";;
"janedoe")
        echo "My name is Jane";;
*)
        echo "Remember Sammy Jenkins…";;
esac
```

In this example, by placing both "janedoe" and "jsmith" together, we are implying a logical OR between the two values. A case statement will then perform a string comparison of $USER to the string "janedoe" and if no match is found, will test against "jsmith", and so on. Once a match is found, it will execute any preceding lines of code until it runs against our break specifier (;;). In the case of janedoe or jsmith, a match would result solely in the execution of the code: echo "My name is Jane". Case statements, unlike if/else statements, do not have access to the more advanced unary or binary operators provided by bash. They are pretty much limited to string comparisons and thus provide only limited (but important) functionality.

For, While, and Until Statements

So, at this point, we have learned how to define the flow of our program through the use of branching statements, expressions, and conditional operators. Automation, however, is rarely about performing an operation once; the benefits of automation lie in the ability to scale production as needed with minimal investment. Automation is particularly well-suited for boring, repetitive tasks that will result in hundreds, thousands, or even millions of iterations. To harness the ability of repetition and iteration, bash provides three looping statements: for, while, and until. The for loop is utilized for iterating over items.

```
declare plistbuddy="/usr/libexec/PlistBuddy"
declare python="/usr/bin/python"

REQUIRED_COMMANDS="$plistbuddy $python"
for COMMAND in $REQUIRED_COMMANDS; do
```

```
        if [ -x  $COMMAND ] ; then
                echo "Command: $COMMAND is installed"
        else
                echo "Command: $COMMAND is missing"
        fi
done
```

Every element of this script is native to bash, and would output the text:

```
Command: /usr/libexec/PlistBuddy is installed
Command: /usr/bin/python is installed
```

> **NOTE:** To determine if a command will result in the execution of an external program, use
> type followed by the name of the function. If the process is external to the shell, it will specify
> the absolute path to the binary (as found in $PATH). For example: type echo returns echo
> is a shell builtin, meaning that bash will use its internal echo ability rather than the
> external command /bin/echo when the echo command is called in a script.

The while and until statements are used for building more customized looping
structures. The and operator allows us to loop while a certain criteria are met:

```
while [ $(ps aux | grep -v "grep" | grep -c "Finder" ) -ge 1 ];
do
        echo "Finder is still running"
        sleep 15
done
```

In this example, there are a few new concepts. First and foremost, whenever we use
expressions, they are primarily expecting string arguments. If we want to call an external
program inside of an expression, we must designate that the text not be treated as a
string, but rather as an external process. To do this, we wrap the entire command
pipeline inside of $(). This wrapper tells the shell to evaluate the contents of the entire
pipeline in a subshell. This same behavior applies if we want to assign the output of a
command to a variable. The following syntax is used to set the value of variable $psTxt
to the output of our ps command chain (this time we will use grep with pipes to
accomplish the same count):

```
psTxt=$( ps aux | grep -v "grep" | grep -c "Finder" )
```

Examining this command chain, we see that we are utilizing the external programs ps
and grep. The ps command lists running processes, and grep is a basic filtering tool.
Because grep is a program, it will sometimes be found in the ps process list, so we must
first filter out the grep line, using the -v flag. Then we do a search for the string "Finder."
The -c flag specifies that we will output the number of matches. If we find one or more
processes, we will proceed through our loop. Next we output a simple text line stating
that the program is running, then we sleep for 15 seconds. At this point, the end of our
loop has been reached and we will once again test for our criteria. If the criteria match,
we will proceed through our loop again, indefinitely, until our criteria fail to match.

The until loop represents a different utility. In bash it does not represent true trailing
logic (as it does in C), but rather serves as an inverse of the while loop. Because of this,

it is of rather limited use. For example, we can pretty easily replicate the logic of the above while loop, simply inversing our conditional logic:

```
until [ $(ps aux | grep -v "grep" | grep -c "Finder" ) -lt 1 ];
do
        printf "Finder is Running\n"
        sleep 15
done
```

> **NOTE:** Bash, like most languages provides control statements for managing individual loop iterations. For instance, the control statement `continue` will instruct a loop to terminate the execution for that particular instance, at which point it will return to its evaluation statement (or the next iterated item in the case of a `for` loop), and continue through the loop. The `break` statement will instruct a loop to terminate completely.

Arrays

An array, sometimes known as a vector, is one of the simplest data structures. Arrays hold a collection of values, generally of the same data type. Each element uses a consecutive range of numbers (integers) to retrieve and store the values. Bash has basic support for one-dimensional arrays. Creating a basic array in bash is pretty simple:

```
## set the variable MY_APPS to an array populated with a directory listing of
/Applications
declare -a MY_APPS=(/Applications/*.app)
```

You can then iterate through these items with a for loop:

```
for APP in "${MY_APPS[@]}"; do
        echo "Application: $APP"
done
```

There are a few things to note in this code. In our `for` statement, we quote the array string `${MY_APPS[@]}` to ensure that individual items with spaces or tabs in the data are escaped. When accessing a specific index in an array, the curly braces are always needed and the index number specified inside them. For instance, here's how to access the first item list in our applications:

```
${MY_APPS[1]}.
```

You can also assign arrays using numeric methodology as well:

```
declare -a USER_NAME[501]=zack
declare -i USER_UID=501

echo ${USER_NAME[501]}
        returns: "zack"
echo ${USER_NAME[$USER_UID]}
        returns  "zack"
```

Arrays are very handy for collating and organizing data. However, their support in bash is a bit limited compared to more robust programming environments. Also be aware that one of the major limitations of an array is that their scope is downward only, meaning you can't export an array between scripts or functions of a script. Basically, arrays are going to only work in your main body of code and not in sub-processes you launch. In practice, this is a major limitation to consider before trying to use bash arrays in a complicated fashion.

Exit Codes

Command-line applications, when implemented properly, will provide what is called an Exit Code, or Return Code after execution. This exit code is internally defined in the program, and is used to signal proper execution, or perhaps a specific error code. When a Unix command-line utility executes successfully, it should return an integer value of 0, which indicates successful operation. Any non-zero value will represent an error condition in the code, and this is a handy way to determine whether a program properly executed. Exit codes vary from application to application and are often referenced in the commands' documentation (192 is also a common error status).To check the exit code of a process, you can test against the special variable $? Immediately after the command has executed:

```
rsync -avu /Folder1/ /Folder2/
if [ $? = 0 ]; then
        echo "The Rsync finished without an error!"
else
        echo "The rsync had problems!!"
fi
```

Alternatively, you can do the same thing on one line:

```
rsync -avu /Folder1/ /Folder2/ && ( echo "Rsync Finished" || echo "Rsync had problems" )
```

When writing your own scripts, It Is important that you follow good practice and properly report the script's status. You do this by utilizing the exit statement in your code, followed by an integer value defining the proper state, remembering to exit 0 on proper execution, and use an arbitrary value of 1 or greater on error. If your script is primarily a wrapper for a different program, it may not be a bad idea to mirror its exit code by referencing the $? variable immediately following the execution of your command. Because $? will change with each process that is run, you will want to save the $? value into a separate variable for later reference in the script, allowing your script to exit with the same value of the original command that you are wrapping your logic around (such as an if or for statement):

```
rsync -avu /Folder1/ /Folder2/
declare -i RSYNC_CODE=$?
if [ $RSYNC_CODE =0 ]; then
        echo "The Rsync finished without an error!"
else
        echo "The rsync had problems!!"
fi
exit $RSYNC_CODE
```

Constructing a Shell Script

In order to be properly processed by a shell, a Unix executable script must specify which interpreter the shell should use to parse and execute its contained shell code. This information is provided via a hash-bang or shbang (#!) specifier, which should always be at line 1 of the script and should precede the absolute path to the file's interpreter. For instance, in this chapter we are primarily utilizing bash scripts. To specify the bash interpreter, we use the following hash-bang specifier at the start of the script:

```
#!/bin/bash
```

> **NOTE:** You can add an -x to the interpreter line of bash scripts to assist with debugging. This will echo the expanded variables and actual runtime code in addition to the more common output vectors like the echo command. For example, #!/bin/bash -x.

Using this syntax, you can also specify atypical shell interpreters, such as Perl (#!/usr/bin/perl), Python (#!/usr/bin/python), or Ruby (#!/usr/bin/ruby), the list goes on. For the most part, OS X, and most *nix variants all utilize the same directory to store interactive user shells in: the /bin/ folder. This folder is defined by BSD as housing: "user utilities fundamental to both single-user and multi-user environments." This folder is very common among the *nix variants, and can usually be trusted to contain at least the Bourne shell (sh), and on most modern systems, the bash shell. However, non-shell interpreters, such as Python, Perl, or Ruby are going to vary greatly from OS to OS. Because of this, if we want our shell to be portable (which these languages provide), then providing a static path is not going to provide much utility on nonconforming systems. If portability is your goal (and certainly it's never a bad one), you may want to forgo specifying an absolute path and instead let the parent shell dynamically determine its location. To do this, utilize the following hash-bang specifier:

```
#!/usr/bin/env python
```

The key thing to know here, is that /usr/bin/env is a very commonly supported binary, and will cause the shell to search through its $PATH to locate the Python executable. If that's found in our path, this executable will be used as the interpreter for the script. The $PATH variable is an environmental variable used by nearly all shells and specifies a number of directories that should be consulted when searching for a binary. This variable contains a colon-delimited string of directories, and will search through them in order of preference from left to right. For instance, if I run the command echo $PATH, I will see all of the directories in my path:

```
echo $PATH
/usr/bin:/bin:/usr/sbin:/sbin
```

Thus, if I were to run the command ifconfig, my shell would first look for the binary ifconfig in the /usr/bin folder, then in /bin, /usr/sbin, and so on until it ultimately finds the command (in this case, in the /sbin directory). If the command is not found after searching the entire path, the shell will terminate execution of the script with an error. On top of this, the PATH variable becomes a good way for a user to inject his own versions of a binary in place of a system binary. For instance, Mr. Joebob Poweruser always likes to have the latest, greatest version of Perl on his system, dutifully installed at /usr/local/bin/perl. However, with a default PATH variable, when Joebob runs the command perl, he will be treated to our localization's binary stored at /usr/bin/perl. To change this, Joebob will want to modify his ~/.bash profile file, adding the line

```
export PATH="/usr/local/bin:$PATH"
```

After doing this, when Joebob starts a shell, the path /usr/local/bin will be the first folder searched in his path. Knowing all of this, it is easy to see how utilizing the /usr/bin/env in your hash-bang line can provide benefits if your script will have a wide audience.

> **NOTE:** With all the variants of Linux and Unix systems out there, it certainly can be a mental exercise to remember each one's folder hierarchy. For this purpose, many such systems provide documentation as to their particular folder eccentricities. On such systems, you can access this documentation via the hier man page by running the command man hier at your Terminal prompt.

With the hash-bang out of the way, we can now start writing our script. Typically at this point in the script, we will do what is referred to as *initialization*. That is, we will define the variables to be utilized by the script. Initializing all of your variables at the beginning of the script provides many benefits. Primarily, it serves as a blueprint for your script. Assuming you adopt good naming conventions for your variables, the general utility and configurability of a script can often be deduced by scanning the variables, at least to an extent. To assign a variable in bash, you simply specify the variable name, followed by an equal sign, and then the value. For instance, in the following line:

```
USER_NAME="hunterbj"
```

With this line, we are assigning the global variable USER_NAME the value of hunterbj. Variables in bash can be uppercase such as PLIST_FILE and can contain underscores PLIST_FILE, and can even be camel case— plistFileNumberThree, the choice is up to you, just be consistent. Notice that during assignment, we do not prepend the variable name with a $ specifier, unlike Perl. However, utilizing the global scope in bash will ultimately make your code less extensible. For instance, if you were to refactor the code into a function, you could have issues with scope conflict. To address this, you can utilize the declare statement, which will initialize the variable only in the local context:

```
declare USER_NAME="hunterbj"
# Beau is available only the local context

declare -x USER_NAME="zsmith"
# Zack is only available to the local and sub shells

export USER_NAME="cedge"
# Charles is available to the local sub shells and parent shells
# (but no type assignment such as array "-a" or "-i" integer)
```

Any local declares will not export to sub-processes or script functions, but stay within the current scope of code running. If you use declare in a function, once the function is complete the variable will no longer be active. This may be advantageous if, for instance, you have a function that contains a password as a variable. If you want to keep a function's variable around after the function is complete, you can use export, as shown in this example:

```
#!/bin/bash

# This is a basic function
littleFunction(){
        declare LITTLE_VAR="local"
        export BIG_VAR="global"

        echo "$FUNCNAME: LITTLE_VAR: $LITTLE_VAR"
        echo "$FUNCNAME: BIG_VAR: $BIG_VAR"
}


littleFunction # This is how we run a function

echo "$0: BIG_VAR: $BIG_VAR"
echo "$0: LITTLE_VAR: ${LITTLE_VAR:?}" # This should error out


$ ./bigscript

littleFunction: LITTLE_VAR: local
littleFunction: BIG_VAR: global
./bigscript: BIG_VAR: global
./ bigscript: line 16: LITTLE_VAR: parameter null or not set
```

While not always necessary, it is a good idea to get in the habit of using declare statements with bash. It will definitely save you time and headaches down the road as you find yourself needing to repurpose code.

One mistake rookie coders make is that they rely heavily on utilizing PATH resolution in shell scripts. That is, instead of typing the command:

```
/usr/sbin/networksetup -getdnsservers "Airport"
```

They actually type the command as:

```
networksetup -getdnsservers "Airport"
```

This won't necessarily prove to be an issue, as networksetup resides in the default path at /usr/sbin. The main problem with this methodology is that PATH variables can be manipulated rather easily. If this script were ever to get called with the sudo command, which escalates privileges to eid 0, then we could potentially compromise a machine simply by injecting our own path variable into the user environment. This way, instead of the system calling networksetup, someone could call our own program identically named networksetup, which might install goodies all over the machine. Modifying a user's PATH is rather trivial to do once a user account has been compromised, and can then be used for local privilege escalation and to ultimately control the box. Several OS X escalation vulnerabilities have been found due to failure to sanitize PATH exploits.

To combat this issue, we have a few options. The first option is to manually specify the PATH variable in our script. This way, we can utilize the dynamic lookup capabilities of scripts and still provide our own known-good paths. To do this, we simply declare PATH in the global scope of the script:

```
#!/bin/bash
PATH="/usr/local/bin:/usr/bin:/bin:/usr/sbin:/sbin
```

By specifying the PATH variable, we are in essence designating trusted paths. Because we are doing this, it is important that we ensure proper restrictions are applied to these paths. We want to make sure that all specified paths are locked down from modification, restricted only to admin users. For instance, the bash /usr/local/bin does not exist by default, so it could theoretically be possible for a user to create this directory, inject his own executables, and then interject those executables into our script. To prevent this, we utilize file system permissions. In the case of /usr/local/bin, a user would first have to create both the local/bin branch. Thus, that user would need to be able to modify the directory at /usr. Luckily, file system privileges are locked down such that a user would need root access to alter any of the specified directories. If they have the ability to alter these system paths, we have bigger issues to worry about.

Specifying a PATH for our shell script doesn't solve all issues. For instance, what if the user installs a copy of a command, which is syntactically incompatible with the options specified in our script? Perhaps only part of what we utilize the utility for in our script actually works with the user's app. In such case, our script would certainly execute abnormally, at best merely failing to execute, but in a worst case scenario, the side effects could certainly prove to be damaging. For this reason, you may want to allow only a specific binary to be utilized for the context of your script. The standard methodology to implement this is to declare full commands as variables, and then call that variable instead of the command. Also, you can use the -x test to see if the command is executable:

```
#!/bin/bash

declare networksetup =" /usr/sbin/networksetup "

if [ -x $networksetup ] ; then
      $networksetup -setv6off "Airport"
else
      echo "$networksetup is missing, is this Tiger(10.4)?"
fi
```

This practice certainly has its benefits. First, we ensure that all binaries paths are hard coded to the system defaults. Of course, ensuring that the system's default software has not been altered is outside of our control. We could certainly calculate md5 sums or check binary version output, but the risk/effort rewards really aren't there; it is perfectly sensible for our script to assume a stock software package, particularly in the context of this chapter.

The second benefit to declaring our commands is that we now have a nice list of all external commands utilized by the script, which is great way to show our users what we are using to make our script work.

Passing Arguments to Shell Scripts

When a script is called, it can have options, much like the options present in commands you run in Mac OS X. These commands are programmatically stored in a predefined variable called a *positional parameter*. The positional parameters are easily identified because they are $1, $2, $3, and so on, with each position the area between a space and the next input. For example, to send a command called foo a variable called bar you would use the command foobar, which would result in being able to use the variable $1 in the script. In the script below, we declare a number of variables and even put the target of the script and the information to change within the script as follows, this is an example postflight script in a package installer. Apple's installer will pass these parameters to a script automatically, but you can simulate them with the following command:

```
sudo /path/to/this_script 1 2 /Volumes/Macintosh\ HD  /Volumes/Macintosh\ HD

sudo /path/to/this_script 1 2 /Volumes/ /
```

> **NOTE:** We are putting the placeholders 1 and 2 here to stand in for what would really be passed during an install. In this case because we don't use $1 or $2, any value here would do, just to make sure the count was right. This is a common way of testing scripts that are destined for Apple package installers.

```
#!/bin/bash
# This script removes the time machine prompt from newly created users
# $1 and $2 are not used in this script
declare -x DSTROOT="$3"              # Installation Volume of mount point.
declare -x SYSROOT="$4"              # The root directory for the system.
declare -x USER_TEMPLATE="/System/Library/User Template/English.lproj"
declare -x PLIST=\
"${DSTROOT:?}/${USER_TEMPLATE:?}/Library/Preferences/com.apple.TimeMachine.plist"

declare defaults="/usr/bin/defaults"
"$defaults" write "${PLIST%.plist}" 'DoNotOfferNewDisksForBackup' -bool 'YES' &&
echo "$PLIST updated successfully"
exit 0
```

> **NOTE:** As you can see here, we are calling the PLIST variable using "${PLIST%.plist}" to remove the plist extension. The defaults command requires this rather odd syntax when referencing a file due to the plist domains concept covered in man defaults.

Scheduling Automations

There will be times when you will need to schedule your scripts to perform various tasks. Maybe you want to periodically run a backup, check and repair permissions, run system maintenance, run updates, or perform whatever it is that you want your machines to do in the wee hours of the morn. No matter, OS X has a scheduler that will fit your need. OS X's scheduling capabilities are rooted both in the past and in the present; its BSD heritage has provided it with traditional *nix schedulers in cron and at. A more modern scheduler is provided with launchd, which brings with it a number of advantages, and a prerequisite to reconsider how schedules are ran.

launchd

launchd is a fairly complex beast, and much more than "just" a scheduler. It provides a job-watching capability, allowing your scripts to loop and even crash and be restarted. It can also watch a folder path or individual file for changes, a very common way of triggering an action. Moreover, launchd allows for items to be created and run by root but also by ordinary users. As we show below, you can even include scripts right in launchd items, making the whole thing self contained. It also presents an interesting solution to the scheduling problem, and as such becomes a very handy tool for scheduling automations. To schedule an automation you must first construct a launchd.plist file. This plist file contains a number of keys that tell launchd how to treat our program. Each launchd.plist file contains a unique label, a series of program arguments, and a schedule defined for that program. When loaded by launchd, the superdaemon will fire your program and specified arguments.

A launch daemon is a plist file that can be deployed in two different domains, which ultimately control the resources that the respective process will have. Launch daemons, installed at /Library/LaunchDaemons and /System/Library/LaunchDaemons are considered system domains, though the latter should not be touched outside of Apple-provided files. The plist file should be named using reverse-domain notation, similar to other preference files in OS X. As the name "launch daemon" implies, most standard UNIX daemons are now handled through launch daemons. For instance, named, OS X's DNS service, can be found at /System/Library/LaunchDaemons/org.isc.named.plist.

A launch agent, on the other hand, is a launchd.plist that specifies a process that will run in the context of the user's environment. For this reason, agents are extremely useful for deploying userland-based automations, but a poor choice for system-level automations. If your process has dependencies on a windowserver process, such as an AppleScript/osascript, launch agents afford you access to that resource. Outside of these differences, all information provided over the next few pages describing launchd.plists are true of both launch daemons and agents, unless specifically stated otherwise.

From a scheduling perspective, launchd allows for two different types of schedules; recurring intervals and specified schedules. The StartInterval key can be used to specify a sleep interval in seconds that will take place between executions of a program. In contrast, the StartCalendarInterval key consists of a dictionary, which can be used to specify regularly scheduled maintenance. This dictionary consists of keys for Hour, Minute, Weekday, and Day (1-31). In both cases, launchd will monitor the processes that it launches and ensure that there are never any overlapping instances.

To create a launchd plist from scratch, luckily we can use our familiar defaults command (assuming a com.318.syncdata defaults domain):

```
sudo defaults write /Library/LaunchDaemons/com.318.syncdata Label com.318.syncdata
sudo defaults write /Library/LaunchDaemons/com.318.syncdata ProgramArguments -array
"/usr/bin/rsync" "-avu" "/Folder1/" "/Folder2/"
sudo defaults write /Library/LaunchDaemons/com.318.syncdata StartInterval -int 3600
sudo plutil -convert xml1 /Library/LaunchDaemons/com.318.syncdata.plist
```

This will create a launchd plist file that performs the following command, every hour (3600 seconds):

```
/usr/bin/rsync -avu /Folder1/ /Folder2/
```

and has the following structure:

```
<?xml version="1.0" encoding="UTF-8"?>
<!DOCTYPE plist PUBLIC "-//Apple//DTD PLIST 1.0//EN"
"http://www.apple.com/DTDs/PropertyList-1.0.dtd">
<plist version="1.0">
<dict>
        <key>Label</key>
        <string>com.318.syncdata</string>
        <key>ProgramArguments</key>
        <array>
                <array>
                        <string>/usr/bin/rsync</string>
                        <string>-avu</string>
                        <string>/Folder1/</string>
                        <string>/Folder2/</string>
                </array>
        </array>
        <key>StartInterval</key>
        <integer>3600</integer>
</dict>
</plist>
```

> **TIP:** You may need to convert the plist file to xml1 format (from binary) prior to viewing or editing. Do so using the syntax plutil -convert xml1 /Library/LaunchDaemons/<file>.plist

As you can see, a program and its arguments are specified in the plist as individual items in an array. Each item will be passed to the command as individual (escaped) strings.

To use a calendar interval, we can specify a StartCalendarInterval dict. First though, we will delete our StartInterval key. While both StartInterval and

StartCalendarInterval entries will be honored, it's not a very elegant way to do automations (though perhaps useful in some circumstances):

```
defaults delete \
/Library/LaunchDaemons/com.318.syncdata StartInterval
defaults write \
/Library/LaunchDaemons/com.318.syncdata StartCalendarInterval -dict Hour -int 3 Minute -int 0 Weekday -int 0
plutil -convert xml1 /Library/LaunchDaemons/com.318.syncdata.plist
```

This will change the automation to fire every Sunday at 3:00 AM. All of these values are strict integer values and no logic is allowed. If you are looking for more flexibility in scheduling, cron might be a good solution.

If you are looking for an easier way to generate launchd plist files, consider the popular GUI tool Lingon, available at http://www.macupdate.com/lingon, which serves the purpose well.

cron

Contrary to the rumors, cron is still alive and well in OS X. The cron daemon itself is fired via launchd. Its plist is found at /System/Library/LaunchDaemons/com.vix.cron.plist. However, this has no impact on the actual operation of cron as you would find on a different system. As with all *nix systems, individual users can configure their own crontab, stored in /var/cron/tabs/. Naturally, each user's crontab runs in the context of that user, but does not necessarily need the user to be logged in (unless a window server connection is needed by the called process). You can edit a user's crontab by running the terminal command crontab -e while logged in. When run, the command will drop you into a vi editor and will open up the user's crontab. A crontab is a file that lists a process and its scheduling information on a single line of text. The schedule is the first part of the line, and includes 5 tab separated values, seen below, that precede the actual cron entry:

```
##Minute Hour  MonthDay(1-31) Month (1-12) Weekday (0-7)   Command
*      *     *        *      *                 /usr/local/bin/myscript.sh
```

> **NOTE:** You can change the default editor from vi to pico by running export EDITOR=pico before you run crontab -e, However, we suggest you give vi a chance as it's a lifesaver when it comes to toolkits.

This code is a valid cron entry. The * designates it will match any condition. Therefore, the above script will fire once per minute, for all of time. Cron also supports ranges and logic:

```
##Minute Hour  MonthDay(1-31) Month (1-12) Weekday (0-7)   Command
*/15    */2   *              *             1,3,5            /usr/local/bin/myscript.sh
```

In the previous entry, the script will run every 15 minutes, every other (even) hour, on Monday, Wednesday, and Friday. While this particular schedule may seem a little silly, it is meant mainly to illustrate the flexibility of the cron scheduling engine. Certain workflows have very particular schedules, and the ability to shape your automations around such schedules is great to have at your fingertips.

Aside from editing individual user crontabs, a global "root" crontab exists, found at /etc/crontab. This file is similar to other crontabs, but it introduces yet another element, the username under which the process will be executed:

```
##Minute Hour  MonthDay(1-31) Month (1-12) Weekday (0-7) User Command
*/15      */2      *            *                1,3,5           root
/usr/local/bin/myscript.sh
```

OS X also has support for the at scheduling engine, though it is disabled by default. For the most part, launchd and cron should be able to meet your needs, but if you must have at, it is there for you. To use it, all you have to do is load its launchd plist file:

```
sudo launchctl load -w /System/Library/LaunchDaemons/com.apple.atrun.plist
```

Now you can use at for scheduling:

```
at now + 1 minute
echo "hello" > /test.txt
job 4 at Tue Jun 9 01:16:00 2009

atq
4       Tue Jun 9 01:16:00 2009
```

Daily, Weekly & Monthly Scripts

Mac OS X ships with a number of scripts that run on a timed interval, including those that run on a daily, weekly, or monthly schedule. These scripts are invoked by entries in the /System/Library/LaunchDaemons directory: com.apple.periodic-daily.plist, com.apple.periodic.weekly.plist, and com.apple.periodic.month.plist, respectively. The periodic scripts are located in /etc/periodic and include the following:

- /etc/periodic/daily/100.clean-logs
- /etc/periodic/daily/110.clean-tmps
- /etc/periodic/daily/130.clean-msgs
- /etc/periodic/daily/430.status-rwho
- /etc/periodic/daily/500.daily
- /etc/periodic/monthly/200.accounting
- /etc/periodic/monthly/500.monthly
- /etc/periodic/monthly/999.local
- /etc/periodic/weekly/310.locate
- /etc/periodic/weekly/320.whatis
- /etc/periodic/weekly/999.local

Triggered Automations

Scheduled automations are nice, but wouldn't it be great to fire certain automations just when you want to? The answer is yes, and the solution is triggers. A trigger is a generic term for any event that can affect, or trigger, the operation of a process. In OS X, there are a number of different triggers that can fire automations. Discussed fairly extensively in Chapter 7, loginhooks are a popular form of userland triggers. Similarly, launchagents can be instructed to run at login. To do this, set the key RunAtLoad to true, using the command that follows.

```
sudo defaults write /Library/LaunchAgents/com.318.syncdata RunAtLoad -bool true
```

Outside of this, OS X has a few facilities we can use to trigger our automations. The most common use of triggers in OS X are filesystem watchers, which fire based on certain filesystem activity. These types of automations in OS X are provided through launchd. Specifically, launchd provides three functions for monitoring filesystem activity:

- *WatchPaths:* An array of file paths that, when modified, will trigger a script.

- *QueueDirectories:* An array of directory paths that will trigger whenever a file is added or removed.

- *StartOnMount:* A bool value that, if set to true, means the script will fire whenever a new filesystem is mounted

For instance, we could utilize this behavior to sync a directory to a volume whenever it is mounted. To perform this task, we will first write our basic script:

```bash
#!/bin/bash

## check for the presence of our volume
if [ "$(df -lh | grep "MyVolumeName" )" ]; then
        rsync -av /Folder1/ /MyVolumeName/Folder1_backup/
fi
```

and then create and edit our plist at /Library/LaunchDaemons/com.318.MyVolumeSync:

```
<?xml version="1.0" encoding="UTF-8"?>
<!DOCTYPE plist PUBLIC "-//Apple//DTD PLIST 1.0//EN"
"http://www.apple.com/DTDs/PropertyList-1.0.dtd">
<plist version="1.0">
<dict>
        <key>Label</key>
        <string>com.318.myvolumesync</string>
        <key>ProgramArguments</key>
        <array>
                <string>/usr/local/bin/myVolumeSync.sh</string>
        </array>
        <key>QueueDirectories</key>
        <array/>
        <key>RunAtLoad</key>
        <false/>
```

```
        <key>StartOnMount</key>
        <true/>
</dict>
</plist>
```

Now, whenever MyVolume is plugged in, the script will fire, pass its test, and perform the sync.

Alternatively, you may want to fire a script whenever a network configuration changes. Network configuration changes occur whenever an interface is taken off or brought online, and therefore can be a good way to trigger a script when a machine first joins your network. This can be handy for initiating client-side backups on laptops that are rarely in the office. By configuring a backup to fire at network change, you can ensure these mostly absent machines don't waste any time in initiating their backup upon returning to the network. Previously this type of script was fired off using a component of the system configuration framework called configd. However, configd kicker scripts are no more, though open source equivalents such as crankd may be useful). Depending on your needs, a simple launchd watcher-called script should suffice for network changes.

Self-Destructing Scripts

In some cases, you may want your script to run only once and then remove all traces that it ever existed on a system. In such cases, you can actually have the script delete itself. Because the entire script is loaded into memory, this won't affect the operation of the script's code, the file will just disappear after execution. This can be very handy if you have sensitive data in the script. For instance, a bind script will likely contain a password and it would be undesirable to leave that sitting around on every machine in the fleet, even if the credentials have extremely limited access. To remove a script when it is complete, you can just put the following line at the very end of the script:

```
srm "$0"
```

The srm command is an Apple-provided equivalent of the rm command but will perform a "secure erase" by writing new, random data over the file's previous data to limit it's recoverability.

The same logic can be applied to launchd items. If you want to deploy a one-time login action, you can make the launchd item itself self-destructing. For example, the launchagent below will enable Apple Remote Desktop (ARD), but when it's done it will remove itself. This is done by chaining multiple commands together via a single ProgramArgument string:

```
<plist version="1.0">
<dict>
        <key>Disabled</key>
        <false/>
        <key>Label</key>
        <string>net.walledcity.enableard</string>
        <key>OnDemand</key>
        <false/>
```

```
        <key>ProgramArguments</key>
        <array>
                <string>bash</string>
                <string>-c</string>
                <string>/System/Library/CoreServices/RemoteManagement/⏎
ARDAgent.app/Contents/Resources/kickstart -configure -access -on -privs⏎
 -all -users adm_mako ;
/System/Library/CoreServices/RemoteManagement/ARDAgent.app/Contents/Resources/⏎
kickstart -configure -clientopts -setdirlogins -dirlogins yes -setdirgroups⏎
 -dirgroups ardadmin ; /System/Library/CoreServices/RemoteManagement/⏎
ARDAgent.app/Contents/Resources/kickstart -activate ;
/System/Library/CoreServices/RemoteManagement/ARDAgent.app/Contents/Resources/⏎
kickstart -configure -allowAccessFor -specifiedUsers -setreqperm yes;
/bin/launchctl unload /Library/LaunchDaemons/net.walledcity.enableard.plist;
/usr/bin/srm /Library/LaunchDaemons/net.walledcity.enableard.plist
sleep 60;
exit 0</string>
        </array>
</dict>
</plist>
```

> **NOTE:** In most UNIX shells, the semicolon (;) can be used to separate individual commands on a single line. When separating commands via a semicolon, once the first command finishes running, regardless of its exit state, the next program will fire.

Automating User Creation from a Third-Party Database

In some cases, you may need to integrate an OS X directory system with a third-party information system, such as an employee database. In an education environment, for example, tens or hundreds of thousands of student records exist, with new records being added every day. All of this user information exists largely in third-party databases, and you may need to ensure that records added to one system can easily be added to Open Directory.

To successfully import the data, you must get it into an acceptable format. Importing data into Open Directory can be performed from the GUI with Workgroup Manager, which supports import of data in a delimited format, with customizable attribute and record delimiters. This makes it a decently flexible tool for importing from third-party databases, as most of these systems can import into a delimited format of some sort, most commonly csv (comma separated values). Once you have a csv file in hand, you can import the file into the system. Consider a csv file with the following data structure:

```
shortname,fname,lname,pass
jdoe,John,Doe,JDo9876
jsmith,Jane,Smith,JDo9876
```

This is about as clean as csv data gets. To import the file, you can open up Workgroup Manager, connect to your OD master, and select Import from the Server menu. From there, you can map the attribute delimiter (,) and the record delimiter (Newline, hex value of 0x0A). If there is a problem with the import, you can check the dsimport log found at ~/Library/Logs/ImportExport/.

> **NOTE:** The delimiter options in Workgroup manager allow for only a single byte of data. Because of this, you can't specify a DOS-style line delimiter, which has an ASCII value of \n\r and a hex value of 0x0D0A and as such, can't directly be imported via Workgroup Manager. You can convert line delimiters to UNIX style (\n, 0x0A) with the following command: perl -p -i -e 's/\r\n/\n/g' /thefile.csv. Some programs such as Excel save csv files with historic Macintosh-style line delimiters (\r). These files can be imported with the delimiter hex value of 0x0D.

However, the premise of this section is to help automate this process, and having to manually specify delimiters each time you do an import isn't the cleanest way to work. Thus, we resort to the command line for automation. Importing data from the command line requires data to be formatted as a dsimport file, a colon-delimited format with an Open Directory-specific header:

```
0x0A 0x5C 0x2C 0x3A dsRecTypeStandard:Users 4 dsAttrTypeStandard:RecordName↵
dsAttrTypeStandard:FirstName dsAttrTypeStandard:LastName dsAttrTypeStandard:Password
```

This data consists of a number of values. In this code, the first value, 0x0A, denotes the record delimiter (a Unix newline \n). The second value, 0x5C, specifies the escape character (a standard backslash \), which is used for escaping the attribute delimiter should its value actually be required for a field. For instance, importing computer data involves importing MAC addresses, which contain a colon. If your attribute delimiter is a colon, you must escape it with the character specified, so 00:50:56:c0:00:08 must be represented as 00\:50\:56\:c0\:00\:08.

The next value in the header, 0x2C, is the attribute/field delimiter (in this case, a comma ,). 0x3A then specifies the attribute value delimiter, used if a particular field/attribute contains more than one value. The next value, dsRecTypeStandard:Users, specifies the record type for import. You can use this tool to import Users, Groups, Computers, ComputerGroups or ComputerLists using those respective values. Next, you specify the number of columns in your import file (4), and the header for each column. The headers consist of dsAttributeStandard entries, which are records abstracted for use by the Directory Services API. These attributes do not correspond to LDAP attributes directly, but rather the abstracted field name. In this example, we are specifying four headers, RecordName (shortname), FirstName, LastName, and Password. A header of IGNORE can be set here to ignore the column of data. Once you specify headers, the rest of the file should consist of record and attribute data conforming to the specified delimiters.

If you have programmatic control over your information system, or if its export options are decently featured, you may be able to craft your own dsimport file. If not, you'll need to process your exports so that they can conform for import. To do so, you have a few options, and luckily one of them is included with this book. In the book's resource section, the csvtowgm Python script can be used to process your own csv-delimited outputs, and convert them to dsimport-compatible import files. The csvtowgm script accepts data from a csv file, or it can read it from the stdin data stream. Its options are best displayed through the program's help page:

```
csvToWGM: converts a csv delimited import file into a dsimport compatible file

Syntax:
    csvToWGM [-i infile] [-o outfile] [-f format] [-h headers]

Flags:
    -i infile        -- path to csv import file
    -o outfile       -- destination path for generated dsimport-compatible output file
    -d delimiter  -- The field delimeter used in your data, default ","
    -h headers    -- specify headers if they are not included in the first line of
                         import file. This should be a comma delimited string.
    -f format     -- Use specified config file. If none is specified, the format
                         "users" is assumed. Supported formats:
                             "users"
                             "computers"
```

In its basic usage, you can simply pass csvtowgm a user import file for processing and an output path to save the file:

```
csvtowgm -i ~/Documents/users.csv -o ~/Documents/users_dsimport.txt
```

csvtowgm will try its best to determine header information from the first line in your file. Optimally, headers will be identical to the dsAttrTypeStandard header. You can find the header resolution determined by csvtowgm by consulting its log file after running the import. The log file will contain an entry specifying the header resolution that was used by the import. Specifically, look for the line:

```
INFO Importing headers: '['realname', ' shortname', ' password']' as: '['RealName', ↵
 'RecordName', 'Password']'
```

Here we are using the csv data specified earlier in this section. We can see the imported headers: realname, shortname, and password, and see their respective mappings. If the system does not properly recognize a header, it will specify a header of IGNORE, and the data will not get imported. To process the file for import, you can specify your headers in comma-separated arguments passed to csvtowgm:

```
csvtowgm -i ~/Documents/users.csv -o ~/Documents/users_dsimport.txt -h↵
 RealName,RecordName,Password
```

This will process the file using fixed headers. You can also use csvtowgm to process computer records. Consider the following computer data file:

```
name,ethernetid
hax.lbc,00:50:56:c0:00:08
helyx.lbc,00:50:56:c0:00:01
```

To import this file, the process is identical to that for users, though we instead specify the computer format using the –f flag:

```
csvtowgm -i ~/Documents/machines.csv -o ~/Documents/machines_dsimport.txt -f computers
```

In some cases, you may need some more advanced features, such as field-data generators or other data-population mechanisms. Currently, csvtowgm simply does basic file conversion and has only basic facilities to generate data. If data generation is a need of yours, consider using Passenger (`http://macinmind.com`), a GUI utility for generating dsimport-compatible files.

Once you have data in a `dsimport`-compatible file, you must import that data into your system. You can do this via the `dsimport` command, which is fairly straightforward and has three mandatory parameters: filepath, nodepath (the target Directory node for import `/LDAPv3/odserver.myco.com`), and the conflict resolution options. A conflict occurs when an existing record contains a record name, UID, or GID that's the same as a new record to be imported. There are five different values that can be provided for conflict resolution:

- *O:* Overwrite an existing record if it contains a matching record name, UID, or GID.

- *M:* Merge data with any existing records. Create the record if it does not exist.

- *I:* Ignore the new record if there is a conflict.

- *A:* Append data to an existing record; do not create a new record if it does not exist

- *N:* Skip conflict detection. This option can be slow and problematic.

So, to import a `dsimport` file into an Open Directory system, use the following command:

```
dsimport ~/Documents/users_dsimport.txt /LDAPv3/odserver.myco.com M --userpreset "Staff ↵
Member" --username diradmin --password 'mydiradmin password'
```

In this example, we are importing a user file into our LDAP directory using a merge. Here, we specify the –userpreset flag, which allows us to set up a preset in Workgroup manager to establish group memberships, home directory settings, and mail and print settings. (You can create presets using Workgroup Manager.) In this command, we also supply our `diradmin` credentials to provide access for the import itself, presenting one of the biggest barriers to full automation for this process: any automated processes will need to have a directory administrator's credentials embedded.

However, embedding administrator credentials in a script to automate import from a csv is not the only issue with a fully automated user-generation process. For instance, say you set up a `launchdaemon` with a `QueueDirectory` entry, which watches a directory for any new files from your information system, passes them to `csvtowgm`, and then uses the resulting file for import via `dsimport`. Such a script might look something like this:

```
#!/bin/bash

PATH=/bin;/usr/bin;/usr/local/bin

## set our variables
declare -x watchFolder="/Library/dsimportwatchdir"
declare -x dirNode="/LDAPv3/odserver.myco.com"
```

```
## create our folder
mkdir -p "$watchFolder" &> /dev/null

## loop through all of the csv files in our watch folder, format them,
## import them, delete the formatted versions, and copy the original
## into an archive directory.
for file in $(ls -1 "$watchFolder" | grep ".csv"); do
        declare -x tempFile=$(mktemp /tmp/dsimport_XXXXX)
        cat "$watchFolder/$file" | csvtowgm -o "$tempFile"
        csvtowgmResultCode=$?
        if [ $csvtowgmResultCode == 0 ]; then
                dsimport "$tempFile" "$dirNode" M -username importadmin -password
'importpassword'
                rm "$tempFile"
                mkdir "$watchFolder/archive/" &> /dev/null
                mv "$watchFolder/$file" "$watchFolder/archive/"
        else
                echo "Error generating import file! error num: $csvtowgmResultCode"
                exit $csvtowgmResultCode
        fi
done
```

This code would get the job done, but it does present numerous concerns. First and foremost, we are trusting the security of our user base to the contents of this folder. By using a merge import, it would certainly be possible for a file to be dropped into our watchfolder that completely trashes our directory, potentially overriding data for admin accounts or simply generating accounts for itself.

Due to concerns such as these, the exact level of desired automation will greatly vary from environment to environment and will depend on the sensitivity of the data housed by the system and the security requirements set forth by the organization. *A fully automated import process such as this is not advisable in any environment where security is a concern.* However, even if the final dsimport is a manual step, simply by generating dsimport-style import files you are greatly reducing the possibility for human error, streamlining the import process, and ensuring more consistent results.

> **Note:** A common automation would also be to tailor this same script to create computers based on imaging events on a live system. For example, an imaged computer can write a text file or copy its computer information into a centralized database to aid in managed preferences. Additionally, the imaged system could automatically connect to the patch management framework you are utilizing. Finally, for larger installations where users are actually created in out-of-band solutions (e.g., Oracle-based Student Management System or SAP-based ERP solution) you can automatically generate user accounts based on events from those databases.

Logging

If your script does anything more than a basic task, it is a good idea to log your output. Logging output can be useful to ensure that any automations are working as they should be, and to catch any errors that are discovered during the operation of your scripts. Likewise, log files can prove extremely handy for historic evaluation of performance and operation.

Depending on your script, you may want to log to ~/Library/Logs, /Library/Logs, or /var/log. So how do you know which to log to? ~/Library/Logs can be used whenever a script is initiated in userland, such as through a LaunchAgent or a user-specific crontab. For the majority of scripts, though, which likely run with root privileges, Apple's addition of a global /Library/Logs to the equation dilutes the situation a bit, as /var/log is the historic logging directory for many Unix and Linux systems and is even utilized by many Apple utilities. For instance, Disk Utility logs disk repair information to /var/log/fsck_hfs.log, and Apple's Installer app and Software Update app both log to /var/log/install.log.

Logging to an output file can be achieved in a couple of different ways. First, you can simply use the echo command and redirect its output to your log file. For instance:

```
logFile="/var/log/myprogram.log"
echo "My Program: starting rsync!" >> "$logFile"
```

This works great for sending updates to a log file, and you can use the same type of technique with any command-line program:

```
rsync -avu /folder1/ /folder1_copy/ &>> "$logFile"
```

Here, we utilize the redirect operator &>>, which redirects both stdout and stderr streams to /var/log/myprogram.log, appending to the end of the file. In this instance, we use this redirection if rsync outputs any errors; we want the errors to be written to our log.

Alternatively, you can redirect all output streams of a script to a certain file in one line. This provides a quick and easy way to ensure logging of all of your script's events. To implement global redirects to your script, add the following line after your hashbang and prior to the implementation of any commands or log statements:

```
logFile="/var/log/myprogram.log"
exec &>> "$logFile"
##From here on, all of our output will be redirected to our log file.
```

It may also be desirable to send log messages to syslog. This provides the added benefit of time-stamping output, and provides you with the ability to integrate your script logging with a more complex syslog system, should your organization employ one. To send messages to syslog, use the logger command:

```
logger -t "$0" -p user.notice -s "hello"
```

The -p flag tells logger to log using user.notice priority, which syslog will output to the system log, /var/log/system.log:

```
Sep  7 21:23:31 helyx /usr/local/bin/myprogram.sh[1461]: hello
```

The priority user.notice is the default priority, and in this case, the entire -p user.notice flag can be omitted; it is added mainly to illustrate how to define custom logging priorities should you want to integrate with a more complex syslog system. The string "hello" is also output to the console, due to running logger with the -s flag. This makes it extremely handy for scripts that might be run by hand. By using logger instead of echo and global redirects, you can ensure that users receive feedback from your program directly in the terminal. In addition, by utilizing syslog, your scripts will be more adaptable, should you adopt a more capable logging system.

Working with Date and Time

There are many instances where it can be beneficial to work with dates in your script. At a terminal prompt, it is really straight forward to grab the date—simply use the date command with no arguments and you will get something similar to the following, including the day, date, time (with seconds), time zone and year:

```
Tue Apr 15 00:40:07 CDT 2009
```

In a shell script, this output can be fairly challenging to parse, especially in cases where you need to do calculations based upon the time. Here we're going to grab the current system date from ESX, OS X, or Linux (or any OS really) and then use a variable, currentdate, to put that date into a pretty standard format, YYYYMMDD:

```
declare -x currentdate="$(date "+%Y%m%d")"
```

This will set the value of current date to:

```
20090415
```

Now, in our shell script, we can create files, add lines to files, and so forth with the shortened date stamp. Some of you will be using log analyzers that depend, for example, on Unix epoch time. To grab the date formatted as such, use the following command:

```
currentdate="$(date +"%s")"
```

Unix epoch time is a numerical value representing the number of seconds since January 1, 1970, UTC. It is extremely useful if you want to perform basic math on time, as this value can be used in base 10 arithmetic. For instance, you can use it in your script to track the amount of time a process takes, and then output as you please:

```
#!/bin/bash
starttime="$(date +"%s")"

## redirect all output to my logfile
exec &>> /var/log/myscript.log

ditto /folder1/ /folder2/

## do our time calculations
endtime=$(date +'%s')
totaltime=$(expr $endtime - $starttime)
```

```
## format time values in human readable format
if [ $totaltime -ge 7200 ]; then
    hours=$(expr $totaltime / 3600)
    adjtime=$(expr $totaltime % 3600)
    hourmsg="$hours hours"
else
    adjtime=$totaltime
fi

min=$(expr $adjtime / 60)
secs=$(expr $adjtime % 60)
timemsg="$min minutes $secs seconds"
if [ "$status" = 0 ]; then
        echo "$instance Finished with no errors! Duration: $hourmsg $timemsg"
else
        echo "$instance Encountered error code: $status Duration: $hourmsg $timemsg"
fi
```

The date command isn't used as much to set time anymore, since most systems rely on a Network Time Protocol (NTP) server to supply date and time information. However, it is worth noting that the date command can also be used to set the time on a computer.

Automating System Tasks

Configuring Local Administrative Permissions

One thing you may notice after working with Open Directory is that there is no good way to define local administrator access to desktops via an Open Directory group. You can add users to the Open Directory Admin group, but due to the way that the DS Search Path is traversed (which is explained in Chapter 2), OS X desktops will search the local admin group for many administrative checks. Unlike the Active Directory plug-in, the LDAPv3 plug-in does not provide the ability to specify a local administrative group mapping. So, you, the administrator, are left to your own devices to accomplish this task. Luckily, we have just what you need. The following script is also available via digital download (file 8_setNetworkAdminRights.sh).

```
#!/bin/bash

###########################
##
## Local Permissioning script for setting local administrative groups
## for system and ARD admin access. Compatible with 10.5, and 10.6
## Uses dseditgroup to modify the active systems group membership. As
## Such, it can only operate on the active system volume.
##
## Written by Beau Hunter
## 04/04/09   beauh@mac.com
##
#########################################################
```

```
declare -x version=08310901
export PATH="/usr/bin:/bin:/usr/sbin:/sbin"

## vars
## localAdminGroup: specify network group to provide local admin access to
declare -x localAdminGroup="od_desktopadmins"

## setupLocalARDGroups: if '1', ard access groups
## will be created in local Directory Services
declare -x -i setupLocalARDGroups=1

## resetARD: if '1', ARD access will be configured
declare -x -i configARD=1

## resetARD: if '1', all ARD access privileges will be reset
declare -x -i resetARD=1

## ardAdminUser: the specified user will be have ARD admin access
declare -x ardAdminUser="hax_admin"

## ardAdminGroup: the specified group will be given ARD admin access
declare -x ardAdminGroup="mobo"

## ardInteractGroup: the specified group will be given ARD interact access
declare -x ardInteractGroup="monitors"


## static and system vars
declare -x scriptName=setNetworkAdminRights
declare -x theDate=$(date +'%Y%m%d')
declare -x -i isTiger="$(sw_vers | grep -c 10.4)"
declare -x -i isLeopard="$(sw_vers | grep -c 10.5)"
declare -x -i isSnowLeopard="$(sw_vers | grep -c 10.6)"
declare -x ARDVersion="$(defaults read ←
/System/Library/CoreServices/RemoteManagement/ARDAgent.app/Contents/Info ←
CFBundleShortVersionString)"
declare -x -i ARDMajorVersion="$(echo "$ARDVersion" | awk -F. '{print $1}')"
declare -x -i ARDMinorVersion="$(echo "$ARDVersion" | awk -F. '{print $2}')"

function getGUIDforGroup() {
    ## outputs a GUID for passed group name
    declare -x theGroupName="$1"
    declare -x GUID="$(/usr/bin/dscl /Search read /Groups/"$theGroupName" GeneratedUID | ←
awk '{print $2}')"
    if [ ! -z "$GUID" ]; then
        echo $GUID
    else
        logger -s -t "$scriptName" "Error! Could not determine GUID for group←
\"$theGroupName\""
        return 1
    fi
    return 0
}
```

```
if [ "$USER" != root ]; then
    echo "Must run as root user, exiting!!"
    exit 1
fi


if [ ! -z "$localAdminGroup" ]; then
        GUID=$(getGUIDforGroup "$localAdminGroup")
    if [ $? == 0 ]; then
        logger -s -t "$scriptName" "Nesting Directory Group: $localAdminGroup into local ↵
Group: admin"
        /usr/sbin/dseditgroup -o edit -a "${localAdminGroup:?}" -t group admin
    else
        logger -s -t "$scriptName" "Error! Could not determine GUID for group ↵
\"$localAdminGroup\""
    fi
fi

if [ $configARD -eq 1 ]; then
            if [ $setupLocalARDGroups -eq 1 ]; then
        if [ "$isSnowLeopard" -ge 1 ]; then
            ardAdminLocalGroup="com.apple.local.ard_admin"
            ardInteractLocalGroup="com.apple.local.ard_interact"
        else
            ardAdminLocalGroup="ard_admin"
            ardInteractLocalGroup="ard_interact"
        fi
            else
            ardAdminLocalGroup=$ardAdminGroup
            ardInteractLocalGroup=$ardInteractGroup
        fi

    ## Process our Admin Group
    if [ ! -z "$ardAdminGroup" ]; then
        GUID=$(getGUIDforGroup "$ardAdminGroup")
        if [ $? == 0 ]; then
                if [ $setupLocalARDGroups -eq 1 ]; then
                logger -s -t "$scriptName" "Nesting Directory Group: $ardAdminGroup into ↵
local Group: $ardAdminLocalGroup"
                /usr/bin/dscl . read /Groups/$ardAdminLocalGroup &> /dev/null || ↵
/usr/sbin/dseditgroup -o create -i 115 -g 2806364B-49F6-4F18-89F9-D159BB93B08C ↵
$ardAdminLocalGroup
                /usr/sbin/dseditgroup -o edit -a "${ardAdminGroup:?}" -t group ↵
$ardAdminLocalGroup
            fi
        else
            logger -s -t "$scriptName" "Error! Failed to create Local ARD Admin Group: ↵
$ardAdminLocalGroup"
            errorCode=1
        fi
    fi
    ## Process our Interact Group
    if [ ! -z "$ardInteractGroup" ]; then
        GUID=$(getGUIDforGroup "$ardInteractGroup")
        if [ $? == 0 ]; then
```

```
            if [ $setupLocalARDGroups -eq 1 ]; then
                logger -s -t "$scriptName" "Nesting Directory Group: ↵
$ardInteractGroup into local Group:$ardInteractLocalGroup"
                /usr/bin/dscl . read /Groups/"$ardInteractLocalGroup" &> /dev/null || ↵
/usr/sbin/dseditgroup -o create -i 116 -g 2806364B-49F6-4F18-89F9-D159BB93B08D ↵
"$ardInteractLocalGroup"
                /usr/sbin/dseditgroup -o edit -a "$ardInteractGroup" -t group ↵
"$ardInteractLocalGroup"
            else
                ardInteractLocalGroup=$ardInteractGroup
            fi
        else
            logger -s -t "$scriptName" "Error! Failed to create Local ARD Interact
Group"
            errorCode=2
        fi
    fi
    ## Process our kickstart commands
    kickstart="/System/Library/CoreServices/RemoteManagement/↵
ARDAgent.app/Contents/Resources/kickstart"
    if [ $resetARD -eq 1 ]; then
        logger -s -t "$scriptName" "Resetting ARD permissions"
        "$kickstart" -uninstall -settings
        "$kickstart" -configure -access -off
    fi
    if [ ! -z "$ardAdminUser" ]; then
        id "$ardAdminUser" &> /dev/null
        if [ $? == 0 ]; then
            logger -s -t "$scriptName" "Setting ARD access for user \"$ardAdminUser\""
            "$kickstart" -configure -access -on -users "$ardAdminUser" -privs -all
        else
            logger -s -t "$scriptName" "Could not resolve user \"$ardAdminUser\""
            errorCode=3
        fi
    fi


    ## reset Directory Services and flush cache
    /usr/bin/dscacheutil -flushcache
    /usr/bin/killall DirectoryService
    sleep 2
    id &> /dev/null

    if ( [ ! -z "$ardAdminGroup" ] && [ ! -z "$ardInteractGroup" ] ); then
        logger -s -t "$scriptName" "Setting ARD access for groups ↵
$ardAdminLocalGroup,$ardInteractLocalGroup"
    elif [ ! -z "$ardAdminGroup" ]; then
        logger -s -t "$scriptName" "Setting ARD access for groups $ardAdminLocalGroup"
    elif [ ! -z "$ardInteractGroup" ]; then
        logger -s -t "$scriptName" "Setting ARD access for groups
$ardInteractLocalGroup"
    fi

    if ( [ $ARDMajorVersion -eq 3 ] && [ $ARDMinorVersion -ge 3 ]); then
        logger -s -t "$scriptName" "Kickstart -configure -clientopts -setdirlogins -↵
dirlogins yes -restart -agent"
```

```
        "$kickstart" -configure -clientopts -setdirlogins -dirlogins yes -restart -agent
    elif ( [ $ARDMajorVersion -eq 3 ] ) ; then
        logger -s -t "$scriptName" "Kickstart -configure -clientopts -setdirlogins -↵
dirlogins yes -setdirgroups -dirgroups $ardAdminLocalGroup,$ardInteractLocalGroup ↵
-restart -agent"
        "$kickstart" -configure -clientopts -setdirlogins -dirlogins yes -setdirgroups -↵
dirgroups $ardAdminLocalGroup,$ardInteractLocalGroup -restart -agent
    else
        logger -s -t "$scriptName" "ARD Version: $ARDVersion not supported!"
        exit 5
    fi
fi
```

Allow Local Users to Manage Printers

You can also provide administrative access to a number of granular functions within Mac OS X by adding a user to the corresponding local group, rather than having a bunch of extraneous administrative users on your system. A great example is one of the ways to allow print queue management in Mac OS X. The Managed Client framework (MCX) has the ability to allow a user to add a printer. The following script was largely created to address an issue with older OS X 10.5-based machines where allowing users to modify printer lists via MCX was sometimes problematic. However, the script is useful to provide granular control to printing functions. Another way to allow a user to add printers and also let them manage queues is to add a user to the lpadmin group, (the group historically used for managing "line printers" that now refers to all printers). The lpadmin group provides capabilities for numerous printing functions, such as resuming print queues, which is not available to standard users. Printing in OS X is supplied via CUPS, which provides granular access to numerous functions. The following script, also available via digital download (file 8_setPrinterAdminRights.sh), adds a specified Open Directory group into the local _lpadmin group, thereby granting directory users lpadmin rights.

```
#!/bin/sh

PATH=/bin:/sbin:/usr/bin:/usr/sbin

## only members of the following group will be given printer admin rights
declare -x printAdminGroup="staff"

## modifies cupsd.conf to NOT require admin group membership to add printers,
## mainly needed for early versions of 10.5 where the equivalent MCX function
## was unstable.
declare -x modifyCupsdDotConf=false


###### script usage vars, should need to make changes  beyond this point. ######


declare -x theDate=`date +'%m%d%y'`
declare -x version="20090721_20:03"
declare -x scriptTag="setPrinterAdminRights"
```

```
logger -s -t "$scriptTag" "Executing $0 v.$version..."


### Add printer admin  ###

## Make sure an admin group was specified
if [ -z "$printAdminGroup" ]; then
        logger -s -t "$scriptTag" "ERROR: No print admin group specified, exiting!"
        exit 1
fi

## Add specified admin group to local lpadmin group
logger -s -t "$scriptTag" "Adding $printAdminGroup to lpadmin group."
dseditgroup -o edit -a "$printAdminGroup" -t group lpadmin
addMemberReturnCode=$?
if [ $addMemberReturnCode == 0 ]; then
        logger -s -t "$scriptTag" "Successfully added $printAdminGroup to lpadmin"
else
        logger -s -t "$scriptTag" "Failed to add $printAdminGroup to lpadmin, returnCode:
↵
$addMemberReturnCode"
fi


## modify our cupsd.conf file if applicable, this gives lpadmin permissions to
add/modify ↵
printers
if [ ${modifyCupsdDotConf:?} == "true" ]; then
        logger -s -t "$scriptTag" "Granting group lpadmin rights to add printers in ↵
cupsd.conf!"
        perl -OOpe 's/(<Limit CUPS-Add-Modify-Printer.*?)(AuthType.*)(Require user)( ↵
\@SYSTEM$)(.*?<\/Limit>)/$1$3 \@SYSTEM \@lpadmin$5/ms' -i /etc/cups/cupsd.conf
else
        logger -s -t "$scriptTag" "cupsd.conf not being touched"
        killall cupsd
fi
```

Home Folder Permission Maintenance

If you maintain a large number of home directories, you may want to periodically flush the filesystem structure on the system to guarantee proper access restrictions are in place. This can be useful, for instance, to protect files and folders that users add directly into the root of their home directory, often with global read access. Unwitting users can place sensitive data inside these folders, not realizing they are exposed to every use in the system. (User home folder structure is covered in depth in Chapter 7.)

The script listed in this section can be used to fix such permissions problems on home folders. The homeDirectories variable defines all root home folders on the machine in question and allows for a customizable depth. For instance, an institution might have two home folder sharepoints on an AFP server, say mapped to /studenthomes1 and /studenthomes2. Inside these folders, each home folder might contain a list of subdirectories denoting the graduation year of a student, each of which contain user home directories. On top of all this, you have the local /Users sharepoint, which we will add to the system as an example. To address these three home folders, we would specify the following homeDirectories value:

```
homeDirectories="/studenthomes1:1,/studenthomes2:1,/Users:0"
```

Using these values, the script will iterate through each of the specified folders, repairing home folders for each user.

You can also use this script to employ ACLs for administrative access, perhaps for a group of users—supervisors —who need read/write access to all User home folders. Alternatively, you might want to give your filesystemadmins group access to all data on the share. This is specified via the aclGroups variable, and allows you to indicate one of three access levels: fc (equivalent to a Full Control ACE), rw (equivalent to a Read/Write ACE), ro (equivalent to Read Only). (See Chapter 4 for more information on ACLs.) Our desired access rights would be accomplished with the following aclGroups entry:

```
declare -x aclGroups="filesystemadmins:fc,supervisors:rw"
```

The script also has a variable removeOrphans that, when set to true, will remove any file or folder found at the specified home folder depth that is not associated with an active user in the system. This check will fail if the name of the folder is not equivalent to an active user's shortname. This can be a very handy function if you have a large number of users to manage and want to ensure that former users' folders are cleaned from the system.

By setting these variables to the desired values in the following script (which is also available via digital download, file 8_cleanupHomeFolders), we can ensure that these groups have the appropriate access to all user home folders, and also that user data has complete confidentiality to the home folder's owner, outside of the ~/Public and ~/Sites directories. The script ensures that these folders have the appropriate access rights.

```
#!/bin/sh

##########  Home Directory Privilege Repair Script ####################
##   Written by Beau Hunter  08/22/08
##   beauh@mac.com
##
##   Script which automates the management of home directory permissions
##   It's typical usage is to ensure proper permissions on every user's
##   home directory. That is, mode 700 to all home folders except ~/Public
##   and ~/Sites. Additionally, if useACLs is set to true, then ACE's will
##   be pushed to each home directory for its respective user.
##
##   On top of this, you can specify global admin groups via the aclGroups
##   variable, in addition to a permission set to apply to each group.
##
##   The tool can be used to cleanup stale home
##   folders for non-existent users by placing the homes in an orphanage
##   folder.
##
######################################################################
```

```
PATH=/bin:/sbin:/usr/bin:/usr/sbin

## homeDirectories: Comma separated list of home roots, specify the
## depth via a colon. For instance, a standard
## OS X local home folder has user homes directly in
## /Users, thus I could specify a homeLoc of
## /Users:0. However, a depth of 0 is the default
## depth so it can be omitted.
declare -x homeDirectories="/testUsers:1"

declare -x repairPrivs=true
declare -x removeACLs=true
declare -x useACLs=true


## $aclGroups Groups sets an inherited ACL across $homeLoc, groups should be
## comma delimited. Access levels can be delimited with a colon,
## supported values are: "fc", "rw", and "ro". Default is rw.
## Example:
## aclGroups="admin:fc,powerusers:rw,rousers:ro"

declare -x aclGroups="admin:fc,staff:rw"
declare -x removeOrphans=true ## Remove non-user directories from the path.
declare -x orphanageName="orphanage" ## the name of the orphanage folder


#### int script vars, probably don't need to make changes beyond this point ####

declare -x date=`date +'%m%d%y'`
declare -x version="20080822_12:03"
declare -x scriptTag="$(basename "$0")"

logger -s -t "$scriptTag" "Executing script: $scriptTag v.$version"


function repairPrivs() {
        ## repair privileges on all items in a particular home folder
        ## expects home profiles based on users shortname.
        ## if the directory name is not resolvable as a user, we skip
        ## A directory path can be passed as a variable, otherwise
     ## executes based on PWD

    declare -x scriptTag="$scriptTag:repairPrivs()"


    if [ -n "$1" ]; then
        declare -x passedDirectory=$1
        if [ -d "$passedDirectory" ]; then
            cd "$passedDirectory"
        else
            logger -s -t "$scriptTag" "structureForOSX() passed directory: ↵
\"$passedDirectory\" does not exist!"
            return 1
        fi
    fi
```

```
        logger -s -t "$scriptTag" "Validating users in \"$(pwd)\" for privilege repair"

        IFS=$'\n'
        for fileObject in `ls | grep -v .DS_Store | grep -v "$orphanageName" | egrep -v ↵
'^\.'`; do
                #logger -s -t "$scriptTag" "Validating $fileObject for priviledge repair"
                id "$fileObject" &> /dev/null
                if [ $? == 0 ]; then
                        #logger -s -t "$scriptTag" " - validation passed, changing ↵
permissions for $fileObject at `pwd`/$fileObject"
                        logger -s -t "$scriptTag" " Validation passed for $fileObject, ↵
changing permissions"

                else
                        logger -s -t "$scriptTag" " Validation failed for '$fileObject', ↵
it is an orphan "

                        ## get our pwd and get our current directory. We
                        ## mimic our structure in the orphanage, this script
                        ## needs more facilities to handle depth properly.

                        declare -x PWD="$(pwd)"

                if [ "$homeDepth" == 0 ]; then
                    declare -x orphanDir="$homeLoc/$orphanageName"
                else
                    declare -x orphanDir="$homeLoc/$orphanageName/$(basename "$PWD")"
                fi

                        if [ "$removeOrphans" == true ]; then
                                logger -s -t "$scriptTag" " - Placing $fileObject in ↵
orphanage:$orphanDir!"
                                if [ ! -d "${orphanDir:?}" ]; then
                                        mkdir -p "${orphanDir:?}"
                                        if [ $? != 0 ]; then
                                                logger -s -t "$scriptTag" " - ERROR: ↵
 Could not create $orphanDir, not moving!"
                                                continue
                                        fi
                                fi

                                mv "$fileObject" ${orphanDir:?}/
                                if [ $? != 0 ]; then
                                        logger -s -t "$scriptTag" " - ERROR: ↵
Could not move user home \"$fileObject\" to orphanage!"
                                fi
                        fi
                        continue
                fi

                #echo chown -R "$fileObject":admin "$fileObject"
                chown -f -R "$fileObject":admin "$fileObject"
                if [ ${removeACLs:?} == "true" ]; then
                        #logger -s -t "$scriptTag" " - removing ACL's"
```

```
                        chmod -f -R -N "$fileObject"
                fi

                ## Apply ACLs to the user dir, we do an explicit ACE at the user's home
                ## and then apply inherited ACLs to children.
                if [ ${useACLs:?} == "true" ]; then
                        logger -s -t "$scriptTag" "  - applying user ACL's"
                        chmod +a "$fileObject:allow:list,add_file,search,delete, ↵
add_subdirectory,delete_child,readattr,writeattr,readextattr,writeextattr, ↵
readsecurity,writesecurity,chown,file_inherit,directory_inherit" "$fileObject"
                        chmod -f -R +ai "$fileObject:allow:list,add_file,search,delete, ↵
add_subdirectory,delete_child,readattr,writeattr,readextattr,writeextattr, ↵
readsecurity,writesecurity,chown,file_inherit,directory_inherit" "$fileObject"/*
                fi

                chmod 755 "$fileObject"
                chmod -R 700 "$fileObject"/*
                if [ -d "$fileObject"/Sites ]; then
                        chmod -R 775 "$fileObject"/Sites
                fi
                if [ -d "$fileObject"/Public ]; then
                        chmod -R 775 "$fileObject"/Public
                        chmod -R 773 "$fileObject"/Public/Drop\ Box
                fi
        done
    ## if we were passed a directory, traverse out of it
    if [ -n "$passedDirectory" ]; then
        cd "$OLDPWD"
    fi
} ## end repairPrivs()

function setACLForGroup() {
        ## passes $directory as first argument, $group as second argument, and
$permissions
        ## this sets an explicit ACL at $directory, with all children receiving an ↵
'inherited' ACL
        ## we accept several different permission types:
    ## "fc"(Full Control)
    ## "rw" (Read and Write)
    ## "ro" (Read Only)
    ## "append" (Append Only)

        declare -x directory=$1
        declare -x group=$2
        declare -x permissions=$3
    declare -x scriptTag="$scriptTag:setACLForGroup()"

    logger -s -t "$scriptTag" "Attempting to apply: ACL to dir:$directory for group: ↵
$group with perms:$permissions"


        ## sanity check our directory
        if [ ! -d "$directory" ]; then
                logger -s -t "$scriptTag" " - ERROR: Could not apply ACL.. dir: ↵
$directory does not exist!"
```

```
                return 1
        fi

        ## sanity check our group
        dscl /Search read /Groups/"$group" name &> /dev/null
        dsclCode=$?
        if [ $dsclCode != 0 ]; then
                logger -s -t "$scriptTag" " - ERROR: could not apply ACL.. group: ↵
$group does not exist! dscl code: $dsclCode"
                return 2
        fi

        ## sanity check our permissions
        ##if ( [ "$permissions" != "fc" ] && [ "$permissions" != "rw" ] ↵
&& [ "$permissions" != "ro" ] ); then
        ##      logger -s -t "$scriptTag" "setACLForGroup() could not apply ↵
ACL.. permissions:$permissions invalid, use 'fc'(Full Control), 'rw' (Read and Write), ↵
'ro' (Read Only)!"
        ##      return 3
        ##fi

        ## deploy our ACL's
        case "$permissions" in
          fc) ace="allow:list,add_file,search,delete, ↵
add_subdirectory,delete_child,readattr,writeattr,readextattr,writeextattr, ↵
readsecurity,writesecurity,chown,file_inherit,directory_inherit";;
          rw) ace="allow:list,add_file,search,delete, ↵
add_subdirectory,delete_child,readattr,writeattr,readextattr,writeextattr, ↵
readsecurity,file_inherit,directory_inherit";;
          append) ace="allow:list,add_file,search,add_subdirectory, ↵
readattr,writeattr,readextattr,writeextattr,readsecurity,file_inherit, ↵
directory_inherit";;
          ro) ace="allow:list,search,readattr,readextattr, ↵
readsecurity,file_inherit,directory_inherit";;
          *) logger -s -t "$scriptTag" "setACLForGroup() could not ↵
 apply ACL.. permissions:$permissions invalid!! defaulting to 'ro' (Read Only)!"
             ace="allow:list,search,readattr,readextattr, ↵
readsecurity,file_inherit,directory_inherit"
             permissions="ro"
        ;;
    esac

        logger -s -t "$scriptTag" " - applying ACL to dir:$directory for group: ↵
$group with perms:$permissions"

    /bin/chmod +a "$group:$ace" "$directory"
        chmodCode1=$?
        if [ $? != 0 ]; then
                logger -s -t "$scriptTag" " - Failed applying ACL to ↵
 top level of dir:$directory code:$chmodCode1... exiting!"
                return $chmodCode1
        fi

        /bin/chmod -f -R +ai "$group:$ace" "$directory"/*
```

```
        chmodCode2=$?
        if [ $? != 0 ]; then
                logger -s -t "$scriptTag" " - Failed applying ACL to dir: ↵
$directory code:$chmodCode2"
                return $chmodCode2
        fi


        return 0
} ## end setACLForGroup()



######### START #############
#############################

## Iterate through all of our specified homeDirectories.
OLDIFS=$IFS
IFS=','
for homeEntry in $homeDirectories; do
    ## check to ensure we have a good homeLoc
    homeLoc=$(echo $homeEntry | awk -F: '{print$1}')
    homeDepth=$(echo $homeEntry | awk -F: '/[0-9]/ {print$2}')

    if [ -z "$homeDepth" ]; then
        homeDepth=0
    fi
    if [ -d "${homeLoc:?}" ]; then
        cd "$homeLoc"
    else
        logger -s -t "$scriptTag" "Fatal error, $homeLoc is not a directory"
        errorOccured=true
    fi

    if [ $homeDepth == 0 ]; then
        if [ "$restructureHomes" == "true" ]; then
            logger -s -t "$scriptTag" "Restructuring home folders for $homeLoc"
            structureForOSX
        fi
        if [ "$repairPrivs" == "true" ]; then
            logger -s -t "$scriptTag" "Reparing Privileges for $homeLoc"
            repairPrivs
        fi
    else
        IFS=$OLDIFS
        for homeDir in `ls | grep -v "$orphanageName" | grep -v "Shared" | ↵
 egrep -v "^\."`; do
            if [ -d "${homeLoc:?}/$homeDir" ]; then
                cd "$homeLoc/$homeDir"
            else
                continue
            fi
            if [ "$repairPrivs" == "true" ]; then
                logger -s -t "$scriptTag" "Reparing Privileges for $homeLoc/$homeDir"
                repairPrivs
            fi
```

```
            cd ..
        done
    fi

    ## Deploy our aclGroups to the root of the home directory
    if [ ! -z "$aclGroups" ]; then
        IFS=$'\,'
        for group in $aclGroups; do
            groupName=`printf "$group" | awk -F: '{print$1}'`
            groupRights=`printf "$group" | awk -F: '{print$2}'`
            setACLForGroup "$homeLoc" "$groupName" "$groupRights"
        done
    fi
done
```

Enabling the Software Firewall

The next script enables the Application Firewall in Mac OS X, which should generally be done in all mass deployments where security is even a minimal concern. The script ends with exit 0, which you may have noticed in previous scripts as well. The script brings in positional parameters from PackageMaker, setting them as variables (discussed in detail in Chapter 6). Then the paths for commands used in the script are declared, with more lines in the script dedicated to declaring variables than to the payload, a common occurrence.

```
#!/bin/bash
declare -x DSTROOT="$3"              # Installation Volume of mount point.
declare -x SYSROOT="$4"             # The root directory for the system.

declare -x PLIST="${DSTROOT}/Library/Preferences/com.apple.alf.plist"

declare -x defaults="/usr/bin/defaults"
declare -x plutil="/usr/bin/plutil"
declare -x chmod="/bin/chmod"
declare -x mv="/bin/mv"

"$defaults" write "${PLIST%.plist}" 'globalstate' -int 1 &&
echo "Plist Edited: ${PLIST}"

if $plutil "${PLIST:?}" >/dev/null ; then
        echo "Plist written successfully"
        $plutil -convert 'binary1' "${PLIST:?}"
        # Not needed , just for good measure
        $chmod +r "${PLIST:?}"
else
        "$mv" "${PLIST:?}" "${PLIST:?}.bad"
fi
exit 0
```

Furthermore, we can build on the logic just introduced. The following script will loop through all of the local users on a system and alter the umask variable for each. Each section is documented accordingly; note the beginning, where variables from the positional parameters are mapped into paths for packages, mount points, and the system root. Having a custom system root allows the script to be run against a non-booted drive, as would be common with InstaDMG style workflows.

```bash
#!/bin/bash
# Standard Package Install Postional Parameters $1 $3 $4
declare -x PKGBUNDLE="$1"        #      Full path to the install package.
declare -x DSTROOT="$3"          #      Installation Volume of mount point.
declare -x SYSROOT="$4"          #      The root directory for the system.


# Command short hand
declare -x awk="/usr/bin/awk"
declare -x chown="/usr/sbin/chown"
declare -x chmod="/bin/chmod"
declare -x basename="/usr/bin/basename"
declare -x dirname="/usr/bin/dirname"
declare -x id="/usr/bin/id"
declare -x ls="/bin/ls"
declare -x plutil="/usr/bin/plutil"
declare -x sudo="/usr/bin/sudo"
declare -x whoami="/usr/bin/whoami"


# Run time varibles
declare -x SCRIPT="${0##*/}" ; SCRIPTNAME="${SCRIPT%%\.*}"
declare -x USER_TEMPLATE="$DSTROOT/System/Library/User Template/English.lproj"
declare -x FINDER_PREFS="$DSROOT/Library/Preferences/com.apple.finder.plist"

# User customized values, also use a file in the same directory <script>.conf
declare -ix UMASK=2
declare -x HOME_PATH="/Users"
# You could change this if you have an external Volume hosting homes
source "${PKGBUNDLE:?}/Contents/Resources/${SCRIPTNAME:-"$SCRIPT_NAME"}.conf"

#       As root is not covered in /Users/* set it here
if [ "$DSTROOT" = '/' ] ; then      #      If Installing on the startup disk
      echo "Setting umask for current user $($whoami):$UMASK"
      $defaults -g 'NSUmask' -int ${UMASK:?}
      #         -g means .GlobalPreferences.plist for the current user
fi


#       This sets the Finder umask, which is not done in umask Doctor AFAIK
echo "Setting Global umask for the Finder: $FINDER_PREF to $UMASK"
$defaults write ${FINDER_PREFS%.plist} 'umask' -int ${UMASK:?}


#       Loop through the homedirectorys in <Destination Volume>/Users/*
loopThroughHomes(){
OLD_IFS="$IFS" IFS=$'\n'
#       Reset the Field Sep to spaces don't hose us.
for USERHOME in "${DSTROOT}${HOME_PATH:-"/Users"}"/* ; do
# Start looping through the path on the destination Volume,defaults to /Users
      test -d "$USERHOME" || continue
      #         Skip anything thats not a directory
      test -d "$USERHOME/Library" || continue
      #         If the loop folder is missing a Library skip it
      #         This will skip Filevault, Shared, Deleted Users etc.
```

```
#       Setup the loop variables
declare USER_NAME="$($basename "$USERHOME")"
        #       Pull the username from /Users/<username>
declare USER_PREF="$USERHOME/Library/Preferences/.GlobalPreferences.plist"
        #       The users Dot Global Preferences file
declare -i NSUMASK=$($defaults read "$USER_PREF" 'NSUmask' 2>/dev/null)

        test ${NSUMASK:?} =${UMASK:?} && continue
        #       If value is already set or to craziness like 0 , then continue
echo "Processing: $USER: $USER_PREF"
echo "Preference file: $USER_PREF"
if [ "$DSTROOT" = '/' ] ; then
        #       if we are running on the active startup Volume
        $id "${USER_NAME:?}" &>/dev/null || continue
        #       Check if the user is valid via DS search policy
        #       Skip if the user's id lookup fails protects against del
$sudo -u "$USER" $defaults write ${USER_PREF%.plist} 'NSUmask' -int $UMASK
#       Actively set the Global preferences as the user to keep ownership
        echo "Configured $GLOBAL_PREF for $USER"
else
        declare OWNER_UID="$($ls -lnd "$USERHOME/Library" |
                                        $awk '/^d/{print $3;exit}')"
        #       If we can't rely on DirectoryService, then pull the parent UID
        $defaults write ${USER_PREF%.plist} 'NSUmask' -int ${UMASK:?}

        echo "Chaining ownership on $USER_PREF to UID:$OWNER_UID"
        $chown "${OWNER_UID:-0} ${USER_PREF:?}"
fi

done
IFS="$OLD_IFS" #        Reset our field separator
return 0
} # End loopThroughHomes()

# Validate plist syntax and ownership and move if they fail the tests
checkPlistFiles(){
declare PLISTS="$@" #  Read in all the given files in the PLISTS array
for PLIST in $PLISTS ; do
declare -i OWNER_UID="$($ls -lnd "$($dirname "$PLIST_CHECK")"|
                                        $awk '/^d/{print $3;exit}')"
declare -i PLIST_UID"$($ls -ln "$PLIST_CHECK"|
                                        $awk '/^d/{print $3;exit}')"
$plutil "${PLIST:?}" 1>/dev/null
done
return $?
} # End checkPlistFiles()

loopThroughHomes
checkPlistFiles
exit 0
```

Managing Items in ARD

Apple Remote Desktop has the ability to use a task server, but not to share databases by default. You can import and export databases and copy information between computers manually from within ARD, but not actually share databases. In com.apple.RemoteDesktop, there is an array called ComputerDatabase. This array lists all of the items in the All Computers list within Remote Desktop. You can view a much less human friendly output of all of the hosts in All Computers by running the following command:

```
defaults read com.apple.RemoteDesktop ComputerDatabase
```

You can push an entry into the list by using the defaults command to write an item into that array in com.apple.RemoteDesktop. Here's a command to do so for a computer with a name of CharlesTest and an IP address of 10.10.10.10. Most of the other fields are extraneous and could probably be removed from the command, but it works as is:

```
defaults write com.apple.RemoteDesktop ComputerDatabase -array-add ' ⏎
{ addedToDOC = 0;collectingAppUsage = 1;collectingUserAccounting = 1; ⏎
docInfoUpToDate = 0;hostname = CharlesTest.local;name = "CharlesTest"; ⏎
ncFlags = 0;networkAddress = "10.10.10.10";preferHostname = 0; ⏎
showCursorForLegacy = 1;uuid = "C8F8966B-ED28-4221-CCE0-E1385D366717"; }'
```

You will need to restart the Remote Desktop services before you can see the new entry in the Remote Desktop application. You can just reboot, or you can restart using a pair of commands similar to the following:

```
launchctl stop `launchctl list | grep com.apple.RemoteDesktop | awk '{print $3}'`
launchctl stop `launchctl list | grep com.apple.RemoteDesktopAgent | awk '{print $3}'`
```

Disk Utilization

df is a great tool for checking the amount of free space on a disk (and the amount that's taken). df has a number of options for viewing the output and can even look at free iNodes and blocks rather than just showing free space. However, df is going to come up short if you're hunting for where all your free space went within a given volume.

For this, look to du, a great tool for checking disk utilization, more at the directory level. For example, the following command shows you how much space is being taken by each application in the /Applications directory:

```
du -d 1 /Applications/
```

Now run the command without the -d 1 parameters:

```
du /Applications/
```

The -d flag limits the depth that the command will traverse. By specifying 0, you'd only see the files in a given directory, whereas if you specify -d 2, you'll see the sizes of the child directories from the path you specified and their children (since that's two). You can go as deep as you want with the depth setting, but the data returned by the command can be too much, at times. Also, the longer it will take for the command to complete as it's calculating more and more data.

Some other flags that are useful are -x and -H. These will traverse mount points and symbolic links, respectively (both of which are not followed by default). This can help to keep your command's output limited to the host and volume of directories underneath the specified parent directory.

If you're interested in seeing way too much information, try just running:

```
du -a
```

If you suddenly have only 1KB of free space available, a series of du commands can turn up information about where all of your data is in no time.

Network Setup

Networking on Mac OS X can be automated. In many environments, system administrators will want to reorder the network interfaces to leverage wired connections over wireless when both are available. Therefore, we're going to go ahead and do two things at once, explain how to configure the interface and show how to automate this configuration from the command line so you can quickly deploy and then troubleshoot issues with this machine-specific part of your deployment.

Before getting started, it is important to note that there is a significant distinction in the nomenclature used in Mac OS X for network *interfaces (devices)* vs. network *services*. An interface is a physical network adapter. These are indicated by traditional Unix names such as en0, en1, fw0, and so on. You can determine which is which in a variety of ways, such as using ifconfig or Network Utility from /Applications/Utilities. A network service, in this context, is an abstraction of a network interface. Each service will have a physical adapter, and a physical adapter can have multiple services, which is how, for example, you would go about assigning two IP addresses to a single physical adapter. Things can get even more confusing when bond interfaces, where you are virtualizing a service to spread across multiple interfaces, in which case multiple interfaces are represented as a single network service.

To get a list of the network services running on your machine, you can use the following command:

```
networksetup -listallnetworkservices
```

And that command might return the following:

```
Ethernet
Airport
FireWire
```

There are about as many naming conventions for interfaces as there are actual interfaces. For the purposes of this example, we're going to patch Ethernet into the network and rename it to WiredNetwork, using the networksetup command again, with the -renamenetworkservice option as follows:

```
networksetup -renamenetworkservice Ethernet WiredNetwork
```

While it's not required to rename your network services, people often do. As you can see, it's quick and easy and can save you a bunch of time in the future in terms of troubleshooting, remote support, and automation facilitation. Renaming is very specific; the command looks for a pattern in the name and replaces it with a new pattern. So Built-in Ethernet would need to be enclosed in quotes, "Built-in Ethernet", and so forth. Now let's go ahead and rename the other services to `WirelessNetwork` using the following command:

```
networksetup -renamenetworkservice AirPort WirelessNetwork
```

Next, we want to make sure that the `WiredNetwork` is listed above `WirelessNetwork`. This will ensure that standard communications DNS, directory services, HTTP management traffic and other unnecessary traffic default to the wired network. To start, let's look at what order the services are listed in. We're going to use `networksetup` yet again, this time with the `-listnetworkserviceorder` option as follows:

```
networksetup -listnetworkserviceorder
```

This should provide a listing similar to the following, though perhaps in a different order:

```
 (1) WirelessNetwork
(Hardware Port: Ethernet, Device: en1)

(2) WiredNetwork
(Hardware Port: Ethernet, Device: en0)

(3) FireWire
(Hardware Port: FireWire, Device: fw0)
```

Here we see that `WirelessNetwork` is listed as the first item in the network service order. Because we actually want the `WiredNetwork` first, we're going to reorder our services using the `networksetup` command with the `-ordernetworkservices` option. Using this option, you simply list each service in order, as you can see here:

```
networksetup -ordernetworkservices WiredNetwork WirelessNetwork FireWire
```

Notice that we include FireWire in the command. This is because you have to include all of your network services for the command to execute successfully. Now we are actually going to disable the FireWire network service (when we do, the interface itself will still function) using the `-setnetworkserviceenabled` option of the `networksetup` command. Because the FireWire service is automatically named FireWire, we simply tell `networksetup` to `setnetworkserviceenabled` to off as follows:

```
networksetup -setnetworkserviceenabled FireWire off
```

Because most environments do not support IPv6 yet, we're going to disable this for both `WiredNetwork` and `WirelessNetwork` using the `-setv6off` option as follows:

```
networksetup -setv6off WiredNetwork
networksetup -setv6off WirelessNetwork
```

Once IPv6 has been disabled, we're going to configure the IPv4 settings for our two network interfaces. For example, `WiredNetwork` might be set up to use DHCP. In that case there's not much configuration that needs to occur. While DHCP should be the default setting used with the controller, it would still be wise to specify it again anyway (just in case), using the next command, where -setdhcp is the option that enables DHCP for the WiredNetwork service.

```
networksetup -setdhcp WiredNetwork
```

While the WiredNetwork could be DHCP, in this case we're going to set it as a static IP address of 10.100.1.11. The subnet mask will be 255.255.0.0 and the gateway will be 10.100.0.1. This is all sent to the service in one command, using the -setmanual option with networksetup. When you use this option, you use the -setmanual option followed by the name of the service to configure, then the IP address that will be given to the service, then the subnet and finally the router (default gateway). In our case, the command would be:

```
networksetup -setmanual WiredNetwork 10.100.1.11 255.255.0.0 10.100.0.1
```

The wireless network is a bit more persnickety. As is typical, we will use DHCP but we will also need to configure a number of proxy services. Use the following command to set the adapter to DHCP:

```
networksetup -setdhcp WirelessNetwork
```

To set the proxies, use a combination of two of the following proxy options per service:

- *Setftpproxystate:* Enables the FTP proxy.

- *setftpproxy:* Sets up a proxy for FTP.

- *setwebproxystate:* Enables the web proxy.

- *setwebproxy:* Sets up a proxy for web traffic.

- *setsecurewebproxystate:* Enables the SSL proxy.

- *setsecurewebproxy:* Sets a proxy for SSL traffic.

- *setstreamingproxystate:* Enables the streaming proxy.

- *setstreamingproxy:* Sets a proxy for streaming traffic.

- *setgopherproxystate:* Enables the gopher proxy (if you are using gopher, please stay after class for a parent-teacher conference).

- *setgopherproxy:* Sets the gopher proxy.

- setsocksfirewallproxystate: Enables a socks firewall.

- *setsocksfirewallproxy:* Sets up the socks firewall.

- *setproxybypassdomains:* Defines the domains that the proxy will not be used for.

To deploy a proxy setting, we'll use two commands, one to enable the option and the other to set it. For each proxy option that can be set, you will add the network service, a host name (or IP address), and a port number that the proxy will run on. Optionally you can then specify (still on the same line of the command) an authentication option (as either on or off) along with a username and password for each proxy service. For example, to set a web proxy for proxy.318.com that runs on port 8080 and requires authentication as username proxyserv with a password of Asimov you would use the following commands:

```
networksetup -setwebproxystate on
networksetup -setwebproxy WirelessNetwork proxy.318.com 8080 on proxyserv Asimov
```

Now that we have the services configured, we need to assign name servers. In order to set up DNS, we will use the -setdnsservers option with networksetup. In this case, our DNS servers are 10.100.0.2 and 10.100.0.3. When using the -setdnsservers option, you simply list the primary name server, followed by the secondary name server and any tertiary name servers. DNS is used on WiredNetwork as WirelessNetwork picks up DNS from DHCP:

```
networksetup -setdnsservers WiredNetwork 10.100.0.2 10.100.0.3
```

At this point you're probably thinking to yourself that you could have done all of this in the Network System Preference pane in about two minutes. Now however, we're going to take all of the commands we used in this example and put them into a shell script, replacing the actual IP addresses with positional parameters for the WiredNetwork and WirelessNetwork IP addresses, so that we can send the script along with the IP address that it will receive to each workstation. The script would look something like this:

```
#!/bin/bash
networksetup -renamenetworkservice Ethernet WiredNetwork
networksetup -renamenetworkservice Ethernet2 WirelessNetwork
networksetup -ordernetworkservices WiredNetwork WirelessNetwork FireWire
networksetup -setnetworkserviceenabled FireWire off
networksetup -setv6off WiredNetwork
networksetup -setv6off WirelessNetwork
networksetup -setmanual WiredNetwork $1 255.255.0.0 10.100.0.1
networksetup -setdnsservers WiredNetwork 10.100.0.2 10.100.0.3
networksetup -setmanual WirelessNetwork $2 255.255.255.0
networksetup -setwebproxystate on
networksetup -setwebproxy WirelessNetwork proxy.318.com 8080 on proxyserv Asimov
```

Now the script can be sent to each workstation. For this example, we're going to call the script setnetworkservices.sh. In order to send an IP address for the WiredNetwork of 10.100.1.12 and an IP for the WirelessNetwork of 192.168.1.12, you would simply send the following command (including the path of course):

```
setnetworkservices.sh 10.100.1.12 192.168.1.12
```

Then, to set up the next host using the same convention you would use:

```
setnetworkservices.sh 10.100.1.13 192.168.1.13
```

If you want to get a bit more complicated with the script, you could add some logic. For example, you might query for en0 and convert a service name to be used with en0 based on the interface, to keep the script from failing due to someone having renamed the service in the past. Because a common issue during setup is to patch the wrong interfaces into the networks (in the case that there are two wired interfaces), you could also use the ping command to test each network to verify it is live and if not (else) go ahead and swap the IP settings and names. You might also go ahead and turn every single setting into a variable to make it much more portable.

Finally, as you are updating this information, you are actually augmenting the
/Library/Preferences/SystemConfiguration/com.apple.network.identification.plist
file. While there are a variety of ways to edit this file directly, I wouldn't really suggest it
because most adapters are referenced by MAC and have generated ServiceIDs (for
example F8166C7E-CCFC-438C-98C6-CB05C7FA13E7). It is far easier to simply use
the networksetup tool than it is to actually use a file drop of the plist or augment this file
directly.

In Mac OS X 10.6 there are three major additions to networksetup. The first is that you
can now use networksetup to import and export 802.1x profiles (and link them to
certificates that you import from pkcs12 into Keychain), which will hopefully ease
implementation burdens for environments with supported 802.1x setups. The second is
that networksetup can now be used to manage a Baseboard Management Controller
(BMC), which is the chip that enables ipmi/Lights-Out Management. The third new
option is the addition of network locations control from within networksetup. This means
that networksetup can now be used to configure basically the entire network stack.

First let's look at the options that have been added to ease the burden of integrating
802.1x. In the Network System Preference pane, if you've enabled 802.1x on a Mac host,
you may have noticed that you have user profiles, login window profiles, and a system
profile. The options in networksetup correspond to these, with -listalluserprofiles and
-listloginprofiles showing available user and login profiles respectively (you can only
have one system profile, so there's no need for listing all one of them). Additionally, any
profiles that you generate will need to be enabled. You will use the -enablesystemprofile
to enable the system profile for a given service. And if you are integrating 802.1x with the
loginwindow you'll need to enable one of the profiles that you listed earlier, using the
-enableloginprofile option to networksetup along with the service, followed by the
profile, followed by an on or off switch. For example, if we wanted to enable a profile
called mycompany for the login window and use the service that we'd set up called
PrimaryEthernet, then we could use the following command:

```
networksetup -enableloginprofile PrimaryEthernet mycompany on
```

But, where are these profiles coming from? Well, the easiest way to get them on
your system is to use the -export8021xProfiles to export all profiles for a given
service on an imaging station and then the -import8021xProfiles followed by
the service to import the profiles into, followed by the path to the export file.
You can also export just the user profiles using the -export8021xLoginProfiles
or the -export 8021xSystemProfiles options to export just the login profiles
and system profiles respectively. TLS will be a bit trickier. Apple includes the
-settlsidentityonsystemprofile and -settlsidentityonuserprofile to assist with
pkcs12 integration (currently the only supported format).

In addition to 802.1x options, in 10.6 you can also now programmatically configure
and control preferred wireless network settings from the command line. Arguments

associated with this functionality are -listpreferredwirelessnetworks, -addpreferredwirelessnetworkatindex, -removepreferredwirelessnetwork, and -removeallpreferredwirelessnetworks. For instance, to add a preferred wireless network "Ansible" with WPA2 personal security, I would use the following command:

```
sudo networksetup -addpreferredwirelessnetworkatindex Airport Ansible 1 WPA2 Secretp4$$
```

10.6 also brings location management to networksetup. Locations have always been pretty straight forward in the Network System Preference pane, and with 10.6 you can now create and change locations programmatically (previously this was provided via the scselect utility). Simply use the -getcurrentlocation option to show you which location is active (if you haven't ever customized network locations this should be "Automatic"). You can see all available locations (not just the active one) by using the -listlocations option. New locations can be created with the -createlocation argument followed by the name to be assigned to the location. By default, the default services will not be included in this location, so use the populate option to add them. As an alternative you can add individual services manually via the -createnetworkservice option. If we were creating a new location called "MyCo Location," with all network services populated, then our command would look something like the following:

```
networksetup -createlocation "MyCo Location" populate
```

To then make that location our active location, use the -switchtolocation option. For example, we could use the following to activate that location we just created.

```
networksetup -switchtolocation "MyCo Location"
```

And to delete it if we did something wrong, use -deletelocation (to continue on with our previous example):

```
networksetup -deletelocation "MyCo Location"
```

> **NOTE:** Mac OS X 10.6 also includes support for automating the deployment of 802.1x profiles. One of the authors of this book did a write-up on doing so that is available at:
> http://www.afp548.com/article.php?story=20090901010221742.

Power Management

Power management can most easily be managed via MCX, as discussed in Chapter 7. However, there may be instances where you need to resort to scripting to deploy your power management settings, and you can use the pmsetcommand line utility to accomplish this. For starters, let's look at enabling the *wake on magic packet*:

```
pmset -a womp 1
```

The -a indicates that the setting will apply to all settings modes for a computer: it will apply to the system when on battery, when we're plugged in, or when we are running on

UPS backup power. You can change settings for only a specific state with the following flags, which fall into the first positional parameter:

- *-a:* all
- *-b:* battery
- *-c:* wall power
- *-u:* UPS

The next parameter you'll pass to the command is the option (argument) for that power setting that you would like to send. Here you can set the number of minutes before the display goes to sleep, the brightness at various power settings, and other options that have a direct effect on power behavior. These include the following:

- *acwake:* Wake when the system is connected to power; it's a 0 or 1.
- *autorestart:* Automatically restart when there's been a power loss (when the system is plugged in); use 0 or 1.
- *disksleep:* Number of minutes before the disk spins down.
- *displaysleep:* Number of minutes before the computers monitor (signal to the monitor) goes to sleep.
- *dps:* Allows the CPU speed to dynamically change with power; 0 or 1.
- *halfdim:* Controls whether the display goes to half- brightness for the power setting in question; 0 or 1
- *lessbright:* Same as above, just not as much
- *lidwake:* Automatically wake the system when the lid is opened; 0 or 1
- *powerbutton:* Allows the box to go to sleep if someone hits the power button. If it's disabled, the system will not go to sleep if someone hits the power button. This doesn't disable powering down by holding down that same power button; 0 or 1.
- *reduce:* Allows reduction of the CPU speed; 0 or 1.
- *ring:* Wakes if someone calls the modem (but since the modern laptops don't have modems, likely not something you'll be using). It's an integer, 0 or 1.
- *sleep:* Number of minutes before the computer goes to sleep (but doesn't spin down the disk).
- *sms:* Controls whether you're using the Sudden Motion Sensor to stop the disk heads from locking down when the system gets jarred (G force math is kewl). It's a Boolean thing, either on or off.
- *womp:* explained previously.

In addition to these, you can also use pmset to get information with the -g flag. Using -g alone will net you all of the available information and while there are other options to limit what it outputs, I normally just use grep for that.

There are also a number of options for managing SafeSleep (maintaining the system state in memory, using the argument hibernatemode) or UPS options (haltvalue for how much battery to trigger a shutdown and halfafterfor when to spin the CPU to 50% of full). If you're trying to manage the system and you have a battery (such as a laptop plugged into a UPS), the settings will not be respected.

Just as in the System Preference pane, you can also control scheduling for when the system sleeps, wakes, powers on, or shuts down as well. These events can be scheduled by using the schedule or repeat arguments, which can be used to set one time power events, or repeated events, respectively. Options for each are sleep, wake, poweron, and shutdown in conjunction with using date, time, weekdays. You can optionally provide a string name of the person setting the schedule for documentation purposes:

```
pmset schedule poweron "09/09/09 9:09:09"
pmset repeat shutdown MTWRF 21:00:00
```

There are also a few other options that you don't have in the GUI. These include force, which doesn't write settings to disk, touch, which reads currently enforced settings from the disk, noidle, which prevents idle sleep (and just spins the disk down when it's ready) and sleepnow, which puts the system to sleep right then. sleepnow is useful when you're troubleshooting why a system won't go to sleep.

For the Xserve specifically, there is also Lights-Out Management (discussed later in the chapter) in the form of the IPMI toolkit from Intel. You can use that to power systems on, power them off, and perform a few other tasks. This must be secured with a password, using Server Monitor. You can then control state through Server Monitor, or through Apple Remote Desktop. Find out more about IPMI on this page over at Intel.com.

ServerAdmin Backups and Change Monitoring

At its most basic, change control can be used in Mac OS X Server by leveraging the serveradmin command. You can use the serveradmin command with the settings option as we've done extensively in Chapter 5 to obtain information about settings and augment those settings in Mac OS X Server on a per-server basis. However, you can also use the serveradmin command to report all of the settings for all of its services. To do so, you use the following command:

```
serveradmin settings all
```

You can then pipe this information into a file. For example, the following command would copy the information from serveradmin into a text file in the /scripts directory of a system called dailyservercheck:

```
serveradmin settings all > /scripts/dailyservercheck
```

It is important to note that any changes made directly to a particular software package's configuration files will likely not be detected through this method; for instance, if a user modified the postfix service's configuration at /etc/postfix/main.cf. To monitor Unix utilities such as these, Tripwire, a change monitoring solution both with open-source and enterprise solutions available (www.tripwire.org and www.tripwire.com), is a better option. That being said, serveradmin is a great way to track changes made through standard Apple tools and therefore certainly does have a purpose.

To fully automate this task, we can use the code listed below, also available for digital download (file 8_sabackuplocal.sh). This code creates a folder specified by variable SABACKUPDIR, and then creates a disk image in the form of a sparsebundle named by the variable SAARCHIVEDMG. Once these assets are created, they will be utilized for the backup. This script will automatically mount the disk image, perform a serveradmin backup, and then check that against the last run to determine if any changes were made. A symbolic link named "Latest.txt" will always be linked at the latest serveradmin output. A more robust version of this script can be found for digital download as well (file 8_sabackup.sh).

```
#!/bin/bash


##########  Server Admin Backup Script ####################
##
##       Written by Beau Hunter, Zack Smith  7/03/09
##       beauh@mac.com acid@wallcity.org
##       Server Admin backup script, equivalent to serveradmin settings all
##       backs up only when config changes, generates diffs with each change.
##
################################################################################

## User configuration
SABACKUPDIR=/Auto\ Server\ Setup

## Serveradmin archive disk image
SAARCHIVEDMG="serveradmin_archives.sparsebundle"
SAARCHIVE_MOUNTPOINT="/Volumes/${SAARCHIVEDMG%.sparsebundle}"

## bin vars
declare -x grep="/usr/bin/grep"
declare -x serveradmin="/usr/sbin/serveradmin"
declare -x defaults="/usr/bin/defaults"
declare -x hdiutil="/usr/bin/hdiutil"
declare -x diskutil="/usr/sbin/diskutil"
declare -x mkdir="/bin/mkdir"
declare -x du="/usr/bin/du"
declare -x date="/bin/date"
declare -x diff="/usr/bin/diff"
declare -x awk="/usr/bin/awk"
declare -x mv="/bin/mv"
declare -x ln="/bin/ln"
declare -x mktemp="/usr/bin/mktemp"
declare -x umount="/sbin/umount"
declare -x sleep="/bin/sleep"
```

```
## Runtime variables
DATE=$("$date" +'%Y%m%d.%H%M_%S')
declare -x REQCMDS="$awk,$ntpdate,$perl,$scutil"
declare -x SCRIPT="${0##*/}" ; SCRIPTNAME="${SCRIPT%%\.*}"
declare -x SCRIPTPATH="$0" RUNDIRECTORY="${0%/*}"
declare -x SCRIPTLOG="/Library/Logs/${SCRIPT%%\.*}.log"

## test for root
[ "$EUID" != 0 ] && printf "%s\n" "This script requires root access ($EUID)!" && exit 1


exec 2>>"${SCRIPTLOG:?}" # Redirect standard error to log file


########## MAIN ##########

## check for the backup dir
if [ ! -d "$SABACKUPDIR" ]; then
        echo "A local directory was not found at path: $SABACKUPDIR, attempting to
create"

        "$mkdir" "$SABACKUPDIR" &> /dev/null
        if [ $? != 0 ]; then
                echo "Failed to mount $NFSPATH to $SABACKUPDIR, exiting!"
                exit 1
        fi
fi

## Check for directory mounted where our DMG should be
if [ -d "$SAARCHIVE_MOUNTPOINT" ]; then
        echo "Directory mounted at ServerAdmin Backup DMG mountpath:
$SAARCHIVE_MOUNTPOINT"
        "$umount" "$SAARCHIVE_MOUNTPOINT"

        ## attempt to remove the local directory
        rm "$SAARCHIVE_MOUNTPOINT"/.DS_Store &> /dev/null
        rmdir "$SAARCHIVE_MOUNTPOINT" &> /dev/null
        if [ -d "$SAARCHIVE_MOUNTPOINT" ]; then
                echo "Could not resolve the issue, please remove: $SAARCHIVE_MOUNTPOINT"
                exit 4
        fi
fi

## Check for an archive disk image
if [ -d "$SABACKUPDIR"/"$SAARCHIVEDMG" ]; then
        ## mount it if it exists
        "$hdiutil" mount -nobrowse "$SABACKUPDIR"/"$SAARCHIVEDMG" >> "$SCRIPTLOG"
        echo "ServerAdmin Backup DMG found, mounting!"
else
        ## here if we need to create our DMG
        echo "ServerAdmin Backup DMG: $SAARCHIVEDMG could not be found! creating..."
        TEMPPATH="$("$mktemp" -d /tmp/XXXXXX)"
        "$hdiutil" create -type SPARSEBUNDLE -size 1g -fs HFS+ -volname ↵
"${SAARCHIVEDMG%.sparsebundle}" "$TEMPPATH"/"$SAARCHIVEDMG" >> "$SCRIPTLOG"
        "$mv" "$TEMPPATH"/"$SAARCHIVEDMG" "$SABACKUPDIR"/"$SAARCHIVEDMG"
        if [ $? != 0 ]; then
```

```
                    echo "Could not move from $TEMPPATH/$SAARCHIVEDMG"
                    exit 3
            fi
            "$hdiutil" mount -nobrowse "$SABACKUPDIR"/"$SAARCHIVEDMG" >> "$SCRIPTLOG"
            echo "Mounting ServerAdmin Backup DMG"
fi


## One last sanity check
if [ ! -d "$SAARCHIVE_MOUNTPOINT" ]; then
        echo "Disk image did not seem to mount! Exiting!"
        exit 5
fi

## and last but not least, dump our settings
echo "Checking for changes..."
"$serveradmin" settings all | "$grep" -v "info:currentTime" > ↵
"$TEMPPATH"/sa_export_"$DATE".txt

"$diff" "$SAARCHIVE_MOUNTPOINT"/latest.txt "$TEMPPATH"/"sa_export_$DATE.txt" &> ↵
/dev/null
if [ $? == 0 ]; then
        echo "No changes were detected, not saving export"
else
        echo "Changes found, saving output and creating diff file."
        "$diff" "$SAARCHIVE_MOUNTPOINT"/latest.txt "$TEMPPATH"/"sa_export_$DATE.txt" >> ↵
 "$SAARCHIVE_MOUNTPOINT"/"sa_export_${DATE}-diff.txt"
        "$mv" -f "$TEMPPATH"/sa_export_"$DATE".txt ↵
"$SAARCHIVE_MOUNTPOINT"/"sa_export_$DATE.txt"
        cd "$SAARCHIVE_MOUNTPOINT"
        "$ln" -s "sa_export_$DATE.txt" "latest.txt"
        cd "$OLDPWD"
fi


if [ -d "$TEMPPATH" ]; then
        "$rm" -rf "$TEMPPATH" &> /dev/null
fi

## if we're still here, then force the unmount (there is no messing around!)
while [ -d "$SAARCHIVE_MOUNTPOINT" ]; do
        let COUNT++
        if [ $COUNT -le 10 ]; then
                echo "Unmounting ServerAdmin Backup DMG: $SAARCHIVE_MOUNTPOINT"
                "$hdiutil" eject "$SAARCHIVE_MOUNTPOINT" >> "$SCRIPTLOG"
        elif [ $COUNT -eq 11 ]; then
                echo "ServerAdmin Backup DMG failed to unmount, forcing!"
                "$diskutil" unmount force "$SAARCHIVE_MOUNTPOINT" >> "$SCRIPTLOG"
        else
                echo "ServerAdmin Backup DMG failed to unmount!"
                 break
        fi
        "$sleep" 1
done

exit 0
```

Xserve Lights-Out Management

Snow Leopard also comes with the ability to manage that Lights-Out Management (LOM) port via the previously discussed networksetup command. To see the LOM settings, you would use networksetup along with the -showBMCSettings option. To set up LOM, use the -setupBMC option, along with the port on which to use it, followed by whether it will be static or DHCP (yes, I said DHCP, but I don't think I'd do that: this is a management interface and should be persistent), the IP, subnet mask, gateway, and finally the admin user name and password (keep in mind those passwords need 8 characters). So let's say that I wanted to configure my LOM interface to use Ethernet 1, using 10.1.1.29 with a subnet mask of 255.255.255.0 and a gateway of 10.1.1.1, with a LOM username of admin and a password of mysecretpassword1. I would then use the following command:

```
networksetup -setupBMC 1 static 10.1.1.29 255.255.252.0 10.1.1.1 admin mysecretpassword1
```

For 10.5 or earlier, or to access additional functionality, you can use the ipmitool command to accomplish the task. To set the IP address on a LOM interface, use the following command:

```
sudo ipmitool lan set 1 ipaddr 10.1.1.29 netmask 255.255.255.0 defgw 10.1.1.1
```

This sets interface one; replace set 1 with set 2 to set it on the second interface. There is some pretty cool functionality here, such as specifying VLAN tagging, backup gateways, hard-coding gateway MAC addresses to protect against arp poisoning, and so on.

If you want to edit the default user account created by Server Monitor, which resides at userid 2, you can do so using these commands:

```
sudo ipmitool user set name 2 myadmin
sudo ipmitool user set password 2 'mypass'
```

> **CAUTION:** Passwords are provided via stdin and are thereby recorded in your .history file.

If you want to create a new user account altogether (on top of an already configured apple user), use the following commands:

```
## get a list of current users to determine the nextuser ID.
## This will output a list of all user's on the system, as well as their user
## id. When creating a new user, we need to make sure we use the next available user id:
sudo ipmitool user list 1

## OS X by default has 2 users, one is a built in system user, the other an admin user
## which is setup typically in Server Monitor. Id 3 is the next unused id
sudo ipmitool user set name 3 mynewadmin
sudo ipmitool user set password 3 'mynewpass'
sudo ipmitool enable 3

## turn on serial over lan for the user on both interfaces (not sure if this ↵
 is needed, but it's used by the default admin)
sudo ipmitool user sol 3 enable 1
```

```
sudo ipmitool user sol 3 enable 2

## set the user as admin for the first LOM port
sudo ipmitool channel setaccess 1 3 callin=on ipmi=on link=on privilege=4

## and then the second
sudo ipmitool channel setaccess 2 3 callin=on ipmi=on link=on privilege=4
```

After running these commands, you should be able to verify LOM management via ARD or Server Monitor by using the newly created user.

Troubleshooting

Regardless of the specific debugging techniques you use (and there are about as many methods for debugging as there are programmers), there are a few general principles to keep in mind as you debug your scripts.

The first task in any debugging effort is to learn how to consistently reproduce the bug. If it takes more than a few steps to manually trigger the buggy behavior, consider writing a script to trigger it. You will be able to debug much more quickly this way.

As you are debugging, you will want to progressively narrow your scope. In many cases, this involves eliminating half the possibilities at each stage of troubleshooting. Analysis is the thoughtful consideration of a bug's likely point of origin, based on detailed knowledge of the code base. In practice, you will probably use a combination of analysis and sheer brute force. A preliminary analysis will isolate the area of your code that is most likely to contain a given bug and then reviewing all of the code within that area will often help to locate it precisely.

Use debuggers, but don't spend an extended period of time getting the debuggers to work. Often, you step through a piece of code, statement by statement, only to find that you accidentally fixed the problem. Stepping through the code is invaluable as the more times you go through it, the more streamlined and commented it tends to become. Becoming more in tune with your code in this way can help to make you a better programmer.

If you are attempting to write scripts just for simple admin purposes and don't wish to spend a lot of time debugging, use a search engine and see if the specific portion of your script has been written before. In the course of writing this book, we found many of our scripts in an almost identical state on the web. In some cases, there are a finite number of ways of writing a script and if someone else has found the way to get the script to work, then learn from their work and build on it.

When trying to isolate a bug, you often want to change only one thing at a time. Debugging is a process where you make changes to code and then test to see if you've fixed a bug. Then you make another change, test again, and so on until the bug is fixed. At each iteration, make sure to change only one thing so that when the bug is fixed, you will know exactly what caused it. If you change several things at once, you risk including unnecessary changes in your fix, which may in some cases cause bugs themselves.

A trace statement is a console or log message that is inserted into a piece of code suspected of containing a bug, then generally removed once the bug has been found. Trace statements not only trace the path of execution through code, but the changing state of program variables as execution progresses. Once you have found the bug, you may find it helpful to leave a few of the trace statements in the code, perhaps converting console messages into file-based logging messages to assist in future debugging.

If you're using a third party server, database, or script, check all of the components and you will often find a good amount of useful information about errors in the log files for each application or operating system. You may have to configure the component to log the sort of information you're interested in.

Sometimes, after you've been hunting a bug for long enough, you begin to despair of ever finding it. When this happens, it can be useful to start from scratch. Create a new script, and bring each function from your old script over one at a time, checking each portion thoroughly before integrating it into the new script. At times, it is also a good idea to break each portion of a script into a separate scripts of its own.

Research shows that bugs tend to cluster. When you encounter a new bug, think of the parts of the code where you have found bugs in the past, and whether they could be involved with the current bug. At times, this is just that the functions you are working with may not be your strongest, or that the code in general is just buggy, but experience tells that where there is one pesky bug, there are likely to be others.

One of the most obscure sources of bugs is from using incompatible versions of third-party libraries. It is also one of the last things to check when you've exhausted other debugging strategies. For example, if version 5.1 of some library has a dependency on version 1.4g of SSL or some other library but you install 1.4b instead, the results may be issues that are difficult or impossible to diagnose. Checking your documentation can help with this.

If all else fails, read the instructions. It's remarkable how often this simple step is . In their rush to start programming with some class library or utility, some developers will adopt a trial-and-error approach to using, for example, a new Perl mod. If there is little or no documentation, this may be appropriate. It's possible that your bug results from misuse of the mod and the underlying code is failing to check that you have obeyed all the necessary preconditions for its use.

When a bug suddenly appears in functionality that has been working for some time, you should immediately wonder what has recently changed in the scripts or software that calls the scripts that might have caused the bug. This is where a version control system can be helpful, providing you with the ability to look at the change history of your code, or re-creating successively older versions of the code base until you get one in which the bug disappears. CVS and Subversion are both great examples of version control systems.

What may be multi-causal problems are often troubleshot as a single-cause bug. When troubleshooting network issues and buggy scripts, it is often hardest to isolate issues that contain multiple errors. In fact, we often do not consider this until trying everything else. But they do happen and if nothing else explains an issue, look for multiple bugs.

Normally you scrutinize the error messages you get very carefully, hoping for a clue as to where to start your debugging efforts. But if you're not having any luck with that approach, remember that error messages can sometimes be misleading. Sometimes programmers don't put as much thought into the handling and reporting of error conditions as one would like, so it may be wise to avoid interpreting the error message too literally, and to consider possibilities other than the ones that are specifically identified.

When you're really stuck on a bug, it can be helpful to grab another programmer and explain the bug to them. Also tell them the efforts you've made so far to hunt down its source. They may offer some helpful advice, but this is not what the technique is really about. It sometimes happens that in the course of explaining the problem to another person, you realize something about the bug you didn't think of before.

Many have noted that solutions come much easier after a period of intense concentration on the problem, followed by a period of rest. Another way to get a fresh look at a piece of code you've been staring at for too long is to print it out and review it. We read faster on paper than on the screen, so this may be why it's slightly easier to spot an error in printed code than displayed code.

After a time you may notice that you are prone to writing particular kinds of bugs. If you can identify a consistent weakness like this, you can take preventative steps. If you have a code-review checklist, augment the checklist to include a check specifically for the type of bug you favor. Simply maintaining an awareness of your "favorite" defects can help reduce your tendency to inject them.

Further Reading

Learn Mac Automation with Ruby Scripting. In this chapter we focused on using the bash shell to script against Mac OS X. However, Ruby is a flexible, popular, and diverse scripting language that can also be used, as is AppleScript. In this book, by Matt Neuberg, you will learn how to translate information between Ruby and AppleScript, which can be very useful, especially if you will be integrating Puppet into your imaging infrastructure. http://www.apress.com/book/view/9781430224938

Beginning Portable Shell Scripting: From Novice to Professional. This chapter has a heavy focus on shell scripting, as we feel that such scripts provide a very accessible, powerful environment, which can be handled for numerous automations. This book by Peter Seebach provides an excellent look into shell scripting. http://www.apress.com/book/view/1430210435

Beginning Perl, Second Edition. Perl is another command-line and scripting tool that can be used to automate almost anything in Mac OS X. In this book, by James Lee, you will learn the basics of programming in Perl. This is often the next step when budding programmers outgrow the capabilities of bash. http://www.apress.com/book/view/9781590593912

Pro Perl. Once you have a good fundamental understanding of Perl, it is time to move on to mastering it. This book, by Peter Wainwright, will guide you through moving from a Perl youngling to a Perl knight. By the end, you will be developing at a level that will have you automating even the most basic of tasks, such as walking the dog. http://www.apress.com/book/view/9781590594384

Beginning Python: From Novice to Professional. Python is another language that people like to try once they master the shell for Mac OS X. Python has a number of options that can be leveraged with Mac OS X. http://www.apress.com/book/view/9781590595190

Chapter 9

Virtualization

When faced with the ultimate goal of integrating Mac OS X clients into the enterprise, the preferred focus should be to provide your OS X users with a native environment whenever possible. There are many benefits to this. First and foremost, your user's lives will be better, which will make your life better. They will have a consistent user interface and a generally smoother experience.

While keeping users in a native environment is preferable, Virtualization is a popular option when deploying Windows and Linux applications on Mac OS X clients, as there are always going to be environments where certain business critical applications are platform dependent. When you have those one or two applications that are business critical to your organizations, but the applications cannot be used natively for the Mac, virtualization is a popular way to deploy non-Apple centric solutions onto Mac OS X. Deploying virtual environments is also a handy way to provide a fall-back when transitioning a user base from a different platform. Having said that, it's important to keep in mind that when you deploy virtual machines, your mass deployment system is now no longer one machine; it includes the deployment and initial configuration of both your host operating system (the Mac OS X operating system that will be housing your virtual machines) as well as the sum of all of your guest operating systems (the operating system running on each of your virtual machines).

Each guest operating system will come with its own deployment considerations, system requirements, long-term management requirements and of course, licensing. Each of these costs adds up to reduce the business case for having Mac OS X in the first place. Therefore, it is highly recommended to look at alternatives before deciding to deploy typical virtualization candidates like Microsoft Windows to all of your Macs, when possible. If you can streamline all of your applications into items available for Mac OS X then your deployment will go much smoother. The paradigm shift to Web-based applications that is occurring in most environments might help you in this regard. If you cannot, consider application publishing to a central server, using a tool such as Citrix prior to considering whether or not to deploy a virtualization application en masse to your end users. If you are transitioning a user base to OS X from another platform, you may have the facilities and licensing already in place to support the former environment. In this case, you have all of the pieces in place to deploy a relatively low-cost, historical window to your old environment—all provided through visualization.

While the mass deployment of only a single operating system in many environments is difficult, this task is made wholly more difficult when you are deploying guest operating systems on top of this. Keep in mind that both operating systems need to be manageable using your patch management solution or may require two different patch management solutions. Each typically needs to have policies enforced, and each will need similar automation logic. They will also need twice the surface space. This sprawl magnifies the need for centralized management and can often lead to the need for a higher staff count in order to deal with support tickets.

OS X is a very capable environment in that it plays well with others. If you are migrating from a UNIX environment, its native support for X11 will likely make you very happy. Common applications available on Windows like Microsoft Office and Lotus Notes are both natively supported. More and more business apps are turning into web applications, where the Mac is (usually) a first-rate citizen. However, the reality of the situation is that many purpose-built business apps are platform dependent in one way or another. Sometimes, there may be a native Mac client for your business app, but after testing it proves to be unreliable and generally unsupported (or perhaps written by the CEO's 16-year-old son, but you did not hear that from us). In some cases, the OS X client may just simply be missing critical functionality. If you need to publish alternative platform applications to users that they can use offline, if you need to allow users to test software, or you find some features of the Mac OS X versions of certain packages to be lacking, then you will likely need to deploy Windows alongside Mac OS X. If you find this reality staring at your face, you need to simply know that the process can work out great, provided that you follow a few specific steps. In this chapter, we will focus on explaining aspects of deployment that are unique to the virtualization environment for Mac OS X, with a general focus toward Microsoft Windows as the guest OS. This will begin with VMware Fusion, Parallels Desktop and Server, Boot Camp (not technically virtualization, but more on that later) and finally Crossover, an OS X native Wine implementation (a Windows API translation layer). We will explain how to deploy the Windows OS to OS X clients, and will cover various aspects used to manage the actual guest operating system. Once the VM has been deployed, we will move into patch management of the guest operating system itself.

Boot Camp

Microsoft Windows can be deployed on a Mac using Boot Camp. Boot Camp will require the system be rebooted between each operating system switch and comes with a host of additional deployment considerations. The Mac doesn't natively support PXE booting and other traditional Windows Deployment options; however, you can deploy Boot Camp through DeployStudio, JAMF's Casper Suite, and by using a number of other solutions. Because it runs on bare metal, we're going to leave further discourse on Boot Camp to Chapter 6.

Thin Clients

Before moving into discussing how to deploy virtualization applications, it is never a bad idea to pose a simple but important question: Why? As we've discussed, deploying multiple operating systems per host can create a large amount of overhead in all facets of your infrastructure, thus increasing the total cost of ownership of your overall environment. Why not deploy applications instead of entire operating system environments? The entire provisioning process occurs faster and upgrades happen centrally, thus there is no need for an additional infrastructure to support these operating systems.

One of the oldest and most stable thin client solutions with a Mac client is Citrix XenApp. Citrix can be used to publish a session, whether that session is an entire operating system environment or a single application. If you are considering deploying virtualization software to supply only a handful of non-native applications to your Mac users, consider Citrix as an alternative.

Microsoft also licensed Citrix technology to include Windows Server. This "Terminal Services" also fully supports a Remote Desktop Connection client for the Mac. You can download the Remote Desktop Connection at http://www.mactopia.com or use the open source CoRD at http://cord.sourceforge.net, which provides you with the ability to tap into multiple Windows RDP sessions concurrently. Terminal Services is going to be less costly than Citrix, but will also have fewer features and is best used when publishing an entire operating system environment, rather than a specific application.

The biggest drawback to a thin client environment is that access requires users to be online. This may or may not be detrimental to your user's productivity, but whether it is will generally be a pretty easy question to answer. With Wi-Fi showing up on flights around the country, high-speed cellular data networks, and a multitude of mobile devices that support the Remote Desktop Protocol (including the iPhone) thin clients are becoming a more and more accessible solution.

> **NOTE:** In addition to publishing Windows environments for Mac users, you can also publish Mac environments for both Windows and Mac users with AquaConnect. More on AquaConnect can be found on their web site at http://www.aquaconnect.net.

VMware

VMware provides a Mac OS X native virtualization client, dubbed Fusion. VMware Fusion is a type 2 hypervisor, meaning that it runs on top of an existing operating system (OS X) as an application. Furthermore, the application currently requires an active user session, which definitely has implications when deploying in a server environment. In such a case, a type 1 hypervisor, or bare metal hypervisor, is typically desirable in a server environment, allowing a system's virtualized operating systems to operate independently of each other. Unfortunately, at the time of this writing there are no true type 1 hypervisor's available for OS X. That said, VMware Fusion does have support for hosting both Mac OS X 10.5 or 10.6 server environments. Where Fusion succeeds is desktop OS virtualization, such as Microsoft Windows. A little later, VMware came on strong with Mac support and provides through Fusion a stable solution with good features and very decent performance.

The best way to deploy VMware Fusion to Mac clients is via an installer package. However, at first glance, the VMware Fusion installer is actually an application, and not an installer package. Never fear, there is in fact a native installer package, it's just hidden inside the application bundle's Resources folder. As such, you can extract this package for mass deployment, without the installer application, to deploy VMware Fusion with very little effort, provided that you do not require any customizations. Many environments will choose to customize the application installer. If you plan to do so then you may need to create a package or use a combination of two packages, one to deploy the actual package and another to deploy the license file. The VM itself will typically warrant its own installer as well. Splitting items up into individual packages can enable you to later replace only specific components on clients, conserving bandwidth, disk space and other resources.

Deploying VMware Fusion on Mac OS X is a three-step process. The first step is to deploy the VMware Fusion application. This is the software that allows you to run a guest operating system in a virtual machine. The second step in the process is to deploy the virtual machines themselves. Each virtual machine will run its own guest operating system which will need its own post-deployment configuration. This final configuration makes up the third step. In many cases, the guest operating system will be able to hook into an existing Windows deployment infrastructure and utilize in-place systems for policy management, and automations. Since this is not always the case, once we cover the initial deployment process, we will review bolting on a new management infrastructure for Open Directory environments.

For those using a package based imaging solution, we typically recommend breaking your VMware Fusion deployment up into three separate packages. The first will be the VMware Fusion 2 installer package. The second will be the serial number (unless you embed the serial number into the installer package) and the third will be the virtual machines, where each likely has a separate package. The more granular the approach, the more work it will seem like you have up front, yet a granular approach will require less work once you move from imaging to patch management.

VMware Fusion in Monolithic Imaging

As described in Chapter 6, a monolithic image will contain all of the items needed to deploy a workstation in a single image and will not typically rely on bolting any additional software. Adding VMware Fusion to a monolithic Mac OS X image is a fairly straightforward process: manually install VMware Fusion on your base image using a volume license. If you don't have a Volume License, then you'll need a post-flight script or package to deploy a new license on each client after they receive the initial software.

NOTE: With any monolithic imaging solution it is strongly recommended that you maintain a change log to track software that has been added or removed from your image. It is also recommended that you list any necessary automations and the utility they provide. Having a detailed change log becomes a key component to the ongoing management of most any imaging scenario, but more so in a monolithic imaging environment.

To install VMware Fusion, begin by mounting the VMware Fusion disk image or launching the installation media that came with the software. Next, double-click on the Install VMware Fusion icon. At the Welcome to the VMware Fusion Installer prompt, click on Continue, as seen in Figure 9-1.

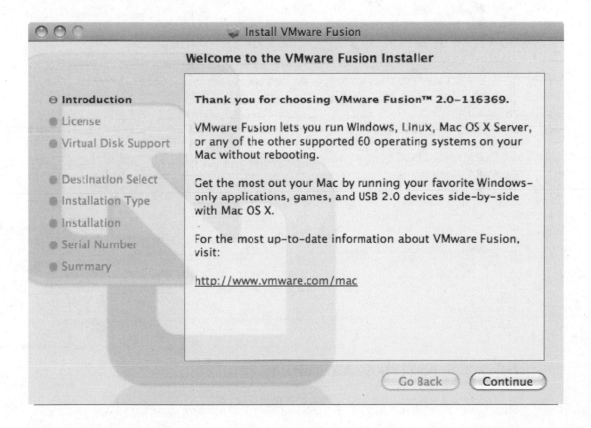

Figure 9-1. *The Welcome to the VMware Fusion Installer prompt*

At the screen for Software License Agreement, read the agreement carefully and then click on the Continue button. This will bring up a dialog box for you to accept the license agreement. If you agree with the licensing terms then click on Agree to continue, as shown in Figure 9-2.

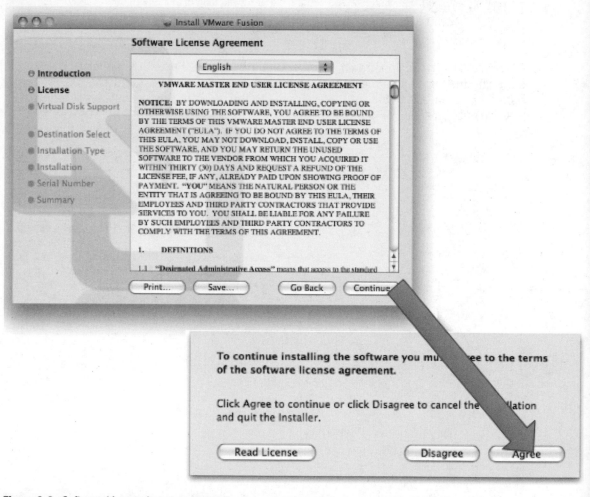

Figure 9-2. *Software License Agreement screen*

Next, you will see the Mount Virtual Disk Support screen, where you will be able to choose whether or not to install the latest version of MacFUSE. This is open-source software that has a plug-in to allow VMware Fusion users to mount volumes used by virtual machines, and it allows a user to browse the file system of a virtual machine from the native OS X Finder, provided the vm is not running. If you would like to enable this feature for end users, check the box to do so and click on Continue (see Figure 9-3).

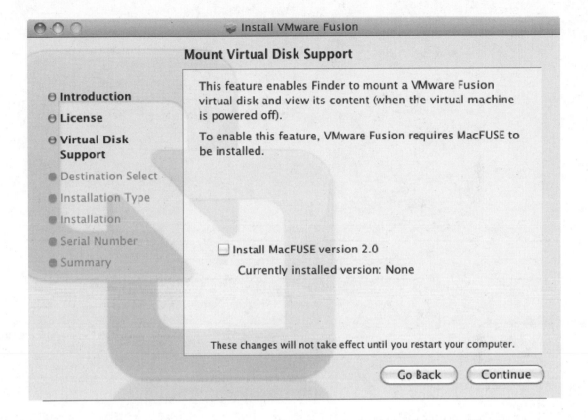

Figure 9-3. *The Mount Virtual Disk Support screen*

At the Standard Install screen (shown in Figure 9-4), you are able to customize which Mac OS X volume VMware Fusion will be installed or you can click on the Install button if you don't wish to perform any customizations. By default, VMware Fusion will install in the /Applications directory of the volume you are currently booted from. If your monolithic image is to be a single volume then this is fairly straightforward. If not, then while you can install it on disks other than a boot volume, you should not do so on a volume that is destined to be a Boot Camp volume nor one that does not run HFS+.

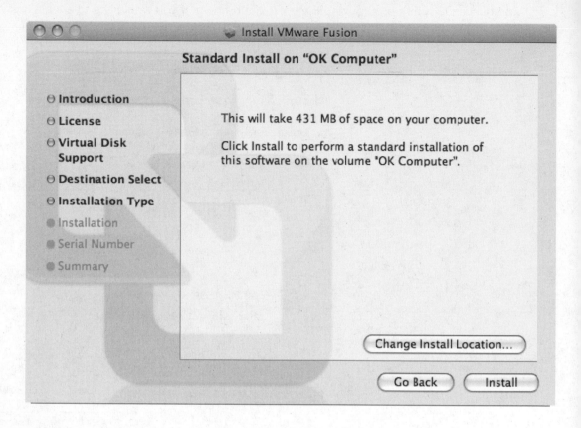

Figure 9-4. *The Standard Install screen*

When the installation process has completed you will need to enter a license. Here, you should enter your Volume License Master serial number (shown in Figure 9-5), clicking on the Continue button when you do so. If you do not have a Volume License serial number, you will need to go ahead and enter a valid serial number, which will subsequently automate the replacement of a separate package.

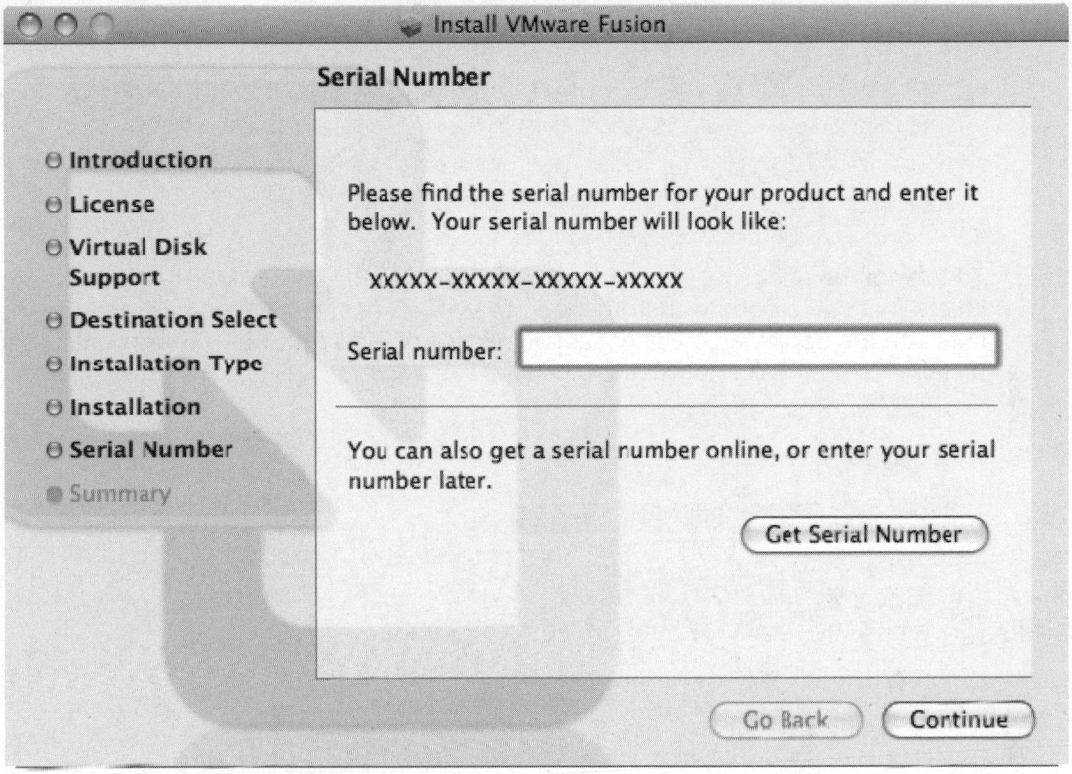

Figure 9-5. *Enter your Volume License Master serial number*

A successful installation will be indicated once the process has finished. At this point, you can move on to creating a virtual machine to install a guest operating system, as described later in this section.

VMware Fusion with a Package-Based Deployment

VMware Fusion 2 is distributed as a package installer that has been bundled inside of an application bundle. They cleverly disguise the .app file with an installer icon, which is confusing to some administrators. When installing Fusion directly onto a client, you can deploy either package or run the application. However, when performing mass installations, installer packages are convenient. Extracting the actual .pkg file will provide you with much better mass deployment options. When you are pushing out the .pkg file, you will then be able to embed a license key in it.

NOTE: It's worth mentioning before we get too much further that some snapshot tools like Jamf's Composer include presets for automatically creating Package installers from the existing installation of VMware. These tools typically (by default) grab all files, including registration, so you may still need to manually separate your serial number files yourself. That said, if you managed to get a volume license key from VMware, this tool may save you a little bit of time by bypassing some of the steps covered in this section.

To extract the package, you will first need to mount the latest VMware Fusion disk image that can be obtained from the VMware web site (you will typically want to make sure you are deploying the latest stable release of most software). Then, control-click on Install VMware Fusion to see the menu in Figure 9-6.

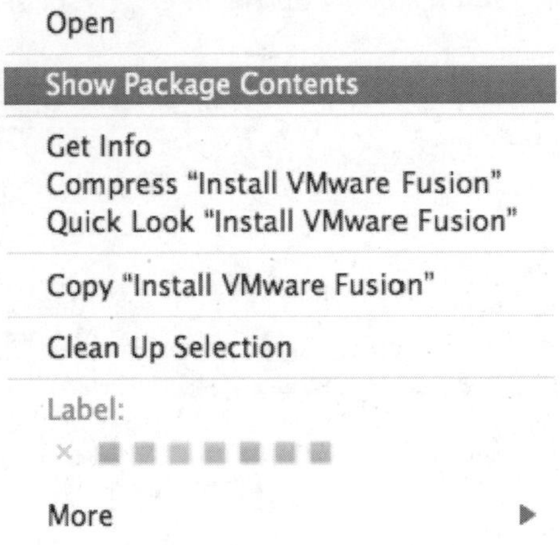

Figure 9-6. *Menu shown while extracting the VMware Fusion package*

Next, click on Show Package Contents and then browse to the Contents folder followed by the Resources folder. Here you will find the Install VMware Fusion.pkg package, which is the actual package installer for Fusion. You can now copy Install VMware Fusion.pkg out into another location, such as the desktop. Once you have completed preparing the package for deployment, you will want to store it in your package repository.

Assuming you have a Volume License Master serial, you will now want to customize the installation package to include the license and therefore fully automate the install. The license can be included inside the Install VMware Fusion.pkg package so that when you go to deploy the package through Apple Remote Desktop or another patch management solution, the installer will not require the end user to enter a serial number—an annoyance that potentially prevents the installation from proceeding (depending on your deployment tool). To embed the license file, first create a file called license.txt. In this file, paste the Volume License Master serial (and only the serial number, because nothing else should be in this file).

Now we're going to place the Volume License Master serial file (called license.txt) into the Install VMware Fusion.pkg package that you just extracted. To get started, browse to the Install VMware Fusion.pkg package and control-click on it, selecting Show Package Contents.

Next, browse to the Contents folder and then to the Plug-ins folder, where you will see the licensingPane.bundle "installer" bundle. A .bundle directory, like an .app or .pkg directory, is simply a collection of related files which is treated by the Finder as a single entity. To once again break this facade, we're going to control-click on it and then click on Show Package Contents. Next, open the Contents folder of the bundle and then navigate to the Resources folder. This is where you are going to copy your license.txt file. The following would achieve the same result in one single step by creating a new text file in the bundle (assuming you copied the Install VMware Fusion.pkg onto your desktop):

```
echo "XXXXX-XXXXX-XXXXX-XXXXX" >"/Users/$USER/Desktop/Install VMware Fusion.pkg/↵
Contents/Plugins/licensingPane.bundle/Contents/Resources/license.txt"
```

One important note about this process is that this installer package relies on scripts and executables that must run under the host operating system. If you use a product that installs packages while netbooted, this type of installer will require you to postpone this installation. This can be accomplished in tools like DeployStudio using the postpone installation checkbox or a reboot policy in Jamf's Casper suite. If you fail to do this, you may find your package installation does not complete correctly or, in the worst-case scenario, may stall your whole imaging process. If you are relying on the Apple Tools for imaging, you may want to create a self-destructing startup item that runs the installer command. More information about this procedure can be found in Chapter 8.

Virtual Machines

Now that you have created a deployment solution for your VMware application, it's time to focus attention on pushing out your virtual machines. Keep in mind that deploying any operating system is equally as complicated as another. You are going to install a virtual machine of Windows, but once installed it will have a unique serial number and other unique information that will need to be removed if that same machine will then be deployed en masse. While this section is meant to be a helpful guide it is by no means a replacement for books and software that are dedicated to this topic. Having said that, according to your task you may need to do little more than install Windows and use the operating system.

To get started, open the newly deployed VMware Fusion application and select New from the File menu (or use the Command-N keystroke). The New Virtual Machine Assistant will now ask you to insert a disk, as can be seen in Figure 9-7. Based on the contents of the disk, the assistant will install an operating system. Go ahead and insert your installation media and complete the Windows Easy Install wizard, which installs Windows along with the required VMware drivers.

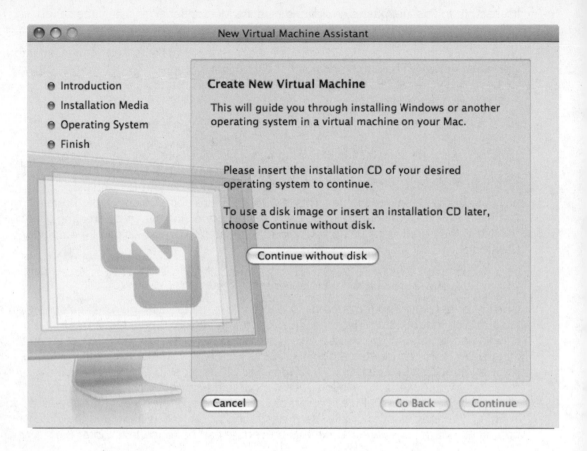

Figure 9-7. *Creating a new virtual machine*

When creating virtual machines you have a number of options for optimizing performance. The default VMware Fusion settings are good for a number of environments, but you should also thoroughly test the performance of your virtual machines and tweak other settings as needed. For instance, in certain environments, guest OS performance may be paramount and settings would then be weighted toward guest OS in terms of RAM allocation and processor priority.

Next, determine whether you want to deploy the guest Operating System's third party software along with the OS in the virtual machine, or as separate packages. If you choose to install all business software into the VM file directly, you may end up pushing out a rather bloated file. However, the abstraction provided in the vmfile itself provides the near equivalent of a block transfer, so it is often desirable to deploy as much software as possible in the VM file right from the start. If you instead choose not to embed your software in the VM file, and opt rather to deploy it through other means after the fact, then you will likely end up building custom installers and further complicating the environment. As with choosing a deployment methodology with Mac OS X, you will want to determine what methodology to take with your Windows virtual machine fleet. There are arguments for either side, but typically it is best left to the incumbent methodology being used for your physical Windows desktops, provided you have one.

Following the initial installation of the virtual machine and any third party add-ons, you will want to manage the systems similarly. If you have an existing solution in place then it is likely best to continue using it. If not, then consider a solution like Microsoft's System Center Configuration Manager (SCCM), LANdesk, or other patch management solutions. At a minimum you will likely want to leverage Microsoft's Windows Software Update Server (WSUS) to cache updates to the Microsoft products installed on your virtual machines.

Preparing the Virtual Machine for Mass Deployment

When building a base VMware image on one machine to be utilized for the purposes of mass deployment, there are a number of measures that need be taken to ensure that each client has a unique environment. In a VMware images .vmx file, there are a number of attributes, which are specific to the host that it is on. You will want to tailor this host-specific information to each destination client during deployment. This is similar to how Mac OS X handles ByHost information such as MAC addresses, but is specific to virtual machines rather than physical hosts. For starters, you will want to change the UUID, or unique Identifier. Luckily, if you simply remove the information from the .vmx file, it will regenerate the next time it is run. Thus, prior to deployment, you will want to clean out all of our host-specific data so that after deployment to a different client machine, the VM settings will auto populate with the relevant data.

Both the virtual MAC address and the UUID information that have been generated for a virtual machine are located in this.vmx file. To sanitize the auto generated information for a virtual machine, right-click on the virtual machine bundle (or cd into it) and select Show Package Contents. Find the .vmx file for the virtual machine and open it in a text editor. Next, remove the lines that contain the following information from the .vmx file:

```
uuid.bios =
uuid.location =
ethernet0.addressType =
ethernet0.generatedAddress =
ethernet0.generatedAddressOffset =
```

You will now want to remove any information about Shared and Mirrored folders, since those can potentially use paths that no longer exist on a host. To do so, open the .vmx file again and look for a line that is similar to the following:

```
sharedFolder1.hostPath = "/Users/cedge"
```

Change the information between the quotation marks to a ~:

```
sharedFolder1.hostPath = "~"
```

Once you have made these changes to the virtual machine, do not power on this VM. If you power on the VM, the settings will be reset to user specific settings and will need to be changed again. Thus, prior to this step, you will want to make sure that the VM host OS is configured full to your liking. Make sure that any customized settings or software has been installed. Once the host OS is setup, we will need to normalize the software install. Similar to our previous cleanup of the .vmx file, Windows has a cleanup process that it must do in order to be suited for deployment to other machines.

Once you are satisfied with everything, cleanup the appropriate values in the .vmx file and then copy the virtual machine to another host. Once copied, you can attempt to open the virtual machine. It should automatically recreate the preceding variables. If so, then the original virtual machine is ready for deployment (assuming the operating system resident on it is ready as well).

You can use VMware to automatically run a script, thus allowing you to rename a guest operating system or automate the binding process.

Virtual Machine Deployment

In addition to deploying VMware Fusion, nearly every organization that leverages it will also want to deploy the virtual machines on which they have installed their guest OS. The virtual machines themselves are stored as .vmware bundle files and while you might think deploying would be as easy as copying these files to workstations, there are a few other steps involved.

As with many other solutions throughout this book, we're going to leverage a package to deploy our virtual machine (more on packages in Chapter 6), which for the purpose of this example will be running Windows XP. Go ahead and open PackageMaker, found in the /Developer/Applications/Utilities directory. Upon launching the program, you will be prompted to specify an organization, which is typically the organization's DNS domain written using reverse notation. This value, along with the package name, is utilized by OS X for package identification. Also, select the minimum operating system on which the package can be installed, shown in Figure 9-8.

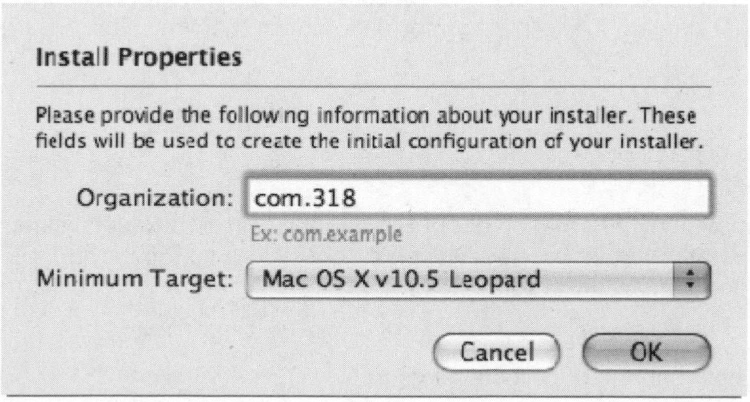

Figure 9-8. *Providing installer information*

Next, provide a name for the package that is unique to your scenario and choose the destination where that the package will be deployed. In this case, you will use the name VMDeploy. As it is the most common option, you'll go ahead and deploy your package onto the volume that contains your System folder, meaning your startup volume. Optionally, you could provide the end user with the ability to choose which directory the package will be installed using the "Volume selected by user" checkbox shown in Figure 9-9. For the purpose of this example, the package will always be deployed in an automated fashion.

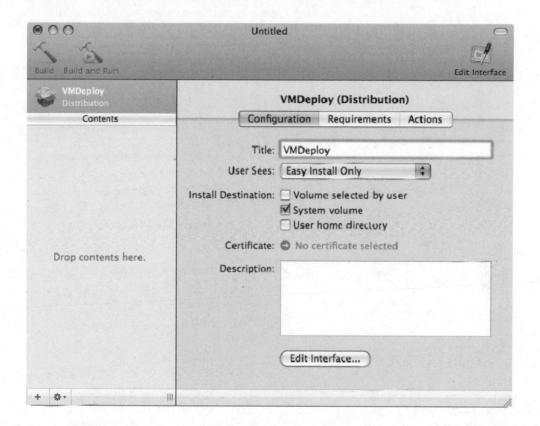

Figure 9-9. *Choose destination for package to be deployed*

Next, click on the Project menu at the top of the screen and select Add Contents to get a window that will allow you to browse for your files (shown in Figure 9-10). Navigate to your virtual machine, select it, and click on the OK button to be placed back at the main PackageMaker screen. You will see a new container in the left-hand pane, which represents our vm file. Enter the folder of the volume selected previously where you want the virtual machine to be located in the Destination: field and optionally provide a version number.

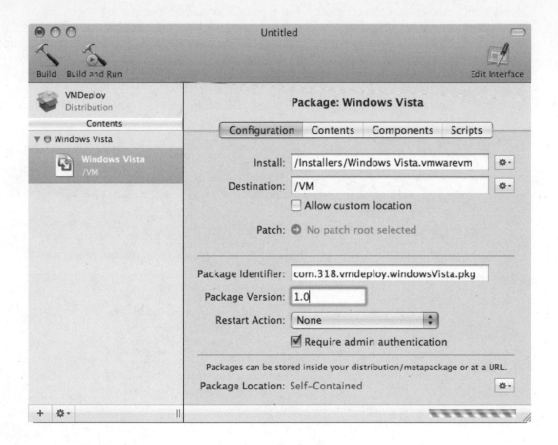

Figure 9-10. *Browse for your files*

Next, click on the Contents tab of PackageMaker and take note of the files. Under the Contents tab, you can view the files to be customized and the permissions as they will be laid down on the installing client. This package is going to be deployed to potentially hundreds or thousands of machines, so use extra diligence to verify everything is in order. Using this interface, you will want to browse through the presented files, verify that you are introducing no permissions-related security holes, and remove any unnecessary files (such as potential cache files) that may be present. When you're done, click on the Scripts tab and then define any scripts you may have to aid you in normalizing the file. For example, if you were to take the information mentioned previously in this section about client-unique attributes specified in a .vmx file, a post install script could be specified, which programmatically removes that data for you. To do so, script a scripts directory located with your project files into the Scripts Directory section, shown in Figure 9-11. Then choose a script to run located within that folder.

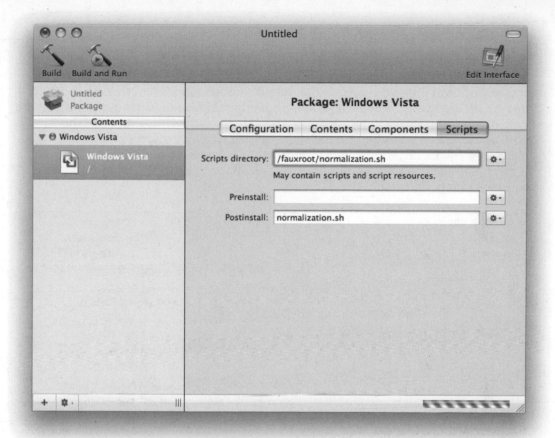

Figure 9-11. *Scripts Directory*

Another appropriate automation for fresh installations is to disable the welcome screen. To do so you would use the following command:

```
defaults write /Users/cedge/Library/Preferences/com.vmware.fusion↵
 VMWelcomeScreenViewed_2.0 -bool yes
```

> **TIP:** The defaults write command needs the absolute path else it will write to the active user domain and if it is being run during imaging it could ergo have unintended consequences. However, it is also not practical to deploy user-centric settings on a base image, as it is unlikely that user home folders will be populated with data at this time. For this reason, it is best to deploy these settings via a system such as MCX, as discussed in Chapter 7.

Populating the Virtual Machine List

Another automation as a post-flight for the package might be to populate the Virtual Machine Library. Once your virtual machine has been placed in the target directory by the package then you can use the defaults command (which is also described further in Chapter 6) to populate the listing of Virtual Machines on clients. If you are only deploying a single virtual machine to each client then you can copy the com.vmware.fusion.plist property list file to their home directory, which is stored in each user's ~/Library/Preferences/ directory. You can also add the file to the English.lproj User Template directory, as shown in Figure 9-12, in order to add it for all users of a given host.

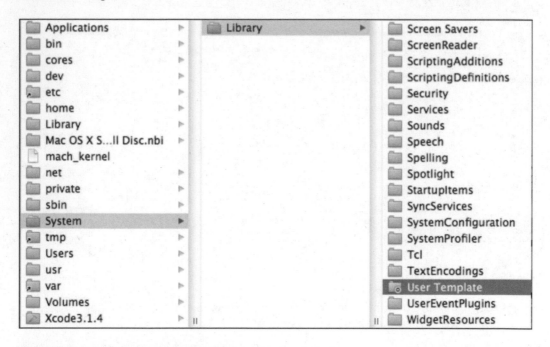

Figure 9-12. *English.lproj User Template directory*

To get started, let's look at the existing contents of the com.vmware.fusion domain.

```
defaults read com.vmware.fusion
```

The list of virtual machines that are available in the virtual machine list is stored in the VMFavortitesListDefaults2 key, which is an array of machine names and paths. You can query for a listing of the machines that are currently available to the Virtual Machine Library by reading the VMFavoritesListDefaults2 key alone:

```
defaults read com.vmware.fusion VMFavoritesListDefaults2
```

Next, you'll use the array-add defaults option to add a virtual machine called "Windows XP SP3" to the Virtual Machine List, assuming it has a local path of /VM/WindowsXPsp3.vmwarevm:

```
defaults write com.vmware.fusion VMFavoritesListDefaults2 -array-add '{name =↵
 "Windows XP SP3"; path = "/VM/WindowsXPsp3.vmwarevm";}'
```

> **NOTE:** Rather than use the array-add option, you could have added a whole listing of virtual machines if you were deploying multiple .vmwarevm bundles by using the -array option.

Assuming that the Virtual Machines List is your final customization to the package, once the post-flight script is added then you can click on the File menu at the top of the PackageMaker screen and then select SaveAs. You will then be able to save the package, as shown in Figure 9-13.

Figure 9-13. *Saving the package from the PackageMaker screen*

Once saved, go ahead and click on Build to generate your package. Now you can deploy it using your mass deployment package or by leveraging a variety of patch management solutions such as Apple Remote Desktop or the Casper Suite.

> **TIP:** We recommend only pushing out one virtual machine per package and then using the array-add defaults option per virtual machine to populate the Virtual Machine Library list.

Parallels

VMware Fusion is only one of a number of virtualization tools available for Mac OS X. Parallels is another, and is also a type 2 hypervisor, running as an Application inside of OS X. Parallels is available at http://www.parallels.com. As with Fusion, you will want to obtain a volume license for Parallels Desktop prior to leveraging the mass deployment options we illustrate through the remainder of this section. To get started, first download the Parallels dmg from the Parallels web site.

Parallels on a Monolithic Image

Installing Parallels on an image that will be deployed monolithically is fairly straightforward. Open the dmg file that you obtained from Parallels and you will see the standard installation screen. Double-click on the package, as seen in Figure 9-14 to start the installation.

Figure 9-14. *The standard installation screen*

The package will then check the Parallels site for updates and verify that the computer meets the minimum requirements. Provided there are no updates and that the computer does indeed meet those minimums, you will next see the Introduction screen of the package. Click on Continue to see the Read Me. Once you've read the Read Me, click on Continue again. You will now see the license agreement, read it and click on the Continue button again. At the pop-up menu, assuming you agree to the Parallels software agreement, click on the Agree button and you will be placed at the Feedback screen. Here, read the contents and click on Continue again, optionally selecting whether you want to be a part of the Parallels Customer Experience Program.

At the Installation Type screen, choose Change Install Location…, if you would like to change the path that Parallels will install onto. Otherwise, click on Install as seen in Figure 9-15 and then enter the username and password to authenticate the Parallels installer.

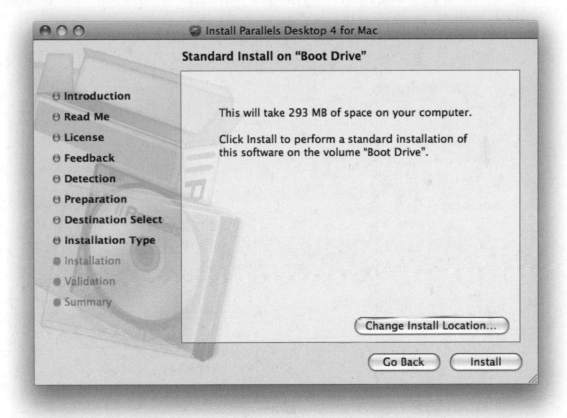

Figure 9-15. *Click on Install then type username and password to authenticate Parallels Installer*

When the installation has completed, click Close. You can now browse to the /Applications/Parallels directory to see the Parallels Desktop application bundle and open it. The first time you open Parallels Desktop it will ask you to Activate the product (enter the serial number). Since you don't want freshly imaged systems to show the Welcome to Parallels Desktop splash screen, uncheck the Show at Startup box, and then click on Start using Parallels Desktop. You will have deployed Parallels to your monolithic image set.

Next, setup the default location that virtual machines will be located. Later, when we move into automated deployment this will become a key component of ensuring the .pvm bundle that makes up a virtual machine is located in the desired location. To do so, open Parallels Desktop and click on the Parallels Desktop menu, selecting Preferences. Next, click on the General preference line item and then enter the default location (/VMs) and then click on the OK button, as seen in Figure 9-16.

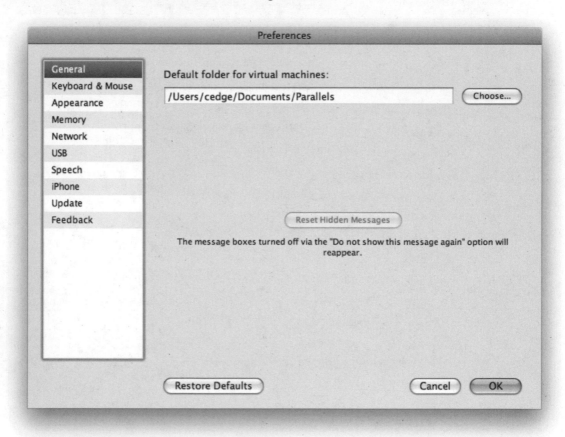

Figure 9-16. *Enter the default location /VMs then click OK*

Virtual Machine Deployment

Within Parallels you can easily invoke the Virtual Machine Assistant, used to create new virtual machine instances. To do so, open Parallels Desktop and then click Virtual Machine… from the File menu. At the Introduction screen of the assistant, click on the Continue button. At the Operating System Detection screen, choose how you want

Parallels Desktop or optionally click on Skip Detection to be prompted to manually choose your installation options such as choosing CD and DVD stand alone "iso" files shown in Figure 9-17.

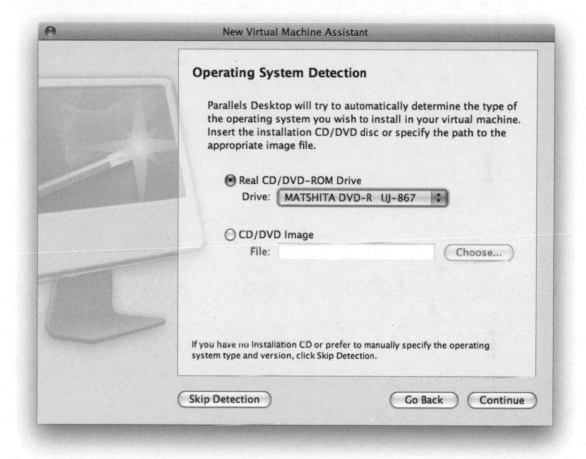

Figure 9-17. *Manually choosing your installation options*

Based on the media in the drive the Virtual Machine Assistant will provide you with an Operating System Type and Version screen so you can confirm the operating system to deploy. Next, you will see the Virtual Machine Type screen, where you can select to customize your virtual machine environment. For the purposes of this example, go ahead and click on Express Windows and then click on the Continue button shown in Figure 9-18.

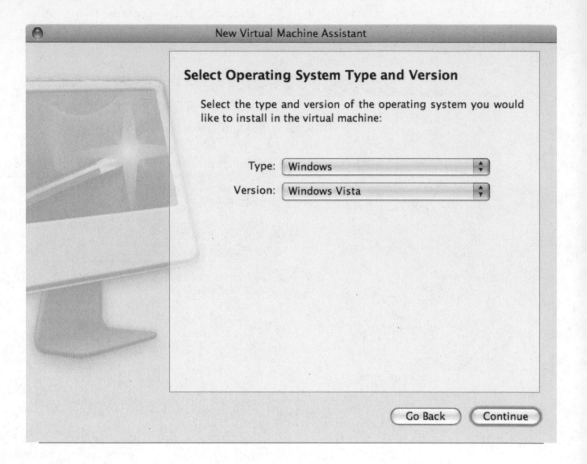

Figure 9-18. *After clicking on Express Windows, click on the Continue button*

At the Express Windows Installation screen shown in Figure 9-19, enter the name, company name, Windows XP serial number, and optionally select whether to install 64-bit. You can then click on the Advanced button to increase the available RAM for the virtual machine to over 1GB and you can even provision more than one processor if you so wish. If you will be running more than an application or two, or if the applications are fairly resource intensive, then it's recommended to go ahead and allocate more resources to the virtual machine. Otherwise, simply click on Continue to move on to the next step.

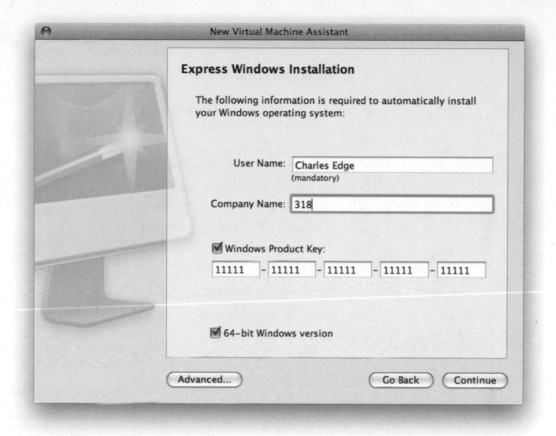

Figure 9-19. *The Express Windows Installation screen*

At the Name and Location screen, as seen in Figure 9-20, provide a name for the virtual machine. Also select whether you will enable file sharing (which will share your Mac home folder to your Windows installation) and user profile sharing (which will share your Desktop and other items between Mac OS X and Windows). Additionally, under the More Options portion of the screen, choose whether to create a desktop icon for the virtual machine, whether to allow other users of the host to access the virtual machine, and finally a custom location for the virtual machine. If you do not choose a custom location, the virtual machine will default to the ~ /Documents/Parallels/ directory. If you are using FileVault then you may want to move the location outside of your encrypted home folder. Likewise, this VM may be utilized by multiple users, so you may want to specify the option to save your virtual machines in the /Users/Shared public directory.

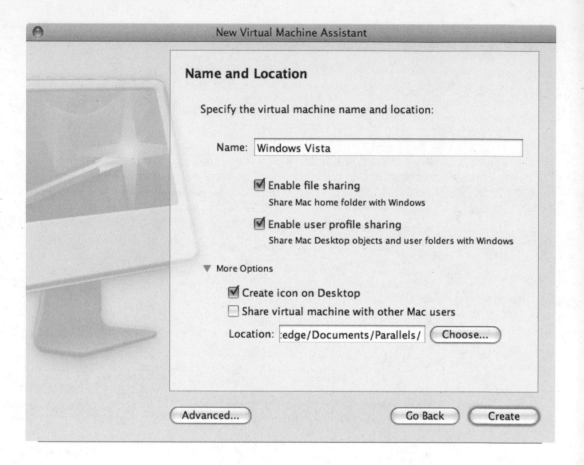

Figure 9-20. *Provide a name for the virtual machine*

Once you click on the Create button you will be in a standard Microsoft Windows installation screen. Complete the Windows installation and then, once you are finished change directories inside the resultant .pvm file that makes up your Parallels Virtual Machine. When you are inside the file from terminal—in much the same way that you did in VMware earlier—you will be able to view the contents of the config.pvs file.

> **TIP:** Once installed you will typically want to install the Parallels Tools software onto the virtual machine. These will allow for integration between the Mac OS X host operating system and the guest operating system that you have just installed. This can be accomplished by selecting "Install Parallels Tools…" menu option from the Parallels Desktop VM menu when the guest OS is booted.

The config.pvs file is the settings file for each virtual machine. As with VMware the virtual machine that you see through the Finder is in fact a bundle, with a number of files inside of it. Parallels have a fair number of settings in the .pvs file, organized by keys. There are multiple UUID keys and a number nested within the Network Adapter key that will need to be changed if you were to mass deploy your virtual machine, although it doesn't have to be that complicated, as we will illustrate in the upcoming section.

Automating the Parallels Installation

Parallels provides a solution to mass deploy their software. In order to leverage the Parallels best practice, to push out Parallels Desktop using a package, go to `http://download.parallels.com/desktop/tools/pd-autodeploy.zip` and download the Autodeploy package. The Autodeploy package will copy the application and virtual machine files for you and regenerate the unique identification information, similar to how you did manually for VMware Fusion earlier in the section "Preparing the Virtual Machine for Mass Deployment."

Once you have downloaded the package, right-click on it and select Show Package Contents, as you did earlier with VMware Fusion. From here, browse to the Parallels folder and find the License.txt file, as can be seen in Figure 9-21. By altering this file, you will provide the Parallels Desktop Autodeploy.pkg file with the serial number to use in an installation.

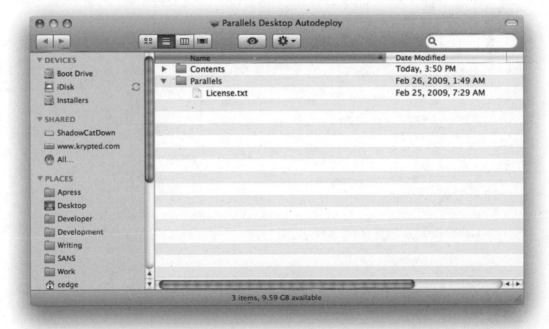

Figure 9-21. *Browse to the Parallels folder*

You will then need to place the Parallels Desktop.dmg file that contains the original package into the Parallels folder as well, which will complete the automated installation of Parallels.

As you are considering automating the deployment of the Parallels software, it is worth noting that there are two property lists that control the application's global behavior across various virtual machines. These are com.parallels.Parallels Desktop.plist and com.parallels.desktop.console.plist, both in the ~/Library/Preferences directory. (These are included with an installation, whether it is the Autodeploy or the standard installer.) The com.parallels.Parallels Desktop.plist file controls screen settings, update preferences, application toolbars, and the Virtual Machine Assistant. The com.parallels.desktop.console.plist controls last used directories. You can now push out the Autodeploy package in order to automate the installation of the Parallels application.

Automated Virtual Machine Deployment

While we covered pushing out the application itself in the previous section we have not yet looked into how to push out virtual machines. To do so, you would first normalize the Windows installation, as we did with VMware Fusion virtual machines and describe in the section "Preparing the Virtual Machine for Mass Deployment" later in this chapter. Once normalized, again control-click on the Parallels Desktop Autodeploy.pkg file and select Show Package Contents. Next, copy the virtual machine bundle from the current location into the Parallels folder of the package, where you previously edited the License.txt file, as can be seen in Figure 9-22.

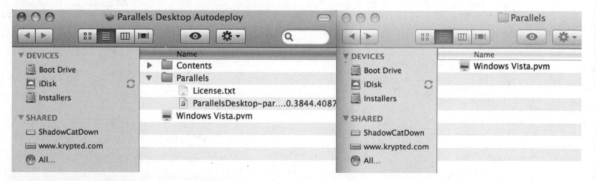

Figure 9-22. *The Parallels folder of the package*

Upon installation of the Parallels Desktop Autodeploy.pkg package, the .pvm file will now be copied into the users ~/Documents/Parallels directory by default. You can now leverage your mass deployment solution (DeployStudio) or your package management solution (Apple Remote Desktop) and the MAC address and all unique identifiers will be recreated without using any complicated scripting.

However, if you are leveraging a solution such as FileVault and you would like to alter the location of the virtual machine upon installation of the package, you will have needed to alter the Default Folder for Virtual Machine Settings when using the New Virtual Machine Assistant, as previously described. Alternatively, by changing the path for a virtual machine in the virtual machines preferences, you will also be telling the automated installer to place it into that location.

Finally, if you are deploying virtual machines after the initial deployment then you will want to register them with Parallels, potentially as a post-flight scripting task to your package. Parallels Desktop has a fairly comprehensive set of command-line tools that can be used to automate a number of tasks, including the registration and deregistration of virtual machines (which would use the register and unregister commands, respectively). See the Parallels Desktop Command Line Reference Guide for more on the Parallels command-line interface at http://download. parallels.com/desktop/v4/docs/en/Parallels_Command_Line_Reference_Guide.pdf.

Managing Windows

Whether you have deployed Parallels or VMware, working within a virtualized environment means that your management surface space has just been doubled. You now have two or more operating systems to manage whereas before you had one. You now have double the security issues, if not more, and a far more complex environment with regards to how each part interacts with the other. In short, your total cost of ownership just shot through the roof! But while your management costs just shot up, they can be kept in check. In the following sections we'll look at various ways to automate deployment and patch management in order to stay a lucid systems administrator.

Sysprep

Similar to deploying Mac OS X, there are a number of automations that you will want to perform on each virtual machine. As previously mentioned, each Microsoft Windows computer needs to be normalized, meaning it will need a unique identifier (SID) and a unique computer name. This means that two computers, whether physical or virtual, should not share an identifier, else they have problems, for example, binding to Active Directory. Other automations often include renaming hosts and, of course, binding machines into Active Directory. The two primary methods for these automations are sysprep or using custom scripts, which typically still involves using sysprep. For many tasks, such as removing machine-specific information and renaming hosts, it will be difficult to justify custom scripting as sysprep has much of the functionality required unless your organization's needs require logic that is beyond the basic sysprep functionality.

To get started with sysprep, first obtain the sysprep for your appropriate version of Windows by either using the optical media, or if you have applied a service pack since the optical media was used, by using the deploy.cab from the /Support/Tools directory. Next, click on the Start menu, select Run, and type sysprep. This will launch the System Preparation Tool, as shown in Figure 9-23. In the resulting window, ensure the checkbox "Don't regenerate security identifiers" is not checked and then click on the Reseal button. This represents sysprep in its basic form. However, most environments are going to require more automation.

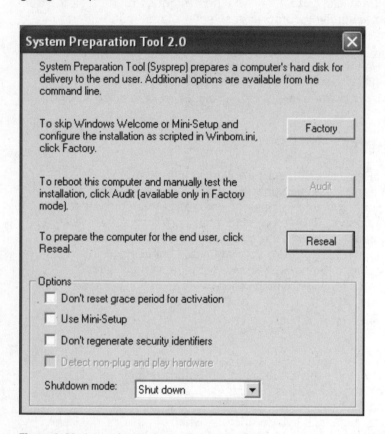

Figure 9-23. *Launching the System Preparation Tool*

Additional automation is provided via the implementation of a sysprep.inf file. The sysprep.inf file can be applied to an OS by placing it into the same directory as the sysprep.exe tool and then using it to reseal the image. However, before doing so from a freshly installed system, first run setupmgr.exe, because it provides a UI for generating your sysprep.inf file. This UI will allow you to set certain parameters, such as machine naming time zone settings and licensing. Once you have tailored the settings to your liking, select Sysprep setup from the option and click on the Next button, as shown in Figure 9-24.

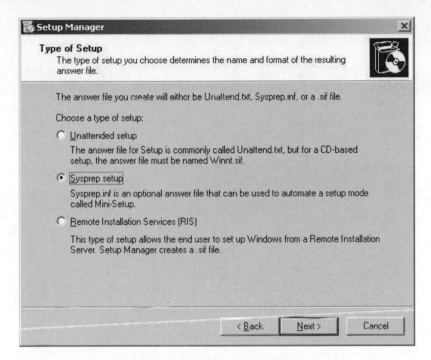

Figure 9-24. *Select Sysprep setup and click on the Next button*

Next, go through each of the options along the left side of the screen and fill in the appropriate information, as can be seen in Figure 9-25.

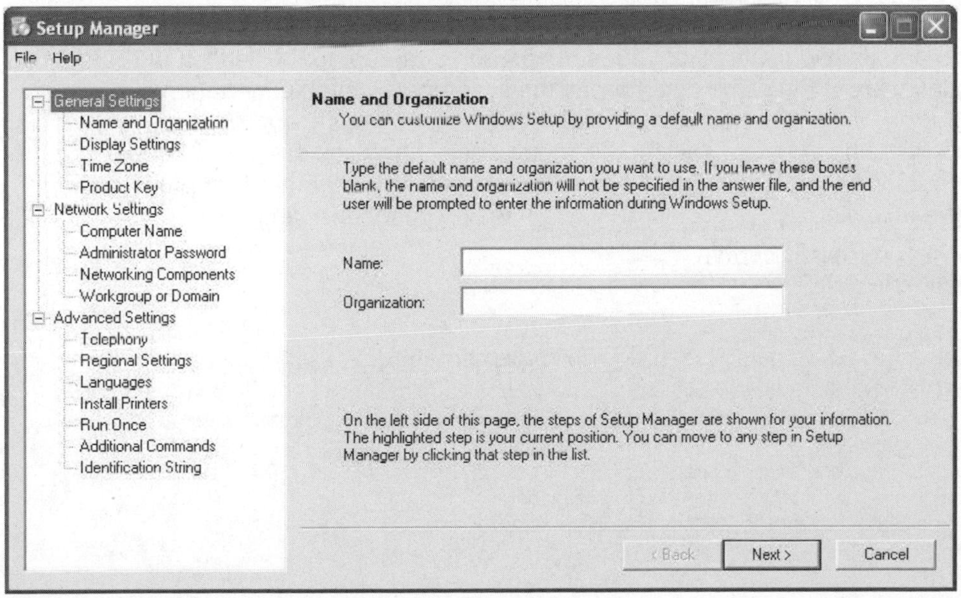

Figure 9-25. *View of the general settings*

When you get to the Computer Name section of Setup Manager (setupmgr.exe) choose to Automatically generate computer name, as can be seen in Figure 9-26.

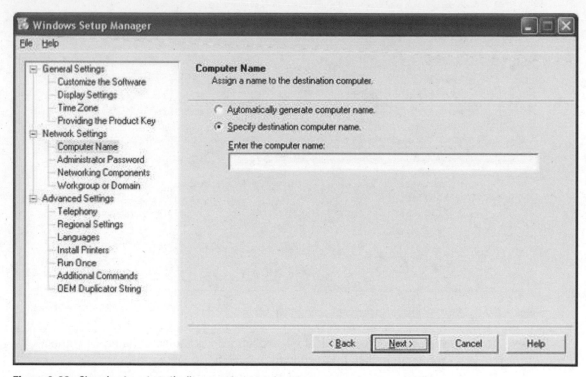

Figure 9-26. *Choosing to automatically generate computer name*

Once you are satisfied with all of your settings, run Sysprep again, verify that the sysprep.inf file is in the same directory as the sysprep executable, and then click on the Reseal button. Even if you use custom scripts for naming hosts and binding, you will likely end up using sysprep, sealing the image again when you are done. Scripts can be easily integrated if you are using sysprep. An example of a renaming script leveraging WMI is the following, which would go in your sealed image for naming:

```
' ------ SCRIPT CONFIGURATION ------
  strComputer = "."
  strNewName = "NEWCOMPUTER"
' ------ END CONFIGURATION ---------
Set objWMIService = GetObject("winmgmts:{impersonationLevel=impersonate}!\\" _
    & strComputer & "\root\cimv2")
        Set colComputers = objWMIService.ExecQuery ("Select * from
Win32_ComputerSystem")
For Each objComputer in colComputers
    errReturn = ObjComputer.Rename(strNewName)
    WScript.Echo "Computer successfully renamed"
Next
```

> **TIP:** After renaming a computer it seems like the very next step most people want to do is to join an Active Directory domain. Joining the Domain can be handled using JoinDomainOrWorkgroup in a Windows Management Instrumentation (WMI) script.

If you run a script at first boot, you can use the registry in combination with the Startup Items for an administrative user. A combination of the AutoAdminLogon, DefaultUserName and DefaultPassword keys can be used in the HKEY_LOCAL_MACHINE\SOFTWARE\Microsoft\Windows NT\CurrentVersion\Winlogon path of the registry to enable automatic logon for the virtual machine. After your automations have completed, you will want to edit the same registry keys, remove the DefaultUserName and DefaultPassword contents, and disable the AutoAdminLogon key, "possibly using the method described further in the next section, Configuration Management."

You can also run a script by passing the script into a command from your virtualization software. For example, the vmrun command could be leveraged to initiate a Visual Basic script as part of an automation. If you have a script that will bind to Active Directory then you can create a post-flight script in your package or leverage a tool, such as Apple Remote Desktop, to send a script through VMware Fusion to your virtual machine and your guest operating system. Assuming the username of an administrator is administrator with a password of SECRETPASSWORD and a path to the Visual Basic script in the c:\scripts\bind.vbs of the WindowsXP host, an example of this command would be the following:

```
vmrun -T fusion -gu administrator -gp 'SECRETPASSWORD' runScriptInGuest "/VMs/Windows XP↩
   Professional.vmwarevm/Windows XP Professional.vmx" cscript.exe "c:\scripts\bind.vbs"
```

> **NOTE:** You cannot run DOS batch files using vmrun.

The vmrun command can be found in /Library/Application Support/VMware Fusion/. You can run the command with no arguments to see pretty thorough documentation on the tool. To give a quick rundown of the above command, the –T flag designates the host type (in this case VMware Fusion). The -gu command and -gp flags designate the.guest host credentials. In order for this command to succeed, an OS X user must be logged in, and the virtual machine will need to be running. VMware Fusion can also use a bootcamp partition as its guest OS. For BootCamp based vm's, Fusion stores the .vmx file in ~/Library/Application Support/VMware Fusion/Virtual Machines/Boot Camp. Use the following command to find output the full path to a user's BootCamp .vmx file.

```
find /Users/*/Library/Application\ Support/VMware\ Fusion/Virtual\ Machines/Boot\↩
   Camp/ -name "*.vmx"
```

Configuration Management

No matter the platform, patch management is a key pain point of large-scale integrations. In many environments this is already handled, and from a virtualization standpoint you need only bind your virtual machines into Active Directory. They will then pick up a Windows

Software Update Service location from a GPO and pull down a number of policies, some of which will automatically install various pieces of software. GPO's, or Group Policy Objects, are Active Directory management policies which are used to manage clients.

> **NOTE:** For more information on Group Policy Objects see the following article on Microsoft's TechNet `http://technet.microsoft.com/en-us/library/cc737816(WS.10).aspx`.

The Windows Software Update Service is a part of Windows Server 2008. If you are already licensed for Windows then it costs nothing extra and, like the Software Update Server built into Mac OS X Server, Windows Software Update Services caches updates for all Microsoft products and allows administrators to control which to release to users. Windows Software Update Services can be configured to mirror the policies that your organization chooses to practice regarding release management of Microsoft software updates. For example, if you need to test every update on each build prior to putting a solution into production, then you can use group policy to configure which patches will be downloaded for a given group, user, computer or other object housed in Active Directory.

As with the Mac OS X Software Update Server, you can run centralize Windows Update using Windows Software Update Services without a directory service. With Mac OS X you update the Software Update Server setting with a key in the system defaults domain (com.apple.SoftwareUpdate) as described in Chapter 5. In Windows, you use the closest equivalent to a key in a defaults domain, a registry key. The server that is used for Windows Update is located in HKEY_LOCAL_MACHINE\SOFTWARE\Policies\ Microsoft\Windows\WindowsUpdate, in the registry, and with the WUServer and WUStatusServer keys. These should read http:// followed by the path of your server instance and the FQDN of your server, respectively. For example, if your Windows Software Update Service were housed on a server called WSUS.krypted.com, then the following settings would be appropriate:

- WUServer =http://WSUS.krypted.com
- WUStatusServer=WSUS.krypted.com

To push these out you could send the following to the guest operating system in the form of a Visual Basic script:

```
Set oshell = CreateObject("WScript.Shell")
        oshell.RegWrite
                "HKLM\SOFTWARE\Policies\Microsoft\Windows\WindowsUpdate\WUServer",↵
                "http://WSUS.krypted.com", "REG_SZ"
        oshell.RegWrite

"HKLM\SOFTWARE\Policies\Microsoft\Windows\WindowsUpdate\WUStatusServer",↵
                "http://WSUS.krypted.com", "REG_SZ"
```

You can also control Windows Update at a more granular level than just setting the server. The following keys are available to control AutoUpdate settings in HKEY_LOCAL_MACHINE\SOFTWARE\Policies\Microsoft\Windows\WindowsUpdate\AU:

- AUOptions
- NoAutoUpdate

- NoAutoRebootWithLoggedOnUsers
- ScheduledInstallDay
- ScheduledInstallTime
- UseWUServer
- RescheduleWaitTime

While you could send out the preceding script leveraging the command-line integration with, for example, VMware, you could also just control the Windows Update service using a group policy object. In Microsoft Windows, *Group Policy* is akin to the managed client framework of Mac OS X. GPOs are policies that, for the most part control a registry key (or more likely a set of registry keys) that control various functions within Microsoft Windows. Group Policies then become the core of using policies to deploy a centrally managed environment. These policies are managed through and enforced by Active Directory (each policy issued will apply to a number of objects in Active Directory).

> **NOTE:** This includes automating the installation of a piece of software leveraging an .msi or an .mst file, which is similar to a .pkg file.

As you'll find with the third-party solutions that were covered in Chapter 6 for patch management, Microsoft Windows also comes with a number of solutions that can manage systems, including the manual release management of software updates. These include applications such as Altiris, LANrev, and FileWave, which are also capable of working with Mac OS X. Microsoft's SCCM should also be looked at thoroughly, although it is not compatible with Mac OS X.

Policies and Open Directory

Group Policies use the registry to define where to pull a policy file from. If a preference manifest in Mac OS X (described in more detail in Chapter 7) is a container of settings, then a Group Policy Object is similar in that a file is created and the unique identification of that file is located in Active Directory. These files are stored in the Group Policy Template (GPT) subdirectory of the Sysvol folder, a directory created by default on all Windows Server Directory Controllers.

> **NOTE:** You can also use the Group Policy Object Editor on a host and apply the policies directly to that system in your virtual machine, which would then apply to virtual machines that are created based on the initial virtual machine; however, you should use the Sysvol as you will be able to centrally manage policies.

To create Group Policy Objects log into a Windows Server (if you are in an Active Directory environment) or a Windows XP computer (if you are applying the policy on the local computer). Click on Start, then Run, and at the Run dialog enter gpedit.msc. The resulting window will show you two types of policies, as can be seen in Figure 9-27, for the Local Computer: Computer Configuration and User Configuration. These control computer based settings and user based settings, respectively.

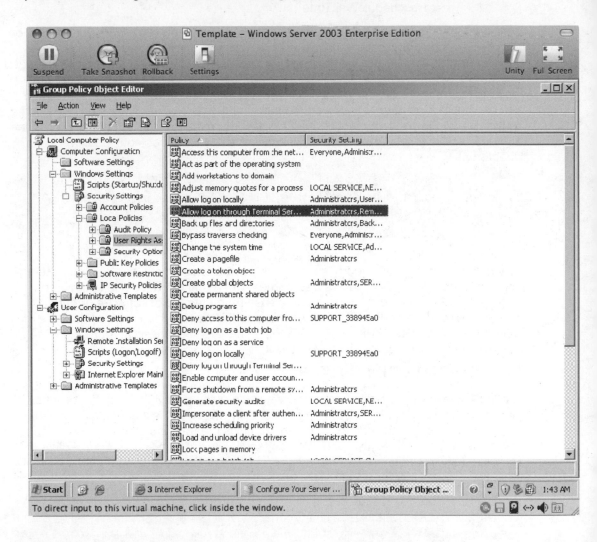

Figure 9-27. *Local Computer: Computer Configuration and User Configuration policies*

Computer Configurations

The Computer Configuration options mostly have to do with rights management. Here you can define which users or groups are capable of performing certain types of tasks and policies that span multiple users.

User Configurations

The User Configuration options are far more granular. Here you can configure various components of Windows, control applications (such as some of the above Windows Update settings) and customize user environments (including settings pertaining to the Desktop, My Documents, Start Menu and the Taskbar, such as whether or not the user has an option to open a Run dialog).

Other Virtualization Solutions

Up to this point we have focused on VMware and Parallels. The primary reason is that most enterprises are going to want to pay for support and are not typically considering free and open source software. However, there are two stand-out applications that can be used in place of VMware and Parallels that can help to keep TCO numbers in check.

The first is VirtualBox, by Sun Microsystems. VirtualBox, like VMware, is cross platform. It can run on practically any operating system and virtual machines can be traded between hosts. VirtualBox comes in a package and can therefore be mass deployed with little fanfare. VirtualBox does not come with some of the slick additional features that VMware or Parallels has, but it is capable of running most operating systems as guests and is a solution that can be deployed inexpensively. For more on VirtualBox, see: http://www.virtualbox.org.

Another free solution is Q, which can be obtained from http://www.kju-app.org. Q comes in an .app bundle and can be copied to client computers as a payload of a package. Bother Q and VirtualBox can have virtual machines deployed alongside the applications themselves in a package or using a separate package, as we did previously with VMware and Parallels.

Wine

Wine is an open source application that allows users of various versions of UNIX, Linux, and Mac OS X to run Windows applications without owning a copy of Microsoft Windows. Wine provides certain Windows apps to run natively in OS X and Linux-based systems by re-implementing the Win32 API. Unfortunately, Wine is not the easiest product on the planet to use and so CodeWeavers (http://www.codeweavers.com) has released CrossOver Mac, a utility that can allow you to leverage Wine without having to use complicated command-line structures each and every time you want to access an application.

Codeweavers does a great job of providing a user-friendly portal to Wine, but the truth of the matter is that it is a very complex task that the Wine project seeks to undertake. The reality is that the project simply cannot guarantee compatibility with every single piece of software out there written for the Windows world. Furthermore, "compatible" isn't really a black and white designation: some apps will function flawlessly, some apps will function mostly, and some apps will barely function. To help address the inevitable "will my software work" questions, Crossovers offers a Compatibility Center (http://www.codeweavers.com/compatibility/), which provides a searchable database of compatable software. This database rates software based upon its reported compatibility and uses a Gold/Silver/Bronze designation to describe software compatibility. The Gold designation is obviously desirable, and should your software be rated Gold, you can be fairly confident that It will function as intended. Silver rated software is mostly compatible, but designates that the vendor will respond and attempt to address bugs in the software. Bronze medallion software indicates the software has compatibility issues and should likely be avoided. Bronze rated software may have serious show stopping bugs, and should be avoided for business-critical usage. In any event, make sure to thoroughly test all business uses of the software before adopting the solution.

If your specific application needs are not present in the compatibility database, that does not preclude it from operation, it just means that no one has tested or reported the application. In such an event, you'll want to download a trial version of Crossover and fully vet your application's functions.

After doing so, you can submit (http://www.codeweavers.com/compatibility/submit/) your findings to Crossover to help share your findings with the community.

Managing VMs and Boot camp Through GPOs

One problem with introducing virtual machines into a mixed platform is that you are also introducing additional complexity. If you are already running Active Directory, then likely you will have bound your Macs into the Directory, as described in Chapter 3. When you introduce virtual machines onto these machines, then you'll be binding the virtual host into AD as well. Suddenly, you have two computer objects per machine. If you have BootCamp partitions not utilized by virtual machines, then this OS instance will also have its own computer record. How do you organize all of these? First and foremost, the naming convention on your OS hosts is paramount to be able to properly differentiate between the respective OS instances. One good practice is to use specialized prefixes or suffixes. For instance, the OS X environment may be jdoe-lt-0435. For this box, VM instances Computer Name might be called jdoe-lt-0435-vm, and its BootCamp partition might be jdoe-lt-0435-bc.

Unless you are using a third-party integration tool, such as Centrify, Quest, or have extended your Active Directory schema for Mac OS X support, then the computer object for your primary OS X instance isn't much good for management on your virtual machine. Its existence is without doubt a requirement, but any GPO's which would normally be applied to a Windows OS are promptly Ignored. Because of this, you can either organize your Mac OS X objects right next to your virtual machine objects, or you can create purpose-specific Computer containers for each purpose: Computers, Macs, MacVM, and BootCamp. Using purpose-specific containers is typically recommended for a number of reasons. First and foremost, in large environments it just helps organizationally. Most importantly, it provides a way to target each specific environment for GPO management.

There are certainly circumstances where you might only want to target specific VM instances, or perhaps only BootCamp computers. For instance, both Parallels and VMware have options to redirect a User's home profile to local folders on the OS X file system. This is similar to a basic redirection deployed GPO, but instead of pointing a user's folders to a network share, you point them to the filesystem on the host OS. This way, when you go to My Desktop on your Windows guest OS, you see the exact same items as you would when you go to your OS X Desktop folder. However, if you deploy GPO's by redirecting a user's My Desktop or My Documents folder to their network profile, those GPO's will conflict with the VM software's redirection, causing unpredictable results. The goal in this scenario would be to terminate redirections specifically on OS X virtual machine instances.

However, Document redirection is a User policy, so computer objects do not have dominion to manage (or prevent) them. Luckily, Active Directory provides a function called User Group policy loopback. When linked to an OU, User Policy application can be directly affected by User Policy GPO's applied to an OU containing computer records. Normally, only the user's Group Policy objects determine which user settings apply. However, if User Group policy loopback is enabled, when a user logs on to this computer, the computer's Policy objects determine which set of User Policy objects are applied. This will effectively allow you to block the inheritance of user folder redirection policies through the use of computer OUs (see Figure 9-28).

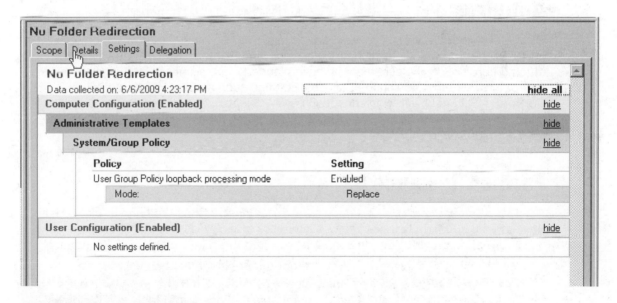

Figure 9-28. *Folder redirection policies*

Configuring your laptops in this way, by allowing your VM's to utilize local storage has numerous benefits. First, the barrier between host OS and guest OS becomes less of a mental challenge when both have access to the same data. This means your users will have less difficulty in comprehending the dual OS workflow. Secondly, it allows for the utilization of OS X-based home directory syncing, which will ensure that both OS X and

Windows altered documents in the user's home folder will get synchronized to the home directory server. This is particularly handy if your users will move back and forth between wired desktops and wireless laptops.

Through the use of OS X network home folders, Windows My Desktop and My Document GPO redirects, and OS X mobile syncing on laptops, you can provide a completely seamless cross platform existence. When the user logs into a wired lab Mac, he will have access to his data. If he then logs into his directory integrated laptop, syncing will ensure any changes made from the lab mac show up on the laptop. The user then opens up a Windows VM on his laptop and modifies some documents. The OS X host will eventually sync that data back to his home directory store as well. Perhaps next, that user logs into a lap running boot camp or even hardware PC's. All changes made on the laptop are right there present on the Desktop, and any changes will be saved back up through the chain.

This integration will be highly desirable in a large cross platform environment. It will help to reduce end user confusion, as they will no longer have to worry about which computer and OS their important data was last left on. It will provide the ability to transition between OS's with minimal burden on the user to understand the complexity that must go on behind the scenes.

AntiVirus

Finally, consider the virus. The Mac (according to the commercials you see on television, and in real life as well) is rarely harmed by malware. But Microsoft Windows, not so much. Therefore, make sure that you have planned for viral infestations on all of your computers. Whether you choose to use a solution such as Symantec's AntiVirus Corporate Edition or a free solution, such as AVG (http://free.avg.com) or ClamWin (http://www.clamwin.com), it is important to run some form of antivirus to keep your environment free from threats.

Further Resources

Virtualization: From the Desktop to the Enterprise by Chris Wolf and Erick M. Halter (Apress, 2005). http://www.apress.com/book/view/9781590594957. For more information on virtualization concepts look into this title, which covers leveraging virtualization overall and is not exclusive to Mac OS X.

Pro Windows PowerShell by Hristo Deshev (Apress, 2008). http://www.apress.com/book/view/9781590599402. Once you are able to work comfortably in a Windows environment, then one of the first things you should do is learn PowerShell. PowerShell is similar to shell scripting in Mac OS X, although nothing like it whatsoever. Confused? Then you need to check out this book, which will fill you in on the basics on managing systems using PowerShell and turn you into a Pro.

Active Directory Field Guide by Laura E. Hunter (Apress, 2005). http://www.apress.com/book/view/9781590594926. Microsoft Active Directory skills are a must if you are going to be centrally managing Windows instances on Mac OS X. This book will help you bridge the gap and take you further than this book can.

Automating Windows Administration by Stein Borge (Apress, 2004). `http://www.apress.com/book/view/9781590593974`. This book, which focuses on WSH, is going to be a little bit dated, but when used in conjunction with the Microsoft TechNet site it will provide a great deal of information on the scripting that will be required to automate your Windows virtual operating systems deployment. The book takes you from basic to complex scripting, and even has a number of scripts that you will likely want to use.

Hardening Windows by Jonathan Hassell (Apress, 2005). `http://www.apress.com/book/view/9781590595398`. One of the hottest topics to likely come up in a cross-platform deployment will be security. This book goes into detail on the security issues and the fixes that you are likely to encounter with regards to your Windows virtual machines. The book covers the security center, firewall, and a number of other features that are musts when deploying Windows. If you are a Mac admin and not a Windows admin, then you should have a resource for security best practices for each platform that you will be deploying.

iPhone

Practically every conversation about integrating Mac OS X into enterprise environments tends to include the iPhone in some way or another. iPhones are a darling of the consumerization set because they're cool, feature rich, extensible and allow for integration with a number of other solutions. The iPhone also has a number of features developed almost specifically for satisfying the needs of large organizations. Most notably is the ability to integrate into Microsoft Exchange. While the iPhone can also be used to support other messaging solutions, its native Exchange support provides the most seamless integration and doesn't require third party software

The iPod touch is similar to the iPhone, but is lacking in some of the core features that are found in the iPhone. Most notably is the fact that it is not a phone—it's an iPod. Physically, the iPod touch does not have a microphone, camera, or Bluetooth. The iPod touch also comes with a different dock, has a headphone jack on the bottom, and older models didn't have a built-in speaker. The iPod touch is otherwise very similar to the iPhone, because they are spec'd similarly performance wise and both run the same software stack. Therefore, the iPod touch makes a good low-cost alternative solution to the iPhone for testing and remote support staff. Throughout this chapter we will note when referencing a feature available exclusively for one.

The iPhone and iPod touch both take advantage of a rich development framework and are b built on a subset of OS X's Cocoa development platform, Cocoa Touch. This is a mobile optimized development environment that allows for the creation of feature rich, user-friendly applications. The numbers of applications that have been published to the App Store, Apple's online marketplace, are a testament to the extensibility of the underlying language. There is definitely a learning curve to writing applications for the iPhone for those without previous development experience. Those with OS X development experience, or experience with other Object Oriented languages, should be able to familiarize themselves with the environment quickly. In some cases, it will be easier to develop applications that can be leveraged using a web browser, thus enabling a number of different platforms to connect to the application and rapid development of portals customized for each type of device that may be supported.

In this chapter we will cover all the burning questions an enterprise organization might ask, given an upcoming mass deployment and integration project. We begin with the basics: how to configure the iPhone and iPod touch for most of the systems found in a large organization. Next, we move on to automating the installation and configuration of the devices. Then we discuss the ecosystem: strategies for making the iPhone and iPod touch as useful in your organization as a desktop computer. Finally, we look at troubleshooting the iPhone and iPod touch.

> **NOTE:** Before you get started with the technical part of this chapter, if you are using an iPhone then you will need to make sure that the SIM card has been installed and that the iPhone has been activated. If your organization uses Microsoft Exchange or VPN connectivity, then you will also need to make sure you have an Enterprise data plan or the iPhone will not be able to leverage ActiveSync.

The iPhone Simulator

The iPhone simulator (see Figure 10-1) is an application that Apple provides as part of its development toolset. The iPhone Simulator provides a means of accessing and testing core features or options on the devices. However, the usefulness is limited to testing web sites in Safari and basic troubleshooting. You cannot configure mail clients, calendars, or install software that you don't have the uncompiled Xcode project for. While the iPhone Simulator is often used as a troubleshooting tool, it's important to keep in mind that it was released as a development tool, and any features that it has (or doesn't have) are meant to aid developers, not to be a replacement for having an actual device.

While limited as a support tool, the iPhone Simulator is a great tool to use for application testing during the development process of an application. While writing an application, you can use the iPhone Simulator for testing the appearance and functionality. You can also check whether or not your organization's site and web-based applications appear and function appropriately on an iPhone or iPod touch.

To obtain the iPhone Simulator, download the iPhone SDK from `http://www. apple.com/downloads/macosx/development_tools/iphonesdk.html`. Once downloaded, install the SDK and then browse to the /Developer/Library/Platforms/ iPhoneSimulator.platform/Developer/ Applications directory and open the iPhone Simulator.

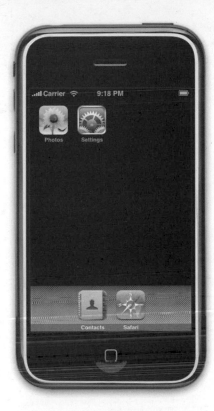

Figure 10-1. *The iPhone Simulator*

NOTE: You also cannot simulate the loss of network connectivity with the iPhone Simulator. The device connects through the active network connection of your computer and can provide mixed troubleshooting results, even if you disable the network connection on the computer itself.

Email

The iPhone's built-in mail client, Mail, supports numerous services and protocols. Compatible with industry standard IMAP, POP, and SMTP protocols, the device also has support for Microsoft Exchange, Mobile Me, Gmail, Yahoo! Mail, and AOL. Of these services, push notifications are available for Exchange, Mobile Me, and Yahoo!. Configuring the email client is a very straightforward process, and an email account likely will have been setup by iTunes during the sync setup.

Email account creation is handled on the iPhone through the Mail, Contacts, Calendars setting pane. To access this, from the iPhone home screen, click on the Settings app. Once the Settings app has launched, scroll down to Mail, Contacts, Calendars, found directly below General.

Tap Add Account. At the Add Account screen, you have to select which type of account that you will be setting up, as seen in Figure 10-2. Read on for information on configuring the app for your specific account type.

Figure 10-2. *Create a new Mail Account*

TIP: If no email account is configured, you can access the Add Account screen by directly opening the Mail app.

IMAP, POP, and SMTP

To setup an IMAP or POP account, from the Add Account screen, tap Other to bring up the interface for manually setting up an Email, Contact, or Calendar account, as seen in Figure 10-3. If you have already setup an account, then use the Settings icon at the home screen of the device and tap on the Mail, Contacts, Calendars entry. Then click on the Add Account… option and tap.

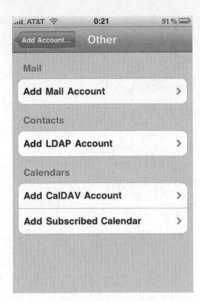

Figure 10-3. *Manually create an Account*

Tap Add Mail Account. At the New Account screen, enter the full name of the user whose email you are configuring in the Name field. This will represent the name shown in the From field when sending emails. After specifying a full name, enter the user's email address in the Address field. Next, enter the Password and a short description of the account into the Password and Description fields respectively, as shown in Figure 10-4. Click Save when you are finished entering the settings into the device.

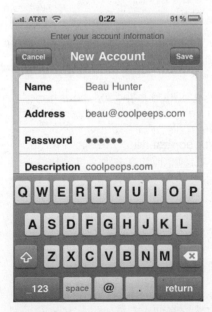

Figure 10-4. *Enter basic account information*

At the second New Account screen, select whether the account should be POP or IMAP by using the top bar to select the desired protocol, as seen in Figure 10-5. Then enter the settings:

■ Provide the server name in the Host Name field.

■ Enter the userID from your mail host in the User Name field.

■ Type the password used to access your email account in the Password field.

■ For Outgoing server, provide the appropriate information, in many cases mirroring the fields from above. For the vast majority of configurations, you will need to supply authentication credentials for your outgoing (SMTP) server as well.

Figure 10-5. *Select IMAP or POP account type.*

When you are satisfied with your settings, tap on the Save button in the top-right hand corner of the screen. The Save button will only be available once you have entered all of the required fields. The New Account screen should then verify your account information. Once complete, open Mail and test sending and receiving.

Setting Up the Exchange Client

The iPhone and iPod touch natively support exchange via the ActiveSync protocol and is officially supported by the Mail app when hosted by Exchange 2003 SP2 or Exchange 2007 SP1. However, the client should work with most third party ActiveSync implementations, such as Kerio MailServer. Configuring ActiveSync access on an iPhone is a very straightforward process. As mentioned, Exchange accounts are configured by adding a new account under the Mail, Contacts, Calendars pane in the Settings app. From the New Account screen, the very first item in the list is Microsoft Exchange (see Figure 10-2). Select it to create a new Exchange account.

Next, you will see some fields to enter your specific user account data, shown in Figure 10-6. Enter the Email address, the Domain, the Username, and the Password. Also, provide a short description of the account that is being added. Click next after you have entered all of your appropriate settings. The iPhone or iPod touch will now verify the Exchange account information you previously provided and often return back to the same screen, but with the addition of a server field. From here the device will try to configure for the environment. If the Exchange server cannot be determined from the provided domain information and DNS, you will be presented to manually specify the DNS name of the Exchange server. Provided that the device can synchronize with the Exchange server, you will now see a list of items to potentially synchronize. These include Mail, Contacts, and Calendars, also shown in Figure 10-6. You can move any of the three to an off slide position in order to disable synchronization for each specific option. When you're satisfied with the options that will be synchronized, tap on the Next button.

Figure 10-6. *Exchange Service Configuration*

You should now have an Exchange client configured and synchronized on the iPhone or iPod touch. If your organization supports Outlook Web Access, configuring synchronization with a Microsoft Exchange environment should occur without much fanfare. Having said this, ActiveSync requires Outlook Web Access to function. If you are in a 2003 environment then this is simple enough, but in 2007 you will need to point your account settings at the server that houses the CAS Client Access Service (CAS) role for the mailbox in question.

Once your initial synchronization has completed, verify that mail, contacts, and calendars work as they should.

NOTE: You can only have one active ActiveSync account configured on an iPhone or iPod touch at any given time.

Installing Certificates

Certificates can be installed on iPhones through a number of means. The easiest way to install a new certificate on an iPhone or iPod touch is by providing the certificate via a web site or by emailing the certificate to the user. In either scenario, the user needs to visit either the web site or tap on the certificate attached in an email. Once you have reached this point, you will be presented with the Install Profile interface. In Figure 10-7, you accessed the organization's root Certificate Authority certificate by opening http://myco.com/myco_ca.cer in Safari, which installs our LBC Certificate Authority root certificate.

> **NOTE:** The iPhone Active Sync client and Wireless configuration can login using certificate-based authentication if your services support it (such as if you are using Windows Server IAS). Typically when using RADIUS or Active Sync authentication you will want to install your certificate along with your wireless or Active Sync configuration at the same time. This will allow you to specify the certificate to be presented during this authentication challenge within the configuration profile.

Figure 10-7. *Install Certificate screen*

At this point, we can verify that it is the appropriate certificate, and then tap on the Install button to install it. If you are using an internally signed Certificate Authority, then you will be presented with an error, as seen in Figure 10-8.

Figure 10-8. *Unverified root certificate*

Click Install Now to add the certificate to the devices local trust. You will be prompted to enter your device password, if one has been configured. The certificate will then be added, and from now on accessing SSL services signed by your Certificate Authority will function without warning.

To modify certificates which have been installed and remove them from the trust, you must use the General pane found under the Settings app. In this interface, certificates will be listed under the Profile section, as seen in Figure 10-9.

Figure 10-9. *Installed profiles*

You can click on each installed profile to view more information. In this interface, profiles can simply be imported certificates, and they can also be configurations created using the iPhone configuration utility, which has a dedicated section later in this chapter. Using this interface, you can remove any installed restrictions, provided you can provide the phones passcode when prompted.

> **NOTE:** As of this writing, the iPhone did not support the Secure/Multipurpose Internet Mail Extensions (SMIME) standard. Messages cannot be signed or encrypted on the phone even if the proper certificate bundle is installed.

Network Connections

The iPhone and iPod touch both support connecting to standards compliant wireless access points and VPNs.

The Wireless network settings can be configured to access a wireless network by opening the Settings application, typically found on the devices home screen. With settings open, tap on General button and then Network. Here, you will have access to configure VPN and Wi-Fi connectivity settings. By tapping on Wi-Fi, you will have options to turn Wi-Fi off completely, or to join a particular network from a presented list of found SSIDs. Select the appropriate network and then enter the required information to connect to it. Alternatively, if you want to connect to a hidden network, tap Other… and then specify the SSID, security type, and credentials. This should be familiar because it is also how you would connect to the same type of network from within Mac OS X (see Figure 10-10).

Figure 10-10. *Configurewireless access*

VPN support on the iPhone includes standard PPTP and L2TP clients. Additionally, you can also connect to a Cisco VPN, because a basic IPSec client built specifically for Cisco Group authentication is included. Oddly enough, this means that native VPN support on the iPhone is actually more robust than that provided by Mac OS X, as the latter has no built-in support for IPsec layer3 tunnels. To access the VPN settings on a device, tap on Settings from the home screen. Next, tap on General and then Network. You will now see Wi-Fi and VPN. Tap on VPN and then tap on the 'Add VPN Configuration' button. From here you will see three tabs, L2TP, PPTP, and IPSec. If you are using any of these, then you more than likely already have a VPN server and configuration will closely resemble configuring VPN settings on any other platform. Configuration of the actual VPN server is outside of the purview of this book, so I will spare you the details about the differences between PPTP and L2TP or what a Group Name is for in IPSec. Enter the appropriate information for your organization and then select whether you want to encrypt all traffic through the VPN. If you do so, network connections will default over the virtual VPN interface. It is worth noting that VPN connections do not persist across different networks—changes between 3g access and Wi-Fi require the VPN tunnel to be re-established (see Figure 10-11).

Figure 10-11. *Configure VPN*

Non-Cisco, IPSec-based VPNs may or may not be supported. Check with your vendor to determine whether support is available. If it supports one of the aforementioned VPN protocols, you will most likely have minimal issues. Many vendors, such as CheckPoint, now have dedicated portals for their iPhone customers (http://www.checkpoint.com/iphone). If your company uses a non-standard VPN technology, such as SSL, then I have some bad news for you. Due to the sandboxed nature of the iPhone software stack, this type of device-wide network control is not possible. Do not hold your breath for third party support of web/SSL-based VPN technologies, at least not until Apple announces some policy changes.

> **NOTE:** As of this writing, Apple officially supports Cisco ASA 550 Security and PIX Firewalls with software version 7.2 and later (version 8 recommended) and IOD version 12.4(15)T or later. VPN 3000 Series are not supported. Also, there was no auto connection functionality of the VPN client. Users must manually connect to the VPN. Keep this in mind for internal web-based applications or those custom applications that require internal resource access (such as databases).

Leveraging the Web Browser

iPhone and iPod touch devices come with the Safari web browser, which is based on the growingly popular OpenSource WebKit engine. Most web sites that function properly in Safari for Mac OS X will also function appropriately in the mobile edition of the browser. However, there are a few key technologies that have not been implemented at the time of this writing. For example, SAML, the single sign on framework used by a number of large SharePoint Portal Server installations is not supported on the iPhone or iPod touch. We recommend that if you are going to be using web applications, such as Software as a Service (SaaS) providers or internal portals that you thoroughly test each business function (and field of each screen) to determine what may or may not need some fine tuning to work seamlessly for the iPhone and iPod touch. For that matter, we recommend the same thing for all of your supported mobile platforms.

Citrix

Custom application development, whether for web portals or for Objective-C, are native to the iPhone and iPod touch and can result in delays in getting applications to market. If you do not need to access your application while the device is offline, and you already have a Citrix infrastructure in place then it is possible to leverage the Citrix client for the iPhone and iPod touch to deploy an application store of your own. Using the Citrix Receiver application from Citrix, you can access any application that has been published from Citrix's XenApp.

To download the Citrix client for the iPhone and iPod touch, first open iTunes and tap on the link for the App Store. Alternatively, you go directly there using `http://itunes.apple.com/WebObjects/MZStore.woa/wa/viewSoftware?id=313735334&mt=8`. Once you have downloaded the application, install it on the iPhone or iPod touch and then look for the Citrix application in your list of available applications. When Citrix is first opened it will prompt you for connection information:

- *Address*: the host name or IP address of the server you will be logging into.

- *Username*: the user account that you will be using on the server.

- *Password*: the password for the user logging in.

- *Domain*: the Active Directory domain name on the server.

- *Sign in automatically*: choose whether to log into the server automatically.

- *Citrix Access gateway*: tapping here opens a new screen with the following settings.

    - Access gateway: controls whether you are using an access gateway.

    - Gateway type: only Standard Edition is supported as of the writing of this book.

    - Gateway authentication: allows you to select No Authentication, Domain Only, RSA SecurID Only, or Domain + RSA SecurID authentication.

Citrix has published a fair amount of information regarding iPhone support, and will likely continue to publish more as the product matures at `http://community.citrix.com/iphone`.

> **NOTE:** The negative side of deploying applications through Citrix to iPhone and iPod touch devices is that the application will require a constant Internet connection and will not be useful to end users while they are not online.

In addition to the Citrix client, there are a few applications available that will allow you to access standard RDP-based sessions being published from Windows (or AquaConnect for that matter). These are as follows:

- *Jaadu Remote Desktop*: allows access to most versions of Windows (or at least those that support Remote Desktop). Available at `http://itunes.apple.com/WebObjects/MZStore.woa/↵ wa/viewSoftware?id=299002339&mt=8`.

- *Remote Desktop:* allows access to Windows XP. Available at
  `http://itunes.apple.com/`↵
  `WebObjects/MZStore.woa/wa/viewSoftware?id=288362053&mt=8.`

- *Jaadu VNC:* Allows remote access to Mac and Windows PC's via the
  VNC protocol. Available at
  `http://itunes.apple.com/WebObjects/MZStore.woa/wa/viewSoftware?`
  `id=288362053&mt=8.`

iPhone Configuration Utility

In the first part of this chapter we looked into how to setup the iPhone to connect to common services that your organization may already have. However, if you've got a project where you need to deploy 100, 1,000, or 10,000 of these devices then you're going to want the set up per handheld to be as automated as possible. In order to streamline deployment, Apple has developed the iPhone Configuration Utility, accessible at `http://www.apple.com/support/iphone/enterprise/`.

Building Configurations

The iPhone Configuration Utility can be used to develop configurations that can be pushed out to iPhones and iPod touches. Once you have downloaded the utility, open and run the application installer. Once it's complete, look in /Applications/Utilities on Mac OS X or by default in C:\Program Files\iPhone Configuration Utility, where you will find the application bundle. Open it up and you will see the initial configuration utility screen. Click on Configuration Profiles, and then click on the New icon in the iPhone Configuration Utility toolbar. You will now see a screen that allows you to configure a number of settings for the iPhone.

The General Configuration Profiles tab is used to describe the profile you are creating. Here, you can enter a name, unique identifier (using reverse domain notation), an organization name, and finally a description of the profile you are creating. Here, we recommend a good naming convention. If you are going to build profiles per-user, consider placing the username followed by the time frame or version of the profile. If you are going to use a generic profile, consider entering a miniature description and/or a version number/date. In this example, you are creating a profile for your executive phones. Specify a configuration name, MyCo Executives, and then your configuration identifier using reverse domain notation: com.myco.executives.profile. Next, enter relevant information for the organization and description as shown in Figure 10-12.

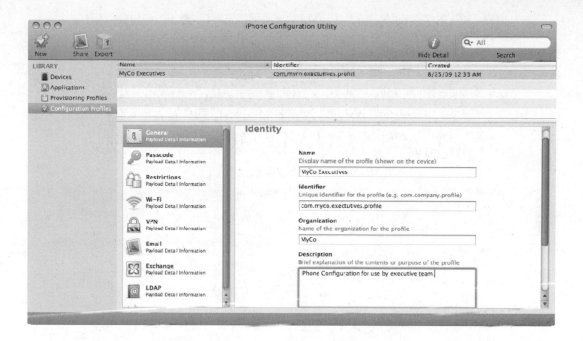

Figure 10-12. *iPhone Configuration Utility: General Tab*

The next section is the Passcode tab, where you can configure password policies, (which the iPhone and iPod touch refer to as passcodes). Shown in Figure 10-13, various settings exist to effect password requirements for sleeping and device power-on. These include pretty standard options, like the ability to set a lock timer, specify password minimum length enforcement, create alphanumeric requirements, and there even includes internal routines to test for weak passwords. You also have the ability to prevent up to 50 previous passwords for re-use, as well as enforce periodic password changes. It's important to note that you do not configure an actual passcode at this time (that's done from the device itself after the configuration has loaded). However, if you wish to configure a passcode policy to be enforced on your company devices, this is the place to do so. First, check the box for Require passcode on device. Next, select the appropriate options that fall within the boundaries of your organization's security policy:

- *Allow simple value*: indicates that insecure character sequences can be used as a password. For example, if you insist on using a palindrome you can use radar as your password using this option.

- *Require alphanumeric value*: requires that at least one alphabetic character exist in the password.

- *Minimum passcode length*: sets the minimum number of characters that a passcode must contain.

Minimum number of complex characters: sets the minimum number of characters allowable in a passcode.

- *Maximum passcode age (in days)*: sets the number of days before a passcode will need to be changed.

- *Auto-Lock (in minutes)*: configures the device to automatically lock and require a passcode to wake from the locked status.

- *Maximum number of failed attempts*: number of times an incorrect password will be used before erasing all of the data on the device.

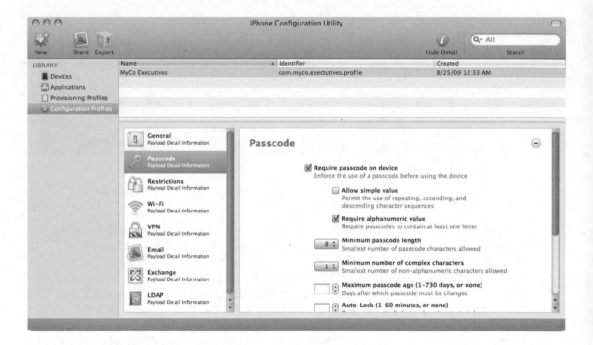

Figure 10-13. *iPhone Configuration Utility: Configuring Passcode Settings*

TIP: If you find that your passcode policies applied in the iPhone Configuration Utility are getting overridden, look into your Exchange Server for potential policy conflicts.

The Restrictions tab, shown in Figure 10-14, allows you to restrict certain activities on the iPhone. This includes disabling built-in features such as the device camera, Safari, YouTube, and the iTunes Music Store. You can also configure restrictions to prevent only elicit content from being watched or heard in the iPod app, and you can prevent additional applications from being installed.

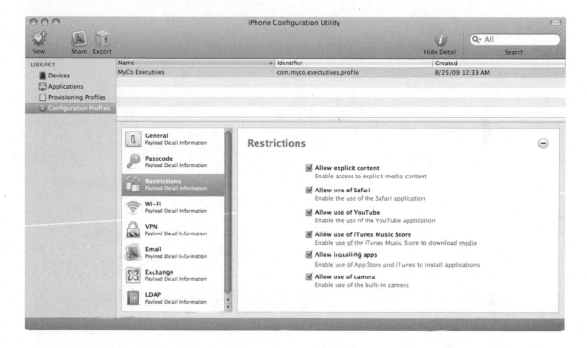

Figure 10-14. *iPhone Configuration Utility: Configuring Passcode Settings*

The Wi-Fi tab allows you to configure an iPhone and/or an iPod touch to connect to a variety of standards compliant VPN appliances and servers. Wi-Fi supports WEP, WPA, and WPA2 Enterprise, which allows support for most modern wireless environments, including those that depend on 802.1x for authentication and authorization. At the Wi-Fi section, click "Configure" to be presented with configuration options. In the resulting screen, shown in Figure 10-15, enter the name of the SSID, the Wireless network's broadcast name. There is not a drop-down menu to select discovered Wireless networks, so you must type the network name by hand. Bear in mind that SSID's are case sensitive. Cycle through all the settings, hopefully matching each one in the iPhone Configuration Utility with those you were able to discover while testing the handhelds.

Figure 10-15. *iPhone Configuration Utility: Wi-Fi*

The Hidden Network field will allow you to connect to hidden networks and must be checked if the network does not publicly announce its SSID. Next, check the Security Type field and find the type of Wireless network encryption that your organization is using. At its most basic, WEP and WPA/WPA2 Personal will not require further configuration. If you select WEP, or WPA/WPA2 options, then the user will need to enter the wireless network password themselves, it cannot be embedded into the configuration file. However, if you select WEP Enterprise or WPA/WPA2 Enterprise then you will need to configure your encryption protocol settings to match the configuration in production.

Under the Protocols tab for your enterprise Wi-Fi connection you will configure the protocol stack for your wireless network. First, use the checkboxes to select the authentication protocols that are supported. Options include TLS, LEAP, TTLS, PEAP, and EAP-FAST. If you are going to be using EAP-FAST then also select the Protected Access Credential (PAC) by first choosing whether to use PAC, and if so, whether or not to provision PAC and whether to do so anonymously.

Finally, select the authentication protocol to be used to access the inner ring (MSCHAPv2) and then click on the Authentication tab of the Wi-Fi screen. As shown in Figure 10-16, use the Authentication tab within the Wi-Fi screen to provide the username to be used to authenticate to networks and whether you want to send an authentication password along with the configuration. Then select a certificate to use for authentication if you have one and provide an outer identity (if required for your organization).

Figure 10-16. *iPhone Configuration Utility: WPA Enterprise User Authentication*

Next, click on the Trust tab of the Wi-Fi screen (see Figure 10-17). Here, you will see the option to provide a certificate that can be used to satisfy the requirement that a client utilizes an SSL certificate to authenticate into the environment. Here, certificates which were added under Credentials tab are listed, which we'll cover later in this section. However, once added, you would check the box for each to trust and present at authentication to the wireless network. To do so, click on the checkbox for each to be sent as part of the configuration. You will also want specify Trusted Certificate names (as defined in the certificates CN). To do so, use the plus (+) icon below the Trusted Server Certificate Names, and then type the name of each certificate to be trusted.

You can also provide multiple preconfigured networks that the mobile device can log into. Using the + and − buttons in the upper-right hand corner of the Wi-Fi screen you can add and remove more networks.

Figure 10-17. *iPhone Configuration Utility: WPA Enterprise Trusts*

NOTE: You can use the "Trusted Server Certificate Names" to bypass the prompt for users to trust dialog when connecting to the wireless access point.

Once you are satisfied with your wireless configuration settings, proceed to the VPN tab of your configuration profile (see Figure 10-18). If desired, click on the Configure button in order to deploy a VPN payload to the device. First provide a friendly name for your end users that describes the connection. Next, select a protocol. You can use PPTP, L2TP, and IPSec (which Apple calls IPSec), much in the same way that you can use the same options in the VPN when configured on a single mobile device, as shown previously in this chapter.

Figure 10-18. *iPhone Configuration Utility: VPN configuration*

The next section, Email, allows for the configuration of non-ActiveSync-based email accounts. Skip to the Exchange section if you have no IMAP/POP based email accounts to configure. Otherwise, click configure to configure the email section, and enter the appropriate information into the following fields (and as shown in Figure 10-19):

- *Account description*: a friendly identifier, you will typically want this to be similar to aid those in your remote support team who may end up providing phone support.

- *Account type*: choose POP if your account uses POP or IMAP if your account uses IMAP.

- *Account name*: the name that will show on sent email.

- *Email address*: the email address that will be used with the POP or IMAP account.

Once you have entered the global configuration information, use the Incoming Mail sub-tab to configure the following:

■ *Mail Server and port*: the host name or IP address of the server that the POP or IMAP account is hosted from.

■ *User name*: the userid for the server entered previously.

■ *Use password authentication*: enables password authentication for the account.

■ *Use SSL*: configures mail to leverage SSL. (If you use this setting then it does not hurt to also add and trust the certificate in the Credentials tab if said ticket was self-assigned rather than originating from a trusted CA.)

Figure 10-19. *iPhone Configuration utilty: IMAP/POP Email*

NOTE: The password here should only be used with encrypted profiles, as it is stored as a string in the `IncomingPassword` key of the file.

Once you are satisfied with your entries, click on the Outgoing Mail sub-tab and assuming your server requires (or at least allows) authenticated SMTP enter the appropriate SMTP information supplied by your mail host, shown in Figure 10-20.

Figure 10-20. *iPhone Configuration Utility: SMTP email settings*

If you wish to deploy Exchange configurations in this profile, you can configure the account settings appropriate for your Microsoft Exchange Server environment under the Exchange section. Only a single Exchange account can be configured on a device. These settings should match those in the Settings screen fairly accurately. To successfully configure an account, you will need to enter the following settings, shown in Figure 10-21:

- *Account name*: the friendly name for the account.

- *Exchange ActiveSync host*: the server that houses the Outlook Web Access role for your organization (your CAS server).

- *User*: the userID for the user in Active Directory/Exchange.

- *Email address*: the email address you will use.

- *Use SSL*: enable ActiveSync over SSL (again, enter the SSL certificate using the Credentials tab if you will be using this option).

■ *Authentication credential*: allows for the specification of a certificate used for authentication.

Figure 10-21. *iPhone Configuration Utility: Configuring Exchange Accounts*

With iPhone 3.0, we also saw the introduction of address lookup via the LDAP protocol. The iPhone configuration utility provides the ability to deploy these settings in mass to users. If you previously provided settings to configure an Exchange account, it is worth noting that the Global Address List (GAL) will be available for searching via the Contacts app as well as in the Mail app when specifying email addresses. However, if your environment does not host Exchange, then configuring iPhones to utilize LDAP services can be very handy. You can deploy multiple LDAP configurations. When deploying a configuration, it is necessary to provide the following information, as shown in Figure 10-22:

■ *Account description*: the friendly name for the account.

■ *Account hostname and port*: the server that houses the LDAP service, and the port which the service is available. By default this is TCP 389, or TCP 636, when using SSL.

■ *Account username and password*: Allows for the specification of an LDAP user for authentication. If your LDAP server does not support anonymous connections, you may want to create a user specific for this cause, such as ldap_iphone.

- *Use SSL*: enable LDAP over SSL, make sure to specify the appropriate port.

- *Search settings*: In this field you can supply multiple search paths which will be searched, as well as the standard LDAP scope options: Base, One Level, Subtree. If a scope of Base is selected, searches will only match against the object specified by the distinguished name provided via the search path. Using "One Level" will search for objects residing directly in the container or organizational unit specified via the search path. In an OS X Open Directory environments, a search path of "cn=Users,dc=myco,dc=com", but can also be "cn=People,dc=myco,dc=com". The subtree scope is the most forgiving, allowing you to search across all leaves of the provided search path. As such, a search path of "dc=myco,dc=com" would find entries both in cn=Users and cn=People. Subtree is also the slowest search pattern; search paths should be refined as much as possible.

NOTE: As of this writing, the LDAP client did not support self-signed certificates.

Figure 10-22. *iPhone Configuration Utility: Configuring LDAP Accounts*

With iPhone 3.0, we also saw the introduction of CalDAV support, allowing the iPhone's built-in calendar app to integrate with CalDAV based calendaring services, with full read/write privileges. Multiple accounts can be configured, and configuration itself of the CalDAV service is pretty basic, requiring only a few fields, as shown in Figure 10-23:

- *Account description*: the friendly name for the account.

- *Account hostname and port*: specify server hostname or IP that houses the CalDAV service, as well as the port over which the service is available. By default this is TCP 8008, TCP 8443 when using SSL.

- *Principal URL*: specify the URL to the user's calendar. You will typically leave this blank, as it is best to let it automatically determine the appropriate URL based upon the user provided username.

- *Account username and password*: specify the username and password to authenticate as. You will likely want to leave these fields blank, which will require the user to enter them upon configuration.

- *Use SSL*: enable CalDAV over SSL, make sure to specify the appropriate port

Figure 10-23. *iPhone Configuration Utility: Configuring CalDAV Settings*

You can also deploy read-only web-based calendar subscriptions based upon the .ics format. These can be useful for publishing information such as staff meetings, holidays, and special events. The payload information for a subscribe calendar is fairly basic and multiple subscriptions can be deployed. The following field information must be provided, as shown in Figure 10-24:

- *Description*: the friendly name for the calendar.

- *URL*: specify the http:// url where the calendar can be accessed.

- *Account username and password*: allows for the specification of an LDAP user for authentication. If your LDAP server does not support anonymous connections, you may want to create a user specific for this cause, such as webcal_iphone.

- *Use SSL*: Utilize SSL via the https protocol.

Figure 10-24. *iPhone Configuration Utility: Configuring WebCal Subscriptions*

The next section, Web Clips, allows you to create an iconified link to a webpage, which is very useful for ensuring employees have quick, easy access to things like the company intranet or help desk system. Deploying web clips is as simple as specifying a name, a url, and an icon. You can also specify whether or not the user can delete the webclip, as shown in Figure 10-25.

Figure 10-25. *iPhone Configuration Utility: Configuring WebCal Subscriptions*

The next section allows you to deploy custom SSL certificates to your iPhone, shown in Figure 10-26. If your establishment uses an internal Certificate Authority, you will need to deploy your CA's certificate to prevent users from receiving SSL errors when using encrypted services. Alternatively, if you are using certificate based authentication for any of the supported services, you deploy them here. Your users will be thankful given that they will need to click on less items to get setup and your support desk will thank you as well, considering they will more than likely get fewer phone calls with users who need help isolating various SSL issues.

To install certificates, click on the configure button in the Credentials section. You will be presented with an open dialog box, use it to navigate to the folder containing your certificates in .cer or .p12 format. With the certificate highlighted, click open. Assuming your certificate is in a supported format, the certificate will then be displayed and added to the payload. You can use the plus (+) and minus (–) buttons to add more certificates or remove certificates, respectively.

TIP: If you browse to an SSL-protected web site from your desktop using Safari or Firefox and accept the certificate, then it will be located in your Login.keychain, accessed via the Keychain Access application. From Keychain Access, you can drag it to the desktop to generate a CER file for the certificate. Alternatively, you can convert a standard PEM style cert (as used by OS X's Servers certificate system) to the DER format used in .cer files using the following command (replacing Default.crt with your certificate):

```
openssl x509 -in /etc/certificates/Default.crt -inform PEM -out
/etc/certificates/Default.cer -outform DER
```

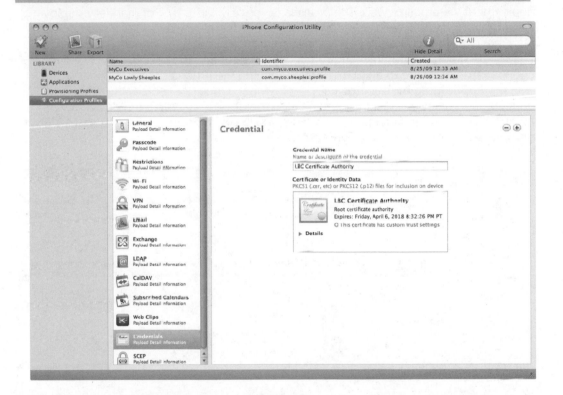

Figure 10-26. *iPhone Configuration Utility: Deploying Certificates*

SCEP allows you to utilize the Simple Certificate Enrollment Protocol for deploying configuration settings and certificates via SCEP, should you have such facilities in place. SCEP allows you to deploy highly customized user or device-specific configurations to iPhones. Unfortunately, setting up the system will require custom development. For more information on SCEP and Over-the-Air enrollment, see Apple's iPhone Enterprise Deployment Guide.

The Advanced section contains settings for the device Access Point Name and cellular proxy settings; they should not be altered unless specified by your carrier.

NOTE: For more information on enterprise deployment, see the Apple "iPhone OS Enterprise Deployment Guide" at
`http://manuals.info.apple.com/en_US/Enterprise_Deployment_Guide.pdf`.

Deploying Configurations

There isn't much of a reason to build a configuration if you aren't then going to apply it to a device. The iPhone Configuration Utility can be used to deploy configurations to iPhone and iPod touch devices directly, or you can export a signed configuration for deployment via email or web. The process is very similar to that of manually deploying certificates, described earlier in this chapter in the Installing Certificates section. To start, assume that you are batch processing a large number of iPhones, and as such, you will be doing the deployment from a central location. The process involves first connecting the device to an admin station running the iPhone configuration utility with the appropriate mobile profile for deployment. Once connected, the iPhone configuration utility will discover and catalog the device, including the device serial number, unique identifier, and the device's public key. Figure 10-27 illustrates an iPhone discovered via the iPhone configuration utility.

Figure 10-27. *iPhone configuration utility: Devices*

From here, you can assign a user to the device, using the Address Book framework, and you can specify an email address, though unfortunately this information isn't used during the deployment. At this point, you can deploy the configuration file to the device. To do so, click on the specific iPhone listed under the "Devices" section, and then select the Configuration Profiles Tab (see Figure 10-28).

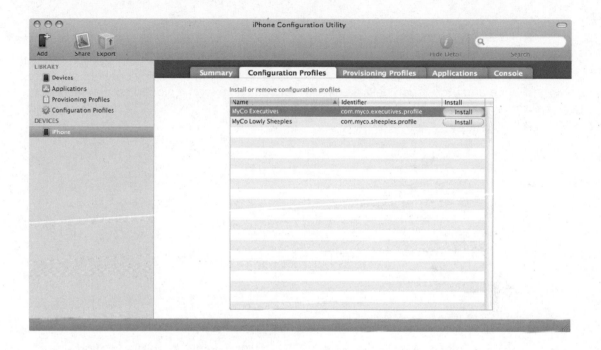

Figure 10-28. *iPhone configuration utility: Installing Configuration Profiles*

With the Configuration Profiles tab selected, you can click Install to install a specific profile onto the iPhone. Doing so will invoke the standard profile installation GUI, which is similar to the process of importing certificates.

When loading a mobile configuration, the first screen that you will see is an overview screen, which displays the profiles intended configuration and trust settings, as shown in Figure 10-29.

Figure 10-29. *iPhone Profile Installation*

Tap on the Install button on the iPhone to install the profile. At this point, you will be queried for any information missing from the mobile configuration. For instance, if you configured a VPN, Mail, or CalDAV payload, but did not specify a username, you will be prompted to provide that information at this point (see Figure 10-30). Likewise, if your configuration contains passcode enforcement, you will need to enter the passcode at the tail end of this process. Therefore, if you wish to batch process your iPhones prior to giving them to your users, your administrators will need your user's passwords, or the account creation process will need to be performed by users. In such a case, you will likely want to provide the configuration via a secured web service. This can be a two step process as well. For instance, the batch process might include SSL certs, generic LDAP connections, and perhaps a webclip towards the webhosted service-centric mobile profile. User's then need only click on the custom icon that you provide, which sends them to the remote mobile configuration file, and thereby directly into the installation screen. While not completely automated, it provides a fairly user-friendly deployment method.

Unfortunately, there is no authentication sharing between the various services, so you will have to enter credentials for each individual service.

Figure 10-30. *iPhone Profile Installation: provide authentication credentials*

There are a number of reasons why importing a configuration profile can fail. If, for example, the profile tells the device to configure an ActiveSync account and one is already present then the user will receive an error when they attempt to install the profile. If the user fails to enter a passcode with the appropriate passcode strength and gives up, then the entire configuration process will fail. Alternatively, if you are deploying Mail accounts which are configured to use SSL that is either self-signed, or signed by a CA which is not included in the iPhone's base trust, then the profile installation will fail, even if it contains the CA root certificate in the profile. For these instances, you may need to build out and deploy two configurations, one with the SSL certificates, and the other with the Account configuration payloads.

> **TIP:** For a list of certificates trusted by default on iPhone 3.0, see Apple Knowledge Base article HT3580: http://support.apple.com/kb/HT3580.

Importing and Exporting Profiles

The iPhone Configuration Utility allows for importing and exporting configuration profiles for distribution via email or web browser. To perform this task, first ensure that you have a configuration polished up and ready to go. Once this is done, highlight the profile, and then select either Share or Export from the toolbar, as shown in Figure 10-31. The former option will email the mobile configuration file, the latter will present a standard save dialog box and allow you to specify the name and location for exporting.

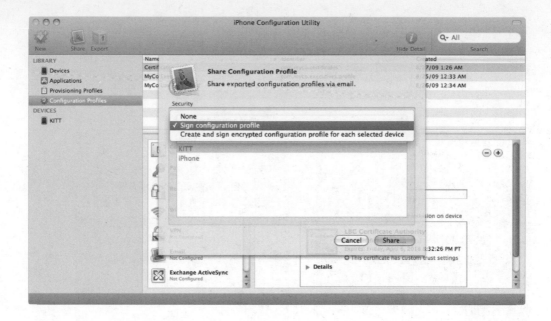

Figure 10-31. *Exporting iPhone Configuration Profiles*

After selecting either option, you will be presented with a dialog asking whether or not you want to sign the configuration, as shown in Figure 10-31. If you are exporting this for deployment, it is highly recommended that you do so. There are a few options here. First and foremost, you can opt not to sign the profile at all. This provides no security on the file, and leaves it open for alteration without any detection capabilities. By signing the configuration, devices which seek to deploy its payload can verify that it is tamper free. Obviously, this is always desirable. Next, it is possible to simply sign the configuration, or we can encrypt it for each registered device. The former option is much more forgiven, and is desirable if you wish to deploy this to an unknown amount of iPhones, and want the task to be as hassle free as possible. Alternatively, if you have all of your iPhones cataloged in the iPhone Configuration Utility, then you can create an encrypted profile for each phone.

The iPhone configuration utility signs exported profiles with a self-signed Certificate authority created when you first open the application for the first time. This certificate authority is used to sign the configuration profiles created by your copy of the application. If you are delegating configuration profile development among multiple members of your staff, you may wish to export this private key and certificate programmatically. The following is an example of perl script that will export this information with the password "pass" to files in the current directory where the script is run. Using this methodology you can keep all members of your group up to date with the latest copy of this certificate and private key.

```
#!/usr/bin/perl -w
# ipcuexport.pl Created by Zack Smith
```

```perl
#
# This script will export the iPhone Configuration Utility certificates and private key
# to files in the current directory with the naming
conventions below.
$certname = "iPCUCertificateAuthority.crt";
$pubkey = "iPCUCertificatePublic.p12";
$privkey = "iPCUCertificatePrivate.p12" ;

open(CERTS, "security export -k login.keychain -t certs|");
my $ifile = "";
my $thisfile = "";
while(<CERTS>) {
    $ifile .= $_;
    $thisfile .= $_;
    if($_ =~ /^\-+END(\s\w+)?\sCERTIFICATE\-+$/) {
        $subject = `echo "$thisfile" | openssl x509 -noout -subject`;
        if($subject =~ m/iPCU Certificate Authority/){
                $crtmodulus = `echo "$thisfile" | openssl x509 -noout -modulus`;
                my $fname = $certname;
                open CERT, ">$fname";
                print CERT $thisfile;
                close CERT;
        }
    $thisfile = "";
        }
}
close(CERTS);
$exportPublic = `openssl x509 -inform pem -in $certname -noout -pubkey > $pubkey`;
open(PRIV, "security export -k login.keychain -t privKeys -f pkcs12 -P pass | openssl
pkcs12 -passin pass:pass -passout pass:pass|");
my $kfile = "";
my $thiskey = "";
while(<PRIV>) {
    $kfile .= $_;
    $thiskey .= $_;
    if($_ =~ /^\-+END(\s\w+)?\sRSA PRIVATE KEY\-+$/) {
        $modulus = `echo "$thiskey" | openssl rsa -noout -modulus -passin pass:pass `;
                if($modulus = $crtmodulus){
                my $fname = $privkey;
                open FILE, ">$fname";
                print FILE $thiskey;
                close FILE;
        }
        $thiskey = "";
        }
}
close(PRIV);
```

The App Store

The iPhone App Store is where users can purchase or download applications for their iPhone. Application development can be a fairly complicated task. If you are looking for a specific function outside of the iPhone's default software, it's never a bad idea to see if such a tool is already on the market before committing development resources to the task. The App Store should be the first place you look. To access the App Store, open iTunes and click on the iTunes Store listing under STORE. Then click on the link for App Store (see Figure 10-32).

Figure 10-32. *The iTunes App Store*

You will now be able to browse, buy, and download applications.

KACE

The KBOX Systems Management Appliances, from KACE, can be leveraged to provide centralized configuration management of the iPhone and iPod touch. KBOX applications can provision, configure, and control policies with more granularity that can be found with the iPhone Configuration Utility. For example, you can leverage groups with your policies, monitor utilization, and application installations and track plans and renewals for the wireless contracts for the iPhone.

More on KACE and KBOX and the ability to manage iPhone and iPod touch can be found at http://www.kace.com/products/systems-management-appliance/ features/iphone-management.php.

Managing iTunes

iTunes provides the best, most seamless interface for users who use an iPhone or iPod touch. You don't have to use iTunes to interact with the device but it sure makes life much easier. If you choose to deploy iTunes as part of your mass deployment, whether it be to Windows or to Mac OS X clients (where it would be installed by default) there are some features that many organizations will certainly want to limit. Luckily, Apple allows you to manage various iTunes features for both Windows and Mac OS X clients. For Windows, there are a number of registry keys that can be used and for Mac OS X there is the ~/Library/Preferences/com.apple.iTunes.plist file.

Using the com.apple.iTunes.plist file you will have the ability to add the preference domain into the Workgroup Manager Managed Preferences (as covered in Chapter 7). Once added, you will be able to set a number of options to manage, including the following keys (which are self-explanatory for the most part):

- allowiTunesUAccess
- disableAppleTV
- disableAutomaticDeviceSync
- disableCheckForUpdates
- disableDeviceRegistration
- disableGeniusSidebar
- disableGetAlbumArtwork
- disableMusicStore
- disableOpenStream
- disablePlugins
- disablePodcasts
- disableRadio
- disableSharedMusic
- gamesLimit
- moviesLimit
- ratingSystemID
- restrictExplicit
- restrictGames
- restrictMovies
- restrictTVshows
- tvShowsLimit

If you have not been allowing your users to use iTunes because of a specific feature having been abused (Radio) then you can now limit many individual features of iTunes, and therefore allow users to still have access to less intrusive capabilities, such as iTunesU and Podcasts. Beware if you don't have a managed environment, and are considering pushing out a new com.apple.iTunes.plist file to your users. The feet will be a little tricky if you want to make sure to preserve any paired devices. Information about iPhones and AppleTVs can be found in this file, so it's best not to perform file drop's (common with package management tools, such as Jamf). If you do wish to push a preference into the file directly, rather than use MCX it will be best to utilize a shell script and the defaults command. For example, to disable iTunesRadio you could use the following:

```
defaults write ~/Library/Preferences/com.apple.iTunes disableRadio -bool true
```

Troubleshooting

It seems like no matter what technology you are talking about there are going to be a number of troubleshooting steps that are always appropriate, almost no matter what the end user's symptom is. For example, is the hardware working as intended? Will the iPhone make a phone call? Is the service plan still active for the device?

If a device will not power on, try plugging it into a power source to check the battery. If the device is on and running, but otherwise unresponsive, you can try to force quit the frontmost application. To accomplish this, press and hold the lock button until the Shutdown Slider appears. At this point, press and hold the home button for a second or two until the front most application quits. This is the equivalent of using Control-Option-Escape in Mac OS X to force quit an application or Control-Alt-Escape in Windows to bring up the Task Manager.

If that doesn't work, reboot the iPhone or iPod touch by holding the sleep button on the top of the device. After a few moments, a red slider appears, press and slide the slider from left to right to shut down the device, similar to the procedure used to wake an iPhone, Press and hold the sleep button to power the device back on. You can also reset the device by holding down the sleep and home buttons until you see an Apple logo. Finally, you can perform a factory reset on a device from the Settings icon on the home screen: click on General ➤ Reset➤ Reset All Settings (make sure you've got a good backup of a device before doing this).

If the device isn't booting at all, you can attempt to boot the device in recovery mode. To do so, first launch iTunes on your admin station. Next, with the device off, press and hold the home button. With the home button depressed, plug the device into your admin station via USB. The iPhone should display that it is in recovery mode, and you can now restore the phone to factory defaults.

With the iPhone and iPod touch, when you are troubleshooting network services then you should always verify network connectivity first. This is critical before you do anything else, as many applications will require the ability to open a network connection to an outside host. If you are having trouble accessing specific services, then provided you can connect to a network, verify that network connections are available between the device you are connecting to and the device you are connecting from. Outside of checking for network connectivity with safari, Apple doesn't really provide a good means for this. You can examine network settings found under the Settings application, but those don't give all the data needed to properly confirm external connectivity. There are some third party applications that can assist here, providing ping and traceroute capabilities. One such app with great polish is Bjango, but there are a handful of others to choose from.

If you encounter problems deploying profiles via the iPhone Configuration Utility, say you receive a generic deployment error when attempting to install a profile on a phone. This can be caused by a few different things. First, verify that the problem is not due simply to a misconfiguration. At times, the issue may be device specific. If this is the case, there may be a problem with your devices configuration file, stored in the folder ~/Library/MobileDevices and named according to the devices identifier. Deleting that file can sometimes resolve your issue. If not, consider deleting the application preferences at ~/Library/Preferences/com.apple.iPhoneConfigurationUtility.plist (make sure it's not running).

Updates

Software and Firmware updates can only be deployed to an iPhone or iPod touch using iTunes. To do so, open iTunes, click on the name of the device in the left column, locating the DEVICES section. Click on the device you are going to update and then click on Check for Update button (as can be seen in Figure 10-33), following the onscreen instructions to completion. Unfortunately, there are no capabilities for over-the-air updates, it all must be user initiated through iTunes syncing. At the time of this writing, Apple does not provide a solution to mass deploy or manage updates to your fleet of devices.

Figure 10-33. *iTunes: iPhone Sync Overview*

Leveraging the Logs

The iPhone and iPod touch store logs that can be useful in troubleshooting the devices. You can access the logs using the iPhone Configuration Utility. Simply plug the device into the computer you would like to review logs for and then click on the device in the DEVICES list. Next, click on the Console tab (as seen in Figure 10-34) and then you will see the logs there. You can then use the Case Insensitive Filter field to search for specific entries.

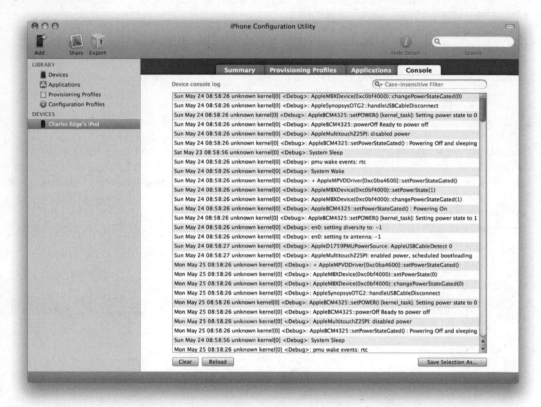

Figure 10-34. *Device Console logs*

Backup and Restoration

Backup and restoration of an iPhone is also a function solely fulfilled client side via USB and iTunes. Unfortunately, there are no centralized management capabilities. A device's configuration, including third party stored data, is backed up whenever it is plugged into the computer. Device media itself is backed up solely according to the iTunes sync settings. This includes the user's music, movies, and pictures. You can also initiate a backup manually by right clicking on your iPhone in the iTunes sidebar, listed under devices. As seen in Figure 10-35, the contextual menu for the device provides several different functions, including transferring songs purchased on the phone to the local computer, backing up, and restoring.

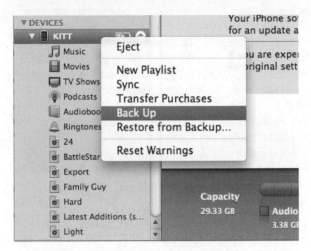

Figure 10-35. *Initiate a device backup in iTunes.*

Device backups are stored at ~/Library/Application Support/MobileSync/Backup on OS X machines, on Windows machines they can be found at C:\ Documents and Settings\username\Application Data\Apple Computer\MobileSync\Backup. Inside of this directory, you will see a directory for each device that you have synced with your system, named after the devices identifier, the same identifier utilized by the iPhone Configuration Utility. Each device will have a primary backup folder, as well as incremental backup folders, which are named after the device's identifier and suffixed with a date string. Inside of the device's primary folder, you will find a number of mddata, mdinfo, and mdbackup files. Each file is a plist file in binary format (see Chapter 7).

Because of the lack of management capabilities, ensuring iPhones are fully backed up largely becomes reliant on user interaction. Because of this, it is recommended to utilize server-side storage whenever possible. For instance, it is highly recommended to utilize IMAP or ActiveSync based mail solutions over POP. Shared calendars should be utilized wherever possible, as should contacts. In any case, strong user education is highly encouraged, users need to be aware to their responsibilities to ensuring their iPhone's are synced to their computers on a regular basis.

Restoring a device that has previously been synchronized to a Mac OS X computer is a fairly straightforward process, making resetting devices a plausible troubleshooting step. To restore a device, open iTunes and click on the Device in the DEVICES section of your list in the left-hand pane. At the Summary page you will see a button to Restore. Click on it and you will then be greeted by a confirmation screen asking if you really want to do this, since after all it is going to wipe out anything that was new to the device since the last synchronization. If you are OK with that, click on OK and the restore will begin, and will take as long as the media you have in iTunes will take to synchronize from iTunes to the device.

Bypassing the Passcode

Cellebrite has a solution that can unlock the passcode on an iPhone or iPod if you have a computer that has synchronized with it. iTunes generates a Security ID for each iPhone or iPod that is synchronized (http://www.cellebrite.com/Cellebrite-Supports-iPhone.html). Cellebrite can use the Security ID file from iTunes to gain direct access to the iPhone data and reset the configured passcode. Cellebrite isn't the only tool though, there are others as well, many of which will allow you to mount the device with or without actually writing data to it. But what if you don't have the passcode or a machine that the handheld has been synchronized with? Jonathan Zdziarski, in his book iPhone Forensics, provides steps to remove the passcode without a Security ID file by doing some fun firmware hacks. Overall, the iPhone Forensics book was a good read, although it seems that things with the iPhone are moving so rapidly that many of the steps have changed (or will very shortly).

Prior to the iPhone 3GS, there was still a big component missing for the iPhone and iPod touch which was the development of a full disk encryption (FDE) solution for the platform. Full disk encryption is actually a feature provided by the 3GS, which works its magic, encrypting all data written to the device on the fly. Apple's solution though, is not without its caveats. First and foremost, it has been demonstrated that the encryption key is actually stored in software on the device, rather than utilizing a hardware-based solution, such as TPM. This means that though the data itself is encrypted, the key to unlock that encryption can be retrieved from the device. The ramification of this discovery means that the encryption provided by the 3GS is relegated to one primary benefit: fast wipes. Fully wiping an old generation iPhone or iPod touch can take several hours, depending upon the amount of data stored on the device. That's a lot of time if you are trying to wipe out potentially sensitive data. Due to the iPhones 3GS's full disk encryption, a remote wipe deletes the encryption key in a matter of seconds, rendering all the data on the device irretrievable. This is certainly beneficial, but an iPhone which has had its SIM card removed isn't likely going to receive the remote wipe command. If the attacker has the toolset to extract the key, then the whole system can be bypassed.

Further Reading

iPhone for Work by Ryan Faas, ISBN # 1-4302-2445-2:
http://www.apress.com/book/view/9781430224457

Apple iPhone Configuration Utilty:
http://www.apple.com/support/iphone/enterprise/

Index

◼D

K

You Need the Companion eBook

Your purchase of this book entitles you to buy the companion PDF-version eBook for only $10. Take the weightless companion with you anywhere.

We believe this Apress title will prove so indispensable that you'll want to carry it with you everywhere, which is why we are offering the companion eBook (in PDF format) for $10 to customers who purchase this book now. Convenient and fully searchable, the PDF version of any content-rich, page-heavy Apress book makes a valuable addition to your programming library. You can easily find and copy code—or perform examples by quickly toggling between instructions and the application. Even simultaneously tackling a donut, diet soda, and complex code becomes simplified with hands-free eBooks!

Once you purchase your book, getting the $10 companion eBook is simple:

1. Visit **www.apress.com/promo/tendollars/**.

2. Complete a basic registration form to receive a randomly generated question about this title.

3. Answer the question correctly in 60 seconds, and you will receive a promotional code to redeem for the $10.00 eBook.

233 Spring Street, New York, NY 10013

Offer valid through 4/10.